CW01149947

SWORD BEACH

www.penguin.co.uk

SWORD BEACH

The Untold Story of D-Day's Forgotten Victory

STEPHEN FISHER

bantam

TRANSWORLD PUBLISHERS
Penguin Random House, One Embassy Gardens,
8 Viaduct Gardens, London SW11 7BW
www.penguin.co.uk

Transworld is part of the Penguin Random House group of companies whose addresses can be found at global.penguinrandomhouse.com

Penguin Random House UK

First published in Great Britain in 2024 by Bantam
an imprint of Transworld Publishers

Copyright © Stephen Fisher 2024

Stephen Fisher has asserted his right under the Copyright, Designs and Patents Act 1988 to be identified as the author of this work.

Every effort has been made to obtain the necessary permissions with reference to copyright material, both illustrative and quoted. We apologize for any omissions in this respect and will be pleased to make the appropriate acknowledgements in any future edition.

As of the time of initial publication, the URLs displayed in this book link or refer to existing websites on the Internet. Transworld Publishers is not responsible for, and should not be deemed to endorse or recommend, any website other than its own or any content available on the Internet (including without limitation at any website, blog page, information page) that is not created by Transworld Publishers.

A CIP catalogue record for this book
is available from the British Library.

ISBN 9781787636712

Typeset in 11.25/14 pt by Minion Pro by Jouve (UK), Milton Keynes.
Printed and bound in Great Britain by Clays Ltd, Elcograf S.p.A.

The authorized representative in the EEA is Penguin Random House Ireland, Morrison Chambers, 32 Nassau Street, Dublin D02 YH68.

Penguin Random House is committed to a sustainable future for our business, our readers and our planet. This book is made from Forest Stewardship Council® certified paper.

For Dad

HMS *Roberts* engages targets east of the Orne River on D-Day.

CONTENTS

Preface	ix
Author's Note	xiii
Understanding the Sources	xvii
List of Maps	xxv
Maps	xxvi
Prologue – 23:15, 4 June 1944	1

PART 1 – THE WAITING — 7
1. A Seaside Resort — 9
2. A Force in Waiting — 21
3. The Waiting Ends — 57

PART 2 – THE ASSAULT — 67
4. On the Midnight Swell — 69
5. Opening Shots — 81
6. H-Hour — 124
7. The Commandos Arrive — 153

PART 3 – THE MORNING BATTLES — 195
8. The Battle of Ouistreham — 197
9. The Race to Pegasus Bridge — 219
10. Building a Beachhead — 236
11. The Fight for Lion-sur-Mer — 249

PART 4 – THE AFTERNOON ACTIONS — 271
12. The German Parry — 273
13. The Slog Inland — 294
14. The Panzer Riposte — 308
15. Darkness Falls — 320

PART 5 – THE FOLLOW-UP FIGHTS 335
  16 Joining Juno, Closing on Caen 337
  17 Securing Sword 342

Epilogue 351

Appendix 1: The Arrival at Pegasus Bridge 355
Appendix 2: Military Ranks 359
Appendix 3: Orders of Battle and Common Abbreviations 361
Appendix 4: Landing Timetable 371
Appendix 5: First Mission Eighth Air Force Targets 373

Notes 376
Glossary 390
Bibliography 393
Acknowledgements 407
Picture Acknowledgements 410
Index 414

PREFACE

EIGHTY YEARS AFTER ONE OF THE MOST WRITTEN-ABOUT BATTLES of the North-West Europe theatre, and possibly of the entire war, it might be construed obtuse to use the word 'forgotten' in the title of any book about D-Day. However you know it – Operation Overlord, Operation Neptune, the Normandy Landings or simply the Sixth of June – D-Day is hardly a forgotten event. Certainly the Allied return to the European continent is an episode even those least versed in the detail of history have usually heard of. How, in this world of movies, websites, podcasts, documentaries and even books, could any aspect of D-Day possibly be forgotten?

The first piece of formal writing I ever did on the subject of D-Day was my GCSE History coursework. I picked a subject I knew about as a result of countless visits to Normandy on the way to the south of France, Spain or Italy for family camping trips. The resulting essay was far from a masterpiece, but it still sits on my bookshelf, a poignant reminder of just how long I've been studying the events of June 1944. Thirty years later, it is a dream come true to have written an entire book on the subject. Admittedly I have picked a single beach to write about, rather than attempted to cover the events of the entire day. Why? Because, quite simply, I believe that Sword Beach is a story that has never been properly told.

My interest began when my archaeological career took me to the National Archives in Kew to research a landing craft. The maritime archaeology unit I was then working for had been commissioned to assess the wreck of a D-Day landing craft tank and establish whether it warranted legal protection as a scheduled monument. Being the only member of the team who knew anything about the Second World War I was given the task of researching its history.

I already knew that there were no published sources that could tell me what I would need to know about this particular landing craft's role. So, needing to build on excellent work already done by the sub-aqua club that had 'adopted' the wreck, I went to the primary source material available to any student of the war. The complicated task of trying to piece together a landing craft's role in Operation Neptune by comparing numerous fleet orders with a myriad of reports, convoy details and landing tables quickly became a fascination. It soon became clear that there was so much more to learn about these often-overlooked vessels.

One archaeological assessment led to another, and before long I was being asked to research specific vessels by a variety of parties, whether the relatives of crewmen, other historians or television production companies. Perhaps unfairly, archaeologically speaking a landing craft's significance is not based solely on its own service but to some degree on the significance of the people who used it. Whether justified or not, a vessel that carried a general might be considered more significant than one that did not. While studying these army units as they crossed the Normandy beaches on their way inland, I began to appreciate the paucity of detail in what had been written about what really happened on D-Day, especially at Sword.

How can this be, when, in the eight decades since 1944, hundreds of books have been published about Normandy? Most of these fall into one of two broad types: some cover the entire campaign from D-Day to the liberation of Paris, while others focus on its most decisive element – the landings on 6 June. The former are understandably brief on the events of the amphibious and airborne assault, but even the latter are constrained by the sheer scale of action on that day, some even more so by concentrating on the preparations in the weeks and months before the landings. Covering the arrival of the equivalent of some twelve combat divisions in Normandy in twenty-four hours,[*] the narrative of events on any one beach must necessarily remain less than exhaustive.

It can be argued that no beach can be written about in isolation, as they are all one part of – and very much influenced by – the undertaking as a whole. With of course the exception of 'Bloody Omaha', to which more attention has been paid than any single Anglo-Canadian beach. There's nothing wrong with good coverage of Omaha, but it comes at the expense of a similarly detailed understanding of the other landing areas.

---

[*] In addition to the six infantry divisions coming ashore on the five beaches and three airborne divisions dropping inland, there is the equivalent of another division of infantry on the Anglo-Canadian beaches, and two armoured divisions across all five. This doesn't include the infantry units attached to the numerous Beach Groups and other specialized formations.

So an authoritative retelling of the story of Sword Beach on 6 June simply doesn't exist. Up to now, Sword has been swallowed up by the greater events of the day, but had it been an isolated battle of its own, as an amphibious landing of the equivalent of nearly two divisions borne by a fleet of more than 700 vessels and with unquantifiable air support, it would have garnered much more attention.

On my bookshelves are some wonderful military history books that cover battles of a similar or smaller scale to Sword. The disastrous Dieppe raid of 1942, for example, is well represented. As is the 43rd Wessex Division's crossing of the River Seine in August 1944. And the 1st Airborne Division's stand at Arnhem is perhaps even more pored over than D-Day itself. These books use primary source information such as war diaries, intelligence summaries and battlefield reports, along with regimental histories, personal accounts and memoirs, to create a comprehensive tale about a battle. Until now no such work has been available on 3rd Infantry Division's landing on Sword Beach on 6 June 1944. Sadly the same can largely be said for the other Commonwealth beaches; so many stories of personal heroism, sacrifice and incredible bravery have yet to be told.

This book, then, is an attempt to rectify an oversight, its focus on the stories that come from Sword, not on the story of how Sword fits into the landings. If there is one aspect of this easternmost beach that is already well told, it is General Montgomery's strategy for the capture of Caen and the prosecution of the Normandy campaign. In this book there are no expositions of generals' plans and the evolution of strategy on either side; the lengthy build-up, the training of 3rd Infantry Division in Scotland and the construction of the numerous defences around Ouistreham and La Brèche are not its concern. *Decision in Normandy* by Carlo D'Este and *Sand and Steel* by Peter Caddick-Adams are excellent introductions to the subject and I cannot possibly hope to emulate them. Rather, it is the story of the events of the day on Sword Beach that is told here, though it starts earlier than the actual landings of course – the landing craft and their crews are as important in an amphibious operation as the men they put ashore.

And there are so many other Sword Beach tales worthy of the telling: the true story of the fighting in Ouistreham; the dogged German defence of Lion-sur-Mer; the commandos who actually led the advance to Pegasus Bridge; and the horrifying defence of the Sole strongpoint. Throughout the day, numerous small unit actions unfolded, all contributing to the greater story of Sword. It is these stories that form the nucleus of this book, told by the people who experienced them, drawn from the various accounts they have left us.

Is this book the definitive account? No. Just as events at Sword Beach were eclipsed by what happened on other beaches, the elements of the operation there, whether the preparation, the landing itself, the advance inland or the link-ups with Juno or 6th Airborne Division, are too numerous for one book. In a situation where so little is known, this narrative can only really aspire to cover the major events and contextualize the battle, but I hope it will inspire a new generation of researchers and historians to look afresh at Sword and dig deeper to discover the people and their stories yet to be told.

Stephen Fisher
January 2024

AUTHOR'S NOTE

THE BRITISH REGIMENTAL SYSTEM MEANT THAT MANY UNITS bore long names, sometimes with multiple numbers and lengthy honourable terms attached. While these names have been used in their first instance, largely for stylistic reasons I have used abbreviations later on. For example, the 13th/18th Royal Hussars (Queen Mary's Own) becomes 13/18 Hussars, while 2nd Battalion the East Yorkshire Regiment becomes 2 East Yorks. Military formations are similarly abbreviated – thus 3rd British Infantry Division becomes 3 Division and 8th British Infantry Brigade becomes 8 Brigade. Such terms may seem blunt, even unnatural, but they were the standard terms used by those formations during the war in their own diaries and reports. At a higher level, army corps tended to use Roman numerals, although Arabic was often used interchangeably. Purely for readability, Arabic numerals are used throughout this book. For a full listing, see Appendix 3.

Similarly, the navy abbreviated many of its vessel types – most especially landing craft – during the war. Again, in the first instance the full name is given, but abbreviations are used afterwards. Thus Landing Craft Tank becomes LCT and Landing Craft Personnel (Large) becomes LCP(L). A full list of abbreviations is included in the Glossary on p. 390.

The British Army and Royal Navy used a well-known system of ranks during the war which remain little changed today. In an ideal world it would be possible to list the equivalent German ranks and positions of command alongside them, but similarly titled German ranks tended to be at least one step higher than their British equivalents and, significantly, German army doctrine placed much higher responsibility on non-commissioned officers. Nonetheless, a list of British and German ranks is provided in Appendix 2.

To ease the flow of the narrative, names of German army formations are presented in English rather than the original German. They are broadly similar to British formations, with a division typically made up of three brigades, each brigade made up of three battalions, each battalion consisting of three rifle companies, and each of those embodying three rifle platoons, along with supporting arms at each level. However, unlike the British regimental system of battalions, a German 'regiment' tended to be the brigade-sized formation. Thus Grenadier-Regiment 736 was a brigade consisting of three battalions within 716. Infanterie-Division. These battalions were styled as I. Bataillon/Grenadier Regiment 736 to III. Bataillon/Grenadier Regiment 736, but in the text are described as 1 Battalion to 3 Battalion 736 Regiment. Companies were named numerically in relation to the entire brigade rather than the battalion, thus Grenadier Regiment 736 contained twelve companies numbered 1. Kompanie to 12, but they appear as 1 Company to 12 Company 736 Brigade in this book (1 to 4 Companies were in 1 Battalion, 5 to 8 Companies in 2 Battalion, and 9 to 12 Companies in 3 Battalion). A kompanie was broadly equivalent to a British company, although while the latter would normally be commanded by a British major, the former would usually be commanded by a German hauptmann or even an oberleutnant. Appendix 3 includes a more comprehensive listing of military formations and their composition.

There are also a lot of measurements used in this book. In the 1940s, Britain still used the imperial system – inches, feet, yards and miles. Today, a hybrid of metric and imperial is usual: most short distances are calculated in centimetres and metres, while our road signs deal in yards and miles. At sea, nautical miles and knots remain the default measurement, but a nautical mile is nearly one fifth longer than a statute mile. During the war (and up to the present day) Germany used a metric distance system of centimetres, metres and kilometres. Metric was also the basis for German armaments and ammunition while Britain tended to use imperial measurements, except when equipped with lend-lease US equipment which tended to be metric.

In the interests of standardization, imperial measurements are used for distances throughout this book, primarily because it was the system used in the vast majority of sources I consulted. I apologize to readers who are only familiar with metric, but conversion is fairly straightforward. For short distances, a foot is broadly equivalent to 30cm, and a yard (3 feet) is just under 1 metre. At longer distances, a mile is 1,760 yards or 1.6km. As a very basic rule of thumb, a distance in miles is two thirds of a distance measured in kilometres (two thirds of 3km is 2, so 3km is roughly equivalent to 2 miles), and a distance in kilometres can be gauged

AUTHOR'S NOTE

by adding one half to a distance measured in miles (2 miles plus 50 per cent is 3, so 2 miles is roughly 3km). This quickly becomes less accurate as the distance increases though. The following table will help to work out rough distances according to whichever type of measurement you are most familiar with.

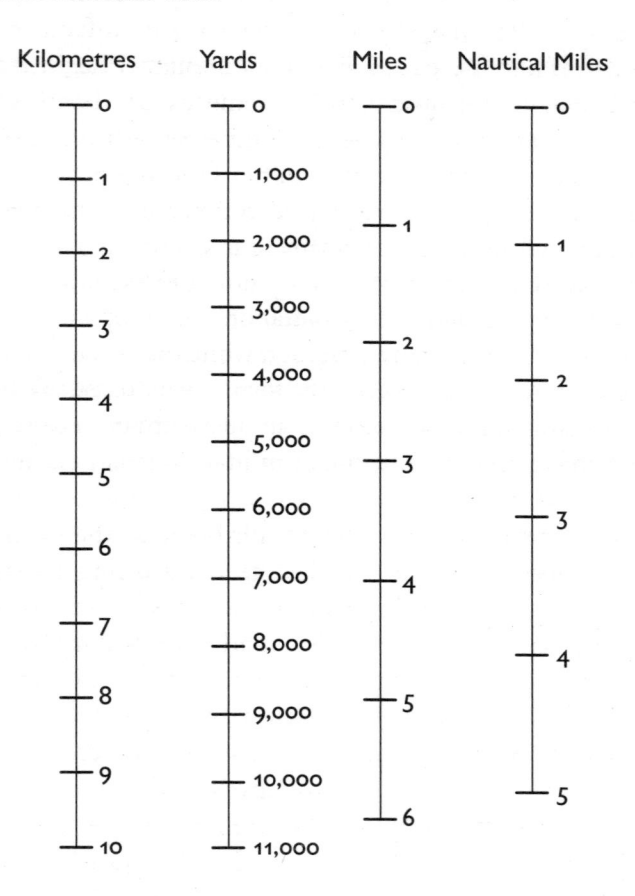

Kilometres	Yards	Miles	Nautical Miles
0	0	0	0
1	1,000		
2	2,000	1	1
3	3,000	2	
4	4,000		2
5	5,000	3	
6	6,000		3
7	7,000	4	
8	8,000		4
9	9,000	5	
10	10,000	6	5
	11,000		

Table 1. Comparison of imperial and metric distances

It is also useful to understand the time zones used in 1944. In the autumn of 1940, Britain did not put the clocks back – a means of preserving a little more daylight in the evenings and saving energy. However, the following spring the clocks were put forward one hour as usual, and in the autumn of 1941 they were put back one hour. This continued for the rest of the war, the net result being that Britain essentially lived one hour ahead of the time it does now. In the winter months today we live on

Greenwich Mean Time (also known as Universal Standard Time or UTC) and in the summer we live on British Summer Time (BST), which is GMT+1 hour. But in the war years, winter was spent in GMT+1 and the summer months were GMT+2 (or BST+1).

All the times used in this book are GMT+2 (or BST+1), the time used by both the invading and defending forces in 1944. This does have the advantage that it is the same time still used in France today. Thus, when the D-Day anniversary is commemorated in Normandy each year there is no need to account for time zone change: 07:26 on 6 June 2024 will be precisely eighty years after 07:26 on 6 June 1944.

There are some less obvious guidelines for reading this book. It is hard to put into written form all the different sights and sounds that dominated the events of D-Day without endlessly repeating oneself. So it is worth remembering that for most of the morning of 6 June, the cacophony of explosions and small arms fire, the roar of overhead aircraft and the revving of tank and landing craft engines were never really absent from Sword Beach. Although the noise faded as the morning wore on, the sound of distant artillery, bombing and the patter of machine gun fire remained, punctuated by closer-at-hand blasts of mines and isolated mortar bombs. But in the first few hours of the landing at least, the reader should imagine an almost continuous din of shot and shell, bright flashes of explosions, and thick, choking smoke and dust.

UNDERSTANDING THE SOURCES

PUTTING TOGETHER THE STORY OF SWORD BEACH ON D-DAY IS like trying to complete a jigsaw the pieces of which are spread across several different boxes, each with a lid that has been recently chewed on by a (once) treasured pet. Some lids are more complete than others, and happily most of the pieces are in the right box. But the pet might have been more thorough on other lids, and perhaps chosen to squirrel away some of the pieces along with your favourite socks and the TV remote, never to be seen again.

Although arguably the D-Day sector that has received the least attention (certainly there's far less published literature on both Sword and Gold than on Omaha, Utah and Juno), there are some stories from Sword that have been told many times before. Being the only beach where Sherman DD (Duplex Drive) tanks were deployed successfully, 13/18 Hussars' swim ashore is relatively well known. 1 Special Service Brigade's advance inland to Pegasus Bridge is perhaps the most familiar story from Sword, while the struggle to secure the Hillman strongpoint is usually included in any account – more often than not in tandem with the failure to reach Caen.

But while these three scenes are familiar, they're often the only bits of the jigsaw to be completed. And sometimes, just occasionally, the wrong pieces have been used to replace the odd missing piece. And of the rest of the giant Sword jigsaw, much of it has never been examined since the pet did their worst, the pieces lying uninspected in their half-eaten boxes. The result is that the full picture of Sword has never been put together.

Resolving this can be easy in some instances, and difficult to the point of near impossibility in others. Some unit war diaries are superbly detailed, providing a comprehensive timeline, names, grid references and even attached reports filed by company or platoon commanders. Others can be simplified to the extent where you might wonder if the unit were even in Normandy on 6 June. In some units many veterans wrote memoirs, recorded oral archives or submitted reminiscences to authors, regimental journals or newspapers. Some of those accounts can be easier to obtain than others, but for other units only the tiniest fraction of those accounts exist.

But finding such accounts is only half the battle. Each and every source, from a war diary written hours after the event to an oral archive recorded seventy years later, can be flawed. These flaws can originate from the point at which the events they record actually happened, or they can be flawed at the point they're recalled. Even worse, they can be flawed at both.

When an event happens, individual spectators are only ever witnessing one aspect of it. They see a singular point of view but may miss other perspectives that are crucial to understanding the event as a whole. Watching a football match, fans usually observe what's going on around the ball. If they are close enough to the pitch they may have a fantastic view of a tackle, but their field of view prevents them from seeing the squabble at the other end of the stadium. Spectators in the high seats may get a better view of the pitch as a whole but are too distant to see the specific reason for a foul. If there are trees, tanks, burning buildings, mortar explosions and machine guns firing over the football pitch (which might be the typical amount of space over which a small unit action is fought), understanding exactly what is happening is that much harder.

None of these events was written down immediately after it happened. Even primary sources such as war diaries, letters home and reports might have been written up to a month or more afterwards, often when men were still in the field. The very best reports might have been written in a candlelit barn with a grubby map to hand, officers trying to relate what had happened to them – or even just what they'd been told – to faint features and contours that might not reveal everything that existed on the ground. Grid references might not be accurate (and frequently can be determined as wrong), and witness contributions might be second or even third hand. And even as little as a week after the event, the recollection of it can be plagued with errors.

Memory is a fickle thing – and a sensitive subject. It can be hard for anyone to accept that their recollection of what they saw, heard and experienced might be flawed, and it is almost frowned upon to question a veteran's version of events, even when photographs, physical evidence or just plain common sense contradicts it. After all, they were there. But we must question any account, whether it was seven days or seventy years ago, because memory is fallible. Any police officer can tell you how haphazard eyewitness testimony can be. Some people genuinely do have excellent observational and recall abilities, but most do not. Unless serious attention is paid and a determined effort made to remember what is happening, numerous errors can creep in.

The order in which events happened can quickly become confused, especially if the settings and substance are similar: one skirmish with an enemy patrol can be easily mixed up with another thirty minutes later in the same wood or field, when the only distinguishing difference might be the wounding of a colleague. Douglas Grant, for instance, recalls the bombing raid that wounded Brigadier James Cunningham on 6 June as taking place on the morning of 7 June, seemingly conflating it with the bombing of 41 Commando HQ. Similarly, the location of specific events or people can be confused. Brigadier the Lord Lovat recalls seeing a wounded NCO with his leg propped up on a chair guarding a group of prisoners on the outskirts of Saint-Aubin-d'Arquenay, when everyone else places him at le Port – as backed up by reports stating that's where prisoners were left.

Such small errors of time and place are completely normal and straightforwardly understood. But as time passes it is easy for these flaws to multiply. The order in which people are killed, and the locations, can start to become conflated; scale (size and distance) can become blurred, along with the inevitable loss of detail – names, times and so on. After a dozen landing exercises, one beach experience can be confused with another, and it becomes easier to mix the events of one landing with another – even to the extent of mistaking events on a training exercise with those of D-Day itself.

The passage of time also allows for a more complex and taboo problem with memory to arise – the introduction of false memories. It is surprisingly easy for this to happen. People possess more such memories than they would care to realize. Memory can be easily led: when someone describes a scene in conversation, many create that scene in their mind, and that can be even more vivid if the location is familiar. Leading questions are a classic example of this: 'Did you see the Tiger tank?' creates an image in the mind that can be more powerful than the memory (to say nothing of audience effects and the pressure to please an interviewer). The more such a scene is recalled, the more it can impose itself as a memory. A museum manager once told me of two veterans who used regularly to attend his museum to talk about their experiences to visitors.

After one passed away, the other continued to recount his friend's experiences, until he began recalling them as events that had happened to him. He had acquired the memories after so much exposure to them.

Finally, there is the least palatable aspect of people's recollections – the imagination. While it is certainly true that some people inadvertently embellish their recollections of events in the manner described above, there are others who do it deliberately, with no care for how it will impact the historical record. It must also be recognized that some people who have recalled their war experiences in public are fantasists, who recount adventures more appropriate to a *Commando* comic. Happily there are very few of them, but just as people do it today (they are often exposed as 'Walts' on social media, and can even be prosecuted[*]), they did it during the Second World War as well.

Reminiscences also vary according to the information veterans had to hand when they compiled them. Some recalled their experiences in isolation – Douglas Grant, for instance, wrote an account of the war as it happened to him and, judging by the visceral nature of *The Fuel of the Fire*, seemingly without the benefit of any other sources (such as war diaries) to help him clarify events. Others clearly wrote their memoirs with access to multiple sources – Derek Mills-Roberts had 6 Commando's war diary and reports as well as other people's reminiscences to hand when he wrote *Clash by Night*. Some recollections vary with age, and in ways that can be surprising and should encourage caution. Peter Masters recounted his D-Day experiences four times – first for Cornelius Ryan's *The Longest Day* (1959), then for Ian Dear's *10 Commando* (1987), again for Stephen Ambrose's *D-Day* (1994), and finally for his own 1997 memoir. The amount of specific detail increases with each retelling. For instance, during the final approach to le Port, in 1959 Masters described moderate firing in the village; in 1987 one of the other cycling commandos was hit, and in 1994 he was killed; and in 1997 he was a red-haired man, shot through the head. A search through all of 6 Commando's fatal casualties on D-Day reveals no obvious candidate.

The result is that every source, primary or secondary, should always be treated with caution, and this is borne out by the fact that rationalizing the huge amount of literature relating to Sword on D-Day can be tricky. Accounts rarely agree on every detail, and forensic analysis has been

---

[*] After Walter Mitty – the character created by American writer James Thurber – who enjoyed a rich fantasy life.

necessary to present the version of events in this book. In many ways I have had it much easier than the people whose reports and recollections I've used. I've had the benefit of a large desk over which to spread maps, unlimited tea, and access to far more material, both historic and modern, than the officers writing their reports or war diaries and the veterans recounting their experiences in the following years. I am familiar with the entire area about which I am writing, having had the benefit of the freedom to cycle Normandy whenever I wanted without being shot at. If I forget the exact location of a building, I have immediate online access to digital maps and photography of every road in the area.

This makes it possible to establish what was happening and where to a level that has not previously been achieved at Sword. For instance, Private James Kelly's description of the large house he defended, its gateway and its view of a tree line 400 yards away in Lion-sur-Mer, along with the war diary's grid references and historic aerial photographs, means the building can be precisely identified (it is now the Résidence Blagny, a school group hostel). Similarly, the farm that Sergeant Thomas Kilvert approached on the outskirts of Hermanville-sur-Mer can be easily identified, and being able to see the farm's layout makes it possible to better understand his assault on it. The route that F Troop 4 Commando took into Ouistreham can be identified from the film shot by Sergeant George Laws and matched to the written description given by Lieutenant Murdoch McDougall, as well as aerial photographs taken on D-Day showing the Sherman DD tanks of 13/18 Hussars, while the earlier troops' route (and F Troop's intended route) can be determined from their briefing maps. 6 Commando's route inland to Pegasus Bridge can be determined by film taken of their briefing model, which aligns with the grid references provided in the reports filed by 2 and 3 Troops. As their detailed narratives, along with Mills-Roberts's memoir, unfold, their journey from one German defensive site marked on the intelligence maps to another can be readily followed. Their route is especially interesting, as the route taken by Lovat and 1 Special Service Brigade HQ is different, but Lovat's is the one most usually used to describe the commando advance on Pegasus Bridge. In fact the accounts of Lovat and Piper Bill Millin are those most frequently used to describe this journey and 6 Commando's has rarely been portrayed, despite it being far more significant.

Being able to place events makes it easier to establish the chronology, and in this way small variations in various accounts can be identified and understood. For instance, a grid reference in 41 Commando's war diary places B Troop at the road junction immediately outside the grounds of Château de Lion-sur-Mer. No change to this location is detailed until the general withdrawal to the church, but James Kelly's account shows that B Troop either fell back to A Troop's position before the general withdrawal, or perhaps had never even advanced quite as far as the war diary suggests.

On some occasions it is easy to spot where someone's reminiscences contain an error of time or place, and that error can be rectified – the event can be reinserted into its correct place in the chronology. Sometimes there is no corroborating evidence for someone's recollection – there are no other witnesses, the building they describe can't be identified, the burned-out tank is not visible on aerial photographs. But in the main, in the absence of contradictory information, it is only fair to take these accounts at face value. Corporal John Scruton describes coming across two burning Bren Carriers between Colleville-sur-Orne and strongpoint 14, and Lionel Roebuck refers to one burned-out carrier somewhere just north-west of Colleville. It's almost certain that they saw the same thing at different times. Aerial photos are unclear, no one else describes the route in detail, and the unit that the carriers might have belonged to cannot be identified. There is nothing to disprove the accounts. It is possible that one got the location wrong, but sometimes it's only fair to accept what veterans say.

On the other hand, some sources can be roundly rejected. In one account a navigator sailing with 1 Minesweeping Flotilla claims to have sailed at night on 5 June and passed a brightly lit V (for Victory) shining from the Nab Tower outside the Solent, waxing lyrical about how this show of defiance confirmed that the seas and skies were now totally out of bounds to the enemy. A quick look at Force S's orders and reports reveals that this is nonsense. The flotilla sailed at 14:00 on 5 June and passed the Nab Tower in broad daylight. The idea that after imposing a complete blackout on the invasion fleet the Admiralty would allow such a pointless gesture is beyond all common sense. How this account, dating to fifty years after the landings, has come about is unclear, but it may be a misplaced memory, perhaps mixing an account of sailing after dark on or after VE Day, when a port may well have finally thrown off the restrictions of the blackout and illuminated a giant V outside their harbour. Whatever the reason, such false memories are red flags, and after more detailed analysis the rest of the account can quite often be found to be in error as well.

Thus, trying to make sense of the events at Sword on D-Day has been achieved with careful analysis of a combination of sources. On many occasions these sources have disagreed on key details and facts. If two equally valid sources state an event happened at a different time and there is no weight one way or the other, I simply cannot specify one over the other and the detail has had to remain necessarily vague. But on just as many occasions a wide variety of sources completely unconnected to one another have happily agreed on key details and events. A fine example of this is the small action between 6 Commando and 4 Company 736 Regiment outside Colleville-sur-Orne where Major Bill Coade was injured (see Chapter 9). The report filed by 2 Troop, Mills-Roberts's memoir, the account by Josef Häger and even his retelling of Ferdinand Klug's experience, the brief report given by Wilhelm Dohmen and the layout of the location as shown in period aerial photographs and intelligence maps all agree on the key details. This small action has never been retold in such context before, but it shows the possibilities open to historians with the rich resources that are available to us eighty years later.

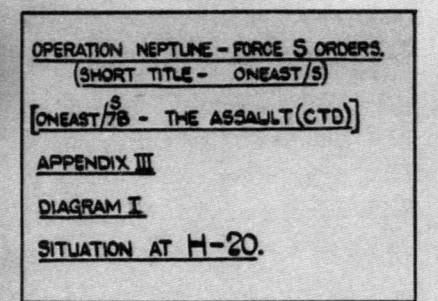

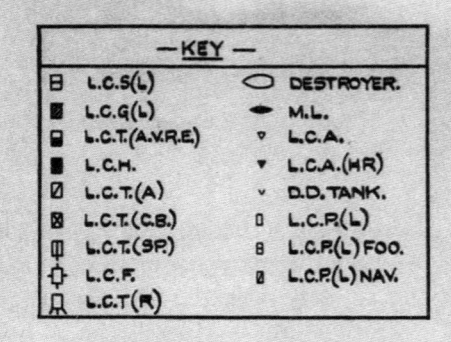

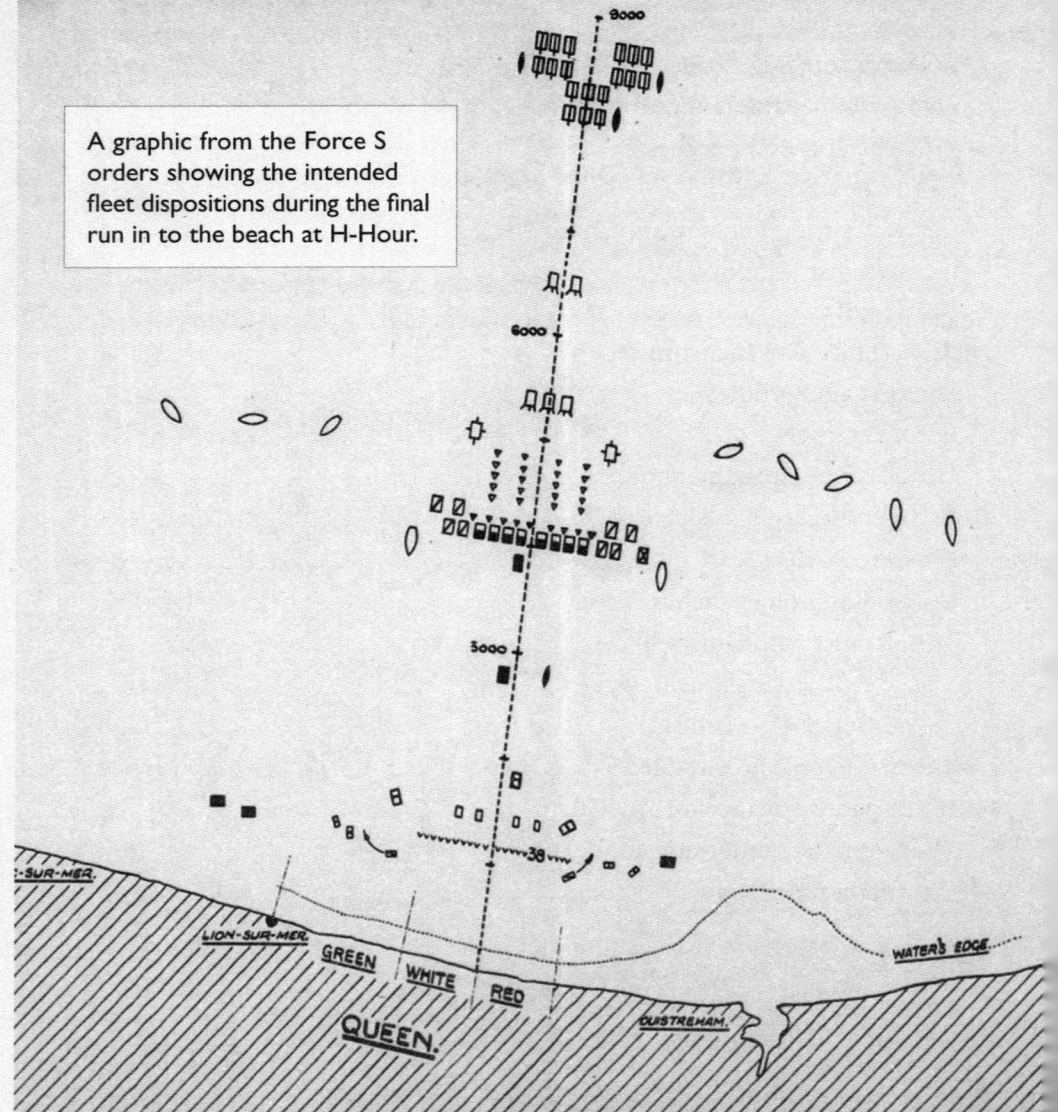

A graphic from the Force S orders showing the intended fleet dispositions during the final run in to the beach at H-Hour.

LIST OF MAPS

The invasion area	xxvi
Distances in statute miles from the centre of Queen, White and Red Beaches	xxvii
Sword area Beaches	xxviii–xxix
German strongpoints in and around Sword area	xxx–xxxi
German dispositions	xxxii–xxxiii
Beach exits	xxxiv–xxxv
Allied objectives in Sword sector	xxxvi
Force S sailing routes	xxxvii
Force D targets	xxxviii–xxxix
Destroyer bombardment berths and targets	xl–xli
Bomber targets in advance of H-Hour	xlii–xliii
H-Hour	xliv–xlv
S3 Assault Group beaching areas	xlvi–xlvii
The advance into Ouistreham	xlviii–xlix
The advance to Pegasus Bridge	l–li
Expanding the beachhead	lii–liii
The battle for Lion-sur-Mer	liv–lv
185 Brigade's advance inland	lvi
The German counter-attack	lvii
Overnight positions	lviii

THE INVASION AREA

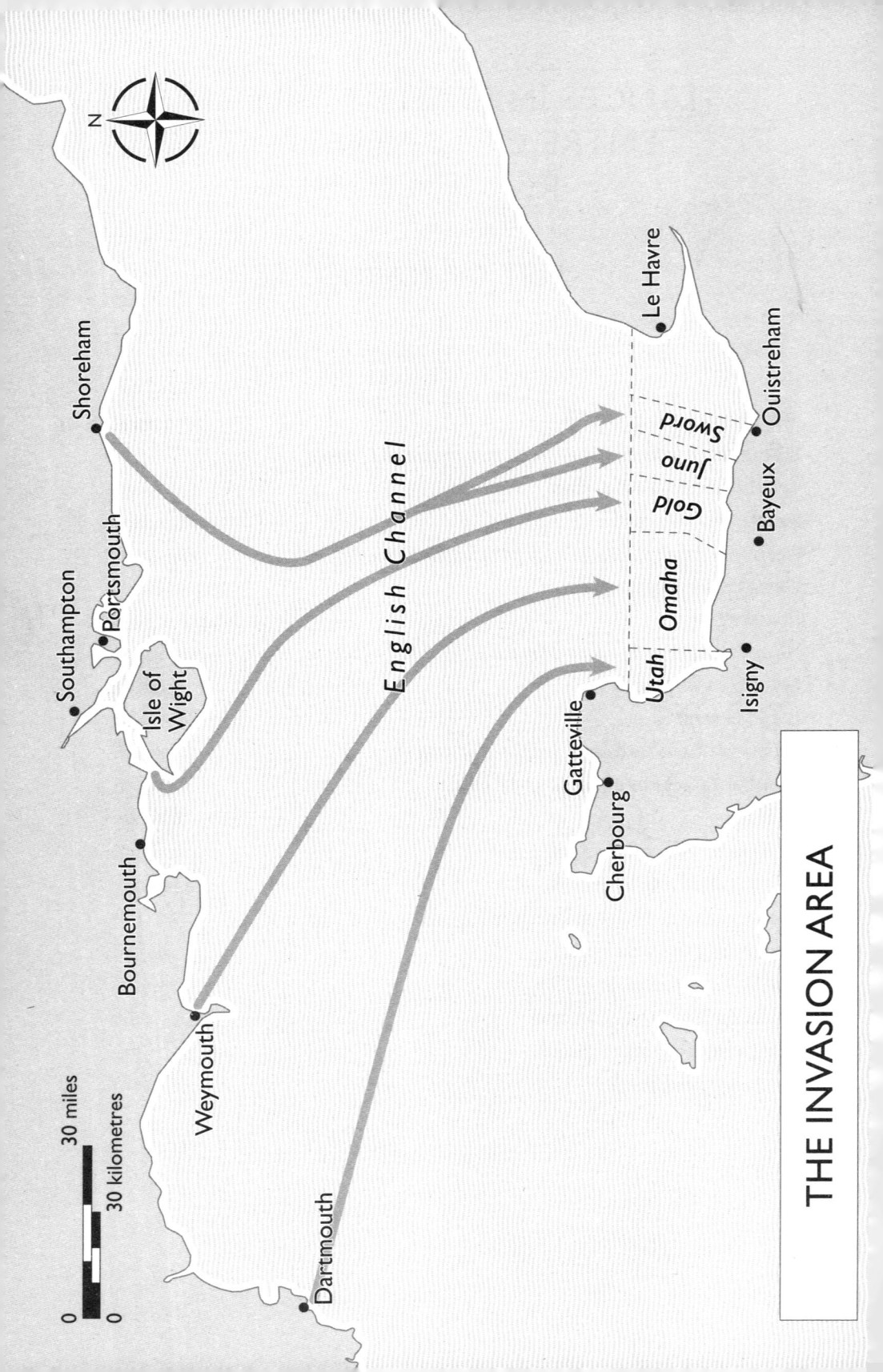

DISTANCES IN STATUTE MILES FROM THE CENTRE OF QUEEN, WHITE AND RED BEACHES

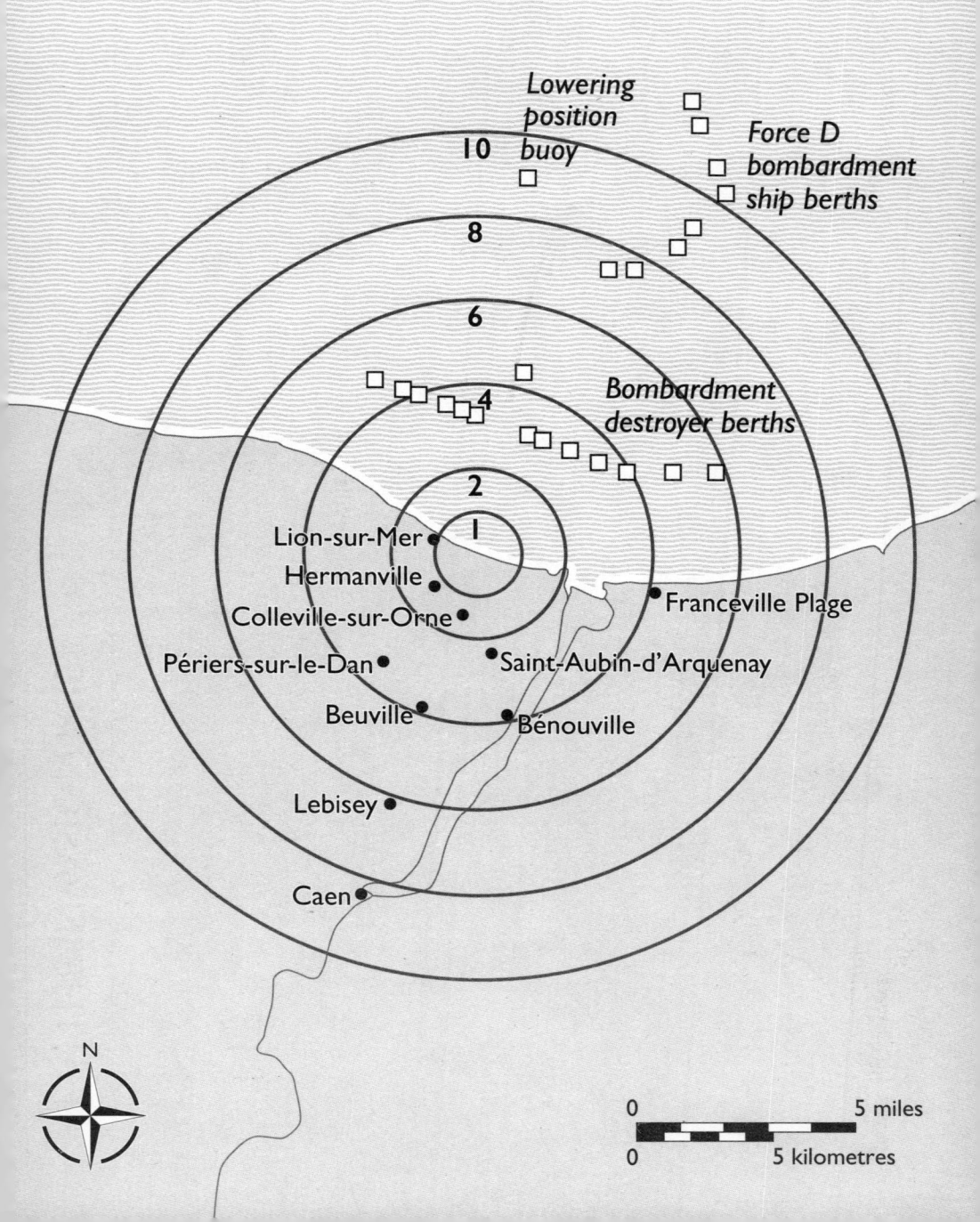

Lowering position buoy

Force D bombardment ship berths

Bombardment destroyer berths

Lion-sur-Mer
Hermanville
Colleville-sur-Orne
Franceville Plage
Périers-sur-le-Dan
Saint-Aubin-d'Arquenay
Beuville
Bénouville
Lebisey
Caen

JUNO

Oboe

Saint-Aubin-sur-Mer

Luc-sur-Mer

Douvres-la-
Délivrande

SWORD AREA BEACHES

The division of the coast from Saint-Aubin-sur-Mer to Ouistreham into landing sectors.

SWORD

Peter
Queen
Green
White
Roger
Red

Lion-sur-Mer
Hermanville-sur-Mer
Colleville-sur-Orne
Ouistreham
Saint-Aubin-d'Arquenay

Map base © Google

WN 27
WN 26
WN 24
WN 25
WN 23
WN 21 Trout
WN 22
WN 20A
StP Douvres II
StP Douvres I
WN 19
WN 16 Morris
WN 17 Hillman
WN 21A

Map base © Google

GERMAN STRONGPOINTS IN AND AROUND SWORD AREA

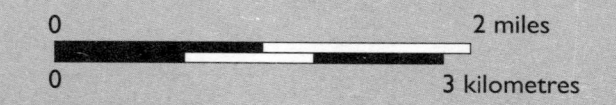

StP 20 Cod
WN 18 Skate
WN 10
StP 8 Bass
WN 03
StP 02
StP 14 Sole
WN 05
WN 09
WN 07
WN 04
WN 12 Daimler
StP 06
WN 01
WN 15
WN 15A
WN 11
WN 13

KEY
WN: Widerstandsnest ('Resistance nest')
StP: Stützpunkt / ('Strongpoint')

- 8 Company 736 Regiment HQ
- 2 Battalion 736 Regiment HQ
- 9 Company 736 Regiment HQ
- 12 Company 736 Regiment HQ
- 11 Company 736 Regiment
- 2 Battalion 736 Ration Train
- 3 Battalion 736 Regiment HQ
- 1 Battery 989 Heavy Regiment
- 11 Battery 1716 Artillery Regiment
- 7 Company 192 Regiment
- 3 Battery 155 Artillery Regiment
- 2 Battery 155 Artillery Regiment
- 2 Company 716 Engineer Battalion
- 3 Battalion 736 Ration Train
- 2 Battalion 192 Regiment HQ
- 1 Battery 155 Artillery Regiment
- 736 Regiment Staff HQ
- 5 Battery 200 Assault Gun Battalion
- 1 Company 716 Anti-Tank Battalion
- 5 Company 192 Regiment
- 6 Company 192 Regiment
- 716 Division HQ

Map base © Google

GERMAN DISPOSITIONS

German unit dispositions on the eve of D-Day (for more information see Appendix 3).

- 10 Company 736 Regiment HQ
- 1 Battery 1260 Coastal Artillery Battalion
- 1 Company 642 Ost Battalion HQ
- 3 Company 642 Ost Battalion HQ
- 1 Company 736 Regiment HQ
- 2 Company 736 Regiment
- 4 Company 736 Regiment HQ
- 1 Battalion 736 Regiment HQ
- 1 Battery 1716 Artillery Regiment HQ
- 2 Battery 1716 Artillery Regiment
- 4 Battery 1716 Artillery Regiment
- 3 Company 736 Regiment HQ
- 736 Regiment Battle HQ
- 1 Battalion 736 Ration Train
- 642 Ost Battalion HQ
- 2 Company 642 Ost Battalion HQ
- 3 Battery 1716 Artillery Regiment
- 4 Company 642 Ost Battalion
- 1 Company 716 Engineer Battalion
- 2 Battalion 125 Regiment HQ
- 8 Company 125 Regiment

0 — 2 miles
0 — 3 kilometres

BEACH EXITS

Beach exit numbers allocated to the lanes leading off Queen White and Red Beaches.

Queen Green

Queen White

9 10 11 12 13 14 15 16 17 18

Map base © Google

Queen Red   Roger Green

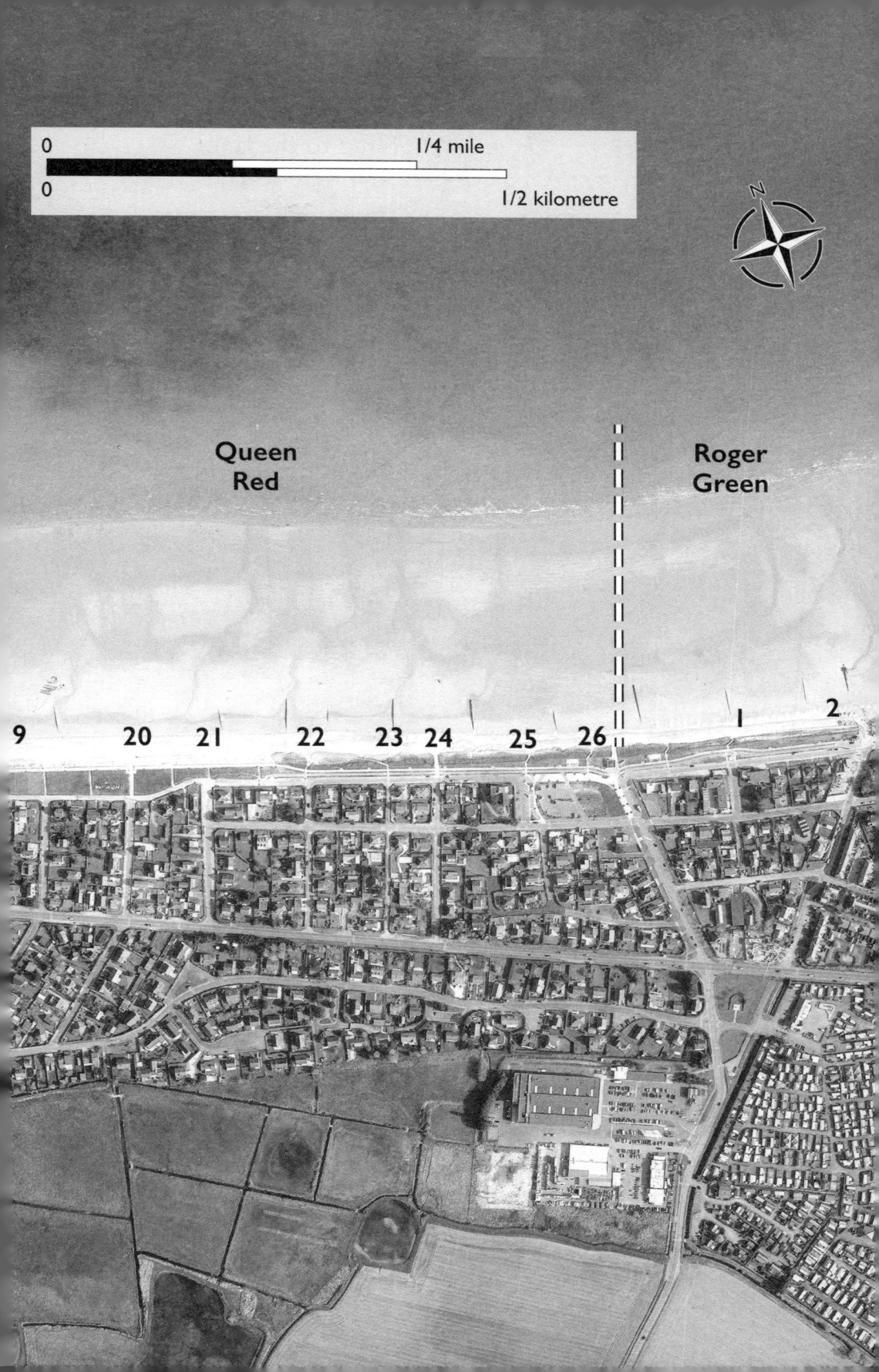

9   20   21   22   23   24   25   26   1   2

ALLIED OBJECTIVES IN SWORD SECTOR

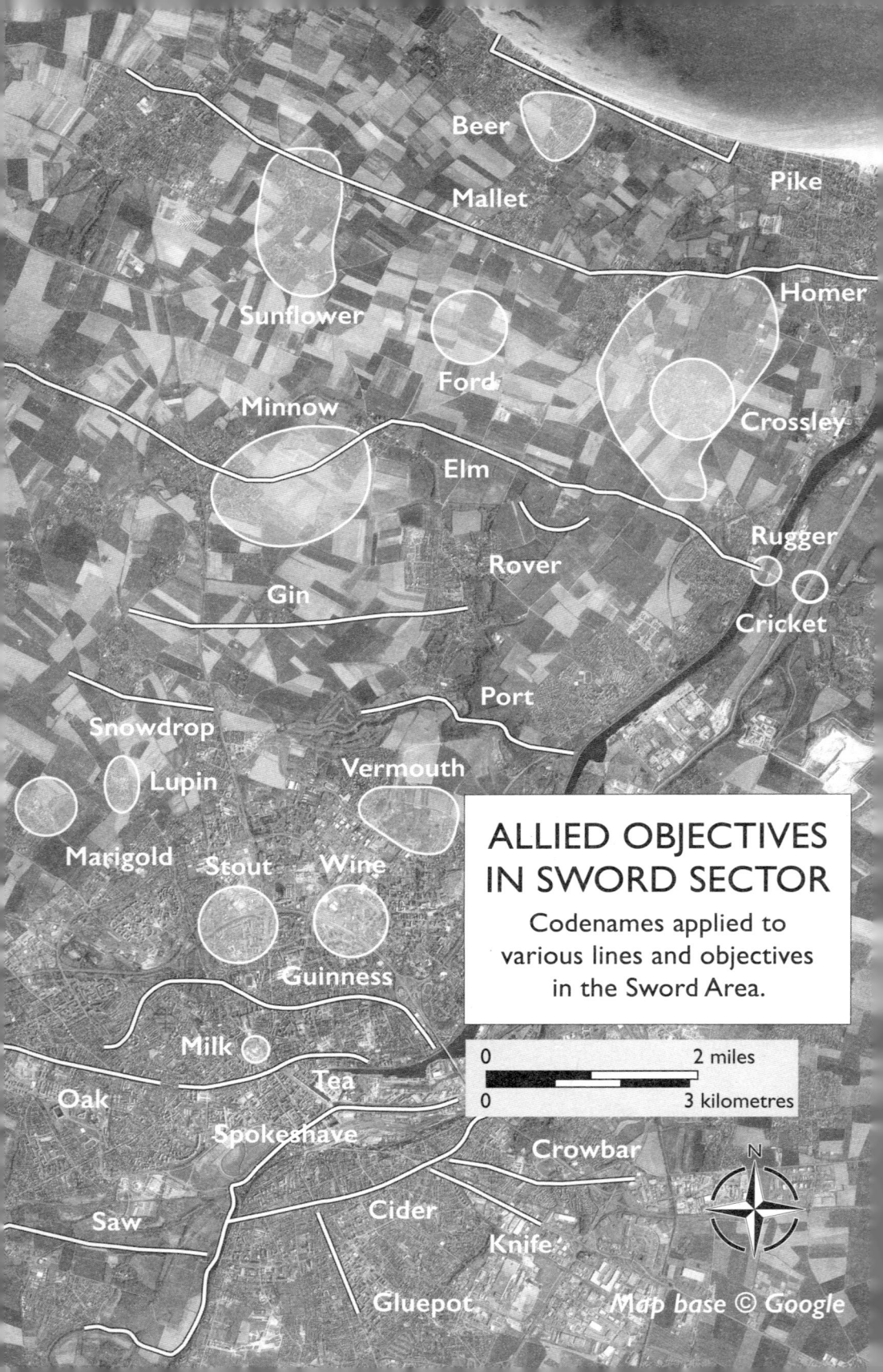

Codenames applied to various lines and objectives in the Sword Area.

0 — 2 miles
0 — 3 kilometres

Map base © Google

Beer
Pike
Mallet
Homer
Sunflower
Ford
Crossley
Minnow
Elm
Rugger
Rover
Cricket
Gin
Port
Snowdrop
Lupin
Vermouth
Marigold
Stout
Wine
Guinness
Milk
Oak
Tea
Spokeshave
Crowbar
Saw
Cider
Knife
Gluepot

FORCE S SAILING ROUTES

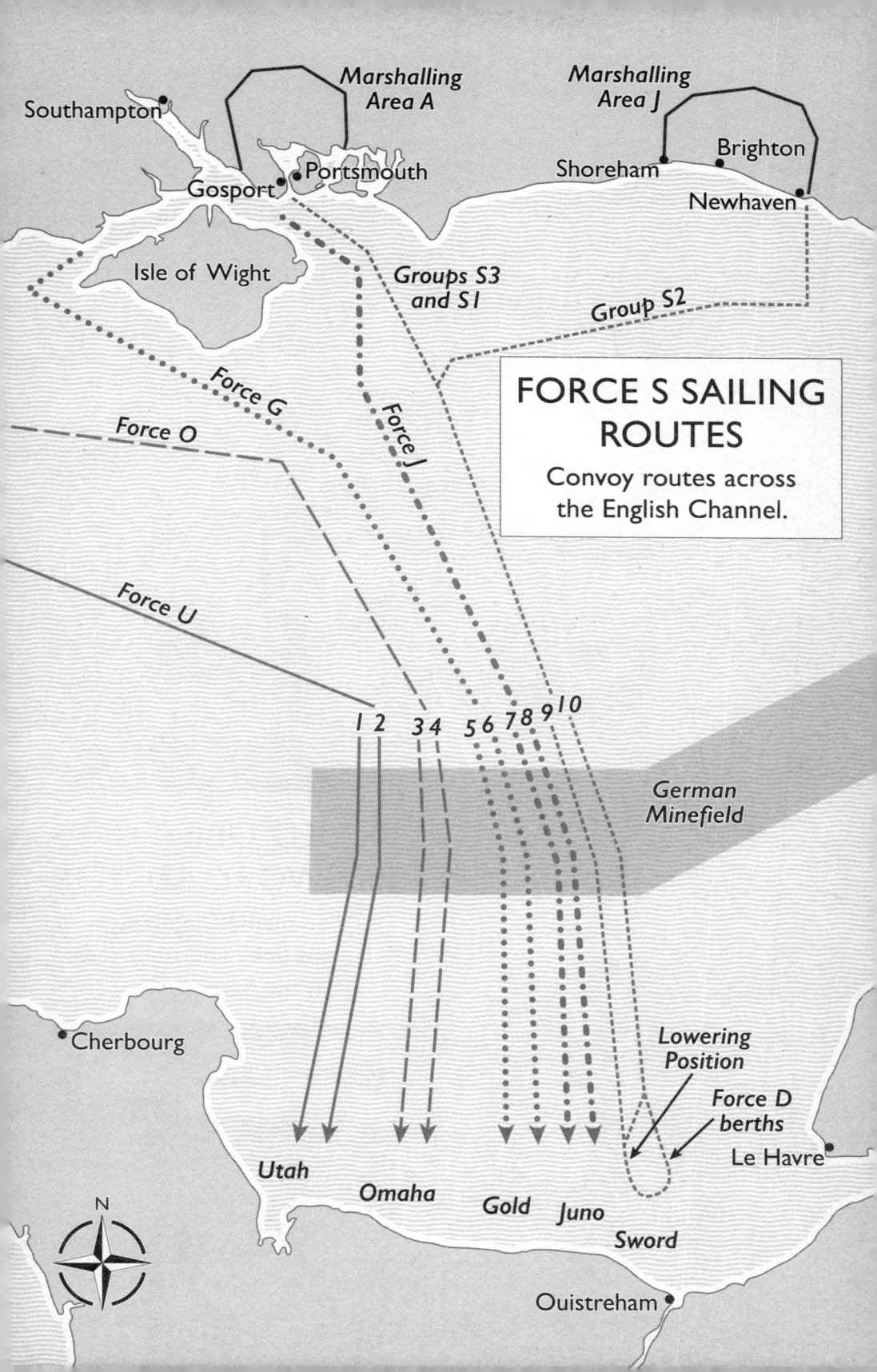

Convoy routes across the English Channel.

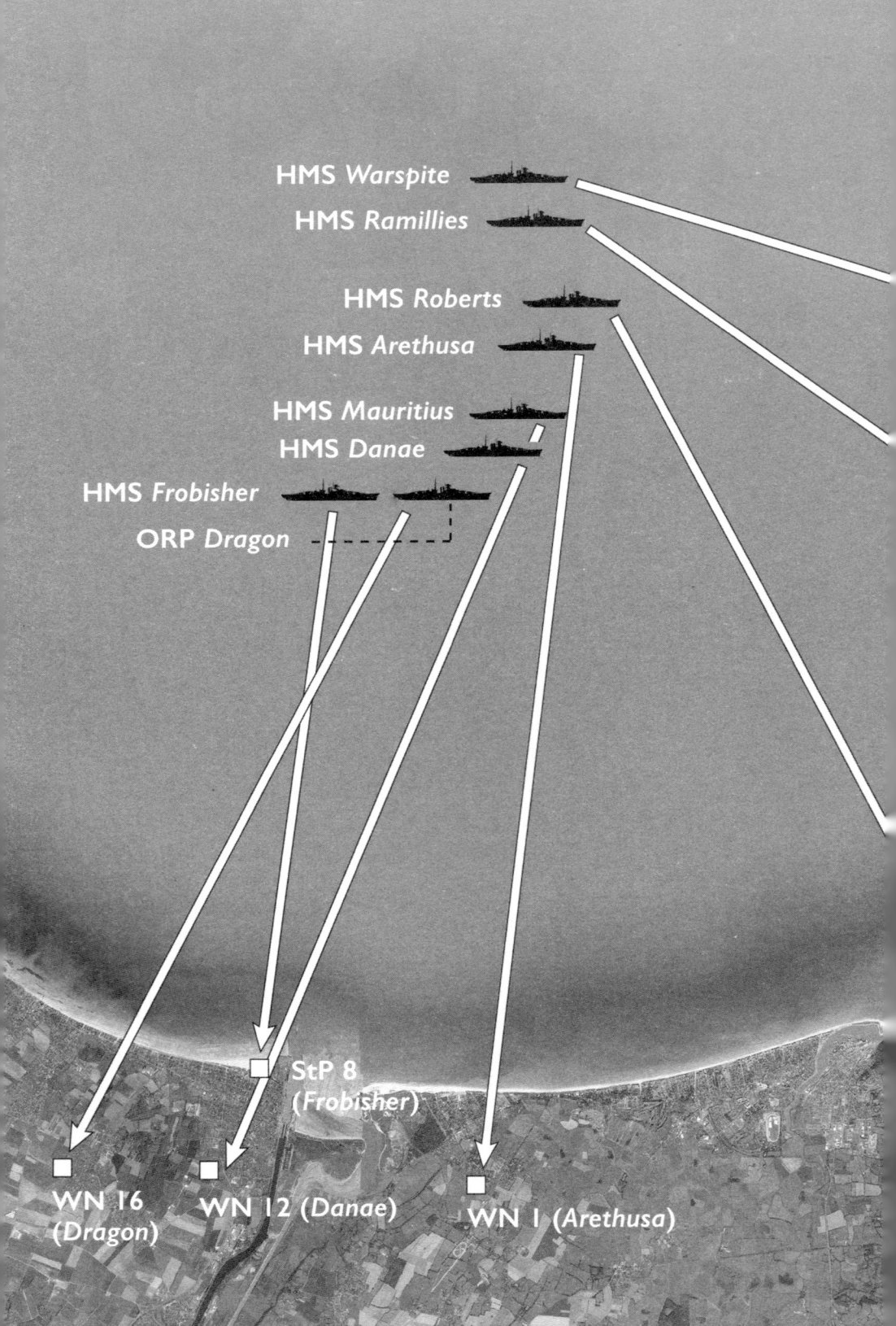

HMS *Warspite*
HMS *Ramillies*
HMS *Roberts*
HMS *Arethusa*
HMS *Mauritius*
HMS *Danae*
HMS *Frobisher*
ORP *Dragon*

StP 8 (*Frobisher*)
WN 16 (*Dragon*)
WN 12 (*Danae*)
WN 1 (*Arethusa*)

FORCE D TARGETS

Initial targets for the warships of Force D during the pre-landing bombardment.

0 — 5 miles
0 — 7 kilometres

N

● Villerville
(*Warspite*)

● Bennerville
(*Ramillies*)

● Houlgate
(*Roberts*)

Map base © Google

1
2
3
4
5
6
7
8
9
14

Luc-sur-Mer

Lion-sur-Mer

Queen White
and Red Beaches

Ouistreham

DESTROYER BOMBARDMENT BERTHS AND TARGETS

Force S destroyer positions off Sword Beach and their allocated bombardment areas prior to H-Hour. The positions are plotted from the coordinates given in the Force S fire support orders (DEFE 2/403).

KEY

1. HMS *Eglington*
2. HMS *Kelvin*
3. HMS *Virago*
4. HMS *Verulam*
5. HMS *Serapis*
6. ORP *Ślązak*
7. HMS *Middleton*
8. HMS *Scourge*
9. HNoMS *Stord*
10. HMS *Scorpion*
11. HMS *Saumarez*
12. HMS *Swift*
13. HNoMS *Svenner* (did not reach berth)
14. HMS X-23

Franceville Plage

Caborg

Map base © Google

Map base © Google

BOMBER TARGETS IN ADVANCE OF H-HOUR

German positions to be hit by RAF bombers (from 05:00) and USAAF bombers of 3 Division Eighth Air Force (from 07:00) (see *Appendix 5* for more details).

KEY TO TARGETS

- A – Ouistreham Battery
- B – Merville Battery
- C – Houlgate Battery
- 16 – Chokepoints 3 and 4
- 17 – Strongpoint 28
- 18 – Strongpoint 27
- 19 – Strongpoint 21A
- 20 – Strongpoint 24
- 21 – Strongpoint 21 (Trout)
- 22 – Strongpoint 20 (Cod)
- 23 – Strongpoint 10
- 24 – Strongpoint 5
- 25 – Strongpoint 3
- 26 – Battery
- 27 – Strongpoint 16 (Morris)
- 28 – Strongpoint 12 (Daimler)
- 29 – Battalion HQ
- 30 – Divisional HQ
- 31 – Regimental HQ
- 32 – Strongpoint 17 (Hillman)
- 33 – 88mm Battery
- 34a – Chokepoint 1
- 34 – Chokepoint 2

KEY TO ICONS

- ▪ USAAF Target
- ◉ RAF Target

H-HOUR

The approximate beaching areas and beach exit clearances of the LCTs carrying the Armoured Vehicle Royal Engineers of 77 and 79 Assault Squadrons.

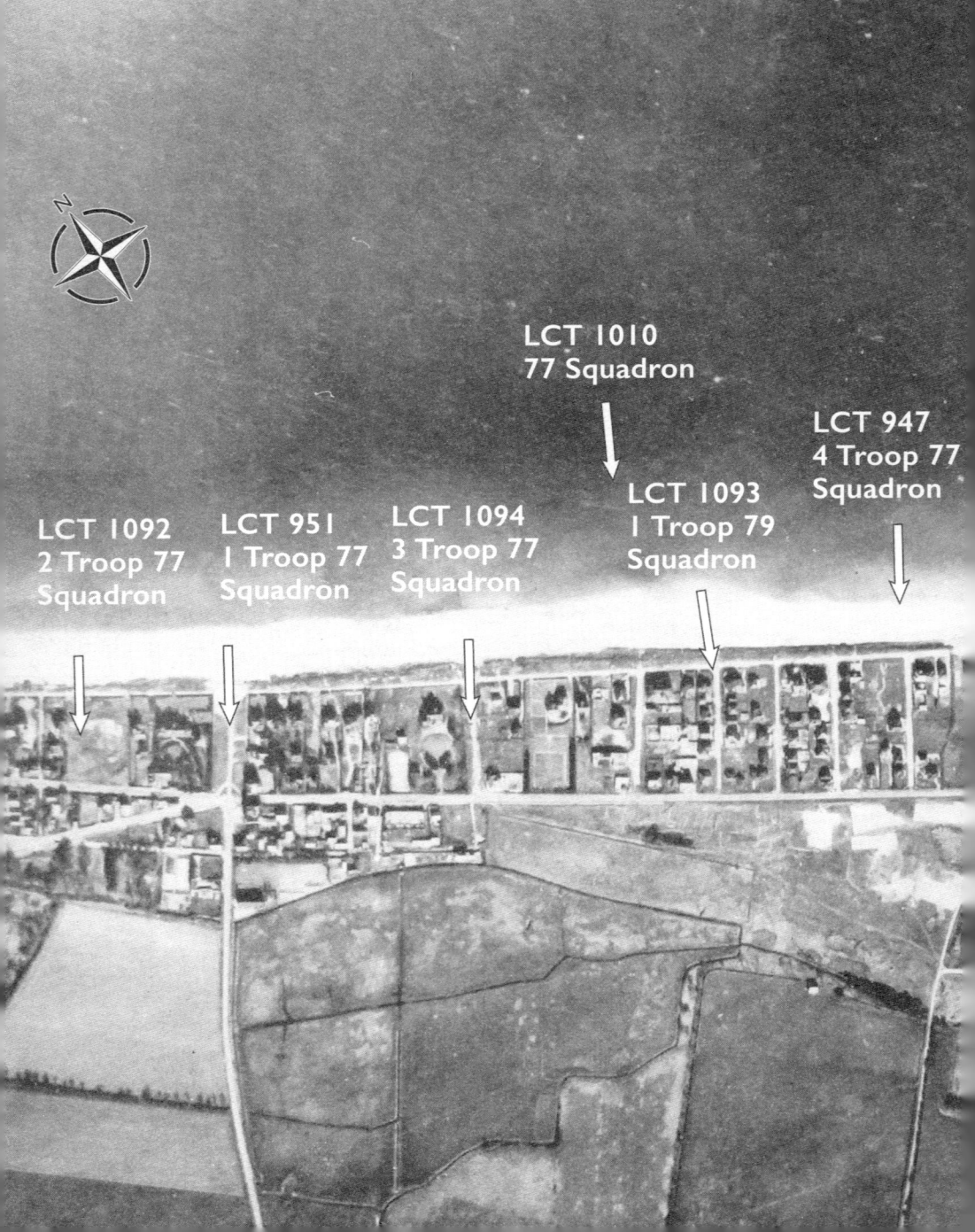

LCT 1010
77 Squadron

LCT 947
4 Troop 77 Squadron

LCT 1092
2 Troop 77 Squadron

LCT 951
1 Troop 77 Squadron

LCT 1094
3 Troop 77 Squadron

LCT 1093
1 Troop 79 Squadron

0 1/4 mile
0 1/4 kilometre

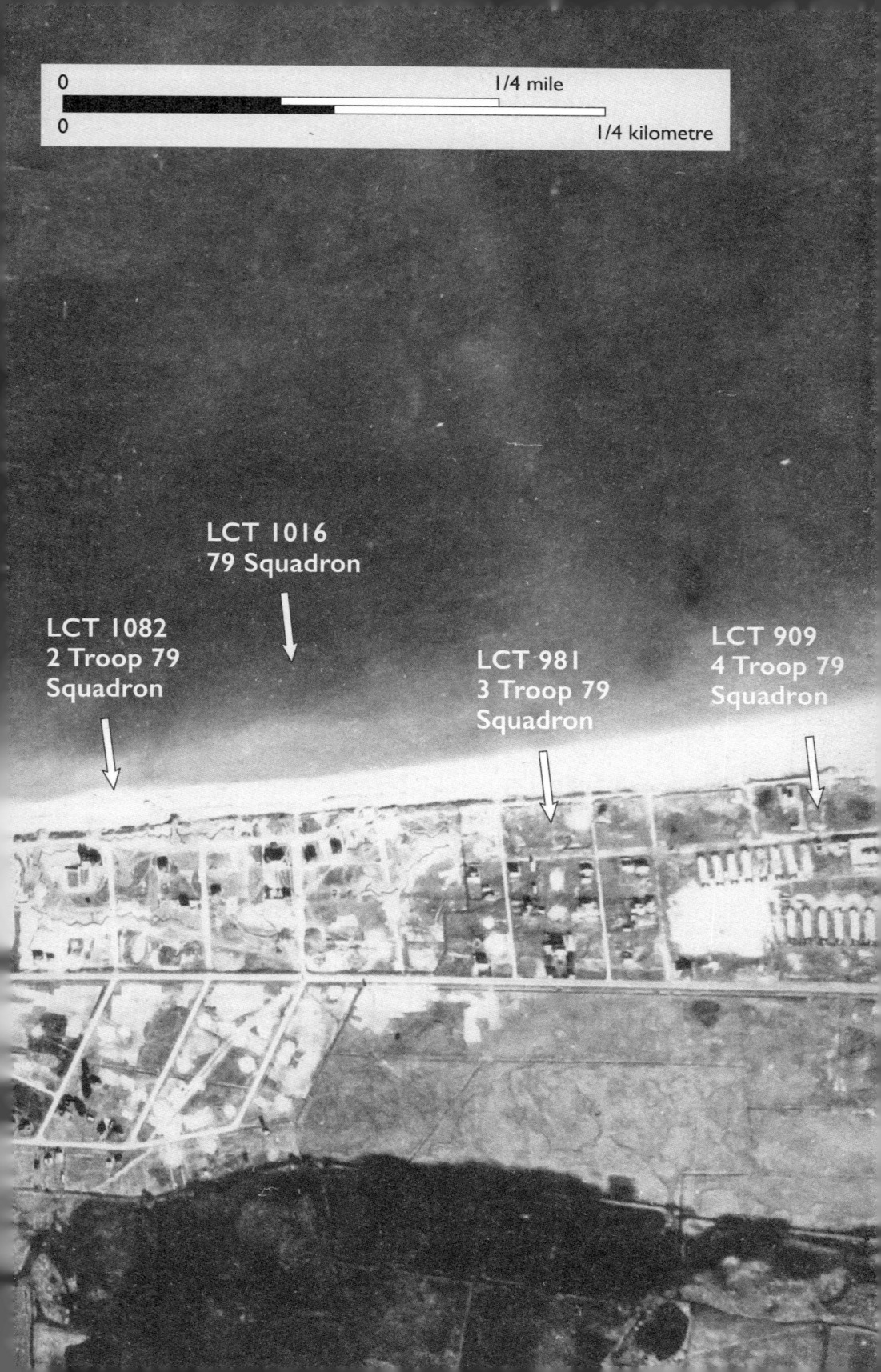

LCT 1016
79 Squadron

LCT 1082
2 Troop 79
Squadron

LCT 981
3 Troop 79
Squadron

LCT 909
4 Troop 79
Squadron

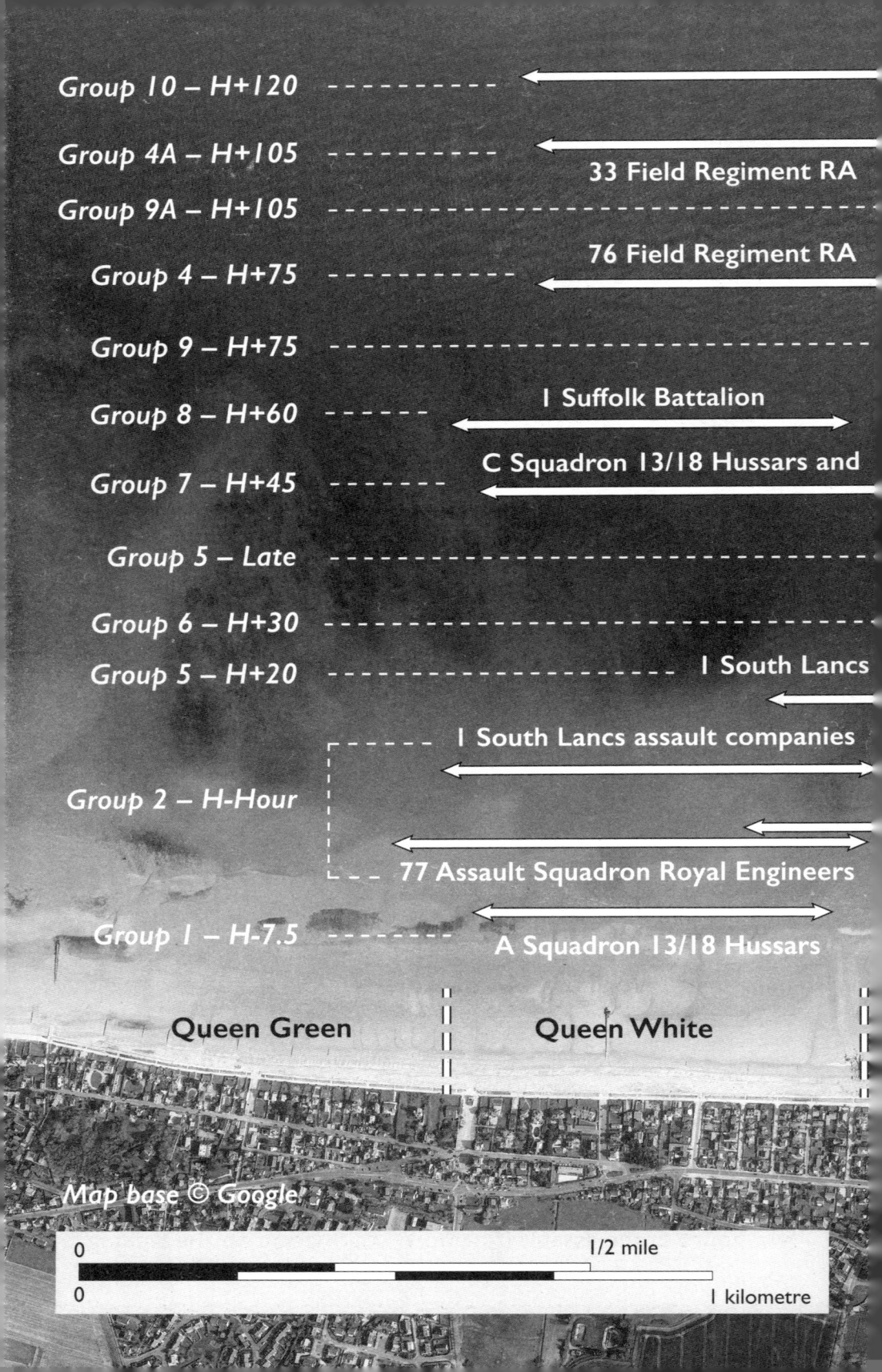

Group 10 – H+120
Group 4A – H+105
33 Field Regiment RA
Group 9A – H+105
Group 4 – H+75
76 Field Regiment RA
Group 9 – H+75
Group 8 – H+60
1 Suffolk Battalion
Group 7 – H+45
C Squadron 13/18 Hussars and
Group 5 – Late
Group 6 – H+30
Group 5 – H+20
1 South Lancs
1 South Lancs assault companies
Group 2 – H-Hour
77 Assault Squadron Royal Engineers
Group 1 – H-7.5
A Squadron 13/18 Hussars

Queen Green | Queen White

Map base © Google

0 — 1/2 mile
0 — 1 kilometre

Stores and second priority vehicles

45 and 3 Commandos

6 and 41 Commandos

first priority vehicles

2 East Yorks reserve companies

4 Commando

reserve companies

2 East Yorks assault companies

79 Assault Squadron Royal Engineers

B Squadron 13/18 Hussars

Queen Red　　　　　Roger Green

S3 ASSAULT GROUP BEACHING AREAS

The approximate location of each wave's landing during the first two hours of the assault (for more information on the landing timetable, see Appendix 4).

4 Commando landing area

8 Troop

Bag Drop

N

Map base © Google

0 — 1/2 mile
0 — 1/2 kilometre

THE ADVANCE INTO OUISTREHAM

4 Commando's advance into Ouistreham, commencing at approximately 08:20.

Strongpoint 10

Strongpoint 8

Casino

I Troop

Tram Station

C, D and A Troops

B Troop

Anti-tank ditch

E and F Troops

Ouisterham Locks

Hotel de Normandie

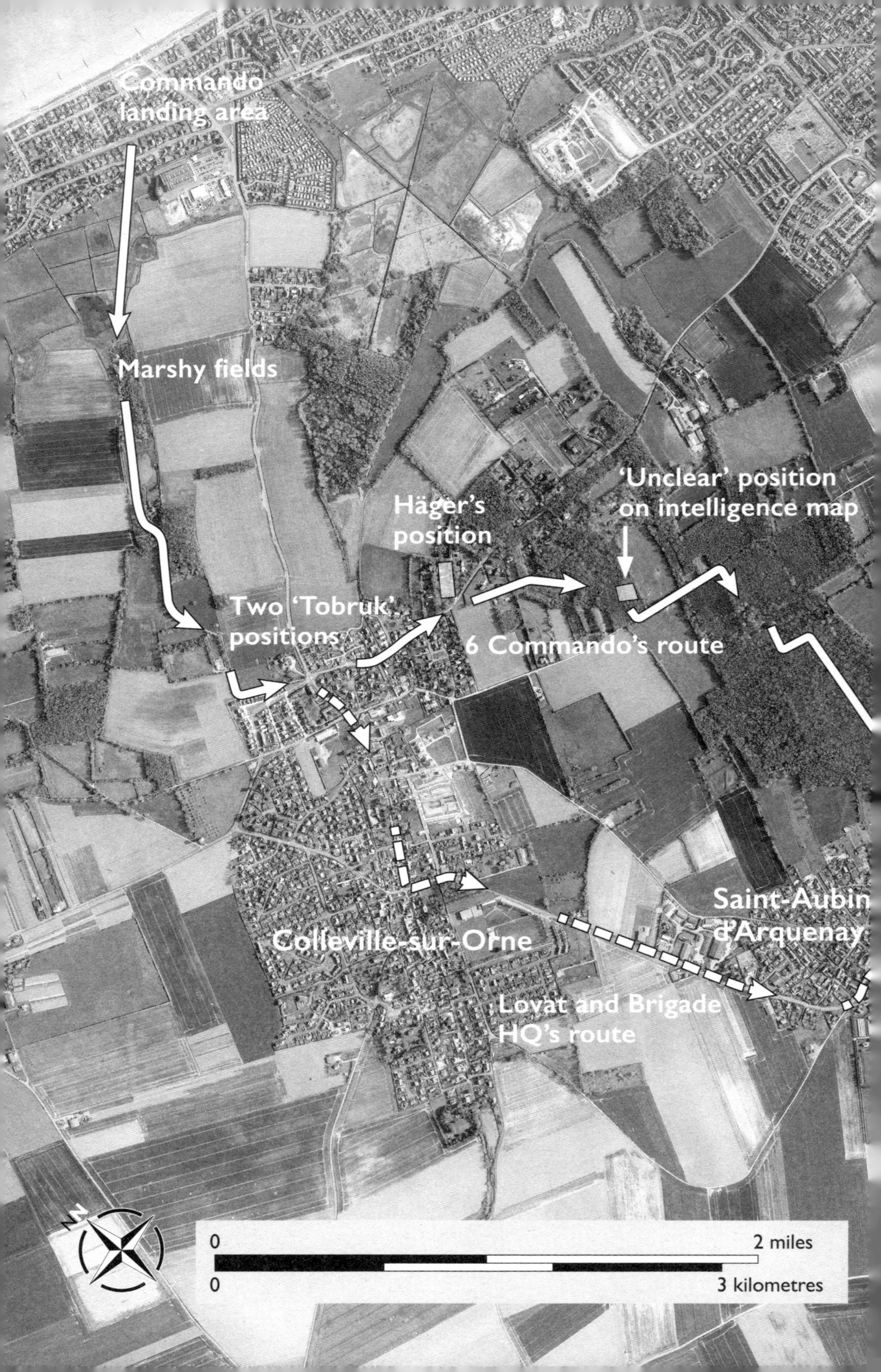

Commando landing area
Marshy fields
Häger's position
'Unclear' position on intelligence map
Two 'Tobruk' positions
6 Commando's route
Saint-Aubin d'Arquenay
Colleville-sur-Orne
Lovat and Brigade HQ's route
N
0
2 miles
0
3 kilometres

THE ADVANCE TO PEGASUS BRIDGE

6 Commando's advance on Pegasus Bridge, commencing at approximately 09:00.

Approximate position of battery

Pyman's route

Masters' route

le Port

Pegasus Bridge

Map base © Google

1 Suffolk's landing area

Planned 1 Suffolk forming-up position

Lieutenant Madden's orchard

Hermanville

1 Suffolk's route

2 East Yorks' route

D Company

Colleville-sur-Orne

Strongpoint 16 (Morris)

B Company

A and C Companies

Strongpoint 17 (Hillman)

0 — 1 mile
0 — 1 kilometre

EXPANDING THE BEACHHEAD

1 Suffolk's and 2 East Yorks' routes to the German strongpoints inland.

East Yorks' landing area

Strongpoint 14 (Sole)

Strongpoint 12 (Daimler)

Saint-Aubin-d'Arquenay

Map base © Google

THE BATTLE FOR LION-SUR-MER
1 South Lancs' and 41 (RM) Commando's advance inland.

Hermanville

1 South Lancs' advance through Hermanville

12 Platoon

Farm attacked by Sergeant Kilvert

Lieutenant Wilson and 12 Platoon

1 South Lancs

41 (RM) Commando's and A Company 1 South Lancs' advance through Lion-sur-Mer

Lion-sur-Mer

Exit 1

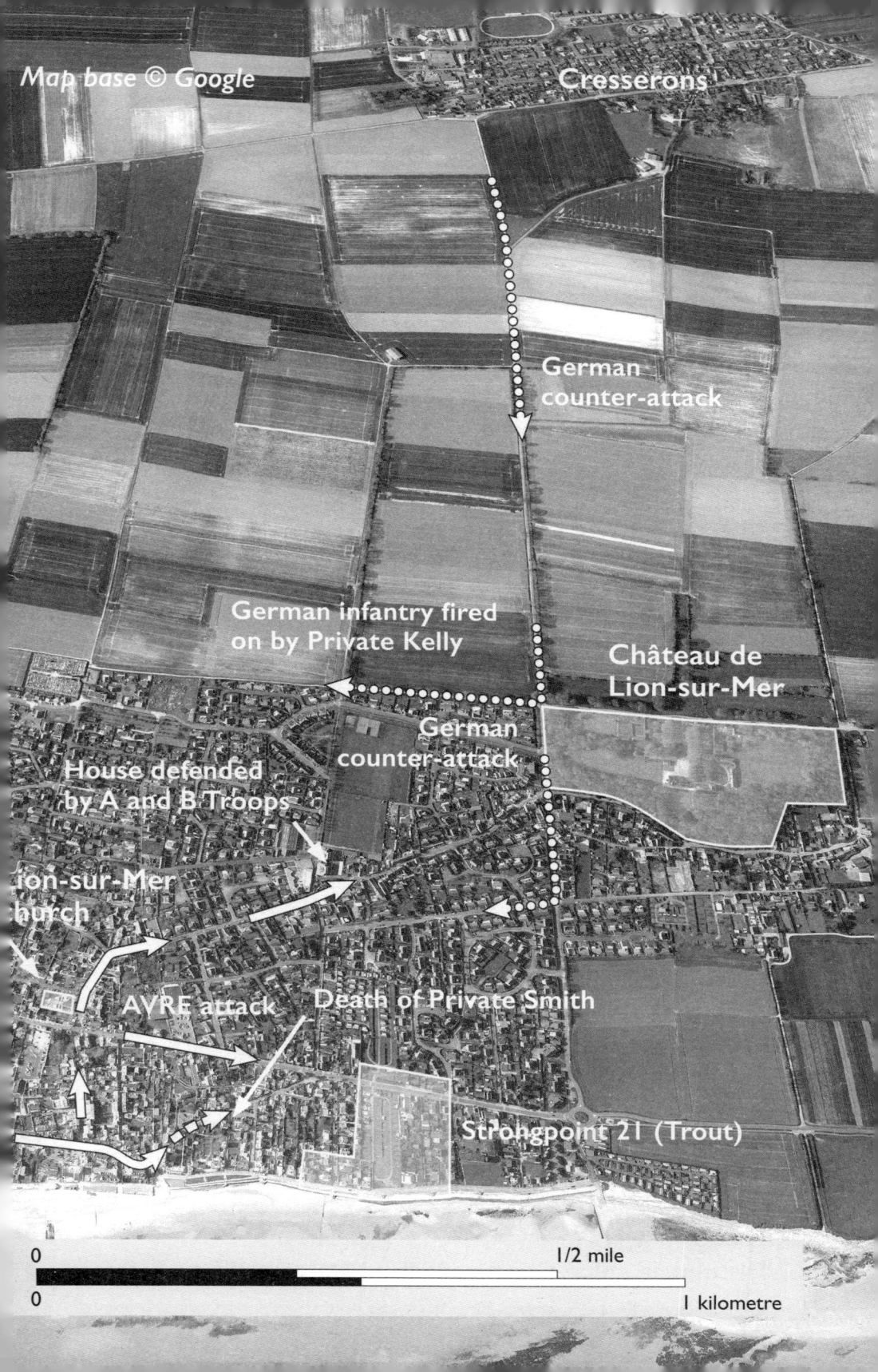

Map base © Google

Cresserons

German counter-attack

German infantry fired on by Private Kelly

Château de Lion-sur-Mer

German counter-attack

House defended by A and B Troops

Lion-sur-Mer church

AVRE attack

Death of Private Smith

Strongpoint 21 (Trout)

0 — 1/2 mile

0 — 1 kilometre

185 BRIGADE'S ADVANCE INLAND

The mobile column's advance from Hermanville to Lebisey.

THE GERMAN COUNTER-ATTACK

21 Panzer Division's strike north for the coast.

Map base © Google

Lion-sur-Mer

Douvres-la-Délivrande

Hermanville-sur-Mer

Cresserons

Oberst Rauch's battlegroup

B Squadron Staffordshire Yeomanry

Périers-sur-le-Dan

Mathieu

Beuville

Major von Gottberg's battlegroup

A Squadron Staffordshire Yeomanry

Biéville

Cambes

C Squadron Staffordshire Yeomanry

Epron

Oberst Oppeln-Bronikowski's battlegroup

Lebisey

0 — 3 miles
0 — 5 kilometres

OVERNIGHT POSITIONS
3 Infantry Division unit locations on 6/7 June.

Map base © Google

- Lion-sur-Mer
- 2 Lincoln
- 41 (RM) Commando
- Hermanville-sur-Mer
- Cresserons
- 101 Beach Group
- Ouistreham
- 1 South Lancs East Riding Yeomanry
- Colleville-sur-Orne
- 1 Suffolk
- Saint-Aubin-d'Arquenay
- Z Company 2 KSLI
- 1 KOSB
- Periers-sur-le-Dan
- 2 RUR
- 2 East Yorks
- 1 Norfolk
- Beuville
- Bénouville
- Biéville
- D Company 2 Warwick
- 2 KSLI Staffordshire Yeomanry
- Blainville-sur-Orne
- 2 Warwick
- Lebisey

0 — 3 miles
0 — 5 kilometres

Commandos of 1 Special Service Brigade HQ take cover during the advance towards Saint-Aubin-d'Arquenay. This may be during the ambush on I/736 Regiment's ration train.

An X class midget submarine surfaces in Holy Loch, Scotland in January 1944. At a mere 51 feet long, the submarine was not easily spotted even when surfaced.

PROLOGUE

23:15, 4 JUNE 1944

IN THE SWIRLING WATERS OFF THE COAST OF NORMANDY, 3.7 nautical miles north of the seaside town of Ouistreham, a dark metal hull suddenly broke the surface. Pitching and rolling in the swell, it did not look like any conventional boat – had anyone been around to see it they might have mistaken it for wreckage. But even if someone had been around it is doubtful that any but the keenest eyes would have seen this small object, even if it surfaced directly underneath them. A storm swept across the English Channel and dark clouds blotted out almost everything around. Barely a foot above the surface, and with waves breaking over it every few seconds, this diminutive little vessel was almost invisible.

Inside, hands weakened by inactivity grasped a wheel. With a creak it turned until a slight hiss emanated as the airtight seal was broken. The hatch was thrown open, and an exhausted figure clambered up and flopped his torso out on to the narrow deck. Cold sea air rushed into the interior of HMS X-23, followed by a cascade of spray. Feeling a little giddy from the rush of fresh air in his lungs, the midget submarine's commander Lieutenant George Honour lowered himself back through the hatch.

The other four occupants of X-23 lounged on the cramped deck within, breathing in the fresh air. But there was no time to lose. Once the stale, repugnant atmosphere inside the submarine – the result of more than nineteen hours underwater – had blown away, the hatches were closed and the submarine's motor was started up. Dead reckoning navigation had led them to the coast in darkness and, having taken several position fixes through the magnified periscope during daylight hours, Lieutenant Geoffrey Lyne RN, part of Combined Operations Pilotage Party (COPP) No. 9, had worked out their exact location from landmarks on the shore.

Ouistreham's lighthouse and church, along with the spires of the churches at Langrune-sur-Mer, Douvres-la-Délivrande and Saint-Aubin-d'Arquenay, revealed them to be a mere 1,000 yards from their intended target. Quickly the submarine motored north-west on the last leg of its mission and dropped its anchor.

Cautiously the hatches were opened again, enough to let the tiniest amount of cool night air filter into the submarine's compact interior. It was sufficient – any fresh air was an improvement on the thick, foul fug that prevailed. On the outside X-23 was 51 feet long, but inside the crew had a cabin barely 8 by 5 feet and just under 6 feet high. The only way to survive such a long period underwater was to periodically release pure oxygen, increasing the air pressure each time they did so. With so little space there had been no chance of any strenuous activity; conversation and anything that might use up precious air was kept to an absolute minimum anyway, and smoking was impossible. All the submarine's five occupants had been able to do was lie on the cramped deck and hope to sleep.

Now, somewhat revitalized, the men sat crouched, listening to their radio receiver. No message had come during the allotted time from 23:30 to midnight, but as the clock ticked towards 01:00 and the second listening watch, the men were quietly confident that they'd hear the confirmation signal that the operation was on schedule. So they sat, eagerly awaiting the codeword: Pomade.

Finally, not long after the hour, a broken transmission could be heard, but was barely intelligible. Honour ordered the gyro repeater compass to be switched off and the faint transmission could be heard fractionally more clearly. Silence descended inside the submarine as the five men listened anxiously to the message as it repeated.

'Hullo Padfoot, this is Niton,' said the crackling voice. 'Have message for you, message addressed 3 ALU from 3 EVO. Message reads Pretty.'

The crew were stunned. 'Pretty' meant that the operation had been postponed by twenty-four hours. Honour was appalled – what could possibly have gone wrong, he wondered?

While the crew absorbed the news, Honour knew they needed to get moving again. With no friendly ships coming for them that morning, they needed to submerge once more and put the submarine on to the seabed. Knowing they'd be there until 23:00 that night he took the opportunity that darkness presented and, one by one, hauled out the crew. Weak with tired and cramped muscles, some of the men had to be dragged through the hatch. The rough sea gave some clue as to the cause of the postponement, although that did nothing to improve the crew's mood. Sprawled on the submarine's hull, holding on to whatever they could, the men gulped in fresh air while Honour willed more of it into the submarine's interior.

Finally, just after 02:00, the men crawled back below, salt encrusted on their stubbly pale faces and around their bloodshot eyes. The hatches were sealed, the men went through the procedure to dive, and the submarine slowly descended through the waves. At 03:00 X-23 hit the seabed and the crew spread out as much as they could and prepared themselves for another long wait.

The decision to postpone D-Day had been made some twenty-one hours before, at an 04:00 meeting on 4 June at Southwick House, SHAEF's command post just north of Portsmouth in Hampshire. Weighing up the advice and opinions put to him about the weather, it was clear to the Supreme Allied Commander General Dwight D. Eisenhower that he had little choice but to postpone the overall operation. The timetable set for radio transmission watch on X-23 meant that there was no earlier opportunity to convey this to the men on board the midget submarine (nor, for that matter, her sister submarine X-20, lying off Juno).

But even before X-23 had surfaced late on 4 June, at 21:00 Eisenhower and his chief officers had sat down in the conference room at Southwick House once again. Group Captain James Stagg, one of the senior meteorologists, opened by explaining that the decision to postpone had been sound – sea conditions off the coast of Normandy were already worsening and an attempted landing on the morning of 5 June would surely have ended in disaster. Then Stagg offered some hope. A vigorous cold front was pressing south, even now approaching the south coast of England. From tomorrow afternoon it would most likely introduce much calmer weather over the Channel and well into Tuesday, 6 June. Winds would significantly decrease, cloud cover would probably be about 50 per cent and no lower than 2,000 feet. From Wednesday the weather may become unsettled again, but interspersed with considerable fair intervals.

The officers at the table leaned back in their chairs as they digested this news. Commander in Chief of the Allied Naval Expeditionary Force Admiral Bertram Ramsay spoke first, highlighting the need to signal the fleet almost immediately if those task forces with the longest journeys were to sail on time to make H-Hour (the time at which the first units would touch down) on 6 June. The pressing deadline hastened the conversation, and at 21:15 Eisenhower leaned forward. 'Well, I'm quite positive we must give the order,' he said, 'the only question is whether we should meet again in the morning. I don't like it, but there it is. I don't see how we can possibly do anything else.' General Bernard Law Montgomery, overall commander of the forces that would be landing in Normandy, opined that the only decision the weather experts could make at 04:00 the next morning was the position of the next depression. The other officers agreed, but all the same it was decided to confirm the decision in seven hours' time.

And so at 04:00 on 5 June, only three hours after X-23 had received the Pretty signal and an hour after she had settled on the seabed for her long wait, the senior officers tasked with delivering Operation Neptune gathered in Southwick House's old library. Stagg's predictions remained little changed, as did the opinions of the assembled party. Eisenhower sat in silence for a moment, turning over the various factors in his head while the weight of responsibility bore on his thoughts. After a few dozen seconds, he looked up.

'OK, we'll go.'

TOP SECRET

ONEAST/S.7B
Page 5.
21.5.44

ONEAST/S.7B - THE ASSAULT (Ctd.)

'SNAG-LINE' SWEEPS (Ctd.)

(a) 5¾ Knots = 750 RPM
(b) 7 Knots = 850 RPM
(c) 8+ Knots = 1000 RPM.

26. The safe distance for craft in the wake of craft using these sweeps is 250 yards.

27. Sweeps are to be hauled in as late as practicable before beaching and, if it can be avoided, are not to be cut or slipped owing to the danger of fouling the screws of succeeding craft.

POLICY FOR BEACH AND UNDERWATER OBSTACLES CLEARANCE.

28. An appreciation of the obstacles on QUEEN and ROGER Sectors, affecting landing craft, based on the latest information to date (May 1944) is given in ONEAST/S.18.

29. Commanding Officers of craft in the leading groups must necessarily be guided in their actions by what they find, but the policy to be followed should be as in paragraphs 30 and 31 below.

30. If the obstacles are thin enough to be overcome, no alternative landfall is necessary.

Action

(a) Major Landing Craft, proceeding at full speed, avoid obstacles if practicable; if not, 'bust' through.

(b) Minor Landing Craft avoid obstacles if practicable; if not, follow through the gap made by craft in (a) above. L.C.T.(AVRE), L.C.T.(A) and L.C.T.(CB) will have scrambling nets over their quarters to assist infantry in L.C.A. landing across them if necessary.

31. If all attempts to force the obstacles fail, an alternative landing must be attempted on an adjacent beach.

Action

(a) D.S.O.A.G. 'One' makes codeword "SCRUB" (See ONEAST/S.1 Appendix II) prefixed 'EMERGENCY', which will be re-broadcast by Naval Commander, Force 'S'.

(b) Succeeding Groups of Assault Brigade stop.

(c) Landing Craft of Group 2 haul off under cover of close support fire, and will be ordered by S.O.A.G. to assault again at a different place.

Men of C Squadron 13/18 Hussars wait by their tanks on Gravel Hill, Clanfield, while moving into their embarkation area on 31 May 1944.

PART I
THE WAITING

I
A SEASIDE RESORT

GENERALFELDMARSCHALL ERWIN ROMMEL STEPPED SMARTLY from his staff car and took the salute of Generalmajor Edgar Feuchtinger, commander of 21 Panzer Division. He walked with him down a track into the woods behind the small village of Lebisey, north of Caen, the two officers discussing the situation in France and the concerns of their superiors before they came upon the first ranks of 192 Panzer Grenadier Regiment.

Rommel inspected the regiment's units, patiently listening as various vehicles and weapons were explained. Radiating confidence, he strode upright and erect through the ranks of men, stopping to examine French vehicles that had been converted into armoured cars and self-propelled guns. The men were impressed by their leader, his presence providing some comfort despite their misgivings. It had not escaped their attention that they had been formed up in a wood rather than an open field as they once would have been – it told them all they needed to know about air superiority over Normandy.

Satisfied with what he had seen, Rommel and his entourage returned to their cars and motored north. Their journey took them into the valley below Lebisey, through the twin villages of Biéville and Beuville, and up on to the Périers-sur-le-Dan Ridge, passing vehicles parked in woods, gun batteries and strongpoints as they approached its broad crest. Ahead of them the land gently rolled away below and the view opened up to a stunning vista overlooking the coast, the blue water of the Seine Bay sparkling behind the green and light brown fields that ran down the coast.

The column drove on into Lion-sur-Mer, sweeping past the twelfth-century church and along the main road into strongpoint 21, the principal

German defence post in the town. Rommel and his party walked the last few hundred yards to the coast, where they found an armoured vehicle already parked on the track above the beach, positioned alongside the strongpoint's reinforced houses and coastal gun positions. The late morning sun was shining brightly, warming the men as the sea breeze gently cooled them. Tuesday, 30 May 1944 had turned into another fine day in Normandy.

The vehicle they had come to see intrigued the party. A heavily converted French Somua gun tractor, much of its bodywork had been refitted and the driver's cab replaced with an enclosed cockpit, complete with vision slits that could be closed to seal it. Behind the canopy was the reason for such precautions: a large rocket launcher, mounted on a rotating and elevating platform. Rommel eyed the launcher curiously, then joined his party a few yards away in front of one of the reinforced houses. The vehicle crew took their posts, loaded a dozen stubby rockets on to the rails and trained the launcher. There was a pause and then, with a magnificent whoosh, the rockets raced out to sea. The party watched as they tore through the sky, the cluster slowly fanning out and then arcing down until they crashed into the sea 500 yards away, hurling up great geysers of steaming water as they detonated. Impressed, the party inspected several more weapons among 21 Panzer Division's arsenal, but time was marching on and there were more sites to visit in the afternoon.

The officers returned to their cars and took a short drive to the Château de Lion-sur-Mer just outside the town. A grand fifteenth-century residence, it was now the reserve HQ of 10 Company 3 Battalion of 736 Regiment, part of 716 Infantry Division which defended this section of coast. When not in the comfortable château the men of 10 Company occupied three strongpoints on the coast, including 21 and, a little further east, 20, where Leutnant Nessel had his forward HQ. The officers lunched in the grounds outside and admired another modification of the Somua gun tractor: this time a bank of twenty 81mm heavy mortars had been fitted on to a turntable behind the cab.

Surrounded by senior officers from the two main divisions based in and around the coast north of Caen, Rommel took the opportunity to share his expectations with them. 'Gentlemen, I know the English from Africa and Italy, and I tell you that they will choose a landing site where they think we do not expect them to land. And that will be right here, on this spot . . . But it will not take place during the next two or three weeks.'

General Erich Marcks, commander of 84 Corps, listened, somewhat unconvinced. A few days later he shared his thoughts with one of his staff officers: 'From my knowledge of the English, they will go to church again next Sunday [4 June] and then come on Monday. For after Tuesday the next favourable tides will not come until 28 and 29 June.'

While the officers dined in the warm May sun, the men under Rommel toiled to complete the defences he had ordered. Oberschütze Ysker,[*] a tank driver in 1 Platoon 2 Company 100 Tank Regiment, had not seen his senior commander that morning – his entire platoon had been detached from 21 Panzer Division to assist with the construction of beach obstacles. So had the entirety of 315 Independent Company; previously attached to 100 Tank Regiment, they were now at strongpoint 18. Günther Fischer, like Ysker only nineteen years old, was contemplating deserting by now. An unenthusiastic soldier with little love for the Nazi regime, Fischer preferred to listen to Soldatensender Calais (the British propaganda radio station) than to read the propaganda coming out of his own country. At least the British played decent German music. Other men were even less willing: Franz Penewitz had been caught asleep on guard duty and now the private from 1 Battalion 192 Panzer Grenadier Regiment had joined fifty other men in a defaulter party digging defence positions around strongpoint 18.

Every day the men of the detached units toiled in the heat, dragging timber from the woodlands inland and raising great log ramps and stakes on the beaches. In front of the villas that lined the shore west of Ouistreham lines of steel, concrete and wood ran parallel to the coast. About 250 yards from the back of the beach were two rows of ramps – 10-foot-high timber tetrahedrons with the longer edge facing to the sea, ready to pitch an approaching landing craft on to its side. Behind the ramps, approximately 200 yards from the back of the beach, were two rows of erect timber stakes, each tipped with a jury-rigged explosive – usually a land mine or an artillery shell armed with a primitive contact detonator. Finally, just below the high-water mark, steel 'Czech hedgehogs' and concrete tetrahedrons threatened both landing craft at high tide and vehicles at low tide.

To the occasional French civilian who might be able to get close enough to the beach to see them, the obstacles looked impressive. To Fischer's commanders, they did not. The defenders had already stripped most of the suitable timber from woodland within a few miles of the

---

[*] An oberschütze was a senior private.

coast and they were running short. Similarly, there was simply not enough steel or concrete to thicken the defences to anything like the number desired to create an impenetrable barrier. With the defences stretched along miles of Normandy sand, the gaps between them were up to 60 feet in some places, enough space to drive a bus through. Or a landing craft.[1]

The last time Ouistreham had been invaded was in the eighteenth century and towards the end of a previous global conflict – the Seven Years' War, fought largely between France and Great Britain. On the night of 12/13 July 1762, a small British squadron appeared off the coast at the mouth of the River Orne. Boats were quietly lowered into the water and marines carefully clambered into them. Jack Tars and redcoats took up the oars and rowed into the river estuary, coming ashore at Sallenelles, where they quickly overpowered a small redoubt. Just as another party prepared to land across the river at Ouistreham the sound of cannon fire awoke the town's inhabitants. Stirred from his slumber, Michel Cabieu, a sergeant in the local militia, realized what the sounds meant and grabbed his musket. Rushing towards the shore he came across a drunken colleague and, realizing he was of no use to him, relinquished him of his drum.

For the next few hours Cabieu ran around the neighbourhood, shooting at any redcoat he saw, beating his drum and constantly changing his position to confuse the enemy. Worried and uncertain of the enemy facing them, the British advance faltered. As the flash of gunpowder continued to light up the sky the British detachments panicked, withdrew to their boats and rowed back to the warships. By morning the squadron was gone – the British incursion had been seen off.

Just how much of the defence of Ouistreham can really be attributed to Michel Cabieu is uncertain. There may have been – and probably were – several other members of the militia involved. Even the location of his defence is vague, with some accounts placing it in Sallenelles and Franceville, others in Ouistreham and still more in the Colleville marshes behind La Brèche – literally 'the Beach' – just west of Ouistreham. But whatever the truth of the matter, Cabieu became a hero, feted locally and even nationally. Even thirty years later French generals wished to make his acquaintance. After his death in 1804, streets in both Ouistreham and Caen were named after him, and even today Ouistreham's cinema carries his name. But a more significant legacy had come to the area in 1778 when, recognizing the threat to the Normandy beaches, King Louis XVI ordered the construction of three reinforced masonry redoubts: one at Franceville Plage, one in Ouistreham (both overlooking the river estuary) and another at La Brèche. By 1780 the three horseshoe-shaped redoubts were complete. But the British didn't return to Ouistreham. Instead the most significant event the forts witnessed was a visit by Napoleon in 1811. After he was exiled to Saint Helena in 1815 and peace settled across the Channel, they fell into disrepair. By 1840 they were in such bad condition that restoration was ordered, but their only occupants after that were the French customs service.

In the 1800s new visitors came to Ouistreham. In the first half of the century a canal was dug alongside the River Orne, reaching from the town into the heart of Caen. Merchants became much more frequent arrivals and the town grew. But in the second half of the century a different trade established itself. Only 120 miles from Paris and facing the sheltered Baie de Seine, Ouistreham was an ideal coastal resort. A villa was built on the shore in the 1860s – allegedly called Belle Rive ('beautiful shore'); the name eventually transposed itself on to the surrounding area as Riva Bella. As Ouistreham's popularity grew, so too did the villas along the shore, and eventually the length of the sandy dunes between Ouistreham and Lion-sur-Mer became populated with ornate wooden and masonry summer residences. By the end of the century a narrow-gauge railway connected the two towns and carried on to Luc-sur-Mer, and by the early twentieth century Ouistreham was a highly regarded destination. Spared from the destruction of the First World War it flourished, the addition of a municipal casino in 1929 only serving to heighten its attraction to French vacationers.

But from then on dark clouds began to gather over Europe, and when the British finally returned to Ouistreham in 1940, there was no chance of them staying. On 16 June, Lieutenant Cyril Cox answered the telephone in Milton Barracks to hear a voice ask how quickly the Royal Engineers could put together special demolition parties and get to Normandy. It could be done quite quickly, he reassured his caller, and early the next morning he awoke off Cherbourg with a small team under the command of Lieutenant Commander Grindle RN. Once ashore, the officers sought out the local French naval authorities and explained their mission – to deny the numerous oil storage facilities between Cherbourg and Caen to the advancing Germans. The French were unwilling comrades in this endeavour and the frequently changing situation to the east did little to temper emotions, but eventually Cox was given permission to take a small party to Ouistreham. After further delays in securing vehicles the small party set off with stores and men in a lorry, while Cox travelled in a requisitioned car with Second Lieutenant Arthur Barton. The authorities in Caen were even less helpful than those in Cherbourg and, sensing that he could achieve more in the port, Cox returned, leaving Barton and his men to drive into Ouistreham.

In Ouistreham, Barton was at least able to make more progress and, after careful and delicate discussions with the French authorities, received permission to destroy the oil storage facilities on the Caen Canal. Leaving his men on this wrecking mission, he was eventually able to get through to Cherbourg by phone and report his success to Cox, only to be informed that the German advance was sweeping up to Caen and that he should make all speed for Cherbourg. After patching up their failing lorry the party beat a hasty retreat along the bumpy coastal roads, past La Brèche and its fine villas overlooking the beach. Behind them, clouds of dense black smoke billowed into the air over the town, a harbinger of the doom that was to come.[2]

By 1944, the residents of Ouistreham were reluctantly accustomed to the new way of life that had begun four years earlier. Once France had surrendered and German occupation forces moved in, they had quickly made their presence felt. In Caen, the historic Caserne Lefèbvre became the central military establishment, the French evicted from their barracks so that the occupiers could move in. In the surrounding countryside and on the coast, châteaux were requisitioned to become headquarters for the various regiments deployed in the area.

Initially seen as something of a quiet sector, the Normandy coast had become more and more important as the years progressed. In 1942 and 1943 there had been some small-scale Allied raids along the shore of Seine Bay, and its position on the English Channel guaranteed plenty of naval action to the north. Even so, the anti-invasion defences in Normandy remained somewhat simple – the much-publicized Atlantic Wall had concentrated on strengthening the ports of Cherbourg and Le Havre into fortresses. When he was appointed Commander in Chief West[*] in the spring of 1943, Feldmarschall Gerd von Rundstedt ordered a comprehensive review of the defences along the coast of the Low Countries and

---

[*] Oberbefehlshaber West, usually abbreviated to OB West, which became the general name of the HQ itself.

France. The subsequent report was scathing, highlighting the near complete absence of defences anywhere except in Pas de Calais. In November, having accepted von Rundstedt's findings, Hitler took steps to improve the situation. His most immediate action was to appoint Rommel General Inspector of the Western Defences. In 1944 he was given command of 7 and 15 Armies.

Rommel set to work with his customary energy, inspecting hundreds of miles of coast, visiting units and assessing the best way to counter an amphibious landing, and lobbying for improved fortifications and beach obstacles. The dawn of 1944 saw new defences springing up all along the European coast. Engineer battalions became a more common sight in the Normandy countryside, soon to be accompanied by labourers from around Europe.

The principal of defence used on the coast needed to account for a lack of manpower. It was not possible to fortify every single yard of seafront, as there were simply not enough men to man that. Instead the defences took the form of a chain of strongpoints primarily centred on areas without natural defences (like cliffs or mudflats). While being independent, these strongpoints would be mutually supportive, with fields of fire that enabled neighbouring fortifications to contribute to each other's defence. A group would usually consist of a company-sized strongpoint and numerous platoon-sized resistance points.* Typically these fortifications were covered by batteries a little further inland that could engage both amphibious forces at sea and land units once they were ashore.

In the area around Ouistreham the principal elements of the much-vaunted Atlantic Wall in 1943 were the large coastal batteries. In front of Ouistreham itself, six 155mm guns on open emplacements guarded the mouth of the Caen Canal and River Orne. This was the westernmost battery of a chain that ran along the coast to Le Havre, with similar-sized batteries at Houlgate, Benerville and Villerville. At Le Havre itself even the Grand Clos battery's 380mm gun had sufficient range to fire on Ouistreham and its approaches.

As the fortification programme was stepped up in late 1943 and early 1944, concrete defences started to spring up all along the coast west of Ouistreham and in the countryside behind. The open artillery positions

---

* A group of strongpoints was a stützpunktgruppe. Stützpunkt referred to a company-sized strongpoint and widerstandsnest to a platoon-sized resistance point.

were slowly replaced with fully enclosed bunkers to protect the guns and gunners from plunging shells or bombs. A string of strongpoints emerged along the coast, the gaps between filled with thickets of barbed wire and thousands of skull-and-crossbone signs warning of minefields. Behind them new batteries, again with reinforced bunkers, emerged from the ground and the surrounding fields were sown with mines and clusters of tall timber posts designed to prevent gliders from landing.

While these works progressed, the units that would man them moved into place. The entire area fell under 7 Army, whose responsibility covered the part of France from Caborg (just east of the River Orne) inland as far south as Le Mans, and then west to Saint-Nazaire. The 45 miles of coast between Caborg and Carentan were initially the responsibility of 716 Infantry Division, first raised in Bielefeld in 1941. Never intended to be a mobile fighting formation in active combat areas, it was created as a static formation to defend the coast of France and as such lacked many of the typical formations of a combat division. It only ever had two regiments,[*] many of its men were generally poor quality, old or very young soldiers (in some companies up to half of the strength was made up of eighteen- to twenty-year-olds), and those who proved themselves able were frequently transferred. Over time, replacements came not just from Germany but occupied countries as well, and very few of its men had any combat experience. After deploying to France in 1941 it was posted to various parts of the north-west coast before it was assigned to 7 Army and Normandy. In 1943 it received a new commander, General Wilhelm Richter.[†] A veteran of the Great War and the Eastern Front, Richter took command just as the division found itself based around Caen with responsibility for the Seine Bay coast from Caborg to Carentan.

In March 1944 it was joined by 352 Infantry Division, which had been formed with the intention of deploying to the Eastern Front, but instead found itself in Normandy helping to prepare anti-invasion defences. Aware that 716 Division's area of responsibility was considerable, Rommel chose to split the zone into two, with 716 based around the 'Divisional Coastal Defensive Section: 7 KVA "H1" – KVA Caen zone'[‡] and 352 Infantry Division facing the 'Bayeux zone'. The Caen zone was further

---

[*] A regiment in the German army was equivalent to a brigade in the British.
[†] In 1943, Richter was a generalmajor, equivalent to a brigadier in the British Army. In April 1944 he was promoted to generalleutnant, equivalent to a major general.
[‡] Küsten Verteidigung Abschnitt 7 KVA 'H1' – KVA Caen zone.

subdivided into the Riva Bella and Courselles sectors, with the former then broken down into Luc-sur-Mer and Orne sub-sectors.

By May 1944 the defences in the Riva Bella zone were considerable. Between Ouistreham at the east end and Saint-Aubin-sur-Mer (Juno sector) in the west were no fewer than ten coastal strongpoints. Strongpoint 7 defended the locks where the Caen Canal met the sea, with a number of bunkers and reinforced machine gun positions covering all the approaches. Strongpoint 8 had encompassed the original coastal battery at Ouistreham and added a number of smaller artillery pieces, machine gun nests and strong personnel shelters. Work was continuing to construct fully enclosed bunkers for the six 155mm coastal guns, although several of them were still on open emplacements. The whole site was surrounded by thick rings of barbed wire, and a deep anti-tank ditch blocked access from the landward side. Should a landing be made in front of the strongpoint a number of flamethrowers had been installed at the top of the beach, ready literally to provide a hot reception. The strongpoint also incorporated the old beachfront casino, which had been demolished to ground level and the basement turned into a reinforced fortification.

A little further west, strongpoint 10 placed a reinforced 75mm anti-tank gun facing west along the shore in the direction of La Brèche, supported by a 50mm gun with a more open field of fire. A little over 1,000 yards west of this, strongpoint 18 replicated the arrangement, with its 75mm gun providing flanking fire for the much larger strongpoint 20 a short distance west. This sizeable stützpunkt consisted of more than twenty individual gun positions, bunkers and machine gun and mortar pits, connected by a network of trenches and surrounded by a veritable jungle of barbed wire. Almost 400 yards from east to west, strongpoint 20 dominated La Brèche with a 75mm gun, two 50mm guns, a 37mm gun and 81mm mortars. Strongpoint 20A, a little further west, was a strongpoint in name only, but a number of gun pits and reinforced houses presented no small obstacle. Further west, strongpoint 21 placed another 75mm and 50mm gun on the coast, while a 50mm gun inland covered the main coast road. Strongpoints 24, 26 and 27 defended Luc-sur-Mer, Langrune-sur-Mer and Saint-Aubin-sur-Mer respectively.

Artillery support came in the form of two batteries. Strongpoint 12, behind Ouistreham, housed a handful of artillery pieces, while 16 housed 100mm guns. Both were in the process of being reinforced, and at least two guns at each battery had been installed in thick concrete casemates.

But the planners tasked with defending Normandy realized that more than a simple line of beach defences was necessary, and with the Riva Bella zone lying directly north of Caen, many more defences sprung up in the fields behind the beaches. The northern approaches to the town of Colleville-sur-Orne were peppered with personnel pillboxes and bunkers, while a little to the east strongpoint 14, a more substantial command post, was installed on a small area of high ground and controlled the road between Colleville and Ouistreham. Alongside the Caen Canal a nest of bunkers was installed in an old quarry at strongpoint 11. Elsewhere, urban areas were assigned strongpoint identities, although little had yet been done to enhance them.

The most significant addition inland was strongpoint 17. Sitting on the Périers-sur-le-Dan Ridge it had visibility over almost every route south from the beach. Like strongpoint 20 it housed a collection of individual personnel bunkers, machine gun posts and mortar pits, all surrounded by barbed wire and minefields. It was also the main battle HQ of 716 Division's 736 Regiment, just forward of their more ornate headquarters in Beuville Château.

By the start of May 1944, Richter's 716 Division had a total strength of a mere 7,770 men. The Riva Bella zone was largely the responsibility of 736 Regiment, commanded by Oberst Ludwig Krug.* Consisting of three battalions, each of four companies, the regiment fielded several thousand men, although this was still far short of the ideal numbers required to defend the sector. 1 Battalion was awkwardly split across the River Orne, with 1 and 3 Companies defending the beachside resorts of Merville and Franceville Plage on the east side, while 2 and 4 covered Ouistreham and Colleville-sur-Orne on the west. The arrangement was far from practical, as the only means to cross the river and canal was at the bridges nearly 4 miles inland.

2 Battalion was in the Courselles sector alongside the sister 726 Regiment. 3 Battalion was stretched across nearly 6 miles of beach, from La Brèche all the way to Saint-Aubin-d'Arquenay. While 11 and 12 Battalions were inland at Cresserons and Douvres-la-Délivrande respectively, 9 Company covered almost 4 miles from Saint-Aubin to the western edge of Lion-sur-Mer. 10 Company, approximately 160 men, were tasked with defending Lion-sur-Mer to La Brèche. This meant splitting the three platoons along 2 miles of beach in strongpoints 20, 20A and 21, with the

---

* Oberst was equivalent to a full colonel in the British Army.

result that strongpoint 20, a company-sized fortification, was defended by little more than a platoon of infantry.

The infantry had support from 716 Division's artillery units which manned the guns at strongpoints 12 and 16, and operated several self-propelled and towed gun batteries, and by 1260 Coastal Artillery Regiment, which manned the guns at strongpoint 8. Additional infantry support of a sort came from 642 Ost Battalion (literally 'East Battalion'), formed of conscripts from occupied Eastern European countries, primarily Poles. The battalion was not officially part of 736 Regiment but was assigned to support it, and already many men from the unit had been transferred into 736 Regiment's companies.

Further inland, more substantial support was based around Caen. As well as enhancing Normandy's physical defences, Rommel had thought hard on the best German response to an invasion. Von Rundstedt believed that any invasion could not be held back at the beach and that the best counter was to hold armoured formations well inland and use them in traditional counter-attacks on land battlefields, where all the advantage of terrain and encirclement could be capitalized upon. Such a strategy had the advantage of holding the valuable armoured divisions well out of range of Allied naval bombardment, but after his experience at the end of the North African campaign, Rommel knew that Allied air superiority was an even greater threat. To his mind the only way to successfully repel an amphibious assault was to do so with massed firepower on the beaches. When both ideas were put to their leader, Hitler wavered between the options, finally deciding on a solution that pleased no one. The main armoured reserve, 1 Panzer Corps, would be held near Paris. Of the armoured divisions under von Rundstedt's command, he turned three over to Rommel, but this was a wretchedly small number for the amount of coast his armies defended.

In April 1944, Rommel had Edgar Feuchtinger's 21 Panzer Division transferred to Caen, where they would be in a better position to respond quickly to an invasion in the Caen and Bayeux zones. Although 21 Panzer had fought under him in Africa, this was a completely different formation: the original had been destroyed in Tunisia and a newly raised armoured division had taken the name in 1943. By 1943 German industry was incapable of producing enough armour to supply all its divisions, so instead the division was to be primarily equipped with vehicles captured from the French in 1940. Tanks, half-tracks, gun tractors and armoured cars were all converted for new functions, principally as infantry carriers, mobile artillery and anti-tank guns for the two regiments of mechanized infantry. The division also fielded a panzer regiment that was partially equipped with German Panzer Mk IV tanks – a tried and tested model that was the most numerous in the German army – alongside French models. 21 Panzer Division was therefore at least a true division in size and fielded some 17,000 men, although like 716 Division, many of these were young and at least 15 per cent were Volksdeutscher conscripts from occupied countries. Most of the division's units were dispersed south of Caen, but at least one battalion of motorized infantry, some artillery and engineer units and the entire anti-tank battalion were positioned behind 716 Division, north of the city.[3]

For four years the occupants of Normandy had watched their German occupiers with varying attitudes. But even in the darkest days of the occupation there was an undercurrent of hope among the Normans. When Mademoiselle Pigache, a retired schoolmistress from Bénouville, visited a shop in Ouistreham she collided with a tall, smart German officer in the doorway. As her parcels scattered across the pavement, the officer apologized profusely and bent down to gather them up. Evidently embarrassed, he quickly thrust the parcels into Pigache's hands, clicked his heels, saluted and strode off. Inside the shop Pigache tried to collect her wits, confused by the officer's abrupt behaviour. Then it hit her – the officer had apologized in English. When she heard a rumour in early 1944 that a high-ranking visit to a German position at Sallenelles had been duplicated a week later, causing considerable suspicion that the first visit might not have been made by genuine Germans, she thought of her confusing encounter, and secretly clung to the thought that perhaps the British had been there all along.[4]

2
A FORCE IN WAITING

CAPTAIN BUSH EYED THE YOUNG RNVR OFFICER STANDING IN front of him with faint disdain. At twenty-five, Lieutenant Philip Barber was almost half Bush's age and – so it appeared – lacked the experience needed to instil discipline in his crew. The young officer had only been in command of HM Landing Craft Flak 34 (LCF 34) for two months, yet in sailing up the east coast to Invergordon had lost four men from his Royal Marines detachment who had deserted not once, but three times. They were now locked in the forward well deck of LCF 34 and, somewhat predictably, were refusing to follow orders. By all reports the rest of the Royal Marines detachment were barely any better.

Eric Bush had been busy since his war had begun at Dunkirk in 1940, when he was Captain Auxiliary Patrol and responsible for minefields in the Dover Straits. Having taken command of the cruiser *Euryalus* in early 1941, he had spent two and a half years in action in the Mediterranean. Now, only two weeks after his return to the UK, he found himself in the cold of Scotland's east coast and appointed Senior Officer Assault Group (SOAG) S3, part of the mysteriously titled Force S. Under him were hundreds of officers like Barber, hostilities-only men who were yet to see any action. A cursory glance at his file told Bush all he really needed to know: after commissioning as an officer, Barber had spent most of his time either studying or working at the various Combined Operations training establishments on Scotland's west coast; all his previous commands had been in training flotillas.

To Bush's mind the only problem on LCF 34 was Barber. Knowing what was needed, he proceeded to tear a strip off the young officer, lecturing him on the subject of discipline. What the men on the landing craft needed was proper command, an authority figure to keep them in line. A disciplined ship was a happy ship.

Barber bristled as Bush spoke, waiting patiently for sufficient pause to interject. His time on Scotland's west coast had at least taught him a thing or two about confronting senior officers, especially regular Royal Navy officers who might perhaps feel a certain superiority over their lesser 'Wavy Navy' colleagues.* When at last the captain finished and leaned back in his chair, he took a deep breath and laid the conduct sheets of his Royal Marines detachment on the desk in front of him. In a calm voice that belied his nerves he made his defence: 'I accept full responsibility for the discipline in my ship, Sir, but I request that before making your judgement you will look at these conduct sheets. You will note, Sir, that every man has been in detention since joining the Corps. Some even have been in civil prisons. The four deserters now being held in my well-deck have all served time for serious crimes. With a detachment where I can trust only the NCOs what more can I do, Sir, in a small ship where these men constitute the majority of the crew? You'll also note that none of my sailors have been in trouble since I took command.'

Bush frowned and picked up the sheath of papers. As he flipped through each conduct sheet the true horror of Barber's predicament became plain. Words like theft, assault and desertion were repeated almost endlessly – the four deserters had indeed all served serious time. His heart sank. A few malingerers could be expected on any vessel, but not an entire crew, not all on one ship. Bush looked up at the young lieutenant much more sympathetically. 'I'm sorry, Barber, I appear to have misjudged you. You seem to have done your best in an impossible situation. Leave these sheets with me. I intend to phone the Admiralty immediately and get to the bottom of this. No small ship should have been sent this detachment. Return to your ship and I will arrange for your four deserters to be put into detention here ashore.'

Much relieved, and somewhat taken aback by the fact an RN captain had just apologized to him, Barber crisply saluted and strode out of the room. In fact, the Royal Marines detachment who would man the anti-aircraft guns on board his converted LCF really were the dross of HMS

---

* Wavy Navy is a reference to the wavy cuff lace used in the Royal Naval Volunteer Reserve. During the war, almost every officer commissioned into the Royal Navy was actually commissioned into the RNVR. Any officer with the straight lace of the RN (like Bush) was almost certainly a pre- or early war regular officer.

Westcliff, the corps' manning station at Southend-on-Sea. Faced with a collection of petty criminals and malingerers, the commanding officer had quickly got rid of them as soon as the opportunity presented itself, despatching them all to the next LCF to be commissioned. Bush's investigation saw the base's commanding officer and sergeant major dismissed from the base and reduced in rank.[1]

Such were Britain's armed forces in 1944. Led by a high-calibre cadre of pre-war and battle-hardened professionals, the Royal Navy, British Army and Royal Air Force had absorbed hundreds of thousands of volunteers and conscripts, very few of whom had any experience in the roles into which they were thrust. Some had acquitted themselves well, while others were just competent. But recruiting from the entirety of British society meant that many were simply incapable, and others were the scrapings from the bottom of the barrel. The armed forces were a true cross-section of the British population. And now they were preparing for the invasion of North-West Europe.

In the autumn of 1943, no one in Force S yet knew where this invasion would take place – it was only known to a relatively small planning team under Lieutenant General Frederick Morgan and the senior officers he reported to. Morgan had optimistically been appointed Chief of Staff to the Supreme Allied Commander (COSSAC), even though the Supreme Allied Commander had not yet been selected, and been tasked with establishing the feasibility of an invasion and identifying the most suitable time and location for it to take place. Working within a framework that limited the likely forces available for such an operation, Morgan's team had finally identified the coast of Calvados, Normandy as the most suitable area. Nestled in the waters of the Baie de Seine, its broad beaches offered a relatively sheltered area for amphibious operations. Although without any major ports, Cherbourg and Le Havre might be captured by ground forces relatively quickly. It was within the range of fighter cover flying from the south coast of England, and crucially was only 100 miles from the Solent, the south's largest sheltered anchorage.

Morgan's outline plan had been accepted at the Quadrant Conference in Quebec in the summer of 1943 and given the codename Overlord. With an intention finally established, planning began to ramp up quickly to launch an invasion of Normandy in May 1944, which would require new strategies, tactics and equipment. It would also require significantly more landing craft than there were available in 1943.

Morgan's team had identified three stretches of beach on the Calvados coast suitable for landings, and envisaged landing three divisions on them in a preliminary assault. Codenamed 313, 308 and 307, their boundaries roughly corresponded with what would eventually become Omaha, Gold and Juno sectors respectively. By September 1943, 21 Army Group had allocated Force S to 307 sector, where they would land the 3rd British Infantry Division so that they could drive on to the Norman city of Caen – Calvados's capital and a vital communications centre, with roads stretching out from it like spokes from a wheel hub. 3rd Canadian Division would land on 308 and secure high ground along the Caen–Bayeux road, while an as yet unspecified US division would land on their right flank, probably also in 308 sector. Morgan cautioned that three divisions did not seem adequate for the task, but he was hamstrung by the limits set by the chiefs of staff.

Even in December, planning was still on the basis of a three-division landing in May 1944. However, that was about to change. More than 1,400 miles away in Morocco, the first seeds of doubt were sown in the mind of General Bernard Montgomery. Having just been informed that he would take charge of the land campaign in the coming invasion of North-West Europe, he arrived in Marrakesh on the evening of 31 December where he met with General Dwight D. Eisenhower, himself just appointed as the Supreme Allied Commander. The two only spoke briefly – there was little time to review the COSSAC plans for Overlord in any detail, and Eisenhower had only seen them in scant detail himself when he was shown an outline plan in October. Eisenhower too felt that three divisions were insufficient for the task, but as he would fly to the US early the next morning he instructed Montgomery to go to London and communicate his misgivings about the size of the landing force to the planners. He was to analyse and revise the plans and have his new proposals ready for Eisenhower's arrival in the UK in mid-January. Later that day Montgomery met Winston Churchill, who had been taken ill after the Tehran Conference and had remained in North Africa. Churchill asked Montgomery to give his early thoughts on the plans and, not known for his wild antics at parties, Montgomery spent the night of New Year's Eve studying them before providing the Prime Minister with a short paper the next morning. The following day he started back for the UK and began planning. Just under three weeks later, on 21 January 1944, Eisenhower arrived in the UK and approved his plans.

In essence, both Eisenhower and Montgomery felt it essential to expand the landing area from a three-division to a five-division front. History judged them right, but at the time this caused a minor panic for the Royal Navy. The large expansion of the invasion and uncertainty about the availability of ships of all types caused considerable anxiety. Even in the joint naval plans issued in February, convoy details had to be left blank, and it wasn't until 20 March that there was sufficient certainty to allow the allocation of vessels to the invasion plan to be finalized. The expansion of the landing area was also a problem for the planners. Looking again at the work done by COSSAC and using new intelligence being gathered by stealthy raids and reconnaissance along the coast, new sectors were identified.

On 1 February the first new plan was issued, under the codename Neptune.* In it, three sectors were identified – the East Cotentin Area at the base of the Cherbourg peninsula, the Caen Area from the Vire Estuary to the Orne Estuary, and the South Seine Area from the Orne to Villers-sur-Mer, approximately halfway between Ouistreham and the Seine Estuary. At the same time the number of naval task forces increased to seven. Force O became part of the Western Task Force and was joined by Force U and follow-up group Force B. In the Eastern Task Force, Forces J and S would now be joined by Force G and Force L, the follow-up force.

Fortunately, the expansion of Operation Neptune had also led to its postponement. It was immediately accepted that there would simply not be sufficient landing craft available for a five-division landing in May. A delay to June would free up more landing craft from the Mediterranean theatre and allow both the US and the UK to complete more LSTs and LCTs in their shipyards.

As the plan was revised, the landing areas became more focused. The Western Task Force became the primary American contribution while the Eastern Task Force was British.† On 2 March a new boundary was established at Port-en-Bessin, delineating these two areas of responsibility.

---

* While Neptune is often described as the naval plan behind Overlord, in fact both codenames were for the same thing – to secure a lodgement on the continent from which further offensive operations could be developed. In essence, Overlord was the intention, while Neptune was the detailed plan to achieve it.
† No slight is intended upon Canadians in this distinction. British and American sectors were the terminology of the time, and 3rd (Canadian) Infantry Division operated as part of 1 Corps, a British formation. Additionally, when factoring in the British units that landed at Juno on D-Day and the primarily Royal Navy force that put them there, Juno quite possibly had a larger British presence than Canadian.

The western extent of the old Caen Area was renamed Omaha and the East Cotentin Area became Utah. The eastern half of the Caen Area became Gem, and the South Seine Area became Band. In a series of meetings the final landing areas for each task force were hammered out, and on 13 April Gem area was divided into three new areas – Gold, Juno and Sword.*

Technically there was no 'Sword Beach'. Sword was one of the six 'areas' along the Normandy coast (from west to east Utah, Omaha, Gold, Juno, Sword and Band). The entirety of this coastline had been divided into smaller 'sectors' based on a phonetic alphabet – hence Able, Easy, Jig, Mike. The allocation of Able to Roger sectors to the original Caen Area suggests that these names were initially allocated by COSSAC, or at least before 1944 when Montgomery revised the plans. The South Seine Area (Band) received a new allocation from A to D and East Cotentin Area (Utah) P to W, suggesting these two areas were given sector identities later. At any rate, Sword Area had four sectors: Oboe in the west (alongside Juno), Peter, Queen and then Roger up against the Caen Canal and the west edge of Band. Each individual sector was further divided into beaches, with Green to the right (starboard) as the amphibious force faced it from seaward (and therefore on the west side of the sector), and Red to the left (port, and east). In some cases, where the beach was particularly wide or its geology needed further division, a White Beach would sit between the Red and Green Beaches.

Sword Area had not been entirely ignored by Morgan and COSSAC. The beach itself between the Orne Estuary and Juno was as good for landing on as the rest of the beaches in the Eastern Task Force area, but there were other factors that counted against it. Offshore a significant rocky bank restricted landings in front of Lion-sur-Mer, and further west, steep 15-foot limestone cliffs prohibited any landing closer to Juno. To the east the beach was much flatter, which would force landing craft to touch down much further out to sea. The town of Ouistreham also presented a formidable obstacle to landings: not only would the town be

---

* Although not overtly stated, it is evident from the chronology of the plan amendments that Utah and Omaha were named for the existing Forces U and O in March, and Gold, Juno and Sword for the existing Forces G, J and S in April. No reason for these names is given in the amendment, but clearly they utilized the letters of the task forces when choosing them. Interestingly, there is nothing in the amendments to suggest that Juno was ever intended to be called Jelly, and although Band remained as a designated area, no task force was assigned to it.

easier to defend, but it would be much harder to pass through and advance inland. There was also a significant coastal battery in front of the town, known to the defenders as strongpoint 8 and codenamed Bass by the British planners. As well as Bass, Sword Area and the sea in front of it also fell within the range of no fewer than five other heavy coastal batteries, including those at Le Havre, a problem that was not as severe further west at Juno, Gold or Omaha.

COSSAC had suggested the possibility of landing commandos close to Ouistreham, possibly supported by airborne forces, to neutralize Bass. But landing an entire assault force was a different matter and would require significantly more space. The planners pored over the available intelligence for the area, inspecting maps, aerial photographs, and even people's holiday snaps and postcards for every detail that could make each metre of beach useable. Beach gradients, obstacles, German defences, roads off the beach and their quality, the terrain behind the beach road and roads inland, all was inspected as thoroughly as possible, until the planners were satisfied that there was an area capable of landing a division upon. The selected area – Queen Red and White Beaches – was small, measuring only 1,585 yards (or 0.9 miles) from east to west. Although this could be expanded on to Queen Green and Roger Green – depending on the tide and as obstacles were demolished and defences neutralized – such a narrow landing area for the initial assault meant that there was only space to land one assault force or one infantry brigade at a time. In contrast, at Juno and Gold there was space to land two brigades side by side simultaneously. The narrow front was a considerable handicap. Only being able to land one brigade at a time limited the speed at which men and vehicles would be able to advance inland and secure their objectives. It would also be a considerable hindrance to the Royal Navy – there was less flexibility for their landing craft if Queen Red and White became unusable. If some of the landing craft waves were slow to clear the beach, or their wreckage obstructed it entirely, there were few alternatives to turn to. In the final orders, issued shortly before D-Day, the designated alternative beach was Juno. Even without any hindrance, it was realized that the incoming tide would significantly narrow the landing area as the day wore on. It would be important to get as many troops and vehicles off the beach and inland as quickly as possible.

Rear Admiral Arthur Talbot was appointed commander of Force S on 11 October 1943. A career officer and veteran of the First World War, Talbot had commanded no fewer than three aircraft carriers in the early years of the Second World War and served as naval aide-de-camp to King George VI. His experience on the staff of the Royal Navy's War College and as director of the Anti-Submarine Warfare Division gave him more than enough experience of planning and he was well thought of by Admiral Bertram Ramsay.

Force S was not the most inspiring name for a new naval task force, but it followed a well-established pattern in the Royal Navy. Force H, formed in 1940 and operating from Gibraltar, had achieved considerable fame during the pursuit and sinking of the German battleship *Bismarck*, but had primarily been created to provide escorts for Mediterranean convoys before it was disbanded in 1942. Force Z had sailed to Singapore just before Japan attacked Pearl Harbor, and then been destroyed only a few days later when bombers sank HMS *Prince of Wales* and *Repulse*. Force J had been created as an amphibious assault force for Operation Rutter in July 1942. Rutter was eventually cancelled but its basic premise was carried out as Operation Jubilee (the raid at Dieppe) in August. Although Force J was cut down to little more than a bare staff team following the raid, it was reconstituted in 1943, and along with Force S and the newly created Force O it was instructed to prepare for an invasion of North-West Europe in 1944.

There was little to Talbot's new command at first: a headquarters was set up at Cameron Barracks in Inverness and various buildings around the Moray Firth were acquired, but there was little in the way of repair facilities, supplies, amenities or even accommodation for his fleet. All of these would have to be found – and quickly. The following month the headquarters of 3 Division moved up to Scotland and joined Talbot in Cameron Barracks. On 12 December, Brigadier Thomas Rennie, a competent officer who had commanded 154 Infantry Brigade in North Africa and Sicily, was promoted to major general and appointed General Officer Commanding 3 Division. For the next few weeks the various regiments of the division moved up to join their HQ and a variety of ships sailed into the firth.

Despite the long build-up to the invasion, the entirety of Force S would only ever come together when it reached the French coast. But the true heart of the task force had been able to assemble in Scotland – the landing craft. Almost every type so far invented in the war would take part in Neptune, and Force S employed almost all of them. The landing craft were almost entirely Royal Navy vessels with some support from the US

Navy, but the crews represented a far broader range of nationalities, with many Commonwealth men who had joined the Royal Naval Volunteer Reserve serving on board.

The landing craft were purpose-designed for different loads and tasks and could principally be divided into two types – major and minor landing craft. Major landing craft were generally capable of crossing the English Channel by themselves, while minor craft would need to be carried in the davits of larger ships or towed across. In the main, minor landing craft carried infantry, while major landing craft might carry infantry or vehicles.

The oldest landing craft used at Sword was still the navy's principal assault vessel, appropriately named the Landing Craft Assault (LCA). Designed in the late 1930s by Thornycroft for the Inter-Service Training and Development Centre (ISTDC, a forerunner of Combined Operations) with the infantry platoon in mind, the 41-foot boat could carry a load of thirty-five fully equipped men in addition to its four-man crew. With its small bow ramp it was limited to infantry only, but it would be the type used by the assault companies landing in the first wave and, as such, seventy-eight LCAs were assigned to Force S. A similar-sized boat was the Landing Craft Personnel (Large) – LCP(L) – an American design. The boat was slightly shorter than the LCA and lacked a bow ramp, so they would not be used to land assault infantry. Nonetheless, twenty would be employed with Force S as despatch boats and navigation leaders.

LCAs and LCP(L)s were organized into flotillas, the size of which was usually determined by the parent ship that carried them. They were too small to cross the Channel themselves – for D-Day they would be carried in the davits of larger troopships, classified as Landing Ship Infantry (LSI). Unlike purpose-built landing craft, LSIs tended to be pre-war ferries and passenger liners that were converted to become troop carriers. One of the largest LSIs in Force S was HMS *Glenearn* – at nearly 10,000 tons, she could carry up to twenty-four LCAs and around 1,500 men, more than double the capacity of some of the smaller LSIs.

The other infantry carriers in Force S were major landing craft. The Landing Craft Infantry (Small) – LCI(S) – which could carry 102 men in addition to its seventeen crew was basic in the extreme, built by wooden boatbuilders to designs created by Fairmile, more famous for their motor torpedo boats. The Landing Craft Infantry (Large) – LCI(L) – could carry 250 fully equipped men in seats, or accommodate 185 men on bunks in addition to nineteen crew. Both disembarked men over gangway ramps that would be pushed over the high bow of the landing craft once it had hit the beach, which was far from an ideal way to get the men ashore. According to the manual, with practice the full load of an LCI(S) could be disembarked in one and a half minutes and 250 men could be unloaded from the LCI(L) in a mere three and a half minutes. The men landing from them on D-Day would find these to be wildly optimistic figures. Two flotillas of twenty-six LCI(S)s and five flotillas totalling forty-two LCI(L)s were assigned to Sword although technically, even though they would be sailing with Force S, the LCI(S)s were part of Force J.

The most important type of major landing craft used on D-Day was the Landing Craft Tank (LCT). First developed in 1940, the LCT went through a rapid development which accelerated when the US came into the war. By 1944 there were six marks of LCT, four of which were used on D-Day and three in Force S. The LCT Mk 3 was somewhat outdated by 1944, and crucially was not designed to operate on Norman beaches. Built in 1941, it was meant to operate on a beach gradient of 1 in 50 and it was only later in the year, when serious planning for a return to Europe commenced, that it was realized that landings would probably be conducted on beaches with gradients between 1 in 100 and 1 in 200. Accordingly the LCT 4 was designed to operate on a 1 in 150 beach gradient and was much better suited to the long shallow beaches of Normandy. When the US came into the war they had no LCT of their own, but quickly began building a new design drawn up by Thornycroft which became the Mk 5. Perhaps unsurprisingly the LCT 4 was the most numerous LCT deployed on D-Day, with just under 400 taking part – nearly 50 per cent of the entire LCT force deployed, and 117 of which were assigned to Force S. LCT 3s were still of use, and had more space for the top-secret swimming Sherman DD tanks on their deck. As they were not intended to beach, they were perfect for carrying and launching the 13/18 Hussars' DD tanks, and nine were assigned to the task force. The Mk 5 would see service as well, primarily for the Royal Marine Armoured Support Group (RMASG). A raised ramp was built on the fore end of the tank deck, allowing the Royal Marines' Centaur tanks to fire over the bow ramp as the landing craft advanced towards the beach.

Much larger than the LCT was the Landing Ship Tank (LST), a vehicle carrier with an enclosed tank deck and space for vehicles on the upper deck. With its bow doors and high freeboard the LST was an ocean-going vessel and was, like the LCT, vital to D-Day's success. Such was their significance that the loss of two LSTs and the damage caused to another two from Force U when German Schnellboote (E-boats) attacked Convoy T5 in April 1944 prompted concerns they might derail D-Day. LSTs were too big and slow to land in the immediate assault wave and would be used to unload vehicles once the beach was captured. To save them from becoming stranded on the beach, most towed Rhino ferries which would be used to transport their load to the shore without the LSTs needing to run on to the beach themselves.

Vast numbers of other landing craft had been converted to fulfil specialist roles. Experience in the Mediterranean had shown the value of dedicated HQ ships with sufficient communications facilities to command and control the fleet and individual assault waves. In Force S, Talbot would sail in HMS *Largs*, a former French merchant ship that was acquired by the Royal Navy after France fell. After conversion, with dedicated spaces for commanders, map and operations rooms, radar and extensive wireless facilities, she had already served as an HQ ship at Operations Torch and Husky in the Mediterranean. Other HQ ships included HMS *Dacres*, a converted *Captain* class frigate. To fit her out as an HQ ship her aft gun turret and all her depth charge gear were removed to provide additional accommodation for officers and staff. Originally intended to serve as the HQ ship for S3 – the assault wave – shortly before D-Day her forward motor room flooded. The cause couldn't be determined and, such was the concern that there might have been foul play, a police investigation was launched. No satisfactory explanation was forthcoming, but the damage was sufficient for *Dacres* to be swapped with HMS *Goathland*, a *Hunt* class destroyer originally intended to sail with S2 – the intermediate wave. To control individual assault waves in S3, two LCI(L)s were also converted into Landing Craft Headquarters (LCH). Troop space was turned into signals offices and operations rooms, and antennae were installed in a large dome for the Type 970 radar, mounted in a large tripod mast above the bridge that looked like it might threaten to capsize the boat.

The LCT was ideal for conversion to a number of roles. Its shallow draught and large tank deck made it an incredibly suitable platform for mounting artillery that could be placed close inshore to pound shore installations. The Landing Craft Gun (LCG) was one such conversion, with two 4.7-inch naval guns on the deck crewed by Royal Marines detachments. The Landing Craft Flak (LCF) was similarly designed to carry 2-pounder and Oerlikon anti-aircraft guns. Primarily used for AA defence in the Mediterranean, there was an expectation they would also engage shore targets on D-Day. Perhaps the most fearsome conversion was the Landing Craft Tank (Rocket) – LCT(R) – which covered the entire tank deck of an LCT Mk 3 with 1,044 5-inch rockets. These could be launched in twenty-four salvoes at targets ashore as much as 3,500 yards away, saturating an area up to 1,000 yards in depth. A similar modification was made to the much smaller LCA, equipping it with twenty-four 'Hedgehog' spigot mortars (usually fitted to convoy escorts as an anti-submarine weapon) intended to be launched at a beach to detonate minefields. Fittingly, the conversion became known as the Landing Craft Assault (Hedgerow), or LCA(HR).

Far more vessels would ultimately sail with Force S. 1 and 15 Minesweeping Flotillas, with their *Halcyon* and *Bangor* class minesweepers, would clear passages through the German minefield running the length of the English Channel, while the *Catherine* class boats of 40 Minesweeping Flotilla and the smaller wooden motor minesweepers and BYMS of 115 and 165 Minesweeping Flotillas would lead bombardment ships to their berths off the coast of France. These bombardment ships included thirteen destroyers, the majority of which were the seven modern S class ships of 23 Destroyer Flotilla, which itself included two destroyers commissioned into the Royal Norwegian Navy. The minesweepers would also lead the separate Force D bombardment force, consisting of the Royal Navy battleships HMS *Warspite* and *Ramillies*, as well as the monitor *Roberts* and five cruisers, including the Polish ORP *Dragon*. Convoy escorts would include frigates, sloops and corvettes, motor torpedo boats, motor launches and anti-submarine warfare trawlers.

Although the supporting vessels of Force S had numerous objectives – to clear sea lanes, to dominate the seas and to neutralize enemy shore positions – the bulk of the task force was an amphibious assault force whose primary objective was to land 3 Infantry Division on Queen Red and White Beaches.

The first British infantry divisions were formed in Portugal in 1809 during the Peninsular War. Until then the infantry brigade had been the de facto army formation, but in 1809 the Duke of Wellington combined these to form larger units complete with their own dedicated supporting arms, organizational staff and supply services. In effect the new divisions were small armies under a single commander who answered directly to

Wellington. Although the size of the constituent formations, the technology of the supporting organizations and the division's place in the British Army's structure have changed considerably over the last 200 years, the division as a basic military organization remains much the same.

3 Infantry Division (3 Division) could trace its lineage back to the first formations of 1809. Although all of the divisions formed in Portugal had winked in and out of existence for varying periods after the Peninsular War came to an end, 3 Division had remained active longer than most, seeing service at Waterloo and in the Crimea and South Africa. Then, just over a hundred years after it was created, it was thrust into action in France in 1914. Although it had been known since Waterloo as 'The Fighting Division', under the command of General Aylmer Haldane at battles such as Ypres and the Somme it acquired the name 'The Iron Division'.

Four days before Germany invaded Poland and started the Second World War in Europe, 3 Division received a new commander. A veteran of the First World War, Bernard Law Montgomery had remained in the army through the 1920s and 1930s, and after organizing an amphibious landing exercise in 1938 had impressed General Sir Archibald Wavell enough to be promoted to major general and given command of a division. After briefly commanding 8 Division in Palestine he returned to the UK and his new command, just in time to take it to France as part of the British Expeditionary Force (BEF).

Having previously commanded 9 Infantry Brigade, which along with 7 and 8 Brigades made up 3 Division's infantry strength, Montgomery was no stranger to the division. Even so, when he took command he was horrified by some of the ill-discipline he found, to say nothing of the state of the entire BEF. By October 1939, Montgomery had issued new memorandums on discipline, and while the division waited for action during the inappropriately named Phoney War in the winter of 1939/40 he instigated a rigorous training regime, making sure the men were well prepared for their role when the time for action came. Determined to instil a sense of pride in them, he also revived the division's 'Iron' nickname and devised a new divisional insignia of three black triangles, representing the three infantry brigades, surrounding an inverted red triangle. The nickname and divisional insignia remain in use to this day.

When Germany finally attacked the Low Countries and France in May 1940, 3 Division and the rest of the BEF made their planned manoeuvre and advanced into Belgium. When the Germans made a second, surprise push through the Ardennes, 3 Division, along with the rest of the BEF and several French divisions, were cut off from their allies to the south and, as the German net tightened, they retreated to the west. In several defensive actions, at the River Escuat, Roubaix and the Yser Canal, the division fell back on Dunkirk. Holding the line at Furnes, just inland from La Panne, 3 Division covered the evacuation for two days before embarking on ships at Dunkirk. Despite all they had gone through, the Iron Division had maintained its cohesion to the end, remaining as a complete unit despite the chaotic nature of the evacuation and re-forming in Frome, Wiltshire by 10 June. In the materiel-starved climate of the time there was no means to re-equip the entire BEF. Instead almost everything the army had was issued to 3 Division, with the intention of sending them back to France to continue the fight. Only the French capitulation on 17 June prevented the division's redeployment to Normandy.

In July 1940, Montgomery was promoted and moved up to 5 Corps. Two years later he found himself in North Africa and fame quickly followed as he led the Eighth Army to victory in the desert. But while their former commander travelled widely, spearheading the British advance in the Mediterranean, for four years 3 Division would not leave the UK.

In early 1943 rumours circulated that they would be deployed to the Mediterranean to take part in Operation Husky (the invasion of Sicily), but before they had moved to Scotland to commence training the frustrating news came through that they had been ousted by 1 Canadian Division. It was a blow to the division that had sat through endless stories in the press about the success of other divisions, but despite the temptation to seek a transfer to another unit very few men did, certain that eventually their time would come. Later in the same year, the division received an assurance that they would be a spearhead formation in the anticipated invasion of North-West Europe. To avoid confusion with the Canadian 3rd Infantry Division, which would also be an assault division, the British formation assumed the title 3rd British Infantry Division for the rest of the war.

In 1944, the heart of 3 Division was its three infantry brigades – 8 Infantry Brigade (under Brigadier Edward Cass), 9 Infantry Brigade (under Brigadier James Cunningham), and 185 Infantry Brigade (under Brigadier Kenneth Pearce Smith) – represented by the three black triangles of the divisional insignia. These were standard brigades, each comprised of three infantry battalions, a small HQ comprising staff and administrative groups, a single platoon for defence and a light aid detachment to assist in the recovery of vehicles and equipment from the lower formations. 8 and 9 Brigades had been with 3 Division since before the First World War, but 185 Brigade had only been raised in 1942 and transferred to 3 Division in early 1943.

As a result of British military tradition the infantry battalions each had their own identity, based on the regiments of the army. These were much older formations than the division, dating to a time when aristocrats or professional soldiers would form and recruit their own military units. Unsurprisingly, many of these came to be identified by the English counties they came from, and over time the battalion emerged as the standard unit formation for a regiment. It was frequent for a regiment to raise more than one battalion – especially in wartime – but less frequent for battalions of the same regiment to serve alongside one another. The East Yorkshire Regiment, for example, had four battalions before the war and raised another three during it. 1 Battalion served in the Far East, 2 served with 3 Infantry Division, 4 (there was no third battalion) was captured in North Africa, and 5 landed on Gold Beach with 50 Infantry Division on D-Day. The 6 and 7 wartime battalions served in the UK, and 50 was assigned to 46 Infantry Division in the Mediterranean.

Although names and traditions varied considerably among these regiments, their basic structure was much the same. Led by a lieutenant colonel, a battalion consisted of an HQ company, four infantry companies and a support company. The HQ company was largely managerial, consisting of signal and administrative platoons to support the battalion's commander. The rifle companies were each commanded by a major who had his own small HQ section, including signallers and snipers, that oversaw three thirty-seven-man infantry platoons. Each platoon was overseen by a single officer, usually a lieutenant or second lieutenant, assisted by the platoon sergeant. Three ten-man rifle sections were each commanded by an NCO who had six riflemen and a Bren gun team under him. Each platoon also had a signaller and an orderly, often employed as a runner and usually the officer's batman. A three-man team carried the platoon's 2-inch mortar and ammunition and usually a PIAT anti-tank weapon issued by the company. The battalion's support company was equipped with all the vital supporting arms the regiment needed. Perhaps the most important was the anti-tank platoon, equipped with six 6-pounder anti-tank guns and twelve Loyd carriers to tow them and trailers of ammunition. Although not as powerful as the 17-pounder anti-tank gun, the 6-pounder was more than capable against most armoured vehicles, although it would struggle to penetrate the frontal armour of some of Germany's latest tanks. The mortar platoon had six 3-inch mortars and the carrier platoon thirteen light machine gun-equipped Universal Carriers (often described as Bren Carriers). The pioneer platoon had two specially trained assault sections for tackling obstacles and fortifications, and a pioneer section with men trained in various trades useful in the field, including skills such as carpentry, stonemasonry and even bricklaying. At full strength an infantry battalion was about 850 men strong.

Within 3 Division, 2nd Battalion the East Yorkshire Regiment (2 East Yorks), 1st Battalion the South Lancashire Regiment (1 South Lancs) and 1st Battalion the Suffolk Regiment (1 Suffolk) formed 8 Infantry Brigade. 9 Infantry Brigade was made up of 2nd Battalion the Lincolnshire Regiment (2 Lincoln), 1st Battalion the King's Own Scottish Borderers (1 KOSB) and 2nd Battalion the Royal Ulster Rifles (2 RUR). Finally, 185 Brigade consisted of 2nd Battalion the Royal Warwickshire Regiment (2 Warwick), 1st Battalion the Royal Norfolk Regiment (1 Norfolk), and 2nd Battalion the King's Shropshire Light Infantry (2 KSLI).

The division was much more than just the infantry brigades, though. In keeping with the original Napoleonic concept of a small army, it fielded artillery as well. The Divisional Royal Artillery consisted of three field regiments, each of twenty-four guns, providing the division with a total of seventy-two guns – in 3 Division these were 7, 33 and 76 Field Regiments. Although lacking the colourful names of the infantry battalions, each regiment was individual and composed of three independent batteries, each made up of eight guns split into two troops. In some regiments these might be towed artillery pieces – in 3 Division's case they were equipped with 105mm self-propelled 'Priest' guns. In addition was an anti-tank regiment with four batteries, each with twelve anti-tank guns organized into three troops of four. In 3 Division's case, 20 Anti-Tank Regiment was equipped with forty-eight M10 tank destroyers – 3-inch guns mounted in turrets on top of a tracked vehicle, almost indistinguishable from regular tanks. 92 (Loyals) Light Anti-Aircraft Regiment completed the Royal Artillery's contribution to the division. In addition, 2 Middlesex Battalion was the division's machine gun and heavy mortar battalion.

Four Royal Engineers units were attached to the division – three field companies and a field park company. The field companies were organized in a similar way to the infantry companies, but their work was minesweeping, bridge building, obstacle clearance, demolition and ordnance disposal. The men were not intended to fight as front-line infantry, but they were naturally trained to fight, and in 3 Division the men of 246 Field Company would be landing at H-Hour with the assault infantry. 15 Field Park Company provided more rear-echelon support in the form of engineers, labourers, builders, even decorators. Divisions also fielded Royal Army Ordnance Corps (RAOC), Royal Army Service Corps (RASC), and Royal Army Medical Corps (RAMC) units for logistical and medical support. Numerous additional companies were attached to 3 Division for D-Day.

Principal armoured support for 3 Division came from 27 Armoured Brigade, an independent brigade made up of former cavalry units that had been converted to armoured formations early in the war and by 1944 were equipped with the ubiquitous Sherman tank. Formerly part of Major General Percy Hobert's 79 Armoured Division, the brigade became an independent formation in late 1943 and was attached to 3 Division for the assault. The structure of an armoured brigade was in some ways similar to an infantry brigade with three regiments (broadly equivalent to battalions) – in 27 Armoured Brigade these were 13/18 Royal Hussars (Queen Mary's Own), the Staffordshire Yeomanry (Queen's Own Royal Regiment), and 1 East Riding Yeomanry. Each regiment was organized into an HQ squadron and three fighting squadrons, with each squadron made up of four troops, each usually of four tanks. The HQ troop might swell the squadron up to twenty tanks in total. The regiment's HQ was a substantial formation in its own right, consisting of the commander's tank, Royal Artillery observation post tanks, a reconnaissance platoon of eleven light tanks (Stuarts in 27 Armoured Brigade), an anti-aircraft platoon of eight tanks equipped with anti-aircraft guns instead of the main armament, a liaison platoon of five to ten armoured cars, and an administration platoon of some twenty trucks carrying fuel, ammunition and spares. The structure of 27 Armoured Brigade meant it could easily be broken up to support the three infantry brigades of 3 Infantry Division. 13/18 Hussars would support 8 Infantry Brigade, the Staffordshire Yeomanry were allocated to 185 Brigade, and the East Riding Yeomanry would land with 9 Brigade.

But there was considerably more armour attached to 3 Division for the assault. The Royal Engineers allocated two assault squadrons from

79 Armoured Division to Sword Beach, each squadron made up of four troops of four Churchill tanks modified to become AVREs (Armoured Vehicle Royal Engineers). Joining them were twenty-six Sherman 'Crab' mine-clearing flail tanks of 22 Dragoons, and together these vehicles would clear the beaches of obstacles while the AVREs could use their 29mm Petard mortars to demolish walls and even concrete gun emplacements (as long as they fell within its range of some 100 yards). 5 Royal Marine Armoured Support Group added a further four troops of five tanks that would primarily be used in the initial assault.

Also accompanying 3 Division were the commandos. Their organization differed from the regular infantry, reflecting their intention to be a light, mobile fighting force. Each unit (confusingly called a commando) was commanded by a lieutenant colonel and was broadly similar to a battalion, but smaller and lacking vehicles and many supporting arms. The commando HQ included signals, intelligence, administrative and a small transport section. Below them were five troops, the equivalent of a battalion's companies. Each was led by a captain with a small HQ team and below him were two sections, each commanded by a lieutenant and consisting of two assault teams, a mortar group and sniper. Support for the commandos came from the heavy weapon troop's 3-inch mortar section and a machine gun section. Sometimes equipped with Vickers medium machine guns, for D-Day most commandos were equipped with the lighter and more versatile Vickers K-gun and had been liberally issued with PIATs and even Boys anti-tank rifles, often considered obsolete by 1944 but still with its uses. At full strength a commando was approximately 460 men. No fewer than five commandos would accompany 3 Division to Sword Beach – 3, 4 and 6 Army Commandos of 1 Special Service Brigade under Brigadier the Lord Lovat, accompanied by 41 and 45 (RM) Commandos of 4 Special Service Brigade, the former attached to 3 Division and the latter to 1 SS Brigade, and elements of 10 (Inter-Allied) Commando.

To bring order to the inevitable chaos on the beaches, 101 Beach Sub Area was attached to the landing forces. This formation was principally responsible for organizing naval and land traffic on the beaches and for setting up the primary Beach Maintenance Area, consisting of storage dumps of ammunition, fuel and supplies that were arriving from the sea. 101 Beach Sub Area consisted of two Beach Groups (5, the primary group, and 6, the reserve), each made up of personnel from all three arms of service. The Royal Navy commando units would be responsible for managing the arrival of landing craft while the RAF Beach Flights oversaw the passage of RAF supplies necessary to establish advanced landing grounds. The army supplied an entire battalion of infantry along with RAMC, RAOC, RASC and RE units to work the beaches. Each Beach Group added several thousand more men to the landing force and by the time the army's assault force for Sword was complete it had swelled to the size of nearly two full divisions of men and vehicles.

Operating high above Sword, support would come from both the Royal Air Force and the US Army Air Force. 3 and 6 Groups of Bomber Command, primarily equipped with Lancasters and Halifaxes, were tasked with overnight raids to neutralize enemy coastal batteries both in Sword sector and along the coast to the east, while the US Eighth Air Force's Third Bombardment Division consisting almost entirely of B-17 Flying Fortresses would hit batteries, strongpoints and lines of communication just before the landings began and again throughout the day. On the night of D-Day the RAF would return to hit enemy targets inland of the beaches.

The Second Tactical Air Force would provide principal air cover during the day, with squadrons of fighters, fighter bombers and light bombers prowling the skies and attacking targets of opportunity. Squadrons were allocated schedules to ensure there was constant coverage over the beaches – as one squadron departed to refuel, another was just arriving to take their place.

All through the winter of 1943/4, 3 Division and Force S trained together. Although no one realized it yet, the coast around the Moray Firth and at nearby Burghead were ideal training grounds, with wide shallow beaches that fairly represented the shores they would land on in Normandy. In Exercises Burger 1 and 2 they practised making an amphibious landing and the Beach Groups studied the methods of marshalling the troops within the beach sub-area. Exercise Smash was due to be conducted in January 1944 but when foul weather blew up it was first postponed and then cancelled. When Exercise Grab was conducted a few days later the weather turned equally bad, but this time COs Arthur Talbot and Thomas Rennie decided to proceed and land 3 Division at all costs. Troops were violently ill and landing craft smashed on to the beach to disembark soaking, freezing men who waded through the icy waters seeking shelter from the elements. But the exercise proved that even in the worst conditions they could get the job done.

Exercise Crown in February was conducted along the expected lines of the assault when Force S landed in France. 8 and 185 Brigades would land alongside each other, each with two assault battalions up front followed by their third in reserve, in effect placing four battalions in the first waves; when they had cleared the beach, 9 Brigade would come ashore. But once Eisenhower and Montgomery agreed to expand the invasion area from three beaches to five, Force S was moved to the narrower beachfront near Ouistreham. Accordingly Exercise Anchor, conducted later in the month, tested the idea of landing the three brigades one at a time – 8 followed by 185, with 9 in reserve.

In between the group exercises the units trained individually. Night marches were followed by mock street fighting and navigation exercises. Individual battalions would sail the Moray Firth and practise disembarking in different conditions, while tanks practised on the ranges and 13/18 Hussars' crews practised sailing the most unlikely of vessels. But these exercises were not without risk and a number of their secret vessels, along with their crews, were lost in the Moray Firth.

The final group exercise held in the Moray Firth was Leapyear, carried out in late March. Effectively the final test for all the units that were present in Scotland, it was also affected by the weather to the extent that after navigating in the North Sea to practise the passage, the invasion force put into Cromarty Firth for a brief postponement. After a day of idling on ships the troops eventually approached the beach the following morning and, despite the delay, the landings were conducted without any serious problems. Both Force S and 3 Division prepared for their move south in confident spirits.

The final exercise was less about training and more of a rehearsal for the invasion. Exercise Fabius was designed to replicate not only the landings but also the embarkation of the thousands of men and vehicles for all five assault forces landing on D-Day. For the first time the troops practised the process of moving from their camps and barracks inland to marshalling camps near the coast, then trundling in convoys to specific embarkation points to meet the ships that would take them to the landing beaches. After a lengthy navigation along the south coast, Force S deposited the men on the beaches between Littlehampton and Bognor in Sussex.

As COSSAC's plans had been passed through the grinder of 21 Army Group and then Montgomery's amendments, the plan for Sword emerged in a series of spurts, changing priorities, learned experiences from training exercises and inevitable compromises that saw the final plans only completed in May: Force S's naval plan, arguably the most important, was only completed on the 21st, two weeks before D-Day. According to 1 Corps' Operation Order the overall objective for the forces landing at Sword sector on D-Day was, along with 3 Canadian Division, to secure a covering position inland roughly in line from Putot-en-Bessin (inland of Juno) to Caen (roughly along the line of the Caen–Bayeux road), and then along the River Orne to the sea. To achieve their part in this plan, Force S was to land 3 Division on Queen Red and White Beaches so that the ground forces could advance inland to secure Caen and a bridgehead over the Orne south of the city. In this they were considerably handicapped by Queen Red and White's narrow landing area and the restriction of landing one brigade at a time. In any amphibious assault it is practically impossible for a formation to deploy its full strength at once, but at Sword it would take longer than at Gold or Juno, where there was sufficient space for a two-brigade front.

Force S's plan was complex but intended to deliver the ground forces as quickly as possible. Along with the rest of the invasion force, Force S would begin loading troops and vehicles at the end of May. The very first regiments would embark vehicles five days before D-Day (D-5), although the vast majority of the invasion force would embark on D-3 and D-2. Embarkation would continue on some ships on D-1, even after the first elements of the force had sailed.*

The bulk of the embarkation would be carried out in the Solent, with troops primarily loading from six specially built embarkation ramps in Gosport and from piers and quaysides in Portsmouth, Hampshire. One part of the assault group, S2, would embark further east at Shoreham-by-Sea and Newhaven in Sussex, while the bulk of the commandos would embark further west at Warsash on the River Hamble. Force D, the bombardment force, would meet Force S in the Channel after sailing from Greenock, Scotland, through the Irish Sea and around Land's End. One convoy would sail from Dover, while some of the elements of Force L (the follow-up force) bound for Sword sector would load at Tilbury on the Thames; others would sail from Portsmouth behind Force S.

On Sunday, 4 June, the main force would sail in a number of separate

---

* When the orders were issued and the embarkation was carried out, the intended date of D-Day was 5 June. As such, D-5 was 31 May and D-1 was 4 June.

convoy groups, although they would not be the first to make their way to Normandy. The lead vessel of Force S would not be a battleship, a sleek destroyer, a landing craft or even a minesweeper. Two days before the main force sailed, it was X-23, the midget submarine with five men aboard, that would be towed halfway to the invasion beaches by a tug. Once it had reached the German minefield that ran the length of the English Channel it would continue independently to a position off Queen Red and White Beaches and wait on the seabed. On D-Day its task would be to surface and signal to the incoming amphibious assault force in order to ensure they made an accurate landfall.

The first of the assault convoys to leave the south coast would depart the Solent at H-21 hours 40 minutes (i.e. twenty-one hours and forty minutes before H-Hour, the time at which the first units would touch down). With H-Hour and D-Day provisionally set for 06:20 on Monday, 5 June, the earliest departure would be at 08:40 on 4 June.

The average speed of the landing craft convoys would be approximately 5 knots, so in the middle of the English Channel the faster minesweepers would take the lead, even though they departed later. Commander Harry Nicholls' 1 Minesweeping Flotilla, operating *Halcyon* class ships, would carefully clear channel number 9 through the minefield, while Commander Herbert Lewis's 15 Minesweeping Flotilla and their *Bangor* class ships would sweep channel number 10 (channels 1 to 8 were assigned to the task forces bound for the other four beaches to the west). The entrances to these two channels were marked by two Harbour Defence Motor Launches (HDMLs) so that the assault forces could safely follow the sweepers through, and they would remain behind them until they reached a position approximately 9 nautical miles from the beach. This position would become the primary staging area for the amphibious assault force, known as the 'lowering position' on account of it being where the larger landing ships would lower their minor landing craft into the water. Moving into position on their eastern flank, Force D would take up positions from which to bombard enemy coastal batteries behind the landing area and east of the River Orne. As they did so, five squadrons of Lancasters of 3 Group RAF would bomb Ouistreham to neutralize the coastal battery at strongpoint 8, codenamed Bass, while 6 Group bombers would hit batteries along the coast leading to Le Havre.

Force D would take over once the bombers had departed, and while they suppressed the gun batteries, the amphibious assault force would deploy to begin the invasion. To help them to the beach, an area of flat land with few natural distinguishing features, they would be guided by members of the Combined Operations Pilotage Parties (COPPs), experts in navigation and reconnaissance. As well as being embarked in the lead ships, a COPP party was waiting in X-23. While the landing craft made their approach to the beach, a screen of destroyers positioned approximately 2.5 nautical miles from the shore would commence a bombardment along the length of the coast, targeting strongpoints and bunkers. In this they would be supported by Eighth Air Force's Third Bombardment Division, which would hit targets on the beach and inland just before the landings began.

The main landing force was divided into three assault groups, each landing one infantry brigade and one armoured regiment as well as numerous attached units. Group S3 under the command of Captain Eric Bush would carry the main assault force, primarily consisting of 8 Infantry Brigade, 13/18 Hussars, beach clearance teams of the Royal Engineers, the commandos and the Royal Artillery. The navy would land them in nine separate waves over the course of the first two hours of the invasion.

The structure of an armoured regiment meant that it could be easily divided between the battalions of an infantry brigade. A Squadron 13/18 Hussars would support 1 South Lancs, B Squadron were allocated to 2 East Yorks, and C Squadron to 1 Suffolk. To facilitate their role, A and B Squadrons had undergone additional training with Duplex Drive swimming tanks and were both equipped with these experimental amphibious vehicles. The initial landing would be made by both these squadrons, which would launch from eight LCTs of 14 LCT Flotilla some 7,000 yards out at sea and then swim into the beach. Behind them and on either flank more support craft would pour fire on to the landing beaches. Destroyers, LCGs, LCT(R)s and the RMASG would pound positions on the actual landing area, while the seventy-two Priest guns of the division's artillery regiments would follow in another wave of landing craft and fire their 105mm guns over the leading vessels to hit the beach.

Mere moments before the DD tanks were to touch sand, the bombardment would cease, and as they came ashore the tanks would deploy in the surf and fire on enemy positions. At H-Hour, the first wave of landing craft would touch down. Ten LCTs of 45 LCT Flotilla would land the AVREs of the Royal Engineers and Sherman flail tanks of 22 Dragoons while another five LCTs of 100 Flotilla would land the Centaur tanks of the RMASG. Immediately behind, twenty LCAs of 536 and 535 LCA Flotillas would bring in the assault companies of infantry – two companies of 2 East Yorks on the left flank on Queen Red, and two companies of 1 South Lancs on the right on Queen White.

The task of the initial wave was to secure the beach. While the AVREs and flail tanks cleared safe paths up the sand and created exits along preselected lanes leading to the main lateral road behind the beach, 2 East Yorks were to secure strongpoints 18 and 20 on Queen Red, codenamed Skate and Cod respectively. One company of 1 South Lancs was to assist in the capture of Cod, while the other was to push through the western end of the beach and establish a position leading into Lion-sur Mer. Twenty minutes later, the assault companies would be joined by the battalions' reserve companies along with beach clearance groups and Landing Craft Obstacle Clearance Units (LCOCUs). While the beach parties worked on the obstacles, the infantry would aid in their battalions' missions and push further inland. 2 East Yorks would advance on two more German positions – strongpoint 14 codenamed Sole, and the coastal battery at strongpoint 12 codenamed Daimler, which was believed to house up to four 155mm guns. 1 South Lancs would advance into Hermanville-sur-Mer and establish a beachhead, codenamed Mallet, through which following waves could pass.

At H+30 minutes, the first of the commando units would land on the eastern end of Queen Red: 177 Free French commandos from 10 (Inter-Allied) Commando would land from two LCI(S)s, while 4 Commando would touch down in fourteen LCAs from 500 and 514 Flotillas. Both units would then advance into Ouistreham to secure German strongpoints 10 and Bass, the major coastal battery.

Fifteen minutes later, at H+45, the remaining squadron and HQ formation of 13/18 Hussars would land conventionally from landing craft of 41 LCT Flotilla, and fifteen minutes behind them, the entirety of 1 Suffolk would land from three LCI(L)s and LCAs of 538 and 537 Flotillas and advance inland to occupy Colleville-sur-Orne and capture the adjacent German coastal battery at strongpoint 16, codenamed Morris, and the significant strongpoint 17 on the ridge codenamed Hillman.

Another fifteen minutes after that, at H+75, the leading elements of 1 Special Service Brigade would touch down on Queen Red in LCI(L)s of 200 and 201 Flotillas, while 38 LCT Flotilla would deliver 76 Field Regiment RA to the beach. Thirty minutes later at H+105 the rest of the commandos would land while 32 LCT Flotilla delivered 33 Field Regiment RA. But although they would land in the assault wave on Queen Beach, the bulk of the commandos' task once ashore was to leave Sword

Area as quickly as possible. The mission of 3, 6 and 45 (RM) Commando was to advance to two bridges, codenamed Rugger and Cricket, across the Caen Canal and River Orne respectively and nearly 4 miles south of the beach. These would hopefully have been captured by airborne forces overnight, and after crossing them, the commandos would deploy east to help secure the larger airborne bridgehead east of the Orne. Once they had completed their assault on Ouistreham, 4 Commando would follow, while 41 (RM) Commando would head west and force a passage through Lion-sur-Mer and strongpoint 21, codenamed Trout, and link up with 48 (RM) Commando, landing at Juno.

Finally, 43 LCT Flotilla would land priority vehicles carrying supplies, ammunition and equipment for 8 Brigade. The first two hours of the landings would see some 8,500 men and 1,200 vehicles put ashore. Once the brigade's infantry and vehicles were landed it was intended that they would be able to secure the Périers-sur-le-Dan Ridge that ran from the Caen Canal to Plumetot, a line codenamed Elm by the British.

Thirty minutes later, Group S2 would begin landing the intermediate force – 185 Brigade and the tanks of the Staffordshire Yeomanry. With the assumption the beach would now be secure, the intention was to land these forces much more quickly, with the entirety of the infantry brigade coming ashore from 263 Flotilla's LCI(L)s at H+150. Thirty-five minutes after that the entire Staffordshire Yeomanry would come ashore from the LCTs of 40 Flotilla, to be followed by 7 Field Regiment RA landed from the rest of 32 Flotilla. At H+215, the first American forces would approach the beach: six US Navy LCI(L)s would land the first large parties of Beach Group personnel, followed fifteen minutes later by another eight LCI(L)s of 251 Flotilla carrying more of the same. At H+250, eighteen LCTs of 42 and 48 Flotillas would land 185 Brigade's vehicles along with supplies and stores.

185 Brigade and the Staffordshire Yeomanry were tasked with leap-frogging 8 Brigade and rushing the advance south. To effect this, 2 KSLI and the Staffordshire Yeomanry were to rally just behind the beaches and form the nucleus of a mobile column, with the infantry riding on the tanks. This column would press south past the lines held by 8 Brigade, through the villages of Beuville and Biéville and on to the next ridge at Lebisey, codenamed Vermouth by the British. 1 Norfolk would advance across the ridge on the left flank of 2 KSLI and mop up any defences the mobile column had bypassed, while 2 Warwick would follow on the right flank and, to lend support to the mobile column, send one company

ahead by bicycle. Once the mobile column reached Vermouth they would assault further south, clearing the approaches to Caen. Various contingencies allowed for potential flanking attacks by 1 Norfolk and 2 Warwick, but the key objective was to reach the city's outer limits. An assault would follow and then the entire brigade would consolidate the city, securing its southern approaches across the River Orne.

Relief for 185 Brigade was due to come from 9 Brigade, which would land from Group S1. Their task was to quickly move right after landing and secure the western flank, passing through the villages of Mathieu and Cambes to Saint-Contest. Their advance would secure 185 Brigade's right flank and, if the intermediate brigade failed to capture Caen, 9 Brigade's axis of advance would allow for an alternative direction from which to assault the city. They would also cover 3 Canadian Division's left flank and hopefully effect a link-up with their forces inland while 41 (RM) Commando did so on the coast.

Throughout the day air support would dominate the skies and be on hand to offer ground attack options to speed the advance. At sea, the Royal Navy's bombardment forces would remain on station off the coast ready to pour shells on to a target if requested by the Forward Officer Bombardment (FOB) spotters who would go forward with the infantry.

The plan for Sword was both grand and ambitious. Based on the available intelligence about the beach strongpoints, it was clear that the weight of some 27,000 men landing in one day would overwhelm the German defences. What was important was how quickly this could be done. The narrow beach did not make this any easier: with Cod sitting almost dead centre in the landing area, with only two battalions of infantry able to come ashore in the first thirty minutes and with little space, it would be harder to outflank and secure the strongpoint, and it might not be a quick task to silence the defence and allow following units to quickly and cleanly clear the beach so that they could continue with their own missions. Inland, Sword had some of the thickest defences in the entire invasion area, with coastal batteries and strongpoints some 2.5 miles from the beach. Strongpoints like Hillman, positioned on high ground, were able to dominate most of the intended axis of advance of the infantry, armour and commandos.

The advance inland relied on a minimum of interference. If there were problems capturing objectives, contingency plans for attacks by alternative units were in place, but it seemed there was little recognition of the delays that implementing those contingency plans might cause, and the impact it would have on the following phases. For instance, if enemy armour was found to be west of 185 Brigade's line of advance it was expected that 2 Warwick would switch to a position east of 1 Norfolk while the Staffordshire Yeomanry paid closer attention to their right flank. This was a sensible approach, moving the infantry away from the armour and leaving the tanks to cover that flank, but it would inevitably hamper the advance. Similarly, if the mobile column failed to take Lebisey, 2 Warwick would make an attack from the right flank and, failing this, 1 Norfolk from the left flank. But in the following phases there was little contingency for a delay.

In reality, the original plan was an optimistic best-case scenario – it would be difficult for a single battalion and tank regiment to capture an entire city and no easy feat for a single brigade to hold it unless relieved quickly. Where the plan was flawed was in its scheduling and lack of flexibility in the event of delays. This would come to be the crucial problem on D-Day.[2]

Even when these comprehensive orders were issued they came with pages of amendments with endless modifications that would need to be made by hand. The issuing of such voluminous documents created a headache for senior officers: for those on warships it was relatively easy to store the documents under lock and key as instructed, but the bulk of Force S consisted of landing craft and other much smaller vessels like motor torpedo boats (MTBs).

For Lieutenant Commander Anthony Law, commander of 29 (Canadian) MTB Flotilla, merely finding room for them was problematic enough. His orders to sail for Portsmouth had just arrived when he was summoned to Dover Castle from the harbour, where he was issued complete sets of orders for every boat in his flotilla – eight in all. But these couldn't be issued to individual skippers until the Admiralty signalled the start of the operation, so they would have to remain on his boat, MTB 459, until then. After cramming them into a car for the journey back to the harbour, he found the only place they could be stored under lock and key was in the compact wardroom heads.* After ramming them in and locking the door, the flotilla prepared to sail and departed Dover early the following morning, arriving in the Solent to find ships of every type and size waiting at anchor or busily traversing the limited navigation channels. Even when the orders were issued to his skippers, the

---

* The officers' toilet.

headaches didn't go away. As well as needing to absorb more than 200 pages of instructions relating to Force S, there were specific orders for each flotilla to memorize and summaries of the other invasion sectors to understand. On top of this, the eight pages of amendments needed to be implemented. Law and his MTB skippers stayed up most of the night making sense of everything and ensuring the navigational details were up to date.

The sheer magnitude of the task led many skippers to make their own decisions on how to handle the top-secret information they had been entrusted with. On 1 June, Lieutenant Commander William Clouston gathered only four of his officers together in his cabin on HMS *Scorpion* to outline the ship's role in the coming operation on a strictly need-to-know basis, showing them only the most basic information but enough to ensure they understood the outline plan. But on sister ship HMS *Scourge*, Lieutenant Commander Ian Balfour revealed everything to all his officers – even the midshipmen – and had them all assist in making the necessary amendments.

At about the same time as the Force S orders were issued and senior naval officers learned their mission, senior army officers were briefed on their final destination. The final Operation Orders for the various brigades and regiments were issued in late May and the plans the officers dissected were comprehensive and complex. Nothing had been left to chance that didn't have to be and as much as could be imagined had been mitigated for. So big and so detailed was the overall operation at Sword that no man could ever know the entirety of the plans. The naval officers were more concerned with what was happening at sea while the army had very little interest in the movement of ships as long as they were landed in the right place at the right time. While the senior commanders knew the major objectives and who was tasked to achieve them, the individual tasks of companies and platoons were the domain of the battalion and company commanders. And while those men knew what their units would be doing, they would only know in outline detail the tasks of other formations.

But while naval officers were becoming privy to the final destination, for the troops they would carry, the secret was maintained. Although many senior officers had been informed of the actual location in May, battalion commanders and below were unlikely to learn their final destination until they were aboard their ships. Those who needed to know the true location of objectives, roads, rivers and enemy strongpoints – after months of exercises manoeuvring around generic landscapes and attacking theoretical targets – were issued their first maps of Sword sector. Only those who had been to Ouistreham or Caen would have had any chance of recognizing the target though, as the place names of every town and river had been changed. Ouistreham became Oslo, Caen became Poland, the Caen Canal was Portugal and the neighbouring River Orne was Prague. Lion-sur-Mer became Ganges and Hermanville became Mexico. Even so, some had no difficulty recognizing where they were bound, in particular Commandant Philippe Kieffer's[*] French commandos, many of whom knew the coast well. Sergent Guy de Montlaur, on recognizing that his mission was to attack the site of a casino in Ouistreham, remarked to Kieffer, 'It will be a pleasure – I have lost several fortunes in that place.'[3]

Fabius had not been a universally popular exercise. Captain Julius Neave of C Squadron 13/18 Hussars found the process of marshalling to be absurd and infuriating, with his men and their tanks chivvied from camp to camp without any apparent reason, then split into tiny groups separating friends and colleagues and stripping the squadron of any cohesion or communication – all while staff officers submitted them to the pettiest restrictions imaginable. Neave was far from alone in his assessment that for many men the days spent in tented accommodation in early May, with only the most basic amenities and food served by unknown catering units, were an even worse experience than their time in Scotland's inclement weather.

What none of the men could possibly appreciate was the full scale of Operation Neptune and the logistical nightmare that getting all of them across the Channel entailed. The airborne forces were easy enough – they were fewer in number and could be spread around camps close to airfields inland, as far north as the Midlands. But for the seaborne forces it was a different matter entirely.

Logistically, the planners faced three essential problems. The embarkation would need to be carried out as close to D-1 (when the fleet would sail) as possible, and as quickly as possible. This was because it was impossible to place an army of men on ships and leave them there for any

---

[*] Kieffer was a lieutenant de vaisseau or ship-of-the-line lieutenant, broadly equivalent to a lieutenant in the Royal Navy. However, as the commanding officer, he was almost universally known as Commandant Kieffer, even by Lord Lovat in his recommendation for a decoration.

more than a few days. Although the troops on the large LSIs, equipped with mess facilities and beds, could be left for a few days, eventually the ships would run out of food and the men, deprived of space and room to exercise, would become fatigued. For the troops who would be embarking on landing craft the problem was even more acute. LCIs only had the facilities to maintain their passengers for twenty-four hours – they would need to be loaded shortly before they sailed or the men would be trapped below decks for too long and left in no condition to make an amphibious assault. On the LCTs there was plenty of space for tanks and vehicles, but no dedicated space for their crews at all. Men would need to sleep in or under their vehicles, or beg whatever space they could from the LCT's crew. It was estimated that the vessels could probably accommodate the men on board for forty-eight hours, but any longer would be too much. The embarkation needed to be carefully choreographed in order to load the men on to their vessels according to the length of time they could remain on them.

The second problem was the need to marshal the men as close as possible to the south coast. This was in part because the timetable could not afford to accommodate lengthy journeys to the embarkation areas, but also because the vehicles could not make such journeys anyway. In order to achieve an amphibious landing, it was essential that vehicles were suitably waterproofed. This was conducted in three stages, the first requiring a significant disassembly of the engine and limiting the vehicle to 200 miles of travel before it overheated. The second stage took the best part of a day to achieve and limited the vehicle to no more than a few dozen miles of travel. The third phase took thirty minutes and could be done once the vehicle was embarked on its vessel, but the final bits of wading kit would have to be removed as quickly as possible once the vehicle was safely ashore on the other side of the Channel. It was the second stage that was the most important, requiring facilities to accommodate the troops for long enough to complete the work that were close enough to the coast that the engines wouldn't overheat afterwards. As a result, the entire south coast became home to dozens of marshalling camps, temporary tented facilities in which men could be accommodated and processed on their way to the coast. Marshalling so many men in such a narrow strip of land would put great strain on space, transport facilities and security.

The third problem was the difficulty in making sure the correct men were at the correct embarkation point at the correct time in order that they got on to the correct vessels to take them to the correct piece of beach in France. This was perhaps the most vexing conundrum. On D-Day some 132,700 personnel and 14,000 vehicles would be landed from the sea, but on specific sectors of beach to a carefully planned timetable. It was essential they were transported on the correct vessel whose crew knew where they were meant to land and when.

Fortunately, planners had been working on the solutions to these problems for the last two years. In early 1942 Combined Operations HQ, working with the War Office and the Admiralty, had begun the construction of dozens of embarkation ramps along the south coast. Simple facilities that utilized prefabricated concrete matting, they turned a sandy beach into a solid slipway upon which a landing craft could drop its ramp and vehicles could embark without risk of bogging down. Come D-Day, these embarkation ramps made up two thirds of the embarkation points used to load men on to vessels. Inland, roads leading to the points of embarkation had been significantly improved. Unpaved roads were widened and relaid in concrete or covered with tarmac. Where necessary, this involved requisitioning land or even demolishing homes if they prevented a road from being widened, or stood on the corner of a junction that needed to be enlarged. At various points along these roads hundreds of laybys were installed, places to move vehicles on to should they break down, or to provide refuge for a desperate car suddenly faced with an incoming convoy. As the full scale of D-Day became clear, such work continued until May 1944 in order to ensure the road network could cope with the traffic it would shortly experience.

The most important solution was the one that so infuriated the soldiers who experienced it. In order to match men and vehicles to specific craft, a whole system of tables for each invasion beach needed to be worked out. Called landing tables, the documents detailed the exact load of each craft landing on D-Day, including the vessel type, the precise number of men and vehicles and their units that would embark, and where and when they were due to land. These vessel loads, known as landing serials, were each assigned a 'landing table index number' (LTIN), a unique identifier within the entire Eastern Task Force. Force S was assigned the numbers 100 to 999, while Force J took 1000 to 1999, Force G used 2000 to 2999 and Force L had 3000 to 3999.

The benefit of the landing serials was that each man only needed to know the one number to embark on the correct vessel, rather than needing to know the identity of that vessel. As such, should the vessel they were due to embark on break down shortly before embarkation, it could be quickly replaced and the LTIN simply assigned to its replacement. It also made troop marshalling easier: each landing serial could be organized in the relative comfort of the marshalling camps and travel together to the embarkation area. Hence the splitting of units that so infuriated Neave. In the camps the various craft loads were divvied up to different camps and despatched according to a strict schedule, necessary to ensure the efficient movement of traffic along the roads between the camp and the specific embarkation points. Men from each battalion might find themselves on totally different vessels that might land some time apart, and therefore some would embark on their vessels much earlier than others. The division of units from their own means of supply meant that each marshalling camp needed to operate a 'hotel service', providing accommodation and messing facilities for each man staying.

The embarkation of the invasion force was a logistical challenge of underappreciated proportions. But despite the complexity of the task it was achieved almost seamlessly.[4]

The bulk of Force S's passengers were marshalled in Area A, a large area of east Hampshire stretching from the South Downs to Gosport and Portsmouth. Within it were eighteen marshalling camps in addition to Portsmouth and Gosport's barrack facilities and nine separate points of embarkation. Meanwhile, Force S2 would embark 185 Brigade and its attached units, including the Staffordshire Yeomanry, from the Sussex ports of Newhaven and Shoreham-by-Sea in Marshalling Area J.

Towards the end of May the men started to make their tentative way to these marshalling areas. In woods and the grounds of stately homes all along the south coast, the infantry of the invasion gathered under canvas. There was an air of expectation and uncertainty – was this the build-up to another large-scale exercise like Fabius, or were they about to embark on 'the Great Crusade'?

Late on 25 May, Admiral Ramsay ordered the signal announcing the commencement of Operation Neptune to be promulgated to the fleet. The original intention was still that D-Day would be 5 June, but he held off issuing this information for now; it was enough that the commanders opened their secret orders and understood the task first. At midnight the order was passed around the marshalling camps that they were to be sealed with immediate effect. From now on no one except senior officers would leave their camp, except to move to another or to travel to their vessel.

For the next few days the men of 3 Division and its attached units were variously shunted around the camps; units were butchered as companies, platoons, sections, vehicle crews and even single individuals were mysteriously scurried away to new locations. Staff cars and jeeps whizzed around Hampshire's country roads as officers moved from camp to camp, briefing subordinates, finding misplaced groups and encouraging their men.

Then, on 31 May, the roads became alive with traffic. The first convoys left their camps when the artillery regiments departed for Gosport to load their Priest self-propelled guns on to their LCTs. Driving down to the Gosport ferry terminal, they skidded the Priest's tracks around on the concrete hard and, one by one, reversed their vehicles on to the LCTs of 32 and 38 Flotillas where 'porpoise' ammunition sleds were fitted to drag behind them. Once each craft was full it backed away to be immediately replaced by the next, while the gun crews boarded trucks back to their camps. Over the next few days the embarkation ramped up. More and more convoys filled the roads between the South Downs and Portsmouth Harbour as trucks and tanks made their slow progress to the coast.

On 3 June, 'Guns' officer Sub Lieutenant Tony Ditcham was taking afternoon watch on the bridge of HMS *Scorpion*. They had idled at anchor for several days now, watching the coming and going of all manner of landing craft and despatch boats hurrying around the Solent and making their way into Portsmouth Harbour, while larger troopships and LSTs glided along the central navigation channel between the vast anchorage areas. But after several days it was no longer spectacular to Ditcham, and he simply sat in the gentle breeze, wishing the time away.

Eventually, he noticed a motor launch gliding towards *Scorpion* from the west. At first he thought they might have visitors, but as the launch neared he realized there wasn't room to attempt to turn alongside; it merely intended to make a close pass. Given the amount of sea around him this seemed a touch unnecessary and he fixed the launch in his binoculars as it closed on *Scorpion*'s bow. As he adjusted the focus, the figures on the small bridge became clearer and he took a sharp intake of breath. He dropped his binoculars to his chest and jumped up on to the ASDIC cabinet so that he stood over the top of the bridge. Bracing himself, as the launch drew level he made a crisp salute. Below him on the bridge of Rescue Motor Launch 516, one man looked up and admiringly returned the salute, then raised his hand with a defiant V sign, maintaining it as he passed the length of the destroyer.

The bridge telephone rang and Ditcham picked it up – it was the quartermaster down at the gangway station. Expecting to speak to the signaller on the bridge, the voice asked, 'Here Bunts, who was that rude old bastard just went by?'

'Quartermaster,' replied Ditcham, 'this is the Officer of the Watch, and that was the Prime Minister.'

Fresh from inspecting 50 Infantry Division as they embarked in Southampton, Churchill and his entourage had sailed down Southampton Water to find 3 Division. After passing *Scorpion*, RML 516 made its way into Portsmouth Harbour and eventually came alongside HMS *Largs*, Talbot's HQ ship, where Churchill, his chief military assistant General Hastings Ismay, Field Marshal Jan Smuts and Ernest Bevin, Minister of Labour, jumped aboard. Talbot and Rennie proudly welcomed the party while the Prime Minister busied himself looking around the ship and observing the preparations.

Elsewhere in the harbour, other ceremonies were taking place. On HMS *Glenearn*, Lieutenant Colonel Charles Hutchinson, CO of 2 East Yorks, presented Captain Colin Hutchison, *Glenearn*'s captain, with a silver bugle inscribed with the regimental crest. In exchange, Hutchison handed over a Royal Marines badge to fix to the blade of 2 East Yorks' headquarters pike, and an anchor was sewn on to the regimental colours.

At the same time as Churchill signed the visitors book on *Largs*, Lieutenant Commander Rupert Curtis was writhing in discomfort on his bed in the sick bay of HMS *Tormentor*, the shore establishment at Warsash on the River Hamble. Laryngitis was taking its toll and he had developed a fever. Under his pillow he kept the top-secret orders for D-Day close at hand so that no one else could access them, even taking them to the toilet with him when he needed to go. Aware that his condition might worsen, only the previous day he had written out his own instructions to his LCI(S) commanders and passed them on to his staff to be typed up and issued when the fleet sailed, just in case he was not with them.

Late that evening Surgeon Lieutenant Geoffrey Potts came into the sick bay. Sitting down next to Curtis he studied his CO's face carefully for a while, then told him in no uncertain terms that he was on the verge of forbidding him from sailing. Equally, he said, there was no pressure on Curtis to sail if he did not feel fit enough. Curtis did not even consider the possibility – he knew that without question he must sail on this operation. Tomorrow he would get up and sail with the fleet that evening, whatever his condition.[5]

But other factors were at play, most notably the weather. The decision to postpone D-Day was made so late that the news nearly didn't reach the task forces anchored in the Solent in time. Some convoys of Force G actually began to make their way past the Needles before despatch vessels raced after them, urgently flashing signals to turn back. For the men of Force S already aboard their vessels the news was received with mild frustration. For the men on the LCTs it immediately became apparent that they would spend another night cramped on board. Nonetheless, the long training in Scotland had stood them in good stead for such hardships and they made the best of what they had aboard.

Not even everyone was aboard their vessels, though. The troops of 9 Infantry Brigade had been due to embark throughout 4 June from Southsea Pier, but by the time most of them arrived there the postponement order had only just reached the embarkation hardmasters, and the infantry were duly bussed back to their camps. The troops of 1 Suffolk who would cross on the LCI(L)s had embarked early in the morning though, and by the time the notification came through all three of their landing craft had already sailed into the anchorage. Simple vessels, the LCI(L)s could not accommodate and feed the 200 men aboard for an additional twenty-four hours, so the infantrymen on board kicked their heels until the afternoon, when they were able to disembark and return to their barrack accommodation in Portsmouth.

Another significant force that had not yet embarked were the commandos of 1 and 4 Special Service Brigade, who would be crossing the Channel in the small boats of 200 and 201 LCI(S) Flotillas. Cramped when filled with a hundred men, and lacking even the most basic facilities to cater for them, the commandos would have to load at the last minute before sailing.

At 10:00 the men of 3, 6, 41, 45 and 48 Commandos gathered for the interdenominational church parade on Southampton Common. 'Eternal Father Strong to Save' echoed across camp C18, the lyrics floating over the trenches cut into the heath and through the open windows of the neighbouring houses. As the final verse died away on the breeze the commandos sat down on the earth banks of the trenches, their legs dangling into the ditches that they had spent the last few weeks training in. The Reverend Derrick Williams, recently attached to 45 Commando, approached the temporary dais and launched into his sermon with full evangelical gusto, portraying the coming fight as one fought for God, and warning the men of the carnage yet to come. As he went on, Lieutenant Colonel Derek Mills-Roberts, 6 Commando's CO, frowned. The imagery of death and destruction Williams portrayed was not to his liking – nor to the men's either it seemed. A morbid silence began to descend over the heath as the reverend declaimed about the divine destruction ahead of them, and Mills-Roberts sensed the unhappy mood among his men. Shortly after the congregation broke up, news of the twenty-four-hour postponement filtered through and morale slumped further.

That afternoon complaints began to make their way up to the senior officers of the brigade and it quickly became clear to Lovat and Lieutenant Colonel Norman Ries, 45 Commando's CO, that the new reverend was bad for morale. Williams was summoned and, as gently as possible, informed that he wouldn't be accompanying the men to Normandy. Devastated, the priest returned to his tent. He had dedicated himself to the war effort and even earned the nickname 'the fearless padre' after his frequent rescue work during the Blitz, helping to dig out survivors from bombed houses, extinguish fires and comfort the bereaved. On the eve of invasion, to be denied the chance to join the men he had been tasked to serve was too much. Early the next morning, he pressed a pistol against his temple and pulled the trigger.[6]

3

THE WAITING ENDS

EARLY ON MONDAY MORNING, 5 JUNE, A FLURRY OF SIGNALS emanating from Southwick House arrived all along the south coast. On HMS *Goathland*, Captain Eric Bush received the notification and immediately ordered the necessary code to be sent by hand or wireless to the senior officer of every convoy under his command, with instructions for them to promulgate it among their ships. The notification quickly passed through the fleet waiting at anchor in the Solent. On HMS *Vernon*, Lieutenant Commander Anthony Law received the instruction by hand aboard MTB 459. The knowledge that the invasion was finally going to happen filled him with a strange overwhelming emotion. The build-up had been so long. Some men were more prosaic. Having been handed the signal 'Carry out operation in execution of previous orders', William Clouston stalked the decks of HMS *Scorpion* until he found someone to tell. Coming across Tony Ditcham on the fo'c'sle he simply told him, 'The party's on,' then strode back towards the bridge.

At 09:00, Lieutenant Commander Cecil Jeff on board HM Motor Launch 196 signalled nine LCTs and eight LCMs moored just to the south of the entrance to Portsmouth Harbour to prepare to get underway. Fifteen minutes later the landing craft slipped their moorings and Convoy S4, codenamed Pannier, slowly proceeded towards the submarine barrier guarding the eastern Solent, passing through the narrow northern entrance on schedule at 09:45. An hour later, as the convoy passed the mass of small boats east of the Isle of Wight, the trawler HMS *Northern Sky* slipped her mooring and scuttled over to join them. Force S was on the move.

For the next twenty-six hours, the various convoys of Force S would make their way out of their home ports and start their slow journey across the Channel. Some wouldn't even leave until after the invasion had started. On HMS *Largs*, lying just south of Stokes Bay, Rear Admiral Talbot watched with pride as line after line of vessels sailed past him. As well as Force S, Force J was departing the anchorage alongside them, doubling the traffic heading east towards Spithead. As magnificent as the spectacle was, Talbot's eye was drawn to the distinctive green bands around the bridges and funnels of 'his' ships, and he noted with pride the black and red iron triangles of 3 Division's insignia, emblazoned on the bridge or funnel of every vessel in the force. For their part, the signallers on each vessel that sailed past *Largs* communicated the signal flying from her masthead to their skippers – Good Luck: Drive On. When 45 LCT Flotilla sailed out of Portsmouth Harbour, Lieutenant Colonel Arthur Cocks, commander of 5 Assault Regiment Royal Engineers, hurried one of his men to the side of LCT 947 and instructed him to play 'The Last Post' on his bugle. His men stood to attention on the side as they steamed past Gosport and Old Portsmouth; civilians and WRENs waved enthusiastically and even the passengers on the little Gosport ferry, which had to take immediate action to avoid being run down by the impressive force of LCTs bearing down on it, waved to the soldiers and shouted good luck.

But while some ships sailed, others still needed to embark their men. Southsea Pier, extended with extra scaffolding walkways and berths to accommodate additional vessels and men, became a hive of activity as twenty-one of the fleet's LCI(L)s busied themselves embarking the infantry battalions of 9 Infantry Brigade and the Beach Groups that would land late in the afternoon of D-Day. Just ahead of them, nosing into the pier at 08:30, the two LCHs that would guide the leading waves into shore picked up their last passengers. Lieutenant Cook gently conned LCH 185 alongside the pier, while striding down it came all manner of high-ranking officers: Commander Edmund Currey, Deputy Senior Officer Assault Group One (effectively Captain Bush's second in command), led Brigadier George Erroll Prior-Palmer, CO of 27 Armoured Brigade, Lieutenant Colonel David Board, CO of 5 Battalion the King's Regiment (the infantry battalion of 5 Beach Group), Commander Rowley Nicholl, Deputy Naval Officer in Charge Sword Area, Lieutenant Commander Donald Amer and Lieutenant Donald Slater of COPP 6, and Lieutenant Commander Edward Gueritz, Principal Beachmaster of Fox Royal Navy Beach Commando. The veritable who's who of military personnel trooped aboard accompanied by Royal Navy ratings of F Commando, while R Commando went aboard the neighbouring LCH 269. The two LCHs backed away and almost immediately a group of LCI(L)s moved in to take their place, ready to embark the infantry who had been turned away the previous day.[1]

Seventeen miles away on Southampton Common, at 10:30, Lord Lovat stood in front of the assembled ranks of 1 Special Service Brigade. Aware that the unpopular sermon the previous day and the subsequent suicide of Reverend Williams that morning had created a certain amount of despondency, he focused on the simple facts but weighted with appropriate encouragement. First he congratulated his men on past achievements that had led them to be selected for this important role and formed as a complete brigade for the first time. Their challenge was greater this time, but if they succeeded, as he knew they would, their achievement would be all the greater for it. He told them that it would be better to attack than to defend. The shoreline they would land on would be pulverized; they would double across the land behind and to the bridges to reinforce the airborne division east of the Orne. The brigade would make history and he had complete confidence in every man taking part. He ended with a recommendation: 'If you wish to live to a ripe old age, keep moving tomorrow.'

Then Lovat turned to the 177 Frenchmen attached to 4 Commando. In colloquial French he addressed them less comprehensively but no less seriously. 'You are going home. You will be the first French soldiers in uniform to punch the bastards in the mouth in France itself. To each his own Boche. You are going to show us what you can do. Tomorrow morning we will have them.'

Lovat's pep talks had some success in restoring morale where it was needed. At 14:00 and in high spirits, the brigade marched out of the marshalling camp on Southampton Common for the final time and boarded lorries parked along Highfield Lane. In a long convoy, 3, 6, 41, 45 and 48 Commandos (the latter bound for Juno), accompanied by the 177 French troops from 10 (Inter-Allied) Commando, set off for Warsash. Simultaneously the thirty-six LCI(S)s of 200, 201 and 202 Flotillas fired up their Hall-Scott engines and slowly crept along the River Hamble to Warsash, near the river mouth on Southampton Water. In the lead, on the bridge of LCI(S) 519, Rupert Curtis admired his command. With an additional day to recover, he had got his way.

At Warsash, the lorries pulled up on the lane leading to the Rising Sun pub and the pier jutting into the water. The men spilled out, gathering on Strawberry Fields, where 3 and 6 Commando engaged in a football match on the public pitch.* Spotting bagpipes, one of the commandos called for a tune and Piper Bill Millin, recently appointed by Lovat as his personal piper, obligingly shouldered his pipes and wandered the field, entertaining the various groups of commandos as they sprawled on the grass.

Meanwhile, on the landing craft, the skippers called their crews and revealed the big secret. On LCI(S) 527, Able Seaman Jim Brooker heard the call to muster on the mess deck. Lieutenant Charles Craven made some brief small talk, then announced that this was the big event. Tomorrow, he told his men, Allied armies would invade Normandy, the first step on the road to liberating Europe. Their task, along with LCI(S) 523, was to land Free French commandos. Off the Normandy coast they would rendezvous with twelve LCAs carrying 4 Commando and lead them into the beach, landing just thirty minutes after the first assault wave. After specifying a few details he wished his men luck, then hurried off to the bridge to prepare. Sensing the mood of tense anticipation, Freddie Cranshaw headed for the galley and prepared a hearty meal while the crew made the ship ready.

One at a time the commando units embarked on their specified LCIs from the pier in front of the Rising Sun, the heavily burdened men hauling their heavy rucksacks across the lines of boats. Others manhandled bicycles down the ramps from the pier, sweating and grunting as they dragged them across the numerous fixtures and fittings on the landing craft decks. Ushered below by the crews, the men stowed their gear wherever they could in the troop spaces and found what room they could claim as their own to make themselves comfortable. As Commandant Kieffer's men loaded on to LCI(S) 527 they were cheered to hear a gramophone on the bridge playing rousing French melodies.

By 18:00 all the commandos were aboard, pressed between their luggage in the troop spaces on each landing craft. Thirty minutes later the landing craft fired up their engines once again and slowly pulled away from their moorings, jostling for space as they manoeuvred on to the river. As LCI(S) 516 pulled away from the pier, Lieutenant Denis Glover, Royal New Zealand Navy Volunteer Reserve, pulled out a record and slipped it on to the gramophone on his bridge. After a brief crackle the stirring chords of 'Hearts of Oak' rang out over the rumbling engines.

---

* The score is not recorded.

Moored against the pier, LCI(S) 519 was one of the last to pull away, but the other landing craft were obediently waiting for their flotilla commander to take the lead. Millin stood on the deck with his pipes, suspicious that Lovat might request a tune. He looked around – Lovat was deep in conversation with Curtis on the bridge, but moments later another commando approached him. The brigadier would like a tune as they sailed down the river, he told him. Millin looked over at Lovat again, who raised his head and nodded at him. Moving to the bow as the landing craft slowly started to make its way down the river, he started to blow up his pipes' bag and then launched into 'The Road to the Isles'. While 519 turned out of the river and on to Southampton Water one of the crew managed to broadcast Millin's music over the boat's loudhailer, and as the flotilla sailed past the assembled ships of Forces J and G the instantly recognizable melody of 'The Skye Boat Song' echoed across the waves. From the decks of LSIs and LSTs still waiting their turn to sail, hundreds of sailors and soldiers roared their approval as the landing craft flotilla sailed by in a single long line, men leaning over the railings to catch the last few notes on the wind as 519 steered into the Solent and sailed to its holding berth at Stokes Bay.[2]

By now the leading convoys were making their way well into open water. Out of the shelter of the Isle of Wight they found themselves sailing through the very weather that had caused D-Day to be postponed for twenty-four hours. Heading south-south-east the flat-bottomed, heavily laden landing craft were tossed around on the seas, disrupting their station keeping and doing little for the comfort of the men on board.[*] Things were not going well for Convoy Pannier. By now the wind had moved round to the west and was blowing a force 5, although on board LCT(A) 2012, Lieutenant Martin Van Heems estimated it might have even been 6 or 7. Great green waves rolled over the tank deck, and even up on the bridge his charts were soon soaked, despite their protective canvas

---

[*] It's often stated that after sailing, all the vessels bound for Normandy converged on a specific area codenamed Area Z (and known to everyone as Piccadilly Circus), south of the Isle of Wight. In fact, although Area Z had been swept of mines in time for the sailing of the assault convoys, its marker buoy was only laid on the morning of D-Day – after the assault convoys had passed. On D-1 each task force sailed along separate channels; only Force G passed directly through Area Z (but navigated on different buoys). Simply put, there was no Area Z or Piccadilly Circus on 5 June.

dodger. A few of his crew took seasickness tablets, but they did little to reduce the ill effects. On LCT(A) 2191 Jack Tear, one of the RMASG tank crews, found the swell almost rhythmic as it swept the landing craft up and down. But every few minutes a steeper wave would throw the bow up on to a crest and suspend it there, the deck beneath him groaning as if it might snap under its own weight, before it dropped back down into a trough with a slam.

At 17:15 LCT(A) 2432 came to a complete standstill as water leaked into the fuel tanks and disabled all three engines. For Lieutenant Commander Edward Foster this was particularly grieving as he watched the rest of his flotilla continue south while his own vessel dropped out of station. Fortunately help was at hand, and a quick signal to an attendant motor launch brought it alongside. Grabbing a few possessions and order documents, Foster made his way down to the side deck and, as the ML pitched and rolled alongside the disabled landing craft, threw himself across on to the Fairmile's deck. With an apologetic look at his stranded crew, the ML whisked him forward and deposited him with little grace on the side deck of LCT(A) 2123. After several hours trying to effect repairs, LCT(A) 2432 was taken in tow back to Portsmouth.

Pannier had sailed early in the expectation that they would probably be the slowest formation to cross the Channel. It was assumed that 5 knots would be well within their ability, but the rough seas they encountered on leaving the shelter of Spithead had so far prevented them from even making that speed, and now they were starting rapidly to lose ground when they needed to be clawing it back.

Behind them, things were little better for Convoy S3 Purify. Once comfortable aboard LCH 185, Edmund Currey had located the eight LCT Mk 3s carrying 13/18 Hussar's DD tanks and their three accompanying LCGs in their anchorage south of Portsmouth Harbour. The crews were already attaching towing lines to the LCP(L) despatch boats and navigation leaders they would tow across the Channel, and at 12:10 the group had slipped their moorings and made their way to east. Now, exposed to the rough seas in the Channel, they too were struggling. At 16:15 the first tow parted and an LCP(L) was left bobbing in the seas behind its LCT as the crew desperately fired up their engines and prepared to make their own passage. One by one the tows snapped until, by nightfall, only four LCP(L)s remained attached to their mother ships. The rest proceeded into the grey seas under their own power, but as darkness descended

LCP(L) 272 drifted in front of an LCT and was smashed to bits by the landing craft's slab-faced bow.[3]

It was late when the large LSIs prepared to sail. Moored in Area 25 just south of Stokes Bay, the men aboard had enjoyed a grandstand view of the landing craft of Forces S and J heading out of the Solent; now the soldiers crowded the railings to get their last glimpse of home. As the big ships started to make steam and prepare to depart, the army and naval personnel in Stokes Bay waved their goodbyes. In the distance, too far to be seen by the men aboard, civilians in Portsmouth and on the Isle of Wight waved at them too: the sheer number of sailings that day had left many of them in no doubt that these ships were bound for somewhere in continental Europe. One by one they steamed out of their anchorage. Talbot waited until all six had passed and then HMS *Largs* proceeded after them. Four destroyers and four MTBs took up escort positions with the convoy and four MTBs, three US Coast Guard cutters, two LCI(S)s and a requisitioned RAF high-speed launch, all intended for rescue work, fell in astern. At 21:40 the largest convoy of Force S passed through the Spithead Gate between the Victorian island fortresses of No Man's Land and Horse Tail Sands.

No sooner had the convoy reached open water than the soldiers aboard were reminded of the least palatable part of their training – swell. By evening the wind had reached force 5 blowing in from the west, hitting the ships beam on and rolling them left and right as they steamed south. Even though 3 Division's troops had trained in the rough North Sea since December and despite the issue of seasickness tablets, many men were laid out by the sea state. Nor were they alone: Talbot noticed that a significant part of HMS *Largs'* crew were unwell. But the ships themselves, with powerful turbine engines and streamlined hulls, were more than up to the task and much better than the landing craft that preceded them. They made up speed and headed for Channel 10, where they would follow the Bombarding Force D's warships.

Shortly after Purify had sailed they were overtaken by a faster convoy of sleek minesweepers from 1 Minesweeping Flotilla. The sweepers passed little collections of vessels as they hurried on their way south, their regular ship hulls much more comfortable in the swell. Behind them, two diminutive Fairmile Bs struggled through the waves – MLs 137 and 141 needed to keep up with the larger ships, for they were soon to lead them. On board ML 137 the navigator, Sub Lieutenant Brendan Maher, was irritated to find himself feeling seasick for the first time in his life, despite having spent the last year at sea. After violently emptying his stomach he felt much better, but the pitching seas under leaden skies, with his greatcoat and helmet weighing him down as he struggled with his charts, did nothing to make the passage enjoyable.

As the sky got progressively greyer, ML 137 hustled alongside HMS *Harrier*, the flotilla leader, and took station on her port beam. At 20:30 the flotilla spied a single vessel ahead of it. Commander Harry Nicholls studied her from the bridge of *Harrier* – flying from her mast was the simple pennant for the number 9. To make doubly sure, as the sky continued to darken, an Aldis lamp blinked out four dashes and a single dot. Harbour Defence Motor Launch 1415 was in position on the north side of the German minefield, marking the entrance to Channel 9.

The flotilla quickly adopted the 'G' sweeping formation. The minesweepers thrust out their sweeping gear to port and assumed positions behind and to the left of the next ship ahead. Each vessel was thus protected by the sweep of the vessel in front of them, which should cut any moored mines in its path. Between them the flotilla would be able to carve a channel 2 miles wide through the minefield. MLs 137 and 141 scurried up to the front of the formation – their task was to sweep in front of the leading ship; now they would be at the forefront of Force S's convoys as they sailed south. 137 took position in the lead with 141 just astern and both threw out their sweeps. Some ninety minutes later 15 Minesweeping Flotilla passed HDML 1416 and began sweeping Channel 10 a few miles west.

Behind them the convoys ploughed steadily on. As the night had progressed the skippers on the bridges, by now maintaining their alertness through a combination of tea, adrenalin and Benzedrine, estimated the wind had at least abated a little to force 3 or 4 and the swell had dropped to 3 or 4 feet, providing some relief for those on the landing craft. Force S had experienced far worse conditions in the winter off Scotland's coast, but combined with expectations and nerves, the swell was enough to bother crew and passengers alike. Even so, most of the troops turned in as darkness fell, hastened by their commanders who reminded them they would need all the rest they could get. Soldiers went to their bunks on the big LSIs, or found whatever space they could in their cabs or under their vehicles on the LCTs. On LCT 979 Lieutenant Eric Smith, commander of

4 Troop of C Squadron 13/18 Hussars, crawled under his Sherman and rolled out a mat on the deck of the LCT. Despite the swell, the monotonous droning of the engines and their vibration through the deck below was enough to lull him into a comfortable sleep. But not all of his men were so lucky and throughout the night a steady stream of them made their way to the sides after failing to hold down the remnants of the late-night tins of self-heating soup they had consumed.[4]

At 23:15, X-23 broke the surface once again. The submarine had sat on the bottom for just over twenty hours, her crew silently waiting and praying for the time to pass. Now they desperately hoped they wouldn't have to do it again. The radio was warmed up and the men, gaunt with exhaustion, gathered around and listened for the flicker of noise that would reveal a transmission. At 23:55 a faint broadcast was picked up from the Niton transmitter on the Isle of Wight, but it was too weak to hear. George Honour ordered the gyro repeater compass switched off again and the crew listened even more intently for a repeat of the transmission. Then, in spite of the weak sound and static, the men heard the faint codeword Pomade. They looked at each other – it was on. There was little time to lose, and after flushing the submarine's interior with as much fresh air as possible, X-23 slipped back beneath the waves.

A mix of Beach Group personnel and infantry from 8 Brigade shelter in front of strongpoint Cod at approximately 08:30. The buildings in the background are next to exit 20.

PART 2
THE ASSAULT

4

ON THE MIDNIGHT SWELL

IN THE MIDDLE OF THE ENGLISH CHANNEL THE DARKNESS brought new problems for the convoys. In the lead, 1 Minesweeping Flotilla continued their steady passage, their sweeps primed to snag and cut the moorings of mines. Behind them came the danlayers – trawlers converted to lay buoys in the minesweepers' wake. Every mile two new buoys were laid, one on each side of the swept channel, their hooded lights faintly glowing northwards, red on the port side of the channel, white on the starboard. But the minesweepers had to maintain a speed of 7.5 knots in order for their sweeps to remain taut enough to cut moored mines, and at that speed the landing craft would never keep up. The only solution was for the minesweepers to reverse their course when they got too far ahead, return to the landing craft and then turn south again. Carried out in the dark, it was a difficult task, made more complicated by the inability to make any signals by wireless or Aldis lamp. Shortly after midnight Sub Lieutenant Brendan Maher notified ML 137's skipper, Lieutenant Leslie Hutchins, that the time of the pre-planned manoeuvre was approaching. On every bridge in the flotilla, all eyes focused on the dark shadow where HMS *Harrier* should be, and at 00:26 their strained gazing was rewarded with a faint pinprick of light at masthead height. A relieved Lieutenant Hutchins quickly rapped orders to his crew. Tired seamen hauled in the sweeping gear, just in time for the pre-planned turn. At the appointed time each ship turned to port and sailed back through the swept channel, the motor launches now astern of the larger ships.

Feverishly, the navigators on each ship calculated their position in the Channel, basing everything on dead reckoning yet having to account for the tide and wind and their effect on their own speed through the water.

It was vital they maintain both their schedule and their formation with the rest of a flotilla they could barely see. Precision was essential now: carry on too far north and they risked running into the landing craft heading south; turn too early and the manoeuvre would have been for nothing. Almost an hour after they had made the first turn, the navigators instructed their skippers to come about and, almost as one, the flotilla turned south. No sooner had they assumed their new course than their revolutions decreased and the flotilla came to a halt in the middle of the sea. The tide had shifted by now, and the sweeping gear had to be redeployed to starboard with the prevailing flow. Finally, at 01:55, the flotilla got underway again, heading south for Normandy, each crew justifiably proud of their successful manoeuvre.

But behind them the convoys were struggling. S5 Lignite had followed Pannier out of the Solent a few hours behind them. Composed of no fewer than forty-seven landing craft and two MLs it had quickly become strung out on the rolling seas, obliging their escorting MLs to hurry back and forth along the line, chivvying the backmarkers on. The convoy's most important component was the ten LCTs carrying the Royal Engineers' AVREs, which would land immediately behind the DD tanks and moments ahead of the assault infantry. The seas battered the landing craft and on the bridges the skippers constantly had to correct their course, shouting instructions down the voice pipe to the cox'n below in order to keep on the right bearing. Some found the only way to make the correct course was to steer 40° to starboard, into the swell, crabbing the landing craft forward. On board, even the crews were worn out by the weather, but for the Royal Engineers it was purgatory. On LCT 1094 Lieutenant Ivan Dickinson was alarmed by the constant creaking of rivets as the LCT crested each wave, and the landing craft's involuntary 'shimmy' along its tank deck. Inexplicably it made him think of Carmen Miranda, the notorious 'Brazilian Bombshell' dancer. But that was a pleasant memory and the sensation on board was most definitely not. Its effects were even worse. When the tank commanders gathered in the wardroom for a meal and Orders Group, it was not long before one of the men could contain himself no longer. To the revulsion of the assembled party, a stream of the dinner they had just consumed reappeared. Once it had begun there was no stopping it, and soon a basin was being passed around. The O Group was cancelled.

With their heavy load of 1,044 rockets raised high above the centre of gravity, the five LCT(R)s suffered as their crews struggled to keep them on course in the slow convoy. Two had to drop out with engine trouble, but remarkably, despite one requiring the replacement of a cylinder head in the cramped, pitching engine room, both managed to effect repairs and regain their positions in the convoy.

592 LCA(HR) Flotilla suffered even more. Special towing eyes had been fitted to the lower hull of the modified LCAs along with rigid spans so that the small boats could be towed by the AVRE LCTs with their crews on the larger boats. The rough swell quickly played havoc with the arrangement and the first tow snapped barely 5 miles outside the Solent. As her crew watched from the safety of LCT 1092, LCA(HR) 1001 drifted away astern. ML 200 dutifully raced to the abandoned craft and a rope tow was fastened to her, but in the swell this soon parted and the LCA foundered. Over the course of the passage the rest of the LCA(HR)s suffered the same fate, straining at their tows and shipping water. LCA(HR) 977's bottom was ripped out by the towing gear and what was left of the craft plummeted below the waves. On board LCT 1016, Lieutenant Lumb could see his little command filling with water. He conferred with Lieutenant Nix on the bridge and the LCT skipper allowed Lumb to bring his craft alongside. But as the towing gear was hauled in, LCA(HR) 1070 banged against the LCT's metal hull and her fragile timber gave way, caving in a hole on the starboard bow. Water poured in and reluctantly the tow was cut. On LCT 1082, Lieutenant Edwards of the South African Naval Forces grew increasingly concerned as LCA(HR) 1064 filled with water. Soon the little boat in tow was acting like a makeshift sea anchor, dragging the LCT off course and schedule. Reluctantly Edwards called Lieutenant Chandler to the bridge and told him he had no choice but to cut the boat loose. 1064 floated astern and was quickly lost to the dark waves.[1]

Seven hundred feet above the water, Pilot Officer William Kirkham peered into the gloom ahead of him. The clear skies over most of the Channel were now darkened by a growing cloud bank above, and only occasional breaks let through the slimmest shafts of moonlight that glittered on the sea below.

Kirkham could no longer see the other fourteen Albemarles of 295 and 570 Squadrons that he knew were nearby. On board each were ten paratroopers of 6 Airborne Division, their task to secure Drop Zone V, just west of the village of Varaville, some 10 miles north-east of Caen and well to the east of the Caen Canal and the River Orne. Kirkham and his fellow crews' job was to drop them there. But now, with so little light, Kirkham was almost totally reliant on Flying Officer Ernest Brown navigating them towards the enemy coast from his little table in the nose space below.

In most of the aircraft were men of C Company 1 Canadian Parachute Battalion. Their task was to secure the drop zone and protect the paratroopers in the leading planes: a platoon of men of 22 Independent Parachute Company, Pathfinders who would use flares and beacons to guide larger forces to the drop zone. Four more Albemarles lagged a little behind, each towing a Horsa glider with additional equipment. Thirty minutes behind them and still flying over England were the rest of the Canadian battalion and 9 Parachute Battalion. While the Canadians would demolish bridges over the River Dives and secure high ground to defend against German counter-attacks, 9 Battalion would storm the Merville Battery and prevent it from firing on Force S in a few hours' time. Accompanying them was Captain John Thompson of the Royal Artillery. Along with a small party of naval ratings, his task was to report the outcome of the attack to HMS *Arethusa*, so that the cruiser could take additional action if necessary.

As they approached the coast, Brown provided a reassuring commentary over the intercom, and five minutes from the drop zone Kirkham ordered 'Action Stations'. Sitting in the fuselage, the parachute stick's leader, Lieutenant John Madden, commander of 9 Platoon, slipped off his flying helmet, donned his parachute helmet and fumbled with the hatch bolts. After sliding them back he heaved the two hatch doors up, opening the 2-metre-long gap in the bomber's floor. Cold air rushed into the plane and Madden looked down on to the dark waters of the Channel. Carefully he manoeuvred into place, leaning over the gap, his hands firmly gripping the hatch doors to hold himself above the abyss. Within minutes surf could be seen, and then, at approximately 00:25, the black blur of land. In a few moments the navigator would switch on the red light and, fifteen seconds after that, the green. Madden couldn't see the light, so he waited for Private Beirness to alert him from behind.

The seconds ticked by.

'Green on!'

'What?' yelled Madden over the rushing of the wind and the snarl of the propellors. 'Did you say green?'

'Yes I said green – go!' Beirness shouted angrily.

There was no time for further questions. Madden pulled his arms in and let himself plunge almost horizontally out of the fuselage. Quickly his men followed him, Beirness, Belec, Pidleburg and Sergeant Keel tumbling into the night. Sixth in line, Corporal MacDonald lurched towards the gap but just as he was about to launch himself one of the doors fell shut. A frantic heave opened it enough for him to jump through, but behind him the door slammed shut again. As the remaining paras struggled to open it Kirkham, knowing they had long overshot the drop zone, circled round. By the time the four men jumped, there was no telling where they might land.

At strongpoint 17, Oberst Ludwig Krug and one of his officers emerged from the network of underground bunkers to smoke cigarettes. Standing on the exposed hillside overlooking the coast, a strong north-westerly wind whipped at the commander of 736 Regiment's uniform as they chatted. In the distance, somewhere near the coast, they spotted spirals of flak ascending and the muted rattle of gunfire carried on the breeze. Air raids were not uncommon – the very reason Krug now lived in the damp bunkers of the strongpoint and not in the much more comfortable château at Beuville was the near constant threat from the skies. Now, yet again, the faint sound of engines droned somewhere to the east. As he looked around, Krug could have sworn he saw aircraft swooping out of the sky. Then, barely visible, he saw pale specks descending. 'Parachutes,' he hissed, and hurried down into the bunker to raise the alarm.*

Seconds after he left the plane, the static line yanked Madden's parachute out of its pack and it billowed open above him. Swinging beneath his silken canopy the Canadian descended the 700 feet in a mere thirty seconds. He could spy the odd farm building and some woods, but no landmark he could use as a point of reference. A line of flak ascended disconcertingly near to him but then he was down, landing on soft pasture. The cold night air was replaced with earthy smells and the feeling of damp ground.

The source of the flak was only 200 yards away, still spitting tracer high into the sky. Madden shrugged free his parachute harness and quickly

---

* Later in June, Krug gave some differing accounts of the night. He told his Allied interrogators he saw parachutes (WO 208/3590) but told fellow PoWs that he saw a fiery glow over his sector followed by up to forty gliders descending (WO 208/4618). The former is probably more likely.

moved to a nearby hedge where, a few minutes later, Privates Beirness and Belec emerged from the darkness. They waited a little longer, but no one else came. Reasoning that the slight delay in jumping might have carried them as much as 1,000 yards beyond their drop zone, Madden decided they should head north. They crossed the pastureland into a cornfield and immediately dropped down into the shallow camouflage the crop provided. Three men were heading their way. The paratroopers' fingers tensed on their triggers, silently waiting as the men closed in. Then an urgent whisper in an unmistakable Canadian accent – Keel, MacDonald and Pidleburg had found them. But other voices carried across the field – German ones. The men lay still until they faded away and then quickly moved in the opposite direction. Now with a slightly more comforting party to accompany him, Madden carried on towards Varaville. The small group looked intently for distinguishing landmarks – crossroads, clusters of buildings, streams, anything that looked like something they'd memorized from the reconnaissance photographs they had studied so intently. But there was nothing. Slowly it dawned on the men that they had absolutely no idea where they were.

Somewhere nearby, Sergeant Earl Rice of 8 Platoon hung from a tree watching German troops scurry around below. Barely daring to breathe, he waited until they departed and only then cut the straps holding him and clambered down the tree. He'd spied a village as he descended from his Albemarle and cautiously made his way towards the outskirts where, to his relief, he found five of his men. Circling the village they found the remaining four. Not one of them had been able to spot a distinguishing feature as they descended to earth.

Little did the two groups of Canadians milling around in the dark realize, but they were in fact the first Allied forces to land in Sword sector on D-Day. Just a few miles east they had been pipped to the post of the record of being the very first men to land in Normandy by Major John Howard and his small party of glider-borne infantry.[*] Even as the Canadians wandered around unfamiliar fields, in one of the most daring actions of the war Howard and his men seized the two bridges over the Caen Canal and River Orne. Over the coming hours thousands more men would fall from the sky, forming a tentative bridgehead to the

---

[*] There is some debate as to whether Howard's party were beaten to this record by US paratroopers behind Utah. At any rate, Howard's men were the first to land in the Eastern Task Force area.

east. But they would need support from the sea if the bridgehead were to be held.[2]

At strongpoint 17, telephones rang, pulling bleary-eyed men from their sleep. As he arrived back at the strongpoint after driving an officer to strongpoint 14, Obergefreiter Hans Sauer was informed by the gate guard that he had seen a parachute a little to the north. Inside the strongpoint chaos already reigned and Sauer quickly mustered a patrol. Nervously the men headed back out on to the dark road into Colleville, out of the protective comfort of the strongpoint. Advancing slowly and silently they reached the southernmost houses of the town and turned west into a meadow, heading in the direction the guard had seen the silken canopy descending. There, in the centre of the field, lay a discarded parachute. The patrol checked the hedges around the meadow, wary that the owner could be watching them closely, but after a few minutes of half-hearted searching the anxious men decided to retire to the strongpoint. Sauer retrieved the parachute and the group made their way back across the field.

Reaching the lane that ran parallel to the west of the high street, they suddenly stumbled into a group of armed men in the darkness. Hearts thumped with adrenalin and panic, and weapons were raised at point-blank range as the men began to shout. It was only when they realized they spoke the same language that the weapons were tentatively lowered. Angry but relieved, their nerves almost shattered, Sauer's patrol hurried back to strongpoint 17.

Inside the strongpoint's command bunker Krug and Leutnant Hanke[*] studied a map of the Normandy area, trying to make sense of the reports just received from Bénouville. Allied soldiers had landed there and were even now in charge of the bridges across the Caen Canal and River Orne. Confused reports of further fighting east of the bridges started to trickle in, and at 00:45 Krug put his regiment on alert. Fifteen minutes later his corps commander, General Erich Marcks, called the strongpoint. Krug outlined what he knew, then gave voice to his own suspicions.

'It's the invasion,' he told the general.

'It's possible, but let's wait to find out more,' Marcks told him. Even so, the general placed 84 Corps on high alert.

---

[*] Leutnant was the lowest officer class and broadly equivalent to a second lieutenant in the British Army.

General Wilhelm Richter studied the new reports coming into his HQ bunker in the old quarry at St Julien, just outside of Caen. There was no doubt now that the airborne attacks were real, but what did they actually mean – was this a raid or the long-expected invasion? At 01:42 Richter got through to Edgar Feuchtinger's HQ. He knew that 21 Panzer could not be committed without Rommel's orders, and right then Rommel was in Herrlingen in south Germany on leave. But he could request that the units of 21 Panzer within his division's sector be temporarily transferred to his command. In fact elements of 125 Panzer Grenadier Regiment positioned east of the River Orne were already engaging the airborne forces of 6 Division.

Three hundred miles south near Bordeaux, Vize-Admiral Theodor Krancke,[*] commander of Naval Group West, was abruptly woken from his sleep when his aide rushed into his hotel room shortly after 02:30. 'Landings have begun in the Cotentin near Caen,' he breathlessly told him. Krancke sat up and looked quizzically at his assistant. Only a few hours previously, before he had left his headquarters in Paris, he had recorded in the command's war diary that it was unlikely the Allies had yet assembled a fleet large enough to invade France. Even when his intelligence chief reported a BBC radio broadcast that appeared to be a coded message to the French Resistance, he attached no significance to it. Now it looked like he might be wrong. 'Oberbefehlshaber West[†] insists that this is a diversionary attack and not the real invasion. We are of the opinion that this is the real thing. Shall we send out the codeword?'

'Yes,' replied Krancke, 'send out the code immediately.' He quickly got dressed while the codeword Grosslandung ('large landing') was flashed across his commands.

In Le Havre, Konter-Admiral Hans-Udo von Tresckow[‡] had already been monitoring incoming reports for several hours when he received the signal from Naval Group West. Immediately he put his command at a state of readiness and began to contact his various subordinates. It did not take long – von Tresckow's only significant operational unit was 5 Torpedoboot Flotilla which, after the loss of one boat less than two weeks

---

[*] A vize-admiral was equivalent to a rear admiral in the Royal Navy.
[†] Commander in Chief West, Gerd von Rundstedt's command, with overall authority for the defence of western Europe.
[‡] Konter-admiral is a rank that broadly falls between a commodore and a rear admiral in the Royal Navy.

ago and another in dry dock, could only muster three ships. In addition he had five boats of 38 Minesweeping Flotilla, a collection of whalers adapted to serve as patrol/escort boats from 15 Vorpostenboot Flotilla, and a number of small minelaying and sweeping boats from 10 Räumboot Flotilla. Outside the weather was not particularly favourable for sailing, and after hurried discussions with Korvetten-Kapitänen[*] Palmbern and Rall, it was clear that their 38 and 15 Flotillas would be of little use at sea, while the Räumboote were far too small.

At 03:55 von Tresckow got through to Korvetten-Kapitän Heinrich Hoffmann. There was little in the way of hard facts he could pass on to the commander of 5 Torpedoboot Flotilla. There had been heavy aircraft activity all night and paratroopers were reported in the area south of Ouistreham but it was not possible to see what was happening at sea – aerial spotting in the dark was impossible and only a handful of radar stations were operational. Ominously, those that had not been destroyed by enemy bombing reported that they were being jammed. Nonetheless, confused reports referred to unidentified ships near Port-en-Bessin. Hoffmann was to take his flotilla and investigate.

Hoffmann hurriedly alerted his captains and started to prepare. Information continued to filter into his bunker, but with little in the way of useful facts. More ships were reported at the far western edge of the Seine Bay but there was no specific information on the enemy's location, type or strength. He hurried down to the quayside and boarded T28.[3]

At sea, 1 Minesweeping Flotilla's temporary course reversal meant that the neighbouring flotilla pulled ahead of them – the convoys following Channel 10, which included Force D, were much faster and easily able to keep pace with the sweepers. And so at 02:50, Commander Herbert Lewis in HMS *Fraserburgh* led 15 Minesweeping Flotilla into the lowering position, the anchorage area that Force S was bound for. Guided by his navigator he carefully manoeuvred the flotilla to a position 9 miles north of the coast and a danlayer dropped a buoy to mark the centrepoint. But the sweepers didn't stop and rest on their laurels – Lewis continued in a broad curve to the east and the sweepers started carving out a channel for Force D's bombardment positions.

In the convoys following them, for those who had finally slipped into

---

[*] A korvetten-kapitän is broadly equivalent to a lieutenant commander in the Royal Navy.

fitful sleep only a few hours ago, the respite was brief. Reveille on the LSIs was 04:30, giving the men time to have a last meal on the mess deck and then prepare their kit before they embarked in the LCAs. On the LCTs men crawled out from under their vehicles while the chains holding them in place creaked and strained menacingly as the vessels wallowed in the seas. Officers who had begged floor space in the tiny wardrooms emerged on to the bridge to find the first glows of twilight on the northeast horizon, while Benzedrine-fuelled skippers with bloodshot eyes stared into the dark gloom ahead. Awakening on the deck of LCT 1094's wardroom, Ivan Dickinson's first trip was to the railings on the aft deck. Nor was he alone – in each convoy a curious wake of vomit lay behind each landing craft. But slowly the fleet was coming back to life again.

On HMS *Glenearn* infantrymen swung themselves off the metal bunks and tramped down the ship's passages as each unit was called to breakfast in the mess hall. In the troop spaces men played pontoon for invasion money, others read or gossiped, many lay in their bunks trying to ignore the pitching and rolling. Those that could ate their meal. In D Company 2 East Yorks' troop space a section commander placed his loaded Sten gun on a table, but as the ship rolled the gun slid to the edge and fell to the deck. The sudden clatter of a machine gun firing spat around the room, sending men diving for cover as several bullets ricocheted off bulkheads and deckheads.* The sound of the shots echoed away and men cautiously got to their feet in a tirade of bad language. Then someone noticed the blood spurting from Sergeant Eric Ibbetson – a bullet had smashed into his right thigh and cut his femoral artery. Men rushed to try and put pressure on the wound while others ran off to find medical officers, but within minutes the life had literally drained out of the sergeant. Two other men were in the sick bay with wounds that would stop them going ashore that day.[4]

Lost in the Norman countryside, Lieutenant Madden had decided the best thing to do was speak to a local and work out where they were. His small band of men were crouched by a deserted lane leading to a collection of dilapidated buildings, but as he outlined his plan of approach in hushed whispers, a cyclist suddenly appeared like a spectre. The blackened features of the Canadians stared up into the face of a slightly puzzled

---

* The Sten was notorious for accidentally discharging if dropped, a result of the open bolt design.

German soldier as he pedalled past and carried on his way. Wide-eyed, Madden quickly decided not to tempt fate. He signalled his men and they scurried across the lane and into some shadows, just as a cry broke the silence: 'Halt!' Madden looked back – the cyclist had turned and was heading back towards them. At any moment he would be close enough to see the paratroopers, and they were unlikely to pass a second inspection. Tightly gripping his Sten, Madden waited until the cyclist was closer. He squeezed the trigger.

For a fleeting moment, the true situation registered with the German and he made to veer away, but a few quick bursts were all Madden needed. The bike wobbled then fell with a clatter and the rider collapsed into the road. The burst of gunfire echoed away but the silence of the night was now gone. Hurried footsteps and the rattling of equipment came from the farm and the paratroopers fled across a field and sought shelter in the dark hedgerows.

The Canadians' wanderings led them across a marshy pasture, their irritation at the wretched terrain tempered by the protection the tall grasses this small patch of wilderness offered. They emerged, exhausted, into a small wood on the other side. Now, with dawn's early glow illuminating the sky to the north-east, Madden knew it would soon be too light to risk moving. They settled into the cover of the trees, and while Sergeant Keel took the first watch, the lieutenant fell into a blissful sleep.[5]

At 04:45, X-23 emerged from the waves once more. In their original instructions their next act would be to move south to within 3,000 yards of the beach, where Lieutenant Jim Booth would launch a dinghy and from there signal with a lamp for the invasion force. Once X-23 had returned to her position 7,000 yards offshore to do the same, the two signal lamps would form the perfect guideline for the DD tanks and landing craft, leading them directly to the centre of their landing area. But down on the seabed, Lieutenant Geoffrey Lyne and Booth had discussed the plan. Their observation through the periscope on 4 June had led them both to realize that an approach that close to the coast, and then surfacing to launch a dinghy, was a risk too far. They were almost certain to be seen from the shore, which could compromise the entire invasion. Booth was crestfallen.

And now a new problem presented itself. Repeatedly switching the gyro repeater compass on and off had caused it to become unsettled. Based on the crew's dead reckoning, it appeared to have developed an error of 150°. It was effectively useless, and without its bearings Lyne had no means of accurately checking their position after they had repositioned in darkness the previous night. Once again he turned to the magnified periscope and looked at the landmarks he had previously observed. Even in the hazy morning light they could be made out quite clearly, but being unable to check their exact bearing, he couldn't triangulate their position precisely. He looked at the signalling lamp on the deck behind him. In his gut he knew they were in the right place and pure pride made him want to affix the amber shade to the lamp, a signal that the submarine was positioned accurately. But his professionalism took over. His lengthy training at the Royal Navy's school of navigation, the high standards and the sense of duty they had instilled told him what he must do. He knelt down and carefully fixed the green shade to the front of the lamp, the signal that the submarine was within 300 yards of the planned position. He donned as much wet-weather gear as he could and then, aided by his colleagues, clambered up on to the deck and mounted the lamp on a binnacle.

In spite of the churning seas, overhead Lyne could hear the roar of aircraft. The noise provided some comfort, but when he looked north, as far as he could see they were alone on the seas. Still, he hoped someone was there.

At 05:08, X-23 started signalling the flashing green light to seaward.[6]

5

OPENING SHOTS

IN THE DAWN TWILIGHT 3 GROUP'S MASSED STREAM OF LANCASTER bombers headed south over the Channel. Sitting in the nose of 'G' George, flying at 12,000 feet, Flight Sergeant Bob Armit concentrated on his usual task of watching for fighters. A dense mass of cloud billowed below him, obscuring his view of the waters below.

As they flew steadily closer to France, Flying Officer Murdock counted down the miles to the coast. Making landfall was usually a navigational matter and Armit's job was to look for useful features on the ground to help obtain exact fixes of their location. But this time landfall *was* their target. As long as their course was correct they should be able to bomb as they crossed the coast and then return directly to England.

'Twelve miles, skipper,' Murdock reported.

Armit glanced down at the cloud again – hopefully it didn't go too far down or they'd be bombing blind. As the bomber passed a bulbous pillar of wispy white on its port side, a slight gap exposed itself behind and Armit was suddenly staring down at the sea, a dark pit in the grey surround. As he stared he became aware of dozens of pale streaks, looking for all the world like little white tadpoles in blackened water. With a start he realized these were the wakes of dozens of ships, slowly making their way to the coast. And then the cloud closed again and they were gone. Now there was no doubting that this really was 'the big show'.

'Ten miles, skipper.'

Squadron Leader Derek Stewart slowly started to lose height. 'G' George lowered itself into the cloud and tears of water streaked across the Perspex nose in front of Armit until they emerged above the English Channel. It was darker down here – the glow of the sun below the horizon was subdued by the heavy clouds. There was no obvious sign of the fleet that Armit had just spied; instead, he saw two dark blurs in the water to port, and tiny twinkles of light slowly climbing towards him. Lazily they closed on the Lancaster until, at the last moment, they seemed to accelerate and flew past the nose like an express train. The Lancaster lifted as Stewart returned them to the cloud immediately above, then dropped back out thirty seconds later. Flak still arced into the sky behind them, but 'G' George was no longer the target. Turning ahead, Armit concentrated on the bomb run – they would be over the target in less than two minutes.*

Stewart dropped to 10,500 feet. As they closed on the shore the cloud base darkened and fluffy bands of cumulus hung all around, exposing and then concealing the sea below. At first Armit could make out very little, but as his eyes adjusted he scanned to the east and could discern the dark line of the coast around the Seine Estuary. He followed the dark line westwards, trying to keep the dark ridge of land in sight until he was facing directly ahead – and there the Orne Estuary materialized in front of him. Then the wisps of another cloud closed around the Perspex and it was gone. Emerging on the other side, the faint glares of the Pathfinder flares started to reveal themselves, and columns of bright flak licked randomly into the sky.

Barely 3 miles from the target, Stewart and Armit could make out the dark shadows of more bombers dawdling ahead, directly on the path to the target indicators. There wasn't much chance of a clean pass over them so Armit looked east, where the clouds were a little more dispersed. The estuary was clearer now; he could see the river mouth and just to the right of it the rigid lines of a canal. The water widened as it entered a port area, and as he looked, a series of locks revealed themselves. That would do nicely.

Behind him the long bomb bay doors opened, revealing the collection of 1,000lb and 500lb bombs within. 'Left a little,' Armit coaxed his pilot. 'Right, just a fraction . . . steady . . . steady . . . bombs gone!' At 05:10 the Lancaster lifted gently as the bombs tumbled out of the bay. Armit watched them fall and saw a geyser erupt below, the spray clear against the dark water. Then another, then a flash as a bomb struck the ground – to Armit's eyes a direct hit on one of the locks. To their right other flashes

---

* In all likelihood, Armit had probably spied Hoffmann's group of ships as they sailed west.

lit up buildings and trees below as the rest of 3 Group laid a carpet of bombs on the seaside town.[1]

Just below on the avenue Michel Cabieu, named after Ouistreham's last saviour, Odette Mousset was sheltering under the main staircase of the Hôtel de Normandie. She'd been awake since shortly after midnight when the first air raid sirens had sounded and the low rumble of distant aircraft had been joined by the sound of nearby flak. Not long after that, hammering had led her to the front door, and two breathless Germans who had only been drinking inside a few hours previously urged her to leave. 'Die Engländer kommen,' they warned her.

She had stayed of course, but now, as hundreds of bombs fell on Ouistreham, she started to wonder if it was the right idea. Thunderous explosions shook the hotel, the convulsions throwing clouds of dust off the stairs and plaster from the ceilings. On and on the roaring continued, rattling the windows. An ornament fell from a mantelpiece, shattering on the tiled floor below.

Just as the explosions seemed to be dying down, there was an almighty blast at the front of the hotel, shattering all the windows and collapsing timbers. Stunned, Mousset huddled tighter under the stairs until the noise eased. Then she nervously emerged from her makeshift shelter and made her way to the front of the building. The entrance hall was ablaze, flames lapped at the walls and a burning timber crashed down from the ceiling. There was no hope of extinguishing the fire. Mousset ran through the back of the hotel and into a wood on the triangular patch of land between the houses opposite and the main locks. Turning round, she watched as flames licked up through the roof of her hotel.[2]

3 Group's raid had lasted a mere ten minutes, during which time the five squadrons' 106 Lancaster bombers dropped approximately 500 tons of high explosives on Ouistreham. Most squadrons reported between 50 and 100 per cent cloud over the target, and that the Pathfinder's markers appeared to have been dropped a touch east of the main battery at strongpoint Bass. Nonetheless, as the battery's garrison emerged from their shelters they found a near lunar landscape around them. Craters littered the shore and fires inland spoke of burning buildings. Several of the open gun emplacements had been damaged by near misses and an ammunition magazine had suffered a direct hit. To the relief of the garrison, its contents had not detonated.[3]

As 'G' George banked left and climbed back into the cloud, Sergeant Patrick Moakler looked back at Ouistreham from his tiny rear turret. The town was encased in a thick cloud of smoke and dust, within which explosions and fires glowed and pulsated. Glancing across the Channel, he could just make out small flashes of light as the battle at sea got underway. Then the Lancaster was swallowed by the welcome embrace of the clouds.

At 05:10, perfectly on time, Convoy Purify arrived at the lowering position. Scanning through the twilight gloom with his binoculars, Commander Edmund Currey spotted 15 Minesweeping Flotilla's buoy and, satisfied they were in the right location, turned to study his collection of vessels astern. The shadows of the large LCTs of 14 Flotilla, the three LCGs and accompanying LCS(L)s were all present and correct, but only a handful still towed the smaller LCP(L)s of 704 and 707 Flotillas – even now the crews were busy separating themselves from their parent craft. But as he peered more intently into the grey waters behind, at the scene slowly being revealed by the dawn light, he was pleased to see the small blobs of the various LCP(L)s whose tows had parted in the night as they gamely sailed through the heavy swell to join his party. The first landing craft had arrived off Sword.

At exactly the same time that Purify arrived off the coast, at his command post just outside Caen, General Richter received a new report from 736 Regiment's 2 Battalion at strongpoint 23. Paratroopers were dropping near Tailleville and attacking north towards Bernières-sur-Mer. Hauptmann Deptolla, 2 Battalion's commander, had already ordered 8 Company and 2 Company of 441 Ost Battalion to advance north to engage this new threat before they encircled Bernières. In the event, no reports would ever be received from these units.*

At strongpoint 17, Ludwig Krug had enjoyed a sleepless night full of confusing reports, uncertainty and confusion. Looking at his watch he realized dawn wasn't far away and took the opportunity to leave the bunker. Uneasily clambering on to the roof, he looked north. If anything was coming, it would come from there, he reasoned. To the north-east, in

---

* Richter speculated that they had been wiped out by the paratroopers. Given there were no paratroopers there, it's fair to assume they were overwhelmed by Force J and 3 Canadian Infantry Division's attack a few hours later.

the exact direction the sun should rise that morning, an orange glow illuminated Ouistreham. Krug quickly realized it was a false dawn, the flames from the bombing raid fuelling the thick smoke that might be mistaken for dark clouds.

Krug studied the town through his binoculars. The raid must have been heavy to have caused such damage – more evidence that this was no normal morning. He turned his eyes away from the flames and allowed them to adjust to the gloomy horizon at sea. The haze slowly lifted and his eyes began to focus when, with horror, he realized there was something there. Dark smudges on the water moved slowly and unnaturally, and as his eyes adjusted he became certain he was seeing ships. Within a few moments he knew for sure. The dark shadows of vessels manoeuvred far out at sea, some of the larger smudges on the water possibly capital ships. He hurried back below.[4]

Harassed, tired and confused, Heinrich Hoffmann led his warships to sea. If this was an invasion, he couldn't rate his chances too highly. Of his three ships, *Möwe* and *Jaguar* dated to the 1920s and their design was better suited to the First World War than the Second. Although as big as some Royal Navy destroyers, the German navies of the twentieth century had placed much more emphasis on the torpedo attack role the destroyer had first evolved from, and more properly classified their boats as Torpedoboote.* Designed to make massed torpedo attacks on fleets of enemy capital ships, the type had succeeded at Jutland twenty-eight years previously, but *Möwe*, *Jaguar* and their inter-war sisters were now mainly employed as escort vessels in the English Channel and North Sea, with little chance to use their six torpedo tubes. Although they had given solid service, by 1944 their hulls were tired and in frequent need of repair. Hoffmann sailed in the much newer T28, launched in 1942 and fresh from a four-month refit. Although her slab-sided bridge made her somewhat less attractive than her older sisters, she was at least fitted with more modern weapons and equipment. All three sported 10.5cm guns, although *Jaguar*'s were of a type that was never fully adopted into the Kriegsmarine and for which there was a chronic ammunition shortage. The crews too were less

---

* This classification has frequently caused the three ships to be misidentified as Schnellboote, commonly known as E-boats – the German equivalent of Royal Navy motor torpedo boats. In reality the only Schnellboot sorties on D-Day came from Cherbourg.

than ideal. Regular operational deployments meant that there was little time to train the young sailors and junior officers who had been drafted in to replace the more experienced men, who had been transferred to U-boats. But although Hoffmann didn't yet realize it, D-Day would be the torpedo boats' great opportunity to fulfil their original role.

At 05:00, as they ploughed on into the freshening seas, the crews could just make out the vast formations of 3 Group's aircraft through gaps in the cloud above them, and the occasional hopeful burst of flak was sent their way. But at sea level, in the dawn's gloom, the view ahead was far from clear and was about to become decidedly worse. A few miles east of Force S, flying just above the waves and dead on time, Wing Commander Maher banked his Douglas Boston and pointed its nose north. With a flick of a switch, acrid titanium tetrachloride began pouring from the cylinders enclosed in the bomb bay. As soon as it came into contact with the damp sea air it hydrolysed, creating a thick white cloud of smoke that billowed behind the aeroplane like a sea fog. Behind Maher, the rest of 88 Squadron RAF made passes every ten minutes, thickening and lengthening the spectral screen.

Now Hoffmann's little force approached the great white curtain in line ahead at 28 knots, their anti-aircraft guns flicking tracer at any Boston that came within range. There was no single smokescreen now – each successive aircraft created a new cloud that billowed and blended with the previous ones drifting east. At sea level wind whipped the smoke this way and that, dispersing it more quickly than the Allies had hoped. Nonetheless, the Germans could see nothing ahead of them as they entered the pungent fog. Choking fumes curled around the warships, and on the open bridges and gun positions men pulled scarves and sweaters over their mouths and closed their eyes to the stinging smoke.

At perhaps 05:11, a gap in the cloud allowed the torpedo boats to see ahead of them. Blinking clear their tear-filled eyes, the crews looked out expectantly. The sight was overwhelming – majestic, awesome, entrancing and terrifying all at once. Hoffmann gaped – almost the entire horizon appeared to be alive with shipping, now illuminated by the morning light. His men reported at least six battleships and twenty destroyers. What could his three boats do? He felt as if he was sitting in a rowing boat.

Snapping back to his senses, Hoffmann quickly rapped out orders. Despite the incredible display of enemy firepower ahead of him, he had to keep his little force ploughing onwards for a few more minutes. Attack, not retreat, was the first thing that came to mind, but he had to close the range. On the three ships, the crews nervously eyed the closing warships. This was a death ride in the truest sense of the term. Surely they couldn't survive this encounter?

In fact, Hoffmann had caught the invasion fleet at its most vulnerable moment, during the critical phase when the lead convoys were manoeuvring themselves to their various dispositions. HMS *Warspite*, *Ramillies* and *Roberts* were slowly heading down Channel 10 to their intended bombardment berths – these venerable capital ships were now the easternmost vessels of the invasion fleet. To the south, the cruisers *Arethusa*, *Mauritius*, *Danae*, *Dragon* and *Frobisher* were still being led by their attendant minesweepers on the loop connecting the two swept channels. Due west of the battleships, the densely packed convoys of the amphibious assault force were heading into the lowering position. There was barely a gap in the lines of vessels now heading south.

Warspite's radar operator had been tracking Hoffmann's little band, but the smokescreen – meant to protect them from German interference – now sheltered their enemy. There was no contingency for the warships to contact the Bostons of 88 Squadron – they had no frequency to reach them by wireless and they could only watch helplessly as each successive aircraft began laying a new protective screen in front of the advancing German vessels. The Royal Navy cursed the aircraft as they strained their eyes to the east.

Finally, HMS *Ramillies* sighted the enemy. Shortly after 05:15 a low boom echoed over the Eastern Task Force as she opened fire – the first shots to be fired by the Commonwealth fleet. The Germans too opened fire and the bow-mounted 10.5cm guns pounded away ineffectually at the enemy warships, while the lighter AA guns continued to engage the Bostons still laying smoke only a few hundred feet away. Minutes later, Hoffmann decided enough was enough. Estimating the range at 6,500 metres, he ordered his force to turn. At around 05.25, as they came broadside on, the command was given – 'Torpedo los!' Each warship fired its full complement of torpedoes. On T28 two of the torpedoes failed to launch, nonetheless sixteen of the 21-inch weapons slipped into the water and accelerated towards the Allied fleet.[*5]

---

[*] There is a huge variation in the distances reported during this opening battle at Sword. 88 Squadron reported laying smoke 1.5 miles (2,400 metres) east of HMS *Roberts*, Hoffmann's estimated range to the battleships when he ordered the torpedoes fired was 6,500 metres, and HMS *Warspite* recorded opening fire at an

The clamour of battle increased as HMS *Roberts* launched her opening salvo on Houlgate Battery at 05:23. Two 15-inch shells sped from her outsized turret and arced across the sky towards the enemy coast. Perched high on the hill just outside the seaside town of Houlgate, the battery was a significant threat to the invasion fleet and had been bombed some weeks prior. Already two of its six 155mm guns were out of action, but the remaining four could pour destruction on to the Allies at Sword and Juno. Slowly, methodically, *Roberts* shelled the battery until it was entirely obscured in smoke and dust and even the spotting aircraft couldn't see the fall of shot.

Suddenly, lookouts on either side of the bridge reported torpedoes to port and starboard. In horror, the crew searched for more ahead of them, but as far as they could see there was no immediate danger. The two torpedoes passed harmlessly on either side of the monitor. A few minutes later, lookouts on *Ramillies* spotted four torpedo tracks astern of them, but no further threat seemed to be inbound from the east. But having passed through the wide gaps of the big gun ships, the deadly torpedoes were closing on the denser shipping in the swept channels.

Due west of *Ramillies* lay 23 Destroyer Flotilla. Captain Peter Cazalet, following his orders, had assembled his flotilla to a near stop alongside the main swept channel, where they waited for the minesweepers of 165 BYMS Flotilla to sweep the path to their various anchorages in front of Sword Beach. Looking ahead and astern he couldn't help but glow with pride to see his flotilla in line. All modern S class destroyers, well armed with 4.7-inch guns and capable of 36 knots, the ships were veterans of the Arctic convoys – most had been present at the sinking of the *Scharnhorst* only five months earlier. Two of the ships were crewed by Norwegians: HMS *Shark* and *Success* had both been officially handed over to the Royal Norwegian Navy and recommissioned as HNoMS *Svenner* and *Stord* respectively. Now *Svenner* led the flotilla, her bow pointing south towards France. Behind her lay *Swift* and then Cazalet's own ship, *Saumarez*.

---

estimated range of 14,000 yards (12,800 metres). In all likelihood, 88 Squadron were further east than estimated, and Hoffmann was still among the clouds drifting eastwards when he fired, rather than completely clear of them. Hoffmann also estimated the time to be at 05:35. However, as most reports from the Allied fleet agree that *Svenner* was struck at around the same time, it seems likely that Hoffmann was in error. Assuming he was approximately 7km plus from *Svenner* when his ships fired, it will have taken at least six minutes for the torpedoes to make this distance.

Astern lay *Stord*, then *Scorpion* and *Scourge*, which had just joined them after escorting convoys. Over to the west he could see *Serapis*, now detached to carry out her own work on the starboard flank.

The flotilla bobbed in the rolling seas and watched as the convoys passed alongside them. Suddenly the relative calm on the bridge of *Svenner* was shattered as a lookout reported a torpedo track. Bringing his binoculars to his eyes, Lieutenant Commander Tor Holthe looked to port and saw, to his horror, the telltale line of bubbles rapidly extending in his direction. He quickly issued a series of orders: 'Hard a port, full ahead starboard, full astern port!' The only hope was to turn towards the torpedo, presenting the narrow bow of the ship rather than her full length. By throwing the boat round to port, reversing the port engine and accelerating with the starboard, they might just make it. Meanwhile the signalling pennants for 'torpedo port' were rushed up the mast. But it was too late – even before *Svenner* had got underway, the torpedo had closed to less than 100 metres. To Lieutenant Desmond Lloyd, one of the Royal Navy's liaison officers on the bridge, the only thing that came to mind was how high he would be thrown into the air.

Just after 05:30, the torpedo slammed into *Svenner*'s hull, perfectly amidships and between the ship's boiler rooms. The huge explosion pushed her over and she immediately started to list to starboard. There was no time for damage reports – to Holthe the outcome was inevitable, and he gave the order to abandon ship.

All around *Svenner* was chaos. On board HMS *Largs*, Rear Admiral Talbot had observed Hoffmann's bold attack with great admiration, but now watched aghast as a burst of steam erupted from the Norwegian destroyer and her funnel fell away. Meanwhile the bridge crew spotted another torpedo on the port bow and went into immediate reverse. Slowly the flagship shuddered to a stop and began to move astern; seconds later the torpedo passed just a few feet across her bow. Now its course took it straight towards the destroyer HMS *Virago*, leading Convoy S7 to the lowering position. But, having seen *Svenner*'s signal at the last moment, Lieutenant Commander Archibald White had quickly ordered the ship full ahead and, her siren sounding short warning bursts, *Virago* quickly accelerated out of the way, followed by *Kelvin*, *Serapis* and *Verulam*. Their bridges were scenes of pandemonium as the ships jostled for space to avoid the torpedo, the captains giving quick orders to avoid a collision. The deadly weapon passed astern of *Virago* and then came to the end of its run, slowly sinking to the seabed.

On HMS *Swift*, Lieutenant Commander John Gower[*] ordered his ship to close with *Svenner*. By now she was settling quickly and he could see the crew coming up from the lower levels of the destroyer, falling-in on deck, and then abandoning ship in orderly fashion. As he watched, the ship started to break in the middle. Holthe, certain now that nothing could be done, jumped into the sea, and as he treaded water he watched, devastated, as his ship broke into two. The centre slipped beneath the water and the bow and the stern lifted themselves above the waves, forming a perfect V. To Captain Kenneth Wright of 4 Commando, who had just come on deck as HMS *Princess Astrid* sailed past, it looked like 'the two ends folded together, as if it were a pocketknife closing'. But help was at hand as first HMS *Swift* then the yacht-cum-headquarters ship HMS *St Adrian* and LCI(S) 522 arrived and began picking up survivors. In total, eleven officers and 161 enlisted men were plucked from the water. *Swift* picked up fifty-seven of them, including Desmond Lloyd, before she had to move to her bombarding position. As he sat on the deck of his rescuer, Holthe reflected bitterly on his crew's greatest opportunity to strike at the enemy, now lost. *Svenner* hadn't even fired a shot.[6]

Hoffmann, meanwhile, had no idea what the effect of their attack had been. Steadying their turn only long enough to launch, the warships had manoeuvred again as soon as their torpedoes were away, putting their sterns to the enemy and racing back into the welcoming cloud of caustic fog. By now more shells were falling uncomfortably close, and as Hoffmann looked around him, the great water geysers erupting around his flotilla glowed with shades of pink, green and yellow.[†] The concussion knocked out T28's lighting and radio, but all three ships were soon protected by the swirling clouds of the Allied smokescreen. Then, in a clearing, lookouts spotted more ships, but these were coming towards them from the east. Korvetten-Kapitän Viktor Rall's 15 Vorpostenboot Flotilla was about to enter the fray.[‡]

If Hoffmann's torpedo boats had had little hope against the Allied fleet

---

[*] Uncle of the famous cricketer David Gower.
[†] Some Royal Navy capital ships had dye bags in the shell caps of their ammunition, making it easier to distinguish water columns produced by their own shells from those of other vessels.
[‡] For his actions in the early hours of 6 June, Korvetten-Kapitän Hoffmann was awarded the Knight's Cross of the Iron Cross. He later received the Knight's Cross with Oak Leaves in recognition of 5 Torpedoboot Flotilla's efforts in the Bay of Seine, which saw all of the torpedo boats sunk.

arrayed against them, Rall's six Vorpostenboote (Vp) were positively useless. Dozens of Vp flotillas had been formed by the Kriegsmarine during the war, mainly using converted trawlers. Equipped with a couple of deck guns and depth charges and manned by a naval crew, they were hardy craft, very capable in rough seas and extremely useful as convoy escorts. The Royal Navy employed such vessels judiciously and both sides even built their own armed trawlers to naval specifications. 15 Vp Flotilla was formed early in the war using whalers, each of between 350 and 400 tonnes, that had provided stout service in the North Sea and English Channel – every ship they had escorted between Hoek van Holland and Cherbourg had made it safely. Painted on the bridge of Vp 1509 alone were the silhouettes of twenty-one aircraft and three MTBs that Oberleutnant zur See Karl Schulz and his crew believed they had destroyed.*

As the war progressed new boats were added, sometimes larger, sometimes smaller, until in 1943 the flotilla started to receive significantly larger PA boats. These would have been familiar to Royal Navy sailors – the PA boats were *Flower* class corvettes being built in France at the outbreak of the war. Captured on the building slips when France fell, they were finally completed several years later and commissioned into the Kriegsmarine. But in June 1944 only PA 2 was serviceable, and now Rall used her to lead five of the elder sisters, Vps 1505, 1506, 1507, 1509 and 1511, to investigate landing craft reported off Caborg and Ouistreham.

If Hoffmann sent a warning, Rall didn't receive it in time. Moments later, as the whalers pressed on through the smoke, the clouds parted and they saw the full extent of the Allied vessels they had been sent to investigate. There was only one course of action open to Rall; his little force could do nothing in the face of such might. As the bow guns on the whalers opened fire, he ordered a 180° turn. Laboriously, the little ships began to make for the shelter of the smoke now blowing away behind them.

By now, *Warspite*, *Mauritius* and *Arethusa* had joined *Ramillies* in targeting the enemy vessels, and their shells threw up great geysers around the retreating ships. In *Warspite*'s radar room, the operator watched the little dots of the ship's 15-inch shells as they raced across the radar screen towards their targets. This broadside was perfectly aligned – the shells were headed directly towards the echoes of the enemy ships. They

---

* Although this was almost certainly a considerable exaggeration of their actual successes, Vp 1509 could at least claim some part in the sinking of MTB 201 in June 1942.

streaked closer until, at approximately 05:45, they intersected with one of the dots and disappeared. On the bridge, Commodore Marcel Attwood watched with satisfaction as a shell plunged into one of the enemy boats.

On the bridge of Vp 1509, Schulz had no warning of the shell that tore through his ship. With an explosion and a great column of water, the whaler briefly disappeared from view. The crews of the other boats stared, open-mouthed, as spray cascaded down around them. When the view cleared, 1509 was already heeling over to starboard and slowly sinking by the stern. Bravely, Oberleutnant zur See Helmut Steinjan steered Vp 1511 towards the chaotic scene. As it came alongside the doomed vessel, scrambling nets were hastily thrown over the side and shattered men were pulled from the water. But even as Schulz was hauled to safety, all around more geysers were thrown up and jagged shell splinters arced across the sea, striking 1511 and killing her own crew. After ten minutes, with casualties mounting, Steinjan had no choice but to break off the rescue. As 1511 pulled away, eight men still waiting on a rescue float pleaded to be saved, but it was too late. 1509's stern slipped below the waves and the bow rose skyward, while the surviving whalers made towards the shelter of the smoke and set course for Le Havre.*7

The Kriegsmarine's sole action of the day at Sword did not create the sort of disruption to the invasion that Hoffmann's high command might have hoped. Even while his torpedo boats had made their attack, undistracted,

---

* Rall attributed 1509's loss to a mine. However, *Warspite*'s crew were certain they had struck an enemy ship, which was observed on radar and from the bridge. To Attwood's mind it was an *Elbing* class destroyer, although none was present and none of Hoffmann's torpedo boats were sunk. However, Attwood's description of the boat sinking by the stern is in accord with Rall's report of 1509's fate, and there can be no doubt that is what Attwood actually saw. If it did fall victim to *Warspite*, in all likelihood the 15-inch shell simply passed straight through the whaler's flimsy hull and didn't detonate – had it done so, 1509 would have been completely obliterated. However, Captain Middleton of *Ramillies* believed the kill may have been from their 6-inch guns, while *Mauritius*'s log suggests they thought their shells scored hits, and more accurately identifies the victim as a trawler. For their actions at Normandy, Korvetten-Kapitän Rall and Oberleutnant zur See Schulz were awarded the Knight's Cross of the Iron Cross, and Oberleutnant zur See Steinjan the German Cross in Gold. 15 Vp Flotilla found itself in action several times over the following days, but was hopelessly outgunned by the Royal Navy. After the loss of six more vessels the flotilla was withdrawn to Norway, rebuilt with surviving boats from other units, and remained there until the end of the war.

the first group of boats were pulling away from the lowering position. At 05:20 LCH 185 led the landing craft of Purify – now Assault Group 1 – south. At the heart of the formation the eight LCTs of 14 Flotilla carried the first of the innovative weapons it was hoped would win the beach: forty of the 13/18 Hussars' swimming DD Sherman tanks. On the flanks, the gunners on the three LCGs and three LCS(L)s studied the shore and surrounding seas intently. Around them buzzed half a dozen or so other craft, hurriedly collecting COPP personnel from the motor launch and LCH that had towed them most of the way across the Channel.

Behind them, more and more landing craft and assault ships were arriving at the lowering position. At 05:30, just as *Svenner* was hit, HMS *Largs* led Convoy Abner into the gathering mix of ships, bringing with her the vital six troopship LSIs carrying the assault infantry. *Svenner's* loss reminded all who saw her that this was the real thing, but even as they stared at her gruesome V for Victory, the men on board every ship that passed her knew that while their own ship was afloat, they would carry on.

Three minutes behind schedule, at 05:33, the anchor on board HMS *Glenearn* was let go and it tumbled into the sea below, its chain paying out behind it with a rumble that reverberated around the ship as the infantry filed towards their stations. As *Glenearn* swung on her anchor the men sorted themselves into their platoons and tramped across the deck to their allotted LCAs, swinging in the davits as the RM crews prepared them. Each platoon was allocated to a specific LCA, one that would take them to their part of the beach. Having trained with the men of 535 and 543 Assault Flotillas incessantly over the last six months, the soldiers and sailors knew their partners for the final show, and one by one the infantry clambered across the gunwales of the small assault craft, taking their allotted seats on the narrow benches so that they could disembark from them and on to the beach in the correct order. Once each vessel had completed its loading it was lowered into the water, electric motors straining as they took the 13.5-ton weight of a fully laden LCA. Dropping into the churning surf below, the boats became buoyant and thrashed around on the rough seas as the crews fumbled to release the hoisting hawsers. On board, the soldiers suddenly felt the movement of the much smaller vessels as they bobbed and rolled like corks. The sudden rise and fall of the boats as they simultaneously pitched forward and back and swung side to side quickly made an impact on the infantrymen and many of them regretted having eaten breakfast.

As the two assault companies of 2 East Yorks boarded the LCAs of 536 Flotilla in the davits of *Empire Cutlass*, the voice of Major Charles 'Banger' King, CO of A Company, came over the ship's tannoy. A popular officer who was known for inspiring his troops, he proceeded to read excerpts from Shakespeare's *Henry V*. As the men clambered into their assault craft his words echoed around them, occupying minds that might otherwise have dwelled too long on what lay ahead.

> And Crispin Crispian shall ne'er go by,
> From this day to the ending of the world,
> But we in it shall be remember'd;
> We few, we happy few, we band of brothers;
> For he to-day that sheds his blood with me
> Shall be my brother; be he ne'er so vile,
> This day shall gentle his condition:
> And gentlemen in England now a-bed
> Shall think themselves accursed they were not here,
> And hold their manhoods cheap whiles any speaks
> That fought with us upon Saint Crispin's day.

Dropping hundreds of small vessels from the sides of much bigger ships could never proceed without incident. On the other side of *Empire Cutlass*, LCA 791 reached the water and quickly became buoyant. As the hawsers above them slackened the crew moved to unshackle them while Marine Geoffrey Bett turned to his two engines and went through the start-up procedure. But to his disgust one refused to fire up. They had been problematic engines since he had been assigned to the boat and now, on the big day, they were playing up again. Reluctantly he informed Corporal Foden in the cox'n position, and Foden took them away from the ship on the one engine. But behind him Bett finally managed to get the troublesome engine working again. 791 turned and headed further away from *Glenearn*, and as they approached the rest of the flotilla, Foden called back to reduce engine revolutions on the first engine, unaware that the second was operating. Despite calling for slower speed, Foden suddenly realized they weren't losing any and LCA 993 was directly in their path. Desperately he turned the rudders in an attempt to clear her, but it was too late and 791 slammed into the back of her sister boat. The impact opened a large hole in the waterline below the ramp and the luckless LCA instantly began shipping water. Quickly the soldiers of 1 South Lancs on board removed their helmets and began baling for all they were worth.

All around them dozens of other LCAs formed into their respective flotilla formations and began their passage through the growing assortment of ships. As LCA 1383 pulled away from *Glenearn*, Captain Reginald Bateman, in charge of the Royal Marine crews of 543 Flotilla, smiled as Lieutenant Colonel Hutchinson ordered his bugler to play the general salute back to their parent ship. As they headed south they heard the strains of 'Roll out the Barrel' drifting across the waves from a passing motor launch. Hutchinson ordered his bugler to play 'Cook House' in reply.[8]

Just like the landing craft, most of the bombardment ships hadn't let themselves be distracted by Hoffmann's attack. At 05:30, an hour and a quarter ahead of schedule, HMS *Danae* opened fire on the 155mm gun battery at strongpoint 12 – Daimler – south of Ouistreham. The ammunition handlers passing the shells from the magazines to the hoists and the gunners in the turrets sweated as more broadsides were loaded. Busy with their work, they couldn't hear the cursing of Captain John Haines, bemoaning the warship's inability to make contact with their spotter aircraft. The first shells to fall on Sword were ragged and ineffectual.[*] A mere minute later, Captain Thomas Brownrigg on HMS *Scylla* decided to join in. *Scylla* had no allocated target, but on board Rear Admiral Philip Vian was privy to all the targets across the entire Eastern Task Force assault area. Ouistreham was visible to the south and Vian watched with delight as the ship's 4.5-inch guns registered hits on the shore.

Even as Helmut Steinjan pulled alongside the doomed Vp 1509, HMS *Roberts* shifted her fire on to Gonneville Battery, and as the German warships moved out of range *Warspite*, *Ramillies* and *Arethusa* returned to their tasks. Villerville Battery reluctantly came into action and a few geysers erupted ineffectually among the bombardment ships, but the German guns were almost immediately silenced by salvoes from *Warspite*. Flying high above the battery, Lieutenant Dick Law of the Royal Navy's 886 Squadron observed *Warspite*'s fall of shot and passed corrections back to the ship. As he soared north of the target, his Seafire

---

[*] Aerial photos taken on D-Day show a marked absence of shell holes around Daimler.

suddenly trembled, and as he glanced outside his cockpit he was horrified to see a shell flash past him on its way to the target. Quickly he flicked his aircraft away from the line of fire and resolved to stay clear of it for the rest of his sortie.* Meanwhile, *Ramillies* brought her guns to bear on Benerville Battery and soon orange winks of flame erupted from the hilltop on which four 155mm guns were positioned. *Frobisher* joined in, sending six salvoes arcing across the sky to join those from *Scylla* landing at Ouistreham. On board HMS *Arethusa*, the bridge crew anxiously looked towards the Merville Battery, straining to see any sort of signal from the paratroopers, while the wireless operator listened for contact from their Royal Artillery liaison officer. They had no way of knowing it, but Captain John Thompson was even then wandering north-west from Caen, where he had been misdropped during the night. Unsure of who now controlled the battery and aware that they might be shelling their own men, Captain Dalrymple-Smith ordered his crew to seek out alternative targets. At 05:50 *Arethusa*'s 6-inch guns joined in the melee of destruction at Benerville.†

The residents of Ouistreham listened to the increasing tempo of the bombardment with a mix of terror and hope. About twenty people were now cowering among the trees in the little wood with Odette Mousset, grateful at least that the bombers had passed. Even so, they could hear the occasional whistling of *Danae*'s shells passing over the town, and the thud of explosions a mile to the south-west as they erupted around Daimler. The burning hotel cast an eerie false dawn and unnatural streaks of orange light penetrated the thick fog of dust hanging around them. Timbers popped and sizzled as flames engulfed them, a surreal percussion accompanying the deep bass of the warships' guns. By now it was

---

* Stephen Ambrose (pp.268-9) relates a similar account to Law's, attributed to Wing Commander L. Glover of 26 Squadron RAF. However, Ambrose moved Glover's account of a post-D-Day event (recorded in Tute, p.167) to the morning of D-Day. A look at 26 Squadron's logs reveals that Glover did not actually fly with *Warspite* on D-Day.
† In fact, a small portion of men from 9 Parachute Battalion had executed a daring raid on Merville Battery in the early hours of the morning and had successfully suppressed the garrison. But they were unable to occupy it and lacked explosives to destroy the guns. Although German forces reoccupied it later in the day, 9 Battalion's actions neutralized the battery at the most crucial moment of D-Day.

clear that there must be a sizeable Allied force at sea, and that this was much more than just another air raid.

At 06:10, HMS *Scorpion* approached its allocated anchorage 5,000 yards north of the town. As reports came in from around the ship confirming each station's readiness, William Clouston studied the coast through his binoculars then examined his watch with equal seriousness. In theory their orders were to commence the bombardment at 06:45, but it was only just approaching 06:20. Clouston frowned and looked astern. Through the haze, 7,000 yards to the north, he could see the flash of *Danae*'s guns. Turning back to the south, he waited patiently for the shell's endpoint and was shortly rewarded with a cloud of smoke from somewhere inland. If Haines was firing, why shouldn't he?

Orders were rapped around the ship. In the director control tower, Sub Lieutenant Tony Ditcham studied the landmarks on Ouistreham seafront through the powerful rangefinder. Tracking right from the lighthouse he spotted the low white building with the tower, the town's old semaphore station, and further west the numerous concrete emplacements of Bass. 'Target in sight!' he called to the men in the transmitting station in the bowels of the ship. Circuits buzzed as elevation and bearing were transmitted to dials at each gun position and the crews lined up their weapons on the target. Shells and cartridges were rammed home, breeches and firing circuits were closed. Four little lights illuminated on a panel in front of Ditcham and he pressed the telephone buzzer to the bridge to report all was ready. The ship waited on the order to fire.

Clouston smiled approvingly. 'Let's begin, shall we?' he said to his number one, Lieutenant Stephen Beresford. Beresford picked up the telephone and with typical composure informed Ditcham, 'You may open fire.'

'Shoot!' called Ditcham to the men crammed around him in the tower, and the director layer pressed the firing button. At 06:26 the ship's four guns fired as one. The 4.7-inch shells streaked south, spinning wildly as they raced through the air.

Even though it hadn't done as much damage as they might have hoped, the RAF's bombing of strongpoint Bass only an hour previously had badly shaken the defenders. Now, some of the men might have hoped that the next blow would fall elsewhere. But as they squinted through the embrasures of their bunkers, some saw the dark shadows in the haze as the destroyers manoeuvred only 3 miles out at sea. Then they saw the twinkle of gun flashes in the gloom.

Less than seven seconds after they'd left *Scorpion*, the first shells crashed down around Bass. Men dived into shelters and bunkers as the explosions threw up vast clouds of sand and earth. Unteroffizier Helmut Schmidt[*] abandoned his 20mm flak gun and lay as flat as he could at the bottom of his trench as the debris fell back down like rain across the strongpoint. The blasts rumbled and echoed, bouncing off the buildings behind the beach and slowly receding as the sound waves raced out to sea. Then, less than a minute later, it happened again.

On *Scorpion*, the crew went through the steady, repeated motions of bombardment enthusiastically and without interruption. As each broadside threw up bursts of flame and dirt, Ditcham sought out new and more visible targets, and Clouston watched contentedly as the beach in front of Ouistreham erupted. On board HNoMS *Stord*, Lieutenant Commander Storcheil brought his crew into action and her 4.7-inch guns joined in the destructive fray, doubling the number of blasts along the beach. As he watched the impact on Bass from his Norwegian guns, Storcheil must have thought briefly of Holthe. But the loss of the *Svenner* aside, so far everything was proceeding just like an exercise. In fact, no one on shore seemed to be firing back.

For men like Clemmens Bonna, a twenty-year-old mailman conscripted from West Prussia who had arrived in Normandy in February, there was some comfort. Holed up in one of the strongpoint's bunkers with his commander Unteroffizier Guswich, the 4.7-inch shells were no threat to the 2-metre-thick roof and walls – as long as he didn't venture outside he should be safe. All the defenders of Bass could do was sit and wait for the tumult to end. And so very few of them could see what was unfolding offshore.[9]

Slowly the landing craft heading south organized themselves into formation. In the vanguard, with the landing craft of Assault Group 1, LCH 185 pulled forward to the very point of the spear. Now, effective control of the entire invasion's eastern flank temporarily rested with Commander Edmund Currey. Currey had joined the Royal Navy in 1920 at the age of fourteen and by the time war was declared was a lieutenant commander

---

[*] An unteroffizier is broadly equivalent to a corporal commanding a section or squad.

in charge of the destroyer HMS *Wrestler*. Commanding destroyers for most of the war, he had won the Distinguished Service Cross when *Wrestler*, along with HMS *Firedrake*, crippled the Italian submarine *Durbo* and captured key intelligence information before it sank. He was also awarded the Polish Cross of Merit in 1943 when his later command, HMS *Musketeer*, rescued some of the crew of the Polish warship ORP *Orkan* when she was torpedoed by a U-boat.

This marked the end of Currey's destroyer war – his next appointment was to HMS *Monck*, the Combined Training HQ, where he prepared for D-Day. In due course he was appointed to Force S as Deputy Senior Officer Assault Group (DSOAG) One, effectively second in command to Captain Eric Bush and tasked to take over his role if his commander was incapacitated. Among his responsibilities, he was in charge of Assault Group S3's Support Squadron, the armed landing craft that would be firing on the beaches in support of the first wave. Sailing on the foremost headquarters vessel during the initial landing, at the very tip of the point of the invasion force, authority was also devolved upon him to signal the codeword 'Scrub' to the fleet behind. Once this was broadcast, the entire assault on Sword would stop.

Now, pressed into the little available space between the compass binnacle, map table and flag locker on the narrow bridge of LCH 185, with Brigadier Prior-Palmer waiting intently by his side, Currey put the worst-case scenario to the back of his mind. His immediate task was to decide whether the DD tanks should be launched, and if so, how close to the beach. He studied the view south through his binoculars. Sunrise was minutes away and in the morning light, visibility was already improving. But clouds of smoke and mist over the beach made features on the shore hard to distinguish.

Fortunately, his navigating officer Lieutenant John Stephenson and LCH 185's navigator Lieutenant Shephard had done an excellent job. Ahead of them the bridge crew suddenly saw a winking green light – a long dash followed by two quick flashes. Standing on the narrow deck of X-23, waves washing around his ankles, Lieutenant Lyne continued to flash his signal to the north with his shaded Aldis lamp. Although no one on the bridge of 185 could see the midget submarine itself, the bright green light was a relief – Lyne had marked the intended launching position of the DD tanks within 300 yards. Looking at the swell around them, Stephenson felt it would have been impossible to be any more accurate.

Currey was also carefully studying the sea state, as the full weight of his responsibility began to bear down on him. The DDs were meant to launch almost 4 miles from the shore, but if the conditions were too rough they could be swamped by the waves long before they reached the beach. If they didn't launch, the tanks would be too late to provide the first waves of infantry with the support they'd need. Driving his LCTs directly on to the beach at H-Hour wasn't an option – there would be enough landing craft in the surf without the ill-equipped LCT Mk 3s getting in the way. If the DDs didn't launch at sea, Currey's orders were to haul the LCTs out of line and beach them at H+45. Deprived of sufficient armour, the infantry might not even survive for three quarters of an hour, let alone clear the beach. His choice might decide the success of the first wave and possibly the outcome of the entire operation on Sword, to say nothing of the safety of the 200 men who would sail the tanks to the shore.

Beside him, Currey could sense Prior-Palmer's agitation. The swell that rolled 185 beneath them was a reminder that, as he later described with some understatement, 'the sea conditions were not very favourable'. On the other hand, the two men reasoned, they were not so bad as to rule out the DDs' use altogether. For his own part, Prior-Palmer was eager to get the DDs into the sea.* His resolve strengthened by the officer's eagerness, Currey made the vital decision. At 05:35 he turned to his signaller and ordered the signal for 'Floater' to be raised up the mast. The DDs would launch.†

Eagerly, Prior-Palmer ordered the same signal to be broadcast to his tank crews. For the first time that morning, radios crackled into life as 'Floater' was transmitted across the army net. Final preparations were hurriedly made – the last bits of equipment were stowed and the crews boarded their vehicles. On each tank the compressed air cylinders were opened again and the canvas pillars supporting the skirt stiffened until they felt as hard as rock to the touch. Lance Corporal Patrick Hennessey

---

* Rear Admiral Talbot had already observed that the brigadier 'would swim his tanks if it was humanely possible'.
† In his history of the 13/18 Hussars published in 1949, Miller attributed the decision to launch the DDs to Captain Bush and Brigadier Prior-Palmer. This has been repeated many times since, with Prior-Palmer often being relocated to HMS *Goathland*. From the task force orders and Currey's own reports, there is no doubt that Prior-Palmer was on LCH 185 and that, while he was consulted, the ultimate decision to launch was made by Currey.

could feel his LCT roll as waves slapped against the hull and nervously he rechecked the thin struts supporting his tank's skirt. If they failed, those waves would overwhelm his unlikely little vessel in seconds.

On 185, Currey anxiously studied the waves. Ahead of him, the smoke that obscured the beach occasionally cleared and revealed the landmarks they were looking for. Lieutenant Commander Donald Amer and Stephenson diligently looked for the church spire at Lion-sur-Mer which was starting to become faintly visible, and to the east the water tower near the centre of the landing beaches occasionally showed itself between clouds of dust. Those crewmen who could, anxiously strained their eyes towards the shore. To Chief Engine Room Artificer Denis Muskett, the beach looked entirely peaceful. It reminded him of a country village where even the dogs and hens slept until suddenly the church clock struck seven, then windows would shoot open, bedding was thrown over the sills and the people walked about like a toy town.

Currey too was struck by the surprising lack of activity on the shore. In fact, no gunfire was being directed at his group at all. He studied the water ahead of him again. If they could get closer in where the waters would be even calmer, the tanks would spend less time in the swell and they'd save fuel. Prior-Palmer concurred, and the signal 'Floater 6000' was quickly relayed to the vessels behind.

Now the vessels formed up into their assault positions. From two lines of four, the LCTs manoeuvred into a smart line eight abreast, each approximately 150 yards from its neighbour, with the LCGs on the flanks. In front, the Fairmile LCS(L)s and the LCP(L)s formed a forward line, while the smoke-laying LCP(L)s 285 and 286 neatly took up position on either side of 185's bow. On board 286, however, Captain Weedy RM was silently cursing HMS *Tormentor*, the base at Warsash where the LCPs had been prepared for the operation. Their wireless equipment, supposedly overhauled and checked at the base days before, wasn't working: the suppression capacitors that prevented excessive interference on the sets were defective. The complete wireless silence imposed on the invasion fleet had prevented testing right up until now – the point when the sets were most needed. As it was, neither boat could receive audible signals.

Currey wasn't unduly concerned. He was only to screen his force with smoke if absolutely necessary, and still there was no significant reaction from the enemy on the beach. The force steadily pressed nearer . . . 9,000 yards . . . 8,000 yards . . .

'Smoke!' bellowed one of the lookouts on the bridge. Looking forward, Currey saw clouds of acrid gas billowing from one of the LCP(L)s. Urgent signals were made to the offending vessel, which had accidentally released a small cloud. It was quickly brought under control and the puff of smoke dispersed. It was just past 06:00.

7,000 yards ... Currey and Prior-Palmer looked ahead at the still, silent shore. The calmer inshore waters beckoned them closer and the swell rolling LCH 185 this way and that reminded them that every yard could make the difference between success and failure. The Aldis lamp blinked again. On the LCTs, the bridge crews noted the new instruction from 185: 'Floater 5000'.

Things were moving quickly now. As they ploughed closer to the beach than originally intended, the sea pushed the group further east. The tide was running stronger than expected as well – Amer estimated it to be at least 1 knot running east-south-east. To give the DDs the best chance of making landfall at the right place, Currey ordered a correction further west. As they complied with his signal, each LCT began the struggle to turn – their twin right-handed screws made manoeuvres to starboard more laboured, their flat bottoms struggled for purchase in the sea, and the sterns kicked out as the vessels turned. The line started to waver, but each LCT held its position and started to re-form as they pressed on into the final few thousand yards. On the deck of X-23, Lyne watched as the LCTs passed about 1,000 yards west of him. The tall landing craft were obvious to him, but no one on board them saw the tiny speck of the submarine in the wallowing seas.

At 06:15, the group was as close as Stephenson could estimate to be 5,000 yards off the beach, and 185 slowed. On LCT 461, Lieutenant Commander Crichton, 14 LCT Flotilla's commanding officer, and Major Derek Wormald, commander of A Squadron 13/18 Hussars, were squeezed into the tiny open bridge. Beside them, pressed variously against the chart table, the compass binnacle or the flag locker, Lieutenant Ramsey, the landing craft's skipper, struggled to command his vessel and stay out of their way at the same time. All eyes were glued to 185, and as the three men watched, a square blue flag with a central white square was run up her mast. 'Flag zero,' muttered Crichton, and Ramsey quickly busied himself getting the vessel stopped.[10]

On board each of the landing craft the tank crews suddenly felt the vibration of the engines cease, and as the noise died away, the rumble of the distant guns of the bombardment squadron echoed in the distance. As some men clambered up the coaming to see outside their little prisons, the rattle of the heavy anchor chain came from the stern as it dropped into the sea. Then, from the bow, came the screech of metal as the ramp was lowered, the chains jangling and the hawsers screeching as they unwound from the winches. Men jumped from their viewpoints and clambered on to their tanks. Hurried goodbyes were shouted down the length of the deck, Mae West lifejackets were buckled on and cigarettes stubbed out. Captain Peter Lyon, the second in command of A Squadron, bade farewell to Sub Lieutenant Shan Somerset on the bridge of LCT 444 and returned to the tank deck. As he passed each tank he issued a tot of rum to his men, then clambered aboard his own. One by one the tank engines roared into life. At the bow, the landing craft crew pushed forward the special troughs for the tanks that would help guide them beyond the lip of the main ramp and safely into the water.

On Landing Craft Navigation (LCN) 189, Lieutenant Donald Slater of COPP 6 was cursing the state of the small vessel's engine. It had broken down several times in the night and it was only by some miracle that the boat had made it to the lowering position. Still, it worked now and that was the most important thing, so he ordered the boat alongside 185. On the bridge, Amer snatched some final looks at the chart, the sea and the shore before he clambered down to the deck. Hauling himself over the railings, he gingerly made his way down the rope ladder and dropped on to 189 as it banged alongside the larger landing craft's hull. In front of B Squadron, Lieutenant Peter Wild, also of COPP 6, had already leapt from the rolling deck of ML 294 on to LCN 197.

Currey and Prior-Palmer looked back at the line of LCTs approvingly as each raised their answering pennants. Within six minutes all eight were fluttering the flags of reply. In response, 185 raised the red and white 'flag five'.

In each landing craft's leading tank the crew, huddled on the top of the tank with only the driver in his actual position, looked forward over the skirt at the foreboding seas. Metre-high waves broke over the landing craft's ramp and further out the stiff wind whipped up whitecaps. The landing craft rolled, groaning at their anchors, and the tank gently slid on the tank deck as it swayed. Major Wormald looked at the shore. Recognizing a church tower ahead of him, he could see that Currey had brought them to a halt opposite Lion-sur-Mer, a good mile west of Queen Beach.

The sea would carry them towards their objective as they swam towards the shore. As he watched, LCN 189 took position just ahead, ready to lead his tanks in. At the same time 197, over on the left flank, was pulling to the front of B Squadron. Both Donald Amer and Peter Wild were pleased to see their respective targets still appeared quite clear: they could easily distinguish White and Red Beaches even at this range.

At approximately 06:35, the leading tanks crept forward. Unable to see, but only needing to go straight ahead, the drivers slowly manoeuvred their tanks up on to the raised 'whaleback' ramp at the bow of the landing craft. The tracks slotted into the troughs and, like a slow-motion roller-coaster ride, the tank locked into its guides and rolled forward.

The rough seas led the crews to ignore the standard methodology for launching. Captain Lyon's driver went down the ramp in first gear, dipping the clutch just in time to avoid the heavy seas. To Lyon it was instantly preferable over the launching style they had perfected on the sheltered waters of the Solent, using second gear and launching much faster. As the tank slipped into the water it was pushed clear of the ramp by the swell and within ten seconds the propellors engaged and the unlikely little vessel started to pull forward. Behind him, Sergeant Sweetapple and his crew were less fortunate. As they slipped off the ramp and into the water, the propellors failed to engage with the driveshaft. Cursing, the driver desperately hammered the controls, but already the waves were breaking over the skirt of the wallowing tank. Hastily, Sweetapple launched their inflatable dinghy and the crew abandoned their doomed tank, seconds before it slipped beneath the waves.

On LCT 467, the leading tank lurched forward but its tracks slewed in the narrow gap at the ramp. Its skirt hooked on a frame of the landing craft and, with an excruciating tear, was ripped open. The crew jumped down and hopelessly examined the hole. Major Rugge-Price, B Squadron's commanding officer, took one look and knew there was no hope of repairing the skirt in time. Pushing his way along the tank deck, he clambered up the ladders to the bridge and conferred with skipper Lieutenant Corrin. The solution, he thought, was to abandon the lead tank, push it over the bow and launch the remaining four. Corrin demurred and thought of the orders he had spent the last few days memorizing. One crucial line stood out: 'In the unlikely event of the DD tanks being unable to swim, LCT of Group 1 are to touch down with Group 7 at H+45'. The unlikely had happened, and Corrin's duty seemed clear. Rugge-Price objected but the skipper held firm, and seconds later the matter was settled by a signal flashed from LCH 185. Corrin ordered the ramp to be raised and the dejected tank commander went back to his crews.*

Standing on the bridge of LCT 465, Sub Lieutenant Wright watched anxiously as the first tank approached the ramp and steered into the track troughs. One of the two chains supporting the ramp had been torn off in the rough seas and now only the single remaining chain and the two hawsers, which were already screeching with the strain, kept the ramp above the crashing waves. The first tank edged off successfully and rolled into the water, followed by the second and then the third. The tension on the bridge was starting to ease as the fourth tank edged along the ramp when suddenly, inevitably, the second chain snapped. The ramp jerked and then fell into the sea as the two cables snapped a split second later. The tank dropped into the waves near vertically, not nose first as was intended. But despite the unorthodox entry, the skirt just remained above the water. Shocked and relieved, the crew engaged the propellors and moved off. Behind them, Lieutenant Anderson and his crestfallen crew in the fifth tank looked down at the ramp in front of them. There was no way they could launch now, and, even worse, with the ramp flapping uselessly in the sea there was no way Wright could beach either. The crew hauled up their anchor and turned north, back to England.

By 06:40, the tanks were all in the water. As they formed up behind the LCNs, the stress of the launch now behind them, they suddenly became aware of a new noise. All around them, a ripple of booms played out in a line from left to right as close support fire began to bombard the landing beach.[11]

Behind 14 Flotilla's LCTs, the following assault waves had been forming up. Steaming into the lowering position a few minutes behind schedule, Commander Kenneth Sellars on LCH 269 quickly led Convoy S5 Lignite straight past the anchored troopships to port and towards the shore. Lignite had had an awkward passage. By the time they had reached the lowering position, only one of 592 Flotilla's boats remained, LCA(HR) 976 clinging doggedly to the stern of LCT 981.

---

* Corrin was later commended by Captain Bush, who praised his quick thinking. Rear Admiral Talbot, on the other hand, felt that Corrin had failed to launch four tanks that were expressly tasked with covering the initial landing at H-Hour. Commander Currey records that Corrin was ordered to beach, something seemingly unrealized by either of the senior commanders.

Fortunately the twenty-eight LCTs in the group had survived the passage. The gun crews of 7, 33 and 76 Field Regiments RA, sheltering in and under their Priest self-propelled guns, had disgorged nearly all their stomach contents into the sea or on to the slippery wet tank deck during the night, but their vessels had all managed to keep station. Now the LCTs fell astern of LCH 269, ready to form up as Assault Group 4 behind the LCT(R)s that made up Group 3.

Driving through the anchorage, Sellars, known to his brother officers as Monkey – a nickname acquired as an international rugby star before the war – searched for the rest of his assault group. Somewhere up ahead he should have been able to see the LCT(A)s bearing the Royal Marine Armoured Support Group waiting for him. But Convoy Pannier's passage had been even worse. After LCT(A) 2432 had broken down, 2042 had also fallen by the wayside. Eventually the convoy had split and only four LCT(A)s were able to maintain something approaching their schedule. Even so, they arrived late and now were driving hard behind Sellars to catch up. The remaining three were a few more minutes behind.

The LCT(A)s weren't the only boats Sellars needed to shepherd into his group, but happily he could see the others patiently waiting for him. At the head of the line of LSIs on his port beam, he could see the LCAs of 535 Assault Flotilla formed up alongside HMS *Glenearn*, waiting to take station behind him. Frustratingly, in line behind *Glenearn* he could see the LCAs of 536 Flotilla still lowering from the davits of SS *Empire Cutlass*. They would have to make up the time themselves, he decided, and Assault Group 2 proceeded through the anchorage, the ten LCAs from *Glenearn* quickly and efficiently taking station behind. A few minutes later 536 Flotilla set off and, throwing their engines to their maximum revolutions, quickly made up the gap. Snatches of heartening songs drifted over the sea as the men on board steadied their spirits.

While Group 1 had been advancing towards the beaches, the remaining destroyers of Force S had completed their move into position off the French coast. Now arranged in a long line running between 4,000 and 5,000 yards from the shore, all their turrets brought to bear on the beaches, the crews waited expectantly for the order to fire.

The minutes ticked by, slowly closing on 06:40 when the orders instructed them to open fire. On the bridge of HMS *Saumarez*, Cazalet watched *Stord* and *Scorpion*, only 1,200 yards west, blazing away at

Ouistreham. They were early of course, but it was easier to think that Clouston had his reasons. The orders did allow for the ships to adjust their fire to the circumstances and the enemy response, so there was no need to rein him in. But looking at his own targets east of Ouistreham, there was no sign of an enemy response. If something – anything – opened fire on *Saumarez*, a high rate of fire could quickly be brought to bear on it – drenching it in shellfire should quickly silence the offender. But their supply of shells was finite and they had to husband their ammunition until the vital moments – laid down in their orders as 07:05 to 07:25 – when the invasion force was at its most vulnerable. But the enemy had yet to respond at all.

Puzzled and frustrated by the inactivity, each captain agonized over what to do. But the orders stated the bombardment would begin at 06:40 and, with a low rumble of booms, the destroyers commenced firing. On *Swift*, Gower must have seen *Saumarez*'s guns belch flame and instantly ordered his own to join in. Eruptions peppered the beaches east of the Caen Canal. A few minutes later the destroyers at the western end of the line opened fire. On HMS *Virago*, Lieutenant Commander Archibald White ordered deliberate fire from his four 4.7-inch guns as they targeted stützpunkt 21, codenamed Trout. As opposed to quick fire, deliberate fire called for maximum precision, with the fall of shot observed and corrections made before another barrage was fired. It was slow and methodical, but it conserved ammunition. Watching from the bridge, White felt completely unhurried – the enemy were still not replying.

In the middle of the line ORP *Ślązak* and HMS *Middleton* were separated by 2,300 yards, leaving a gap large enough for the assault forces to pass through. *Middleton*'s captain, Lieutenant Ian Cox, had already had a scare as he manoeuvred to their position – X-23 had emerged from the haze, barely visible at waterline level and with the green lamp turned away at the vital moment. Rapid instructions prevented a painful end to the midget submarine's exploits that morning.

In the director control tower, Lieutenant Victor Chappelle studied the coast for the first time, marvelling at its similarity to the model he had pored over so intently in Portsmouth. Every single detail was there, including the distinctive pair of houses nicknamed the twin villas. These two holiday villas, named Quinquin and Tancrède, would be a familiar sight to everyone at Sword, situated as they were directly in the centre of the landing area. They also sat at the western end of stützpunkt 20 – Cod to the Allies – and had been reinforced as part of that strongpoint. Now Chappelle lined up the villas for *Middleton*'s 4-inch guns.[12]

Sailing alongside the DD tanks, Captain Hendrie Bruce of the Royal Artillery had no warning of the sudden outpouring of vomit from the Royal Marines pressed in beside him. Cramped into the tiny interior of the landing craft, the fifteen men on board LCP(L) 282 had long since dispensed with buckets and the deck was awash with the contents of most men's stomachs, now considerably diluted by seawater. He tried to focus and repress his own urge to regurgitate. He had long since voided his own stomach but the landing craft's pitching, the sight of his companions' latest meals and the unholy smell meant his own suffering was far from over.

Bruce was the Forward Observation Officer (FOO) for 7 Field Regiment RA and his task was to direct the fire of the regiment's twenty-four M7 Priest self-propelled guns. The Priest mounted a 105mm gun on a tank chassis, creating an artillery piece that was more mobile than the traditional towed howitzer. The gun was also forward facing, a far more practical arrangement which also enabled the artillery to fire from their landing craft on to the beach. Along with the forty-eight guns of 33 and 76 Field Regiments, this enabled a considerable concentration of shellfire to be dropped on to the beach just ahead of the leading wave. Now all seventy-two guns were following approximately 6,000 yards behind him, carried on eighteen LCTs of 32 and 38 LCT Flotillas.

Things were not going well, though. His LCP(L), and those of the FOOs of the other two regiments, had been towed across the Channel by the LCTs carrying the DD tanks. Taking his passage on the larger landing craft, Bruce had watched his little boat – with a skeleton RM crew on board – detach from the tow in rough seas no fewer than three times during the night. At 05:00 they had finally gone aboard and cast off, but less than an hour later were summoned to another of 14 Flotilla's LCTs. 33 Field Regiment's FOO's LCP(L) had been lost in the night and now their three-man team and the four RM crew joined 282. A few minutes later 76 Field Regiment's commander contacted the landing craft to report that their FOO had not been seen or heard from all morning. Bruce's one vessel would now need to direct the fire of all three regiments.

Carefully, and with much difficulty as the craft swung and gyrated, the wireless operators netted in the three wireless sets to communicate with the gun batteries behind them. Bruce tried to study the coastline through his binoculars and compare what he could see to the wavetop photograph booklet of the beach, but as the landing craft lurched over each wave and the bow swung in different directions every few seconds, he became more violently ill. At 06:30, as they entered calmer waters some 3,000 yards offshore and the haze lifted, he finally managed to identify strongpoint Cod. The air hummed with radio traffic as Bruce passed bearings and ranges to ML 197, sailing alongside 7 Field Regiment's LCTs. Powered loudhailers broadcast commands across the waves, and on LCT 859 the gunners of A Troop loaded several salvoes of white phosphorus smoke shells into the breeches and fired. After several misses, at 06:43, Bruce observed the first hits on the foreshore. He passed a few corrections to bring the impacts closer to strongpoint Cod and then called 'fire for effect'.

At 06:50 the seafront at Hermanville erupted as *Middleton* and *Ślązak*'s first dozen 4-inch shells and the combined weight of seventy-two 105mm artillery rounds fell on to strongpoint Cod. Shockwaves raced down the trenches joining the bunkers and barbed wire was hurled into the air, cascading on to the men unlucky enough to be sheltering in the slit trenches. Even those in the bunkers weren't safe: unlike the thick concrete less than 2 miles away at Bass, Cod's personnel shelters were small and weak. The noise from a nearby impact threatened to blast the thin walls away as if they were made of twigs, and the vibrations sent concrete dust cascading down from the ceiling. Inside the command bunker, Obergefreiter Toni Kresken's wireless set vibrated almost incessantly.[*] Hauptmann Mikisch at 3 Battalion HQ was less than 3 miles away in Cresserons – just within range for the set's telephone communication – but no one could be heard through the receiver.[†] Kresken could usually transmit up to eighty words a minute in Morse, but it was a useless skill now – his telegraphy went unanswered as well. Leutnant Nessel couldn't even raise 10 Company's other platoons further along the coast at Lion-sur-Mer – he had no means to communicate with his men or his superior.

---

[*] Obergefreiter was a senior enlisted rank but not an NCO rank. However, the level of responsibility was similar to that of a lance corporal in the British Army.
[†] A hauptmann is equivalent to a captain in the British Army. Mikisch was identified as 3 Battalion commander by at least two PoWs of 10 Company during their interrogations shortly after D-Day. The same PoWs identified Leutnant Nessel as the CO of 10 Company (WO 208/3621). However, some secondary sources refer to a Major Pipor as 3 Battalion's commander, Kurt Mikisch as 9 Company commander and a Hauptmann Heinrich Kuhtz as 10 Company commander.

The bombardment had already severed all communication in and out of stützpunkt 20.

Out at sea, LCNs 189 and 197 gamely ploughed through the waves, leading the lines of swimming tanks behind them. They were pulling ahead of *Middleton* and *Ślązak* now, and the boom of the guns was joined by the sound of shells whistling and whining above them. Looking left, Peter Wild saw LCG(L) 9 firing her two guns in rapid fashion, clouds of smoke billowing around one gun and then the other, back and forth with almost rhythmic timing. On the right flank LCGs 10 and 11 were similarly bombarding Queen White Beach, their shells mixing with those of *Ślązak* as she shifted her fire to targets not encased in clouds of smoke.[13]

Very few people in the leading landing craft or on the beach could hear anything above the din of the guns firing, the screaming shells overhead or the crump of explosions. Perhaps a few heard a drone, some may have even been able to tear their eyes off the horizon and look up into the haze of drifting smoke and dust above. Just occasionally, when the dense cloud layer parted, they could see into the brighter morning sky above. What they saw amazed them.

Late at night on 5 June, the bomber crews of the US Eighth Air Force had been called to briefings at dozens of airfields scattered over East Anglia. The late hour was indicative enough of the briefing's importance, but in case anyone was unsure, all men were ordered to carry their .45 Colt sidearms. Some of the aircrew reasoned it was to protect the information they were about to receive, others suspected that it was a touch of bravado to beef them up a little. Suspecting the latter, Frank Scannell, a pilot in 4 Combat Wing's 94 Bomb Group, decided against loading his.

As the briefings unfolded, the full scale of the coming mission became clear to the aircrews. At dawn on 6 June, 1,361 of the Eighth's four-engine B-17 and B-24 bombers would attack forty-five targets at Omaha, Gold, Juno and Sword. To the west, another 542 twin-engine bombers of Ninth Air Force would attack Utah. To be able to strike their targets just before the landing craft hit the beaches, the US bombers – more used to flying their missions entirely in daylight – would depart in darkness, with the earliest take-offs in just a few hours' time. Most bombers would carry 100lb HE bombs armed with nose fuses to minimize the chances of cratering on the beach and roads, which might make them impassable to vehicles. Wide-ranging restrictions suggested the scale of the aerial armada: guns would be manned but no test firing was permitted; other aircraft were only to be fired on if they were attacking; most importantly, no second runs on targets would be carried out – an entire stream of bombers circling above the invasion zone was asking for trouble in the crowded airspace. Once bomb runs were complete, the squadrons would continue a few miles inland then bank west and cross the coast near the Channel Islands. Any aircraft banking left and returning to England east of the invasion area was liable to be shot down. At Knettishall, home to 388 Bomb Group, the briefing concluded, as it always did, with a prayer led by the chaplain.

The first bombers of the Eighth Air Force's Third Bombardment Division had started lifting off from their bases in East Anglia just after 02:00, and aircraft had continued to bump down the darkened runways for nearly three hours afterwards. Third Division was the easternmost of the groups attacking Normandy – their targets were the beach defences and inland strongpoints at both Juno and Sword Beaches. But such was the aircraft activity that night that, as the first bombers ascended into the dark night, their first direction was north-west, over the Wash and as far north as Harrogate. Searchlights beamed into the sky, providing navigators with vital reference points as the pilots strained their eyes searching for fellow fliers in the murk. Other squadrons flew a series of jerky patterns across East Anglia, filling time while waiting for the final groups to get airborne.

At 02:45 Frank Scannell powered B-17 *Ordnance Express* down the runway at USAAF Station 468, known to the men as Rougham airfield or, if they needed to contact it on wireless, Chairleg. Below him in the nose section, navigator Abe Terkowitz plotted their complicated series of twists and turns over the English countryside. After a seeming age they finally ascended through the clouds, up to 14,000 feet and into a brightly moonlit sky. Flares popped in the sky, beacons to aid the bombers in seeking out their own formation. Setting course south, as the white light of the moon gave way to early twilight, Scannell's crew marvelled at the assembly of aircraft around them, each sporting a series of new black and white stripes around the wings and fuselage. In the cockpit, Scannell had little idea of just how great the formation of bombers was – flying in 94 Bomb Group's A Flight, low squadron, he was near the very front of 4 Combat Wing's lengthy column. In the tail gunner's position, Marion Weston watched spellbound as the lengthy streams of aeroplanes of 45 Combat Wing on their starboard side and 13 Combat Wing on their port slowly closed on their own. As they approached the English coast the

457 bombers of the Third Bombardment Division formed three near adjacent columns across 6 miles of sky.

At 06:26, Terkowitz radioed his pilot and informed him they were crossing the coast. Looking down through the nose, bombardier Art Dignam had to assume the navigator was right, for both ahead and below there was nothing to see but cloud. Scannell was concerned too – the cloud base below them seemed to get higher and denser the further south they pressed. Then a sudden break exposed the dark grey sea still below them, and the crew collectively gasped. Endless lines of ships, small dots leaving white V-shaped wakes, could be seen plodding along to starboard. To Scannell it looked like there were more ships in the Channel than he could have imagined in the world.

Just a few dozen miles ahead of Scannell and below the clouds, Flying Officer Richard Rohmer of 430 Squadron Royal Canadian Air Force kept one eye on his leader, Flight Lieutenant Jack Taylor, and another on the sky. Nine months of practice watching for German fighters was hard to shake off, but all he could see were formations of Allied fighters, their white and black stripes clearly visible. Sufficiently comforted, Rohmer allowed himself the pleasure of taking in the incredible sight below him. Endless groups of ships, their mottled camouflage colours blending with the grey sea's foaming whitecaps, steamed south. Landing craft chugged slowly in lines, rocking in the waves, while barrage balloons trailed above and behind them like children's toys above a pram. Rohmer was sure no larger fleet had ever sailed the Channel.

Flying only 200 yards apart, the two Mustangs zoomed over the sluggish ships until, at 06:30, they approached the Normandy coast. They could see the tiny flashes of the bombardment ships to port, but something more concerning caught Rohmer's eye – the cloud base that for most of their journey across the Channel had hung about 10,000 feet above the sea dropped to perhaps as little as 500 feet over the coast. There was precious little room between the ground and the cloud to manoeuvre, and no chance of carrying out their task of photo reconnaissance unless they could gain more altitude in a clearer sky. More seriously, any German aircraft could quickly hide itself in the grey leaden cloud, while the Allied bombers would struggle to find their targets.

Taylor accelerated to 400mph and led Rohmer down, below the clouds. Zipping across the coast just above Queen Beach they could see explosions erupting around Ouistreham, but below them all was quiet. Zooming across the Norman countryside they arrived over Caen two minutes later where, to their relief, the cloud above broke up and rays of sunshine filtered through from the north-east. The Mustangs danced up into the sky, relieved to be back in their natural environment, leaving the dark grey clouds swirling behind them.

At the front of Scannell's flight, leading the 120 B-17s of 4 Combat Wing, their commander Colonel Frederick Castle frowned at the cloud below. There was clearly no break that would enable a visual bombing run to be made, and now his entire wing was reliant on a mere twenty-seven Pathfinder bombers fitted with GH radio navigation and H2X radar. Both systems were acceptable for navigating to and bombing a large area, as had frequently been required on previous missions over Germany, but Castle knew they were of little use when hitting pinpoint targets like strongpoints. Worse still, shortly before take-off he had received fresh orders from headquarters, amending the bombing tactics in the event of cloud cover. Concerned by the possibility that bombs might fall on to the troops landing unseen below, Eighth Air Force's Operations Staff issued, at the last moment, instructions that the Pathfinder aircraft were to delay dropping their own bombs, depending on how close to H-Hour they were. If they arrived at the target between fifteen and twenty minutes before H-Hour, the Pathfinders should overfly the target by five seconds, with the delay increasing for every five minutes closer to H-Hour they were.

It seemed absurd to Castle that a bombing mission that was supposed to be the final element of a complex beach bombardment was already timed up to thirty minutes ahead of the landings. Bombing by H2X was nowhere near as accurate as visual bombing as it was, but delaying dropping the bombs even by just five seconds could see them overfly the target by some 1,000 feet, which would nearly guarantee the targets would be missed. But Castle knew that there was far more to this operation than he was privy to. His superiors, with access to far more information than he, would have their reasons for the instructions.

His thoughts were interrupted by the navigator reporting in with bad news: his group of eighteen bombers of 94 Bomb Group A Flight were ahead of schedule, and if they continued on their current course and speed they would be over the target much too early. Quickly addressing the flight, Castle pulled his B-17 into a series of S curves, twisting the flight left and right in an effort to kill time.

Crouched on the edge of the small wood his men had established themselves in, Lieutenant Madden looked north. Sergeant Keel had woken him at dawn and now the morning light revealed their true location close to the coast – perhaps only 1,000 yards away. The flat terrain and near horizon were evidence enough, but at 06:50 the confirmation came in the form of hundreds of shells falling to the north. At first Madden watched impassively as small pinpricks of light in the distance heralded the launch of another shell, and a few seconds later bright flashes lit up the beachfront. But all too quickly stray blasts came closer to their wood and the paratroopers quickly flattened themselves to the ground. Short and tall columns of flame rent the earth around them, throwing dirt into the air.

Then, overwhelming the noise of the stray blasts, came a new noise, and Madden instinctively looked to the sky. The rumble of large formations of aircraft was far from alien to the paratroopers, but they knew that these were not more airborne infantry coming to reinforce them. Hurriedly, the men tried to dig shallow shell scrapes to afford themselves some additional protection from what was about to come.

Some 14,000 feet above, Art Dignam sat in the nose of *Ordnance Express* intently watching *Tommy*, the lead bomber of A Flight's low formation. Below them a sea of grey cloud absorbed the early morning sunlight and blotted out any chance of an observed bomb run. His own bombsight was useless now; all he had to do was release his bombs when *Tommy* did. 'Crossing coast now,' Terkowitz suggested on the intercom, and Dignam instinctively wanted to flick the bomb release switch. But knowing that the navigator could only estimate their position, he quietly counted to five, sure that the lead would release any moment. As he watched, the first black cylinders tumbled out of *Tommy*'s bomb bay. His thumb flicked the switch beside him. 'Bombs away!' he called over the intercom, and in the cockpit Scannell and his co-pilot Ed Reed pushed gently forward on their control columns as, freed from more than 3,500lb of high explosive, *Ordnance Express* suddenly sprang higher into the air.

At 06:55, as the rumbling of aircraft came directly overhead, the falling bombs screeched in the ears of Madden and his men. A chain of explosions ripped up the ground outside the wood and the earth shook, threatening to tumble the trees above them. Almost as suddenly as they'd started, the explosions ceased, but the rumble above was incessant. Instinctively the paratroopers hacked into the ground again, using the precious couple of minutes to gain a few more inches' depth. But all too quickly the shriek of bombs returned and the men pushed themselves against the cold earth once more and waited. The ground heaved again as more explosions erupted in the near and middle distance.

Above the clouds the steady stream of Third Bombardment Division's B-17s droned over their targets. Crouched in the cramped nose of *GI Jane*, bombardier Bob Simmons looked down at the thick cloud beneath 388 Bomb Group's B low squadron. Below him – he hoped – was Luc-sur-Mer and target number 20, a German coastal strongpoint. Glumly, he flicked the bomb release switch as his group leader did and watched as the bombs tumbled down into the clouds. Other squadrons ignored the coast, their leaders taking them to targets inland. 388 Bomb Group's C low squadron roared towards Caen to attack Richter's divisional headquarters in the quarry at St Julien, but by the time they arrived, thirty minutes after Richard Rohmer in his Mustang, the cloud had shifted again and, finding themselves without any way to see the target, they overflew and dropped on a secondary target on their way out. 94 Bomb Group's C Flight headed towards the Périers Ridge to attack the headquarters of 736 Regiment – the forward HQ at strongpoint 17 (Hillman) and the staff HQ in the château at Beuville. As the various squadrons around them filed off to their targets and roared upwards once their bombs were released, the two squadrons of C Flight suddenly found themselves alone. Worse still, they had not been allocated any Pathfinder aircraft to lead them to their target. Helplessly, the navigators, working on dead reckoning, estimated their likely path over the two HQs, but there was no break in the grey layer beneath them. Cursing, the bombardiers closed the bomb bay doors and the pilots accelerated into a westerly curve to take them back home.

On the east flank, 13 Combat Wing was attacking targets around the Orne Estuary. Over the course of a mere eight minutes, seventy-three bombers of 95 and 390 Bomb Groups dropped 940 bombs as they passed over Franceville. Meanwhile, to their west the entire 100 Bomb Group was tasked to attack Ouistreham. In the leading aircraft, Colonel Thomas Jeffrey scowled at the cloud that covered the coast. The only saving grace was that as the target was actually on the shore, it should be plainly visible to radar.

Whether through a mistaken assessment of the target or an expectation that 3 Group RAF had already pulverized strongpoint Bass, the USAAF target was the small strongpoint 10, just to the west of the coastal battery. As Jeffrey led the first squadron over at 07:03, the last-minute instructions from headquarters played on his mind. There was no danger of dropping short, but who knew where the ground forces might be beneath all that cloud? What if they were already on the beaches below?

The seconds ticked by, dragging them closer to the target and simultaneously closer to the time window that would require them to delay dropping by five seconds. Twenty-four aircraft waited on his bombs to fall, with another eighteen following over the next ten minutes.

The whine of shells overhead, the rumble of distant large-calibre explosions, the blast of nearby smaller-calibre shells and the popping and hissing of the burning hotel created a hellish soundscape for Odette Mousset and the small group of French townsfolk sheltering in the little wood behind the Hôtel de Normandie. Lying as flat to the ground as they could, they prayed for the seemingly endless cacophony to be over. 100 Bomb Group's 507 bombs were about to join the destruction, but there was no way of separating the whine of bombs from naval shells now – the source of each explosion was a mystery. The only hope was that each one might be the last, and would bring this hellish experience to an end.

The end, when it came, was not what they had prayed for. A sudden burst among the cowering residents assaulted the senses – a ball of bright light, a flash of burning heat and a deafening roar was the last thing thirteen of their number would remember. For those who survived, the rumble of the explosion echoed against the nearby building walls, drowning out all other noises. But when it receded there came a strange silence; the bombardment that had terrorized them for so long seemed muffled, distant. And then came intense pain, and a new noise: the terrifying sound of screaming.

Beyond the horror in the little wood, Norman residents in nearby farms and villages also heard the monotonous drone of aircraft slowly recede as each squadron of bombers pulled up and away to the west to begin their journey home. They left behind them a scene of utter destruction across acres of countryside. Small, shallow bomb craters peppered farmers' fields, and the limbs of trees, splintered and stripped of foliage, lay shattered in copses and orchards. The tortured, pitiful wails of dying cows echoed across grassy meadows.

Eighth Air Force headquarters' last-minute changes to the mission's execution, while effected with the best of intentions, had essentially guaranteed the failure of a plan that already had only a very limited chance of success. Even if the skies had been clear over Sword that morning, the chances of the Third Bombardment Division successfully striking their targets were low. The Eighth Air Force was well practised at flying in large formations and laying carpets of bombs over a wide corridor, but trying to pinpoint individual strongpoints, especially when their formations might be flying 200 yards or more apart, was always going to be difficult. The cloud cover significantly altered their chances: relying solely on H2X radar was haphazard, and effectively useless when trying to hit specific targets. Technically described by the USAAF as the overcast bombing technique, it was with good reason that it was known among the crews as blind bombing. The change in orders to avoid bombing their own troops as they landed, and the uncertainty it created in the minds of the bomber crews, was the final nail in the coffin of the aerial bombardment. A total of 224 aircraft dropped 3,494 bombs in the thirty minutes before H-Hour on Sword Beach, but the vast majority fell into empty fields. Even those that hit their targets did little damage: 1,139 were 100lb HE bombs and 2,205 were 500lb HE bombs. While both were effective against targets in the open, the former was useless against concrete installations and the latter only marginally better. Thousand-pounders had a better chance against the Atlantic Wall, but only 150 were dropped – and most missed.[14]

At La Brèche, the entire seafront rocked under the bombardment from sea and air. In their requisitioned villa, Oberschütze Ysker and 1 Platoon had heard the earliest shots of the bombardment and now, as it increased in intensity, their commanding officer ordered them to fall back inland towards strongpoint 14 while Franz Penewitz and his defaulter party withdrew to Colleville. Other units were not so lucky – 3 Company of 21 Panzer Division's 220 Pioneer Battalion were all but annihilated, the few survivors scattering among the various defences along the coast.

At Cod, the hail of shells coming from the sea continued. In a whoosh of flame a small machine gun post overlooking the beach was obliterated, the blast collapsing the concrete roof and destroying the trench network leading to it. A single shell hit the 8-inch-wide embrasure of an observation post at the front of the strongpoint, felling the periscope and killing the men inside. Another fell on the corner of a shelter on the south side of the strongpoint, fracturing the reinforced concrete and unleashing a hail of splinters that cut down the occupants within. Crouched in the corner of another bunker, Franz Koza, a young Polish Volksdeutscher, did not enjoy the experience. 10 Company's morale, like that of the other units in 736 Regiment, was low enough at the best of times. Rations were insufficient, entertainment was poor, leave was scarce. Now, under a near continuous and seemingly never-ending bombardment, it probably would not have improved Koza's mood to learn that even his own countrymen were firing at him.[15]

At sea, it was not just the Poles of ORP *Ślązak* firing now. Although still unable to reach their spotter aircraft, at 07:02 the men on ORP *Dragon*, eager finally to take the fight to the enemy, opened fire on strongpoint 16 (Morris) outside Colleville-sur-Orne. A few minutes later the LCS(L)s on the flanks of the leading waves finally found the beach in range of their 6-pounder AT guns. Training their turrets – cannibalized from Valentine Mk X tanks – on to the visible strongpoints on the beach, they began to pour a steady, unrelenting fire into the maelstrom of destruction ahead of them.

Lieutenant Commander Robert James had led 45 LCT Flotilla and their cargo of AVREs through the destroyer line now, and obediently *Middleton* and *Ślązak* had fallen in on their flanks, advancing alongside while their forward guns continued to methodically fire on the beach. The four LCT(A)s that had managed to catch up had now assumed positions on the ends of the LCT line and behind them the twenty LCAs had assumed a tight formation, ready to deploy in a line in the last few hundred yards. But the slow progress of Group 1 meant that 45 LCT Flotilla now found itself gaining on LCH 185 and, ahead of her, the DD tanks. The swell had indeed proved less severe closer to the shore, but it was still enough to delay the DDs. As they yawed in the open water, having to steer as much as 40° off course to correct for the tide and swell, they failed to make their intended 4.5 knots. Most struggled to make 3, and slowly, inexorably, the LCTs gained on them. Wary of the fragile DDs and the spray of debris falling from the barrage overhead, James signalled the flotilla to decrease their engine revolutions. As each LCT obliged, the gap between the two groups opened a little – but this was immediately apparent to Captain Bush, following a few thousand yards behind in HMS *Goathland*.

Bellowing into the electrically powered loudhailer fitted to *Goathland*'s bridge, Bush instructed Commander Sellars on LCH 269 to keep the LCTs moving. They couldn't risk delays – even if the first wave was late it shouldn't force the following waves to be, or the whole timetable would quickly slide into chaos. The LCTs needed to resume their planned speed, even if it meant them getting ahead of the DDs. Sellars passed the instruction on to his charges and the flotilla increased its speed again, quickly bearing down on the wallowing DDs. Minutes later the landing craft were passing between the disorganized diminutive little tanks, their steel hulls looming over the tank crews as they passed within yards of them. Then with a certain inevitability, an unsighted DD crumpled under the bow of one of the LCTs, its canvas skirt instantly collapsing under the weight. Standing on top of the hull, Captain Noel Denny was thrown into the water as the tank was thrust aside and rolled over on its beam. Gasping for air and grateful for the RAF-issue Mae West lifejacket the tank crews had been issued with, Denny spluttered to the surface just as the underside of the tank slipped beneath the waves in the bow wake of the LCT. He looked around for his crew, but in the churning waters they were nowhere to be seen.*

The seemingly endless destruction on shore continued. Individual explosions were impossible to distinguish: the sound was just one endless and hellish rumble. Black smoke spilled into the sky, obscuring the flames below. On board HMS *Serapis*, Midshipman Colin Lawton, a South African by birth whose family had emigrated to Britain in the 1930s, found the non-stop pounding of guns from the line of ships completely shattering. The beach was like an erupting volcano, red flames spurting up from the ground while flashes flickered in the murk overhead like lightning in an ash cloud. Soon there was so much smoke on the beach that every detail was obscured. Then, as the pungent smell of cordite drifted over the fleet, Lawton was suddenly startled by a bright flash closer to the shore.

Ahead of the destroyer line, Lieutenant Tom Phillips's five LCT(R)s had followed the AVRE LCTs into the shore but at 07:00 allowed them to pull ahead. As they arrived at the 3,500-yard line, Phillips studied the beach intently through his binoculars, but there was little to see. Shouting up the voice pipe, Electrical Lieutenant J. Cowan RCNVR reassured his skipper that LCT(R) 457's radar had a clearly defined view of the target and the landing craft were carefully conned on to the target area, yet again centred on Cod. At 07:15, with shrieks that penetrated even the thunderous fire of guns and the deafening explosions from the shore, the first three LCT(R)s launched their opening salvoes. In a bright flash, the first thousand or so rockets were fired into the air. Seconds later the three vessels fired their second and third salvoes – over the next two

---

* Denny was picked up after approximately thirty minutes in the water, but his crew were never seen again.

minutes each of them launched almost all of their 1,044 rockets. Minutes later the remaining two LCT(R)s joined in the bombardment. In all, 5,163 rockets were sent towards the shore.

Launched at almost 45°, the rockets screeched into the air like giant menacing murmurations propelled by an unnatural energy. As they reached the zenith of their ascent, the sheer density of the concentration led many to strike each other in mid-air and several toppled out of formation, falling like spent fireworks. Much more was falling from the sky – short artillery rounds, shrapnel, even spent bullets at the end of their flight, falling like metallic drizzle into the sea. The disorientated rockets tumbled down and fell among the mixed LCTs, LCAs and struggling DD tanks below. On *Goathland*, Captain Bush watched through his binoculars, horrified, as splashes erupted around the tiny wallowing tanks. One giant geyser appeared just 10 yards away from a DD and as he watched the tank started to wander off course. From what he could see there appeared to be soldiers struggling on top of the tank, but the canvas skirt did not appear to have failed. On board the tank, the crew were struggling to treat Lieutenant Roy Burgess, the commander of 3 Troop B Squadron, who had been struck by a splinter. As some men applied pressure to the mortal wound, another grabbed the tiller and coaxed the DD back on course.* More rocket splinters fell on to the decks of the LCTs. As Lieutenant Colonel Cocks discussed the landing with his tank's commander at the back of LCT 947's tank deck, a splinter suddenly crashed into the unfortunate Sergeant James Wingate, killing him instantly as Cocks stood in front of him.

Meanwhile the thick clouds of rockets continued their course towards the beach. But despite Cowan's best efforts the rockets started to descend, en masse, fractionally west of their target. Thousands shrieked into the ground, causing small explosions among the houses on the shore of Queen White and still more harmlessly in the fields behind.[16]

At the same time as the rockets ascended, the Royal Marine Armoured Support Group added the final touch of destruction to the proceedings. Lieutenant Cameron Badenoch clambered into the turret of his Centaur tank, suddenly aware of just how exposed he was. The large platform on the tank deck raised the turret well above the height of LCT(A) 2012's bow and he was head and shoulders above the turret. But he was

---

* Burgess died of his wound two days later.

reassured by the view of destruction he had just enjoyed from alongside Martin Van Heems on the bridge of 2012. Nothing, it seemed, could survive in the great cloud of smoke and dust billowing from the shoreline. As 07:15 approached the crew prepared to open fire, while Badenoch sought out targets on the beach. But it was a fruitless task – there was too much smoke and their landing craft pitched too wildly to have any hope of targeting anything accurately. The 95mm fired sporadically into the fog ahead, adding its fury to the maelstrom.

Then Badenoch heard the unmistakable zip of bullets as they whisked past him. The ping and clank of metal striking metal echoed from the tank hull and with sudden shock he realized someone was firing at him. He ducked down into the turret as more bullets struck the tank, rattling like hail against a greenhouse.

Almost everyone in the assault groups had observed the complete absence of any enemy reaction, so when it came, it was almost a surprise. As the LCTs closed on the beach and narrowed the distance to less than 1,000 yards, enemy gun positions suddenly, finally, sprang into life. Mortar bombs fell into the sea, spurting up geysers of water among the landing craft, while bullets crisscrossed through the air, the occasional flash of tracer starkly visible against the dark background. The fire was sporadic and random – it seemed to be done in hopeful exuberance rather than aimed at any particular vessel. Nonetheless, any hopes that the German defenders might have already been annihilated were quickly dashed.

One by one the tankers on their landing craft lowered themselves into their positions. Sitting in the co-driver's seat of *Temeraire*, one of the two Centaurs on LCT(A) 2191, Jack Tear pulled the hatch above him shut, and one of the ammunition handlers outside crawled forward to seal it with asbestos wax, even as the 95mm above them boomed out to sea. As the LCAs closed behind them, the cox'ns pulled into a line, eagerly looking for the gaps between the lumbering LCTs. As they shouted the range to the troops behind them, the men tensed, eager to leave, desperate to stay. They had stopped singing now.[17]

Behind them a new roar thundered overhead, although the noise was barely audible over the melee of the bombardment. Twelve Typhoon fighter bombers of 440 Squadron Royal Canadian Air Force raced over the fleet, ready to add the coup de grâce. Even though he had spent a near sleepless night on an uncomfortable camp bed next to his aircraft at RAF Hurn near Bournemouth, Flying Officer Ramsey Milne was wide awake and staring from his cockpit at the barely comprehensible spectacle below. The long lines of landing craft steadily steaming south seemed endless, but so tiny in the swelling sea. His one hope was to do something to help them.

Ahead of him, Squadron Leader William Pentland eyed the bright red and yellow explosions erupting from the shore. At least they were in the right place, although identifying their exact target through the fog of the bombardment was another matter. He looked intently at the land behind the smoke, looking for features and roads that matched those he had studied on aerial photographs most of the night. As they neared the shore the scene became familiar enough for him to spot their primary target, already engulfed in smoke and flame.

Quickly, Pentland altered his course to bring strongpoint Cod into a position off his beam and adjusted his sights in preparation. Slowing his Typhoon to 250mph, he watched the target slowly come into line with the leading edge of his wing, then threw himself into a roll to bring it into his forward sights. He dropped into a shallow dive, keeping the smoking cluster of concrete defences in sight just above his aircraft's nose. The Typhoon thundered down until, at nearly 1,000 feet, Pentland flicked a switch on his control column and released his two 500lb bombs. Pulling back on the stick, his Typhoon raced back up into the sky while the two bombs screeched down, their momentum carrying them like missiles straight towards Cod. Just a few seconds later, as Pentland rolled away to the north, they slammed into the ground, detonating among the buildings and bunkers in bright bursts of flame. Hot on their heels came the two black eggs of the next Typhoon in line, and over the next minute twenty-four 500lb bombs plastered the strongpoint. As they raced back into the sky the Typhoons circled over the beach before Pentland led them inland to continue their destructive journey.[18]

Behind them, the smoke from their bombs mixed with that of the thousands of other bombs, shells and rockets that had hit Queen Beach over the last forty-five minutes. But the Canadians' addition was the last act in this great display of firepower. Across the fleet, almost in unison, hundreds of commanders looked at their watches and called for their gunners to cease fire. One by one the last shells arced across the sky, and after a few final blasts only the echoes of this final hurrah were left to roll across the audience. To Philip Barber, still some miles to the north on LCF 34 as it plied its way south, the sudden silence that followed was almost as terrifying as the bombardment had been, an eerie precursor to whatever lay behind the clouds of smoke.

LCHs 185 and 269 pulled away, their work done and under instruction not to beach themselves. 45 LCT Flotilla had passed through the DDs but slowed as they adjusted their own course, and the tanks were making up ground again, intermingling with the big landing craft. But up ahead the two little LCNs remained in the lead, guiding Force S to the beaches. On 189 and 197, Donald Amer and Peter Wild had their eyes intently fixed on the shore, even though there was nothing to see. Black smoke rolled over the beach, obscuring almost everything ahead of them. Quick fixes to port and starboard, where Ouistreham lighthouse and Lion-sur-Mer's church were still visible among the dust and fumes, reassured them they were still heading to the right area, but it was imperative they get their respective squadrons to the correct bits of beach. Finally, at about 1,000 yards, as Amer squinted through his binoculars while they advanced, the drifting smoke cleared just enough for him to spot some of the distinctive houses on the seafront. Five hundred yards to his left, Wild spotted his main landmarks. Quickly, the two navigation specialists made minor corrections to their course and new bearings were hurriedly signalled to the tanks astern before the two LCNs led them in for the final run. Behind them on LCT 947, Robert James – one eye on the LCNs, another on the shore – spotted his target and ordered his flotilla to full speed.

A few hundred yards off the beach 189 stopped and a sounding pole was thrust over the side. As Major Wormald in the lead DD passed by, Amer shouted the depth and final bearing over to him. Then the little DDs flooded past with the LCTs of 45 Flotilla lumbering up behind them and, in their wakes, the LCAs of the assault infantry.[19]

6

H-HOUR

AT 07:26, ONLY ONE MINUTE BEHIND SCHEDULE, LCT 947 SHUDDERED as it ground up against the sand, its momentum and the choppy waves pushing it up the shallow beach. Within two minutes, seven more LCTs of the flotilla started to scrape ashore and in between them the gallant little DD tanks. With great relief, the drivers felt the tracks bite into the sand and pull them up and out of the crashing surf. Seconds later the first of the twenty LCAs carrying the assault infantry arrived, manoeuvring into the already crowded shoreline. With their shallower draught many ploughed ahead of the LCTs that had grounded with several feet of water in front of their bows. In the space of a little over ten minutes the entirety of Group 2 arrived at the Queen Beach waterline – thirty-seven vessels with some 120 vehicles and 1,400 men.[*]

As ramps lowered into the surf the defenders of strongpoint Cod poured fire into the landing craft. The barrage, which had looked so impressive from the sea, was primarily intended to suppress the defenders; it would have been extraordinary if it had succeeded in destroying them completely. The thicker anti-tank gun bunkers of Cod, Trout, Skate and strongpoint 10 were practically impervious to the shells and small bombs that had dropped on them, and once the barrage lifted the defenders, realizing that they would now have to fight for their lives, had rushed to their weapons to fire shot and shell at the invaders. Grenadiers emerged from the personnel shelters and manned the 81mm mortars and the

---

[*] Approximately 114 tanks/AVRES, six D7 bulldozers and at least one Universal Carrier, some 620 crewmen, 500 infantry and engineers, and in the region of 280 RN personnel. Information drawn from the Force S landing table and individual war diaries, although these cannot be considered definitive figures.

machine gun pits. Where communications survived, observers raised the batteries inland and ordered immediate bombardment of pre-sighted areas of coastline. The names of German towns Engers, Füssen and Freiburg – denoting three sections of beach in front of strongpoints 18, 20 and 20A respectively – buzzed across the airwaves and batteries sluggishly moved into action. Within a few miles of Queen Beach, 1716 Artillery Regiment's 2 Battery at Morris, 4 Battery at Daimler, and 11 'Graf Waldersee' Battery at Plumetot brought their guns to bear. Further behind them 1 and 2 Batteries of 155 Artillery Regiment 21 Panzer Division at Périers-sur-le-Dan and 1 Battery of the independent 989 Heavy Artillery Battalion at Basyl would all eventually come into action against Queen Beach. But deprived of clear communication and observers, their fire was ragged and not the saturation of the shore that had been envisaged.

LCT 947 had beached almost exactly where intended, opposite exit 17 on the far eastern edge of Queen White Beach. Unfortunately this put her within 100 yards of the edge of Cod and she quickly became the primary target for the gunners on the strongpoint's west side. 947's crew had started well: the ramp was down into the surf almost the moment the LCT had stopped, and within seconds Lieutenant Donald Robinson of 22 Dragoons instructed his driver to advance. Bullets pinged on to the Sherman Crab flail's hull as it emerged from the sloping bow of the landing craft, rolled down the ramp and into the surf. The driver gunned the engine and *Stornoway* waded through the breaking waves. Moments later the large drum suspended between thick metal arms protruding from the tank chassis started to spin. As it quickly picked up speed, the centrifugal force kicked the heavy metal chains out and soon they were lost in a blur of steel spinning around in front of the tank. The Crab emerged from the waves and the chains smashed into the soft damp sand as the Sherman started up the beach, searching for landmines to detonate and sending gritty spray in all directions.

But behind Robinson, things were going badly wrong. No sooner had the first Crab descended the ramp than Corporal Ernest Brotherton ordered his driver to advance, but as she manoeuvred between the two winch houses on either side of the bow, *Dunbar* became exposed to the defenders on the beach. In a second a bright flash illuminated the front of the tank and the men behind saw it judder with the blast of an explosion; the engine covers behind the turret blew open and the whole tank was barged sideways. As men quickly leapt out of their turrets and ran forward to the stricken tank, more shells pounded into the port side of

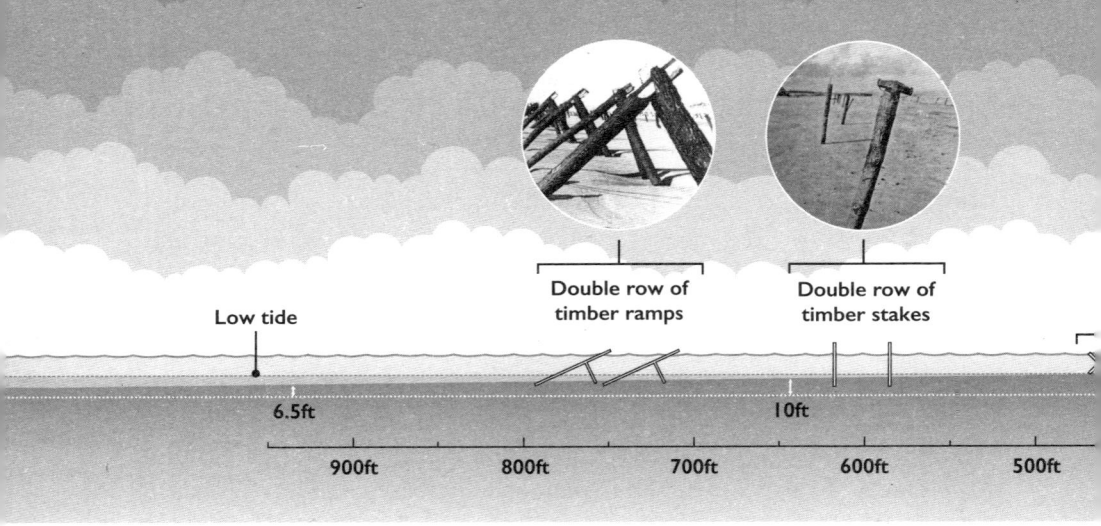

| Low tide | Double row of timber ramps | Double row of timber stakes |

6.5ft   10ft

900ft   800ft   700ft   600ft   500ft

LCT 947.* Lieutenant Colonel Arthur Cocks rose out of the turret of *Battleaxe* to see what was happening ahead, just as a shell struck the Boase Bangalore frame at the front of *Barbarian*, Captain Thomas Fairie's AVRE alongside.† A shattering red blast enveloped the front of the LCT as the 25lb of explosive detonated and screams echoed across the tank deck, audible even over the clamour of battle and the growl of the tank and LCT engines. Inside *Battleaxe*, Sapper Joe Williams felt a massive compressive wave squashing him, forcing the air from his lungs. Even before the blast had finished, Cocks, killed immediately, fell back into the turret alongside him, while driver Frank Winstanley was peppered with mortal shrapnel wounds in his back, wine-red blood stains instantly expanding across his battledress.

On the tank deck, confusion reigned. Screams emanated from Cocks's tank and dazed sappers approached, looking for the source. A cry for morphia brought Lambton Burn, a journalist attached to the Royal

---

* The source of the shells that hit 947 is not clear. While it may have been the 75mm anti-tank gun in the concrete casemate at the west end of Cod, this gun would have been firing on the absolute limit of its traverse and might not have been able to hit the landing craft. It is possible it was the 50mm gun in the centre of the beachfront, which is roughly the same distance away as Captain Fairie estimated the range to be, suggesting he may have sighted the offending gun. However, on the bridge, Lieutenant Commander James thought the damage was caused by mortars, as did journalist Lambton Burn.

† The Boase Bangalore consisted of two Bangalore torpedoes placed on a lightweight frame at the front of an AVRE, designed to be pushed into sand dunes or barbed wire and detonated to clear a path.

A cross section of Queen Red Beach, based on Allied intelligence and reports written after D-Day. The beach at La Plage has a very shallow gradient, so it can be very wide at low tide but quickly floods as the tide comes in.

Double row of Czech hedgehogs and tetrahedrons

High tide

Anticipated high water, 6 June, approx 85ft from datum

Barbed wire

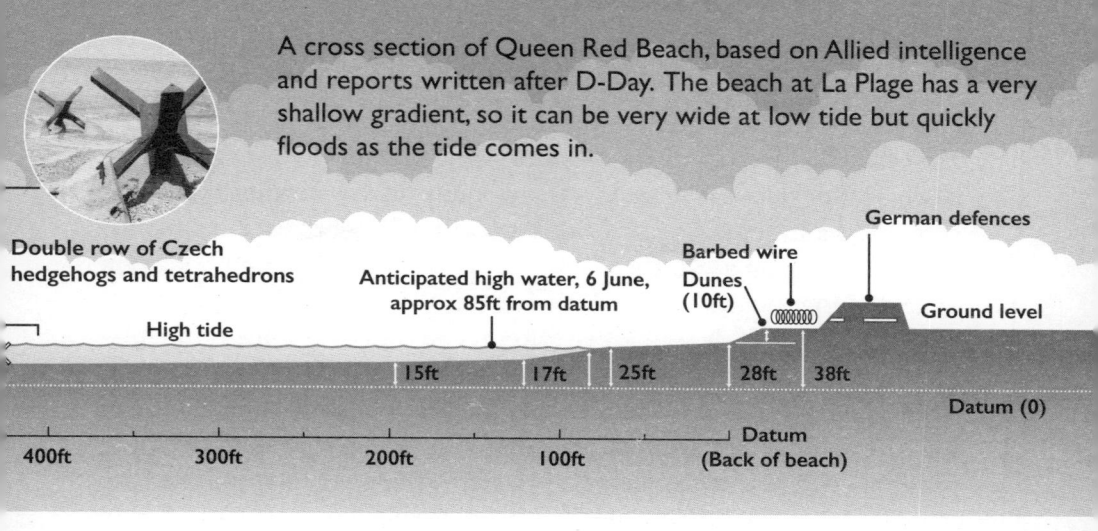

Dunes (10ft)

German defences

Ground level

15ft | 17ft | 25ft | 28ft | 38ft

Datum (0)

400ft | 300ft | 200ft | 100ft | Datum (Back of beach)

Engineers, down to the tank deck, where he quickly squeezed a dose into the sweaty arm of a wounded sapper. Ignoring fusillades of bullets and the ever-present explosions all around, men clambered on to the hull of *Dunbar* and slowly extricated Brotherton from the turret. His faint pulse belied his shattered back, torn asunder by the first blast, and despite the men's best efforts he died almost as soon as he was laid on the tank deck. Winstanley was pulled from *Battleaxe*'s driver's compartment, but it was obvious to the shocked sappers that he too was beyond their help.

Even though it was their tank that had been hit, miraculously no one on *Barbarian* had been hurt. Fairie quickly dismounted and ran forward to inspect *Dunbar*. It was immediately apparent from the smoke that billowed from the engine that the tank wouldn't be going anywhere under its own power. It was also jammed between the two winch houses on either side of the LCT's bow. Fairie called *Barbarian* forward and tried to use the AVRE's weight to push the tank forward, but it was stuck fast. *Barbarian* pulled back and men jumped into its place; chains and tackle were attached to the Crab's hull, and logs were cut from the carpet on the front of Fairie's tank to try and lever *Dunbar* out of the way. Sweating profusely as bullets continued to strike the hull, men and machines strained to free the tank, all to no avail.[1]

Outside LCT 947's chaotic little world the other assault groups were advancing up the beach, but they too were doing so under fire. Just a little west of the stricken 947, two LCAs carrying A Company HQ and 9 Platoon of 1 South Lancs beached in the surf, albeit much further east than they had intended as a result of being buffeted by the heavy seas. Major John Harward dashed off the ramp of his landing craft and through the surf, pausing at the obstacles as enemy fire swept across the beach, kicking up sand. Up ahead, Lieutenant Bill Allen and 9 Platoon were dashing forward to the dunes where, above them, Harward could see the tall wall of dense barbed wire. As he watched, some of the platoon crawled forward, sliding across the tussocky sand, clutching the long cylindrical Bangalore torpedoes. The first 5-foot pole was slid under the wire and the men grabbed at a second, screwing it on to the first and pushing the whole thing further forward. A third pole was screwed on, then the firing fuse, and the whole 15 feet of explosive was bodily shoved beneath the wire. Pulling the fuse, the three men scampered away alongside the cliff that offered a modicum of shelter from the sprays of machine gun fire, and the assembled men nearby ducked to the ground, waiting for the inevitable blast.

The seconds ticked by. At first, time seemed to be passing slowly, but soon one man, then others, raised their heads, wondering what had gone wrong. Harward jumped to his feet, telling the platoon to wait while he investigated. Crouching low, he was jogging forward when a sudden kick struck him in the back, and he grunted loudly in pain and frustration as he collapsed to the ground. Private William Lockett saw the burst of machine gun fire hit his company commander and immediately dashed forward, but he too was hit in the back, bullets striking his pack but penetrating with sufficient force to near paralyse him. In agony he raised his head towards the barbed wire and saw Harward lying on the sand. To Harward, the force of the blow felt like it was still pinning him to the ground, but ahead of him the Bangalore remained inert. Summoning his strength, he half crawled, half dragged himself to the sandy cliff edge. Feverishly, he reached up to the fuse. Lockett watched as Harward fumbled with it, then saw the puff of smoke as it ignited. His company commander collapsed back on to the sand making no effort to get away before the torpedo exploded just seconds later. A huge blast shook the dune and threw sand into the air that fell back like hail. 9 Platoon rose from the sand and charged forward into the gap as machine gun bullets danced in the sand around them. Lieutenant Bill Allen never made the gap, some of those bullets felling him with mortal wounds.

As he closed on his company commander, Private Bill Wellings saw Major Harward look up. Through gritted teeth, his face sweating, and trembling with pain, he told him, 'Carry on, Wellings, I'll catch up later.'[*2]

The DD tanks came ashore in small clusters, squeezing between the LCTs and LCAs. Standing on the hull of his tank, Lance Corporal Patrick Hennessey felt the tracks below him suddenly jar and then bite into the shelving sand of the shore. His crew jumped down to the corner struts of the canvas screen and watched as the water level dropped, agonizingly slowly, until the base of the screen was clear of the rolling surf. The struts were broken and the screen collapsed. The crew hurriedly jumped into their hatches and prepared for action.

Hennessey was already scanning for targets. Along with most of A Squadron he had come ashore on Queen White as planned and had begun the search for any familiar landmarks from the photographs he had studied so intently over the last few days. But there was no time for that now – spotting a weapon protruding from a house just ahead he shouted instructions over the intercom: 'Seventy-five, HE. Action. Traverse right, steady.' His gunner dutifully traversed the turret until the 75mm barrel was pointing towards the house. 'On. Three hundred, white-fronted house, first-floor window, centre.' The gunner and loader acknowledged, and after a final snatch of a look through his periscope, Hennessey called out, 'Fire!' With a sharp crash the gun fired, the recoiling breach rocking the tank backwards as the 75mm shell raced towards its target. Hennessey watched as a brief puff of flame followed by a cloud of smoke and dust erupted from the white house, then immediately began searching for another target.

Alongside them more of the DDs were coming ashore. Standing in his turret, Major Derek Wormald searched for the other tanks of A Squadron. As he looked down the beach a neighbouring tank appeared to touch off one of the explosives mounted on the beach obstacles, the blast rupturing the canvas screen before the tank was out of the water. Another was swamped by the surf, the crew scurrying from the hatches as the waves crashed around them.

It may well have been Hennessey's tank. As he continued to direct his gunner's fire, the lance corporal suddenly heard his driver's urgent voice

---

* Harward died of his wounds early the next morning. He is buried in Hermanville War Cemetery.

calling out, 'Let's move up the beach a bit – I'm getting bloody wet down here.' Looking behind the tank, Hennessey was alarmed to find the tide was rising faster than expected and already water was lapping around the driver's hatch nearly 6 feet above the sand. But before he could order an advance a large wave cascaded across the tank's hull, water pouring into the hatches and the engine compartment. The engine spluttered briefly then died. The driver and co-driver clambered out of the flooded hull, coughing up seawater and cursing their luck, though with the turret still safe Hennessey continued to direct his gunner on targets. But they were fighting a losing battle against the tide, and as the water level rose inside the turret he suddenly focused his attention on his immediate surroundings. The swirling surf surrounded them now – his tank was no longer on the shore – and the waves were breaking on to the beach several dozen yards ahead of them. It was time to leave, so Hennessey ordered the crew to abandon the vehicle. The crew unshipped the tank's Browning machine guns, grabbed cases of belted ammunition, bundled them into their emergency life raft and struck out for the shore.[3]

Lieutenant Edward Jones leapt forward towards his LCA's bow ramp as it dropped open. As commander of 8 Platoon A Company 1 South Lancs his position was at the front of his men and he was glad to get off the unseaworthy shoebox anyway – all his men had spent the journey from *Glenearn* vomiting. With a final step he went into the water and instantly dropped deeper than expected. As the water came up to his waist a wave pushed the LCA forward and the metal ramp was shoved into his back, pushing him below. Just as it seemed the LCA might crush him the cox'n, seeing what had happened, coaxed his craft back a little and the next wave pushed it alongside the unlucky officer. Jones staggered up as his men leapt into the water alongside him and pressed on through the obstacles in front of them.

Wading up the beach, he was struck by its similarity to the waterfront at Blackpool – a gently sloping golden sandy beach; even the obstacles looked like the defences he had seen when he had last been at the English seaside town. More frighteningly, the villas at the top of the beach seemed intact, not the demolished structures they had expected the bombardment to have created. He looked along the shore: to his right Lieutenant Robert Pearce's 7 Platoon were spilling out of their landing craft nearby, and behind him the Royal Engineers' AVREs were trundling off LCT 951, but to the left there was a sizeable gap between him and the next nearest landing craft. 9 Platoon weren't there either, and nor could he see any of the DD tanks they had expected to support their landing.

The infantry moved forward through sporadic machine gun fire and the muffled detonation of mortar bombs around them. But it was clear that the greater resistance was to their left, and the men sprinted up to the dunes as a relatively intact formation. Crouched down at the foot of the sandy cliff below the dunes, Jones took stock. Just beside them was beach exit 11 – they'd landed in the right place, but a thick wall of barbed wire loomed over them on the top of the bluff; in some places it looked to be at least twice his own height. Jones called for a Bangalore torpedo and word went down the line of men huddled below the cliff, but the response soon came back that they'd all been lost coming ashore. Jones grimaced and looked up again at the entanglements blocking their path while he pondered what to do.

On LCT 951, Captain George McLennan had long since decided that no meaningful plan was possible for the landing – it would soon come undone. Instead he'd briefed 1 Troop 77 Assault Squadron to get their AVREs into the water and wait, hull down in the surf, for the Sherman Crabs to clear a lane up the beach to their exit. To his relief, Sub Lieutenant Vale had brought his LCT perfectly in line with their desired exit – exit 11, which led straight on to the road to Hermanville, at the far western end of Queen White.

The ramp dropped just as mortar rounds began to bracket the boat, and without wasting time Lieutenant David Knapp drove the lead Crab off and straight into some 7 feet of water. Corporal Plimer cursed as the Sherman nearly stalled with the force of water blocking them, but he deftly nursed the Crab forward until they emerged in the surf. Knapp peeked through his periscope, relieved to see that despite the lines of obstacles running along the beach his path to the beach exit ahead was clear. He ordered his gunner to fire an armour-piercing shell through their 75mm gun – an effective way to remove the canvas waterproof cover over the muzzle: he'd heard a rumour that the cover was sufficient to detonate an HE shell as it was fired and had no desire to find out if it was true or not. The drum at the front of the tank began to rumble and soon a deafening roar obscured almost all other noise as the whirring chains smashed into the sand. Behind Knapp, Corporal Applin led his Crab just behind and to the right of Knapp, and together, crawling along at one and a half mph, they beat a 16-foot-wide path up the beach. Knapp tensed, waiting for the sound of a detonation, but none came.

Emerging behind the Shermans, McLennan in *Busaco* led the Royal Engineers into the water where they waited, the surf lapping against their hulls, while eyes strained to see the progress of the Crabs ahead of them. Enemy fire started to fall among them and Lieutenant Charles Tennent was obliged to keep his own AVRE, *Balaclava*, constantly moving, the steel box girder bridge on the front of his chassis a rangefinder's dream. Sergeant Thomas Kilvert in AVRE *Blenheim* had been separated from his troop at embarkation and had now just come ashore from LCT 1010 some 350 yards east. Kilvert was unsure how safe his vehicle was – they'd already been hit just as they prepared to leave the landing craft and again in the shallow water, but this was no place to hop out and inspect for damage, so he gamely pressed on as long as the tank would move.

Up ahead, Knapp had reached the top of the beach without incident. In front of exit 11 the sandy dunes were easy to traverse and he pressed on, the Crab's wildly flailing chains smashing through the line of barbed wire strung across the entrance to the little square beyond. Watching from the surf, McLennan signalled his troop to advance and the three AVREs emerged from the water like ancient monsters crawling from the sea. Seeing the safe route that Knapp had already taken through the dunes, the captain lowered his deadly Boase Bangalore on to the beach. Crawling the final few hundred yards up the sand, McLennan came to a stop near the dunes, just as Kilvert's luckless *Blenheim* hit a mine behind him. A bogie was blown out of the tracks, but the tank remained mobile enough to pull up behind *Busaco*, just before they detonated a second mine on their left side. Two bogies collapsed under the blast and the broken track flopped uselessly on to the sand.*

In front of them, Sergeant Lynn and Lance Corporal McNamara had crawled out of *Busaco*'s side hatches to set up a windsock to mark the beach exit, but a quick inspection revealed it was missing, presumably knocked off in the surf. McLennan called back to Kilvert on the wireless to erect his and dutifully Sergeant Vaughan and Lance Corporal Walter Fairlie clambered out. Wary of the constant soundtrack of machine gun fire and explosions, Fairlie jumped down on to the sand and jogged towards the back of the tank. A sudden blast rocked *Blenheim* and Vaughan saw a cloud of smoke and sand on the other side of the tank. Fearing the worst, he ran round to find his crewmate, but instead saw

---

* Kilvert believed he had hit mines, but the beach itself was not actually mined at all. He was most likely hit by mortar or artillery fire.

Left: Allied bombs fall over the lock gates at Ouistreham on 19 May 1944.

Below: Rommel inspects 21 Panzer Division's 200 Assault Gun Battalion, formed up in Lebisey Wood, 30 May 1944. The self-propelled gun is a 10.5cm leFH 16 (Sf.) auf Geschützwagen 39H(f), a First World War German artillery piece mounted on a 1930s French Hotchkiss tank chassis.

Right: A Somua gun tractor converted to carry twenty 81mm mortars, displayed for Rommel at the Château de Lion-sur-Mer on 30 May 1944.

Rommel and his fellow officers watch as rockets explode in the sea in front of strongpoint 21 (Trout) on 30 May 1944.

Above: Strongpoint 20 (Cod) at La Brèche. This aerial reconnaissance photograph shows the scale of this strongpoint, with numerous bunkers, weapons pits and personnel shelters connected by a trench network and surrounded by barbed wire.

Below: A view of Ouistreham taken in 1945. The locks on the Caen Canal can be seen on the left. The coastal battery at strongpoint 8 (Bass) sits behind the beach in front of the town, including partially constructed casemates. The remains of the casino are on the right in front of the town.

A view of Queen Red Beach taken in 1945. Strongpoint 18 (Skate) sits between the triangle of roads on the left behind two wrecked LCI(S)s, and strongpoint Cod is on the right behind a wrecked LCT.

A view of Queen White Beach taken in 1945. Strongpoint Cod on Queen Red can be seen on the left. Exit 11 on to the Fontaine de Gravier and the road inland to Hermanville can be seen on the right.

Rommel inspects beach defences in April 1944. The ramps are similar to those constructed at Queen Beach, albeit more densely arranged here.

Above left: Photographed in Belgium in 1942, this is the popular impression of a German machine gun post on the Atlantic Wall — a reinforced position equipped with modern MG 34 or MG 40 machine guns.

Above right: The reality was often quite different. Photographed on Juno Beach, this machine gun position was similar to several of those found at Cod on Queen Beach. Note the wooden door used to shore up the trench through the dune. The various machine guns used in these positions might even be of First World War vintage.

Tanks of C Squadron 13/18 Hussars embark on to landing craft of 41 LCT Flotilla at Gosport Ferry (GF) embarkation hard, 3 June.

Major General Thomas Rennie wishes the crew of an M10 self-propelled gun good luck as they wait to board their LCT in Gosport, 3 June.

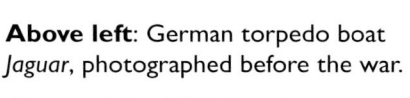

Men of 3 Commando embark on their LCI(S)s at Warsash, 5 June.

Force S sails. Lieutenant Peter Wild of COPP 6 captured the scene as Convoy Purify departed Spithead. LCP(L) 197 bobs around under tow while in the background LCTs of 14 Flotilla, carrying the DD tanks of 13/18 Hussars, pass by Spithead Fort.

Above left: German torpedo boat *Jaguar*, photographed before the war.

Above right: HMS *Scorpion*, photographed on 14 June 1944.

Left: HMS *Warspite* opens fire on German batteries east of the Orne early on the morning of D-Day.

A sequence of three images taken by Lambton Burn from LCT 947 as it came into the beach at H-Hour. Beside the LCT are DD tanks of A Squadron 13/18 Hussars, and LCAs of 535 Flotilla landing men of 1 South Lancs.

A photograph taken by Lieutenant Peter Wild (COPP 6) of LCT 1094 (carrying 3 Troop 77 Assault Squadron) coming ashore for the second time after initially hitting an obstruction at H-Hour.

Above: HMS X-23 arrives at HMS *Largs* after the successful completion of her mission. The midget submarine was a mere 51 feet long.

Above: Leutnant Nessel's HQ bunker at the south-west corner of strongpoint Cod, camouflaged to look like a civilian villa.

Left: The 75mm bunker at strongpoint 18 (Skate) that faced west along Queen Red, photographed in July 1944. The impact of numerous shells can be seen just above and to the right of the embrasure – shells almost certainly fired by Corporal Johnson from his Sherman Crab.

Below: Medics attending to wounded in the lee of *Cheetah*, a Churchill AVRE from 3 Troop 79 Assault Squadron Royal Engineers.

Above left: The interior of the 75mm gun bunker at Skate. The 7.5cm FK 231(f) was a modified late nineteenth-century design still in service in France and Poland when the Second World War broke out. Thousands were used by the Germans along the Atlantic Wall.

Above right: Heavily laden men from 4 Commando advance through the ruins of the holiday camp on Queen Red Beach.

Left: Self-propelled 105mm Priest guns disembark from an LCT. These are most likely guns of 76 Field Regiment Royal Artillery coming ashore just west of exit 13.

Below: Photographed from LCT 610 looking towards the twin villas of Quinquin and Tancrède. In front of them Lance Sergeant Bartley's AVRE burns after being hit, most likely by the 50mm anti-tank gun ensconced in the low mound immediately above the bulldozer to the left.

only a smoking crater and a stream of petrol gushing out of the tank's engine compartment and draining into the sand. There wasn't any time to lose, and Kilvert ordered his crew out. The men grabbed small arms and haversacks while Kilvert pulled a sheaf of codeword papers and the slidex card out of a file and destroyed them. Jumping down on to the beach, he beckoned his men to take cover then made his way around the tank. Petrol was spilling into the crater faster than it could soak away and now a lethal puddle was starting to form. Keeping low, he searched for Fairlie, expecting at least to find some remains of the unfortunate lance corporal. But there was nothing to be seen and, grimly, Kilvert returned to his crew and led them up to exit 11.*

With Knapp's clearance of the barbed wire, Jones now had a route off the beach and quickly led his platoon through it, just as more ranging artillery started to fall. A large house on the left corner of the exit overlooking the square and the beach was the next objective, as well as a potential shelter from artillery, and Jones ordered Corporal Walsh to clear it. The platoon's other two sections were already pouring fire at the windows as Walsh burst in through the door of Les Marmousets, a tall half-timbered home with imposing pavilion roofs. As Jones followed with the rest of his men, the building's occupants emerged wearily from the cellar – a collection of somewhat dishevelled men who had been sheltering from the bombardment. Jones suspected that many were Eastern European conscripts. But their appearance presented a sudden problem that until now Jones had not considered – what to do with them? It occurred to him that he had received no instructions on how to handle PoWs, so at a loss, the men were disarmed, returned to the cellar and locked into one of the rooms.†

As LCT 951 had come in to beach, LCT 1092 had been perfectly on station just east of her. Captain Arthur Low, commander of 2 Troop 77 Assault Squadron, had been on the bridge with Lieutenant Wigley spotting for landmarks when they had both seen the large villa that was their

---

* Fairlie's remains were never identified. He is commemorated on the Bayeux Memorial, although it is possible that he lies among one of the 103 unidentified burials at Hermanville War Cemetery.
† It is worth noting that very few of the Operational Orders issued at brigade and battalion level mention PoWs at all, despite detailing tasks, objectives, administrative details like post and pay, captured stores and even refugees.

target next to exit 12. Smoke rolled over again as the LCTs accelerated to the beach, and it was only when the scene cleared at 300 yards that they saw they were too far to starboard. But now their gap was closing: LCT 951 was moving to port to hit her exit and on their left LCT 1094 was drifting across to their bit of beach. At that moment Sub Lieutenant Harold Surtees was struggling to manoeuvre 1094, which had come aground short of the beach. Hollering commands into his voice pipe, he fought with the craft to find a clearer section of beach to come on to. Wigley and Low quickly conferred – there was little time for much more than a shouted suggestion and an acknowledgement before 1092 swung out to the right, clearing 951's stern, and raced for the shore approximately 100 yards to her starboard. Bullets pinged against the bridge and Low took his cue to leave. As he raced down to his AVRE, Wigley looked up the beach – there was no one further west than they were.

The ramp fell on to the beach just as Low climbed into his tank, *Barbaric*. Ahead of him, Sergeant Walter Smyth ordered Trooper John Hogg to advance and the first Sherman Crab lumbered forward and down into the water. Peeking through his periscope, Smyth could see an anti-tank gun on the dunes directly ahead of him, its attention seemingly distracted by LCT 951 to his left. As his flail drum started to rotate, Smyth drove his Crab forward, making a beeline directly for the gun. Too late, the gun crew realized their mistake in concentrating on the target to their right; desperately they tried to turn the gun, but its wheeled carriage was difficult to manhandle. Just as the gun was brought to bear on Smyth's Sherman, the crew saw that the tank was practically upon them and dived out of the gun pit. Sparks flew and metal shrieked as the gun was twisted aside like a child's toy by the flailing chains.

As Smyth turned round to widen the path behind him, Low brought his AVRE up behind, his Boase Bangalore ready to deploy. As he reached the dunes he saw an ideal exit a little to the right of the gun position and pressed the entire frame and its explosive charge into a 6-foot dune. The two prongs of the frame slid into the sand and the power of the AVRE pressed it deep into the sand, but as the crew tried to release the rope tackle holding it to the tank, it jammed. The charge couldn't be detonated until it was freed. Low raised his head out of the turret hatch, but the clanging of bullets on the tank's chassis quickly forced him to retreat.

Behind him, Sergeant Albert Myhill brought *Brutal*, the AVRE bridgelayer, up the path flailed by Smyth. The gun position provided a perfect and stable structure on which to lay the box girder bridge so that following vehicles could ascend the dunes. Guiding his driver, Myhill directed *Brutal* into position and lowered the bridge, which fell with a clang on to the 75mm gun. The holding hooks were released and the AVRE went to back away, but as it did so it tugged on the bridge. Realizing they were still attached, Myhill climbed out of the tank and ran forward to loosen the hook by hand. Bullets ricocheted off the tank and bridge as the defenders targeted him, without success. Once the bridge was free, Myhill dashed round his tank to grab his windsock and mark the exit, but it was missing. He jumped back into the safety of the tank and *Brutal* advanced over the bridge.

As grenades started to bounce off *Barbaric*'s hull, Low called Corporal Gregory forward and *Brawny*, the next AVRE in the column, pulled up at the bridge. While Gregory's crew erected a windsock and deployed yellow smoke to indicate the beach exit, Low managed to spot the offending grenadier and a quick burst of machine gun fire was sufficient to silence him. Quickly he popped out of his tank and freed the Boase Bangalore, before ordering the driver to reverse. As they pulled away from the torpedo a burst of fire suddenly detonated it prematurely. A huge explosion of sand and smoke enveloped the tank and cast the body of the dune into the air, hurling it back down across the beach and houses behind. Low looked through his periscope as the sand cloud subsided – fortunately they had just got out of range, although the sandblasting had done little for *Barbaric*'s paintwork. Ahead of them he was satisfied to see a broad path cut through the dunes.

Myhill advanced along the track on top of the dunes and into a large garden. Passing abandoned mortar positions, he made for a gate that led on to the lateral road to find British infantry making their way west. Turning right, he joined them for a short distance, spraying the way ahead with his co-axial machine gun until a radio call from Low called him back to concentrate on the main exits. He returned to the bridge, but his CO was nowhere to be seen. Dropping out of *Brutal*, Myhill set off on foot to locate Low when a burst of machine gun fire killed him where he stood.[4]

C Company of the South Lancs had come ashore much further east, their task to secure the left flank of Queen White and support 2 East Yorks' clearance of strongpoint Cod. Major Eric Johnson led his company across the beach with mercifully few casualties. Behind him raced Private Raymond Bush. Having nearly drowned when he jumped into deep water, he had managed to grab some kit from a corpse on the beach. Now, as he ran up the beach dodging bullets while shells burst all around, men shouting orders or screaming in pain, he was astounded to come across a beachmaster[*] calmly directing men off the beach. 'Don't stop for anything,' the naval officer told him as Bush stared in shock and admiration at a man willing to be a non-moving target among the whirlwind of fire on the beach.

Johnson led his men through the wire defences on the dunes and into the small lanes between the houses leading off the beach. Carefully they threaded their way through the houses until they were looking at the outer lines of barbed wire surrounding strongpoint Cod.

One of the most significant German strongpoints in the entire invasion area, Cod dominated the entire western half of Queen Red Beach with fields of fire over the eastern half of White. The 75mm housed in a concrete bunker at the strongpoint's north-west corner barked continuously, firing shell after shell at the landing craft and tanks to the west, its crew impervious to the fire striking the bunker's outer walls. At the centre of the strongpoint's beachfront the 50mm anti-tank gun traversed east and west, firing at targets as quickly as its crew could reload it. Inside the strongpoint, those who could had emerged from their bunkers once the bombardment had lifted and were now handling machine guns and mortars, bringing as much fire to bear on the landing craft and the men running up the beach as they could.

Coming ashore on Queen Red, five LCAs of 536 Flotilla brought East Yorks' A Company to the centre of the beach, at the eastern end of Cod, so that they could attack the strongpoint from that side while the South Lancs attacked it from the west. Major King was in one of the first LCAs to grind into the sand, and as the ramp dropped into the surf the A Company commander vaulted forward, closely followed by his batman Private James Blenkhorn.[†] To Blenkhorn it had looked like the beach had been hit with every explosive there was in England during their approach, so terrific had been the bombardment. As he dashed up towards the first

---

[*] Almost certainly one of the assistant beachmasters with F Commando who landed with the first wave.
[†] In his correspondence to Blenkhorn and Blenkhorn's mother, King spells his batman's name thus. In his own oral archive entry with the IWM it is spelled Blinkhorn.

beach obstacles, the whistles of machine gun fire quickly revealed that the bombardment had not been everything he'd hoped for. Just ahead of him, King dived behind one of the tall timber posts. Looking behind, he saw that Blenkhorn was still standing. 'Get down, you bloody fool!' he hollered at his batman, just as a bullet grazed the private's arm. Suitably persuaded, Blenkhorn made himself as low as possible and slapped a dressing over his arm while intense fire swept the ground around him. As more men moved up from the LCAs, they sheltered behind the obstacles. Seeing their hesitancy, King yelled back at them, 'Keep going, you bloody fools, keep going!' and in spurts small groups of men dashed further up the sand. Those who made it flopped gratefully in the shelter of the dunes, but when they looked behind them they saw the small mounds of wet battledress and webbing, indicating those who would never make it that far.[5]

Further east, the other five LCAs of 536 Flotilla brought B Company to the shore close to strongpoint Skate, which needed to be neutralized before 4 Commando arrived thirty minutes later. On the flotilla's far left, almost at the very east end of Queen Red, the men of 10 Platoon B Company watched, horrified, as their LCA's cox'n weaved them through the line of tall posts, each with a mine at its top. Then they felt the hull shudder beneath them as the boat started to ground and the cry 'Down ramp!' summoned them to attention.

The metal doors at the bow were pushed open and Lieutenant Reginald Rutherford led the first section that spilled out of the LCA into 4 feet of water and a cascade of enemy fire. Almost at once, barely a few feet from the bows of the landing craft, men were cut down, their bodies falling into the surf, and the waves pushing and twisting them forward like drunken marionettes. The rest of the men heaved themselves through the deep water while waves broke across their backs and threatened to push them under. Holding 3 Section's Bren gun above him, Private Ron Major heard the uncomfortable snap of bullets passing close by his head and saw small spatters of water kicking up all around. More men alongside and ahead of him were similarly struggling to move forward, some of them collapsing under the waves as bullets continued to rake the water. Mortar shells whined overhead and subdued booms threw up small geysers as they came down.

Despite the LCA crews' best efforts there was still a collection of beach obstacles barring the progress of the platoon as it advanced up to the water's edge – the incoming tide was already lapping around the bases of staggered rows of Tetraeder and Tschechenigel 'Czech hedgehogs', many with large mines mounted on top. Reaching the obstacles, Major temporarily sought cover behind the barricade, briefly disregarding the fact that if a bullet touched off a mine it wouldn't be pretty. Then, taking a deep breath, he pushed on until the deep water gave way to breaking waves and he found himself on the sand. Immediately he dropped down into a prone position and brought his Bren to bear up the beach. Concentrating on the view ahead for the first time, he suddenly became aware of the number of bodies already littering the beach, men he knew but now violently transformed into anonymous scraps of khaki on the wet sand. He fired some sporadic bursts up at buildings ahead, then pulled himself up and ran a few more yards ahead. As bullets scoured the sand around him he dropped again, fired a couple of bursts, then leapt forward a few more yards. Despite the noise and clamour he felt strangely calm, his actions automatic. Besides, he reasoned, there was nowhere else to go and he didn't fancy being back in the water. After a few more sprints he flopped down at the low sandy cliff at the top of the beach.

Lieutenant Rutherford was already there, taking stock of his platoon's predicament. Heavy fire was coming down the beach from the left – a smokescreen would be an ideal way to reduce the pressure, but the mortarman was nowhere to be seen.* He crawled over to a Bren gunner just in time to see the man suddenly crumple beside him. Lance Sergeant Robert Fenwick lifted the Bren from the body and Rutherford grabbed a magazine, but just as he slapped it on to the gun a bullet smashed past it, shattered the backsight and slammed into Fenwick's head. As the sergeant rolled away, Rutherford scrambled further into the lee of the dunes. His men were now spaced out in a thin line along the foot of the low ridge with bullets whipping up the sand alongside them. Ron Major lifted his Bren to bear on a target when he suddenly felt a heavy thwack and dropped the gun. Looking down, he saw dark red blood spurting from a large hole in his right wrist, the shattered bone rendering his hand completely useless. He fell back into the dunes and clamped a field dressing over the wound, holding it tight as it turned red and warm blood oozed between his fingers.

Around Rutherford his men were cursing as they tried to clean wet

---

* This was probably Private Samuel Williams, whose body would not be found until the following day.

sand from the breeches of their rifles. Slowly some withering covering fire started to be returned. Rutherford looked for a suitable place to cross the barbed-wire entanglements running along the top of the ridge. There was only a single 5-foot Bangalore torpedo available to them now – the second was somewhere in the surf – but it should suffice. Quickly, the infantrymen fitted the firing fuse and pushed the explosive tube under the thicket of steel wire just above them; someone pulled the fuse and the men threw themselves to the ground. A loud explosion blew several feet of barbed wire up and into the air, slashing it into several pieces. As the sand fell down around and on to the East Yorks the wind blew the smoke away, revealing a gap of several feet. Clambering up the ridge, Rutherford led his men on to the gravel road behind the wire. A mine detonated, encasing two men in flame and smoke. Scrabbling for cover, the remaining men ducked into the scant protection afforded by the undulating ground, ditches and low walls. Rutherford looked around. Of the twenty-nine who had followed him off the LCA, only eleven had got off the beach.*[6]

Behind them the AVREs of 79 Assault Squadron were advancing up the beach in small groups. Lieutenant Edwards and his crew had managed to beach LCT 1082 just a few dozen yards to the right of exit 19, the road adjacent to Quinquin and Tancrède villas. Immediately the ramp dropped, the two Sherman Crabs of 22 Dragoons had moved on to the beach and cleared a lane up to the dunes. But as Corporal Agnew's tank turned to widen the lane back down the beach it became a target for the gunners manning the 50mm anti-tank gun at the centre of Cod. In quick succession three shells slammed into the Crab's engine compartment, flames started to lick around the hull, and the crew immediately baled out, just managing to avoid the attentions of the German machine gunners. The next shell hit Sergeant Cochran's turret, killing one of his crew and forcing the rest to abandon the tank.

Behind them, 2 Troop were making their way through the water. An AVRE fired on the 50mm gun, but the range was too great for the 29mm Petard mortar and it fell short, exploding harmlessly in front of the bunker. In the leading AVRE, Lance Sergeant Bartley drove up the lane, but realizing the dunes were only low he decided against using his Boase

---

* Of the thirty men of 10 Platoon who landed at H-Hour, six were killed and fourteen were wounded on D-Day, almost all of them on the beach.

Bangalore. Just as he started reversing his tank to reposition to the right of the two knocked-out Crabs, Captain Geoffrey Desanges's AVRE bridgelayer behind him was hit, the shot detonating the small explosive charge that released the bridge from the front of the Churchill. It crashed down on to the beach immediately behind Bartley, whose AVRE quickly became entangled with the steel frame and jammed there.

Inside the concrete bunker the gunners swung the 50mm at this new and inviting target. The first two shells struck the AVRE's left-hand storage panniers and a third hit the turret ring. As the crew desperately struggled to free themselves the fourth shot blew up a box of explosives and machine gun ammunition. The blast enveloped the tank, wounding most of those inside and leaving it ablaze across the hull, providing more than enough motivation for the crew to bale out.

Desanges jumped from his own AVRE and started to release the fallen bridge, wrestling it from its mounts by hand and freeing his tank. But as he looked towards the gap he realized it was too badly blocked by the wreckage of the bridge and tanks. Returning to his turret, he summoned Lieutenant Nicholson, his second in command who had landed on the neighbouring LCT 1016. The only way to clear a lane off the beach was to use a handheld mine detector, and cautiously Lance Sergeant Purkiss dismounted Nicholson's AVRE and made his way forward, the clumsy apparatus slowing his progress. As he neared the tanks, intense machine gun fire kicked at his heels and he was forced to seek shelter behind the wreckage. Instead, Desanges directed Nicholson to use his Petard to detonate any mines alongside the wreckage, but as he prepared to do so his gunner reported that his hatch was jammed and he couldn't open it to reload the weapon. Nicholson clambered out of his turret to free the hatch, but despite his labours it remained firmly closed. It was then that he realized the turret itself was jammed too, victim of no fewer than four hits and stuck on a steel hawser jammed under the turret ring, so he gave up the pointless task.

Looking to report to Desanges, Nicholson spotted him going forward on foot with Sappers Price and Darrington. Running to join them, the four men dug three shallow pits. Explosives were placed inside, ready to be detonated to flatten the sand dune and create an exit, when Nicholson realized they needed more detonating cord. As he dashed back to his tank, a machine gun turned its attention on the dune and Desanges was felled in a hail of bullets. Ducking and weaving to avoid the maelstrom of machine gun fire, Nicholson returned and started to connect the charges.

Shouting warnings to men of the South Lancs lying in the shelter of the dunes, he lit the fuse and ran, but just as he neared cover a burst of bullets struck his arm and torso and his world went dark.* Behind him the dune exploded and sand showered down across the beach.†

On the far left of the landings, LCT 909 came ashore just in front of the ruins of a French holiday camp, some 200 yards west of Skate. Lieutenant John Allen directed his Sherman Crab down the ramp, but the LCT was too tempting a target for the 75mm gun housed in Skate's thick concrete bunker and before his tank was even clear of the water three shots had struck the hull. Inside, the impact of the HE shells scattered metal fragments throughout, felling Allen and three of his crew with fatal wounds. The tank burst into flames and Lance Corporal Pummell, the gunner, threw himself from the turret and into the sea to extinguish his flaming uniform.

His Crab still sitting in the water, Corporal Johnson had been watching for muzzle flashes, and as shells slammed into his commander's tank he spotted their source. Traversing the turret, he brought the 75mm to bear on Skate's concrete bunker and unleashed a flurry of shells. Flame, smoke and concrete dust billowed from the structure, the steel girder over the top of the gun embrasure fell, and shrapnel peppered the gun, collapsing its carriage, damaging the barrel and incapacitating the crew. Johnson waited for a moment to make sure the gun didn't fire again, then began to thrash clear a new lane. Behind him, 4 Troop of 79 Assault Squadron began deploying their AVREs in the surf.[7]

Back on LCT 947, in desperation Captain Fairie had called Lieutenant Robinson to return to his landing craft and try to pull *Dunbar* off the front of the craft. But by now, Commander Currey on LCH 185 could see that 947 was an obstacle on the beach that needed to be removed if the following waves were to land. Robert James was signalled to get clear and, reluctantly, he ordered the landing craft astern. Even so, despite the fact 947's port winch house was now a collapsed wreck, the port side coaming was a jumble of wrecked steel and water was flooding in

---

* Although knocked out, Nicholson survived his injuries.
† Lieutenant Tom Phillips, whose own AVRE had by now been knocked out, commandeered Nicholson's and over the next thirty minutes used it to tow the bridge and Bartley's AVRE out of the way. An armoured bulldozer finally cleared the lane.

through dozens of shell holes in the bows, seeing that LCT 1094 was also struggling to beach, James conned his landing craft west. But just as he closed on the seemingly stricken landing craft, Harold Surtees finally got it ashore. Relieved, James pulled away from the beach and headed out to sea.

From 1094, Ivan Dickinson saw the charred remains of the tanks on 947's deck. He had seen the Boase Bangalore detonate when 1094 had first grounded and now, seeing the outcome, he was reassured that he had made the right decision in ordering his men to cut their own torpedo away, thinking it was more of a hindrance than a help. Greatly relieved, his men had pulled the assembly down and thrown the explosives over the side.

As the crew scrambled back into their tank, Surtees had conned 1094 back among the obstacles. To his consternation, the first row of vertical poles was already in deep water – even with the delay caused by their first grounding, he knew there was no way the tide should have come in quite this quickly. Carefully, 1094 threaded its way through the first line and then the second and the crew finally brought the LCT to a rest alongside a ramp obstacle, itself in 4 feet of water. The bow ramp dropped and the first two Sherman Crabs advanced into the water, struggled through the surf and on to the sand. The drums were started up and soon both Shermans were beating a path to the dunes.

Behind them, Captain William Carruthers drove his AVRE into the waves and followed them on to the sand. Popping his head out of the turret hatch, Carruthers chanced a look behind: the three other AVREs had followed him, but one, carrying a bobbin on its hull, was stopped in the water. No time to worry about that now. He turned around and stared, startled. Seemingly oblivious to the whines of bullets and the muffled explosions of mortar bombs impacting the sand, three German soldiers came running down the beach with their hands high in the air. Somewhat dumbfounded, Carruthers waved them on and then watched, astonished, as they carried on past his tank and into the sea, still with their arms in the air.

Ahead of him, the two Crabs had reached the gap in the dunes that led on to a lane leading inland. Carruthers moved up behind them and prepared to lay his log carpet, creating a firmer surface for all the vehicles that would follow. But when the gunner went to blow the small charges that would release the rolled carpet, the bundle declined to fall forward.

Carruthers realized his turret was jammed too, so jumping out of the hatch with a knife he went forward and began cutting at the ropes holding the carpet on to the front of the AVRE. Finally the ropes gave way, but as the bundle fell forward its tubular shape collapsed. Disgusted, Carruthers knew that the carpet was unlikely to unroll if the AVRE pushed it forward – now it was more of a hindrance in the gap than a help. As he pondered this exceedingly irritating turn of events, a blinding flash and bang solved the dilemma for him. He came to on the sand alongside the AVRE, his world a fizz of lights, colours and noise. His crew attended to him as he gathered his senses – a grenade had been thrown from one of the overlooking windows, they explained. A Crab had offered the sender a 75mm shell in return.[8]

On the eastern flank of the landings came 100 LCT(A) Flotilla and the Royal Marine Armoured Support Group. Although still lagging behind the rest of Group 2, the lead landing craft managed to hit the beach only five minutes after 45 LCT Flotilla. On board LCT(A) 2123, Lieutenant Gibbons conned his vessel through the first row of obstacles under the watchful eye of the flotilla's CO, Lieutenant Commander Foster. The ramp was dropped and two Centaur tanks of S Troop disembarked, closely followed by the Sherman of their CO, Captain J. D. Scott. Alongside them the rest of the troop disembarked from LCT(A) 2012 and the five tanks formed up in the surf just below the waterline and proceeded to fire on the enemy strongpoints they could see. Behind them the two LCTs backed away from the beach when 2123 juddered to a halt. Ropes – probably tidal detritus that had wrapped itself around the beach obstacles – now entangled all three propellers of the landing craft. Leading Motor Mechanic Robinson jumped over the side and stood in chest-deep water to free a propellor while the LCT lay stranded on the beach. A veritable bullet magnet, shots pinged off the hull around him and wounded some of the crew before Robinson was able to clear a single shaft, and Gibbons gratefully reversed into deeper water.

On the far left flank, east of every other vessel, came LCT(A)s 2052 and, to her left, 2191, between them carrying the five tanks of Captain Edward Elliott's T Troop. As they neared to within 3,000 yards, heavy mortar fire began to fall between the two LCTs, supplemented by equally heavy machine gun fire as they got nearer to the shore. 2052 ploughed through several obstacles that failed to impede the craft until, just as it came to a stop on the shore, the vessel touched off a mine near the bow that blasted a 5-foot hole in the bottom. Regardless, the ramp was dropped into the water and the first Centaur trundled down it. Behind it, Sergeant George Jones ordered his tank forward, but as it descended the ramp it jammed against something. Heavy gunfire started to sweep across the tank, and as machine gun bullets clattered against the hull, Elliott spotted the delay, jumped from his Sherman and ran forward. Hearing his commander calling him, Jones stood up in the turret – well above the height of the landing craft's bows – and relayed Elliott's instructions to his driver, slowly manoeuvring the tank back and forth. Beautifully silhouetted above the landing craft it was only a matter of time before he caught the eye of a German gunner and, just as the tank was extricated from its trap, a bullet struck the sergeant in the head. Staggering under the blow, Jones remained standing until the tank was safely on its way again, then dropped down into the turret, blood trickling from a flesh wound.* Elliott scurried back to his tank and the Sherman followed the Centaurs into the water while gunfire continued to pepper 2052's bow, wounding the first officer, Sub Lieutenant Francis.

Jack Tear couldn't see anything outside *Temeraire* but felt the Centaur lurch down LCT(A) 2191's ramp and heard the sound of churning water as they entered the sea. All too suddenly water sprayed through the edges of the hatch beside him and he realized with horror that the ammunition handlers had forgotten to seal it. Seawater continued to pour in until the tank moved forward enough to put the hatches above the waterline, but even so the intercom was put out of action and for the rest of the day all instructions would have to be shouted over the roar of the engine and the pounding of the gun.

Further along the beach, other strongpoints had found the range of the two LCTs behind the tanks and methodically they started to pound them with shells.† While 2052 started to back away from the shore, rounds smashed into the bridge tower and shrapnel slashed at the occupants of the wheelhouse – Albert Smith recalled a loud bang, and when he came round he saw that most of cox'n Norman Hannah's head had been blown clean away. Another rating rolled on the deck groaning and blood poured from Smith's own head wounds. 2052 detonated another

---

* Jones was awarded the Military Medal for his actions.
† One of the witnesses refers to a German tank or mobile gun, but it is more likely these shots came from strongpoint 10.

mine at the stern and on the bridge Lieutenant Woodham could see the vessel was in dire straits. Unable to raise the engine room, he descended the ladder and went below himself, finding Stokers Parkinson and Piggot in nearly 3 feet of water and near darkness. The port and starboard engines had been knocked out, but the centre engine was still running and couldn't be stopped. Eventually Piggot shut the valves to bring it to a jarring halt but by then the landing craft had driven itself back up on to the beach.

The incoming tide had swept 2052 a little further east along the beach and it once again came alongside 2191. While Woodham had tried in vain to keep 2052 afloat, Sub Lieutenant Julian Roney had had no time to respond to the fire coming at 2191 from positions on their port side. A shell struck the bow with such force it swung the front of the vessel to starboard and probably killed Sub Lieutenant Sidney Green and Wireman Edward Trendell in the port winch house instantly. As the landing craft turned broadside to the beach the stern became exposed to the enemy gun and the next shell struck the back of the bridge, the flames and shrapnel shredding Roney and Sub Lieutenant Richard Thonber and blasting signaller Peter Hutchins to the deck. When he came to his senses it was immediately obvious to Hutchins that there was nothing to be done for the two officers, their burned duffel coats already turning dark red as blood soaked into them. The blast had reduced the bridge to a viewing platform – its controls, compass and voice pipes were obliterated – and Hutchins scrambled down the ladder and into the wheelhouse. 2191 was adrift now, the tide pushing her down the beach sideways, waves breaking against her starboard side. Cox'n Francis Lemon had staggered out of the wheelhouse after the blast, blood gushing from his throat, and was even now making his way towards the beach. As Hutchins staggered inside he saw two of the crew running across the deck towards him. Able Seaman Robert Bryson and Stoker Victor Orme were probably the last men on board.

The two men clambered up to the aft deck and into the wheelhouse but just as they entered another shell struck the landing craft, decimating the small party. Hutchins was amazed to find himself still standing, but looked down and realized with horror that his right ankle was smashed and his foot was dangling hopelessly from his leg, connected only by a single tendon. Bryson and Orme lay on the deck, their wounds serious. Hutchins pulled Orme clear of the wheelhouse, but Bryson was stuck and in his weakened state the signaller couldn't get him out. Delirious and only able to crawl, he searched the stern of the ship for other wounded before shuffling towards the bow to find help.[9]

While the infantry and armour fought to control the beach, the next wave of landing craft was coming in. But Group 5, intended to land at 07:45 – twenty minutes after the first waves – was already badly dispersed. While the two reserve companies of the South Lancs bore down on Queen White, and the Royal Engineers and beach units headed into Red, the two reserve companies of the East Yorks were nowhere to be seen.

No sooner had the first wave of landing craft pulled away from Queen Red than the eight LCAs of 538 Flotilla raced between them and made for the shore, five minutes ahead of schedule. Major Frederick Carson, CO of 629 Field Squadron Royal Engineers, looked over the bow of his LCA, grimly surveying the obstacles ahead. The first row of ramps was deeply immersed – he estimated only one quarter of the timber was above the surface, and probably some 6 to 8 feet of obstruction lay below. Shells and mines perched on top of the ramps and the upright poles behind were now just above sea level, the perfect height to blow their fragile boat to kingdom come. But Carson had no intention of letting the craft get in among the field of timber and concrete – his squadron's mission was to clear the obstacles on the beach, starting with the first row. Technically they weren't on the beach any more, but behind him stood Lieutenant Colonel Ronald Urquhart, 3 Division's Commander Royal Engineers. There would be no changing the plan now.

The LCA slowed and a rating pushed open the armoured doors and kicked the ramp down. Gingerly, he leaned over and prodded a depth pole into the churning sea, cursing as it dropped further and further until finally he felt it touch bottom. 'Seven foot, sir,' he called over his shoulder. Carson winced – far too deep for the men. But the explosives ahead of them were too dangerous to leave where they were. He looked round at Urquhart. The senior officer was already stripping off his kit. Carson knew what came next.

'Right men, into the water!' he shouted above the din.

The twenty Royal Engineers dutifully started to unbuckle their assault jackets, their relief at dropping the heavy, water-soaked cotton canvas jerkins tempered by the thought of jumping into the menacing waters around them. Now stripped of his heavy gear, Urquhart looked doubtfully at the bow, tossing up and down in the swell, the cox'n struggling to maintain a position off the obstacles – not the safest way out, he thought.

Slipping a pair of wire cutters into his pocket, he clambered up on to the hull and turned to the men behind him. There was nothing they could do to demolish the obstacles themselves, he told them, but they could at least get the explosives off.

Grumbling men fumbled with their kit, pocketed knives and pliers, clambered on to the sides of the LCA and slipped into the sea, gasping as the cold water tightened their chests. Ever wary of the other landing craft nearby and trying to remain oblivious to the mortar bombs falling around them, the men struck out for the obstacles, fighting the swell and waves that tried to steer them in any direction other than the one they actually wanted to go in. Gagging on seawater, Urquhart reached one of the ramps. An AA shell was fixed to the upper section of the ramp, crudely secured with straps nailed into the timber. A push igniter faced seaward, ready and waiting to be hit by a vessel, and the whole assembly had been coated in a black molasses-like sealant in an effort to waterproof it. Fumbling with his wire cutters, his hands already trembling with cold, Urquhart set to work cutting the straps and cables holding the shell in place. The rusting metal wires gave way easily, and carefully lifting the shell clear, Urquhart dropped it into the sea. Briefly it occurred to him that it might well explode when it hit the seabed, but after a few seconds it appeared he was safe.

Waves crashed against him as he held on to the slippery timber, almost reluctant to let go. But on the next obstacle he could see a crazily perched Teller mine, just waiting to welcome another landing craft. Gamely he released his grip and swam on.[10]

Meanwhile, on Queen White, seventeen LCAs of 536 and 537 Flotillas fanned out into a long line, jostling for space as they approached the first obstacles. Behind them LCA 791 made her own chaotic journey to the shore. Despite the large hole in her bow, the efforts of the soldiers with their helmets had kept the little boat afloat over 8 nautical miles of sea. Now Corporal Foden desperately hoped that one final effort would see them ashore.

Looking through the narrow view slit in the small armoured cox'n position on LCA 704, Corporal Jas Oddie could see the sterns of two great LCTs manoeuvring ahead of him.* There wasn't a great deal of space

---

* It's uncertain which LCTs Oddie saw, but they must have been from 45 LCT Flotilla.

between them so he hauled his little landing craft to port and into slightly clearer water. Just as he thought he was clear of the left-hand LCT and passed it about 25 yards away to starboard, another LCA came across his bows from port. 'Full stop!' he shouted through the voice pipe to the stoker in the stern of the boat and simultaneously hauled his boat to starboard so that he didn't barge the errant LCA into a ramp obstacle ahead. With a crash, the small boat collided with a tank coming down the ramp of the LCT, knocking a jagged hole through the flimsy hull and sending water cascading through, soaking the cursing infantry.

Oddie just managed to wrest back control of the LCA as the surf battered it. 'Give it all you got!' he shouted to the stoker, and briefly the LCA surged forward; but then, over the cries of the shouting soldiers, he heard the muffled voice of his stoker through the voice pipe: 'Starboard engine burnt out!' The LCA struggled into the shallows, and just as Oddie could feel the hull scraping the bottom, an LCA ahead of them went into reverse and smashed into their port side. Limping the shattered LCA forward just a touch more, few options now remained available to the crew. They dropped the ramp, manhandled the armoured doors open and the South Lancs gratefully piled off into 3 feet of water.

Just as the last of the infantry cleared the bows, the surf pushed the LCA into another ramp obstacle. As he turned around Oddie saw the menacing timbers above them, and froze as he spotted a mine on top. Another wave crashed them against the ramp a second time and, almost in slow motion, Oddie saw the timbers collapse. The mine started to fall – Oddie knew where it was going even as he followed it down. But the inevitable explosion didn't come: the mine smashed into the stern and through the deck cover, dislodging the port engine and snapping the shaft. Wide-eyed and breathless, the stoker scrambled out of his small compartment. There was no longer any hope for LCA 704 and the crew quickly followed the infantry into the water.

As each LCA beached, the men on board rushed from the ramps, and thanks to the good job the crews had done of driving up on to the beach most ran into only 3 feet of water. 791 eventually made it to within 50 yards of the shoreline, close enough for the tired soldiers to wade towards the beach, the deeper water barely bothering them after their soaking efforts to save the craft for the past hour. But her job completed, Foden realized there was little to be done for the broken vessel and he led the crew off. Spotting LCA 792 nearby, they jumped aboard to hitch a lift home.[11]

But the cox'ns' efforts to negotiate the obstacles in the eastward-drifting tide brought most of them ashore much further left than intended. B and D Companies of the South Lancs hit the sand on and around the boundary between Queen White and Red Beaches – in front of strongpoint Cod. D Company landed directly in front of the strongpoint. When his ramp went down, Lieutenant Wilfred Lacy leapt into the churning seas to lead 16 Platoon ashore, but the LCA was still drifting forward. As Lacy plunged into 3 feet of water, it was carried by the waves further forward and promptly knocked him down. The metal ramp pinned the luckless officer to the sand and he gasped for breath between each breaking wave that immersed him. Despite his violent struggles there was no way to free himself. Just as it dawned on him that this might actually be how he died, the weight on his back lifted and he rose a little, enough to raise his head out of the waves and gulp some air. A little dazed, he looked around – ahead of him his men were already dashing up the beach while behind him the LCA was backing away. Of his steel helmet and Sten gun there was no sign. He stumbled to his feet, the surf threatening to knock him back down again, and staggered for the shore. As he reached the waterline he saw a crumpled figure and, reasoning that the man's equipment was of no use to him any more, relieved him of his helmet and Sten.

The two LCAs carrying the battalion HQ staff came in, as intended, between the two companies. Unperturbed by the rain of fire kicking up sand on the beach, Lieutenant Colonel Richard Burbury strode forward, carrying in his hand a small flag with the battalion colours to help rally his men. Seeing their commander advancing, soldiers from the surrounding landing craft chased him up the beach. Mortar bombs landed among them and men were thrown to the ground, rolling and writhing in agony from their wounds. Seeing others rush to their comrades' aid, the battalion adjutant, Captain Arthur Rouse, hollered at them to keep going. 'They'll be looked after,' he tried to reassure them, before he dashed after Burbury.

Reaching the dunes, Burbury flopped down in a slight lee below the seaward-facing Quinquin and Tancrède villas on the north-west corner of Cod. Seconds later Rouse crashed down beside him, and not long after that Lieutenant Eric Ashcroft,[*] the battalion signals officer, ducked down

---

[*] Father of businessman and former deputy chairman of the Conservative Party Lord Michael Ashcroft.

with them, his right arm bleeding from a wicked shrapnel wound. All around them men were taking cover in the dunes, their progress now blocked by the barbed-wire boundary of Cod, while mortars screamed overhead and machine guns raked the beach. As Ashcroft fumbled for a dressing, Burbury pulled his map out and studied it intently, then sat up and looked around, trying to find a recognizable landmark.

He turned to Rouse. 'Where are we, Arthur?' he asked.

Before Rouse could say anything in response there was the sudden thud of a bullet impacting Burbury's chest. His jaw began to spasm as his body fought an all too brief battle for life, then he collapsed on to the sand. Realizing he would need to find the battalion second in command, Major Jack Stone, Rouse took Burbury's maps. Wary of the flag, which might well have been his late commanding officer's undoing, he left it on the sand.

B Company, expecting to land on the western side of Queen White behind A Company, instead found themselves coming ashore behind C Company and next to a strong enemy defence nest. 10 Platoon's landing craft was zeroed in on by enemy machine guns and as they raced off the ramp men stumbled and fell into the surf, bowled over by bullets. The company CO, Major Robert Harrison, was struck almost the moment he hit the sand and collapsed, mortally wounded.* Witnessing the fate of his commander, Lieutenant Robert Bell-Walker immediately took charge of the company and, dashing forward, led them across the sand and up to the relative shelter of the sea wall. But even here a small machine gun emplacement with a line of fire along the beach kept them pinned down. Pulling a grenade from his webbing, Bell-Walker dashed forward until he was underneath the pillbox and thrust his bomb through the slit above him. His men watched as he ducked down and counted for a few seconds before a muffled blast erupted from within, blowing smoke and dust through the slit. Bell-Walker rose, ran round to the back of the pillbox, raised his Sten and began to empty his magazine through the doorway. Just as he completed this classic battle school attack, a burst of machine gun fire from somewhere within Cod stitched a line of bullets across his back and he fell, dead, into the pillbox.

Bell-Walker's sacrifice was not in vain. Seeing the lieutenant's attack neutralize the pillbox, Rouse led the men of the battalion's HQ along the beach, crouching to stay below the height of the dunes and the sandy

---

* Harrison died of his wounds the following day.

cliff, bypassing Cod on the west side. While machine gun fire rattled above them and ricochets from stone walls spat into the sand at their feet, he searched for a route inland, eventually being rewarded by the sight of a narrow track devoid of enemy attention. Charging across the dunes and into the shelter of the buildings behind them, the South Lancs HQ made their way off the beach.[12]

When sufficient men of the East Yorks had gathered at the shallow cliff east of Cod, Major King led them through the barbed wire and they swept into the outer defences of the strongpoint. The east end of Cod had been ravaged by the bombardment – the trenches along the outer wire had been caved in by the shelling and the small concrete shelters they led to had been utterly pulverized. Inside the main wire, shelters had collapsed into themselves under the weight of fire and bodies lay distorted and mutilated on open ground and along the trenches, just short of the protection they had sought.

A Company pushed through the south-east corner of the position, first storming a machine gun nest near the outer wire. With the position secure, King led his company to the 50mm anti-tank gun position at the south-east corner of Cod, overpowering the defenders before tackling the next set of trenches. Further down them, Obergefreiter Herbert Sommer and some of his friends had already given themselves up. He had long since decided not to resist, and anyway, his rifle breech was full of sand.

In just over twenty minutes nearly two entire battalions of infantry and more than a hundred armoured vehicles had come ashore on Queen Red and White Beaches. These units absolutely dwarfed the limited Axis presence on the beach, which was largely confined to the 150 or so men of 4 and 10 Companies sheltering in Skate, Cod and strongpoint 20A. While the nature of an amphibious assault tends to favour the defender – especially those in pre-prepared positions – the sheer weight of the landing at Sword meant that unless reinforcements arrived soon the strongpoints would quickly be surrounded and subdued. Already the East Yorks and South Lancs were nibbling at the edges of Cod, their men bravely overpowering the positions up against the outer wire and making their way further into the trench network while the tanks and AVREs pounded the strongpoint from the beach. In the 75mm bunker at Cod's north-west corner, the crew heard only the briefest shriek of a shell and, for a fraction of a second, the crump of an explosion before their senses expired.

An anonymous tank had managed to plant a shell straight through the open embrasure, silencing the gun that had already caused such chaos on Queen White.

Huddled in the command bunker, Toni Kresken knew that there was little chance of help coming – ever since the bombardment he had been quite unable to raise anyone outside the strongpoint. Some weak transmissions had reached him, but they did not offer any good news. Paratroopers appeared to have cut them off to the rear, so the chances of anyone reaching them even if they could be requested were slim. Above him the thin walls of the bunker's second storey, designed to make it look like a villa rather than a headquarters, had already collapsed under the weight of fire coming from the beach. It was only a matter of time before their level came in for similar punishment.[13]

7

THE COMMANDOS ARRIVE

WHILE THE ASSAULT BATTALIONS SOUGHT TO DISENTANGLE themselves from their numerous small actions, two more landing craft came up to the beach. Much larger than the LCAs, LCI(S) 527 and 523 carefully nosed their way between the beach obstacles, wary of the shells and mines displayed like ugly fruit on macabre trees standing in the water. On 527, Lieutenant Charles Craven thought the jungle of timber and concrete might be sparser further east and signalled Sub Lieutenant John Berry on 523, suggesting they redeploy. Berry replied in the negative – he was too committed on his line now and even then was swinging the bridge telegraphs to demand full power from the engines. After passing instructions to Kenneth Dawson on the wheel, Berry shouted at the men on deck to get down as the landing craft lurched forward and between the obstacles. The Free French commandos dropped as low as they could and held on to anything at hand as the LCI swung one way and then the next, holding their breath as the obstacles with their dangerous add-ons passed by mere feet away from the gunwale. Then, with a violent crash that threatened to throw the men forward, the LCI grounded on the beach. It was 07:50, five minutes earlier than intended.*

---

* It is often stated that Lieutenant Colonel Dawson of 4 Commando allowed the French commandos the honour of landing ahead of 4 Commando. Dawson himself observed that the French commandos themselves gave Dawson this credit, but by his own admission he had little choice in the matter as the two LCI(S)s surged ahead of his LCAs. It hadn't occurred to him to make this sort of arrangement and when he thought on it much later he reasoned it would have been impossible to arrange anyway. Nonetheless, he hoped the Frenchmen carried this belief to their graves. His observation, written in a letter to Ian Dear, has seemingly gone

Almost immediately the ratings at the bow slid the two long gangways forward and they tipped down into the water below. But before the commandos could file towards them, a whining shell crashed down ahead of them, the blast twisting one of the ramps away and knocking a hole in the fragile bow. Unperturbed, Officier des Équipages Alexandre Lofi,[*] commander of 8 Troop, beckoned his men to the remaining ramp and within moments the first Free Frenchmen were wading ashore on their homeland.

Berry watched with satisfaction as the Frenchmen moved quickly down the ramp. Turning, he looked over to see 527, which had beached at almost exactly the same time, but instantly realized there was a problem: her ramps were missing. As they had charged through the obstacles Craven's worst fears had been realized – his propellers had become fouled on an obstruction just as he was beaching and 527 failed to get as far up the beach as 523. Then shells crashed into the sea in front of the landing craft and carried away the two ramps, leaving just the detritus of one hanging uselessly from the bow.

Impatient to get ashore, the hardier Frenchmen were dropping into the sea, and scrambling nets were hastily thrown down the sides of the landing craft. Enseigne de Vaisseau Guy Vourc'h,[†] commander of 1 Troop, jumped over the bow and splashed into the water 6 feet below. Clambering to his feet he yelled with joy and exhorted his men forward as he staggered through the surf and on to the sand of his native country. But after taking no more than a few dozen steps an ear-splitting roar from behind hurled him to the ground. He lay, numb and disorientated, on the sand, at first clueless as to what had happened. Then an aching pain shot through his back and his right arm and the reality of what had occurred dawned on him. Cursing, he watched as his men raced past him for the dunes. He bitterly regretted not being able to follow them.

On LCI(S) 523, Berry watched the last of his passengers heading down the gangway. Looking across at 527 he could see dozens of men still lined up on the deck and he certainly couldn't blame them for not jumping

---

unpublished until now, fortunately a full year after the last French commando passed away.

[*] Lofi was an officier des équipages 2ème classe, broadly equivalent to a lieutenant in the Royal Navy.

[†] An enseigne de vaisseau, or 'ship-of-the-line ensign', is broadly comparable to a sub lieutenant in the Royal Navy.

down into the sea with the weight of equipment they carried. His next task was immediately obvious, and as the bow party hauled in the ramp he was cheered to feel 523 starting to become buoyant again on the rising tide. Quickly, orders were rapped out and the engine telegraphs were pulled back to order full astern. To his mild surprise the landing craft started to reverse – against his expectations, the propellers had survived the beaching intact. Passing commands to Dawson, Berry gently coaxed the landing craft back into deeper water and then forward again, towards 527. There was no time for niceties and 523 roughly scraped alongside her sister craft as Berry once again drove her hard on to the beach, forming a bridge between 527 and the shore. The ramp was once again run out and willing hands stretched out to receive the commandos on to 523's empty deck. The Frenchmen threw themselves across the narrow gap between the two boats and sped for the bow, ushered on by the impatient crew.

Vourc'h was not the only man to fall as the Frenchmen pounded up the beach. Commandant Philippe Kieffer was sprinting forward when a mortar knocked him down and a fragment of metal embodied itself in his left thigh, fortunately missing all the vital muscles and not seriously impeding his progress. When he reached the dunes he discovered that he was far from the only casualty. Lofi was busy organizing 8 Troop to clear the wire, but 1 Troop had taken heavy casualties. Still, as he looked around he was relieved to see the men of 4 Commando storming up the beach alongside them.[1]

Even as 523 came to her sister's rescue, fourteen LCAs of 500 and 514 Flotillas were milling around them, bringing ashore 4 Commando to whom the Free French troops had been attached. Lieutenant Higham, 500 Flotilla's CO, studied the coast as they headed in and observed LCT(A)s 2052 and 2191 lying on the beach. Reasoning that they provided some cover from enemy fire and shelter from the tide, he steered the flotilla towards them.

Heavy machine gun fire was flung at the boats as they made their final approach, bullets pinging against the armour plate almost as frequently as the spray. Crouched in the back of his LCA, Captain Joseph Patterson, 4 Commando's medical officer, peeked above the gunwale just as a small explosion lit up the starboard bow. A bottle of rum was making its way around the LCA and even above the racket of gunfire he could hear snatches of the hoarse strains of men singing 'Jerusalem' in one of the neighbouring craft. They were manoeuvring through the obstacles now and the cramped men tried to contort themselves into positions from which they could pull their heavy Bergen rucksacks on to their backs. Pushed against the back bulkhead, Patterson decided to wait until there were fewer people aboard.

As a result of having to pick their way between the beach obstacles the small boats were prevented from making a full-speed run on to the shore. Patterson felt the hull beneath him bump and grind on the sand before the LCA twisted, slewing round until he feared it might end up sideways on the beach. 'Ramp down!' came a cry from the bow, and ahead of him the densely packed commandos started to push their way forward. As the crush in front of him began to ease, Patterson rose and swung his Bergen on to his back. His small party had already rushed forward, leaving two stretchers at the stern, so he grabbed both and hobbled awkwardly to the bow where he flopped into 3 feet of water. Cursing the two cumbersome stretchers, he waded for the shore.

Within moments the full reality of the situation on the beach hit him. A body swung lazily against a tetrahedron as the waves pushed it back and forth, the dead man's uniform snagged on the barbed wire at its base. To his right, heavy shellfire was pounding the waterline and one of the LCI(S)s still beached there was struck. Ahead of him figures lay prostrate on the beach. Some were clearly already dead, blood and organs flowing out on to the wet sand and draining towards the waterline. But some were moving, and Patterson quickly realized he was needed.

The first casualty he came to was one of his own men. Lance Corporal Brian Mullen, 4 Commando's unofficial war artist, lay in the surf, the weight of his pack pinning him down and threatening to drown him. With numb hands Patterson pulled out a pair of heavy-duty scissors and got to work cutting away Mullen's equipment and webbing. As one of his orderlies crashed down beside him and started work on the other side of the wounded man, Patterson suddenly felt a heavy whack across his backside. He swore loudly, but a quick feel around his back revealed no obvious wound and he carried on his work. The two men dragged Mullen clear of the water and further up the beach, then rushed back to the water's edge, horrified by the speed with which the incoming tide was immersing wounded and immobile men.[*]

Wading ashore, 4 Commando's adjutant Captain Donald Gilchrist thought the beaches looked shambolic: bodies in the surf and on the

---

[*] Mullen died of his wounds later in the day.

sand, blazing tanks and landing craft at the waterline, puffs of flame as a mortar bomb fell to earth and thick black smoke drifting across the battlefield. He ran up towards the dunes, spying the derelict buildings of the holiday camp just beyond, when suddenly a hit to his torso knocked him down and he fell to his knees. Clutching his chest, he found his hand gripping a small piece of red-hot shrapnel no bigger than a coin. But to his shock no blood oozed from his uniform – the fragment had presumably hit his webbing and failed to penetrate. In his bewildered state he heard his CO, Lieutenant Colonel Robert Dawson, ask if he was OK. Unsteadily he rose to his feet and ran on, but even as he did so Dawson buckled as a piece of shrapnel whacked into his leg. Gamely he staggered on to the dunes.

Behind him, F Troop section commander Lieutenant Murdoch McDougall felt numbed by the hellish din that assaulted his senses and left him dazed. He looked around, trying to identify individuals among the men moving forward, but crouched over with their heavy Bergen rucksacks uppermost everyone looked alike. It was only when he spotted men ahead without the distinctive Bergens that he recognized men who were not commandos. Several lay in a line, and as he closed he saw one of them jump up and run forward, only to be cut down within a few yards. As he passed the line of men he kicked at one and snarled at him to get up and get moving. It was only then that he saw the men were either dead or wounded.

McDougall flopped down next to the barbed wire in front of the main bunker of Skate, where he was quickly joined by his troop commander Captain Len Coulson. A gunner in a small gun pit behind the main bunker was spraying machine gun fire across the sand just above the lip they sheltered behind, pinning most of the men down. Returning fire over the dune and into the recently knocked-out 75mm gun embrasure in hope more than expectation, they attempted to suppress it, but the occasional stick grenade and burst of fire showed their efforts were unsuccessful.

As McDougall pondered what to do, wary that between the wire and the gun pit might possibly be a minefield, Coulson called out and pointed to Captain Carr, the commander of B Heavy Weapons Troop. 'What the hell's Knyvet up to?' The men watched as the officer slid under the wire then in a half crouch ran in zigzags forward and up the slope of the bunker. A Bren gunner immediately started firing controlled bursts at the gun pit to try and suppress the defender, and as soon as he was close enough, Carr bowled a grenade like a cricket ball. The commandos watched, electrified, as in slow motion the grenade dropped into the pit. A split second later it detonated, an earthy blast churning up sand and silencing the gunner. Carr turned but slipped and rolled down the slope of the bunker, finishing up in front of it just as a stick grenade was tossed out. It detonated feet away from the troop commander but miraculously did no damage and, as he got up and patted himself down, the commandos forced their way through the wire and swarmed the bunker. Two men inside were mown down as the commandos raced to the entrance, and a few others scarpering down the trench network were cut down by the combined fire of all the men who could target them. With Skate cleared, the commandos pressed forward, into the dunes surrounding the old fort built more than 150 years ago.

Back on the beach, after dragging several men clear of the incoming tide, Patterson came upon Lieutenant Donald Glass, one of B Troop's officers, and started to clear away his equipment. As he feverishly cut at the webbing he suddenly became aware of a line of bullets stitching the sand alongside him, but before he could react it completed its journey across the beach and a bullet smacked into his right knee, the force of the strike pushing him over and on to a cursing Glass. Momentarily stunned, Patterson tried to move his leg and found, to his surprise, that it still worked. Ignoring the throbbing, he and an orderly rolled Glass on to a stretcher and together they manhandled him to the relative safety of the dunes.[2]

Lieutenant Commander Edward Gueritz was still thinking about how unduly cheerful Commander Currey had been when he had told him that it was time for him to go ashore. Looking down from LCH 185's bridge, Currey and Lieutenant Cook had watched out for a suitable LCA returning from the shore that they could requisition, careful to allow those with the bloodied bodies of wounded lying on their decks to sail past them. Eventually a suitable-looking boat had appeared alongside and Gueritz, along with Lieutenant Colonel David Board of 5 King's Regiment, jumped aboard, hastily followed by their batmen-cum-bodyguards.

Now, just over half an hour after the first landing craft had ground up against the sand, Gueritz's LCA approached the beach. Fox Royal Navy Beach Commando's Principal Beachmaster noted with some concern the immersed beach obstacles, already under far more water than they had expected. With a grinding vibration the landing craft struck the sand and a rating pushed open the armoured doors. The party jumped off the ramp and immediately regretted it as they dropped into deep water, Gueritz and Board's 6-foot frames proving the saviour of their much shorter batmen, who nearly staggered under the waves beneath the weight of their kit.

Wading through the surf and bearing only a blackthorn walking stick, Gueritz looked around him. To his left he could see two blazing LCTs and knocked-out tanks. Broken LCAs swayed in the breaking surf and all around were inert bodies and detritus. Smoke drifted across the sand, filtering the colour out of the day like a film noir. Small arms fire rattled away but was almost drowned out by the scream and crump of mortar bombs and shells falling all around. Saying his goodbyes to Board, he hurried along the beach to find Commander Rowley Nicholl, who had gone ashore with the first wave.[*] Keen to find the advance elements of the Beach Groups, Board strode forward for the dunes, his batman hot on his heels. As they reached the elevated ground a German machine gunner swivelled his weapon to face them and stitched a line of bullets across their torsos. They fell, hidden among the beachgrass.[†]

The Beach Groups themselves were far from ready to undertake their immediate tasks – the advance elements of 5 King's who had already landed were even now fighting for their lives. Lieutenant Peter Scarfe, CO of A Company's 9 Platoon, had come ashore with B Company of the South Lancs but now, like them, found himself some 500 yards from where he expected to be and with strongpoint Cod looming over him. Seeing one of his men stumble as a bullet struck him, Scarfe rushed to his side and started to drag him up the beach, only to be hit himself. Scowling in pain, he rapped out orders to his sergeant to take his small advance party up the beach, then looked for the source of the bullets. The flash of machine gun and rifle muzzles highlighted a small German position at the top of the dunes and, ignoring the pain from his wound, he scrambled forward, breaking into a run as he closed on the position. Spraying his Sten as he rushed the position, several of the defenders fell before their comrades could turn their guns on the new threat. But the outcome

---

[*] According to fleet orders Nicholl should also have sailed in LCH 185. Gueritz does not refer to him being on 185. It is possible he was of course, although it's also possible he sailed in a different vessel.
[†] The 5 King's war diary states that Board was missing until his body was found two days later in the dunes. Gueritz recalls finding him later on 6 June and that he hadn't a mark upon him, and had probably succumbed to a shell. The war diary's record is considered to be the more likely version of events.

was inevitable, and as Scarfe fell, mortally wounded by a hail of bullets, his enraged men charged. Overwhelmed by this new threat, several more German defenders fell before the remainder quickly threw their hands into the air.

Gueritz carried on along the beach, heading west towards Queen White in the hope of contacting Nicholl. He was pleased to see that the assistant beachmaster parties who had landed in the first wave had managed to conduct their recces and place flags to mark the beaches, although many of them had been wounded as a result. Men of his own Fox Commando were now coming ashore, bringing with them larger signs to show the beach extents and exits, although it was clear that the beach was still contested and he couldn't see any obvious exits yet. AVREs ground around in the dunes, but they appeared to be more involved in fighting than clearing routes off the sand.

Sticking close to the waterline, Gueritz made his way past Cod and finally spotted Nicholl ahead of him. Blood oozed from an evidently serious wound in his commander's shoulder, but Nicholl brushed aside Gueritz's concern and proceeded to outline the situation to him. Gueritz listened patiently, then gently pleaded with his commander to consider making his way to an aid post. Nicholl was reluctant, so Gueritz switched to light dishonesty, assuring Nicholl that the situation was well in hand. Eventually Nicholl was persuaded and Gueritz set off to wrest some order from the chaos around him.[3]

Lieutenant Philip Barber was late. He had been busy enough maintaining LCF 34 on the right course and speed for the past hour, and could do little to hasten the small boats behind him that were being buffeted by the heavy seas. 543 Flotilla, carrying C and D Companies of the East Yorks and bound for Queen Red, were the final part of Group 5 – the rest of which had already landed. The flotilla had been significantly delayed after their late departure from HMS *Glenearn* and had failed to meet up with 538 Flotilla, with whom they should have gone ashore. They had at least found LCF 34, and now they wallowed behind the larger landing craft like ducklings following a mother. But Barber was an unhappy mother duck. The bombardment of the beach, while impressive, had served to obscure every single landmark that he needed to make sure he led the LCAs to the right bit of beach. As black smoke rolled over the sea for miles to east and west he could rely only on a compass bearing and pray it would lead him to Queen Red.

But once the bombardment ended, devoid of the explosions that had fuelled it the haze slowly drifted away and, as Barber studied the beach through his binoculars, the shapes of buildings and the ghostly shadows of LCTs were revealed. There was little in the way of landmarks to see, but the presence of the landing craft and the evident signs of battle were enough to show Barber that they were at least on the beach. Steering fractionally east to come into the left-hand side of the beach, Barber hung on until, looking behind him, he saw sand being stirred in his wake. It was time to go. He swung his tannoy around to face his brood of ducklings. 'Here you are, lads, and the best of luck!' He switched his attention to the voice pipe into the wheelhouse below and LCF 34 swung out of line and away from the shore.

On board LCA 1383 the stench of vomit was oppressive. More than half the soldiers aboard had thrown up in the last hour, bits of their breakfast floating in the shallow pool of sloshing seawater in the bottom of the boat. Captain Bateman looked ahead, but being even closer to sea level than Barber had been there was little to see to confirm their exact position. Beside him Lieutenant Colonel Hutchinson was conferring with his signaller – the assault companies were reporting heavy opposition on the beach and their CO was itching to get ashore with the badly needed reserve companies.

The LCAs nosed their way towards the outer row of obstacles. Sensing his last opportunity to properly survey the scene before they beached, Hutchinson looked ahead and asked Bateman if they could slow down a little. Bateman obliged, and frantic signals brought the line of LCAs to a wallow in the swell while the East Yorks' CO studied the shore. There were several LCI(S)s on the beach, roughly where he wanted to go. But there was a gap further east, right of some broken LCTs. This would do. Thanking Bateman, he turned back to his men as the LCAs accelerated. After carefully negotiating the outer obstacles the landing craft surged for the beach, narrowly avoiding the poles and concrete tetrahedrons closer to the shore. Eschewing their kedge anchors, the LCAs drove hard on to the sand and dropped their ramps at 08:05 – twenty minutes behind schedule. Within moments the East Yorks had plunged into the water, relieved to find the flotilla had managed to get them ashore in less than 2 feet of water – a relief instantly tempered by the sudden racket of a pitched battle all round them.

Most of the flotilla had come ashore 100 yards or so east of Queen Red, close to strongpoint Skate and right where 4 Commando had arrived only ten minutes earlier. As Hutchinson and his staff raced out of LCA 1383, Bateman noted with unease that the enemy's artillery fire was disturbingly close – shells and mortar bombs fell across the beach and among the men charging up it. Nearby, LCA 171 was hit by a bomb and wrecked while 1216 was hit by shellfire, blowing the LCA upside down and killing Marine Stanley Fox instantly. None too soon, Hutchinson's men were off 1383 and the stoker ran the engines into reverse. But just as they eased off the sand, with a jarring crash LCA 604 smashed into their stern and the hapless LCA was thrust forward on to the shore again. The cox'n, Corporal Maurice Bicknell, quickly inspected the rudders, noting that they were pretty badly knocked about and the guards bent out of shape. But given how unhealthy a place the beach was, efforts were quickly made to refloat the vessel and the LCA juddered backwards. Almost inevitably the guards twisted into the propellors, fouling them. The LCA floated off and Bicknell made futile attempts to steer his craft, twisting the wheel one way and the other, ordering the stoker to adjust the revs on each engine in an effort to wrestle some manoeuvrability out of the craft. But the LCA largely went where it wanted, while the cursing crew willed it to get to open water.

Private Arthur Smith leapt from his LCA straight into waist-deep water, which instantly made him fear for the platoon wireless set he carried on his back. He quickly took stock and realized he had a considerable wade before reaching the beach. His opposite number, Private Arnie Moore, stood nearby – Smith was relieved to see him as his friend carried all of his kit. Together they struck out for the shore, the breaking waves threatening to suck them back out to sea. Idly, Smith wondered why the men who had been knocked over by the current didn't stand back up and fight against it. It took him a few moments to realize that the waves were not the cause of their lethargy. As his eyes affixed on the shoreline ahead he realized that there were just as many men who had made it out of the water but not beyond the beach.

Corporal John Scruton of C Company's 15 Platoon found himself with some 30 yards of waist-deep seawater to push through, the beach obstacles and floating bodies complicating the task immensely. To his left an LCT(A) blazed furiously and to his right a tank had met the same end. Lance Corporal Arthur Thompson, a section commander in D Company's 16 Platoon, found his way barred by a petrified soldier standing in front of him in the landing craft so, with no one behind able to get off, he brusquely pushed the young lad off the ramp and charged into the surf. Very quickly he found himself rushing past dead and wounded bodies. Morbid thoughts ran through his mind almost as quickly as his legs carried him up the beach, where he threw himself into the dunes. Already men from 4 Commando were engaging the strongpoint east of him while the rest moved west and into the vague shelter afforded by the ruins of the holiday camp.

As they raced up the beach, Smith and Moore heard a cry from one of the mounds of equipment nearby and quickly realized it was a wounded man. Recognizing him, Moore dashed over to help, ignoring all the instructions he'd been given to get off the beach. Smith realized the man was in a very bad way and as a stretcher bearer raced past he implored him for help, but the medic already had far more cases to tend to than he could handle. One of those was his own superior, the battalion's medical officer Captain James Laurie. He was hit as he waded through the waves, and as he tried to rise he was struck again and collapsed into the sea.*

Arthur Thompson once again found his path barred, this time by thick barbed wire. As he contemplated trying to find someone with a Bangalore torpedo, a shell crashed into the dune and smashed a gap in the wire. Without waiting for another one to land any closer, Thompson rushed through the gap with his colleagues, tearing his uniform on barbs as he went. No sooner were they through than they realized they were next to a pillbox and Thompson quickly instructed a Bren gunner behind him to lay oppressive fire on the entrance and keep the occupants' heads down.

A small group was forming around Thompson and the men took up defensive positions while they waited for an officer to come through. He didn't know it, but it would be a while before any did. D Company's commander Major Robert Barber had been leading his HQ section ashore when a mortar bomb had fallen among them, killing and wounding almost the entire party. Mortars continued to plaster the sand around them, and at length Thompson decided it was safer to move inland. He nudged the Bren gunner but got no response – turning to him he found he was unconscious. A mortar blast exploded close by, raining sand upon him, and as the smoke cleared he saw two broken corpses next to the new crater. Pausing only to put the Bren gunner's helmet under his head to

---

* Laurie later died of his injuries.

stop him from suffocating in the sand, Thompson rushed towards the inland road.

Hutchinson led his HQ group directly up the beach and into the dunes, moving right towards the collection of ruined buildings that made up the holiday park. The commandos were already advancing through them and, clear of any enemy infantry, he started to corral his men. Seeing Lieutenant Hugh Bone, the battalion signals officer, emerge through the beachgrass he quickly ordered him back to the beach to try and find more of the HQ staff – so far only one boatload of the HQ had arrived in the holiday camp. Far from being fearful of returning to the fire-swept shore, Bone felt oddly elated about his experiences so far and jogged back on to the sand to see who he could find. Returning to the shoreline, he witnessed the sheer number of men lying in shallow water, unable to move under the crippling effect of their injuries and the weight of their equipment. He went to pull one body from the waves but quickly appreciated the fruitlessness of the attempt. He had to concentrate on the able-bodied men and get them moving to the rally point. Jogging along the beach, he found a number of East Yorks sheltering alongside a burning tank. Bawling over the din of explosions, he told them to get moving to the holiday camp until, as he got closer, he saw that most of them were dead or badly wounded. Shamefaced, he nonetheless sorted the living from the dying and shook the men into action. Leading his small party along the beach, he found Reverend Victor Price and the adjutant and took them with him back up to the dunes and soon had sufficient men to move some of the battalion's bulky wireless sets up to the main road behind the beach.

Even as the commandos and reserve companies of the East Yorks pounded up the beach, the tanks and landing craft of the first waves were still disentangling themselves from the surf and beach obstacles. *Temeraire*, along with the other three Centaurs and Captain Elliott's Sherman, stayed in the water and fired on the emplacements of strongpoint 18 in front of them. A little further east, Victor Orme and Robert Bryson lay grievously wounded at the aft of LCT(A) 2191. Both slipped into periods of unconsciousness as the sounds of battle echoed around them. Knowing that his shipmate was less badly hurt than himself and could get off the wrecked vessel, Bryson implored Orme to leave and save himself, but Orme refused and tried feebly to free his friend. But by now 2191 was ablaze, flames licked around the mess deck below them, and the metal they lay on was growing hotter. A sudden blast erupted from below;

whether machinery exploding or another hit from a German gun, it made no difference now – but it finally brought Bryson's suffering to an end. Still drifting in and out of consciousness, Orme knew only that he would rather drown than burn, so he crawled aft, where he allowed himself to fall, splashing hopelessly into the sea. Despite his wounds he managed to stay on the surface and allowed the tide to carry him on to the shore.

Captain Bateman had given up trying to steer back out to sea and decided the only thing for it was to beach and try to repair their steering gear later. Seeing two crippled LCTs on the beach, he directed Bicknell to steer as best he could for them, hoping to land in what little shelter they might provide. The landing craft drove hard ashore but, wary of the constant rattle of machine gun fire and pounding of guns up the beach, Bateman decided the best course of action was to remain aboard and lie low. Even so, when they spotted the broken figure of Victor Orme nearby, they hauled him aboard and waited for the bombardment to ease.[4]

Lingering at the back of Group 5, the cox'ns of LCAs 352 and 780 desperately tried to hold station just off the immersed beach obstacles, the rising surf pushing them one way then the other. Raising his head above the armoured door of 780, Captain Archibald Jackson surveyed the scene ahead glumly. At the water's edge broken landing craft were being bashed by breaking waves, while geysers erupted all around. Bodies floated around them, turning the foaming waters red with their blood. The screech of shells and rattle of machine gun fire continued unabated and his LCA tossed and twisted as Jackson pondered what best to do.

Jackson's small command consisted of a mere twenty-one men of Royal Marine Landing Craft Obstacle Clearance Units 7 and 8. Their unenviable task was to echo the work of the Royal Engineers ashore, creating clear zones through the immersed obstacles by removing them with explosives and marking the routes for follow-up waves of landing craft. Some of the men were wearing rubber immersion suits – their even less desirable task would be to slip into the water from the bow of the landing craft and place timed explosives in the hard-to-reach nooks and crannies of the obstacles.

Anxiously the teams watched the shore, waiting for the engineers to mark the paths they had cleared on the beach so that they could extend them north into the sea. In the pleasant conditions of training the task had been rehearsed a dozen times, but now the reality of D-Day made the situation quite different. As the LCA crews fought to maintain position, more mortar and small arms fire zeroed in on them. On 352 the situation was made doubly difficult by the failure of one engine, and when a mortar bomb exploded alongside, 780 was similarly reduced to a single functioning propeller to battle the tide.

Finally the teams spotted the Royal Engineers' flags and posts on the shore, although there was only one marked lane on each beach. Clearly things were not going as well as they had in training. Wallowing in the surf, the LCAs moved into positions parallel to the lanes. The armoured doors were opened and the ramps dropped so that the men could heave buoys into the water, their anchors quickly sinking and leaving the orange floats straining their hawsers as the surf washed over them. Coming alongside two semi-submerged LCAs floating 100 metres in front of the obstacles, the Royal Marines leaned over the bow ramp and started attaching obstruction flags, their numb fingers furiously tying the ropes as breaking waves threatened to sweep them into the sea.

Their initial task complete, Jackson eyed the front row of obstacles ahead of them. They'd marked the channel leading to the cleared lane ashore – now they had to make it good. Desperately shouting commands back to the stokers to curtail their speed while they fought to steer, the cox'ns tried to approach the first row of obstacles, but the thick swell threatened to accelerate them into the obstacles without a second's hesitation. As each wave crashed across the stern, the pathetic little craft fought to stop themselves smashing into the obstructions. As if to mock them further, the lumbering LCTs of the following groups were now surging forward, crashing through the obstacles they couldn't navigate around.

Ruefully, Jackson accepted that there was no way his hamstrung LCAs could maintain a position next to an obstacle, much less put a man into the water to attach explosives. Even if the obstacle didn't sink their landing craft, the LCA would probably run down the man. And anyway, the cox'ns were now fully occupied making sure the LCTs looming up from behind didn't run them down. There was little those bigger vessels could do to avoid the small wooden boats as they made their final run into the beach, and if they hit them they would smash the flimsy LCAs like matchwood.

Reluctantly, Jackson gave the order to abandon the task – and even then it was nearly too late for 352, as a wave flung her against an obstacle. Gingerly, the cox'n made for the shore while 780 pulled away to clearer water. The following waves of landing craft would need to deal with the obstacles as best they could.*5

On the beach, the Royal Engineers struggled to remove the obstacles that had not yet been totally immersed. The death of Lieutenant Colonel Arthur Cocks had deprived the entire Royal Engineers beach clearance team of their leader, and once he had come ashore, dripping wet from his endeavours in the surf, Major Frederick Carson of 629 Field Squadron assumed overall command. The situation was not good: the racing tide had now reached the upper line of obstacles and those furthest out to sea were no longer accessible. The Crabs and AVREs that had been assigned to beach clearance were, in the main, still occupied working on creating exits off the beach, and the intense artillery fire and sporadic small arms fire still targeting the area made their work extremely hazardous. Worse still, their planned method of obstacle clearance – 3lb plastic high-explosive charges – simply wasn't viable on a beach that was now so crowded and on to which landing craft were coming ashore almost continuously. Slowly the tide was overwhelming the obstacles entirely. Braving the churning waters, the Royal Engineers removed what explosives they could from the tops of the accessible obstacles and then concentrated on what they could achieve above the tide.

In the infernal din of a pitched battle, the high-altitude drone of sixty-two B-17 bombers flying above the clouds went entirely unnoticed by the men on the ground and on the sea. High above them, the crewmen of 384

---

* It is interesting that the LCOCU teams abandoned their task while elements of 629 Field Squadron RE went well beyond the requirements of their own. There are two possible reasons for this. First, Lieutenant Colonel Urquhart went into the water some time before Captain Jackson decided against it – Jackson had been forced to wait for the engineers ashore to mark lanes before his task could begin, and then had to mark the channels before any demolition could take place. By then the sea could have been much rougher, and more landing craft were pressing into the beach. Second, the LCOCU task was to completely demolish the obstacles, a much harder mission than simply removing the explosives. The swimmers needed to fit explosives underwater and would need to remain close to their landing craft, which were crippled by engine failure. For Urquhart, swimming was a difficult but suitable means of achieving his objective. For Jackson, his task was almost completely impossible whatever means were used to try and achieve it.

and 303 Bomb Groups peered out of their windows and gun ports, eagerly searching for a view of the beach battles below. But almost complete cloud cover entirely obscured their view and, dismayed, they returned to the job at hand.

Both bomb groups were on their way to Caen, their targets two bridges across the River Orne. These two 'chokepoints' had been identified as crucial to German communications. Both bridges, one on the rue de Vaucelles and one on the rue de la Gare, were major routes in and out of the city and knocking them out would hinder any German attempts to counter-attack the forces landing at Sword. But they were less than 1,000 yards from the centre of this historic city and any effort to bomb them was bound to result in civilian casualties as well as military.

In *Shoo Shoo Baby*, Captain Robert Sheets was aware of his extra passenger standing just behind the cockpit – an excitable young United Press International journalist by the name of Walter Cronkite. He had been attached to the bomb group at the last moment: his initial assignment had been in London, but on 5 June a visit from a friendly public relations Eighth Air Force officer had led him to Molesworth in Cambridgeshire and now to here, the skies above Normandy. He had peered down excitedly at the small ships in the English Channel, but like the rest of the crew was now despondent to see so much cloud below. It seemed unlikely they would even be able to see their target. No one in the sixty-two B-17s knew it, but ninety-seven B-24 bombers that had been sent to hit two further chokepoints in the city just minutes ahead of them had all aborted. The dense cloud cover and a lack of H2X-equipped aircraft had left them entirely blind and reluctantly they had turned west and headed for home.

Now the deputy commanding officer of 303 Bomb Group Lieutenant Colonel Lewis Lyle faced a similar predicament. Sitting in the bombardier's position on *Scorchy II*, he listened as Lieutenant Myles Walsh, in the navigator's seat just behind him, sang out the various landmarks they were – in theory – overflying. But below there was only a continuous grey-white sheet. Fortunately they had H2X aircraft in their formation, but already one of them had reported that their equipment had stopped operating. Still, with no break in the cloud visible, there was little choice. Lyle ordered his groups to bomb by radar.

Just ahead of them, 384 Group were already over the target. Two H2X aircraft in the lead carefully counted down the seconds until they were – in theory – over the Pont de Vaucelles, closely watched by twenty-eight bombardiers sitting in the noses of their aircraft, waiting for the sign to release their destructive cargo. As the aircraft droned over Caen the first black eggs fell from the leading B-17s, and within seconds they were joined by hundreds more. Three hundred and sixty 500lb bombs and fifty-five 1,000lb bombs tumbled from thirty aircraft into the clouds and out of sight as the B-17s pulled away to their right and began the journey home.

Hot on their heels, 303 Group arrived over the city. The gunners searched the sky around them, peering into the cloud and expecting enemy fighters to break through at any moment. But nothing came. No lines of flak raced into the sky either. Only the distant sight of the occasional rocket soaring through the clouds showed that there was any enemy within dozens of miles.

As they closed on their target, the rue de la Gare bridge, the bombardiers in each formation focused their eyes on the leading Pathfinders. In *Shoo Shoo Baby*, Cronkite watched the bomb bay doors open, the cold wind whipping through the aircraft interior and tugging at his flight jacket. Down below the cloud mocked the crew, goading them to do their best job in the near impossible circumstances it had set. In the nose, Lieutenant Umphress watched the lead bomber dispassionately, waiting for the sign. But as the seconds ticked by it became painfully obvious that the Pathfinder had already overflown the target and wasn't going to drop any bombs. In the nose the navigator was still cursing his H2X set that had failed them over the Channel, its sweep arm no longer updating the display and hiding the world below from view as effectively as the cloud. Reluctantly, the formation overflew the target and *Shoo Shoo Baby*'s bomb bay doors whined as they closed again. Cronkite tried to mask his disappointment – this would not make good copy for the newspapers.[*]

Lyle's formation had better luck and seventeen bombers dropped 202 500lb bombs and twenty-eight 1,000lb bombs into the sea of cloud below

---

[*] It is worth noting that in his 1997 memoir *A Reporter's Life*, Cronkite claims that his flight was as part of a squadron's last-minute mission to hit a German 'heavy artillery emplacement that commanded Omaha Beach. It would go in just as the troops were landing and, to ensure accuracy, it would attack at low level.' 303 Bomb Group's records are clear that Cronkite was with them, and he even names Lieutenant Colonel Lyle in his memoir. Caen was too far away to be a problem for Omaha and both groups bombed from between 16,000 and 17,000 feet. Whether Cronkite's memory was failing him fifty years after the event, or whether a raid on a German battery simply seemed more palatable than an attack on a French city, we shall probably never know.

them. Then the B-17s began their lazy turn to starboard and set course for the Channel Islands and their route home.

Hundreds of bombs crashed into Caen and its surroundings. Buildings erupted as they were hit, their strong ancient stone construction suddenly weak and pliable in the face of modern warfare. Earth was thrown into the air and scattered around surrounding fields while gigantic splashes erupted from the River Orne and the city's docks. The bridges remained undamaged.

The terrified residents of the city, most of whom were already hiding in basements and bomb shelters when the bombers passed over, hesitantly emerged from below ground once the raiders had passed. Scattered around the streets, some still floating down in the dusty air, they found hundreds of sheets of paper, printed with a message in French from the American airmen. It warned the civilian population that they should, wherever possible, evacuate the city. The bombers would be coming back later that day.[6]

Back at the beach, the next wave was coming in. Almost on top of 543 Flotilla came Group 7, the thirteen LCTs of 41 LCT Flotilla under the command of Lieutenant Commander Herman Poucher RNVR, bringing with them C Squadron of the 13/18 Hussars and priority vehicles of the assaulting formations. The same station-keeping difficulties that had bedevilled most of Force S's convoys had caused them to arrive at the lowering position fifteen minutes behind schedule, but, undaunted, Poucher drove his flotilla straight through the melee of ships and sped south. Now, as they headed to the beach, they were perfectly on time.

On LCT 898, Sub Lieutenant Charles Flynn RNVR cursed as an LCH suddenly steamed across the front of the formation. His morning had started badly when an errant German shell had come down alongside, throwing up a geyser of water that cascaded down on to the bridge, soaking him, Able Seaman Porter and two army officers. The blast blew in a sea inlet suction valve in the engine room and in the bowels of the landing craft Petty Officer Flynn (no relation) and Stokers Swordy and Hutchings were desperately working to fix it. Worst of all, the torrent of water had destroyed Flynn's breakfast, which had only just been placed on the chart table. Now, with the remains of his meal splattered across the bridge's deck, Flynn realized that he was on an intercept course with the LCH passing in front of his colleagues to port. Indignation gave way to duty and he ordered reduced speed and an alteration to port. As 898 dropped out of the line and fell in behind the adjacent LCT, Flynn's anger was at least assuaged as the LCH flashed 'Thank you' to him.

Flynn couldn't grumble too loudly – he felt lucky enough just to be there. LCT 898, his first command, had only been added to the invasion fleet at the last moment. A week earlier, Poucher had broken the bad news that only twelve of the flotilla's fourteen LCTs were needed, and both 898 and 1084 would be left behind. They'd still get to Normandy, Poucher had assured him, but not on D-Day. Flynn had been crushed, but only a few days later came respite. After the flotilla had embarked its armoured contingent and moved out into the Solent, the sheer weight of C Squadron's Sherman tanks and their additional equipment had proved too much for their three LCTs, which wallowed dangerously in the Solent. That afternoon 898 was summoned to the embarkation hard next to Gosport's ferry terminal. The overladen vessels unloaded some of their tanks which, to Flynn's delight, backed on to his own LCT.

Smoke still obscured the view ahead, and on 789, Poucher was anxiously scanning with his binoculars, searching for a recognizable feature. Finally, about half a mile from the shore, the view cleared and to Poucher's relief the key landmarks were quickly sighted – they were exactly where they were meant to be.

On each of the thirteen bridges, eyes were glued to the beach. Burning vehicles flickered in the haze and explosions threw up great clouds of sand and smoke. Small figures sprinted and fell, sometimes rising again, sometimes not. The tide was coming in quicker than expected and already most of the beach obstacles were partially underwater. The double row of stakes looked like toothpicks emerging from the waves while behind them the tetrahedrons looked to be at least half immersed, meaning the depth was already up to 3 feet. The LCT crews desperately searched for gaps through which to manoeuvre to the shallower water, but there were none. The order to 'bust through' loomed large in the skippers' minds.

As the LCTs closed to the last 400 yards, German machine gunners ensconced in their trenches and strongpoints along the shore switched to this new threat. Bullets pinged against the hulls of the landing craft and crews nervously ducked behind shields as more fire began to zero in on the lumbering vessels.

Now all thirteen LCTs arrived at the obstacles. Calling down the voice pipe to Leading Seaman Tyson in the wheelhouse below him, Flynn delicately steered his vessel through the two rows of stakes.

Ahead, surf broke against tetrahedrons on either side of the bow, but the LCT gently glided between them until, unsighted, they struck another. Fortunately this one did not appear to be mined and did little to impede their progress.

At 08:15 Flynn slammed the buzzer on the bridge that activated the siren at the bow, instructing Sub Lieutenant Willis and his crew to lower the ramp. The brakes on the port and starboard winches were eased off and jerkily the ramp began to fall forward. In the tank waiting at the head of the vehicle deck, the commander instinctively lowered himself deep into his turret as the view opened up ahead of him.

Suddenly, with a bright flash, a shell crashed through the starboard side of the bow, zipped across in front of the leading tank and passed straight through the port winch house on its way out of the vessel.* In the small winch compartment, Seamen Batty, Wells and McKinnon, dazed and with their ears ringing, picked themselves up from the floor and examined themselves for injuries. They had been lucky – shrapnel had struck all of them, but the wounds were minor. The winch was still operable and, gamely, they returned to their post, ready to lift the ramp as soon as ordered.

On the bridge, Flynn had barely had time to see the smoke on the tank deck clear before two shells landed alongside 898, the great geysers swamping the bridge and threatening to overwhelm the engine room pumps. Spluttering, almost knocked out by the weight of water that had fallen on them, Flynn and Porter pulled themselves up and surveyed the tank deck. The vehicles were moving off now, one by one funnelling through the space at the bow. Then, in slow motion, Flynn spied a mortar bomb as it finished its arced journey through the sky and landed squarely on the port foredeck. He ducked as flash and flame erupted, sending smoke and shrapnel over the top of the tank passing through the exit.

Inside the port winch house the already wounded crewmen were encased in a blast of noise and heat. Searing flame rushed through the deckhead above them, driving a cloud of fragmented metal that cut into all three men and threw them down on to the deck. Smoke billowed as McKinnon got to his feet, his lungs choking. Wells, his wounds quite serious, struggled to his post only to find the winch mechanism quite

---

* Flynn describes a shell passing diagonally through the LCT from starboard to port. This will most likely have come from one of the two sea-facing guns at strongpoint 21 (Trout), approximately a mile to the west.

wrecked. Together they searched the blackened space for their crewmate, but Lawrence Batty, a senior rating who had refused offers of further advancement to remain a part of 898's company, was unrecognizable. His torso had been ripped asunder and there was a giant hole where his stomach should have been. What was left of his head rolled around on the deck several feet away.

Outside the shattered little cabin, there was no let-up. A shell struck the starboard bow, showering Willis and his team in the starboard winch house with splinters. Flynn sent Porter down to help his devastated winch crews and now, alone on the bridge, he forced himself to stand, exposing his full upper body to the continual cavalcade of enemy fire. Leaning forward, he could see only one tank still on board and hollered at them to get away. Agonizingly slowly the Sherman jerked forward, every yard of the tank deck seemingly taking minutes to traverse. Finally, the tank completed its epic journey and Flynn signalled his crew to back off, just as another shell struck the quarterdeck below him. A scream echoed up the voice pipe as shrapnel peppered Tyson in the wheelhouse. Alone in his little cabin, the cox'n gritted his teeth and gripped the wheel as the LCT began to back off from the beach, its hull shuddering as the two engines pulled it off the sand. Looking at his watch, Flynn was astounded to find it was only 08:22. The seven minutes had felt like hours.

LCT 898 pulled away from the beach, her ramp hanging uselessly from the bow by a single winch cable while the crew fought to secure it sufficiently to head out to sea. Either side of her, the rest of 41 Flotilla had come in for an equally hot reception. On LCT 980, Sub Lieutenant Peter Gurnsey RNZNVR expertly guided his vessel through the first two lines of stakes, but with no gaps ahead of him he deliberately rammed the LCT into one of the tetrahedrons. A bright explosion ripped away a 4-foot section of the bow ramp, but the heavy vessel's momentum pushed them through the defences. At the stern, eighteen-year-old Wireman Denis Garrod cast the kedge anchor behind them as they ploughed on to the beach, then ran forward, along the side deck and down a ladder to the port-side winch house. The tangled ramp was lowered on to the sand and Sub Lieutenant John Tait directed the myriad of vehicles either side of the jagged hole. After a lifetime, they were all away, and Garrod and his colleagues began to winch the ramp back up. As soon as it was clear of the sand, Tait took over Garrod's handle and the wireman clambered out of the winch house to head back to the kedge anchor. Seconds later, a near miss shook the LCT. Stumbling under the blast, Garrod looked back to see Tait on the deck, his head mangled by the piece of shrapnel that had killed him instantly.

On LCT 979, Eric Smith held his breath as a large explosion battered the bow ramp. The smoke was whipped away in the breeze, presenting a mangled but useable exit, and the troop commander breathed again. Agonizingly slowly, the landing craft's crew began to lower the twisted metal and the craft drifted the final 20 yards to the shore. Tank engines rumbled impatiently until, finally, Smith was given the signal to disembark. Trooper Gee put the tank into gear and the Sherman lurched forward, down the uneven ramp and into the sea, immediately in front of the 75mm gun position at the north-west corner of Cod. Standing on the bridge behind him, Sub Lieutenant William Winkley snapped away with his small personal camera, capturing the scene as the tanks rolled ashore.

As his tank pushed a bow wave ahead of it, Smith peered out carefully from the commander's hatch, surveying the beach. Wrecked and semi-submerged vehicles lay either side of him, while up ahead thick black smoke billowed from buildings, tanks and shell holes. Sporadic shells whined overhead and the occasional crack of a rifle caused him to duck still lower into his turret. As they approached the waterline, bloody carcasses became obvious, and ahead of them, four German soldiers with their hands up tried desperately to surrender to anyone who would take them. Smith ignored them and drove on to the sand, where chaos reigned. The tide was driving in quickly now and the beach was concerningly narrow. C Squadron's tanks were massing on the dry sand near the sea wall with little space to manoeuvre. One by one the tanks moved left and right, crawling along the sea wall looking for evidence of an open beach exit. Moving behind one of his compatriots, Smith's tank unavoidably ran across its porpoise, mangling it under his tracks. The troop commander's faux pas was far from unique: C Squadron lost ten of its fifteen porpoises as they clamoured for space on the congested sand.

Behind them, some of the LCTs were still on the shoreline. A mortar bomb fell from above on to 854's tank deck, hitting a Bren Carrier loaded with mortar rounds. They ignited as one and a fireball swept across the deck, quickly engulfing several more vehicles. The LCT's crew raced to connect hoses to the water pipes on the tank deck's coaming, but the pipes themselves had been shattered by the blast. Parked near the back of the tank deck, Captain Herbert Jankel, CO of 20 Beach Recovery Section REME, watched the blaze from the turret of his Beach Armoured Recovery Vehicle (BARV). It was essentially a Sherman tank chassis modified for deep wading and with an armoured hull to help it barge and drag disabled vehicles and obstacles out of the way, so he thought they should be sufficiently protected to be able to pass through the flames. The central row of vehicles had already disembarked, leaving a narrow corridor through the blazing wreckage on the port and starboard sides of the deck, and Jankel gently coaxed the BARV through and triumphantly on to the ramp.

Alongside on LCT 789, Poucher was lucky. When his flagship struck one of the mined obstacles it ripped away the ship's bottom at the back of the tank deck, just forward of the fuel tanks and the engine room. Fortunately the deck plates and the numerous watertight compartments of the double-bottomed hull held firm. Nonetheless, it left the landing craft stuck on the beach for fifty-five minutes, a veritable bullet magnet. Miraculously the crew survived.[7]

While C Squadron 13/18 Hussars desperately sought to find a way off the beach, the dozens of other vehicles that had landed with them ploughed through the waves and on to an ever-narrowing belt of dry sand. Eight Universal Carriers of A Company 2 Middlesex Regiment, 3 Division's attached machine gun and heavy mortar battalion disembarked from 41 Flotilla's LCTs and instantly found themselves needed. Coming ashore opposite Cod, the two carriers of 1 Platoon quickly ripped away the high wading attachments fixed to their carriers, exposing the Vickers medium machine guns fitted inside. Quickly they poured suppressing fire into the German strongpoint, providing valuable cover as troops mingled around on Queen Red and White. Lieutenant Anthony Milne led 3 Platoon's two carriers inland on the left of Cod, but as soon as they reached the avenue de Lion they came under fire. A shell slammed into one of the carriers, disabling it and killing some of the crew, but Milne and his men were able to bring some fire to bear on the strongpoint.*

While 41 Flotilla desperately tried to land their vehicles, Assault Group 8 was coming in behind them. But on LCI(L) 130, one of the three large

---

* The war diary states that Milne's two carriers came under fire from an anti-tank gun on reaching the avenue de Lion on Queen Beach's left flank. It is possible that this was the 50mm AT gun on the south-east corner of Cod, although this would appear to be the gun position taken by Banger King and his men a little earlier. It is possible the gun was reoccupied, but it is perhaps more likely that Milne's carrier was knocked out on one of the tracks inland next to the Maison de la Mer and photographed by Sergeant James Mapham there. Lieutenant Hutchinson of 79 Assault Squadron believed it was knocked out by mortar fire.

LCI(L)s carrying the reserve HQ of 1 Suffolk as well as troops from 5 King's and the Beach Groups, all was not well. When Lieutenant Commander C. Wall had found Major James Gough, 1 Suffolk's second in command and the designated officer in charge of troops on board, he was shivering and sweating, his body convulsing as it tried to retch up the contents of a stomach long since emptied. In his feverish seasick state, Gough assured Wall he had handed his duties for disembarking the men to one of the other officers, but a search through the compartments of groaning men had only revealed more seasick officers with no one willing to take responsibility for organizing the troops. And now the three large landing craft were closing on the beach, eighteen LCAs bobbing busily in their wakes, anxious to get to the shore. Wall warily eyed the beach through his binoculars. 41 Flotilla were under heavy shellfire at the west end of Queen White and there wasn't much room between their large LCTs. Cautiously, he led Group 8 a little further to port, to the east side of Queen White.

In the LCAs, Lieutenant Colonel Richard Goodwin glanced at Captain John Sykes as the flotilla officer directed his cox'n to port in the wake of LCI(L) 183. Together they looked through the viewing slits of the watertight doors; just to the right, the Suffolks' CO could see some of the landmark buildings they had picked out in their briefing. But with the beachfront there blocked by the LCTs, the beach ahead would suffice to get the men ashore. Glancing ahead again, Goodwin was horrified to see the dark stakes projecting through the surf with ugly explosives strapped to their peaks. Sykes yelled a series of commands at the cox'n, the sailor rapidly altering his course to avoid the obstacles. The sprightly LCAs were surging past the lumbering LCIs as they raced towards the surf. The turret of an abandoned tank loomed ahead, the cox'n deftly spinning his wheel to avoid it, and then, with a bumping grind, the LCA hit bottom at 08:23, two minutes ahead of schedule.

Within seconds the watertight doors were thrown open and the ramp at the bow splashed down into the surf. Goodwin ran off, exhorting his men to follow, dropped into knee-deep water, kicked through the surf and led his HQ section on to the sand. To his right were the two houses he had hoped to land in front of, ablaze but recognizable enough for his men to rally towards before they pushed inland. Other buildings burned fiercely around them, as did tanks on the beach and landing craft in the surf. The stench of cordite and burned metal was overpowering. Platoons were dashing from the LCAs alongside now and the enemy began to direct shells and mortars their way. Moments after LCA 870 had ground on to the beach a mortar bomb slammed into the port bow and detonated, the frightful blast spitting chunks of metal and timber splinters across the open ramp. In his tiny cox'n position on the starboard side Corporal Gerald Dean was cut down instantly, while Royal Artillery Captain Glyn Llewellyn, whose feet had only just touched sand, was blown forward and lay, crumpled, on the beach. Seeing 1 Suffolk's attached Forward Officer Bombardment – whose task was to call for fire support from HMS *Kelvin* and ORP *Dragon* – desperately wounded, ratings pulled him aboard another LCA, hopeful they might get him to a hospital ship.* The rest of his party, sporting minor wounds and with their transmitters smashed, hobbled up the beach. Behind them more of the LCAs foundered as they crashed into obstacles in the boiling surf and more sailors fell dead or wounded. But they had done their job magnificently, and in good order most of their passengers raced up the beach and into the lee of the sand dunes beneath the burning houses.

Although they had led the LCAs in, the deeper-draught LCI(L)s had grounded in deeper water. On 130 the naval personnel had tried desperately to sort their passengers into some sort of sensible groupings, but having little idea of their units and composition it was a difficult task. As it came into the beach, 130's bow had struck a beach obstacle, bringing them to a violent halt. The two bow ramps were pushed down their rollers and into the surf, but both almost immediately snagged on neighbouring obstacles. As the surf buffeted them they were pulled from the bow, their fixing wires snapping. Now, the army personnel, expecting to land from the bow, jammed the deck in disorganized parties. Angry sailors pushed through them, shouting and cursing at them to make space so that they could access the scrambling nets and drop over the side, while ladders were pushed towards the bow. For fifteen minutes, 130 sat stationary in the surf. Then, just as it seemed men might start to disembark, the enemy's artillery found them. A shell screeched into the sea along the port side and a jagged hole was torn below the waterline. Seawater rushed into one of the troop decks and nervous men crowded the ladders, pushing up towards the men on deck who still had nowhere yet to go. Even

---

* Llewellyn was taken to HMS *Serapis*, where he died of his wounds. Although buried at sea, his body was later re-interred at Tilly-sur-Suelles (presumably his body was not sufficiently weighted and returned to the shore in later years).

when the sailors finally completed the nets and ladders, the soldiers baulked at clambering down the vessel's tall hull with their heavy kit.

Not far to their port, LCI(L) 183 was making better progress and most of her men disembarked in good time, but further over, LCI(L) 131 was little better off. The Beach Groups were unwilling to carry their heavily laden handcarts down the ramps and the crew had to manhandle them down instead. Fifteen minutes after it had been rolled over the bow, the port ramp was smashed by a mortar, and fifteen minutes after that the starboard ramp suffered the same fate. Half of the passengers still waited to disembark and, equally heavily loaded, they refused to use the scrambling nets. Lieutenant Baker tried to cajole them off his vessel, but most of the army officers had already landed and he found he could do little to control the enlisted men.

As the navy struggled, the Suffolks gathered at the top of the beach and organized themselves. Goodwin spied Major Jack Stone of the South Lancs and quickly pressed him for information, but there was little the harassed officer could tell him, and already the beachmasters were shouting at the newly arrived men to move off the beach. Company COs rapidly searched for their platoon commanders to get them despatched inland, even as bullets continued to kick at the sand and shells screamed overhead. Beach personnel were already laying tape down some of the lanes leading inland, showing safe routes for an advance, and quickly the men filed down them. Their enforced landing further east actually placed them closer to their rendezvous inland, and the men marched briskly east along the avenue de Lion. Wary of the signs of battle around Cod, they scurried on to the track leading south and made their way inland.

At approximately 08:30, two more fighter aircraft appeared in the skies east of Sword. A convoluted schedule saw RAF Spitfires, Mustangs and Typhoons flying continually over the beaches, with one squadron scheduled to arrive over the fleet just as another had to return for fuel. At any one moment there should be a multitude of fighter cover, reconnaissance and ground attack aircraft protecting the beachhead, while twin- and four-engine bombers flew further inland.

But these two fighters were not on the Allied schedule, and had anyone studied the aircraft they would have recognized them as Focke-Wulf Fw 190As. In the cockpit of the lead plane, Oberstleutnant Josef 'Pips' Priller[*]

---

[*] An oberstleutnant is broadly equivalent to a wing commander in the RAF.

studied the scene below him. The view of the vast fleet to the west of Le Havre was stunning – ships of all different sizes moved around like toys on a blue bedsheet, battleships, cruisers, destroyers, troopships and the tiny dots of hundreds of small landing craft. Priller longed for more aircraft, but his entire 26 Fighter Wing had been transferred south only the previous afternoon and now he had only himself and Unteroffizier Heinz Wodarczyk. He cursed the Luftwaffe high command again, then focused on his attack. Looking above he could see thick fighter cover, and below the sea covered with ships and a beach blackened with men and vehicles. There was really only one course open to him – a strafing attack along the length of the beach. He figured one pass might be possible, although it was highly likely that he and Wodarczyk would be shot down by fighters or flak.

Slightly ecstatic with the thrill of what was to come, Priller called into his radio. 'There's everything out here – everywhere you look! Believe me, this is the invasion! Wodarczyk, we're going in! Good luck!' With that he dropped his nose and led his wingman in a screaming 400mph dive towards Ouistreham. Only a few dozen feet above the beach he levelled out and pressed the gun button on his control column. There was no time or room to aim, he could only flick his fighter fractionally to direct the stream of bullets down. As he flashed past he saw men drop to the sand, among tanks and trucks. Some were burning, others were firing, while in the water dozens of little craft disgorged yet more men and machines on to the beach. And then, within fifteen seconds, his Focke-Wulf screamed past the last of the landing craft and he saw only a deserted beach below him. Scarcely able to believe they hadn't been hit by flak from the dozens of vessels they had just roared over, the two pilots quickly swung inland and climbed for the nearest clouds.

Despite having almost complete air superiority, even over the beaches Allied aircraft were not necessarily safe. At 09:00 Flying Officer Stanley Barnard, a volunteer from Brazil, was crossing the coast over Lion-sur-Mer after returning from a sweep south of Caen. His three colleagues were flying their Mustangs alongside in loose formation at 3,000 feet when they suddenly saw an appalling explosion and Barnard's fighter simply disintegrated. His aircraft had almost certainly been hit by a shell fired from a warship offshore.[8]

While the Suffolks came ashore on Queen White, another cluster of landing craft was swarming towards Queen Red. Standing on the bridge of

LCI(S) 519, Lord Lovat and Rupert Curtis studied the beach intently through their binoculars, fascinated by the battle scenes unfolding in the distance. Behind them, the eleven other LCIs in Assault Group 9 fanned out into an arrowhead formation, those on the left carrying 6 Commando, those on the right carrying 41 (RM) Commando, while two additional support craft raced along in their wake, ready to rescue craft in need and pick up casualties as required. Lovat was expecting there would be many and had prepared for a rough landing: racing along on their port side on 502, his deputy adjutant Captain Max Harper-Gow commanded a reserve HQ for 1 Special Service Brigade. At least one of them should be able to get ashore. Or would it be easier than that? As they headed south they spied one of the LCTs of 14 Flotilla heading back out to sea.* As they passed close by a rating on the quarterdeck gave the commandos a thumbs up and then cupped his hands to his mouth. 'It's a piece of cake!' he hollered to them.

On the bridge of LCI(S) 516, Lieutenant Denis Glover and Lieutenant Colonel Derek Mills-Roberts searched for landmarks on the coast. Glover was reminded of the toy-like models he had studied in Force S's intelligence room shortly before embarkation began – châteaux, woods and pillboxes had all been so perfectly represented. Now the real thing had an uncanny air of familiarity about it, although the models had been quite far removed from the churning sea, drifting smoke, bright flashes of explosions and the echo of thunderous blasts that assailed his senses now.

'That's surely the château, Colonel, through the smoke,' he opined to Mills-Roberts, pointing to the Château de Colleville. 'A cable to starboard of it is our limit.' Mills-Roberts studied the château – that was it all right, its peculiar high sides quite evident through the smoke. The two officers scanned right, searching for a flat-topped white villa that sat on the exact boundary of Queen Red and Roger Beaches, but there was only a small pile of rubble where it should be. It appeared the villa had been destroyed in the bombardment.†

Ahead of them Rupert Curtis was steering west, fighting the eastward-drifting tide and aiming for an open area of beach in front of the Maison de la Mer. The flotilla followed, bows searching left and right as the crews looked for suitable gaps through the obstacles that they were rapidly

---

* It is quite possible that this was LCT 467, returning from landing its DD tanks directly on the beach.
† In fact the villa had been demolished by the Germans a few weeks previously.

closing in on. As many commandos as could fit had assembled on the decks now, and they crouched down as machine gun fire started to ping off the armoured plates on the hulls and mortar bombs whooshed overhead. Totally engrossed in his task, Curtis kept his eyes glued on the obstacles and, working purely from instinct, gave quiet orders to his cox'n. Sudden but smooth turns led 519 through the first row of ramps, their tops still just visible above the waves, straight between two stakes, and then over some almost completely immersed hedgehogs. Open water then appeared between them and the beach, and a quick flick of the engine room telegraphs thrust 519 forward, Curtis determined to get as high on to the shore as possible.

Just as the LCI started to graze the seabed, two shells crashed through the port Oerlikon gun position, just missing the gunners and the surrounding commandos. Scarcely able to believe their luck, the gunners returned fire at the strongpoint to their left, which still seemed to be in action. Then, with a grinding lurch, 519 came to a stop, perfectly on time at 08:40 and almost exactly halfway between strongpoints Skate and Cod. Almost immediately 502 slammed into the beach right alongside, the gunwales of the two LCIs almost touching. A split second later a shell crashed into her port hull, smashing through four of her petrol tanks, followed moments later by a second that wrecked her port engine. On the bridge, Lieutenant John Seymour and Harper-Gow looked down at the deck behind them, half expecting it to erupt at any moment. It was with much relief that they realized the German gunners were firing armour-piercing ammunition. Had they used high explosive it would have been a completely different matter – the resulting conflagration as the fuel tanks exploded would have engulfed both 502 and 519, and 1 Special Service Brigade would have lost both its HQs and some 200 men. Chastened, Harper-Gow made his way to the ramps.*

As soon as the landing craft stopped, the ratings at the bow pushed the ramps forward on their rollers and they crashed down into shallow water. Lovat was already waiting at the prow, and as soon as the ratings gave him the signal he jumped down the ramp. Standing in the knee-deep surf, he waved his men on as they rushed down the ramps and headed for the sand about 100 yards away. Still on the deck, Bill Millin saw his CO

---

* The source of the shells is not immediately clear, but given that Skate was almost certainly out of action by now, it is quite likely that strongpoint 10's 75mm was firing down the beach, almost at the limit of its range.

down below and filed towards the ramps among the crowd of commandos. The ramp rocked and rolled, both under the weight of the heavily laden men and the swell of the sea, and he staggered down as fast as his legs allowed before jumping off into the water. To his shock, and in contrast to the men he could see ahead of him, he fell into waist-deep water and started to fall backwards as his pack dragged him down. Just as he thought he was going under, kind hands grabbed him and pushed him back up. Relieved, he staggered towards Lovat.

Glover watched with admiration as the first commandos sprinted down 516's ramps. Mills-Roberts turned as he approached the bow, waved his gratitude, and then he too dropped out of sight over the bow. The lead commandos were almost at the waterline now, racing through the surf, ignoring the machine gun fire producing little spurts in the sea all around them. To Glover they looked to be the finest troops Britain could produce.

A sudden burst of machine gun fire arcing past the bridge snapped him back to the immediate matter. At first he thought a following LCI(S) must have fired past him, until a second burst of tracer revealed it was coming from the shore. 'Port gunner! Tall building bearing red one five! Red one five!' he snapped urgently. But already both of 516's Oerlikons were firing back at their attacker. Bright tracer raced shoreward as the barrels cackled away and Glover watched as they smashed into each and every window of the offending building. The machine gun did not fire again.

While 516 disembarked the last of her men, all around the other craft carrying 6 Commando were still unloading. To Glover's port, Lieutenant Christopher Berg, a fellow New Zealander, had just nosed LCI(S) 505 on to the beach. The ratings pushed the ramps down and the first commandos rushed down into a hail of machine gun fire. Men collapsed into the sea under the weight of bullets and the rest dived for cover. As the troops still on the bow did so, the ramps, deprived of weight, were tossed around by the surf and swept away. The first three commandos to disembark from 521 were hit by a mortar bomb, killing them instantly. Nonetheless, 6 Commando quickly raced up the beach. Mills-Roberts noticed that although shells and mortars continued to pound into the sand, there was little direct infantry fire and his men were able to assemble in reasonable order. Accompanied by the swirl of Bill Millin's pipes as he launched into 'Highland Laddie', the troop commanders gathered their men and pushed them through the dunes and the ruins of the holiday camp towards the inland road.

To the west of 519, the five LCIs carrying 41 (RM) Commando had come in slightly further east than Lieutenant Colonel Thomas Gray had wanted. Looking towards Queen White Beach, his preferred landfall, there seemed to be far fewer shells and rockets crashing into the sand, but above the din of the battle, as Lieutenant Frederick Backlog struggled with incoming shells and beach obstacles, there was little 41 Commando's CO could do to influence events. Eventually they beached just west of 519 and five minutes behind them. But there was no neat line of vessels: each of the LCIs struck bottom at different distances from the shoreline, some as many as 200 yards from the sand.

Ramps were pushed out quickly, where they buckled and twisted in the surf. The commandos clambered down them, some thrown from the pitching walkways before they could get to the bottom. Spluttering and cursing they emerged from the water and grabbed hold of the wayward ramps, hoping to secure them for the following men. Corporal Raymond Mitchell carefully cradled his 70lb miniature folding 'parabike' in his arms as he looked down at the swaying ramp and decided to slide down, his backside banging against the batons until he was low enough to drop into the sea. Slowly but surely, 41 Commando got ashore.

Ahead of them was strongpoint Cod. Although it was now fighting for its survival, as several units infiltrated its flanks, there was still a tremendous amount of fire coming from the position. As the commandos doubled along the beach aiming to reach Queen White and turn inland, mortars and shells fell among them. The carefully organized units started to break apart after the chaotic disembarkation and the rush across the sand. Captain Douglas Grant, CO of S Troop, ran back and forth along a line of his men sheltering behind the dunes in front of Cod, bellowing and cursing at them to move even as they floundered under their top-heavy Bergens packed with belts of ammunition. Further west he could see a gap on Queen White leading inland and, determined to get them up there, he shouted over the din of the battle for his men to follow him. Cajoling them on, although he could scarcely hear what he was saying, he led them along the dunes, into the open exit and on to the avenue de Lion. Suddenly out of direct fire, the transformation in their surroundings was astounding. Even more amazing was Grant's discovery that every single man in his troop had made it off the beach.

But the rest of 41 Commando was not so lucky. B Troop found themselves in front of uncleared wire and took heavy casualties from unseen assailants as they tried to negotiate it. X Troop lost half their men as they raced across the sand, including their CO. Hit by mortar bombs and shells as they traversed the beach, casualties mounted. Those who could ditched their heavy loads. Mitchell spied a crew sitting alongside their knocked-out tank and decided they could make better use of his parabike than he could, so he dumped it alongside them and dashed off before they could utter an objection.[9]

Lieutenant Frederick Backlog had brought his LCI(S) on to Red Beach because White was already too crowded. Landing simultaneously with the commandos, 38 LCT Flotilla were bringing ashore 76 Field Regiment, the first self-propelled artillery unit to land. Flotilla Officer Lieutenant Commander Tom Unite, a South African commissioned into the RNVR, watched as Lieutenant Oldham brought LCT 532 into the beach perfectly on schedule. They had enjoyed the artillery bombardment; the pounding delivered by the four Priest SP guns of A Troop on the tank deck below them had been more than impressive. But as they came into the beach they were struck by the fact it was still under fire – this time hostile. The cox'n threaded between the nearly submerged obstacles and turned his bow straight to the beach, but less than 100 yards away from the surf a mortar bomb crashed into the back of the tank deck amid a supply of petrol jerry cans. Unite and Oldham ducked as a fireball erupted in front of them, flames shooting up above the height of the bridge. All at once the fireball burned out and a huge black cloud mushroomed into the sky above. Cautiously, the two officers peered over the bridge: flames licked greedily at three of the vehicles at the back of the tank deck while their crews rushed urgently around searching for hoses. 532's crew were too busy to help: the landing craft ground against the beach and the ship's company quickly went through the well-practised routine of landing. The ramp dropped and with no time to lose three of the Priests drove off, followed by two half-tracks, a Sherman observation post tank and two armoured cars. Their immediate task fulfilled, the crew quickly raced to the fire and turned the hoses on it. By now the petrol had burned out and the remaining flames were doused with seawater. The vehicles appeared to be only superficially burned but, looking around, there was no one the crew could ask to test them. All the artillerymen had gone ashore, leaving only their badly burned colleagues and the body of Lance Bombardier

Robert Drummond. Forlornly, the crew raised the ramp and pulled off the beach.

A mine exploded on the bow of LCT 750 as it drove on to the beach, the blast blowing a large hole through the port side of the ramp, severing cables and mangling the metalwork. Undeterred, the crew dropped the ramp and started to move its heavy extensions out of the way. The first Priest manoeuvred on to it and Lieutenant MacLean ran down ahead and into the surf. Waving his hands one way then another, he proceeded to guide the self-propelled gun down the right-hand side of the ramp, avoiding the jagged hole on the left. Slowly the Priest edged down and into the water, and when its tracks bit into sand it triumphantly raced forward through the surf. MacLean repeated his act for the next gun, but the following half-track stalled as it entered the water. Another half-track attempted to manoeuvre around the hole, but jammed in between the two winch houses. The exit was now blocked.

The two Priests of B Troop joined those of A, while the remaining four troops landed without difficulty. But their woes were only just beginning – Queen White was rapidly becoming jammed with traffic. The tide had driven higher up the beach, leaving barely 40 yards of dry sand for the vehicles that had landed from 41 Flotilla thirty minutes earlier. Most of C Squadron 13/18 Hussars had managed to extract themselves from the beach, but dozens of support vehicles, anti-tank guns and supply trucks lingered there, waiting for exits to appear. Dozens more wallowed in the water, disabled and abandoned. 76 Field Regiment parked themselves in the shallow surf, wirelesses crackling as forward observers with 8 Brigade were summoned, and the guns elevated in expectation of action.

On LCT 750, Sub Lieutenant George Cash watched hopefully as a BARV of 20 Beach Recovery Section REME trundled forward. But as the heavy-duty recovery vehicle neared, it was bracketed with shells, and the crew wisely withdrew back towards the sand. The crew settled down to wait, but Cash was concerned. It seemed their enforced stay on the beach was being observed.

While 750 sat in the surf, 32 LCT Flotilla were bringing 33 Field Regiment in behind her. Lieutenant Ernest Jewsbury cursed as he felt LCT 899 slow, his mechanics even now trying to extinguish the flaming starboard engine they had just reported to him. He watched as the other five vessels slowly pulled away from him, disappointed not to be able to lead his group on to the beach. 899 rumbled on slowly for a few minutes, then a hopeful voice came up the engine room voice pipe. Hesitantly, the mechanic reported that he could get the starboard engine running again, and it would run until it decided to stop. That was enough for Jewsbury. The starboard engine fired up again and 899 resumed its original speed towards the beach.

Jewsbury watched as his five sister LCTs slewed between the beach obstacles. Shells were falling uncomfortably close, and an explosion of flame and black smoke rose up from LCT 887. Squinting at the shore itself, he could see no beach markings to indicate the extents of Queen Red and White – the five LCTs all sought out their own space among the clusters of vehicles seemingly blocking the shoreline. Just before 09:10, a few seconds ahead of schedule, they drove on to the beach, ramps were dropped, and hurriedly 33 Field Regiment's Priests and support vehicles started to drive off. Two minutes later, 899 crashed over a submerged obstacle and ground up against the sand alongside them. As the Priests disgorged over the ramp they found little space on the crowded sands and milled around in the shallows while men went ahead on foot to try and find some way inland.

Running parallel to 32 Flotilla as they approached Queen White, Assault Group 9A were approaching Queen Red. Ten more LCI(S)s bearing 3 and 45 (RM) Commandos raced for the beach, their skippers searching for gaps on the shore where Curtis's flotilla were still trying to disentangle themselves. On LCI(S) 528, Sergeant Ian Grant of the Army Film and Photographic Unit (AFPU) whipped up his cine camera as he spotted a burning LCT withdrawing from the beach, a fresh explosion on the tank deck brightly illuminating the leaden grey sea and sky.[*] He panned his camera around the boat, capturing the tense faces of the commandos kneeling on the deck, and lingered briefly on those who looked at the camera, stern faces trying to stare him out.

On LCI(S) 512, Lieutenant Colonel Peter Young studied the beach through his binoculars. He could see some of his landmark houses, a few looking a touch worse for wear, others partially obscured by the clouds of smoke rolling down the beach. Tanks crept around, evidently manoeuvring hesitantly and probably still under enemy observation. Flashes

---

[*] From the position of the fire visible in his footage (IWM A70 31-2), this may well have been LCT 854 withdrawing after the mortar bomb hit. An LCI(L) can be seen approaching from astern, which tallies with the photographs taken from 854's bridge that show an LCI alongside helping to extinguish the fire.

erupted from a strongpoint further down the beach to the east. Then, as he lowered his binoculars, he realized they had slowed down.

'What are you waiting for?' he asked Lieutenant Peter Whitworth alongside him.

'There are still five minutes to go before our landing time,' replied the skipper.

Young was slightly amused. 'I don't think anyone will mind if we're five minutes early on D-Day,' he gently reproved him.

'Then in we go,' announced Whitworth, and he swung the engine telegraphs forward.

The LCI accelerated, and to port the other four carrying 3 Commando surged forward alongside. Suddenly it seemed to Young that they were entering the inferno. A shell burst overhead and splinters rained down on them, one striking him, albeit after its momentum had decreased sufficiently that it merely struck his battledress rather than penetrating it. He glanced to port and saw the gun in front of Ouistreham fire again.* A geyser of water was thrown up from the craft alongside – a miss or a hit below the waterline? It made little difference now, for their momentum alone would sweep them on to the beach. Young hurried towards the bow at 09:05, and seconds later they thudded into the sand, five minutes ahead of schedule.

Ratings thrust the ramps forward and Young immediately mounted the starboard side. It flexed under his weight and he felt his angle of descent steepen as it sank itself into soft sand, before he dropped into 5 feet of water. Behind him there was a sudden explosion on 512's port side below the bridge, piercing the hull. The blast touched off a commando's pack of mortar ammunition which detonated, felling several men of 6 Troop, wounding a rating and caving in a large section of the hull. Seawater began to pour in, and commandos and ratings quickly descended to pull the wounded out of the rising water. Whitworth quickly realized that they would not be pulling off the beach, and as the last commandos disembarked over the ramps, the crew followed, searching for shelter from the shelling somewhere ashore.

Sailing on the right flank of Assault Group 9A with the five vessels carrying 45 (RM) Commando, Sergeant Ian Grant panned his camera along the beach. Directly ahead of him, John Allen's Sherman Crab continued to burn, the late lieutenant and three of his crew still inside.

---

* Young almost certainly saw the 75mm at strongpoint 10 firing.

4 Troop's AVRE bridgelayer was just getting into position to lay the steel box girder bridge across the dunes next to a dilapidated building. To his right, tanks and vehicles littered the narrow beach, some manoeuvring, others either waiting or already knocked out. The tide was concerningly high.

His landing craft ground into the sand and he moved to the bow to capture the men disembarking down the steep ramps. To the left, more commandos were coming ashore between the Centaur tanks of S and T Troops of the Royal Marine Armoured Support Group, some of which lay abandoned and battered by the surf, while others crawled forward, lobbing shells at high angles to the east. As he filmed, the two ramps at the bow of his craft were caught by the swell and twisted, locking together at the bottom. Commandos were thrown into the surf while others clung to the ramp's rope rails and those already in the water tried desperately to untangle the mess. A member of the Beach Group rushed forward and tried to coax a man down the ramp with his bicycle so that disembarkation could continue.

As 3 and 45 Commando raced ashore, mortar and shellfire continued to pound the beach, but the fire was slackening and the men were able to assemble in good order and make their way to the inland road. Twenty of the twenty-two LCI(S)s that had landed then backed away from the beach – two of their number would never sail again.[10]

Sluggishly, the wallowing LCIs manoeuvred away from the carnage on the beach and, as smoke billowed out from the decks and water poured in through holes in the hull, the flotillas headed back out to sea. But for some their work was not yet over. Having failed to land anyone ashore after almost an hour, LCI(L) 130 had finally backed off the beach, and now, listing badly and still laden with almost all of her passengers, Lieutenant Commander Wall sought to find some way to get them ashore. In desperation he signalled LCH 185 and, spotting LCI(S) 516 heading back out to sea, Commander Edmund Currey flashed a signal to Denis Glover. Somewhat apprehensively the New Zealander conned 516 towards the overladen vessel, eyeing the hole in the port side as the swell rocked it out of the water and then back beneath the waves. He shouted at his crew to throw out every single fender they had, aware that the bigger vessel would inevitably give them a sound bashing once they were alongside.

Gently, 516 pulled alongside and Glover hollered up to the deck above, 'Bad luck, chum. But we'll run the ferry service. All aboard for Margate!'

Stony seasick faces stared back at him and Glover felt a pang of sympathy for the unfortunate soldiers. 130 rolled back and forth, her hull smashing against 516's fenders with a jarring crash each time. But much worse, enemy guns had found their range and shells plopped into the water alarmingly close by. The sailors eyed the geysers nervously – there was nothing worse than being hove to under fire.

As 130 rolled back towards 516, the first troops jumped down from the higher deck on to the LCI(S). Some collapsed on to the deck and had to be grabbed by sailors so they didn't fall between the two vessels as they rolled back again. Major Gough presented himself on the bridge and Glover cheerfully chatted to him. 'Oh I know where it is,' he said, referring to the beach. 'Nothing's a trouble.' Even so, he was painfully aware that it would take time to get almost 200 men aboard.

Meanwhile, briefly free from the distractions of getting their commando passengers ashore, the crews of the other LCI(S)s turned to themselves, treating their wounded and fixing the most pressing damage to the boats. As she limped away, smoke curling up from a hatch to the engine room where a small fire was being fought by the crew, LCI(S) 524 began to be bracketed by German gunfire. Seaman Harold Barton fell to the deck, one of his feet sliced away. As blood pooled around him he cheerfully urged one of his crewmates to tend to more needy casualties and, slipping off his coat, covered the bloody stump from view.

On the bridge, Lieutenant Alan Nigel Cromar willed his craft on and out of the range of the guns. The pock-marked landing craft was now nearly 2 miles from the shore, although the clamour of battle could still be heard over the throbbing engines that were giving their all to speed the vessel to safety. More shells landed alongside, throwing up geysers of water that cascaded on to the decks. Cromar watched the waters subside, hopeful that they might have represented the German artillery's last hurrah. But it was not to be, and in a sudden blinding flash his world went dark.

On the bridge of US Coast Guard Cutter 35, Lieutenant George Clark watched, appalled, as a flash as bright as the sun obliterated his view of 524. Seconds later a thunder-like boom echoed across his boat. Like a blown light bulb, the flash burned itself out to reveal only flames and thick black smoke billowing from the sea's surface, as if an underwater volcano was erupting.

Calmly giving orders to his helmsman, Clark manoeuvred CGC 35 closer to the inferno. The cutter had been assigned to the LCIs as their rescue craft and Clark had promised Curtis that he would be behind them all the way to the beach. Dutifully, the little 83-foot boat had stayed with the landing craft all the way across the Channel and as close to the shore as Clark dared take her without grounding. Now there was no question what he had to do.

But 524 appeared to have been obliterated. As they closed, Clark could make out dark shadows of bits of wreckage, but certainly nothing he could definitively describe as a vessel. The most visible part of her now was her fuel, spread across some 50 metres of sea. Clark knew that his own boat was powered by the same highly combustible petrol: at the back of his mind he knew the fuel itself was less of a problem than the vapours in his tanks, which might erupt at any moment when exposed to the heat of flames. But it never even crossed his mind not to go into the tumult, and gingerly he coaxed his cutter closer. With flames mere metres from the hull, the crew threw the scrambling nets over the side and climbed down to the waterline, so close that some singed their clothes.

Dazed, Cromar had come to his senses to find himself in the sea surrounded by a wall of flame. His arms hung limply in the water and his legs flailed uselessly below him – only his life preserver kept his head above water and, as the flames roared around him, that was cold comfort. Gagging on the seawater and oil in his mouth, he resigned himself to the inevitable. Just as the oppressive heat on his face and the cold, numbing water swirling around his body threatened to overwhelm him, he saw a dark shadow emerging through the smoke. Slowly the welcome sight of a boat materialized through the conflagration. Barely able to comprehend what was happening, he felt himself being pulled up and out of the water. Pain shot through his spine and his arms and legs throbbed incessantly, but all was numbed by welcome relief as comforting hands laid him on the wooden deck.

On the bridge, Clark looked down as his crew heaved five bundles of burned and oil-covered men on to the deck. The flames and smoke had shrunk his world to within a few metres of the cutter, blotting out the sky and sea and threatening to envelop him too. No one else could be seen in the water around him and, knowing that he couldn't stay any longer without endangering everyone aboard, he ordered the helmsman to back away. Slowly they emerged from the heat and smoke, back into the refreshing sea air.*

---

* When he finally reached hospital, doctors discovered that Cromar had fractured both his knees, dislocated his right shoulder and fractured his vertebrae. Despite

After patiently waiting, 516 had taken aboard all of 130's passengers and once again it turned its bow to the beach. Glover looked at the deck, packed with men and just as many below. He could feel the additional weight of double his normal load as the landing craft sluggishly got underway again. With Gough alongside him on the bridge, he picked out a landing spot and directed his cox'n to the gap between two smouldering buildings. 'We've been surf riding here all morning,' he confidently told Gough. 'The beach is ours all right, it's just like home to half the army now.' Even so, mortar bursts started to bracket them as they closed the shore, and the explosive-topped uppers of submerged beach obstacles were occasionally revealed in the troughs of the waves. To Glover it felt more dangerous than the first landing. Or was he just more nervous this time, he wondered?

For a second time 516 shuddered up the beach. The crew quickly rolled out the ramps and then watched, mystified and despairing, as one raced off the craft entirely, its preventer cables shot away. To the soldiers it was almost too much to lose another ramp, but the other one held firm and the crew cajoled them down it. Slowly the men disembarked, while Glover watched, aware that there was nothing to do but wait now. Grimly he watched another LCI(L) coming in alongside – uncomfortably close, he felt, its kedge wire looking like it might be difficult to miss when he reversed off. Up ahead he was astounded to see his impromptu passengers milling around the beach once they got ashore rather than running up it as the commandos had done. Mortar bombs and bullets indiscriminately fell among them.

After an agonizingly long time, the final soldier trooped down the gangway. The crew whipped the surviving ramp back up and both of 516's engines were thrown into reverse, the battered landing craft just avoiding

---

his wounds, he returned to work, this time at a desk, less than a year later. Lieutenant George Clark summarized his rescue of LCI(S) 524's survivors quite simply in his subsequent report, noting only 'Survivors rescued, five. Corpses, none. Comments, none.' The Royal Navy thought differently and Clark was awarded the British Distinguished Service Cross, his citation stating that 'During the landing of commandos at Ouistreham by LCI(S) on June 6, 1944, Lieut. Clark's cutter was detailed to act as escort. HM LCI(S) 524, on clearing the beach after landing troops, received a direct hit and blew up in a sheet of flames leaving a mass of blazing Octane petrol on the water. Although his cutter burned Octane petrol, he did not hesitate to steer his craft into the flames and rescue the commanding officer and some of his men.'

the neighbouring vessel's kedge. Once out far enough, the cox'n spun 516 around and they raced back out to sea, the stiff wind seeming to blow the noise and smoke of the oppressive beach off them.

Glover peered around with his binoculars, looking for any of the flotilla to join up with, but the first one he saw looked to be in a far worse state than them. LCI(S) 517 had struck a mine when pulling off the beach. The crew had done everything they could to hold back the water pouring through the hull once they got away, but now the doomed vessel was foundering. Glover could see her screws lifted out of the water as she went slowly down by the bow. 'Starboard ten,' he told the cox'n, and 516 raced towards the doomed vessel. There was no hope of a tow, and Glover was anxious about even attaching a line – it looked like 517 might nosedive any second. 516 bumped alongside and Glover ushered the sailors aboard, commiserating with Sub Lieutenant Joe Gaunt as they watched 517's bow lurching down even as the last men jumped over. They'd arrived just in time.

Noticing that shells were still falling nearby, Glover decided it was time to get well clear of Queen Beach. 'Number One, we will now go to seaward out of here and find the rest. Issue rum to everybody, and by God, I'll have a tot myself!'[11]

Slowly but surely, strongpoint Cod was wrestled into silence, the sheer weight of numbers pushing against it from all sides steadily overwhelming the defenders. On the sea-facing side, a shell exploded inside the 50mm gun bunker, the blast enveloping the gunners and blasting the barrel of the gun on to the sand outside. Near by, engineers succeeded in creating a ramp up the dunes and into the strongpoint itself. A Sherman Crab drove through the barbed wire, flailing a route above the trench network while its guns sprayed the surrounding area. Soon, offensive fire from the position all but ceased. Hesitantly, British troops pushed through the trench network, searching bunkers and rounding up the defenders, who started to give themselves up in larger groups.

At 10:30, an LCM slid ashore on Queen Red. Its ramp dropped into the surf and a small, semi-amphibious 'Weasel' tracked vehicle, piled high with kit, drove ashore. Behind it strode Major General Thomas Rennie and his staff. It had taken him longer than he had wanted to get here – a vocal argument with Arthur Talbot on the bridge of *Largs* had forced the admiral to remind him that it was the Royal Navy, not the army, in charge of the landings, and the general would go ashore at his discretion.

Eventually the LCM had come alongside and his HQ party had lowered themselves down rope ladders and settled on its pitching deck. Eschewing a helmet and proudly wearing a tam-o'-shanter cap, Rennie surveyed the beach. Bodies rolled in the surf and littered the sand, shells continued to fall, and occasional bursts of machine gun fire and cracks of rifle fire showed that the beach area was not yet completely cleared, but it was at least secure.

Now the fighting moved inland.

Troops from 4 Commando dart behind a DD tank of B Squadron 13/18 Hussars, as they rush along the avenue de Lion into Ouistreham.

PART 3
THE MORNING BATTLES

8

THE BATTLE OF OUISTREHAM

IGNORING HIS INJURED LEG, LIEUTENANT COLONEL ROBERT Dawson strode out from behind the Château de Colleville and on to the avenue de Lion. Looking east towards Ouistreham, he was pleased to see the street was deserted and, more importantly, free from obstacles. But was it safe? The answer came quicker than he imagined, for as he turned back to the château he suddenly heard the screeching last moments of a mortar bomb's flight above him. He dived for the ground just as the bomb impacted nearby, its blast bowling him over. Sitting back up, he felt a throbbing in his head and, putting his hand up to his temple, found that warm blood was already trickling down his face.

Back by the château, the men of Dawson's commando were forming up in groups along the road. The French 1 and 8 Troops were at the front, Commandant Philippe Kieffer having asked for – and been given – the honour of leading the advance. C Troop were behind them, ready to lead D, A, E and F Troops, while B Troop with their heavy weapons were dispersed among them. As he looked along the growing groups of men, Donald Gilchrist turned to see the figure of his commander, blood now streaming from his head and struggling on his wounded leg, just as Dawson's gaze alighted on him.

'What the hell do you think you're doing, adjutant? Get them moving!' Gilchrist opened his mouth to speak, but Dawson didn't give him the time. 'Move, I tell you!'

His adjutant didn't hang around. Charging towards the head of the column, he began shouting in his pidgin French, 'Allez, allez!' The French commandos stared at him. Why was this madman shouting to Allah? Nevertheless the intention, if not the instruction, was clear. Alexandre Lofi shouted an order to 8 Troop and they began to move. Dawson, more congenially this time, waved them off. 'Bonne chance,' he called out to Lofi, watching with admiration while a medic implored him to sit down.

At 08:20, 8 Troop turned on to the avenue de Lion and broke into a jog, the background noise of mortar and machine gun fire quickly supplemented by the sound of hobnailed boots on the hard road and the soft flapping of canvas webbing. The crack of a bullet quickly broke the lines of men into looser formations running along the walls on either side of the deserted street, and 8 Troop scurried up to the first group of farm buildings. Behind them Lieutenant Amaury led the K-gun troop out on to the road, with Kieffer and 1 Troop bringing up the rear of the French contingent. After he was sure the other British troops were nearly ready, Captain David Style ordered C Troop to follow them.

The commando's objective was Ouistreham. Despite the powerful bombardment from air and sea, D-Day planners were aware they could not guarantee the battery of 155mm guns at strongpoint Bass would be completely neutralized. Its proximity to the landing areas meant it could not be continually bombarded throughout the day as the other batteries east of the Orne were; equally, it couldn't simply be ignored. The only way to ensure it would no longer be a threat was for infantry to storm it. 4 Commando would secure and, if necessary, spike the six guns. Dawson was pleased to have the additional support of the French troops, but knew that language was a difficult barrier to incorporating them into the attack. Happily there were two objectives they could tackle independently. At the western end of Bass was a sizeable strongpoint that would need at least one troop to neutralize it. Slightly further west was strongpoint 10. With its gun positions able to hit the landing area in the flank, it had to be taken out as quickly as possible.

Lofi's leading scouts darted up the exposed road. Pairs of men crossed it, gained whatever cover they could find in ditches and bushes, took aim and waited for their counterparts to move ahead of them. Behind them the rest of the troop followed at a crouched run, some by the wall on the north side, others careful to avoid tripping on the narrow-gauge tram track running along the south side. Somewhat incredibly, Lofi's entire troop had got off the beach and now all sixty-five of them, accompanied by half of the French K-gun section, were leading the charge into Ouistreham.

The first objective, about 1,300 yards down the road, was the 'bag drop'. While it would be madness to carry their heavy Bergens during the assault on their objectives, each man carried in his pack a 3-inch mortar bomb for B Troop's three mortars, and they'd be needed in Ouistreham. Already the 80lb weight was becoming a strain, the straps cutting into the shoulders of the men as they jogged forward. And now the enemy were starting to respond. Mortar bombs fell indiscriminately along the road and occasional bursts of machine gun fire kicked up dirt and stones.

All at once the Frenchmen reached the bag drop, just short of the town's main junction with the road to Caen. Barely pausing, Lofi's men unshouldered their packs and turned up a side road leading back to the beach, with two of the K-gun teams on their heels. 1 Troop came up to the same spot as the last of Lofi's men disappeared round the corner and gladly slipped their bags off.[*] More cautiously now, Kieffer led his men further along the avenue de Lion. From here on they were in an urban environment, with buildings on both sides of the road and all the dangers that presented.

Behind them, the British commandos were taking more fire from an enemy alerted by the French commandos' passing. Sporadic houses along the road now became exercises in tactics, even once the first troops had passed them by. The occasional crack of a sniper's bullet sent the columns cascading for cover and a quick hunt ensued. Covering fire splattered around the windows of the nearest house and men dashed forward to clear it. Then came the growl of engines and the rattle of steel tracks on concrete. Fortunately the noise came from behind, and commandos cheered as tanks of 13/18 Hussars B Squadron charged down the road, their canvas skirts bouncing and flapping around their hulls.[†] The bursts

---

[*] There is some uncertainty about exactly where Lofi and his troop turned off the avenue de Lion. In their memoirs, Gilchrist and McDougall suggest the French turned off earlier than the British, which is true. But their indicative maps, not accurate or to scale, appear to have been taken in later publications to show Lofi's turn-off being almost immediately after they set off from the Château de Colleville and then continuing parallel to the avenue de Lion along the boulevard Maréchal Joffre. 8 Troop's exact route isn't recorded by Lofi or Kieffer, but the boulevard Maréchal Joffre was largely devoid of cover and there is no obvious villa, which Lofi describes passing. The more likely route – from Lofi's recollection and basic military sense – would have been along or close to the boulevard d'Angleterre, now the boulevard Winston Churchill.
[†] The tanks aren't identified by the commandos, but Sergeant George Laws' video footage shows them to be Sherman DDs. They most likely came from B Squadron's 1 Troop who, Captain Neave recalled, had reached the lateral road and then turned left towards Ouistreham before anyone could stop them.

of sniper and machine gun fire grew marginally less frequent, and those Germans who did try were quickly dealt with by high explosive.

But other threats remained. By the time the French commandos had reached the 'bag drop', F Troop were only just moving off from the assembly area. While medics treated the protesting Dawson, troop commander Len Coulson led his men forward, jogging to maintain contact with E Troop ahead of them. They hadn't got far when they heard the rushing roar of incoming mortars and, as one, the section dived to the ground. The bombs rained down on E Troop's stragglers crossing the junction ahead of them – a quick shock of blasts with bright flashes and flames, followed a second later by a hailstorm of earth, stones and wooden splinters. Then, all at once, the 'stonk' was over. Murdoch McDougall, automatically back on his feet and running forward, saw prostrate forms, blackened and smoking, lying on the road. Coulson spied a dazed signaller leaning against the wall with his head in his hands. As he drew level he shouted at the man to keep moving, but the signaller only twisted himself back against the wall and, turning towards him, presented an image of mutilated flesh, blood and bone. One eye stared lifelessly at F Troop as they ran on; the remains of the other oozed down what was left of his face.

Nursing his injured leg, Captain Joseph Patterson limped along the road as quickly as he could. One marine carried his rucksack and another supported him by the arm, but neither could speed the lame medical officer across the junctions or between the gaps in the houses, which was where the worst of the fire seemed to be. Coming across the remains of a mortar hit, Patterson found one man dead and another with his head caved in. There was a faint pulse, but there was nothing he could do for the commando and he pushed his helmet over the wound and moved on. Another man lay by a wall with what looked like a shoulder wound, but as he got closer Patterson realized that his arm was almost completely severed and blood was gushing out. Frantically, Patterson pinched his neck to try and reduce the blood flow while a medic bound the wound. Carefully holding on to the injury they got him on to a stretcher and carried on.

Ahead of them, Lofi and his men were already in action. After gratefully shedding their rucksacks the Frenchmen jogged down the deserted side streets with Sous Lieutenant Leopold Hulot's section in the lead.[*]

---

[*] A sous lieutenant is the equivalent of a sub lieutenant in the Royal Navy.

Warning signs pasted on the sides of buildings spoke of minefields, but reluctant to waste time with mine detectors the men chanced their luck and ran on, into the grounds of a château. Their luck had held so far, but as they moved through the grounds the first mortar bombs, fired by an unseen enemy, started to fall. Hulot led his section through a gap in the wall and across open ground, ignoring another 'Achtung Minen!' sign. The enemy response grew more intense – a mortar sent Hulot's section to ground and wounded several, including the lieutenant. As the injured were pulled off the road, André Bagot's section took the lead. As they darted through gaps in the houses, the dunes behind the beach came into view, and now, as they closed on their target, the menacing shadows of the concrete structures of strongpoint 10. In that instant, machine gun fire suddenly sliced down the road. Four men fell wounded and the rest rushed for cover in the nearby houses, the Frenchmen kicking down doors and hammering up stairs to take positions overlooking the strongpoint.

In front of them the commandos found a large blockhouse on the right flank and, about 100 yards west, an anti-tank gun in a concrete emplacement. A low wall ran another 50 yards west to a small shelter and, buried in the dunes, what was clearly another sizeable bunker. Trenches and barbed wire crisscrossed the ground in front of them. To Lofi's dismay the position had been left almost completely untouched by the bombardment.

In the strongpoint, Leutnant Aschenbrenner's small force continued to fire on the landing beach just over 1,000 yards to the west. Their 75mm gun – housed in an unusual casemate with a 23cm-thick steel roof and a much lower profile than most normal gun positions – and their 50mm had been methodically shelling the landing craft for the last hour, but the gunners could see that there were far more vessels than they alone could hit and that it was only a matter of time before land forces reached them. Now, shouts and machine guns firing inland heralded their arrival, and the 50mm was pivoted around to face the new threat.

From their elevated viewpoints in the villas the commandos opened a withering fire on anything that moved in the trenches while Lofi prepared an assault. Sous Lieutenant Louis Hubert's small party from the K-gun troop moved into a shell hole on the right flank and, with Bagot's section, lay down covering fire. Despite his wounds Hulot had returned to his section, and while part of it occupied houses on the left flank, the young lieutenant and some of his men crawled forward until they were close enough to lob grenades. Mills bombs arced through the air and into the trenches and from one of the upper windows a PIAT launched its deadly-shaped charge at one of the bunkers. Bursts of flame erupted and screams echoed from the trenches, but the concrete and armour plate protected the men inside the bunkers.

As Hulot and his men withdrew, the German gunners responded. Heavy small arms fire ricocheted around the Frenchmen's positions and the 50mm blasted a hole through one of the houses. Lofi quickly realized that strongpoint 10 was a tough nut, and even as he watched he could see some of the defenders making their way to the right, almost certainly looking to outflank them. He had to keep the pressure on and disguise the slender size of his own force.

While the PIAT turned its attention to the softer targets in the trenches, Lofi sent Bagot's section further right to block the Germans. As the infantry moved past them Hubert saw the chance for his K-gun section to redeploy. He raised his head slightly out of the crater and looked around for Second-Maître Robert Saeren,[*] but just as his eyes alighted on his second in command, his world went dark. From his position Saeren saw his commander turn to him, the puff of red mist as a bullet struck his head, and his body slump out of sight. While men scrambled to reach the lieutenant, Saeren's problems compounded as first one crew, then the other, reported jams. Hurriedly he ordered them to withdraw to a nearby house to strip and clean machine guns. Taking advantage of the K-guns' absence the German forces edged further around the flank and Bagot's section came under increasingly heavy fire. Bagot himself fell wounded, along with one of his two Bren gunners.

Lofi could see the situation was becoming untenable – he had no idea of the size of the German force and how far they could keep pushing his flank. As his troop desperately tried to win the firepower fight, their own meagre supply of ammunition was getting lower. Knowing that only armoured support could swing the battle he sent his runner, Matelot Guy Laot,[†] himself wounded in the arm, back to the Commando HQ. Then, spying some low mounds behind the houses, he ordered a withdrawal to new positions out of the line of direct fire from the strongpoint. Hurried orders were issued and the Frenchmen pulled back. As he made for the mounds, one of the grenades hanging from Jean Letang's webbing was hit

---

[*] A second-maître is roughly equivalent to a petty officer in the Royal Navy.
[†] A matelot is roughly equivalent to a seaman in the Royal Navy.

by a bullet and detonated, the ensuing blast mortally wounding the twenty-three-year-old. As he lay in dreadful pain, he had just enough strength to wave his colleagues away before he slipped into blissful peace.

As the Frenchmen settled in their new positions, one of the houses they had just abandoned was reduced to a ruin by the 50mm anti-tank gun. It was the last act in a battle that moments ago had been intense, but now suddenly came to an end as both sides gratefully accepted the respite. As Lofi watched Hubert's body being laid in a small garden, alongside that of Marcel Labas, who had fallen to a sniper, Laot returned to report that Lieutenant Colonel Dawson was nearby. Leaving Bagot in charge, Lofi quickly set off with his runner to find him.

Laot led him back to 4 Commando's HQ at the Caen road junction on the avenue de Lion. Dawson, wrapped in a green blanket with his beret perched on top of a blood-stained bandage, greeted Lofi warmly and congratulated him on his efforts. Lofi protested that his mission wasn't complete. He had heard the clatter of tank tracks as he made his way back – with armoured support he would be able to make a final assault. But Dawson shook his head. Lofi had done enough and the commandos had other tasks. Kieffer would be back soon – it was time to disengage and rejoin the rest of the French commandos.*[1]

When Lofi's troop had branched off, 1 Troop took the lead of the long column of commandos. While scouts leapfrogged each other at the front, lines of men jogged down either side of the road behind them. Kieffer had fewer men than Lofi – twenty-eight men of 1 Troop were still on the beach, five of them dead.

As they approached the Caen road junction, ahead of them the commandos could see residents of Ouistreham who had started to gather around four stationary carriages in front of the tram station. The desire to go and converse with their countrymen and women burned deep in the commandos, but they had a mission to complete. A hundred yards

---

* Although strongpoint 10 had not been fully neutralized, it is uncertain how much it bothered the landing craft approaching Queen Red after 8 Troop's attack. Leutnant Aschenbrenner ordered his men to surrender and later in the day they gave themselves up to the driver of a passing British jeep. In all likelihood this was the Red Cross jeep that Joseph Patterson recalls despatching to pick up wounded men, but it came back with fifty prisoners from a surrendered strongpoint instead. The main blockhouse at the east end of the strongpoint is today the base of the 'Monument of the Flame' dedicated to the Free French and 4 Commando.

short of the junction, Kieffer led his men left on to the rue Pasteur.* It was 09:00.

The commandos started moving quicker now, forming into two columns on either side of the road. After passing a small tree-lined park they moved on to a narrower road lined with houses and small pruned trees running along the pavements and here came under heavy fire from ahead. Injured men fell and were dragged into the shelter of gardens and side roads. More civilians had started to emerge now, some gathered in small groups in the lee of buildings. The commandos asked them where the Germans were and they stared back at them, open-mouthed. Who were these English soldiers who spoke such good French? One man snapped away with a camera; another, looking downcast, explained to Maître-Principal Hubert Faure† that he had been working for the Germans on their defences, and now he had lost his job. An older man sporting a generous white moustache hurried over and embraced Kieffer enthusiastically. Introducing himself as a member of the Resistance, Marcel Lefèvre quickly outlined the location of several German positions and minefields nearby, information that was gratefully received.‡

---

* The 4 Commando briefing map shows 1 Troop's intended line of advance up the next road to the west, the avenue Andry. Neither Kieffer nor Guy de Montlaur identify the road used by name, and both roads had anti-tank chicanes at their north end, so it is possible that either was used. Most publications identify the rue Pasteur, and it is noticeable that in an aerial photo taken on the afternoon of D-Day there appears to be more damage at the end of that road.
† A maître-principal is broadly equivalent to a senior petty officer in the Royal Navy.
‡ Over time, Monsieur Lefèvre's contribution to D-Day has become considerably exaggerated. In his post-war account, Montlaur claimed that Lefèvre showed Faure where to cut communication cables connecting a tower with the rest of Bass and to HQs inland at Saint-Aubin-d'Arquenay and Caen. While this might well have happened, Faure does not recall it and Kieffer does not refer to it in his 14 June report or memoir. True or not, the account seems to be the basis of an oft-repeated story that Lefèvre told Kieffer he had snuck up to the German fortifications during the bombardment and cut the control wires of flamethrowers mounted on the beach. McDougall made this claim in 1954, it was repeated by Lovat in 1978 and Gilchrist in 1982, and since then has been widely repeated in books and many more commando memoirs. None of these men were actually present when 1 Troop met Lefèvre but appear to have heard his story 'through the grapevine'. While these flamethrowers did exist, there is no evidence that Lefèvre made any such claims on D-Day. None of the French commandos recall it, including Kieffer and Faure, who only say that Lefèvre told them where some of the fortifications and

The commandos moved into the gardens on both sides of the road and started to make their way north, picking their way across walls and clearing houses as they advanced. Three hundred yards later they were nearing the end of the road and found themselves overlooking an unexpected obstacle. Two large concrete anti-tank blocks, each a short wall in its own right, lay in the road forming a narrow chicane. While a formidable obstacle for tanks, the wall offered the commandos a fair degree of protection as they prepared for the next phase of their attack.

Faure redeployed the two sections and they steadily crept through the grounds of the final few houses until, at the end of the road, they found themselves overlooking their objective – the 'Casino' strongpoint. By now the casino existed in name only – demolished by the occupiers in 1943, only its ground floor and basement survived. Reinforced with concrete and turned into a sizeable blockhouse serving as an HQ and accommodation building, the ramps that once allowed taxis to pull up outside the ornate east entrance to deliver wealthy patrons to the roulette wheels now gave access to the blockhouse roof and a 20mm flak gun.

As they took up positions in the windows and behind the wall, the strongpoint sprang into life. The flak gun, machine guns and snipers put up a heavy defence, forcing the commandos to seek cover. Kieffer quickly instructed Maître Abel Lardennois to get the PIAT teams into a villa on the west side of the road, an exposed position but directly overlooking the casino. Darting across the garden and through the shattered doorway, the crews were injured by the weight of fire coming from the strongpoint even before they'd positioned themselves. Hauling the heavy PIAT launchers up the stairs, they hurriedly got themselves into position on the top floor, a mere 70 yards from their target. The two teams quickly launched their first two bombs together, erupting balls of flame on the casino's rooftop that enveloped the 20mm gun crew. Quickly the Frenchmen reloaded the unwieldy weapons and two more bombs flew across the road, this time hitting the embrasures facing them. In those few minutes the teams had expended their slender supply of ammunition and,

---

mines were positioned. Even if the flamethrower control cables were cut, it would most likely be a result of the bombardment. When he visited the strongpoint shortly after the landings, Steven Sykes identified one flamethrower and followed its control wire back to a nearby pillbox. Cutting cables in this sort of location, in the centre of an elaborate strongpoint during a heavy naval barrage, would have been an impossible task for anyone.

with nothing to be gained by remaining, they made to leave. But before they could escape the vulnerable villa, 20mm shells ripped through the building and Emile Renault fell, blood spurting from his neck. Matelot-Breveté Bolloré* was called for and morphine was administered, but it was too late.

Kieffer could see that 1 Troop's position wasn't strong, and he was worried about the other half of his command. To the west he could hear the sounds of a battle, almost certainly 8 Troop, but he had no idea how they might be doing. Then a possible solution presented itself. Monitoring wireless traffic, his signaller informed him that a number of tanks were ashore and moving inland. Tank support could make all the difference and so, leaving Faure in command, Kieffer set off with his batman Matelot Devager to find one. Retracing their steps back down the rue Pasteur, they jogged past a house just as two women emerged. 'Are there any Germans in your house?' called Kieffer. 'No,' the two women sang out in unison, while simultaneously gesturing back into the building. Kieffer and Devager quickly got up against the garden wall. His batman raised himself just enough to cover the building with his Tommy gun while the women scurried on to the road and Kieffer, stooping low, moved up the garden path. Cautiously he approached the open door, dropped down on to the step and took a deep breath. In a quick movement he leaned forward and swung his pistol in a wide arc around the room. A German soldier turned to face him just as his pistol came level and, without hesitation, Kieffer fired directly into the man's face. The German fell backwards and blood spurted across the floor while Kieffer, wasting no time, returned to the road.

Back at the casino, Matelot-breveté Paul Rollin had just moved to a position in the chicane of the anti-tank blocks when a sniper's bullet struck him in the head. Rushing forward, Médecin-Capitaine Robert Lion broke cover to grab the matelot's legs, while his orderly Bolloré went to grasp his arms. Appalled, the commandos behind them shouted at the two men to get into cover, and as Bolloré turned he heard the thwack of a bullet as it zipped past his face and smashed into the concrete behind him. Instinctively dropping down into cover, it took him a few moments to realize that there had been more than one bullet. Behind him, Lion slumped to the ground.

Commandos rushed forward and under a fusillade of covering fire

---

* A matelot-breveté is broadly equivalent to an able seaman in the Royal Navy.

dragged the men behind the concrete walls. There was nothing that could be done for Lion. The bullet had gone straight through the captain's heart and Bolloré looked sadly at a face that seemed already to be assuming the waxy complexion of a corpse. Rollin still clung to life, but as Bolloré watched he could see his brain starting to ooze out of the wound. He could only administer morphine to ease the young commando's suffering, which ended a few minutes later.

The commandos' mourning was interrupted at 09:25 by the sound of armour to the south. As they watched, a Centaur tank came up the rue Pasteur, and as it closed on them the commandos spotted their commander and his batman riding on the hull.* To the sound of cheers the tank reached the end of the road, but with the anti-tank wall preventing any further progress up the street, Kieffer instead directed it through a wall behind the villa so recently used by the PIAT teams. Crossing the garden the driver turned right, positioning the tank directly opposite the strongpoint, and without a moment's hesitation the gunner fired. Sitting on the tank's turret both Kieffer and Devager were concussed by the shockwave as first one then two shells were directed into the low building. Clouds of cement dust spilled across the road and the machine guns that had so fiercely defended the south side of the casino fell silent. Even so, enough defenders remained to return fire and Kieffer was struck in his right arm. Jumping off the tank, he took cover behind a low wall while he directed the tank's gunners. More 95mm rounds piled into the structure, ensuring the 20mm flak gun's demise, before the tank's co-axial Besa machine gun started to spray the entire building.

While the tank inflicted death and destruction on the defenders of the casino, Kieffer found Faure and instructed him to make the assault. Second Maître Guy de Montlaur took his section behind the tank to attack from the left, while Lardennois took his to the right and simultaneously the Frenchmen charged, hurling grenades and firing as they stormed up to its walls and into the neighbouring trenches. While Montlaur's men made good ground, Lardennois' men came under fire from behind – bullets peppered the road and the commandos dived for cover. Kieffer spied the German gunners on the flak tower and, jumping back

---

* The tank is unidentified, but was most likely a Centaur of T Troop, 5 Royal Marine Armoured Support Group. In *The Longest Day* the tank is depicted as a Sherman, which may be the cause of it often being identified as such in later publications. But in both his report and his memoir, Kieffer identifies it as a Centaur.

on the tank, he guided its crew on to the main coast road and around to the front of the small hill the tower was on. Without hesitation the gunner fired into the tower, and after the loader had swiftly rammed another round into the breech, fired again, and then twice more, the tower fell silent.

Quickly the right-hand section was back on its feet and moving for the casino. On the left, Montlaur's section was already storming inside, finding that the PIATs and 95mm had made more than enough impact to quash resistance. Inside, about ten dejected men were only too pleased to surrender. Outside in the trenches on the right side a similar number quickly raised their hands, but on the west side a small group escaped, scuttling into houses near the seafront. Second-Maître Lanternier escorted the first group of prisoners out of the casino and Kieffer eyed them sceptically. Covered in cement dust, their clothes in rags, and looking thoroughly shocked and miserable, he was not impressed. Three or four were Eastern Europeans, probably Poles. As they were led away, one had the temerity to throw a grenade. Commandos and PoWs dived aside, escaping the worst of the blast, which lightly injured two of the Frenchmen. Without hesitation Tommy guns were turned on the PoWs and three of them did not make it into captivity.

Reports came in that 4 Commando was reassembling on the avenue de Lion and it was clear to Kieffer that their work in Ouistreham was done. The occasional sniper shots became more and more infrequent as the last PoWs were led back on to the rue Pasteur, and the growling and clanking of the Centaur tank receded as it went off in search of its troop. A fragile peace descended over the casino. As the Frenchmen tramped back down the road they passed their chaplain, Capitaine René de Naurois, who remarked to Kieffer, 'Commandant, these men have superb faces.'[2]

While Kieffer's men scored France's first victory on their home soil, 4 Commando were dealing with the main battery. As each troop arrived at the outskirts of Ouistreham they dropped their rucksacks on the growing pile, each with a mortar bomb protruding from the top. Patterson arrived and quickly set up his Regimental Aid Post under some pine trees. His stretchered patient was laid on the ground and the doctor continued to pack the wound with dressings as best he could, but even so he feared the worst until a plasma drip finally brought his pulse round.

While Patterson's small team treated the wounded as they arrived at the RAP, the rest of 4 Commando continued east, each section hugging the sides of buildings and garden walls while the Sherman tanks trundled down the road. As they arrived at the tram station and the Caen road junction, a Frenchman clad in pyjamas with a cigarette clamped between his lips dashed from man to man embracing and shaking hands with whoever he could. A young woman sobbed uncontrollably, causing the commandos to wonder if she was overcome with emotion or mourned the loss of a German lover.

But although the liberation had begun, the war was not over for the residents of Ouistreham. At the head of D Troop, Captain Patrick Porteous VC encountered a distressed Frenchman frantically searching for a doctor to treat his injured wife. Even above the man's pleas, Porteous heard the shriek of a mortar bomb and dived to the ground, just before a blast showered him with earth. He sat back up to see the Frenchman's head rolling to a stop in the middle of the road. Porteous's Troop Sergeant Major Irving Portman had just ordered his medical orderly, Orlando Farnese, to accompany a Frenchman and tend to his brother when a mortar round exploded among them, killing the civilian and medic and blowing Portman on to his face. Sitting back up he checked himself over and found, to his amazement, that he didn't have a scratch on him. A gendarme emerged from a house and offered his assistance to C Troop, advising them on the locations of the strongest German positions and guiding them on the quickest route to the battery.*

Behind them, HQ arrived at the Caen road junction and quickly began setting up their base, signallers establishing themselves as high in the surrounding buildings as they could. The first teams from B Troop arrived, each man gratefully dropping their part of a mortar. Hurriedly the three 3-inch launchers were assembled and the bombs gathered from the pile of rucksacks. Within minutes a small battery was ready to lay down covering fire once the assault began.

Donald Gilchrist had just dropped his bag when he turned to find 4 Commando's second in command, Major Ronald Menday, with a face like thunder. 'Why the bloody hell wasn't I informed that the CO was wounded?' Tired of being the dogsbody, Gilchrist was about to launch

---

* In some post-war accounts this helper is identified as Monsieur Lefèvre. It seems unlikely that he could have been able to help both 1 Troop and C Troop at around the same time, and he was not a gendarme. It's most likely that C Troop's assistant was another patriotic Frenchman.

into a tirade of his own when both of them were silenced by bursts of small arms fire. Men dropped on to the road, some hurriedly searching for targets, others spurting blood. Someone shouted and pointed at a house, and within seconds Brens, Thompsons and Lee Enfields were pouring fire at its windows and doorways. As men started to jump forward under the covering fire, Gilchrist heard a rumbling behind him and turned to see the welcome sight of another one of the Shermans. Instructions were passed to the crew and the tank lurched forward and demolished the building with a well-placed shell, the roof collapsing on the unfortunate occupants.

The streets were more built up now and interruptions became more frequent. As he crouched alongside a low wall, Murdoch McDougall noticed that the muffled blasts of mortar bombs had been replaced with the louder explosions of field artillery shells coming from inland. Ahead of him a man suddenly stood upright, clutching his stomach, then fell forward. As the man in front turned to see what had happened a bullet struck him in the head. The other commandos frantically searched the windows opposite before a tank rumbled past and, barely pausing, put a shell through the window of a house. The enemy fire ceased and the commandos moved on.

Like the French troops, 4 Commando's basic plan was to head east through the town before turning to assault the battery from the south. C Troop would clear the way up to the jagged anti-tank ditch protecting the battery on its landward side and D Troop would then make the initial assault, securing a crossing over the ditch with their portable bridges and neutralizing the immediate defences. E and F Troops would then follow them across and assault the six 155mm gun positions, E Troop taking the three on the east side, F Troop those on the west. Hopefully the bombardment would have taken out most of the battery already, but only the commandos could make that a certainty.

But as C Troop led D Troop to the left at a junction, the tanks continued straight on along the avenue de Lion, and behind them, E and F Troops followed. McDougall looked uneasily at the next junction. It looked more like a track than a road and he desperately tried to recall the aerial photos he had studied on the ship – was this one of the junctions or not? But too late, the column moved inexorably forward, and within a few minutes found itself at the last junction on the avenue de Lion. A line of craters crossed the road and led into the shattered remains of a house on the corner, the masonry of its walls now scattered across the road leading north. Just beyond the junction the buildings came to an end and the road opened up on to the promenade alongside the canal locks. But the end of the houses was also the end of protection, and as the leading tank lurched on to the junction it was suddenly exposed to withering machine gun fire coming from strongpoint 7's bunkers beside the locks. It was pointless to try and get any further east – there was too much open ground and the locks were a distraction from their principal task. The men dived into the rubble-strewn remains of the house while the tanks crunched brick underneath their tracks as they skewed left and into the side road.

A few minutes later F Troop followed E Troop up the road. Picking his way across the broken masonry, McDougall heard the continuous sound of machine gun and rifle fire up ahead. One of the Sherman tanks was off the track, nearly on its side with its gun pointing uselessly at the ground. A dazed and blood-stained figure stumbled back down the road, his fresh dressings already turning crimson as he passed by his companions without a flicker of recognition.

After a short 300 yards the buildings on the right of the road came to an end and with them the only cover from strongpoint 7. McDougall could see Ouistreham lighthouse much closer than expected and realized they had almost certainly come one junction too far. The DD tank had probably succumbed to the Germans' 50mm anti-tank gun at the foot of the lighthouse, perhaps directed by spotters up at the top. F Troop's leading section switched left, across open ground pock-marked with slit trenches and shell holes, and on to the parallel road they should have been on. Bringing up the rear, McDougall's section followed them across, but as the leading men reached the road machine gun fire sent them scattering. McDougall cursed – up ahead he could see the rest of F Troop disappearing into a cluster of houses, but his section was pinned on the road. He couldn't afford to let the troop get split up now, not when they were so close to their objective.

Orders were rapped out to the section. The Bren gunner and his number two darted across the road and ducked down next to McDougall as machine gun fire splattered into the wall behind them.

'There he is, I just saw the flash when 'e was firing at them two,' said one of the commandos, pointing at a small window in a nearby house.

'The range will be about two fifty, keep firing in bursts while we all cross,' McDougall ordered the Bren team.

While the gunners kept the German MG team down, the first

sub-section crossed the road in small groups, then the next sub-section's Bren team crossed and maintained the fire until, some five minutes later, all of McDougall's team were across. Leaving the Germans to their own devices, McDougall led his men at the double across demolished homes and through gardens torn asunder by giant craters.

Up ahead were C Troop, who had cleared most of the opposition on the main route and already secured several buildings in front of the battery's anti-tank ditch. Captain David Style positioned his men to keep the Germans north of the anti-tank ditch under continuous fire. From a window, Sergeant Patrick Byrne carefully lined up a target through the telescopic scope of his rifle. A German helmet bobbed slightly above a wall and Byrne crooked his finger around the trigger, waiting for the owner to appear again. A second later his target revealed himself, Byrne's finger twitched with just the right amount of pressure on the trigger, and with a jolt the Lee Enfield discharged. The German convulsed suddenly and fell. Operating the rifle bolt, Byrne loaded another bullet into the chamber, scanned to another target, and within seconds made another kill.

While C Troop kept the defenders under pressure, A Troop, equipped with K-guns, was moving towards its planned deployment position, a tall four-storey apartment building on a junction just south of the anti-tank ditch. Arriving at the junction, to their dismay the troop found the building behind a high wall with a locked gate. After a few bullets had failed to make an impression on the lock, Sergeant Major Taff Lewis ordered the men over the wall. The commandos dutifully clambered up, but just as they neared the summit of their endeavour, machine gun bullets ricocheted around them and the commandos tumbled back down. Rolling into a gutter, Bill Bidmead opened fire on the building, certain the enemy must be waiting for them inside. Ricochets flew off the stone exterior until Lewis grabbed the rifle and reprimanded the young private. 'Bloody fool, we're being fired at from a pillbox,' he told him.

While the sergeant major pondered their next move, the welcome sound of clanking tracks came from down the road, and shortly after that a tank lumbered into view.[*] Hurriedly getting the commander's attention, Lewis explained their plight. Even as he did so a fresh burst of machine gun fire struck the tank, sparks flying off the turret and around the flaps on either side of the commander, who fell out of view. There was a brief

---

[*] The tank is unidentified but was possibly one of the Centaur tanks of T Troop, 5 RMASG.

moment of despondency among the commandos, who were convinced the unfortunate tanker must have been killed, but their spirits lifted as the turret traversed to its right. A single shot boomed out, blasting dust off the tank's chassis; further up the street a reciprocal boom raised a cloud of smoke. The commander's head appeared again. 'OK chaps, you can go over now.'

Gratefully, the commandos scrambled over the wall and smashed their way into the house. After rushing up the stairs and into the back rooms they cautiously moved to the windows, where broken glass covered the floors and tattered curtains flapped in the breeze. Crouching and ready to drop down lest they were still observed, the men peered over the windowsills and stared in silent amazement at the lunar landscape in front of them. Only 200 feet away was the anti-tank ditch and beyond it a cratered mess of sand and rubble. Only a few buildings were still standing. Most of those that hadn't been pulled down by the Germans had been obliterated by the earlier bombardment. Hundreds of bomb and shell craters of all different sizes covered the area in every direction, huge blankets of light sand and concrete dust carpeting roads, gardens and rooftops around the giant pits. And in the centre of this otherworldly landscape stood a single white tower – the strongpoint's observation and range-finding tower had somehow escaped the lethal destruction.

A Troop hurriedly started deploying their K-guns, the top-floor windows giving them an almost completely uninterrupted view across 4 Commando's objective. Down below, D Troop were deploying in preparation to make the initial assault. Porteous made his way to a position overlooking the anti-tank ditch and cautiously raised his head. His troop had brought with them a pair of custom-designed foot-wide collapsible aluminium bridges in order to cross the anti-tank ditch, and he knew that the destruction of one of them on the beach would severely hamper their assault. How badly he hadn't been able to guess until he saw the obstacle, and as he inspected the ditch the situation looked bleak. It was approximately 10 feet deep and 15 feet wide, with sloping concrete sides. The commandos might be able to crawl down and back up, but it would be difficult. Then, to his amazement and utter relief, he spied a pair of plank bridges already lying across the ditch, almost certainly left in place by engineers working on the ditch or even as a convenience for troops stationed in the battery. Both had been lucky to survive the bombardment – one was only yards from the lip of a sizeable crater. While Portman was glad to see them, he cursed the one collapsible bridge that the troop had struggled to carry for the last mile. The unwieldy apparatus had caused three of its bearers to be hit by snipers, and now it wasn't even needed.

D Troop was poised, ready for the assault. On their right A Troop opened up, the clattering rapid fire of their K-guns pouring fire on to the defender's positions. Flashes of tracer streaked through the clouds of acrid smoke laid by the troop's 2-inch mortars, across the anti-tank ditch and bounced off concrete emplacements as the two assault sections stormed across the bridges and rushed the nearest enemy positions.

Faced with a storm of bullets and a troop of charging men, the German defence was unenthusiastic. Defying the recent order to fight to the last man, Unteroffizier Helmut Schmidt remained in the trench below his 20mm flak gun. Like many of his colleagues, he waited for the attackers to overrun his position and take him prisoner. Others weren't given the chance. Commandos rushed their pillboxes and crouched below the embrasures. Pulling the pins from their Mills bombs, they let the lever flick away and then counted for a second or two before pushing the grenades through the small openings, giving the occupants no time to return them.

Amid the clatter of sub-machine guns and thud of grenades, D Troop quickly secured a slim bridgehead across the ditch. A Very light flare arced through the air to indicate their success and call up the following troops. A Troop ceased fire and watched from their elevated viewpoint as the lead commandos advanced on the concrete tower. From their position they could see Germans moving around on the rooftop, safely out of view from the ground. Sporadic bursts of .303 forced the defenders to keep their heads down, but there was nothing the gunners could do to stop them throwing grenades over the parapet. They watched helplessly as the stick grenades pirouetted through the air. Down below, Porteous looked across to where one of his section commanders, Lieutenant Michael Burness, moved along the base of the tower with his men, seeking an entrance or a way of smoking out the occupants. The German potato masher grenades clattered down among them and in the short blasts and puffs of smoke that followed the young lieutenant was cut down. Porteous, who had been best man at Burness's wedding only a few months before, was crestfallen. Commandos bombarded the tower with PIATs, and wireless calls to the mortar troop on the avenue de Lion brought a pattern of bombs on to it, but the thick concrete walls had barely been dented by the earlier bombardment and they weren't going to crumble now.

E Troop now rushed across the anti-tank ditch and moved through D

Troop's positions on the right of the tower, ready to tackle their three gun positions. Hot on their heels came F Troop, with McDougall's section lagging just behind. As they crossed the ditch McDougall noted with grim resignation the tall concrete tower and the hail of grenades continuing to twirl over the parapet. Ahead he could see the rest of the troop, moving on the tower's left to take the three western guns, commandos appearing and disappearing as they crossed the moonscape of craters. Gamely he led his section on, sliding down the soft earth of a crater and then scrambling up the other side, across a short piece of undisturbed garden and then into the next pit. Small arms fire echoed all around but with no obvious origin to fire back at. Then, just as he dropped into a new crater, the clearer sound of a machine gun announced a hail of bullets that kicked up the soft earth. Quickly looking around, McDougall could see they were now level with the front-facing observation slit of the tower and, out of sight of the K-guns, a German machine gun had been set up to hit the commandos in the flanks. He looked around for his Bren teams, but one was already zeroing in on the tower. Bullets clattered against the concrete around the slit as one, then two Brens sought to neutralize this new threat. Inside, standing on crates so that they could see through the high slit, the German gunners ducked as bullets pinged off the concrete embrasure.

Up ahead the leading sections were engaging the defenders in the personnel bunkers. The various shelters had been well placed to provide supporting fire for one another and were constructed with low profiles so that some positions were only revealed to the commandos when they came under fire from them. Meanwhile A Troop continued to pour fire into the outer defences. Leaning out of one of the upper-floor windows, Bidmead only realized what a tempting target he made when a bullet thwacked past him and into the chest of a commando who had just come up the stairs behind. He wisely moved to another vantage point.

The Bren guns fought their own private battle with the tower and McDougall was plotting the next move when one of his men cried out, 'They're coming back!' He chanced a look over the lip of the crater and sure enough the rest of F Troop were picking their way back across the tortured ground towards him. As they did so a new sound overtook the background noise of small arms fire. In a few seconds a thin whistle turned into a roaring scream and a great explosion rent the ground. More followed, and with horror McDougall realized an artillery bombardment was coming down on them. As Gilchrist dived for cover he saw a small group of men thrown aside like ragdolls, but watched with relief when all but one got back up again and immediately went to the aid of their fallen companion. Fearing the worst, one of the artillery officers attached to 4 Commando tried to get in touch with the HQ ships offshore to call off the bombardment, but such efforts were wasted. The warships had long since moved on to targets further inland – at that moment HMS *Scorpion*, which had fired so many shells so ineffectually at Bass, was trying to reach their own Forward Officer Bombardment for a target, but without any success. Perhaps one of the defenders had managed to get a message to the other German batteries and called for artillery fire on their own position. With the defenders still in their bunkers and the attackers in the open, it was no more dangerous to the Germans than it was to a tank crew if a friendly soldier emptied his machine gun to deal with enemy infantry swarming over the hull.

The commandos scurried from shell hole to shell hole, the undulating landscape protecting them from the blasts and sprays of shrapnel. Captain Coulson dived into McDougall's shell hole. 'Where the hell have you been?' he yelled above the tumult. It was a rhetorical question. 'They've taken the big guns out, so there's nothing we can do here.' McDougall was stunned. No guns? On the eastern side of the battery E Troop had just discovered the same thing. Next to the thick casemates still under construction – one a skeleton of reinforcing steel rods and with timber moulding in place, probably ready for the concrete to be poured that very day – the three open gun positions were empty. In some were dummy guns, simple constructions made from tree trunks and telegraph poles, but good enough to fool a reconnaissance aeroplane.

Back at the main junction an excited Frenchman explained to the Commando HQ that the Germans had removed the guns only three or four days earlier, and placed them a few miles inland. In fact 21 Army Group knew that three had most probably been removed as late as 1 June. The other three had, as the civilian claimed, been removed only days before. Nevertheless the rangefinder was installed in the observation tower, large stocks of ammunition had been left in place, and returning the guns would have been less than a day's work for the gunners of 1 Battery 1260 Coastal Artillery Regiment. It was probably the weeks of aerial bombardment that had persuaded the Germans to withdraw the guns until the new casemates were completed – so in one way the RAF and USAAF had succeeded in neutralizing the battery. In another it hadn't: observers who visited the battery a few days after its capture found that the aerial and naval attacks had not been especially accurate and that very little material damage had been done to the bunkers, magazines and even the open gun positions. Only one of the latter showed signs of bomb damage and it's quite possible that if the guns had been in place some – if not all – of them would have been operational when 4 Commando arrived.

None of this mattered to 4 Commando. As the barrage tailed off they started to mop up the German defenders. Unteroffizier Guswich's squad threw aside their light machine gun and sidearms and emerged from the bunker, the first time it had been safe to leave since 05:00. C Troop had already taken numerous prisoners in the south of the battery including, to the commandos' surprise, Italians – labourers pressed into service by Organization Todt to work on the defences. A number of East Europeans in German uniform also emerged – a quarter of 1260's battery were Poles. Zenon Dushinski gladly surrendered and ditched his equipment as he left. Meanwhile, medics from both sides moved across the battlefield, commandos working alongside Germans even while some of the latter's companions continued to snipe from their hiding places. Occasional shells still came down, making the battery an unhealthy place to remain, and unable to secure the observation post and a few other bunkers, the commandos marched their prisoners across the anti-tank ditch and withdrew. One of the last shells came down behind Bidmead and his section as they carried a wounded man out of their building, blasting them all to the ground. When he got back up, two others didn't. Another stared aghast at his stump of an arm that had just been amputated by shrapnel.*

As they returned to the main junction, Dawson congratulated his men. There was no doubting the quality of Bass as a defensive strongpoint – well designed and built, it was not an easy fortification to overcome. Dawson was pleased that a determined assault had been victorious, but he was to lose his own little battle with Joseph Patterson. The lieutenant colonel was finally persuaded to relinquish full command to Major Ronald Menday and was sent to a Field Dressing Station.

The commandos, exhausted by their endeavours, retired to their packs and rested, taking the opportunity to eat and brew up. Residents started

---

* The defenders quietly remained in the observation tower, their presence seemingly unknown to the British, who occupied Ouistreham later that day. On 9 June an RE party tried to gain access to the tower to recover German equipment and were surprised to find a group of German occupiers waiting to surrender to them.

to come up the street, some bringing libations for their liberators. A man erected a tricolore on his front gate while others fraternized with the French commandos. But Menday knew the men still had work to do, so their rest was brief. Leaving a small detachment to manage the prisoners and assist Patterson and his medical orderlies treating the wounded, he chivvied the troops back to their feet.[3]

As the commandos marched back up the avenue de Lion the noise of battle finally receded and more inhabitants of Ouistreham emerged from their cellars. They searched the rubble of the demolished houses and tended the wounded. The disaster in the woods behind the Hôtel de Normandie was discovered by two members of the civil defence, Leon Tribolet, a barber, and Pierre Desoubeaux, a civil servant and member of the Resistance. Appalled by the destruction, they quickly separated the living from the dead and took those that could be moved to the aid post in the town square near the church.

At that aid post the town's only doctor, seventy-three-year-old Charles Poulain, was assisted by midwife Paule Gérandier and several residents trained in first aid. Blanche Boulet, who worked at the town's bakery, had been trained by the Caen Red Cross, and now she desperately tried to help treat the town's citizens, even while the battle continued nearby. Unfortunately, the chemist's was one of the buildings destroyed in the air raid and there was a shortage of dressings and medicines. Poulain inspected Odette Mousset's injuries as she screamed in agony. They were life-threatening – one leg was shattered and a lung had been punctured by shrapnel. But there was very little he could do to treat her, although there was at least enough morphine to soothe her pain a little.[4]

9

THE RACE TO PEGASUS BRIDGE

ARRIVING AT THE LATERAL ROAD BEHIND THE RUINED HOLIDAY camp, 6 Commando's troop commanders and NCOs quickly moved among their men, sorting out their sections and rousing those who, thinking they could enjoy the briefest of respites, had allowed themselves to sit against the walls and earth banks lining the road. There was no time for rest – already Lovat and Brigade HQ were marching off the beach, Bill Millin's pipes still swirling as they came through the shattered buildings behind them.

First to organize themselves were 3 Troop. Captain Alan Pyman put Lieutenant Donald Colquhoun's section in the lead and sent them straight into the fields behind the road, but as the men dashed into the tussocky grass they soon found themselves in marshy, brackish water. Mud gurgled under their feet and oozed into their boots, replenishing the seawater that still squelched out of their socks with each step. After only 100 yards a large puddle revealed itself to be a deep flooded ditch. Some men attempted to launch themselves across, but their heavy packs held them down and hampered their flight. Others sloshed through, cursing the Norman countryside. A hundred yards further ahead an identical obstacle mocked them, then another, and another. Even the men who had managed to keep themselves vaguely dry, now exhausted by the effort, gave in and waded on.[*]

By now the narrow wood that marked 1 SS Brigade's rendezvous was

---

[*] This was almost certainly the same swamp that Lieutenant Madden and his men had crossed in darkness several hours earlier.

only 400 yards ahead of them, but the sluggish manoeuvring over the boggy terrain made it seem like an unattainable destination. Men moved along the occasional low, weedy hedgerow that offered the flimsiest of shelter from enemy observation, but there was no hope of hiding when they got to the drains. One ditch threatened to drown the first men to enter it and the cumbersome scaling ladders that the troop carried with them had to be deployed as makeshift bridges. Then the enemy added to mother nature's discomfort when they heard ahead of them the low whining of a Nebelwerfer, the mortar bombs falling into the fields east of them.

Their pace quickened. Eventually, soaking and dirty, the commandos reached firmer ground among the trees. A few yards on they found men of the East Yorks resting – some wringing the slimy ditch water out of their clothes – and passed by them and further through the woodland. Pyman didn't give 3 Troop any time to rest; he let the two sections organize themselves into marching order then pressed them on, along a cart track that happily ran in the direction they were going. 'Achtung Minen!' signs were nailed to trees in almost every direction the commandos looked, but there was no stopping for them – Pyman correctly guessed they were a bluff. Then, as the track led them closer to the edge of the wood, the leading scouts spotted two pillboxes in the perpendicular tree line, both covering the open lane to the east that led from La Brèche to Colleville-sur-Orne. This was 3 Troop's first objective.

Pyman briefly studied the two pillboxes through his binoculars. Neither was firing, but they were almost certainly occupied. Scanning the field, he spotted a few dugouts – nothing unusual about that – but in the opposite corner he noticed another apparent strongpoint that covered the rear of the two pillboxes – not one he was expecting. It was obvious it couldn't be ignored, so Colquhoun's section was sent to neutralize it. The commandos quickly and stealthily moved through the trees until they were close enough to assault the strongpoint. Colquhoun studied it briefly – it looked like a work in progress, an unfinished defensive post. But there was no way of knowing if it was definitely unoccupied without getting into it, so under the cover of a flurry of grenades the commandos went in. They found a position that had been vacated in a hurry, equipment and rations still laid out, weapons abandoned. The section raced back to provide support for Lieutenant Marshal Leaphard's men, who were already infiltrating east towards the pillboxes.

The pillboxes were simple affairs, straightforward concrete 'Tobruk' shelters for light machine guns. They were part of the optimistically titled widerstandsnest 19, at the north end of Colleville, guarding the approaches into the town from the lanes from the beach. But unlike the more elaborate strongpoints Cod, Bass, Skate and Sole, 19 was little more than a collection of small bunkers and slit trenches dispersed among the trees outside the town. Occupying them were the men of 4 Company 1 Battalion 736 Grenadier Regiment. The company's organization was dictated by the defences – their commander Oberleutnant Luke[*] had only been able to deploy the men in small rifle or light machine gun groups, rather than complete platoons. Most had spent a sleepless night listening to the alarms and bombing that had started at midnight; the daylight had only brought shells on their positions, and then the sounds and smoke of battle only a mile to the north. Now, scattered and isolated, they awaited the inevitable arrival of enemy infantry. The occupants of the two Tobruks didn't have long to wait – to their horror, the blast of grenade and sub-machine gun fire erupted behind them. The men crouched into the shelter of the concrete pits, expecting the worst.

While a small force provided cover, 2 Section hit the first Tobruk in a wave of grenades. The defenders offered a token resistance but were quickly overpowered when the commandos deployed their flamethrower, which they'd been itching to use. Barely pausing, the commandos rolled over the next Tobruk; this time the terrified occupants surrendered before the flamethrower could be put to use. Pleased with their success, the commandos pulled back to the wood, just as fire was opened on them from a hedge to the east.

Only one field away, Obergefreiter Josef Häger sat in his slit trench. The nineteen-year-old was tired – a combination of the sleepless night and weeks of back-breaking work erecting obstacles on the beaches. He was despondent too: the defences around Colleville that he and his company manned were pathetic. He was only surprised that the bombing hadn't targeted them – just one raid would probably have been sufficient to take out the foxholes and flimsy personnel shelters behind him. Now, with the sound of battle slowly nearing, Häger was unenthusiastic about his chances. But whatever he thought, it was obvious to him that the only way he might survive was if he fought for his life. As soon as enemy troops appeared in range in front of his position he opened fire, spraying his sub-machine gun in their direction, largely indifferent to what it

---

[*] An oberleutnant is broadly equivalent to a lieutenant in the British Army.

might achieve. Occasionally men went down as he fired at them, but whether because of his bullets or in response to them he couldn't tell.

While 3 Troop took care of their objectives, Captain Ronald Hardey's 2 Troop took over the lead of the advance and at 10:15 moved along the track on to the lane from La Brèche to Colleville. As they crept forward they heard the worrying sound of armour somewhere nearby. The commandos went to ground, fingers tensed on triggers and eyes searching for the source. To their relief the sound crystallized from the north and soon, lumbering up the lane, appeared DD tanks of B Squadron 13/18 Hussars.

Time was ticking by, and Lieutenant Colonel Derek Mills-Roberts was anxious to keep 6 Commando moving. Reassured by the armour, 2 Troop advanced on Colleville, moving along the lane towards the houses at the northern end. The reassurance was short-lived as the tanks darted off to attack a mortar position, leaving the troop alone just as a light machine gun opened up from the road on their left. Quickly, as they'd been trained to do, one section provided covering fire while the other moved round the flank and attacked the enemy position with grenades, wiping out the gun crew. But in reaching the gun position, the troop exposed themselves to a stronger position in the woods. Major Bill Coade, 6 Commando's second in command, quickly moved forward and, sticking to tall hedges for cover, led a small party up a narrow track to recce the new threat. Among the trees he spotted two concrete strongpoints, light machine guns poking menacingly through the embrasures while coal scuttle helmets bobbed up and down in surrounding slit trenches. This was a tougher nut to crack. As he briefly considered the best way to neutralize the position, Coade suddenly heard a grenade land nearby. There was no time to react before a flash blinded him and bowled him backwards. He lay on his back, a high-pitched tone ringing in his ears and overriding the muffled sounds of voices and the bark of rifle fire. He opened his eyes, but there was nothing to see. He reached up and, groping around his face, felt warm blood. Then he felt the pain.

Mills-Roberts and his little HQ party had just crept up when the sound of gunfire broke out further down the track. As he closed on the commandos ahead of him, one turned and shouted at him to stop. A few paces more and he would have come level with a gap in the hedge – 'There's a sniper covering that gap,' called his saviour. The CO quickly sprinted across the dangerous opening, but as his batman Eric Smith followed a shot rang out and a bullet thudded into the unfortunate lance corporal's arm.

Mills-Roberts reached Coade, finding a shocking mess of blood and shrapnel wounds. A medic gave him an injection to ease his pain. Then his wireless operator relayed a message: Brigadier Lovat wanted to know the cause of the delay, why had 6 Commando's advance halted? Mills-Roberts knew that while he had his own problems, Lovat's was that the rest of the brigade would start stacking up behind him every time there was a halt. The pressure of being the lead commando, the one chosen to cut through the enemy and forge the path, suddenly pressed on him. Running back to the main road, he found one of 13/18 Hussars' DD tanks and had a quick conflab with its commander. Obediently, the tank moved forward.

Crouched among the small collection of concrete shelters and slit trenches, Feldwebel Wilhelm Dohmen* saw the tank approaching his position. His group of men held an outpost more fragile than the two Tobruks which they'd already seen fall – and there was absolutely nothing any of them could do about tanks. He saw a few men sprinting back from the trenches in the field before he dived into the bottom of his foxhole. Above him he could hear the steel giant crashing through a hedgerow, and then the dreadful boom of its gun.

Mills-Roberts watched as the first shot hit one of the concrete positions, producing a burst of flames followed by a plume of grey concrete dust. Inside, Obergefreiter Ferdinand Klug had just moved to the rear of the small, cramped compartment to find ammunition when the powerful blast smashed into the embrasure and showered him with dozens of metal and concrete splinters. Screaming in pain and shock he fled out of the bunker as, behind him, the tank's turret shifted slightly and then fired a second shot, splitting the pillbox like a rotten apple hit by an arrow. As black and grey smoke drifted across the track the commandos jumped forward, rushing the mediocre defences with grenades. There was no resistance from the shocked defenders – those who survived followed Dohmen's example and gladly raised their arms above their heads.

Josef Häger had abandoned his slit trench and run back to the road that led east to Ouistreham. Between low crouched runs and scrabbles from cover to cover, he turned and sprayed bullets behind him, desperately trying to throw his pursuers off the scent. Arriving at a tall barrier

---

* A feldwebel is broadly equivalent to a senior sergeant rank in the British Army, although a German senior NCO might take on far more responsibility, including platoon command.

of coiled barbed wire strung across the side of the lane, he was appalled to find the body of one of his platoon sergeants, Ruter, who had always delighted in playing the violin for his men. Now his corpse blocked the narrow gap in the wire and Häger, with some revulsion, was obliged to crawl over it to escape. He staggered on to the lane, only to see enemy soldiers to the right. He sprayed his sub-machine gun and raced away once more, round a welcoming bend in the road. After a terrifying run further down the lane, half expecting a hail of bullets to pursue him at any moment, he found familiar faces languishing in a ditch and flopped down beside them. One face was less recognizable – Klug was streaming blood from the dozen tiny metal and concrete splinters that had embedded themselves in his face. The men embraced, until then fearing that the other had almost certainly been killed. Häger spent some time picking the splinters out of his best friend, until Oberleutnant Luke appeared. He was dismayed to find only about twenty men of his company had escaped Colleville but, urging them to make one last effort, he led them to 1 Battalion HQ a little further down the lane at strongpoint 14 (Sole). The trenches and bunkers there would be a safer place to hold out, and he might be able to find out what on earth was happening.

The immediate threat removed, Mills-Roberts helped Coade to his feet and entrusted him to Smith to take back to the beach. 2 Troop were already on the move again, now abandoning the road. A length of barbed wire decorated with numerous 'Achtung Minen!' signs was strung along the verge, blocking the entrance to the small field they needed to pass through. The commandos quickly cut through the overtightened strands, which ruined the blades of a brand-new pair of bolt cutters. The cutters were dumped, along with the flamethrowers and Bangalore torpedoes – now surplus to requirements and an unnecessary burden in the next stage of the advance. Mills-Roberts eyed the minefield sceptically. To his great satisfaction raised square mounds littered the field, evidence of sloppy engineers laying mines and simply replacing the turf without levelling the ground. Two-inch mortars laid smoke as the first troops dashed across the field, dancing between the raised sods of grass.[1]

Brigadier Lord Lovat had watched the progress of 6 Commando as the final troops advanced through the marsh. The Nebelwerfer screamed again, launching its six incendiary missiles into the air. But while the mortar bombs' ear-scything shriek promised much, their accuracy delivered little and the bombs burst into flames, setting fire to the marsh grass, having landed harmlessly short of 6 Commando's men. Somewhere up ahead a machine gun chattered away, the German gunner seemingly firing through any gaps in the trees they were aiming for. Reasoning that 6 Commando would have dealt with it by the time they got there, Lovat led his HQ into the marsh.

Other men were struggling through the wet ground and its bottomless ditches. Lovat came across some wayward troops from 41 Commando, their misplaced landing on Red Beach having led them in completely the wrong direction inland. Even so, Lovat was pleased to see them advancing. Up ahead, threatening tracer whipped across the open ground they needed to cross, barring their advance. For a few minutes they waited in the squelchy sanctuary of a ditch, and it was only when Captain Douglas Robinson appeared behind them that the spell the machine gun had woven was broken. 1 Troop, dragging their clumsy bicycles over the marshy ground and hurling them over the ditches, were undeterred, Robinson encapsulating their mood when he confided to Lovat, 'I'd rather be shot up on a road any day than do this sort of thing.' The occupants of the ditch got out and strode after him. The commandos reached the woodland as the machine gun fire ceased, Lovat deducing that 6 Commando had finally outflanked it. The woods were sparse, most of the trees having been felled after the intelligence photographs they had studied for so long were taken, but some cover was better than no cover, Lovat reasoned, and they began to move forward.

A few hundred yards further on, Obergrenadier Johann Kramarczyk[*] sat among shattered timbers and tree stumps not far from the bunkers he had so recently been ejected from. A farmer from Raciborz in Upper Silesia, Poland, he was far from home but lucky to be alive after the commandos had swept through his position. The streams of men passing by eyed him with varying degrees of mild curiosity, malice and pity, while a nearby guard showed only unwavering alertness, a rifle ready to be used if needed. Presently a taller man appeared, his attendant men including one with a wireless on his back, others with map cases dangling from their shoulders, suggesting he was of some importance. The tall man approached him, conversing with the others in what Kramarczyk recognized as English, but couldn't understand. Another man, pushing a bicycle across the uneven ground, was hailed and the tall man addressed him. The cyclist turned and spoke to Kramarczyk – he recognized it as

---

[*] An obergrenadier is equivalent to a senior private rank.

German, but that was another language he simply didn't understand. He pleaded with the interrogator, stating his nationality as clearly as he could and proffering his paybook. The interrogator flicked through it and frowned, looking a little helpless and despairing before a sudden look of inspiration came across his face. 'Où sont les canons?' he asked. Kramarczyk's heart lifted to hear a language he knew and he started to explain at length his nationality and his story. The interrogator, however, began to look even more helpless and Kramarczyk faltered, but at this point the taller man interrupted, asking a flurry of questions in French. Now it was Kramarczyk who felt helpless. He had no idea where the artillery was positioned – even as they fired over their heads, the positions of the numerous batteries were a mystery to him. He was only a simple farmer – he had been forced into the German army, and the officers had little regard for him and his countrymen; he wasn't privy to information like that. He poured all of this out to the tall man, but already he seemed to have lost interest. After a few more questions about units of which Kramarczyk again had little to no knowledge, they moved on. It was only a little later that he realized the cyclist had kept his paybook.*

Lovat strode on, reaching the outskirts of Colleville to find tanks and infantry of 1 Suffolk milling among the stragglers of 6 Commando, and he stopped briefly to chat to Lieutenant Colonel Richard Goodwin. But 6 Commando were held up to the east and Lovat sent blunt signals to Mills-Roberts, anxious that progress should continue as fast as possible. Time was ticking away and they were already behind schedule.

Up ahead, 2 Troop were moving quickly through the thin orchards behind the minefield. Almost immediately they came under fire from some dugouts further up the lane they had just abandoned. Ronald Hardey quickly led a section in the enemy's direction with the intention of outflanking the position but Mills-Roberts, striding behind him, reined him in. 'Your job is to get on,' he told Hardey. 'We'll look after the flanks.' 2 Troop was to cut a path – the rest of 6 Commando would widen it. Hardey turned his men away and steered them south.

6 Commando continued through the woods, past fresh dugouts and signs of recent felling. Another defensive site was just ahead of them and

---

* The tall man was Lovat and the cyclist was Corporal Peter Masters, originally Peter Arany, an Austrian Jew who had fled to England and joined 10 (Inter-Allied) Commando and was now attached to 1 Troop 6 Commando as a translator.

Mills-Roberts watched approvingly as the lead troop deployed in cover while the following troop readied themselves to move forward. The intelligence map wasn't entirely clear what the site was – which meant that the aerial photographs weren't entirely clear either – and Lovat's schedule burned in the back of Mills-Roberts's mind. But there was little to be gained by blundering into a possible enemy position. A rifle shot followed by a burst of light machine gun fire confirmed the commandos' caution. The advancing troop went to ground while the covering troop opened fire, the chatter of small arms heightening the urgency of the encounter. Up ahead the enemy troops ducked down into their trenches, the weight of fire too much for them to compete with. None of them saw a third troop's grenades as they stormed the position until it was too late.

2 Troop picked up the advance again. It was approaching 11:30 as they turned on to an east-west track, the tree-lined avenue suddenly more open and exposed than the scrub behind them. With a certain inevitability a sniper's rifle sang out and a commando just ahead of Mills-Roberts slumped to the ground. Men on either side of the track dropped to one knee and poured fire forward of them, someone scoring a hit on a shadowy figure in the scrub ahead. Gripping his arm in pain and apologizing to his section, Lieutenant Peter Cruden made his way back to the beach while Mills-Roberts pushed 2 Troop forward. Barely 200 yards further on, movement was spotted in the bushes lining the track and once again the troop went to ground and poured fire forward. Invisible foreign voices shouted and faded as the enemy broke and scattered into the woods.

Saint-Aubin-d'Arquenay was just over 1,000 yards south of them, but the thick scrub and woodland of the Bois du Caprice would necessitate a route along narrow paths of almost a mile. Turning off the track into the dense undergrowth, scouts jogged from bush to bush, ever wary of snipers. The rest of the troop followed in single file, silently manoeuvring down faint paths between gorse bushes, one eye to the flanks, the other on the commando ahead of them, lest they take a wrong turn and find themselves alone. More than once the thin trails marked on the maps failed to concur with the physical reality of the woods, and routes had to be chosen on best guesses. Occasional sniper shots continued to bother them, the enemy optimistically loosing off a shot before withdrawing deeper into the bush. A movement in the scrub once again brought down a hail of fire and a small group of Germans emerged almost sheepishly, happy to surrender themselves. Even so, Mills-Roberts was more than glad of the route they'd chosen. Avoiding the main roads and major settlements, they were making good progress towards the bridges.

At midday, 2 Troop emerged from the densest part of the woods and saw the picturesque rooftops and low spire of Saint-Aubin's church ahead of them. Birds still sang in the woods behind them and for a brief moment the idyllic rural Norman scene appeared totally removed from the events of the day. But then a menacing noise drowned out the gentle sounds of nature. Somewhere ahead of them the low booms of field guns reverberated behind the dense hedgerows.

Moving quickly forward, the commandos identified the source of the disturbance in a field just off their line of advance. Thick bushes and scrub obscured 2 Troop's view of the battery, but equally protected them from observation as they advanced past it and wheeled round to attack from the rear. In a flurry of sub-machine gun fire and grenades they stormed the guns, the shocked crews offering no resistance. To 2 Troop's surprise they found the crews weren't all German or even the Eastern European conscripts they had already come across – among them were Italians, still in their Regio Esercito army uniforms. The guns, part of 1/1260 Battery that only an hour ago 4 Commando had expected to find in Ouistreham, were spiked. Pushing their prisoners ahead of them, the troop continued into Saint-Aubin.

Although it had not been a target either for the navy or the air force, stray shots had hit Saint-Aubin. Here and there smoke drifted lazily from skeletal timber roofs, devoid of tiles that now lay across the road.[*] Even so, the locals were happy to see them and came into the streets. A middle-aged Frenchman pressed a bottle into the hands of 3 Troop's Philip Pritchard, who took a long and willing gulp. But instead of the light refreshing cider he expected, he almost gagged as the raw spirit hit the back of his throat. Somewhat less refreshed than he'd hoped, he handed the bottle of calvados back to the beaming and newly liberated resident.[2]

As 6 Commando spilled into Saint-Aubin from the north, Brigade HQ came into the town from the east.[†] Having escaped Colleville, Captain

---

[*] The most likely cause of the damage was naval fire directed by air spotters who observed 1/1260 Battery.
[†] Lovat's exact route from the north of Colleville-sur-Orne to Saint-Aubin is not explicitly stated in the war diary, his memoir, or the accounts from anyone else in

Douglas Robinson's bicycle troop had mounted their steeds and raced off down the road ahead of them, leaving the small party of footsloggers on their own. As they moved up to the first houses and barns on either side of the lane, Lovat realized that his small forces were out on a limb. Scouts were sent into the town to recce the route ahead, while Captain Harper-Gow was placed at the back of the column with a small rearguard. The entire HQ troop, signallers, engineers, even men of the postal section, gripped their weapons tightly and watched their surroundings intently.

Small arms fire sounded from the other end of the town, indicating 6 Commando's presence ahead of them. But as they moved further into the town, a solitary sniper's bullet smashed into the wall, narrowly missing Lovat's head. Captain Robert Holmes of the Royal Marines Engineer Commando spotted the culprit and, yelling a warning, sprinted across the road to a house on the corner of a junction. Someone threw a grenade through the window and as soon as it detonated Holmes kicked the door in and sprayed the room with Tommy gun fire. There was a pause, then the sound of more muffled fire before Holmes's head poked out from an upstairs window. 'This one was dressed in civvies, but he had a Jerry rifle,' he called. Then his voice became more alarmed. 'My God, I'm coming down. More Huns are advancing over the fields to the south.'

Some hurried spotting revealed a platoon or so of men advancing across the fields on the south-west side of Saint-Aubin, while horse-drawn carts waited in a side street.* They appeared to be oblivious to the commandos' presence, but Lovat realized there was little choice but for Brigade HQ to engage them. The fact they didn't appear to have been spotted gave them a considerable advantage and the best bet, he reasoned, was to let

---

his party. However, Captain Evans, AFPU, was attached to Brigade HQ, and his photos from D-Day suggest that he remained with them on the way to the bridges (his photos depict tanks in Saint-Aubin and a horse and cart, both described by Lovat). Three of his photos show locations leading to Colleville's town centre and from there the only route leading to the bridges is the rue de Saint-Aubin, strongly suggesting this is the route Brigade HQ took. An annotated map among Mills-Roberts's papers (GB0099 KCLMA Mills-Roberts) shows HQ's route on the same path. This matches Lovat's statement that when 'Derek dealt with one end of the long street [in Saint-Aubin], my party came in at the other' (Lovat, p.317). Lieutenant Colonel Goodwin also commented that when he met Lovat at the north end of Colleville, 'a little later he followed up through the village and struck off eastwards' (Nicholson, p.99).

* It seems quite likely that this small force was part of I/736 Battalion's ration train, which was based in Saint-Aubin.

them come in close and ambush them. Men dropped their weighty rucksacks and moved into the gardens facing the fields, a K-gun was deployed in a shed, and several dozen rifles poked through hedges facing the advancing enemy. Lovat's command was passed down the line – wait until they're close and target the identifiable officers and NCOs first.

Once the platoon was within a stone's throw the commandos opened up. Lovat fired away with his American M1 carbine, delighted with its semi-automatic fire, and saw a fair-haired young officer spin around as a volley of shots hit him before he collapsed into the corn.* At least a dozen of the grey-clad figures collapsed with him, easy targets who had unwisely bunched together. The rest dived into the corn of their own volition, occasional rifle shots keeping them there until a few minutes later the rumble of an approaching tank encouraged them to surface again with arms aloft. The commandos rounded them up, finding most of them to be Russians and – judging from the smell – in poor health. But they were willing prisoners and the commandos were happy to liberate their horses and carts, quickly employing them to carry the heavy wireless sets, excess packs and ammunition. Now, with the arrival of a couple of Sherman DDs that had followed them into town, the Brigade HQ continued through Saint-Aubin with a renewed sense of authority.[3]

45 Commando had followed Lovat through the marsh, enduring the random blasts of the Nebelwerfer and the occasional attention of snipers as they crossed the ditches. Stragglers hurried to keep up, and as they struggled across the final few ditches the sound of Captain Brian White's hunting horn echoed across the fields, the tune of 'Gone Away' the rallying call for anyone within earshot.† At the head of 3 Commando, Captain Keith Ponsford's 3 Troop heard the call as they hauled their bicycles over the ditches, a task made even harder by the additional weight of the 3-inch mortar

---

* It's often said that Lovat carried a hunting rifle on D-Day, an image reinforced in *The Longest Day*. In his memoir he clearly recounts carrying a US carbine (p.320). Nor is there any evidence he wore a white sweater, as depicted in the film. Footage shot by Sergeant Norman Clague (AFPU) on 7 June (IWM A70 36-2) shows Lovat in standard battledress and a normal army shirt, with what certainly appears to be an M1 carbine over his shoulder. Curiously, the same film shows Lieutenant Colonel Mills-Roberts with a US M1 Garand rifle.

† Anyone who has seen the film *A Bridge Too Far* will be familiar with the melody of 'Gone Away', which is played by Anthony Hopkins/Lieutenant Colonel John Frost on a hunting horn.

bombs and inflatable dinghies fitted to the racks. Although 3 Commando would bring up the rear of the brigade's advance, 3 Troop's task was to ride ahead of their colleagues and recce a route for 3 Commando, as well as prepare a crossing if the bridges were down. Reaching the rendezvous in the small woods, the men feverishly pulled the reeds out of the chains and wheel spokes, and as soon as they were ready, Ponsford led his troop off. Behind them came Peter Young and his HQ group, leading the rest of the men on foot. In the woods they found 45 Commando, the men crouching as a new barrage of mortar fire from some unseen enemy started to range on them. But while 6 Commando dealt with 4 Company's defences, the following units were forced to wait and endure the bombardment. Young grew impatient and eventually could wait no more. Leaving his second in command, Major Pooley, to lead 3 Commando, Young struck off with a small party to find out what was happening and recce a route. He passed through 45 Commando's men just as they were approaching Colleville, then found a quiet lane into Saint-Aubin.*

Douglas Robinson's 1 Troop of 6 Commando wheeled out of Saint-Aubin and down the rue du Bac du Port. Only 100 yards from the town's last buildings, the low wall on their right ran out and the road continued into the distance, utterly devoid of cover. But there was no other route to take, and the cycle troop pressed their boots into the peg pedals and pushed on. The sun had burned through the clouds and risen high in the sky nearly directly ahead of them, the commandos' berets doing little to shield their eyes from its glare. Their rucksacks, suspended in the handlebar racks, sagged on to the front wheels, and the tyres buzzed uncomfortably as they dragged against the canvas brake. In between hauling the bags back on to the racks, the commandos glanced left and right into fields of greeny-gold corn, interspersed with bright red poppies. This pastoral charm was disturbed when Corporal Peter Masters noticed piles of German Teller mines lying by the side of the road, seemingly left there ready to be laid the moment an invasion began. It appeared that the Allies must have taken the defenders completely by surprise.

Half expecting to be strafed from above, the troop followed the flat and level road until finally it began to curve to the left and, ahead of

---

* Like Lovat's, Young's exact route into Saint-Aubin is uncertain. Lovat believed Young was to his left, suggesting he might have taken the track immediately east of the rue de Saint-Aubin.

them, they could see the slight crest as it dropped into the broad Orne valley. As the panoramic view opened up and the low tower of Église Notre-Dame du Port appeared above the hedgerows, the men let gravity do the work and coasted down the slope. Then the illusion of a carefree ride in the countryside was shattered by the sound of gunfire echoing in the small hamlet below. Robinson quickly ordered his troop off their bikes and the commandos threw them aside as they deployed down the tall hedges on either side of the road. Looking around, Robinson's eyes alighted on Masters, who had been pestering him all morning, asking if there were any tasks he could fulfil.

'Now's your chance to do something – go into that village and see what's going on.'

'How many people shall I take?' asked Masters.

'No, just you alone.'

Masters perused the view ahead. 'OK. I think I'll get into the village along that field over there—' he started to explain.

'No, I don't think you've got the idea,' Robinson interjected. 'I want you to go down the road into the village to see what's going on.'

A morbid thought dawned on Masters. Did Robinson simply want him to reveal the enemy positions by exposing himself to them? He was, after all, a stranger in the troop; an Austrian Jew from 3 Troop 10 Commando, he had been attached to 6 Commando just before embarkation – primarily as a translator – and had ended up with 1 Troop simply because he could ride a bicycle. Still, as the eyes of the rest of the troop watched, there seemed to be little other option. He reluctantly stood up and started down the road.

Masters fingered the trigger of his Tommy gun gently. The hedges on either side of the road were thick and impenetrable, the wall across the T junction ahead of him was too high to vault. With no cover and no idea where the Germans might be, there was only one option left open to him – bluff. As he advanced to the T junction and turned right towards the small crossroads that was the effective centre of the tiny village, he called out in German, 'Come out! Give yourselves up! You are completely surrounded. Throw away your weapons and come out with your hands up. The war is over for you.'

There was no immediate reaction, and Masters nervously eyed the sides of the road. He moved a little closer to the crossroads, where the houses on each corner obscured his view of what lay ahead. A sudden movement caught his eye and he flicked his head round to see a German appear from behind a low wall. There was a quick and random spray of automatic fire from his Schmeisser and Masters dropped to one knee, snapping his weapon up and squeezing the trigger. There was a single judder as the first round fired, before the trigger sickeningly stiffened behind his finger. The gun had jammed. Fortunately, the helmeted figure had already dropped back into cover. Masters frantically cocked and re-cocked the Tommy gun. The German popped up again, barely exposing more than his helmet and randomly spraying his bullets out into the road. Masters tore his eyes off the wall and looked into the breech of his gun, horrified to find two crumpled rounds jammed together. He ripped them out and re-cocked the gun, bringing it to his shoulder.

The crisis felt like it had gone on for an eternity, but in reality it had lasted mere seconds and was already over. Even as he steadied his sights bullets thwacked into the wall and Masters turned to see 1 Troop storming down the road towards him, a tall Bren gunner leading the charge and firing from the shoulder. The commandos swept past him and up to the junction, where the Bren gunner spun on his heel and sprayed to the left, almost at his own feet. Masters quickly recovered himself and moved up to join them. While the others tried to storm a house on the junction, Masters found the Bren gunner's target – a pair of wounded German gunners lying behind their machine gun. From the steadily growing pool of blood it was immediately obvious to Masters that one would not be suitable for interrogation, but the other was already talking. A young man – a boy, really – from Styria in eastern Austria pleaded that he hadn't even fired the weapon in front of him. Masters picked up a belt of ammunition next to the gun.

'The others,' the gunner begged. 'They ran. The feldwebel said stay here, and we did, and he ran away.'

Masters regarded him cynically, but the tall Bren gunner was more sympathetic.

'How do you say I'm sorry in German?' he asked.

'Es tut mir Leid,' replied Masters automatically, then corrected himself to something simpler: 'Or Verzeihung.'

The tall commando stammered the word out, while near by Germans lobbed grenades through windows at his colleagues.[4]

Meanwhile, 3 Troop's pace had quickened as they left the shattered edge of Saint-Aubin. The sun's glow warmed the men's damp battledress, and they tugged uncomfortably at their sweaty and itchy collars. Even as their rucksacks had slowly dried they had steadily become heavier and heavier, and their wet boots dragged at their leaden feet. The bark of rifle shots, the clatter of machine guns and the occasional crump of explosions rolled over the ridge as they jogged onwards, accompanied by the occasional call of a bugle somewhere in the distance.

As the high ground started to descend into the Orne valley and the church tower came into view, the sound of small arms fire echoed through the streets below them.* Captain Pyman quickly decided that le Port's centre was best avoided and led his troop around to the left, following the slope down to the canal on the north side of the village. Jumping from hedgerow to hedgerow they doubled across a last field and at last saw, through small gaps in the trees, the steel girders of the canal bridge. Then one of the scouts spotted something else. Some men were moving around in a hedgeline 200 yards away, and the troop went to ground. Eyes strained for identifying signs and then Pyman, aided by his binoculars, spotted a red beret. He pulled a small Union Jack from his blouse pocket and waved it enthusiastically, at which point the airborne forces cheered and clambered through the bushes.† Pyman led his leading section forward and found to his surprise both a brigadier and a lieutenant colonel. Nigel Poett, commander of 5 Parachute Brigade, welcomed Pyman enthusiastically. 'We are *very* pleased to see you,' he intoned, aware that his men's hold on this isolated position was tenuous. Characteristically adding a touch of melodrama, Pyman looked at his watch and replied, 'I'm afraid we're a few minutes late, sir.' The assembled men smiled, as the first swirl of distant bagpipes carried on the wind.‡

Champing at the bit, Lovat had advanced ahead of his Brigade HQ

---

* It's possible that the gunfire 3 Troop heard was from 1 Troop, although the exact order the troops arrived in is unknowable. It's equally possible that 3 Troop arrived first and heard combat between the airborne forces and the Germans.
† The paratroopers, commandos and all of 2 East Yorks' section commanders were issued with a small Union Jack with which to identify themselves to each other, although it's not clear if other units were also issued with them.
‡ The meeting between Pyman, Brigadier Poett and Lieutenant Colonel Pine-Coffin is recounted in 3 Troop's report, written by section commanders Lieutenants Leaphard and Colquhoun. That the troop met the airborne forces near the canal is confirmed by commandos Sid Dann and Geoffrey Scotson (Barber, p.230), although they do not identify the airborne officers. Sadly neither Poett nor Pine-Coffin recount the meeting in their memoirs. Only 3 Troop's report, submitted on 2 July 1944, recounts Pyman's quip about being a few minutes late. See Appendix 1 for more detail.

with a small party of bodyguards and his piper, Bill Millin. They marched towards le Port, Millin playing 'Lochanside' and following in the welcome wake of the 13/18 Hussars tanks. Small arms fire echoed up the road, its volume gradually overpowering the pipes as they closed on the T junction where not long before Peter Masters had made his lonely walk. Scattered fire came from the right and Millin abandoned his tune, ducking along the wall and up to the gable end of the seventeenth-century barn – the village's northernmost building. Mills-Roberts and his HQ party, who had followed 2 Troop into the village, watched anxiously around the corner of the building towards the crossroads where the cycle troop was already engaged. The tanks were a welcome addition to the fight and the lead Sherman lurched forward on to the crossroads. Commandos enthusiastically pointed out the house that had so recently repelled their assault and the turret turned obligingly, the 75mm gun's muzzle practically next to the stone wall. The gunner stamped on the firing button and the 75mm shell went straight through the wall in a cloud of masonry dust. Fire was coming from the church tower, and the turret traversed again, the barrel elevated, and with a sharp roar blasted open the fragile stonework that had already been damaged in the early morning's fighting. As more commandos came out from behind the tank and moved forward, the scattered German defenders' fire slackened. Airborne soldiers, many down to their last handful of rounds, emerged from their positions and cheered as Millin started to inflate his pipes again.[5]

It had taken the leading commandos some four hours to land on a beach still under fire and make a 5-mile journey through enemy territory – an impressive feat. Their arrival at the bridges provided a valuable morale boost to the airborne troops holding them, as enemy forces had spent the morning probing the thin defences. However, the commandos did not linger and quickly made their way over the bridges and north-east to expand the bridgehead on the Bréville Ridge overlooking Band Beach.

10

BUILDING A BEACHHEAD

LIEUTENANT JOHN MADDEN AND HIS MEN LAY OUT UNDER THE trees, still somewhat dazed from their experience of the barrage. After the bombers had passed there had been only minutes of respite before, like a cry from hell, the rockets had screamed through the sky, thousands of them falling less than 500 yards away. The earth seemed to erupt under their weight and a giant cloud of smoke billowed to the south and rolled across the landscape, carrying with it dirt, debris and wood splinters that fell like hailstones within a tornado. Then the barrage that so far had been largely north of them started to creep south. Shells fell only 100 yards to the east, bright flashes illuminating the clouds of dirt like sheet lightning.

This was the last hurrah of the bombardment, which finally lifted a few minutes later. The booms of heavy-calibre shells echoed away, to be replaced by the rattle of heavy machine gun fire and the dull thuds of smaller anti-tank guns on the beach 1,000 yards to the north. The clouds of smoke thinned and slowly the view became clear, revealing black smoke rising from the small settlement near the shore.

Being under bombardment is a shattering and exhausting experience, and once it had lifted, the paratroopers took the opportunity to recover. Madden lay under a tree trying to process what had happened and comprehend the fact that he had survived it. The fighting on the beach seemed to recede and he lost track of time until, like a voice interrupting a dream, he heard Private Belec calling to him: 'There's a body of men crossing our front.'

The commander of 9 Platoon snapped back into reality. The men took up positions on the edge of the orchard and, with his binoculars, Madden inspected these new figures through the haze of smoke and dust that lingered like a morning mist over the fields, fuelled by the fighting on the beach. At first it looked like German troops withdrawing inland, but as they came closer the olive drab uniforms became clearer. Were they, he thought? Yes, they were – British troops! He fumbled in the pocket of his jump smock for a small Union Jack and waved it above him. In the field, one of the soldiers stopped and waved, then beckoned him forward.[*1]

While 4 Commando attacked one battery in Ouistreham, 8 Infantry Brigade were required to silence two more. After securing Queen Red Beach, 2 East Yorks were to move south, take out Sole (strongpoint 14) and move on to capture Daimler (strongpoint 12) and its 155mm guns housed in thick concrete casemates. Meanwhile, 1 Suffolk needed to advance to Colleville-sur-Orne to secure the town and both Morris (strongpoint 16) with its 100mm guns and Hillman (strongpoint 17) on Périers Ridge.

Having made it off the beach, 1 Suffolk had moved directly down the track behind Cod towards the woods north of Hermanville as planned. Reaching the rendezvous in the first wood shortly after 09:00, Lieutenant Colonel Richard Goodwin had been dismayed – although not entirely surprised – to find that most of the trees had been felled and there was very little cover to be had at all.[†] Seeking alternatives, he had spied an orchard only 300 yards to the south. While not quite as dense as they had hoped for, the trees were still a safer bet than the deforested field they were in. He had quickly issued instructions to the company commanders he was with, a small party was left to guide the following men, and scouts had led the men across a field and through a hedgerow to the orchard.

Goodwin followed his leading troops into the small plantation where a lieutenant presented himself. Unlike his own troops, this man wore the camouflaged smock and helmet of an airborne soldier, and both he and his small band of men seemed delighted to see the Suffolks. Madden quickly explained his story, and although he wasn't expecting to see paratroopers quite so soon, Goodwin wasn't completely surprised to have come across the Canadians. After he had passed on what little information he could, Madden asked exactly where they were. Unfolding a map,

---

* It's not clear if 1 Suffolk were also issued with the small Union Jack flags, and it should be remembered they were not expected to encounter paratroopers. Madden only records that after a cautious wave of his own flag he 'received the proper reply'.
† Almost certainly to provide timber for the obstacles that men like Günther Fischer had been working on.

Goodwin pointed to the little orchard and Madden's eyes widened. They were some 6 miles from their drop zone – more than 8 miles if they wanted to cross the Orne with dry feet. And whether the bridges were in Allied or enemy hands was anyone's guess right now. As there was no immediate hope of rejoining his unit, Madden quickly volunteered his men's services to Goodwin, who gratefully accepted and allocated them to D Company.

The Suffolks had trained extensively for their task, with each company specializing in the roles for which it was required. A and B Companies had practised assaults in detail, assisted by D Company, who had specially trained in breaching techniques to get through the outer defences of strongpoints. C Company had practised urban fighting – in particular house clearance. Now it was time to reap the rewards of all this preparation. D Company's initial task would be to move south to the edge of the woods between Hermanville and Colleville and establish a base of fire from which to dominate Morris. C Company would then move along their left flank to enter the northern end of Colleville and clear strongpoint 19. After that they would sweep south through the village and clear it for B Company who, with a pioneer demolition team and one of D Company's platoons attached as a breaching force, would assault Morris from the east. Once the battery was neutralized, A Company, with another of D Company's platoons and pioneer force attached, with B and C Companies in support, would attack Hillman.

So far there was no visible opposition, but a mortar stonk on the original rendezvous validated Goodwin's decision to leave it. The rest of the battalion was coming into the orchard, stragglers and small groups alongside whole platoons. By 10:00 most of the Suffolks were present, minus Major James Gough and the troops of the HQ company delayed by the calamity that befell LCI(L) 130. To Goodwin's relief it became evident that the battalion had suffered remarkably few casualties on landing, although perhaps the most glaring gap in their ranks was Captain Glyn Llewellyn. Without their Forward Officer Bombardment and his signallers, the battalion was unable to summon fire support from HMS *Kelvin* and ORP *Dragon*. They could, however, call on their two allotted batteries from 76 and 33 Field Regiments, assuming they were able to deploy their guns. Then more relief came up the track behind them: Major Sir Delaval Cotter arrived in his tank to report that C Squadron 13/18 Hussars were ashore and moving up from the beach.

Major Phillip Papillon moved off first, leading two platoons of D

Company through the orchards and copses to the south. Finding a small squad of Canadian paratroopers at his disposal Papillon kept them close, ready to use them as troubleshooters should the need arise. They passed signs warning of the substantial minefields surrounding Morris, but some investigation showed that there was no continuous obstacle, and the men filtered through the dangerous crops and newly fruiting apple trees, along hedgerows and in ditches, until they had an effective position about 500 yards from the battery. Between them, young corn swayed in the breeze in fields scarred by the craters of dozens of misplaced bombs and shells.

C Company followed D Company out of the rendezvous accompanied by Eric Smith and 4 Troop of C Squadron 13/18 Hussars. Spotting cattle grazing in the fields, Major Charles Boycott led his men among them, realizing that a dairy herd wouldn't be released into a mined field. The plan worked, and in due course the infantry and tanks emerged at the south end of the town of Colleville-sur-Orne, with Goodwin and his HQ hot on their heels.

To their surprise, they were met by commandos, their green berets making them easy to recognize. They explained that 6 Commando had just cleared the bunkers on the north side of the town and now they were looking to deal with a Nebelwerfer that had been bothering them. Boycott offered them two of their tanks, which were gratefully accepted, and the commandos scurried off, leading the lumbering vehicles into the fields. Goodwin found Brigadier Lovat marching across a field and on to the road. They exchanged gossip about the landings before Lovat pressed on, looking for all the world to Goodwin like he was out for a country walk.

Advised by the commandos that the north end of Colleville was clear, C Company nevertheless prepared to put their training to use and make certain of the job. In 1944, Colleville was a simple linear town with a single narrow high street running for 1,000 yards from north to south. A lane ran behind the houses on the west side and occasional roads branched off, connecting to Hermanville-sur-Mer and Saint-Aubin. While Smith briefed one of his tank commanders, Corporal Fred Ashby took his section into the town hall at the very northern end of the village. Charging upstairs, they found the top floor offered an excellent view of the churchyard and the fields east of the town, over which the soldiers could project heavy supporting fire as the company advanced. As they set about the task of preparing the rooms for urban fighting, pulling back curtains and turning furniture into weapon supports in front of the windows, Alphonse Lenauld came up the stairs. Far from being distraught at the redisposition of his furniture, the town's mayor brought with him glasses, into which he began pouring generous portions of calvados to toast the liberators.

Meanwhile, C Company began their advance through the town. Lieutenant Smith drove his tank on to the high street while sections of infantry moved down both sides. Men moved through the churchyard too, one team twisting between the irregular tombstones and ducking down, ready to lay covering fire, while the next section leapfrogged past them. Frank Chivers' section was instructed to clear a house. Covered by his colleagues, Chivers advanced to the door, fired at the lock and kicked the door in. The men stormed into the house as they'd been trained, firing through the floor and ceiling, kicking open the interior doors and pouring sub-machine gun fire into neighbouring rooms. The last blast of Sten fire died away into complete silence, broken only by the arrival of the owner, who came to plead that the house was undefended. The soldiers quickly searched the rooms upstairs to be sure, then returned downstairs to find the owner hurriedly serving wine.

In his Sherman, Smith found the town surprisingly quiet. After negotiating a number of dead cattle at the top of the town, all his crew saw as their tank clanked down the high street was civilians, their expressions bewildered and haunted as they stood in the doorways of their homes. Eventually they came across a German, his limp body lying motionless in the road. Smith's driver slowed, reluctant to crush the body beneath their tracks. Smith too felt disturbed by the idea, but if there was a sniper around, a crew dismounting to move a body was just the sort of target they'd want.*

The tanks never needed to fire their guns, but at least one German remained somewhere in Colleville. A shot rang out at the northern end of the town and signaller Frederick Monk fell dying. He was the only casualty suffered during the clearance of the town, although he wouldn't be the only casualty the sniper would cause. The following day shots rang out from the church tower, prompting a fusillade of return fire that included a tank round. The bell tower was partially demolished, and shortly after two dusty Germans emerged to be marched into captivity.

While C Company began clearing the town, Major Papillon had been studying the concrete casemates of Morris closely through his binoculars.

---

* Smith does not record if the body was moved or not.

In Colleville, the HQ signaller's wireless crackled into life and Papillon passed his observations on to his CO. Even though C Squadron 13/18 Hussars had moved up to the right of D Company and were now exchanging shots with Hillman high on the Périers Ridge, Morris was surprisingly quiet. Anxious to avoid missing an opportunity, Goodwin summoned B Company to the northern end of the town, preparatory to making their assault on the position.

Just before midday, Major Dennis McCaffrey led his company, along with one of D Company's platoons attached as a breaching group, up to Colleville. Goodwin quickly briefed his company commander, warning him that although the occupants of Morris might have pulled out before the Suffolks had even arrived, it could well be a trick. McCaffrey went forward to view the strongpoint for himself and the battalion's Forward Observation Officer RA called up 76 and 33 Field Regiments. A few ranging shots landed around the casemates, but there was still no obvious response, so McCaffrey quickly modified his plan to achieve maximum speed and, hopefully, surprise. As there had been no reaction so far, the breaching platoon and pioneers would clear a gap through the outer barbed wire defences and minefield before the artillery bombardment instead of after it. Once a gap was made and the artillery had kept the defenders' heads down, the company would sweep through the perimeter and make the assault.

Quickly the attackers got to work. On the beach the 105mm guns of two batteries of Priests angled to the sky ready to drop their shells. With C Squadron and B Company watching intently, the breaching platoon moved forward to the outer perimeter of the strongpoint. No mines were found and gingerly the first of the Bangalore torpedoes were slid under the outer line of barbed wire. But, just as they were put into place, a white flag appeared from within the strongpoint. Wireless sets crackled to life as the flag was reported and the attack was suspended.

The white flag was soon followed by its bearer, then several more of the garrison emerged from the casemates and bunkers in small groups and advanced to the wire with their hands in the air. McCaffrey, still wary of tricks, led a platoon into the strongpoint, while two others moved forward to secure and search the garrison. It quickly became clear that the sixty-seven men of 2 Battery 1716 Artillery Regiment had no spirit for the fight. Even though the majority of the bombs and shells that had fallen that morning had missed the strongpoint, and the three casemates were almost completely undamaged, the garrison was shaken and unwilling to endure any more. In keeping with the findings of the other battalions fighting their way through the countryside south of Queen Beach, the Suffolks found a fair number of Poles and Eastern Europeans among their ranks. Meanwhile, McCaffrey and his platoon explored the strongpoint, finding the guns in working order but no more crews in hiding. Corporal Eddie Byatt was pleased to find a room well stocked with food and wine, and he and his men enjoyed a meal before hunting for souvenirs.

Morris had fallen without a single casualty to either side. But for the Suffolks there was a far greater challenge to come.[2]

In contrast to the well-ordered marshalling of 1 Suffolk at their rendezvous, 2 East Yorks' had been chaotic. C and D Companies, having advanced across the hectic beaches, had staggered on to the avenue de Lion. Privates Arthur Smith and Arnie Moore moved to their rendezvous behind the Maison de la Mer and found, in keeping with the confusion they had left behind on the beach, that there was no sign of C Company. Instead, men were moving straight into the fields behind and making their way inland, so Smith and Moore joined them. Lieutenant Hugh Bone spied his HQ group in the fields and followed them, where he quickly became entwined in the marsh reeds. Just before Corporal John Scruton set off inland he was amazed to see a horse and trap race along the avenue de Lion at the gallop, its civilian driver standing and waving as he deliriously shouted words that Scruton could appreciate the sentiment of, if not the actual meaning.

Of all the East Yorks' companies, D was the worst off, following the death of their commander Major Robert Barber and the heavy casualties in the company HQ. As the men of the company sought out the rendezvous behind the ruins of the holiday camp they found no obvious command to rally to. As 4 Commando gathered nearby and prepared to march off, the leaderless men loitered or wandered around seeking direction, while some set off into the fields in penny packets.

Just as 6 Commando would discover not long after, those who had started crossing the fields quickly learned that it was a marsh, crisscrossed with drainage ditches. As he struggled across one, Peter Brown of 14 Platoon C Company was horrified to find his feet tangled in barbed wire at the bottom. He struggled to free himself until his corporal produced a pair of wire cutters and reached into the stagnant waters to cut him free. Struggling through the flooded terrain, Hugh Bone stepped into a drainage ditch and sank up to his armpits, which soaked him even more than the trip up the beach. He cajoled, pushed and dragged his signallers through the ditches, desperately trying to keep the wireless sets above water level. To make matters worse, mortar bombs started to fall among them, making the boggy environs even more hazardous to the men's health. Just after his men left a particularly deep ditch behind, a number of bombs bracketed it, throwing up small geysers and hurling deadly shrapnel across the reeds.

As they staggered south, converging on a narrow wood, Bone realized there were other men mingled among them – soldiers with green berets and cumbersome rucksacks. His platoon emerged from the swamp dripping with mud and cursing, and found Lieutenant Colonel Hutchinson and the battalion HQ among the trees. Gratefully they flopped down to rest while the commandos streamed past towards Colleville. Bone inspected the battalion's wireless set, but it hadn't survived the journey across the marsh. They had managed to keep it out of the sea and swamp, but the rough journey and mortar blasts had taken their toll. Fortunately, the company sets still worked.

After thirty minutes, once 6 Commando had passed through, the troops of the battalion that had so far assembled set off with C Company and their CO Major David de Symons Barrow in the lead. The East Yorks advanced to the end of the woods, across the northern tip of Colleville-sur-Orne and on to the road to Ouistreham. Briefly following in the path cut by 6 Commando, they pressed on along the road.

At strongpoint 14, Oberleutnant Luke had deployed what little was left of his company in the trenches west of the main command bunker. The enemy fire had barely relented during their retreat down the road – at one point it appeared that even the French were firing at them from one of the buildings on the outskirts of Colleville.[*] Inside the bunker Hauptmann Gundlach[†] coordinated the defence. Acting as an administrator for Major Wallrabe who had fallen ill only a week previously, he now found

---

[*] Josef Häger's account states they were fired on from buildings close to stützpunkt 14. There were no buildings close to the strongpoint, and only one on the road from Colleville. He may have confused the location of these events. If it was in the vicinity of Colleville, it could just as easily have been British troops that had occupied the buildings.
[†] A hauptmann is equivalent to a captain in the British Army.

himself thrust into the role of combat commander of 1 Battalion. But of the battalion's four companies, he was in contact only with one – and that was because 4 Company had withdrawn to his position. What little information he had managed to get from across the river overnight suggested that 1 and 3 Companies had been engaged in battle with paratroopers. There was no word from 2 Company in Ouistreham, nor from regimental HQ at strongpoint 17. All the lines out of the bunker had gone dead several hours ago, and in the corner, Obergefreiter Bosseler desperately tried to summon 'Spinach' (736 Regiment HQ at Hillman) or 'Powder Box' (716 Division HQ) over the wireless. From the reports of the stragglers who had come back from the seafront, it was clear a major landing was underway. Heavy shellfire had fallen on strongpoint 12 only 700 yards south-east for several hours, and the sound of battle emanated from La Brèche and Ouistreham.

But despite the daunting odds facing him, Gundlach firmly believed in the Nazi cause.* He had been director of the Battle School in Caen and was commandant of the Caserne Lefèbvre, Caen's historic citadel and the Germans' principal centre of resistance in the city. He was not lacking in determination to defend his battalion headquarters. The bunker had been sealed for battle, and with air only coming through the ventilation system the atmosphere was already becoming stifling. It was made worse by the large number of wounded and shell-shocked men, along with civilian members of the Zollverwaltung (the German customs and border guard service), who were gathered inside. When 4 Company arrived, Gundlach placed the one cohesive unit he had in the trenches, while other able-bodied men crewed the bunker's machine gun positions.

Some 500 yards to the west, C Company of the East Yorks were cautiously advancing along the road, using the shelter of the trees but wary of the shrubby ground on either side. They had reached the abandoned slit trenches just cleared by 6 Commando, where John Scruton looked admiringly at the apparently new weapons abandoned in haste by the defenders when a single rifle shot barked out. The East Yorks dived for cover, pouring fire in the direction of the shot, and methodically a

---

* In the UK, Gundlach's interrogators noted he was 'thoroughly indoctrinated in Nazism', and Häger described him as somewhat fanatical in his defence of the strongpoint.

Right: Photographed from LCT 610, vehicles on the tank deck of LCT 854 burn after being hit by a mortar bomb.

Below: A photograph taken by Sub Lieutenant William Winkley from the bridge of LCT 979. His LCT has come ashore just west of exit 18 – the mound of the anti-tank gun bunker at the north-west corner of strongpoint Cod can be seen on the left. Just in front of the ramp are the four surrendering Germans seen by Lieutenant Eric Smith as he disembarked.

Left: Sherman tanks of C Squadron 13/18 Hussars come ashore. In the background are the buildings between exits 15 and 16.

Below: At approximately 08:30, troops and vehicles advance up Queen Red Beach. The immersed beach obstacles can be seen in the background.

Left: Commandos from HQ 1 Special Service Brigade come ashore from LCI(S) 519. The man in the foreground appears to be carrying bagpipes and is most likely Bill Millin. The man in the water immediately on his left is frequently identified as Lord Lovat, but how this identification has been arrived at is unclear.

Middle left: Commandos race ashore from their LCI(S)s opposite exits 20 and 21. On the right a Beach Armoured Recovery Vehicle (BARV) drives ashore.

Bottom left: As the LCI(S)s carrying 45 (RM) Commando advance towards the beach, Sergeant Ian Grant shoots film of an LCT bursting into flames as it heads away. This was probably LCT 854.

Bottom right: Lieutenant John Allen's Crab burns fiercely as 45 (RM) Commando come ashore.

Above: Infantry advance down exit 23, passing a wrecked DD tank of B Squadron 13/18 Hussars and a Universal Carrier of 2 Middlesex Regiment.

Below: The 75mm bunker at strongpoint 10. The position faced west along the beach and the gun is probably the one that knocked out LCT(A)s 2191 and 2052.

Right: Major General Tom Rennie clambers down from HMS *Largs* and on to an LCM ready to take him ashore at 09:30.

Below: Photographed from HMS *Frobisher*, this patch of burning sea was described as the remains of a landing craft – almost certainly LCI(S) 524.

Top: Commandos from E and F Troops 4 Commando, supported by DDs of B Squadron 13/18 Hussars, advance towards strongpoint 8 (Bass) at Ouistreham seafront.

Above: The 50mm gun bunker at strongpoint 10 that engaged Alexandre Lofi and his French commandos.

Above: Commandos of 1 Special Service Brigade, supported by tanks of B Squadron 13/18 Hussars, advance east along the rue du Général de Gaulle in Saint-Aubin-d'Arquenay. The rear house survives today, albeit somewhat truncated.

Left: The range-finding tower at strongpoint 8 in Ouistreham. The hit from a naval shell just above the viewing position can be seen, but it caused no damage inside. The tower is now a museum.

Left: Two wounded South Lancs men walk into the square at Fontaine de Gravier from Lion-sur-Mer. The man on the right is almost certainly Lieutenant Robert Pearce. In the background are vehicle waterproofing exhaust trunks at the exit created by 2 Troop 77 Assault Squadron.

Below: At approximately 10:40, LCTs of Group 10 and LCI(L)s of Group 11 try to unload between exits 12 and 13. In the background, LCTs of Group 12 can be seen approaching the beach.

Bottom: At approximately 10:50, tanks of the Staffordshire Yeomanry are disgorged from LCTs of 40 Flotilla on to the beach on either side of exit 11. Most would remain on the sand for at least an hour.

Above: A self-propelled 105mm Priest gun of 33 Field Regiment Royal Artillery, probably in the woods north of Hermanville.

Above: An M10 self-propelled gun of 20 Anti-Tank Regiment stops on the avenue de Lion to engage a target to the south.

Right: British infantry, possibly 2 KSLI, advance past a First World War memorial in Hermanville.

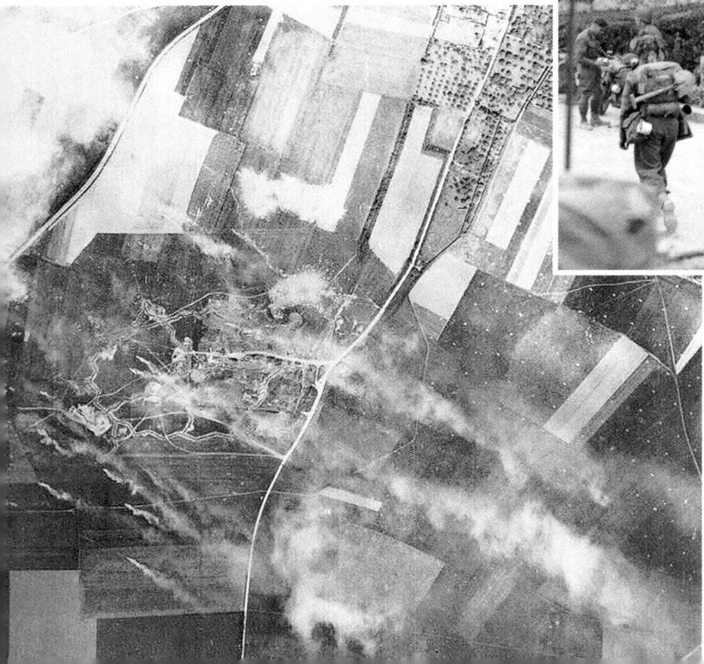

Left: At approximately 13:10 the Suffolks' attack on Hillman begins with an artillery barrage.

Left: Anti-tank gunners of 1 South Lancs set up in front of the rue de la Croix Rose at the southern end of Hermanville-sur-Mer.

Below: Sherman tanks of the Staffordshire Yeomanry advance across the fields south of Hermanville.

Bottom: Troops and vehicles advance inland from beach exit 18 on the west side of strongpoint Cod. It was down this road that the Suffolks advanced on 6 June and that Captain Roger Wietzel walked on 9 June.

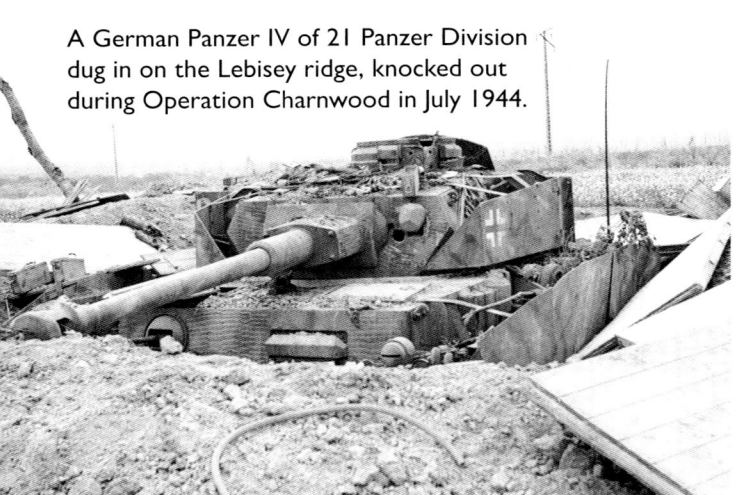

A German Panzer IV of 21 Panzer Division dug in on the Lebisey ridge, knocked out during Operation Charnwood in July 1944.

Above: A photograph taken by Lieutenant Peter Wild (COPP 6), probably on the afternoon of D-Day. The 75mm gun bunker at the north-west corner of strongpoint Cod is on the left. In the centre of the photograph, LCA 1381 of 538 Flotilla carried units of the Beach Groups in Assault Group 5. She was damaged on landing but later salvaged.

6 Airlanding Brigade on their way across the anchorage off Sword at approximately 20:50. The ships visible from left to right are *Warspite*, *Serapis* and *Ramillies*.

section started to flank the suspected sniper's hide. Within a few minutes the troops were on the move again and support now materialized behind them – B Squadron 13/18 Hussars had successfully moved up from the beach and were now arriving in Colleville, although losses on the beach and the disappearance of 1 Troop into Ouistreham had reduced their number to only eight tanks.

Creeping forward, Scruton closed on two Universal Carriers stopped further along the road. The interior compartments blazed like furnaces and bright flames licked the curling paintwork on the chassis. The crews, some in their seats, some sprawled on the road, were blackened like burned wood. They had almost certainly succumbed to gunfire from Sole, now only 100 yards away. The time had come for C Company to abandon the road, and the men quickly moved into the shrubland. Major Barrow briefed his two platoon commanders: the most sensible approach was to flank through the shrubs and orchards on the west side of the strongpoint with one platoon, and the tanks laying down fire support while one platoon made the assault. To prepare the way, 76 Field Regiment were already ranging their 105mm guns on the target.

The remnants of 4 Company had barely had any respite from the assault that had chased them out of Colleville. Sniper fire and mortars were ranging on them and among the trees they could see infantry moving forward. As the enemy flanked them the pressure became more intense, but even so the German infantrymen maintained a stout defence – perhaps for more than an hour, and even against armour.[*] But as the enemy closed, the defences started to buckle. Grenades started to burst in the trenches and the German soldiers were forced back until they were in the single communication trench leading to the HQ bunker. Realizing there was little hope of their survival outside the bunker, Gundlach beckoned them in and the men gratefully tumbled down the short flight of stairs into the protection of the 2-metre-thick concrete walls. The outer door was sealed behind them and the gunners of the two machine gun embrasures covering the entrance waited for the enemy's inevitable onslaught.

---

[*] Häger refers to an attack by two tanks and that one was knocked out and the crew killed. 13/18 Hussars' tanks were certainly present, but no source mentions a tank being destroyed. It is possible Häger saw the Universal Carriers that Scruton recalled, although there are no other witnesses to clarify what happened.

Inside, Häger was astonished to find the bunker already full.* Wounded men lay on straw mattresses and bloody sheets in the main room and a random assortment of soldiers from different units cluttered the short corridors and side rooms. Both Ysker and Fischer had found themselves crammed inside after their headlong retreat from the coast. The HQ had seemingly promised a refuge, but instead was rapidly becoming a living hell. An air of terror filled the bunker, men cried out, the wounded moaned continuously, and in the corner Bosseler desperately pleaded, 'Come in, Spinach . . . come in, Spinach.' The ventilation system struggled to provide enough air and the atmosphere was unbearable, hot and thick with choking fumes. With barely room to squat, the men squeezed themselves into whatever space they could find and tried not to move.

Outside, the East Yorks systematically moved through the trenches of the strongpoint, finding the Tobruks empty. They closed on the main bunker at the end of the last trench and Captain James McGregor, a Canloan† in command of 14 Platoon, approached the entrance. As he stepped into the space at the top of the entrance steps, a machine gun burst from one of the two embrasures struck him and he fell, badly wounded. His platoon angrily hurled grenades into the entrance passageway and moved to surround the last holdout.‡

Inside, taking advantage of the small apertures in the bunker's steel cupola on the roof, a soldier observing events gave a running commentary of what he could see. His voice carried across the cries of the wounded, the rattle of Hauptmann Gundlach's machine gun and the

---

* Exactly how many men were inside the bunker is uncertain. Häger estimated at least thirty people, possibly in addition to his own company. The 13/18 Hussars war diary (WO 171/845) refers to thirty to forty prisoners, Hilfszollassistent Nimz (a member of the customs service who had retreated to the bunker) estimated forty to fifty men (WO 208/3590), and Günther Fischer approximately sixty (WO 208/3621). However many it was, the Type 634 bunker had only approximately 38 square metres of internal space and considerable machinery, furniture and equipment within that. With several stretcher cases taking up more floor space, the bunker will have been incredibly cramped.

† A Canadian officer 'on loan' to British forces. Many Canadians were assigned to British battalions in the Canloan scheme, four to 2 East Yorks alone.

‡ McGregor is recorded to have died the following day. Interestingly, his grave concentration record suggests he was buried at Sole, which would suggest the possibility that he actually died on 6 June.

blast of grenades at the door – then he shouted urgently that the soldiers outside were blocking the ventilation system. Almost immediately it started to get hotter inside and the men struggled to breathe in the cordite-filled rooms. In desperation, Oberleutnant Luke shouted above the clamour, 'We'll breathe all together when I say in, and expel when I say out.' The noise of the fighting became interspersed with the hoarse, gulping breaths of the strongpoint's occupants and Luke's shouted instructions.

Meanwhile, Gundlach continued to fire through the embrasure, safely protected from return fire by the armour plating around it. Watching him, Häger realized the hauptmann had become detached from the events behind him. Eventually Luke addressed his senior officer in an effort to make him see the hopelessness of their situation: 'Sir, we can't carry on . . . the wounded are suffocating. We must surrender.'

'Out of the question,' replied Gundlach. 'We'll fight our way out of here if we have to.'

The men cramped into the bunker were shocked and appalled. There was a chorus of objections, and with a sense of despair mixed with defiance some of them pulled the bolts out of their rifles. Then the observer in the cupola screamed above the din, 'My God, they're bringing up a flamethrower!'

Now there was panic inside the bunker. Soldiers screamed to be let out, others gagged in the thick air, some fainted. Luke continued to shout, 'In . . . out!' Bosseler implored Spinach to answer his transmissions. One soldier, paralysed with fear, simply repeated the only English phrase he knew: 'Hello boys, hello boys!' Then, above it all, the men heard the crackle of the flamethrower outside. Instinctively one soldier grabbed a blood-stained sheet from a mattress. It was passed through the bunker and pushed through one of the apertures in the cupola on a stick. The din of small arms outside faded and faint shouts could be heard. Eventually a voice called over the roof, 'All right then, come out!' The soldiers looked at Gundlach, still staring out of the embrasure. Finally, he turned round and looked at Bosseler.

'Have you made contact?'

'Nothing,' replied his radio operator simply.

Gundlach suddenly seemed to comprehend the hopelessness of the situation and, as the blood drained from his face, he dropped his machine gun.

Shortly after 13:00, one of the soldiers opened the bunker's door and waved a white sheet.* After a pause, he hesitantly stepped out to find the East Yorks standing on either side of the trench above him. They beckoned him forward, and as he passed the first of the imposing British figures someone fired a short burst of bullets into the ground behind him. Someone else motioned for him to remove his helmet and webbing, and soon a pile of discarded equipment had built up as each German was led to the end of the trench and made to lie down. Finally, after dozens of men had marched out, Gundlach emerged, exhausted and pale. Immediately he was out of the doorway, a medic went in behind him to tend to the wounded.

C Company were elated and watched with satisfaction as the prisoners were marched back along the road in the direction of Colleville. Coming the other way was the rest of the battalion, A and B Companies having now cleared the beach. Even so, stragglers from all four companies continued to wander in all afternoon.[3]

---

* There are no consistent times given for the capture of Sole. The East Yorks war diary doesn't record a time at all and PoW accounts vary wildly. The 13/18 Hussars war diary records the position secured at 15:45, but this is probably when they received a report. The most reliable and likely time comes from the 8 Brigade war diary, which records that '2 E Yorks reported the defences on the left of the bridgehead cleared' at 13:30. As the next entry at 14:30 describes the wounding of Lieutenant Colonel Hutchinson (see chapter 13), the 13:30 entry must refer to Sole.

II

THE FIGHT FOR LION-SUR-MER

ON THE FAR RIGHT OF THE LANDINGS, CAPTAIN GEORGE McLENNAN and *Busaco*'s ride off the beach and through the exit cleared by Lieutenant David Knapp in his Crab had led them on to the square at Fontaine de Gravier. Charming half-timbered chalets bordered the roads where the wide boulevard from the beach met the avenue de Lion as it split into two at a Y junction. The rue du Pré de l'Isle continued the lateral road behind the beach and led to the seafront town hall in Lion-sur-Mer, while the avenue Henri Gravier (named after a past mayor of Lion-sur-Mer) led a little inland in the direction of the town's church, taking the tram lines with it. To the south, the lane to the main town of Hermanville ran past La Brèche's small church and away to the south.

Parked in the square, McLennan was relieved to see Sergeant Thomas Kilvert and his crew advancing behind him, brandishing the weapons they had salvaged from *Blenheim*. They quickly formed a small defensive group around *Busaco* while Lieutenant Knapp brought his Crab up and on to the square behind them. In the absence of any opposition, Knapp decided to proceed inland and began beating his flail along the centre of the square and up to the junction proper. While McLennan's gunners watched the surrounding houses, Kilvert and his crew hesitantly advanced behind the Crab until they were among the chalets and across the tram lines. Seeing nothing in the fields beyond, Knapp pressed on, beating a path along the dusty lane south. The mechanical drum swung the chains violently around, their weighted ends pummelling into the hard ground with a thunderous pounding beat. The crew sat, tensed, waiting for the sound of an explosion, but none came. Three hundred yards later, as the road started to bend out of sight of the beach, Knapp stopped and jumped off the tank to consult his escorts. Kilvert came up and the lieutenant advised him there didn't appear to be any mines. Knapp took his Crab into the fields on the west side of the road and rumbled around, sticking to the hedgerows for cover while sampling the field for any threats. Eventually, pleased with their success, they stopped and brewed up tea in the meadows.

While his small force waited by the road, Kilvert jogged back to the junction and briefed McLennan, who had now been joined by Lieutenant Charles Tennent in *Balaclava*. Finding 3 Troop's Lance Sergeant Freer and his AVRE crew also on foot, he took them and a couple of infantrymen who had got ahead of their own platoons forward and, assuming the two AVREs were following, returned to his crew. Once assembled, this little squad set about advancing on Hermanville. With Kilvert's crew on the left and Freer's on the right, the men leapfrogged their way up the road, slowly following its curve until the beach exit behind them was out of sight. Up ahead they could see the long stone wall of the farm that lay north of the town, so familiar from the maps and aerial photographs the sappers had studied back in the UK.

They moved up to the corner and then along the wall where Kilvert split his small squad into three, one to cover the road, one to assault the farm and – having realized the AVREs hadn't actually followed them – one to cover the rear. They advanced along the wall, keeping close to it to avoid being seen from the buildings behind, but as they closed on the main gate the chatter of a sub-machine gun came from ahead. The sappers dived to the ground and fired up the road, seemingly silencing the invisible enemy, and Kilvert jumped up and forward to the heavy wooden gates. As they resisted his first hearty shove, he fired his sub-machine gun at the lock and kicked them open, then charged into the courtyard covered by Freer and two others. The men opened fire at the farmhouse, spraying bullets at the walls and windows, then rushed forward to lob grenades through the broken glass. The crump of explosions blew out dust and smoke, and the sappers kicked open a door and charged inside. They searched the house from top to bottom looking for any occupants, but found only the bodies of those they'd just killed. Emerging from the farmhouse, they searched the outhouses and orchards, where they discovered the trembling farmer and his family hiding in a shelter. A few hand gestures reassured them that they weren't in any danger and Kilvert called for Sapper Hand, who spoke fluent French. The stunned family stared at Hand as he explained who they were, then pressed them for information. Where were the Boche? he asked. The family pointed south in the direction of the manor 400 yards away – there were some 200 Germans in Hermanville, they explained.

Kilvert frowned – that was a bit more than was comfortable. The squad quickly made their way back to the road, half expecting to see the German army advancing along it. Relieved to find it much as they had left it, Kilvert despatched two runners back to the beach while the remainder of the force took up positions along the wall and in the ditch opposite. Very soon after they were rewarded with a small patrol advancing down the road. Almost immediately Sapper Vaughan opened fire with his Sten and the rest of the squad joined in, felling at least two of the grey-clad figures before the rest beat a hasty retreat.[1]

While Kilvert and his private little army continued their fight at the farm, the men of B and D Companies 1 South Lancs moved up to the avenue de Lion in small parties, some searching vainly for Lieutenant Colonel Richard Burbury's assembly flag, little realizing that it lay in the sand behind them. Lieutenant George Wilson found himself gazing across the fields behind Queen White Beach in the direction of their next objective, Hermanville-sur-Mer. The fields looked a more attractive route than the road that led inland from the beach a little to the west, but on the other hand there was a rather conspicuous sign nearby with the dreaded words 'Achtung Minen!' emblazoned on it. While 12 Platoon sought cover in the roadside ditches, one of the mine clearance teams that had accompanied their company in the LCAs came off the beach behind them.[*] Wilson asked them to have a quick look across the field and the two men smartly moved forward and started to search the ground. After he'd watched the two Royal Engineers carefully sweeping their detectors through the tussocky grass for a few minutes, Wilson decided the warning sign was most likely a bluff and, thanking them, he led the first section of the platoon into the field.

With lumps in their throats, the men bent low and raced across the field, watching and waiting for an explosion. To everyone's great relief they arrived safely at the first hedge and deployed while the other section caught up. A new section took the lead and led them into the next field, then the next until, in leaps and bounds, they drew level with the farm

---

[*] Almost certainly men of 1 or 3 Platoon 246 Field Company RE.

outside Hermanville. Advancing through orchards to the town, they passed a small group of sheltering civilians and Corporal Gordon Penter was faintly amused to hear them call out, 'Vive les Américains!' 'Je suis Anglais!' the troops called back as they hurried past. Cautiously they advanced along the main road, past rustic stone-walled houses, their dilapidated window shutters closed and uninviting. Up ahead they could see the church tower, painfully aware that their view of it would be reciprocated and anyone inside would have clear sight of them as well. But as they rounded the gentle curves of the road and the church came into view, Wilson was relieved to see Captain Arthur Rouse in the churchyard.

Having led the battalion HQ off the beach, Rouse had headed right until they found the lane leading to Hermanville and followed it to the small town, relieved to find 77 Assault Squadron's AVREs already manoeuvring along it. Cautiously entering the town, they found it appeared to be undefended.* Now his small party impatiently waited, hoping the companies would follow them in soon and allocating positions to each group as they arrived. 12 Platoon was a welcome arrival and Rouse quickly instructed Wilson to undertake a recce of the town's east side.

Wilson led his men along a lane opposite the church and into a small copse, beyond which he could see a cornfield through the well-spaced trees. Replicating the advance through the fields north of Hermanville, he quickly deployed two sections along the edge of the copse to provide cover and prepared to lead the remaining section through the corn to flank around the side of the town. Men busied themselves readying their weapons, the Bren teams picked positions with good outlooks to the south, and the loaders prepped magazines. Wilson looked around and, satisfied everything was ready, stepped beyond the cover of the trees and into the field. Widely spaced, the section followed and advanced into the waist-high crop, pushing through the green sheaths with their eyes fixed forward.

The men hadn't got far when the first bark of a rifle was heard, followed by a few more sporadic shots. Wilson glanced along his section and saw men fall wounded, while the rest dropped down. Men peeked

---

* It may be that the garrison the French civilians reported had moved out much earlier in the morning, or they may have withdrawn after Kilvert's force reached the outer approaches of the town. Hermanville was the base for 3 Company 642 Ost Battalion.

through the weaving heads of corn trying to spot where the fire was coming from, but their helmets presented targets and brought fire on them. More men fell wounded and Wilson ordered them back to the tree line while he tried to find a target. Then the section corporal spotted the flash of rifle fire and called out to Wilson, who directed the Bren team to join the NCO. At a crouched run they moved across, but almost instantly brought down more fire on themselves. Soon the gunner and corporal were wounded too and joined the growing number of men crawling back to the rest of the platoon.

Just as he realized that practically all of his section were retiring with wounds, Wilson's batman was hit, and then he felt a hammer blow in his own left arm. He looked down to find blood oozing through a tear in his battledress and realized it was time to go. As he prepared to turn around he suddenly heard a guttural cry and looked up to see several figures in dark grey uniforms only 20 yards away and charging through the corn towards him. Instinctively he snapped his Sten up and fired a burst, realizing that his aim – such as it was – was probably too high. But the figures went down anyway and Wilson raced back to the trees while his men fired a fusillade of fire at the invisible enemy.

Safe in cover, Wilson recovered his breath while the gunfire petered out. The enemy didn't resurface, but a new group of men appeared from behind. Relieved to see familiar uniforms, Wilson discovered a group of 1 Suffolk moving up behind them. He quickly briefed their officer before they moved on, into the adjacent copse.*

Meanwhile, a relieved Rouse had welcomed more of B and D Companies into Hermanville and deployed them further into the south of the town. By 09:00 there was a reasonable force in occupation and, aside from Wilson's brisk engagement, no enemy resistance had been encountered. The locals had started to emerge from their houses and jovial conversation echoed down the narrow streets. C Company were starting to move up from the beach. Soon their vehicles would start to arrive, Universal Carriers bringing with them anti-tank guns and ammunition,

---

* Butler suggests Wilson's recce of Hermanville went right, effectively to the west (p.52), but they must have gone east in order to encounter men of 1 Suffolk, who were most likely D Company moving up to their position in preparation for the assault on Morris. The German force may have been remnants of Hermanville's garrison – 3 Company 642 Ost Battalion – or a squad from Morris making a recce of the surrounding area.

and in another few hours reserves would start to arrive to fill the gaps in their ranks. But there had been no word from A Company – only the faint sounds of battle a mile to the north carried on the morning breeze.[2]

7 and 8 Platoons had methodically moved through the houses on either side of exit 11 after clearing the beach. After locking his first group of prisoners in a cellar, Edward Jones's 8 Platoon had swept through a series of dugouts lining the left side of the square at Fontaine de Gravier using grenades. On the other side, Lieutenant Robert Pearce led his platoon through the houses behind the high wall on the square's west side. Advancing through the gardens alongside the impressive La Brèche villa – the house that had started Ouistreham's new life as a beach resort – his men came upon several mortar pits, the occupants so focused on their task that they didn't even see the South Lancs until their rifle muzzles were levelled at them.

The two platoons emerged cautiously on to the square. Unfortunately for the South Lancs the junction was an obvious target for German artillery, and as Lieutenant Jones caught his breath after the drive through the houses and gardens, a shell crashed into the ground nearby. Jones doubled up in pain, clutching his stomach, and Pearce rushed over, expecting the worst. As the two officers fumbled through the webbing and battledress, the men found a tiny lump of shrapnel had gone straight through a torch on Jones's belt, the webbing and the battledress, and stuck in his flesh. Red hot, the shrapnel was intensely painful, but not life-threatening, and Pearce flicked it away.

A short while later the remnants of 9 Platoon and company HQ had joined them and, on learning of Major John Harward's injuries, Pearce took command of A Company. Their next task was to push out the landings' right flank and clear the route into Lion-sur-Mer, ready for 41 (RM) Commando to advance through them and secure strongpoint Trout.

The company set off, following the quieter roads away from the beach. Although their orders only required them to reach a small wood some 600 yards down the road, their journey took them further into the town. To their surprise, locals started to emerge from their houses, some even appearing to be heading to work in the fields. They passed the woods and moved on along the coastal road towards the town centre, past the grand town hall and a woodyard on a small square.

Private Leslie Smith moved down the road alongside his platoon commander. There was no obvious enemy presence, but as they went further west the lanes became narrower and some of the houses looming over them appeared to have been stripped of their homely commodities and converted into blockhouses. The roads twisted in long curves, reducing their visibility ahead, and some of the side streets had been blocked with tall walls of barbed wire several yards deep. Smith moved more cautiously now, keeping to the edge of the road. For a split second he heard a rifle crack and then felt a sudden blow to his face. Jones too heard the crack and a millisecond later he was showered in bits of brain and bone. He glanced right and to his horror saw Smith collapse, a bullet hole right between his eyes that had blown the back of his head out. Before Jones even had time to process what had happened another shot rang out and the soldier on his left collapsed. As one, the platoon dived for cover.

A Company had reached the outer defences of Trout and now the enemy gunners poured heavy fire down the road. The South Lancs quickly pulled back down the curving road and Pearce led them south to try and flank the position on the left. Heading down a narrow lane, they emerged at a small farmstead and barged their way into its buildings, securing viewpoints out to the west overlooking the strongpoint. But there was little a single company could achieve against the defences – securing it was the responsibility of 41 (RM) Commando.[3]

When he had studied the objectives his commando had been given, Lieutenant Colonel Thomas Gray decided to split his force into two groups, one each to tackle the most significant German defences. He would command 'Force I', consisting of P and Y Troops, and would assault strongpoint Trout; Major David Barclay would command 'Force II', B and X Troops, who would move directly to the Château de Lion-sur-Mer a little inland and west of Trout, attack and occupy it. A Troop would be in reserve and S Troop's jeep-mounted heavy weapons would land forty-five minutes after the infantry and be distributed between the forces as necessary on arrival. Once Lion-sur-Mer was secure, Force I would move along the coast road to Petit Enfer and Force II along the lateral road to Luc-sur-Mer, both just over a mile west, and together attack strongpoint 24. By then, 48 (RM) Commando landing on Juno Beach should have entered the seaside town from the west and together the two units would assault Douvres-la-Délivrande.

Gray's plan hadn't lasted much beyond the beach. The landing on Red Beach instead of White sowed confusion among the troops, who arrived at the planned rendezvous in irregular groups. P and one section of A

Troop formed up quickly and, noting the chaotic nature of the beach, Gray quickly decided to move them on to the lateral road. By 09:20 they were just inland of exit 11, but the arrival of the other troops was painstakingly slow. Penny packets from X and Y Troop arrived, mainly bearing bad news for Gray about their officers. Then someone informed him that they'd seen Barclay killed when a shell came down close to him. Sensing that his plan was already coming undone and with his schedule falling away, Gray decided to move with what he had. An hour after they'd landed, Captain Basil Sloley led P Troop down the rue du Pré de l'Isle at pace, reasonably satisfied that 1 South Lancs would have cleared the initial approach to Lion-sur-Mer from the landing area. Y Troop came behind, followed by what there was of A Troop.

Free of the burden of his weighty parabike, Corporal Raymond Mitchell felt almost skippy and he broke into a run along the lateral road towards the Y junction where 41 Commando should be. He approached a soldier slumped against a wall and quickly noted there was little treatment he could offer for his shattered leg, but he slowed long enough to enquire if there was anything he could do for him. 'I'm OK, but I wouldn't mind a fag.' Mitchell lit one for him and put it between the injured man's lips. 'I'm OK, better push off and catch up with your pals.' At the junction, confusing crowds of people moved in different directions, seemingly making order out of the disordered groups and colourful collections of shoulder patches. He looked around hopefully for a familiar green beret, eventually finding two in a ditch, where their owners were debating which of the two roads into Lion to take – the left-hand road bordering open country inland, or the right-hand lane along a narrow street overlooked by houses. Overhead the whine of shells urged them to make a decision and, erring on the side of caution, the men jogged along the lateral road, hopeful that their colleagues would have made the same choice. They passed the remains of the outer defences of strongpoint 20A, an AVRE bridge now lying across the 75mm gun position. Tanks ground around in the garden, emerging through a shattered wall and ditching their wading trunks on the pavement.

They hadn't gone far when another clutch of shells fell into the road ahead of them, as if to mock their choice. But the commandos had picked their poison now and, trying to reassure themselves that like lightning, shells don't strike twice, they ran across the shallow craters in the hard road and pressed on. Five hundred yards later, as the road narrowed and gently curved, they caught up with the commando's HQ troop, the men crouched below the walls waiting expectantly for an order to move forward again. Mitchell crashed down beside them, panting and sweating in the June warmth, but within seconds the expected order came, and the commandos rose up and moved on.

The road seemed continually to narrow as the houses on the landward side grew taller and the bushes and trees behind the wall opposite grew thicker. The pavements vanished and the sounds of battle somewhere out at sea gently reverberated off the walls. Then the road opened up to reveal a magnificent town hall, its stately windows overlooking a green that ran down to the sea. Beyond, in the grey waters, some nearby warships flickered as they fired their armament, and further towards the horizon small dots moved sedately left and right. But there was no time to enjoy the charming scenery of this seaside resort and soon the road had plunged them back among the tall buildings. Then, a few dozen yards further on, they emerged at a small square where excited locals approached them. Between embraces and toasts to their liberators, they explained that the Germans had vacated the main town much earlier in the morning.

The troops halted briefly and Captain Douglas Grant quickly took the chance to organize the heavy weapons of S Troop and deploy their 3-inch mortars in a woodyard off the square. Behind them, Mitchell and his sweating comrades flopped down, grateful for the opportunity to administer some vitally needed personal care. Boots were removed to be drained of sand and socks wrung out of seawater. Webbing was readjusted and weapons cleaned. Cigarettes were produced from under green berets, where they'd been stashed to keep them above the water. At the urging of colleagues, Mitchell was despatched to a shop across the road to obtain matches. He entered the small tabac to be met by a young girl and an elderly lady waiting behind a counter. In schoolboy French he asked for some 'allumettes' and duly handed over a note of Allied Military Currency. The lady took it and issued some change. Awkwardly Mitchell thanked them and backed out of the shop, wondering at the regularity of this transaction made with a new currency while naval gunfire boomed outside.

Up ahead, P Troop had moved on and Gray had received more bad news. B Troop had caught up, but section commander Lieutenant John Sturgis brought with him the news that Captain Morris was still on the beach, wounded. Only a handful of X Troop had arrived and Captain Stratford was not among them. Without Force II's commander or either of the troop commanders, Gray decided to take command of both forces, but still try to tackle both objectives. Then more bad news came. Captain Peter Dixon arrived but regretfully informed Gray that none of his signalmen had got off the beach and that although he had his wireless set with him, it was damaged. A commando signalman quickly got to work on Dixon's set, but until it worked or a new set arrived, there was no way to contact ORP *Ślązak* or HMS *Verulam* offshore. Worse still, none of the Centaur tanks of the RMASG had made it off Queen White beach. Wireless contact was at least established with A Company of the South Lancs, who reported they were held up by the strongpoint, and even now Gray could hear small arms fire echoing down the road ahead of him. Then P Troop reported in, revealing it was their small arms – they had arrived at Trout.

By now it was 10:20 and time was slipping away. Gray quickly rapped out orders. Sturgis was told to take what there was of B Troop up to a road junction 500 yards short of the château and try to contact the South Lancs. A Troop would follow in support and hopefully the combined force could outflank the strongpoint. Sturgis quickly led his men down to the avenue Henri Gravier and into the lanes to the south, passing the church and turning right on to the rue Victor Hugo that led to the château some 800 yards away. Here the shelter of the buildings came to an end. Ahead of them telegraph wires lay across the rural lane like broken spider webs, and on their left a water tower poured its contents on to the road like an industrial waterfall. The men hurried forward, sticking close to the sparse hedges for cover, and approached the tiny hamlet set around their objective. Sleepy Norman houses closed up against the lane once again and the pace slowed as the men warily examined windows and doorways. But there was no obvious sign of anyone, least of all the South Lancs.

By now B Troop had managed to get around the south side of Trout, its barbed wire now about 300 yards to the north-east. The corner of the château grounds was only about 300 yards to the west, but as they tentatively advanced down the lane a little further, towards the end of the collection of rustic houses, gunfire suddenly opened up from the buildings next to the château's grounds. The commandos dashed into the houses, kicking open doors and bounding up the stairs to secure positions overlooking the road and fields. Sturgis rushed up the stairs of a small farmhouse and went to a window overlooking the yard, where he saw, to his alarm, a German NCO opening a gate to lead his men in. Instinctively he brought the only weapon he was carrying – a Browning automatic pistol – to bear and blasted several shots through the window before ducking back down. When he next looked through the window the Germans had gone, but as his men set about fortifying their position and bullets started to ricochet off the stone walls, it became clear that any advance would be difficult. Both sides settled down in stalemate across the 100 yards of no-man's land between the two tiny hamlets.

Back at the strongpoint, German mortars were taking their toll on the South Lancs' position. The infantry had quickly realized that they weren't alone in the farm when a small German force had attacked them from one of the other buildings, but the company's Bren teams were able to break it up. Once the enemy had dispersed, the two platoons attempted another flanking manoeuvre to the south, but here their luck ran out. As they carefully advanced down a narrow sunken lane a stonk of bombs fell on them. The high earthen banks offered little opportunity to take cover and the men dived to the ground as the bombs burst among them, erupting shrapnel and flames and spilling earth and broken branches over them. Once it was all over, Edward Jones found a number of men had been killed or wounded; worse still, both Robert Pearce and his own platoon sergeant were among the latter. Quickly the South Lancs withdrew and formed a new position behind a stone wall. By now there was only the equivalent of a single platoon of men still fit to fight, and Jones was the only officer.

Gray had moved over to the avenue Henri Gravier and set up his small HQ in a little green behind the church. Grant's mortars had redeployed to a park across the main road from the church and now intermittently dropped their bombs on to Trout. But their ammunition was finite and already running low, and both the South Lancs and P Troop were still heavily engaged by Trout and unable to advance any further. Gray decided to shift the axis of attack to the main road. Y Troop would move down the avenue Henri Gravier and hopefully locate the South Lancs and advance through them into Trout.

Then, finally, some good news arrived. 41 Commando's jeeps were arriving on the beach, and with them more ammunition. But something bigger was also rumbling along the road in their direction.[4]

At Hermanville, 77 Assault Squadron's AVREs had started assembling in the orchard opposite the farm that Sergeant Kilvert had assaulted. Now that they'd cleared their gaps off the beach, the squadron was free to fulfil its other obligations and support the advance out of the beachhead. Major Furguson arrived and instructed Captain Arthur Low and

Lieutenant Charles Tennent to recce Lion-sur-Mer and see what support the South Lancs and 41 Commando required. Returning to *Balaclava*, Tennent found his crew looking forlornly at the Petard mortar, which was now out of action. After a quick word with Captain McLennan, Tennent jumped into *Busaco* and set off behind Low in *Barbaric*. They moved back towards their beach exit, dodging oncoming vehicles, and turned left at the junction, following the main road into Ouistreham. Near the church they came across 41's HQ and the commander disembarked to consult with Gray and his staff.

They quickly discovered the situation was not promising. The commandos were held up by the strongpoint, actually some distance outside of it where German infantry occupied numerous houses on the main road. Machine guns in the strongpoint itself dominated the main approach along the avenue Henri Gravier. P Troop had moved into the houses on either side of the road but heavy mortars and snipers continued to take their toll and, to make matters worse, the commandos' slim supply of mortars was already expended. But Gray was optimistic that armour could swing the battle and if they supported Y Troop in their coming assault they could probably gain entry to the position and overrun it.

Tennent's run of bad luck was continuing – *Busaco*'s turret was now jammed, facing right over the side of the tank. Low sent him back to the squadron to fetch a new AVRE and rustle up another or two. Tracks ground on the kerbs of Lion-sur-Mer's tight streets as *Busaco* turned and raced back to the squadron as quickly as Tennent could manage, while Low went forward on foot to recce the ground. He cautiously made his way along the road, wary of the strongpoint only 400 yards away. Ahead of him the main road gently rose to a low crest, where he could see the occasional flash of a green beret moving among the houses – the strongpoint was somewhere beyond there, but the straight road and elevation prevented any visual assessment of it. There was little room for manoeuvre; the side streets were narrow, probably too narrow, Low thought, for an AVRE to safely negotiate. The best approach, possibly the only approach, was for the AVREs to lead the infantry along the main road, providing an armoured shield to protect them from the machine guns.

Low returned to the church to find his crews chatting and smoking with the commandos. Lieutenant Tennent had returned in another borrowed AVRE, along with Captain McLennan, who had similarly borrowed *Barracuda* from Captain Carruthers. They found Captain Peter Howes-

Dufton of Y Troop and together they worked out the plan. McLennan would lead the convoy, advancing along the main road with a section of Y Troop behind him. Low would follow 20 yards behind, leading another section, with Tennent bringing up the rear with a third section.* It was as simple as it was bold, but the AVRE was a Churchill tank in all but name, and its thick armour would be good protection. The only weakness was their Petard mortars, which greatly reduced their fighting range and meant they'd practically need to get into the strongpoint before they could engage targets. But this introduced another weakness: there'd be no rushing up the road to smash their way into the strongpoint; they would have to move at the speed of the infantry in order to protect them.

Nevertheless, at 11:00 the column set off, advancing up the road towards P Troop's positions. As they approached the low crest, McLennan ordered his crew to test-fire their Besa machine guns and they sprayed some of the houses ahead. All seemed quiet and there was no sign of the enemy as yet. But behind them, the German infantry in the houses on either side of the road opened up on Low's AVRE, their rifle bullets bouncing ineffectually off the hulls. As soon as they identified targets, the Besa gunners in Low and Tennent's AVREs poured fire into the houses and soon the splatter of heavy machine gun fire on their positions forced the German infantry to take cover. McLennan trundled on and, with the defenders around him subdued, the column managed to penetrate about 250 yards beyond P Troop's position.

Then all hell broke loose.

McLennan's AVRE finally began to attract attention and a lucky rifle shot struck the Petard bomb loaded in its launcher, which burst into flames with a loud boom. Just at that moment *Barracuda* moved into the line of sight of a 50mm anti-tank gun positioned next to the road but until now shielded by a house. As the front of the turret burned, the first shell smashed into the AVRE's driver position, striking the visor and wounding the driver although not penetrating the tank's thick armour. A series of small explosions echoed around *Barracuda*'s interior before a huge explosion detonated inside the turret. Whether the Petard round had exploded or another anti-tank round had struck, the result was the same. The tank rapidly filled with sparks and smoke as equipment burned

---

* It would appear that Y Troop took what little there was of X Troop with them for their attack. The war diary suggests that this happened after the attack, but at least one member of X Troop recalls participating in it.

and McLennan ordered the crew to bale out. As they abandoned their doomed vehicle, the crew saw German infantry clutching grenades rushing towards them and moved back behind the tank, through the thick swirling smoke that enveloped the road. 'Tell Mr Low we've been knocked out,' called McLennan from the turret before he dropped down beside the tank, but no sooner had he hit the road than he was felled by a grenade. The surviving crew ran back towards Low's AVRE while he covered them with machine gun fire.

In the swirling smoke, and with German infantry now counter-attacking the lead AVRE and mortar bombs raining down, the lead commandos dived for the houses, dragging some of the wounded sappers with them. Howes-Dufton had tried to push on, but fell to a burst of machine gun fire that struck him in the stomach. He rolled on the ground screaming and cursing in pain until slowly his life ebbed away, blood pooling around him on the road. Low advanced *Barbaric* using McLennan's burning tank for cover, while Tennent moved up on his right and prepared to advance around him. Heavy fire now began to come from a house on the left and Low traversed his turret a little and ordered the gunner to fire. He watched as the bomb flew out of the barrel and arced in a shallow curve ahead of them and right into the wall of the target house, which collapsed in a bright explosion.

Now Tennent pulled out from behind Low's tank and came up on his right, but once again the loaded Petard proved their greatest hazard and it burst into flames as bullets hit the exposed explosive charge at the front of the launching barrel. As flames engulfed the front of the turret the 50mm anti-tank gun fired again, the round adding to the melee in the turret and killing the radio operator. Tennent ordered his driver to move out of range and, needing no second bidding, the man threw the AVRE into reverse and began backing away, but the gun crew up ahead were faster and a second shot slammed into the front of the vehicle. With flames pouring from the Petard and the crew wounded, Tennent ordered his men out and they fled to the nearby houses.

Once it had been reloaded, Low made one last effort to advance and knock out the anti-tank gun with his Petard. Moving around the burning *Barracuda*, he ordered his driver forward, but before they could close the range the 50mm spoke again and a round slammed into the co-driver's position, wounding one of the crew. The driver made to reverse, but another round struck almost immediately, wounding him and damaging the controls. The gunners opened up on the position with their Besas, but it was well entrenched and shielded and the bullets ricocheted off harmlessly. Unable to move or neutralize the gun, Low realized they had no option but to abandon the tank. The crew started to clamber for the hatches when a third round struck the gun mantlet and sparks and shrapnel showered the inside, killing their gunner. The rest of the crew spilled out into the street and jumped behind a wall with some of the commandos.

It had been no better for Y Troop, who had managed to follow the AVREs for a short distance but were quickly pinned down as soon as the advance stopped. Although the German forces withdrew to their defensive positions, the commandos, their commander dead and their armoured support soundly defeated, realized the hopelessness of the advance against a strongly entrenched enemy. Unable to hold their slim spur into the enemy strongpoint, the commandos withdrew a few hundred yards down the road. Low looked back at McLennan's pitiful body, but he knew there was no way to get to it without more men dying, and grimly he followed the commandos through back gardens and over walls to a new line of defence. Then someone asked if all the wounded had come back with them and Low, accompanied by a marine, ran forward again. No one had been left, and the two men gratefully returned to the modicum of safety provided by their new front line.[5]

While Y Troop had been trying to subdue Trout, a new threat was coming from the south. For several hours, 11 'Graf Waldersee' Battery of 1716 Artillery Regiment at Plumetot had been bombarding the predetermined defensive fire targets at La Brèche – Engers, Füssen and Freiburg. Equipped with six 15cm self-propelled artillery guns, the battery looked on paper to be well armed. In reality, their self-propelled guns were First World War-era 15cm sFH 13 howitzers mounted on small French Lorraine 37L armoured gun tractors. The resulting 15cm sFH 13/1 (Sf.) auf Geschützwagen Lorraine Schlepper(f) looked every inch as convoluted as its name, a huge gun perched on a chassis only 157cm wide and sitting so far back it looked like it might topple the vehicle backwards at any moment. But despite its ungainly appearance, the 15cm gun had been a significant artillery piece in the First World War, and was no less lethal in the Second.*

---

* 11 Battery had a complicated lineage. Its self-propelled guns were originally part of the independent Graf Waldersee Battery, which was later reclassified as

At 10:00 their commander, Leutnant Rudolf Schaaf,* had been contacted by Hauptmann Mikisch at 3 Battalion 736 Grenadier Regiment HQ. Although the battalion had lost all contact with strongpoint 20 at La Brèche, 10 Company were still holding strongpoint 21 at Lion-sur-Mer. But if the enemy advance was to be curtailed, they needed reinforcing, and soon. The battery was to advance with infantry support to Lion-sur-Mer and counter-attack the enemy forces there.†

Schaaf was not enthused by the idea. Once out of the town of Cresserons their advance would take them across almost one and a half miles of open flat fields where it would be impossible to avoid being spotted and fired on both from the sea and the air. But what could he do? Gathering his men around him, he outlined a rough plan. There were only a few substantial tracks from Cresserons to Lion-sur-Mer, all of which passed by the château. Their infantry support was limited to what was immediately available. Mikisch only had one company to hand – Leutnant Hans Gutsche's 11 Company in Cresserons – that would support the guns, but it was a pitiful little band to counter the huge force Schaaf had seen assaulting the beaches.

Nevertheless, he had his orders. The gun crews replenished their small ammunition stocks in the tractors and loaded more supplies on to trucks. Moving along the narrow lanes between high stone walls, the six guns wound their way to Cresserons, where the infantry waited for them. With an air of foreboding, the advance north began.[6]

B Troop had taken up an all-round defensive position among the houses, but now mortar fire rained down on their little hold-out, snipers restricted their movement, and somewhere to the south-west – beyond the château – was what looked like a self-propelled gun. There was a wireless link to HQ, but no defensive line back to them – they were out on a limb. HQ had little good news either: they were out of 3-inch mortar ammuni-

---

10 Battery 1716 Regiment. The battery was then re-armed with 15.5cm towed howitzers, and the self-propelled guns were issued to a newly formed 11 Battery, which then reclaimed the name Graf Waldersee.

* A leutnant was broadly equivalent to a second lieutenant in the British Army.

† In his reports, General Wilhelm Richter makes no mention of who ordered the counter-attack, but does record that the 'Graf Waldersee' battery was placed under 3 Battalion's control. This instruction most likely came from either himself or Ludwig Krug, but it was most likely Richter who gave the orders to attack Lion-sur-Mer.

tion and could provide no direct support. Gray could only advise the troop to hold their position for the time being.

Meanwhile A Troop had managed to reach the crossroads 100 yards behind B Troop, but no sooner had they arrived than sniper and mortar fire began to rain down on them too. The troop started to occupy the houses around them when Captain Caryll Powell noticed that some of the bombs ranging on them were much heavier than standard mortars. Another shell fell but rather than exploding when it hit a wall it went straight through it. Ordering the troop into cover, Powell spotted Private James Kelly, one of the troop's Bren gunners, seemingly with nothing to do. Grabbing his Bren gun, he gave Kelly a simple mission – get back to HQ and tell them that the troop were being engaged by tanks.

Kelly didn't relish his mission and, expecting that HQ were probably a mile away on the beach, he set off in a stooped run along the rue Victor Hugo towards the houses of Lion-sur-Mer. Rounding the corner, he was relieved to find HQ were only 400 yards behind A Troop in the grounds of the church, where he found Major John Taplin – the commando's adjutant but now acting second in command – and reported Powell's message. But Kelly was less relieved when Taplin told him to return with an instruction for Powell to hold on until they could sort out the overall situation. Cursing his luck, the marine set off back along the lane, keeping as low as possible in the 'marine crouch' and occasionally diving into the ditch alongside whenever bullets zipped past. As he passed a small farmstead he dived aside once more and found himself beside a small trench that led into an air raid shelter. Crawling along the trench he found a French couple hiding inside and in his basic French he explained he was English. Somewhat dazzled by the whole experience of the morning, the civilians silently proffered an open bottle of wine and Kelly took a grateful swig.

Returning to the road, Kelly dashed forward to the small gathering of buildings at the junction. There was no sign of A Troop as he hurried down the lane, bullets zinging off the walls, until he passed a large manor house on his left where a marine stepped out of the gateway and called him in. Darting through it, Kelly found himself standing among A and B Troops' wounded, laid out in the courtyard. Their signaller, still with his wireless strapped to his back, lay twitching on the hard cobbles; men moaned in pain. Running into the manor, Kelly found Captain Powell and passed on Taplin's instructions, whereupon his CO handed back his Bren and pointed to the back of the house with a gruff instruction. The marine made his way through the house and into the garden where unfamiliar faces directed him into a small shelter. Inside he found a young lieutenant studying the tree line at the end of the fields behind the manor through his binoculars. He wasn't one of Kelly's officers, but an officer was an officer whichever troop they were in and he quickly set the Bren up on a step – deploying the bipod at the front, setting the sights and bracing the butt into his right shoulder.

As he observed the tree line 400 yards to the south-west, Lieutenant Sturgis could see small parties of men advancing east along the track, their grey uniforms intermittently appearing in the gaps between the vegetation. A Bren gunner had just set up beside him, and calmly he directed the marine on one of the groups, passing on the range and bearing as he kept his eye on the target. Kelly adjusted the range dial on the side of the Bren, squinted down the sights and, once he was comfortable, fired his first burst. The Bren chattered and the butt juddered back into his shoulder. He let loose another few bursts while Sturgis watched the tracer fly across the field. As the targets moved around, Sturgis corrected Kelly's fire, directing him one way or the other, and although Kelly couldn't always see what he was firing at, after every few bursts Sturgis offered a few words of praise and encouragement. To Kelly it was so ridiculously simple that it felt just like practising on the ranges back in Kent. There didn't appear to be any immediate danger, the targets didn't seem particularly threatening, and his officer companion reloaded the Bren with fresh magazines whenever they were needed. But although neither man could see it, beyond the tree-lined lane a greater threat was materializing.

Five hundred yards behind the commandos, Captain Grant finally had some ammunition and was ordered to bring it down on the château, where armoured cars were rumoured to be gathering. With a signalman he went forward to observe the fall of shot, dodging the attentions of a sniper as they negotiated the treacherous tangle of telegraph wires. They dived into a cottage, scurried up to the top floor, from where they could just make out the château grounds, and summoned down the first stonk. The confusion of noise up ahead made it impossible to tell who was firing at who or if their rounds had made any difference, so Grant prepared to move again and find the forward troops.

Gutsche's 11 Company were steadily moving along the tree-lined lane south-east of the château, drawing fire but still able to penetrate closer to Lion-sur-Mer. Schaaf's self-propelled guns had now advanced into the château grounds, where at least one had been spotted by B Troop, although they had no effective way to respond. The 15cm artillery fell on to Lion-sur-Mer, demolishing the houses that 41 Commando sheltered in. As information trickled back to HQ at the church, Gray, who had no way of knowing the enemy's actual strength, realized that A and B Troops' slim salient was at risk. With the rest of the troops dispersed around Lion-sur-Mer, there was a very real threat of an enemy breakthrough. So close to the beaches, the effect could be disastrous. At 13:10, Gray decided there was little choice but to withdraw his troops and form a blocking line to protect the landings' west flank. Signals were transmitted and runners sent to the outlying positions to pull the commandos back.

Just as Grant reached the next collection of houses on the rue Victor Hugo, two stretcher bearers emerged from a courtyard ahead of him carrying a casualty between them. 'Orders to withdraw!' they shouted as they passed. 'Bloody chaos!' A battered section followed them, their corporal nursing a head wound that practically sprayed blood as he ran, and quickly organized a defensive position around the next house to cover the next group's withdrawal. Another stretcher appeared, this time carried by French men – barely boys, in fact – and an elderly lady supported a commando as he limped down the road.

Inside the manor's air-raid shelter James Kelly had slowly started to realize all was not well. His successful firing, as simple as a fairground shooting gallery, had brought the unwelcome attention of mortars and now, in the lulls between their explosions, he could hear the more frantic sounds of battle. At one point he looked behind him as Captain Powell came forward, but as the officer approached the shelter a shot rang out and a burst of blood blew out from his face. He collapsed then sat back up, a hole in his cheek where the bullet had gone straight through his open mouth.

Sturgis now had to organize B Troop. He laid three grenades on the parapet they were firing from and patted Kelly on the back encouragingly. 'Use them if they get too close,' he said, then headed back towards the house. Kelly stared after him. He had no intention of being around if the enemy got that close to him. Fortunately, a few minutes later Powell ordered him out and the two men pulled back down the road towards the church. By the time they got there the captain had acquired another wound in the leg, the fourth of 41 Commando's troop commanders to become a casualty in only six hours.

By 13:30, the church was the new front line in Gray's defensive position. All four of the troops so heavily engaged near the strongpoint and the château had fallen back to the new line. Somehow a despatch rider from the South Lancs had managed to find A Company and passed on the order for them to withdraw to the rest of the battalion. But in the chaos, one section from 41 Commando's A Troop had gone missing. There was no time to search for them – the growing enemy presence to the west suggested a counter-attack was imminent, and the commandos braced themselves for more action.

Gray moved his HQ back to the small wood closer to the beach – ironically the same wood that A Company South Lancs was originally supposed to secure for 41 Commando to pass through. S Troop's mortars were positioned nearby behind a row of semi-detached villas, but Grant was already back at the church. Together with Captain Dixon he climbed the tall church tower, the two officers cramming their equipment up the narrow staircase that seemed to tighten with each step, while cold stone walls threatened to asphyxiate them in their bulky webbing. On the flat roof a sandbagged position, doubtless an enemy observation post, offered a modicum of protection while they observed the grounds of the château from 77 feet above the town. Vehicles were manoeuvring around the château and Dixon, now joined by Bombardier Hazel 'Dick' Berryman, his reserve signaller with a new wireless set, struggled to contact the ships out at sea. But communications with *Ślązak* and *Verulam* remained ropey and Grant's mortars were the first to hit the enemy. Shortly afterwards a burst of machine gun fire smashed into the twelfth-century stonework and hastened the observers back to ground level.[7]

Whatever they might have achieved, 11 Company and Graf Waldersee were not aware of it. Their drive across the fields to Lion-sur-Mer had attracted attention from the air and strafing attacks had caused the first casualties. One of Schaaf's men, who had only recently been posted back to Germany but lingered in Normandy long enough to go souvenir shopping, died driving one of the ammunition trucks down the hill. The guns did better, reaching the château intact and quickly turning on the offensive, their powerful shells hitting the weakly equipped commandos and demolishing their positions over open sights. Small groups of men were ferreted out of their buildings and, unable to withdraw, were rounded up by 11 Company as they advanced through the small hamlets. As the British line fell back, the attackers were able to link up with the men in Trout.

Now, with the wreckage of the British assault littering the road, they pressed home their own attack along the avenue Henri Gravier. S Troop's machine guns, now positioned in a house looking down the road, poured covering fire past them, bullets thudding into grey-clad forms moving around the knocked-out tanks. One gunner, trembling with irate fury at the fate that had earlier befallen his comrades, called out each time he added another German to his grim tally. The mortars hit the advance hard and the brief German effort expired. Scurrying back to Trout, the defenders left an uneasy peace settling over Lion-sur-Mer.[8]

Troops of 1 Norfolk advance along the avenue de Lion, past strongpoint Cod on the right.

PART 4

THE AFTERNOON ACTIONS

12

THE GERMAN PARRY

ON THE BRIDGE OF HMS *DACRES*, BRIGADIER KENNETH SMITH glanced at his watch. It was already 09:00 and the first complete units of his brigade would start landing in less than an hour. It would soon be time to go ashore, he decided, and Captain Renfrew Gotto, Senior Officer Assault Group S2, looked for a suitable vessel to disembark the brigadier on to. At 09:25 he spied LCI(S) 524 and had his signaller flash a request for a pick-up. The signaller had just picked up his Aldis lamp when a violent explosion obliterated the LCI, a mushroom of smoke and flame slowly dispersing to reveal only a blazing sea. Gotto was appalled to see the sudden end of the ship, but there was no time for sympathy. Spying LCI(S) 505, he instructed his signaller to summon Lieutenant Christopher Berg's craft instead.

Berg manoeuvred his craft alongside the frigate and Lieutenant Colonel Nigel Tapp, CO of 7 Field Regiment, looked down on to the deck of the battered LCI without cheer. A badly wounded man lay groaning on the deck and the HQ party watched as Berg's crew struggled to transfer his stretcher on to *Dacres* as the two craft rolled and crashed against each other. After an uncomfortable wait Berg was ready to receive his new passengers, and Smith and his party jumped down on to the landing craft, stepping over the detritus of twisted hawsers, dropped kit and blood-stained bandages. At 09:55 Berg pulled away from the frigate and started back for the shore.

At that exact moment, Assault Group S11 was touching down on the shore. Nine LCI(L)s of 263 Flotilla had left the lowering position under fire as the German batteries east of the Orne unenthusiastically sent ranging shots back out to sea, sparking a flurry of broadsides from Force D. As they came into the beach, searching right on Queen White for space among the obstacles and wrecked landing craft, fire erupted from strongpoint Trout once more, and mortar bombs plopped into the sea alongside the impatient landing craft, spraying the decks full of waiting troops. Lieutenant Commander Frederick Newman did his best to keep the flotilla as close together as possible, but as they manoeuvred through the obstacles the line became ragged.

Even so, the flotilla touched down on time and in reasonable order. Quickly the ramps were thrust forward and the bulk of three entire battalions of infantry began to disembark. The Norfolks landed on Queen Red, just in front of the now nearly silent strongpoint Cod. On LCI 169 the starboard ramp was lost almost immediately to enemy mortar fire and the troops quickly made for the port side. Major Humphrey Wilson, the battalion second in command, glanced back at the bridge and saw Lieutenant Harrison give him a wave and a thumbs up. The major courteously remembered to salute as he left one of His Majesty's ships and disappeared down the gangway. To his delight he landed in less than a foot of water, so he kicked off the rubber waders his battalion had been issued with and, gathering his little party, set off to place signs at the beach exits to direct the Norfolks inland.

On Queen White the Warwicks had a similar experience, finding themselves landing in shallow water that made the waders redundant. Even so, indiscriminate mortar fire continued to land among them and Lieutenant Colonel Hugh Herdon found both the ramps of his LCI shot away. Obligingly, the skipper pulled away from the shore a little and came back in closer to an abandoned landing craft. The men on deck scrambled down to the wreck and used it as an impromptu pontoon to get ashore.

The King's Shropshire Light Infantry did not have it quite so easy. Coming ashore at the west end of Queen White, the LCIs grounded further out from the beach. As troops poured off LCI(L) 377, the starboard ramp twisted in the surf and rolled over, pitching heavily laden men into the sea. Corporal Robert Littlar moved over to the port ramp and staggered down it in a tightly packed line of men. As he looked down he realized the men ahead were still descending the ramp as they entered the sea. Reluctantly he followed them and found himself dropping into nearly 5 feet of water. It poured over the top of his chest-high waders, and, as they started to fill, his legs became heavier and harder to move. Ratings had attached a rope to the ramp and run it to the shore so that the line of nearly incapacitated men could drag themselves to the beach. As soon as he got to shallow enough water Littlar pulled out a knife and cut away the bottoms of his waders, then went to work on men emerging from the surf with waders swollen like tree trunks. Water drained out as if from a colander and, freed from their unnatural burden, the men dashed up the beach.

As 185 Brigade disembarked, their commander came up to the beach. 505's crew fired their Oerlikons at some houses that appeared still to be resisting as they closed the shore, then Berg brought them up on the sand. The ramps were pushed out a second time and the passengers dashed off, through a couple of feet of water and up the sand to a lane leading inland. After catching their breath and getting their bearings, the party of men wandered down the lane and on to the avenue de Lion.

There they found a breathtaking spectacle – hundreds of vehicles packed on the road, most heading west. C Squadron of 13/18 Hussars was filtering into the rows of Universal Carriers, jeeps, trucks and M10s of 20 Anti-Tank Regiment. Columns of men marched alongside the traffic, some using the narrow-gauge railway line on the south side of the road. Occasional bursts of fire would send them diving into an adjacent ditch or scurrying behind the vehicles, until the moment passed and they set off on their journey again. It was an impressive display of just how much had been landed so far, but it was deeply unsettling to see it all jammed on the road and blocking egress from the beach.[1]

While the infantry of 185 Brigade marched off the beach and snaked their way to their marshalling areas around Hermanville-sur-Mer, their armoured support was approaching the beach. The entire three squadrons and HQ Troops of the Staffordshire Yeomanry were borne by the eleven LCTs of 40 Flotilla. They had had a difficult passage, the heavy tanks reducing the LCTs' freeboard to the extent that most of them had more than half a foot of water sloshing around the tank deck as they approached the beach. Spotting the crowd of landing craft already on Queen White, Lieutenant Commander Frederick Humphrey held his flotilla a mile and a half off the beach for a short while and then contacted HMS *Goathland*. Captain Eric Bush informed him that rather than divert to Queen Red, 40 Flotilla would be better off aiming for the west end of White. Duly informed, Humphrey led the LCTs in.

As they closed, the individual craft skippers could see that there was only limited space at Queen White, and as they got nearer they realized that there was even less room on the beach itself. The black dots of dozens of vehicles sat above the waterline, seemingly so packed in on the narrow band of dry sand that there was no space to manoeuvre. Five hundred yards from the shore Humphrey signalled the flotilla to steer even further to the right flank. In tight turns, the LCTs twisted to starboard and headed to Queen Green.

Although a few landing craft had come ashore beyond exit 11 at the westernmost edge of Queen White, there had not yet been time to clear any of its obstacles, and defenders in the houses further along the shore were still resisting. On LCT 952 Lieutenant Stiles-Cox passed corrections down to Leading Seaman Philip Sharp in the wheelhouse and deftly 952 wound its way through the barely visible obstacles. Standing on the bridge, signaller Able Seaman Ralph McClure suddenly became aware of a pinging noise on the hull and uncomfortably realized that riflemen in the houses nearby were using him for target practice.

Worse still, the LCTs were now much closer to strongpoint Trout – the four LCTs furthermost west were only 1,000 yards away – and they instantly started to attract unwelcome attention from the coastal 75mm and 50mm guns. Even so, the gunners at Trout were acting almost in isolation. On the beach, Cod, Skate and Bass had been overwhelmed and the crews of strongpoint 10 were lying low after the French commando attack. Inland, the gunners of 2 Battery 1716 Artillery Regiment at strongpoint 16 (Morris) were more interested in their own defence as the Suffolks surrounded them. Graf Waldersee were engaged in Lion-sur-Mer, while 155 Regiment's batteries were now targeting enemy forces in Hermanville. Deprived of observation, 1 Battery of 989 Heavy Artillery Detachment at Basly continued to fire at the limit of their range, but like every other battery they were frequently interrupted by attacks from the air.

At 10:30, dead on time, the first landing craft ground ashore. The ramps dropped and the first Shermans of the Staffordshire Yeomanry drove off. At first the commanders were delighted to see that they were making what was in effect a dry landing, with only a few yards of shallow surf to negotiate. But as their drivers skidded the tanks around to the left to find the exits on Queen White, their hearts sank. A wall of stationary vehicles blocked their path. Almost nothing was moving off the beach.

At 11:00, Lieutenant Commander Edward Gueritz, now acting in the role of Deputy Naval Officer in Charge of the Queen Beach until his superior Captain William Leggatt arrived, looked east along Queen Red. Stationary vehicles littered the little band of sand above the waterline.

Even those that could move had nowhere to go. In the surf, dozens of abandoned vehicles lay, mixed with the obstacles, while broken landing craft rolled around with the waves. Only a few exits had been made off the beach and some of those had become blocked by vehicles that had hit mines or been struck by mortar bombs. Gueritz knew that another three groups would be beaching in the next thirty minutes, and he knew that it couldn't be here. Crossing the beach to the newly established naval headquarters in the dunes, he instructed a signaller to make contact with HMS *Goathland*. Reluctantly, he informed Captain Bush that Queen Red Beach was closed. It would be several hours before the beach was clear and open again.[2]

Brigadier Smith walked past the farm that Sergeant Kilvert and his men had assaulted only a short while ago and into the orchard where he found most of his staff waiting for him. Having been separated in the crowds, he had missed his turning off the avenue de Lion and now arrived late for his own Orders Group.

Quickly he issued his orders to his assembled officers. Lieutenant Colonel Maurice and the KSLI were to wait for the Staffordshire Yeomanry to join them in the adjacent orchard, ready to enact their mission as the mobile column. While a couple of the tank troops would lead without infantry, X and W Companies would clamber on to the hulls of the following tanks and the whole column would advance up the Périers Ridge along the road south of Hermanville leading to Biéville. Once they came into contact with enemy positions the infantry would dismount and the combined infantry and armour force would engage together before moving on along the road. Meanwhile, the Warwicks would follow on the right flank and the Norfolks on the left as planned, ready to assist in the capture of Lebisey and then, hopefully, Caen. There was a quick discussion about the start time for the move, but Smith decided they must wait for the tanks. Some of the assembled officers looked back towards the beaches doubtfully. It was obvious they would be late – even as they spoke the Shermans were parked on the sand, impatiently waiting to exit via the Fontaine de Gravier. Nonetheless, Smith insisted.

Major Alistair Cameron, second in command of 7 Field Regiment, found himself overlooking the fields south of Hermanville. To his concern, these were the positions chosen for his regiment, but as yet there were no infantry around them. In fact if they hadn't advanced by the time the guns arrived then 7 Field Regiment would be at the very front of the

Allied line. After contacting the recce party and discussing the best positions for the Priests, he walked back along Hermanville high street, passing dozens of French families standing in front of their homes and pressing flowers and even strawberries into the hands of their liberators.

As he reached the northern edge of the town he stumbled into his CO, Lieutenant Colonel Nigel Tapp. Tapp had been with 185 Brigade HQ and pressed Cameron for any updates on the regiment, but his second in command could offer little in the way of solid information. When he had left his command vehicle and walked into Hermanville, it was stationary on the beach. He promised to return and see what he could do to get them moving, but it would not be an easy task.

Lieutenant General John Crocker, commander of 1 Corps, had commandeered a landing craft and sailed over from Juno Area to Sword to come ashore and see for himself how things were progressing. Pacing down the avenue de Lion, he had quickly issued orders for all traffic to clear the roads. If a unit couldn't get to where it needed to go it shouldn't be stopping everyone else from doing so as well. Cameron was impressed to see his corps commander strolling the road, seemingly unflustered by the situation and wearing a peaked cap instead of a helmet. But Crocker could do little to help him right now and instead he sought out the aid of different caps – the red caps of military policemen. By employing a few he managed to cajole and bully half of the regiment's Priests past some of the traffic on the road, but it was a thankless task and he realized that with the rest still on the beach, more direct measures were needed. Having chased the rest of his regiment after it was diverted to and fro in front of the dunes, he saw them on to the road and then, disregarding the 'Achtung Minen!' signs lining the fields alongside the avenue de Lion, directed them through the corn. Seeing what was happening, a Royal Engineers officer immediately started to remonstrate with him, but Cameron ignored his protestations. As the first gun pulled off the road, the crews and numerous spectators held their breath, waiting for an explosion. As it crawled through the cornfield, the tracks churning the soil, it slowly dawned on the crew that there wasn't going to be one. Just as Lieutenant George Wilson had discovered only hours earlier, the minefield was a dummy.

But now the first mutterings of armoured resistance started to be heard. A French civilian reported that he had seen some forty German tanks in the area around Ansy and Anguerny three days previously. Urgent reconnaissance was asked for, but around midday the early intelligence was signalled to 1 Corps and then back down to 3 Division. At 12:00, Smith called another Orders Group as he ruminated on his brigade's dispositions. Tapp was pleased to report that all of 7 Field Regiment was now in position south of Hermanville, and Smith instructed Lieutenant Colonel Maurice to get the KSLI moving on foot; the Staffordshire Yeomanry would have to make contact once they had moved off the beaches. The Norfolks were to head east to Colleville and start their own move up the KSLI's left flank as soon as Hillman had fallen.

Then he announced the biggest change. In light of the reports of tanks north of Caen, alongside the strong opposition that 8 Canadian Brigade were apparently encountering to the west, and the heavy fire reportedly coming from a position near Périers-sur-le-Dan, he was going to put his alternative plan into effect. Reluctant to expose the Warwicks to a possible armoured thrust on their right flank, the battalion would move from their concentration area near Lion-sur-Mer to the east of Hermanville, preparatory to moving up the Norfolks' left flank. Some of the assembled officers shuffled uncomfortably. Smith had tried the same manoeuvre during Exercise Fabius, which had only led to chaos as the battalions became separated from one another and communication fell apart. Major General Rennie had pointedly asked, 'You won't let this happen on the day will you, KP?' but nonetheless had approved 185's final plan and its alternatives.[3]

Sergeant Earl Rice and the small party he had collected during the night had waited in the darkness south of Colleville all morning. Not long ago they had watched a large group of dejected-looking Germans stumbling their way south along the road to Hillman, and now they spied a following formation of troops in much more familiar olive green battledress. The paratroopers raised their weapons above their heads and stepped into view.

C Company of the Suffolks led the advance out of Colleville, where Lieutenant Colonel Richard Goodwin was startled to find the second group of Canadian paratroopers but pleased to hear that their leader had already seen Hillman. Together they advanced up a narrow track to the edge of a field where, peering over the corn, Goodwin got his first sight of their most important objective. To his surprise he could see an armoured cupola among the concrete positions – not something he had been led to expect from the intelligence documents he had been supplied with in the UK.

In fact Hillman was a substantial strongpoint. Straddling the lane running south out of Colleville, it consisted of seven machine gun positions, three of which were heavily reinforced with concrete and armoured cupolas. A network of trenches connected some twenty bunkers and personnel shelters, including Ludwig Krug's HQ bunker. The entire site was surrounded by two belts of barbed wire – the outer ring some 10 feet thick and the inner even thicker than that – the ground in between thickly sown with mines. British intelligence had believed it to be a battalion HQ and as yet none of the attacking force realized it was a much more significant regimental HQ. Crucially, all previous intelligence about Hillman had failed to identify the reinforced machine gun posts.

Hillman was also more crowded than usual. Units battered by bombardments and decimated by infantry and tank attacks had stumbled away from the front and, in the absence of anywhere else to go, had made their way to 736 Regiment's HQ. The strongpoint which usually housed thirty men – mainly staff and administrative troops – now hosted more than 150. But while Krug was pleased to see his men arriving, as far as he knew this might be all that existed of 736 Regiment. The last reports from 1 Battalion at strongpoint 14 and from 3 Battalion at Tailleville had spoken of heavy enemy attacks before all contact had been lost. 3 Battalion had obviously been heavily engaged on the coast where the main landings appeared to be. Krug could only hope that the companies east of the Orne survived, although he knew that there had been numerous airborne landings there.

Returning to the village, Goodwin found Captain Geoff Ryley who had brought A Company forward for their assault, dodging a short impromptu German artillery barrage on the way. The CO quickly briefed his company commander, instructing him to thoroughly reconnoitre the site and report back. He would post a platoon of C Company to the left of the Colleville road to observe the position's eastern edge while the rest of the company waited by the road. B Company would move to the fields to the right to provide fire support from the north of the position.

Leaving A Company and D Company's breaching platoons in a sunken lane at the southern end of the village, Ryley set off to examine the site. Crawling up the narrow lane with high earth banks and an avenue of trees on either side, he realized he was in perfect cover which would also shield his company as they advanced. Reaching the cornfield, he crawled through the 18-inch-high crop until he was close enough to study the site in detail. Ryley noted the armoured cupolas and the sheer scale of the position, far in excess of what his intelligence maps and documents had predicted. He also noted with dismay that there did not appear to be any damage to the site – supposedly bombed at dawn, the only visible craters were well to the north. This would be a tougher nut to crack than he had first assumed. Turning about, careful not to jostle the corn too much, he crawled back to the sunken lane and made his way back to the village to report to Goodwin.

After studying his maps and absorbing what Ryley had identified, Goodwin formulated his plan. The loss of Captain Llewellyn meant there was still no chance of Royal Navy support, but 76 Field Regiment and the battalion's 3-inch mortars, along with any other firepower that could be assembled, would bombard the position for five minutes before the assault began. Under cover of the bombardment the breaching platoon would make their way to the top of the sunken lane and then, under cover of smoke, crawl to the outer bank of wire and blow it with Bangalore torpedoes. A mine clearance party would move through and clear a narrow path to the second belt of wire so that a second Bangalore team could clear that. With a route into the strongpoint open, A Company would advance and assault the individual positions. At 13:00 Ryley reported that his company was ready, and Goodwin issued the prearranged fire support codeword 'Grab' in plain language over the radio net. C Squadron 13/18 Hussars picked up the message and moved up the road to fire on the strongpoint, adding their weight to the artillery and mortars.

In the HQ bunker's observation cupola, Hans Sauer watched nervously for any sign of movement to the north. He had seen the British take strongpoint 16 outside Colleville so he knew they were near, but as yet he hadn't sighted anyone enter the field in front. Suddenly, at 13:10, he heard the whine of artillery shells overhead and, seconds later, their scream as they descended. He ducked down into the protection of the thick underground bunker as a rain of shells and mortar bombs fell into the strongpoint, throwing up great sods of earth. Less than 300 yards to the north-west, Lieutenant Mike Russell of D Company's breaching platoon led his men up the sunken lane. Staying low, they crawled into the edges of the cornfield and watched the last gasps of the all too brief bombardment. As the final explosion faded away they crawled the last 100 yards through the corn to the edge of the outer wire, while sections spread out on either side and threw smoke grenades beyond the wire to obscure Russell and his men. As soon as they reached the wire the Bangalore torpedoes were screwed together and thrust under the coils. The charge was ignited and the men scurried back a few dozen yards, pressed themselves against the hard earth and waited for the explosion.

In a great blast the barbed wire was thrown into the air and collapsed back to earth, sagging out of its coils like a squashed spring. As the dusty smoke cleared, a neat gap through the wire revealed itself – instantly the mine clearance party were through it and probing for mines. But now the smokescreen became a threat to the breaching team. Aware that an assault was underway, it was clear to the defenders that the smokescreen was obscuring it and indiscriminate fire was directed at the cloud. Under intense fire, the mine clearing party had no time to lift the mines they found and marked them instead, the hail of bullets miraculously missing them. Finally, after fifteen minutes of methodical work, the party had cleared a 3-foot-wide track through the minefield right up to the inner wire. As they slid back, Russell and his team crawled up with the second set of Bangalores and began to assemble them while bullets zipped over their heads. Painstakingly slowly, each torpedo was screwed into the next until it could be slid under the entire thicket of wire. The party retreated while Russell attached the charge then scurried back along the cleared path. He ducked down to the ground and waited.

Nothing happened. Russell looked up and saw that the detonator had failed; the Bangalore lay uselessly under the wire. Cursing, he slid forward on his stomach again, holding a new detonator in his teeth and trying to use the full width of the narrow track to avoid the sweeping machine gun fire. He reached the torpedo and fitted the new charge before crawling back, scraping his body across the hard earth as quickly as his tired limbs allowed. This time the detonator worked: the wire was severed across its width and tossed sideways, opening a route into the strongpoint for A Company.

Corporal Edmund Jones didn't need to wait for an order – as soon as the Bangalore blew he was on his feet and leading his section from 8 Platoon through the outer wire. They rushed along the 3-foot-wide track and through the second wire, where they instantly ran into a storm of machine gun fire. Jones was killed immediately and several more of his section fell, clutching wounds. Lieutenant John Powell raced up with 9 Platoon, but now the machine gun in the cupola less than 30 yards away had an unhindered view of the assaulting troops and poured fire in their direction. The platoon went to ground as bullets scoured the area. Powell called up his PIAT team with their anti-tank mortar. Crawling forward, the team cocked the unwieldy weapon, placed a bomb into the trough at the front, then carefully lined it up with the cupola. The gunner pulled the trigger and the PIAT kicked back into his shoulder, threatening to break it, while the bomb soared forward and smashed into the cupola in a burst of flame. The fire blossomed up and the smoke cleared, but the cupola was undamaged. The team re-cocked the rigid spring and fired another bomb, which exploded equally ineffectively. Now grunting with the effort the team re-cocked again, and a third bomb was launched. The German steel remained unaffected.

The strength of the defences was becoming clear to the attackers, but the PIAT had at least managed to distract the gunners inside the cupola long enough for some of the Suffolks to rush forward to the trenches. One at a time the men darted to a small shell hole and from there into the trench network. Private Eric Rowland passed bodies as he made the desperate run into the strongpoint, but his attention was on the bomb hole ahead and he didn't see what uniforms they wore. In the trench, Lieutenant Powell quickly began organizing his small force when a stick grenade whirled through the air and landed among them. There seemed to be no time to react and the men simply stared at their nemesis. With each passing second came doubt – if only they had dived to the ground immediately they might have survived; now it was surely too late. But as the seconds continued to tick by it became evident the grenade was a dud. Relieved, Powell peeked out of the trench. The strongpoint was on sloping ground so it was impossible to observe the rest of the site. Spotting Rowland, he ordered him to clamber out of the trench and crawl forward to see if there was any value in putting a Bren on the rise ahead of them. Far from delighted, Rowland held his breath and rolled out of the trench. Slithering forward, he realized the ground continued to slope to another rise – there was no real view to be had. He called back to Powell, who beckoned him, and, relieved, the private tumbled into the trench.

Powell realized his little bridgehead was precarious. Only a few men had arrived in the trench and they had little ability to control their position. He ordered a man to run back to the sunken lane and ask for reinforcements. The man dropped his kit, scrambled out of the trench and dashed for the gap in the wire, dodging left and right before a burst of machine gun fire struck him and he fell like a sack of lead. Powell cursed, then called another man forward. Sprinting for all he was worth, leaping left and right as bullets spat around him, the runner rushed for the gap, sprinted down the cleared path through the minefield and tumbled into the sunken lane. Breathlessly he passed his message to Goodwin.

Realizing the attack might falter, Goodwin ordered the second assault platoon forward under the cover of smoke from the platoon mortars. As soon as there was a thick enough white acrid fog over the gap Lieutenant Trevor Tooley led 8 Platoon forward, with Ryley hot on his heels. Frank Varley, Ryley's signaller, stuck close to his CO, the bulky wireless set on his back bouncing as he sprinted through the gap in the outer wire. As machine gun fire whizzed through the corn alongside him he dropped to the ground and into the welcome – if ineffective – shelter afforded by the crop. The wireless set's whip aerial sprung around above him as German bullets zipped through the air, buffeting it one way and the other.

Ryley managed to sprint into the trenches but Tooley and Powell were nowhere to be seen.* Quickly he organized the troops that had made it this far, but they were few in number and the small force couldn't progress any further down the trench network. Without his signaller to call for assistance, Ryley jumped out of the trench himself and started on the dangerous bullet-scarred path back to the sunken lane. Varley looked up as his CO came sprinting back towards him, when a sudden burst of bullets struck the officer and he fell, dead, to the ground.

Powell could now see there was little hope of maintaining their slim bridgehead in the strongpoint. He gathered the small party of men and, seeing smoke once again drifting across the gap in the wire, led them back out and into the sunken lane at the double. Dropping into the cover of the trees, their hearts thumping with adrenalin, the men collapsed, dejected and bitter.[4]

In Hermanville, the KSLI had been sat waiting for instruction in an orchard adjacent to Brigadier Smith's temporary HQ. Desultory shellfire occasionally landed among them, obviously unobserved and based largely on guesswork on the part of the gunners, but even so Corporal Robert Littlar's lance corporal was hit in the foot by red-hot shrapnel, splitting boot leather and flesh in equal measure and depriving him of his section's second in command. No sooner had his lance corporal been carried away than they received orders to move. Every man had brought ashore with him a sandbag packed with extra equipment – sweaters, gas

---

* Tooley was already dead, Powell was alive but out of sight.

masks and extra rations; now they dumped these in large piles to be collected by the battalion's transport later. But Smith's plan was continuing to crumble. Royal Engineers reported a large minefield on the right flank south of Hermanville, so the battalion were to advance along the road leading due south and up on to the Périers Ridge, hopefully with the tanks close behind.

With X Company in the lead, the battalion marched through Hermanville and along the road to Lebisey. As they made their way up the gentle rise between fields of corn, mortar and artillery fire started to fall nearby, slowly getting heavier as the company climbed higher on the ridge. At first Littlar wasn't sure if it was their own artillery and naval support, but as it got closer it started to become painfully obvious they were being spotted by enemy observers. Enemy infantry started to snipe on them from the fields. Lieutenant Harry Jones, commander of 10 Platoon, heard rustling in the field to his left and without thinking stood on the bank alongside the road, at first ignorant of the rifle fire whistling past his head. To his shock he discovered an armed German advancing on him through the corn. Quickly drawing his own revolver he whipped off two shots but in his keyed-up state he paid little attention to his aim and both missed. The German threw his weapon aside and gleefully raised his hands as he closed on the bewildered lieutenant. Suddenly aware of the rifle fire, Jones grabbed the man and dived into the ditch. Lying alongside his first ever prisoner, he relieved him of his paybook then pointed towards Hermanville and in schoolboy German ordered him away. The grateful German jogged down the slope behind him.

The intensity of enemy fire increased. The men nervously spread out to the practised 5 yards between each man and then the leading two platoons spread out and moved through the corn, like beaters flushing prey from the crop. As the small arms and artillery fire got closer still, they dived into the shallow ditches alongside the road. Unfazed, Lieutenant Colonel Maurice carried on up the road, fiddling with his helmet strap and seemingly oblivious to the incoming fire. Watching him, some with admiration, some with incredulity, the men followed his example and got back up and soon X Company was on its way again. As they neared the top of the ridge, Jones saw infantry bundling themselves into trucks and withdrawing, but a machine gun position to the right opened fire on them instead and desultory fire seemed to be coming from Hillman on the left. The men went to ground yet again and Maurice sent W Company around the right flank to clear the machine gun position. As they did so, the first rumblings of tanks came up the hill behind them. The Staffordshire Yeomanry had arrived at last.

The Staffordshire Yeomanry's CO, Lieutenant Colonel Jim Eadie, had sensed the need to get to the high ground on Périers Ridge and ordered C Squadron to race there as soon as they were clear of the traffic chaos behind the beach. Major Patrick Griffin obligingly led his tanks straight through the fields west of the Lebisey road in order to get to Point 61, the high point of the ridge just south-west of Hillman and the KSLI's first objective. B Squadron under Major George Turner MC followed, pushing out further to the right to cover C Squadron's advance. But as they approached the summit of the ridge an anti-tank gun somewhere to the right flank barked; in a flash a round penetrated the hull of the leading Sherman and it juddered to a halt. B Squadron's tanks fanned out but in quick succession two fascine tanks, another Sherman and an Observation Post tank[*] of 33 Field Regiment all brewed up as rounds hit them. Then even the medical officer's half-track burst into flames. The remaining tanks pressed forward, identified the errant gun's location and silenced it, but it was a shaky start to the advance.[†]

Worse was to follow. As C Squadron and the lead companies of the KSLI reached the high point of the road at Point 61, 2 Battery of 21 Panzer Division's 155 Artillery Regiment – positioned at strongpoint 21A and with a completely unrestricted view of the road – began firing their 122mm guns over open sights. C Squadron returned fire while the infantry took cover, but it was clear to Maurice that it would need his men to silence the battery. At 14:25, the advance already well behind schedule, he ordered Major Peter Wheelock to attack it with Z Company.

Z Company had followed X and W up the hill and had received less attention from the enemy fire directed on the lead companies, but even so they lost two men and a third wounded as they summited Périers Ridge. At first Wheelock was uncertain of the exact location of the battery he had been ordered to engage but quickly organized his company

---

[*] A Sherman tank stripped of its armament in order to provide space for map tables and wireless sets from which a forward observer could call on artillery support. The 75mm was often replaced with a wooden barrel in order to give the Sherman the appearance of being a regular tank.
[†] The gun, identified in the war diary as an 88mm, may well have been a self-propelled 75mm of 716 Division's Anti-tank Battalion. 1 company was based in Biéville and, according to Richter, was operating around Point 61.

for an advance west, with 16 and 18 Platoons in the van and 17 following a short distance behind.

Meanwhile X Company pushed forward, advancing through the corn and occasionally flushing out snipers and machine gunners. The view south opened up as they crossed the wide ridge and in the distance, just over 3 miles away, they could see Lebisey Wood on the next ridge. Down below them was the small village of Beuville, nestling at the start of the valley between Périers Ridge and Lebisey. Just in front of it a small stream – little more than a cutting in the ground – wound its way from the fields on the right, through a small culvert under the road and round to the south-east. But as the leading platoon closed on Beuville's few rustic buildings and farmhouses, unnervingly accurate sniper fire started to come their way. Wary of the time, Lieutenant Colonel Maurice came to the conclusion that trying to push the entire battalion through Beuville was a fruitless endeavour and he quickly decided that while X Company pressed on along the road to secure it for traffic, W and Y Companies should bypass the north end of the village and come into it from the flanks. Meanwhile, anxious to cover their west flank lest the rumours of tanks were true, the battalion's 6-pounder anti-tank guns, along with M20s of 20 Anti-Tank Regiment's 41 Battery, were deployed along the southern edge of Périers Ridge from Beuville towards Périers-sur-le-Dan.

Followed by a handful of tanks, X Company's leading platoon kept low and rushed down the slope to the culvert. But as they rounded a bend in the road behind a small copse an incendiary round suddenly struck a soldier's bandolier and the rounds of ammunition across his chest detonated. The platoon dived for cover and started unleashing fire at wherever they thought the shots had come from. Robert Littlar took out all of the visible windows of a farm on the left side of the road, but in truth he had no idea where the round had been fired from. X Company came to a complete halt as they tried to identify their invisible enemy, but the well-hidden snipers proved good shots and soon almost all of the section leaders in the leading platoon were casualties. Major Guy Thornycroft quickly directed the following two platoons to fan out to the right of the road, where they scrambled their way through the corn up the short slope to the village. Once he'd made it to cover, Littlar slipped out his knife again and cut away his corporal stripes. He would not advertise his rank to snipers again in Normandy.

Still grappling with the enemy on the road, Harry Jones decided to try and push through. Grabbing the handset from his wireless operator's set he called up his CO to report, but Thornycroft was way ahead of him and already pinned down behind a low wall further up in the village. Politely he asked if Jones might be able to help extract him. Dashing forward with two of his men, the young lieutenant rushed down the road, zigzagging lest they had been spotted by the snipers. Eventually they found their CO just ahead and lobbed smoke grenades in his direction. As the canisters released their noxious gases a cloud grew in front of the major, enough for him to break cover and sprint back to his saviours. They dashed back down the road towards 10 Platoon, leaving the cloud of smoke behind. No longer obscured, a shot rang out and one of Jones's men fell, a bullet lodged in his head. A second shot brought down a second man. Their lungs bursting, the two officers took a curve in the road and out of sight of the sniper. As Jones caught his breath a Priest appeared along the road. Suspecting the sniper had fired at them from the tower of the small church down the road, he asked the crew if they could deal with the problem and, only too happy to help, the gunners moved down the road. There was a loud bang as their 105mm fired, followed by the mad clanging of the church's bells.

Taking advantage of the trees lining the stream, Major Peter Steel led Y Company out to the left of Beuville and on to the route de Colleville, a track running north and back to Hillman – which even now the Suffolks were still trying to secure. But to the west, W Company quickly became embroiled in the fighting further along Beuville's main road. Major Slatter DCM, seeing that X Company were still locked in a battle with the snipers further back along the road, walked towards the hotspot and engaged in his own personal battle with the snipers, spraying submachine gun fire wherever he thought he saw a rifle poking from a window or from behind a wall. As Jones rounded a bend he saw the major ahead of him, just as a grenade landed at the feet of Private Edward Owen, who had joined Slatter. The stick grenade detonated, killing Owen immediately and wounding Slatter in the arm. Jones darted up and pulled the major out of sight into a small barn to patch him up, and Captain Robert Rylands, the company second in command, took over. But Slatter's action had linked the two companies and X Company were able to advance through the rest of the village and put the snipers behind them. Steadily, the KSLI advanced on Biéville.

Far behind them, Z Company had advanced the mile along the ridge. It was approaching 16:00 when the leading scouts reported back to Wheelock that they had a tough nut to crack: the battery outside Périers-sur-le-Dan was also a minor strongpoint and in addition to the four dug-in guns there were at least three large concrete shelters and several weapons pits and trenches. The company did not have an artillery spotter with them, but Lieutenant Colonel Jim Eadie had a good view of the battery and passed the coordinates on to Major Ian Rae of 7 Field Regiment RA, who was travelling with Maurice's HQ. 7 Field Regiment, their guns now established in the field a mile north, repositioned and elevated their barrels, then unleashed a storm of fire on the target. But watching from the cornfields nearby Z Company were not impressed – every shell missed the strongpoint.

There was no time to waste, though. Lieutenant Frederick Percival led 16 Platoon towards the outer wire. The defenders quickly unleashed a hail of small arms fire and 16 Platoon returned fire as both sides attempted to suppress the other. Eventually the British gained the upper hand and were able to force the gunners away from their artillery pieces, but the Germans simply withdrew to the weapons pits and returned fire from better cover. Although 16 Platoon had been able to halt the battery's bombardment of targets to the north, they couldn't gain entry to the strongpoint. Lieutenant Scarlett led 18 Platoon round the left flank but ran into the same problem, made worse by enemy mortar fire that quickly killed three of the men. Then Lieutenant Percival was felled in a hail of bullets.* It was stalemate.[5]

While the KSLI advanced south, Brigadier Smith visited Colleville to find out what progress the Suffolks were making. By 14:30, 1 Norfolk and 2 Warwick were gathering in the orchards on the east side of Colleville, waiting for the strongpoint to fall so that they could make their advance on to Périers Ridge. With three battalions now gathered in the village and vehicles queuing on the high street waiting to advance, the pressure was increasing.

Having pulled all his men out of the wire around Hillman, Lieutenant Colonel Goodwin was now considering his next move. He decided that tank support was essential, and the apparent absence of any anti-tank guns in the strongpoint made this appear feasible. Accordingly, some of C Squadron 13/18 Hussars' tanks lumbered up to the outer wire and started to fire on the strongpoint. While their machine guns chattered away at anything that moved, the 76mm and 17-pounder guns were

---

* Percival died of his wounds the next day.

directed on the cupolas. Solid shot and HE were blasted at the steel defences, but to the tankers' dismay they did little more than score the thick metal. Goodwin was little better off: it was obvious that the tanks would need to get into the strongpoint in order to subdue it, and in order to achieve that the track through the minefield between the inner and outer barbed wire needed to be widened. As he looked around for a Royal Engineer, his eyes alighted instead on a tam-o'-shanter cap. Striding up the road was Major General Tom Rennie.

Goodwin quickly briefed his CO. Rennie frowned as the predicament became clear: Hillman was taking longer to crack than had been hoped for and now it was holding up three battalions. 'Well, you must get it before dark,' he told Goodwin, 'and in time to allow you to dig in on your consolidated positions. Enemy armour is about and they will probably counter-attack before first light.' Goodwin assured Rennie they'd get it done and the general headed off. Although Hillman was causing trouble, 3 Division was well ashore and in command of a sizeable beachhead. Things were going reasonably well considering they'd just made an opposed amphibious assault.

Captain Arthur Heal of 246 Field Company listened patiently as Goodwin explained his needs. The problem he outlined was solvable, Heal thought – the quickest, easiest and safest way to widen the track was with a Crab flail tank. But, he reasoned, he was here now and a recce was a sensible idea before the armour arrived. Collecting Lance Corporal Boulton, the captain headed up the sunken lane and through A Company. Reaching the field, the two men dropped on to all fours and made their way to the wire. While a squad threw more smoke grenades into no-man's land the two men dropped on to their bellies and set about searching the minefield, gently prodding the ground with their bayonets. Despite the best efforts of the tanks, the machine gun posts in the armoured cupolas continued to fire sporadically into the smokescreen. But Heal was unperturbed – his mind was more fixed on trying to make sense of the minefield's layout. At first his prodding brought no results and he started to think it might be a dummy, until his bayonet struck metal at last. Searching around, he started to find more and had soon identified four rows, each mine about 5 yards apart from its neighbours. The final mine he encountered was unusual – he had successfully identified the others, but the final one appeared much larger. Gently he scraped away the soil until he could see the whole device, and to his relief, he finally recognized it. It was a British Mk III mine, practically obsolete but evidence that the Germans were using anything they had access to. This one had probably been dumped by the British in 1940.

His recce complete, Heal reported to Goodwin. It would take about an hour to clear the gap by hand, he informed the CO. It could be done quicker if he used gelignite charges to detonate the mines, but this would only guarantee a gap 5 yards wide. Goodwin turned to Major Sir Delaval Cotter. It was tight, the commander of C Squadron 13/18 Hussars agreed, but enough. Goodwin ordered Heal back to the minefield.

Even as Heal returned to the strongpoint, new pressures started to come to bear. Brigadier Edward Cass arrived in Colleville to see progress, keen to find out what was keeping 185 Brigade's two battalions from advancing. Goodwin updated him and requested two flail tanks to speed the clearance of the minefield. Cass immediately agreed and promised to get some tanks from the Staffordshire Yeomanry to support the attack. Shortly after, Lieutenant Colonel Eadie despatched A Squadron to support the next attack on Hillman.

Heal had gathered a section of his men and was back in the minefield again. Everyone lay as flat on their bellies as they could, dragging themselves across the corn, which by now was so trampled it offered little cover. Their arm muscles ached with the strain of trying to gently prod the ground and then dig out a mine from such a prone position. But time was marching on and Brigadier Smith had decided that 1 Norfolk simply had to get moving. He instructed Lieutenant Colonel Robert Bellamy to take his battalion across the ridge east of Hillman. Lieutenant Colonel Hugh Herdon would go wider, taking the Warwicks across to Saint-Aubin and south from there. If it was feasible they would follow the Norfolks on to the ridge, but if circumstances dictated they would press on to the canal and follow it south. Even so, Smith declined to release the Warwicks immediately – they would wait until the enemy strength at Saint-Aubin was clear.

Bellamy ordered his second in command, Major Humphrey Wilson, to see if he could identify a route through to their first objective, a building and woods on the high ground of the ridge with commanding views south, codenamed Rover. Wilson headed out to the east of Colleville. Some 1,000 yards further east he could see the town of Saint-Aubin, but that was the Warwicks' objective and they had no idea what strength the enemy might be in there. He jogged along a track leading south, stooping low to keep as close to the level of the surrounding corn as possible, nervously keeping half an eye to his right where sporadic gunfire echoed around Hillman. A little further on he could see that the track forked – one branch struck out up the slope and directly towards their objective.

Pleased with Wilson's discovery, Bellamy ordered him to take A and B Companies through the fields on either side of the track and up to Rover; he would follow with C and D Companies in reserve. Lieutenant Eric Smith and 4 Troop of C Squadron 13/18 Hussars were sent out at the same time to provide support and, if possible, flank Hillman. On no account was the force to get involved with Hillman or Saint-Aubin – they needed to get on south.

The battalion struck out shortly after 15:00, the leading companies keeping themselves widely spaced as they moved through waist-high corn. At first things seemed quiet, but after a quarter of a mile the first machine gun fire started to zero in on them. The Norfolks dropped to hands and knees and started moving on all fours through the fields while the machine guns' bullets whizzed through the heads of the corn. Private Geoffrey Duncan of 10 Platoon B Company found the experience of crawling through the corn exhausting – sweat poured down his face as he moved forward in his own little world, the corn cutting him off from his colleagues, their locations only revealed by muffled shouts and cries of pain. Private Evans in 12 Platoon heard a cry behind him, looked around through the swaying crop and saw one of the company's cooks clutching a bullet wound through the neck. As he pushed on he was struck by the sight of bright red poppies growing among the corn and he remembered his father's stories of the Great War.

Smith and 4 Troop were not having any better a time. An anti-tank gun opened fire – Smith saw the shots aimed at them but was relieved they missed. The following two tanks were hit in quick succession. While one brewed up, the other was still mobile, although the driver was badly wounded. The internal wireless was knocked out, so Sergeant Haygarth clambered out of the turret and directed co-driver Corporal Pickles through his hatch. Despite the AT gun continuing to target them, they managed to get the tank back into the cover of Colleville's orchards with Smith racing in behind them.

By now A and B Companies were taking heavy casualties as Hillman's machine guns scythed the cornfield. As they returned fire and sought to suppress some of the positions firing at them, they became more and more drawn into a battle with the strongpoint. Their axis of advance slowly and inevitably drifted west. Soon they were fully embroiled in a firefight with Hillman.

Bellamy was worried. He ordered C and D Companies to stay on the planned course and sent instructions to A and B to disentangle themselves as quickly as possible and follow them up to Rover. Making their way alongside the track in leaps and rushes through the corn, the two reserve companies briskly got up the slope. At 17:00, after covering just over a mile, they reached a traditional Norman farmhouse on the ridge, thick stone walls enclosing a courtyard with a small idyllic cottage at the back. The two companies were without any support – their mortars and anti-tank guns were still back in Colleville and no vehicles had made it this far with them. Major Robin Dunn, their liaison with 7 Field Regiment RA, had arrived but his wireless set was with the vehicles back in the village, so they could not even call on artillery support. Quickly the Norfolks set about securing the farmhouse and then started to explore the woods on the reverse slope. Small arms fire echoed among the trees as invisible German defenders sniped at the attackers as they tried to secure their tentative hold on Rover.[6]

13

THE SLOG INLAND

GAZING AT THE BEACH FROM THE DECK OF LCI(L) 388, LIEUTENANT Cyril Rand, the commanding officer of 15 Platoon in C Company of 2 Royal Ulster Rifles, felt he was watching some epic film rather than witnessing real events with his own eyes. Burning buildings pumped thick black smoke over the shore, where shells burst in bright flashes of yellow and orange flame among broken bodies and vehicles. At the top of the beach hundreds of vehicles sat nose to tail, apparently stationary, while sporadic small arms fire came down on them from some of the houses.

On the bridge, Lieutenant Francis Willoughby was determined to drive his landing craft as high up the beach as possible. His passengers were heavily laden enough with their kit, but parked on deck were dozens of bicycles with which they were to make their advance. Deep water would not be welcome and so, after they had negotiated the obstacles, 388 crashed ashore at 8 knots at 11:55. The bow pushed deep into the sand, the crew hastily threw out the ramps, ratings rushed down them with lines, and the first troops descended. Rand ran down the ramp in a manner he hoped would inspire his platoon, only to tumble into deep water at the bottom; his men followed, sticking to the port ramp as the starboard side floundered. But for some the burden of the bicycle was one too many and they threw the hated contraptions over the side. On the bridge Willoughby watched with concern – it would take twice as long to disembark everyone at this rate, and the growing pile of submerged bicycles alongside the port ramp did nothing to improve matters.

Then, as if things weren't difficult enough, a new problem came into view. LCI(L) 391 had beached on Willoughby's starboard side and now the tide started to sweep her down the beach. Lieutenant Jack Houghton found himself powerless to stop his vessel from lurching to port and within minutes she was up against 388 and thudding into her hull. As the two craft locked together Willoughby gritted his teeth as he imagined what might be happening to the hull. But there was one bright light to be seen: the Royal Ulster Rifles on his deck had quickly started jumping over to 391 and even now were using her ramps to descend.

On either side of the conjoined landing craft the rest of Reserve Group 16 had come ashore, bringing with them the bulk of the infantry of 9 Brigade. Lieutenant Commander James Harbottell had directed the entire group on to Queen White, and now bagpipes echoed across Sword Beach once again as 1 King's Own Scottish Borderers descended the ramps of LCI(L) 376 and her neighbours. On 387, Sub Lieutenant Williams bit his lip as he watched the Scots stripping off their waders on deck, apparently unconcerned about his need to eventually get off the beach. He looked behind him – the tide was already starting to fall.

Further east along the beach 2 Lincoln came ashore in deeper water, some of them up to their necks and losing kit in the rough surf. As they made their way to the back of the beach they were impressed to see long lines of Germans marching past, their hands on their heads or high in the air. Nearby, while he waited for his platoon to gather, Rand watched with faint amusement as a German officer demanded of one of the beach party sergeants that his men should be taken to a place of safety away from the shelling. Rand could see from the look on the sergeant's face that he was not amused by the irony of the fact it was German shells falling on the beach. Grabbing a spade, he threw it at the German and told him to 'dig yourself a fucking hole then'.

As 9 Brigade's companies came together, they marched down the cleared exits and on to the avenue de Lion where they turned west and headed for their pre-allocated forming-up locations in the fields west of the lane to Hermanville-sur-Mer. Not long after, Brigadier James Cunningham arrived with his HQ party and established a temporary base near the Fontaine de Gravier – the plan was to quickly move off to the west and into Cresserons and Plumetot, where the main HQ would be established prior to the advance on Cambes.[1]

On LCI(L) 388, it had taken well over an hour to clear all the infantry aboard, and looking behind him Willoughby could see the tide had already fallen significantly. The kedge anchor they had dropped on their way into the beach was already poking above the waves. The crew tried running the winch to pull themselves off, but it was too late – 388 was stuck fast. Next door Houghton found much the same problem, exacerbated when they appeared to become the targets for some unwanted artillery fire. He shouted over to Willoughby, and they decided there was no sense in staying aboard. Gathering small arms from the ship's weapons locker and collecting their confidential books, the two crews dashed off their landing craft, suddenly aware that as well as artillery they were receiving unwelcome attention from riflemen in the houses in front of them.

Faced with 1,800 men disembarking from nine landing craft, the few German defenders still ensconced in the houses behind Queen White Beach had wisely kept low. But now that the beaches were relatively quiet again they took the opportunity to take pot shots at the small parties of men waiting in the dunes and the Royal Engineers that had ventured back out to the exposed beach obstacles. But Willoughby's crew were in no mood simply to sit on the receiving end, and Leading Stoker Kelly led Able Seamen James and Barter into a nearby house. A few minutes later they returned with a terrified prisoner and, communicating through the first lieutenant who spoke some German, they discovered he was an eighteen-year-old Pole who had been left in the house after his CO had been killed. Grudgingly they turned him over to the Military Police. Houghton's crew went even further, joining with some soldiers of the beach party to stalk around several villas, eventually driving out seven Germans and capturing a treasure trove of maps, artillery information and intelligence documents. A little later one of the beachmasters enquired if the crew could put their deck Oerlikons to use on some of the more obstinate defenders still holed up in the houses. The gunners of both landing craft were only too happy to oblige and 20mm shells quickly silenced even the most stubborn defenders.

Meanwhile, other landing craft were still coming ashore. Although the shellfire and mortaring had slackened considerably as the various enemy positions inland fell, sporadic air attacks by small groups of Junkers 88s and strafing runs by fighters continued to cause disruption.* Offshore of

---

* In contemporary reports, Ju 88 raids are recorded at 15:35 (by Admiral Talbot) and at 17:35 (LCI(L) 391). Other witnesses, including journalist Alan Melville, report seeing bombers and fighters attacking the beach during the afternoon. It is possible of course that many people witnessed the same attacks but mistook the times, but it is fairly certain that Priller and Wodarczyk in their Focke-Wulfs were not the only pilots to attack Sword on D-Day.

Lion-sur-Mer, Reserve Group 17 were preparing to unload their vehicles. But unlike the landing craft that had gone in to beach, the five LSTs of Group 17 stood 1,000 yards offshore. They were too big to risk beaching as they would in all likelihood become stuck in the sand – this would be dangerous for their hulls, expose them to enemy artillery and air attacks until the next high tide, and clog the beach unnecessarily. Instead, the flat-decked Rhino ferries they had towed across the Channel behind them were cautiously unchained and, rolling in the rough seas, steered around to the bows where the LSTs' cavernous doors opened. Each Rhino was manoeuvred into place and lashed to an LST before its ramp unfolded like a mechanical tongue. One by one vehicles crawled on to the ferry until its deck was fully laden, then it cast off and slowly motored towards the shore.

Despite the rough swell, unloading was proceeding well on the LSTs until, out of nowhere, two Fw 190s descended across the anchorage. Immediately every anti-aircraft gun nearby opened up and long chains of tracer licked hungrily towards the fighters. But the two German pilots held their course and released a bomb apiece over the LSTs before soaring back into the sky, searching for clouds in which to hide. Behind them, the bombs just missed LST 302, falling into the water alongside, but even so the blast was enough to break the electric motor of the lift that carried vehicles from the upper deck down to the main tank deck. While the remaining vehicles on the lower deck filed out on to the waiting Rhino, the crew wrestled with the motor, but to no avail. With the lift out of action there was no obvious way to get the rest off the LST.

Seeing the problem, Lieutenant Commander McReynolds on LST 363 came to 302's aid. Slowly he brought his large and unwieldy vessel alongside until their two hulls were thudding against each other. The crew placed long planks between the two decks while Albert Holmshaw, a REME fitter attached to 7 Field Regiment, looked on in horror. He couldn't escape the fact that the planks were being arranged next to his truck, and as he feared, once the planks were in place he was ordered to drive across them. While 302 and 363 rolled, lifting and twisting the planks, he carefully manoeuvred his truck on to the makeshift bridge. As soon as it seemed steady enough he gunned his engine and roared over to the neighbouring deck, breathing a sigh of relief once his wheels dropped down off the planks. Slowly but surely, the entirety of 302's upper deck was cleared and the vehicles shuttled ashore by Rhinos loading at 363's bow.

As well as mixed support vehicles, the LSTs carried the Sherman tanks of A Squadron East Riding Yeomanry, and even as the Rhinos carried them ashore the rest of the regiment was landing from the LCTs of Reserve Group 18. Tasked to support 9 Brigade, the tanks filed off the beach, trying to negotiate their way past the columns of marching men and nose-to-tail vehicles, seeking out their assembly area near Lion-sur-Mer.[2]

Lieutenant Henry, CO of the Lincolns' 9 Platoon A Company, led his small reconnaissance party out of Hermanville and along a dirt lane leading north-west. Grunting as they pedalled their bikes with legs made heavy by their sodden battledress, the patrol followed their battalion's pre-planned route – the track that ran along the south-west side of Lion-sur-Mer before turning left at the château and advancing up the slope to Cresserons. Henry had no way of knowing that this was the exact route that Leutnants Hans Gutsche and Rudolf Schaaf had taken in reverse when they had counter-attacked Lion-sur-Mer not long before. Even now 41 Commando were withdrawing to their new defensive line around the church.

As the patrol cycled down the track between flat fields barely 500 yards from Lion-sur-Mer, the first desultory fire started to come their way from the town. When it was joined by more concentrated fire from the château ahead of them, the men jumped from their bikes and took cover in the fields. As he studied the way ahead, Henry could see vehicles moving along the very road between Cresserons and the château that he was expecting to take – evidently 41 Commando had run into much more trouble than anticipated. There was clearly no way that the entire battalion could come this way any time soon, not if Lion-sur-Mer was still in enemy hands. Calling his signaller over, Henry made contact with battalion HQ and settled down to await developments.

Less than a mile east of Henry, Brigadier Cunningham and his staff had driven a little way into Lion-sur-Mer and made contact with Lieutenant Colonel Gray. While Gray updated the brigadier on his own precarious position, Captain Grant thought it prudent to mention to 9 Brigade's staff that their truck could almost certainly be seen by the enemy observers who had been bringing fire down on them all morning. He was disappointed to find the officers seemingly resented the intrusion and he watched, bemused, as they spread a camouflage net across the truck, an attempt at concealment that did nothing to hide the vehicle among Norman stone buildings.

After explaining the situation and his new defensive line, Gray departed and Cunningham pondered his next move. With Lion-sur-Mer still in enemy hands and no clear route to Cresserons there was little immediate opportunity to advance as planned. But the assembled officers' thoughts were suddenly interrupted by the scream of a shell. Grant heard it only a millisecond before a bright flash erupted in front of him, flames tickling his face as he was bowled backwards. Half thrown, half twisting, he crawled towards a gutter when more shells rained down, one striking the truck behind him. Then came the distinctive sound of mortars falling around them. Grant scrambled away to his own mortar team and ordered counter-fire on the known enemy positions, and the German barrage ceased almost as quickly as it started.

Men quickly ran to the burning truck, already a blackened shell. Grant found a wounded man sitting against a low garden wall, his head resting on one hand as if he was contemplating what had just happened. He went to tap the man's shoulder but at the slightest touch the body collapsed – he was already dead. So were two other men, and the heart of 9 Brigade's HQ had been gutted – the staff, intelligence and liaison officers all writhed in agony from their wounds. Cunningham himself had broken both his arms and his back and legs were peppered with shrapnel. Captain Cregan, 41 Commando's medical officer, arrived almost immediately although there was little he could do but stabilize the casualties and order their evacuation.

9 Brigade was suddenly rudderless. At that moment Colonel Dennis Orr, the brigade's second in command, was at Bénouville acting as a liaison to 6 Airborne Division. Temporarily Lieutenant Colonel Ian Harris of 2 RUR took command, but even as he tried to find out what was happening the brigade was starting to come under fire from the enemy positions at Lion-sur-Mer. Mortar bombs fell on the fields, disrupting the battalions as they formed up and waited for their vehicles. After he had been on the receiving end of some small arms fire, Lieutenant Rand probed west with a small patrol. Following a ditch, they reached the edge of a field of scrub where they saw two men peering over a bank, apparently observing Lion-sur-Mer's communal cemetery about 500 yards away. They crawled over to see if they had identified the cause of the sporadic fire, growing more concerned when the two men failed to

respond to their hails. On reaching them the horrible truth became clear: both men had neat bullet holes in their foreheads. The patrol scrambled back to the ditch and counted their blessings.

Meanwhile, Major General Rennie was trying to get a grip on 9 Brigade's movements and summoned the battalion commanders to an Orders Group at his Hermanville HQ. Before he left, Lieutenant Colonel Christopher Welby-Everard quickly issued new orders for the Lincolns to bolster the defences facing west. A and B Companies were sent west to strengthen the left flank of the defensive line that 41 Commando had formed in Lion-sur-Mer, with C and D Companies further back in case a withdrawal was necessary. Quickly the two lead companies swept across the fields and up to the communal cemetery, where they positioned themselves along the hedges at the edges of the fields. In front of them the view opened up to the château half a mile west and Cresserons, a mile southwest. With their advance on the church blunted, the German forces ahead of them stuck to their positions and an uneasy stalemate developed, each side sniping or mortaring the other whenever the opportunity presented itself. The only good news was that Captain Peter Dixon had managed to get through to *Ślązak* and even now was calling down fire from her 4-inch guns on to the German positions. So desperate was 41 Commando's position that Dixon simply passed target locations to Captain Booth, the battery liaison officer on the Polish destroyer, without being able to spot the fall of shot to make corrections. On the bridge, Captain Romuald Nalecz-Tyminski knew his orders quite clearly stated that bombardment was only to take place if it was observed, but noting Dixon's exhilarated voice and the seriousness of the situation he decided not to waste time getting permission from HMS *Largs*. Instead he ordered his gunnery officer to start slamming the targets Dixon gave him, and soon a hail of shells were falling on the château and Trout. The bombardments weren't without risk – still nothing had been heard from the missing section of A Troop somewhere in the houses in front of the defensive line.

Meanwhile, Rennie had moved his HQ to Colleville to escape the mortaring at Hermanville. At his meeting with 9 Brigade, still temporarily under the command of Ian Harris, Rennie instructed the brigade to take command of the Suffolks while the Lincolns were handed over to Brigadier Cass's 8 Brigade. Harris needed to deploy his forces to cover the approaches to the Caen Canal and River Orne bridges from the west, to secure the important bridgehead from any German counter-attack that may come from Caen. The Royal Ulster Rifles were ordered to the high ground on Périers Ridge. Following the Beuville road and the litter of the KSLI's advance, the battalion moved up to Point 61, past the sounds of battle still emanating from Hillman but with the comforting sight of B Squadron of the Staffordshire Yeomanry to their right. Once they had reached the summit the men dug in and waited, joined by their CO a little later after Dennis Orr arrived at 9 Brigade HQ. Meanwhile the KOSB were moved east to occupy the village of Saint-Aubin while Brigade HQ moved into Colleville and 1 East Riding Yeomanry were sent to a new assembly area on the east side of Colleville. Most importantly, the Suffolks needed to capture Hillman and occupy the high ground behind it as quickly as possible.[3]

By 14:00 the entire 2 East Yorks Battalion had assembled at Sole and Lieutenant Colonel Hutchinson decided to lead a recce group to their next objective, the 155mm gun battery Daimler. Moving forward along a sunken lane that led east from the southern end of Sole, the small party studied Daimler, only 500 yards away across some open fields. Major David de Symons Barrow paid close attention to the access track to the rear of the strongpoint. It looked to him as though this approach from the south would be the best way to assault the battery.

Meanwhile, back at Sole, the battalion staff had taken the opportunity to hold an Orders Group, and Lieutenant Hugh Bone accompanied the other officers to a small thick wood across the road from the strongpoint. As they chatted and smoked cigarettes, the first mortar bombs started to fall. Targeting their now fallen strongpoint, German mortars fired a prolonged 'stonk' on the East Yorks. Bone hugged the ground: there was nowhere to escape to in the wood and he couldn't dig in – the ground was thick with tangled roots. He curled up waiting for it to end, then saw the provost sergeant, lying 5 yards away, jolt suddenly and cry in pain. He crawled over and found a piece of jagged shrapnel in the sergeant's shoulder, blood oozing from the wound while the man's face turned yellow. He fumbled for his shell dressing and pressed it on to the wound as the ground continued to erupt around him.

On their way to catch up with C Company, men of 13 Platoon were moving down the sunken lane and had just passed by the recce group when the stonk began. Lionel Roebuck was getting tired of throwing himself to the ground every time he heard the explosion of a bomb overhead, his pack slamming into the back of his head and dislodging his helmet each time. By now he'd realized the futility of doing it – once the bomb had exploded he couldn't move faster than the shrapnel anyway. As if to remind him of this, another bomb fell on the lane and a splinter crashed into his pack, fortunately not penetrating it. But across the track a lump of jagged metal smashed into Hutchinson's arm, doing much more damage. The wound was enough to force his evacuation, and command devolved to Major Sheath, commander of B Company.[*]

After his recce, Barrow outlined his plans to his company. 14 and 15 Platoons, who had attacked Sole, would provide fire support this time, but 13 Platoon would make the assault with Major King's A Company. Reinforcements had just arrived in the form of Captain Clive Crauford who brought with him the reserve company HQ. One of the sergeants he brought with him immediately took command of James McGregor's 14 Platoon. Another party of men who had landed as reinforcements with Force S2 had also caught up, bringing some valuable manpower to the assault companies. The main assault would be made along the entrance track at the south-west corner of the battery, the route least likely to be mined. Once through the wire the platoons would fan out, securing each gun position and bunker at a time. The FOO from 76 Field Regiment had just arrived and reported that the Priests were positioned on the beach and ready to bring down fire support.

John Scruton and 15 Platoon crawled forward to positions on the edge of Sole that overlooked Daimler. Two of the strongpoint's fully enclosed gun positions were complete. A third, only just completed and lacking any earth covering, glared white in the daylight, and a fourth, only partially completed, appeared as a great concrete skeleton. Around them low blocks of concrete revealed a number of machine gun posts and personnel shelters. Thick, menacing hedges of barbed wire surrounded the entire site, goading anyone to try and penetrate them.

Radios crackled as 76 Field Regiment's FOO passed bearings and elevations to the gunners on Queen White. Engines were started and tracks skewed in the sand while barrels elevated to face a target 2 miles south-east.

---

[*] Both the East Yorks and 8 Brigade war diaries state that in the absence of the second in command Major Field, who was still on the beach collecting vehicles, command temporarily passed to Major Sheath of B Company. However, the Military Cross citation for Major David de Symons Barrow of C Company states that he took over the battalion. It is feasible that the men briefly shared the responsibility of command of the battalion between them until Field could be found.

A few ranging shots flew through the air, adjustments were communicated and made, and then the command was passed: 'Fire for effect.' Shells screeched overhead and plummeted on Daimler. Explosive bursts of flame erupted from the ground, throwing up dirt and dust that mixed with the thick black smoke. Waiting in the woods south-west of the battery, the assault platoons felt the ground rumble as shells rammed themselves into the earth 500 yards away. While they waited they lightened their loads, ditching their small packs and entrenching equipment, restricting themselves to weapons and ammunition pouches, and once suitably prepared they crept forward until they were almost outside the wire.

After twenty minutes the bombardment started to fade. Watching from Sole, Scruton, who felt relieved that someone else was making the assault this time, opened fire. Vickers and Bren guns chattered and Lee Enfields barked as the platoon sought to suppress the site entirely. Bren gunners with the assaulting force took position on either side of the track and opened fire while the lead attackers dashed forward in single file. At any moment Lionel Roebuck expected German bullets to smash through them – they were easy targets for a fixed machine gun. But to his surprise he reached the wire and the men quickly fanned out. Behind them, Sherman DDs revved their engines as they raced in open formation across the fields behind the battery, firing smoke shells and then engaging any position unwise enough to be spotted firing.

The barbed wire was not as severe as it had appeared from a distance, and the assault teams were able to breach it with relative ease. Ripping his trousers on one barb he had got entangled with, Roebuck rushed towards the nearest pillbox, grenade in hand and ready to assault it. He dropped down alongside the concrete frontage, ready to push his explosive through the embrasure. But as he caught his breath and steadied his nerves, he realized it was empty. He rushed forward to the interconnecting trench network behind the pillbox and moved down it until he reached a personnel bunker. This time the grenade was deployed and, after a satisfying crump, he rushed inside. As the smoke cleared he found himself in a liberally decorated office, complete with stationery and a framed portrait of Hitler, but no people.

All around the attackers were finding the same thing – defensive emplacements devoid of defenders. Slowly they began to converge on the gun bunkers, where Crauford ran round to the embrasure and fired his Sten gun in. There was no reply, and the officer gingerly stepped over the lower wall. At that moment his batman on the roof dropped a grenade into the ventilation shaft. The Mills bomb rolled down the pipe and into the bunker just feet away from Crauford. For a split second he stared at it, then turned and ran. Behind him the grenade exploded and Crauford tumbled out of the bunker. He quickly patted himself all over, shocked to find he was untouched. The gun shield had been between him and the grenade and protected him when it detonated.

Although somewhat chaotic, the final assault was enough for the defenders, who started to emerge from the corners of the gun bunkers they had retreated to when the barrage started. Some seventy gunners of mixed nationalities from 4 Battery 1716 Artillery Regiment came out, their hands in the air – something of a surprise to the East Yorks officers who had expected a coastal artillery regiment. Forcing their way past the droves of surrendering men and into the bunkers, they discovered that the 155mm guns they had expected were in fact only 75mm. Elsewhere some of the attackers made a more interesting discovery: the battery mess was liberally supplied with wine and beer, providing some welcome relief for the tired East Yorks.[*4]

Charles Lefauconnier hurried up the avenue de Lion, determined to see the landings with his own eyes and lend his assistance if he could. As he emerged from the building-lined streets of the town the rhythmic background noise of activity up ahead drifted towards him, steadily increasing in volume and tempo as he closed on the beaches. Men shouted, engines revved, equipment banged and crashed. The occasional crack of rifles or rattle of a machine gun and the crump of mortar bombs came from the shore, and a low-flying fighter roared across the trees nearby. Breathless with excitement he arrived in front of a large tank blocking the road and approached its crew, who stood alongside their vehicle smoking and drinking from chipped white enamel mugs, their olive drab battledresses and faces stained with smoke and grease, goggles hanging around their necks and pistol holsters dangling low on their legs. Lefauconnier embraced his dishevelled liberators passionately and quickly unfolded a large map of his town, explaining that his role as mayor and chief of civil defence had made him privy to useful information and enabled him to

---

* Much like the attack on Sole, there are few definite times given for the capture of Daimler. Once again the East Yorks war diary does not record a time at all, but 8 Infantry Brigade reports the East Yorks' second objective falling at 18:00 and the 13/18 Hussars war diary at 19:00.

make certain observations. Cynically, Captain Eric Pollard took the map, but as he studied it he realized there was much more detail than he might have imagined. Major John Hanson arrived and compared the mayor's map with his own intelligence map prepared in England, while Lefauconnier pointed out two anti-tank guns and explained how to get around behind them.

There was no doubting the mayor's information was good. It was also timely. Not long before, Hanson had been approached by a limping commando, his head wrapped in a thick blood-stained bandage. Despite his injuries he still had determination about him – Lieutenant Colonel Robert Dawson might not have been able to get to the Orne bridges, but he had other missions he wanted to fulfil.[*] Some of his scouts had observed that the locks at the head of the Caen Canal appeared to be operational, and knowing that they were top of the list of facilities to be captured intact, he was searching for someone to do it. Finding the Royal Engineers' tanks parked up in the farm, not far from the crater of the mortar bomb that had put him out of action, he outlined to Hanson what 4 Commando had achieved and what was still left to do. Impressed, and possibly a little daunted, by the senior officer, Hanson promised to take care of it. After he had implored Dawson to return to an aid post, he sent Lieutenant Hutchinson of the Royal Engineers back to the beaches to find the HQ and request some infantry support. Unfortunately 3 Troop's commander returned with orders for 79 Assault Squadron to deal with the locks themselves.

Hanson quickly briefed his crews and then, as his own was still on the beach, requisitioned an AVRE. At 15:30 the column drove out of the farm and advanced cautiously down the avenue de Lion, wary of any German stragglers – or worse, reinforcements filtering back into the town. Instead, the ten trundling AVREs encountered only civilians who cheered them on enthusiastically. Approaching the town they passed scattered rucksacks, dumped there in the morning by men who would not return to retrieve them. Medical officer Joseph Patterson watched them pass. He had remained in Ouistreham after 4 Commando left and driven around in a jeep to collect more wounded – British, German and French.

---

[*] Despite quite serious injuries, Dawson rejoined 4 Commando east of the River Orne on 7 June. He remained with them until the 9th when both he and medical officer Joseph Patterson were ordered back to the UK by 1 SS Brigade's assistant director of medical services.

As they pressed on further east the civilians faded away and the crews buttoned up their tanks. But as they neared the deserted end of the road there was no obvious response and it seemed to Hanson that they might have caught the defenders of strongpoint 7 unawares. His small force moved forward, past the junction where the commandos had turned left, and prepared to deploy according to their instructions. 1 Troop broke to the left, ran behind a small wood and raced across to the canal bank next to the outer lock while the remaining tanks moved on the inner lock and its swing bridge. The German defenders were slow to react and the two Tobruk machine gun bunkers were quickly overpowered by the AVRE's Besa machine guns. Hanson, noting that the two-span bridge across the inner lock was intact, instructed his driver Sapper Edward Beeton to move across it and on to the island between the old and new locks.* Beeton gunned the tank forward and then cautiously edged his way on to the steel bridge. The tracks squealed on the metal while bullets pinged off the hull as the tank slowly advanced.

They were nearly halfway across the first span when there was a blast ahead of them, the bridge shuddered, and metal shrieked as the second span fell on to the lock gates beneath. Fearing an imminent tumble into the canal, Beeton slammed on the brakes, but to the crew's relief there was no second explosion. The first span groaned under their weight and Beeton slowly backed the tank on to the promenade behind.

Meanwhile, the rest of the squadron were mopping up the positions on the west bank and firing on the east.† Pollard directed his gunners to fire their Petard mortars at strongpoints across the locks while Hanson neutralized the last remaining positions on the west bank. For some twenty minutes the crump of Petard mortar blasts and the chatter of machine guns became the soundtrack to the one-sided battle. Suspecting there might be observers and snipers in the lighthouse, Lance Corporal Parsons ordered his gunner to spray the windows with machine gun fire, starting at the top and working down. After a few minutes he was satisfied to see a white flag waving from the door, and hesitantly some

---

* There were two lock channels at the mouth of the Caen Canal. The new lock on the western side was operational, the old lock on the east side was disused.
† The 50mm anti-tank gun that might have knocked out a DD tank earlier in the day does not appear to have been an impediment to the AVREs. It might have lacked the power to penetrate the Churchill's thick armour at this range. The other 50mm guns at strongpoint 7 faced east.

Germans emerged with their arms raised. As he opened the commander's hatch on his turret, a sniper targeted Lieutenant Hutchinson and fired, the bullet striking the tank and the ricochet wounding him near the eye. But he was the only casualty suffered by 79 Squadron, and it was the last act by strongpoint 7's defenders.

Over the next thirty minutes fifty-seven men, including six officers, emerged from their bunkers to give themselves up. Equipping themselves with Bren guns and sidearms, some of the tank crews crossed the canal and set up defensive positions, capturing anti-tank guns and equipment on the other side. Inspecting the locks, Hanson was pleased to see that although one span of the swing bridge over the new lock had fallen, the locks themselves, the pumphouses and all the associated machinery was intact. Whatever Flight Sergeant Bob Armit had thought he saw from the nose of his Lancaster 'G' George after loosing his bombs that morning, it was not the destruction of the locks.

Satisfied with the result, Hanson placed Lieutenant Redmond Cunningham in charge of the locks' defence, with instructions to recheck the area for demolitions and booby traps and hold the site until relief arrived. The rest of the squadron gathered the PoWs and marched them ahead of some of the AVREs back to the beach. Lieutenant Hutchinson was taken to the nearest aid post they could find which, he was startled to find, was staffed almost entirely by French women.*

Elsewhere in Ouistreham, other casualties were being treated. Joseph Patterson was the first Allied doctor to find Dr Poulain at the town square, but lacking plasma and blood there was little he could do to help treat the wounded civilians gathered there. Odette Mousset remained conscious and in agony, but refused to be evacuated when the first RAMC units arrived and started taking the most severely wounded back to the beach for transport to England. She was desperately waiting for her husband Raoul, not knowing if he was dead or alive. In fact he had survived the events of the day and travelled home from Caen on foot and by bicycle, across the ever-shifting front line. When he found their gutted hotel, he searched the town until he found the first aid post. Later that evening they were both evacuated to England.[5]

---

* There are occasional references in post-war memoirs (usually from the 1990s and later) to French nurses on the beach. Hutchinson's account, written in June 1944, is the only contemporary mention. None of the medical units attached to 3 Infantry Division record assistance from male or female French civilians.

14

THE PANZER RIPOSTE

OBERST HERMANN VON OPPELN-BRONIKOWSKI STUDIED THE NEW orders his signaller had just passed him in complete despair. After receiving his first alert eleven whole hours ago he had not received any orders until gone 07:00 when Generalmajor Edgar Feuchtinger had finally arrived at his HQ and issued instructions – seemingly without reference to his superiors. Since then Oppeln-Bronikowski's 22 Panzer Regiment had been advancing up the east side of the Orne to engage the airborne forces reported there. The journey from Falaise had been a struggle in itself; constant attack from the air had forced 1 Battalion to abandon the road and instead go across country, rushing from one patch of woodland to the next whenever the skies appeared to be clear. He had just completed forming up his regiment at Escoville, just over 2 miles south-east of the River Orne bridge, and even now his 4 Company from 1 Battalion was in action alongside his fellow regimental commander Major Hans von Luck with 125 Regiment. Now he was being told to move across the river and drive north to intercept the Allied forces landing west of Ouistreham. It was infuriating, but orders were orders and wearily he called his battalion commanders together. With the bridges between Ranville and Bénouville in enemy hands, the only place to cross the Orne was in Caen itself, or at a small bridge just north-east of the city at Colombelles. He did not relish crossing at either site.

At noon, Oppeln-Bronikowski led 1 Battalion into Caen. The city was chaotic: the bridges over the Orne had so far survived the attacks from the air, but the bombs that had missed them had hit the roads, cratering them in some places and blowing rubble across others. The thoroughfares were jammed with people – civilians fleeing the city, administrative units seemingly moving at random. In between air raids, stalwart officers tried to usher vehicles across the bridges, but the jams on either side hampered their work considerably. As he drove past his stationary companies in his command vehicle, Oppeln-Bronikowski spied a German paymaster, staggering as he swung his legs one at a time in an effort to walk. On either side of him were two young women in the uniform of the Wehrmachthelferin (auxiliary corps) and they were evidently all quite drunk. As he closed he could hear that they were singing – or rather bawling – 'Deutschland über Alles'. The farcical comedy of the scene in many ways echoed his own feelings: a veteran of the Eastern Front he, like many others, thought the war was probably lost already.

As it was evident that none of his regiment would get through Caen, Oppeln-Bronikowski directed them to bypass the city entirely. He led some units south-west to circle the city on its western side while Major Wilhelm von Gottberg took most of 2 Battalion north to cross at Colombelles. The regiment quickly became fragmented, and with radio communication forbidden, Oppeln-Bronikowski could only hope each unit would make it to the new rendezvous north of Caen.

22 Panzer Regiment's redirection had come from much higher up the command chain than just his divisional commander. General Erich Marcks of 84 Corps had realized that with enemy amphibious operations all along his front he had little in the way of reserves to counter them and, with so few units between the sea and Caen, the city itself was under threat. At 09:25 he had contacted 7 Army to request permission to deploy 12 SS Panzer Division, at that moment positioned west of Paris and approximately 80 miles away from Caen. But thanks to Hitler's enforced and convoluted command structure, even that division could not be released. His only card, he realized, was 21 Panzer Division. Fortunately Rommel had by now been alerted to the situation, and passed orders to General Hans Spiedel, his chief of staff, for the division to attack. Overruling the earlier directives made by General Wilhelm Richter and Feuchtinger, Marcks now needed the division to attack the landings from the sea on the west side of the Orne, rather than the airborne landings on the east.

The chaos in Caen meant it was not until 14:30 that the first units of 21 Panzer Division started to assemble north of the city. Tired and harassed, these units began to form up in two hastily assembled battlegroups. Oppeln-Bronikowski had under him both battalions of 22 Panzer Regiment (less the company still fighting across the river), a company of 220 Panzer Pioneer Battalion and 3 Battalion of 155 Panzer Artillery

Regiment, whose sister units were even then engaged on Périers Ridge. He had also been assigned three companies of 1 Battalion of 125 Panzer Grenadier Regiment, motorized infantry that had not yet reached the rest of their regiment east of the Orne when the change in orders came through. But in the chaos that surrounded Caen, Oppeln-Bronikowski was unable to find these additional infantry all day. The elements of the battlegroup that did arrive formed up in the woods and side streets at Lebisey where so recently Rommel had admired 192 Panzer Grenadier Regiment. Oberst Josef Rauch's 192 Regiment now formed the basis of the second battlegroup that Feuchtinger assembled. Stationed much closer to Caen they had had an easier time forming up, although the regular air attacks hampered them as much as their fellow units. Rauch only had 1 Battalion of his regiment available to him, the second company of 220 Panzer Pioneer Battalion and 2 Battalion of 155 Panzer Artillery Regiment, all of whom came together in the orchards around Saint-Contest.

At 15:00, General Marcks came forward to the north of Caen to see the preparations for himself. Finding Feuchtinger nearby, the corps commander proceeded to publicly harangue the 21 Panzer Division CO, criticizing his late commitment to battle and the farcical movement of his units to the front. The two generals bickered but without conclusion, and Marcks left, resolving to take control of the counter-attack himself.

At Lebisey, Oppeln-Bronikowski had found a greatly distressed General Richter pacing up and down in the formation area. 'My troops are lost, my whole division is finished,' he moaned. The oberst tried to reassure him that they would do what they could to support 716 Division and he pulled out a map, asking where the main formations were located. Richter stared at it for a moment, then confessed he had no idea. The full magnitude of what was happening further north began to dawn on Oppeln-Bronikowski, made certain when he witnessed dozens of small parties of men marching south after escaping their overrun positions near the coast. Now he knew that the war could be well and truly lost.

Shortly before 16:00, Marcks arrived at Lebisey to see for himself the final preparations. Seeking out Oppeln-Bronikowski, he greeted the oberst far more civilly than his divisional commander, but had a stark warning for him. 'Oppeln, the future of Germany may very well rest on your shoulders. If you don't push the British back into the sea, we've lost the war.' Oppeln-Bronikowski stifled a gulp, wondering how the future of his country could have fallen so far as to rest on his ninety-eight tanks.

But he gave his corps commander a crisp salute. 'General, I intend to attack immediately,' he assured him. And at 16:20, the advance north began. Oppeln-Bronikowski placed Hauptmann Herr's 5 Company of his regiment in the van with his regimental HQ following – a total of twenty-five tanks. Slowly the tanks advanced through Lebisey Wood, came out the north side and moved down the Biéville road.

The King's Shropshire Light Infantry had just cautiously advanced through Biéville after fighting their way through Beuville, although the proximity of the two villages meant that there was little to distinguish the movement from one to the other.[*] W Company were the first to reach the gates of the château on the main road which they understood to be a regimental headquarters.[†] Supported by a couple of Staffordshire Yeomanry tanks, 8 and 9 Platoons raced into the grounds. Signaller Corporal George Bunting jumped into one of the slit trenches in the grounds only to find the body of a German already occupying it. Helped by another signaller, they hauled the corpse out and took residence, but a few minutes later were aghast to see the dead man sit up, shake himself off, clamber to his feet and walk off. Bunting stared, but decided the 'dead' man must be shell-shocked and let him go. Meanwhile the rest of the platoons were advancing into the château, finding only a handful of dejected Germans rather than any organized resistance. Sergeant Major Roberts rushed into one of the grand dining rooms to find the table set for lunch, with a gently cooling stew still waiting to be served. Evidently they had only just missed the château's last tenants.

While 8 and 9 Platoons occupied the château, Lieutenant Bellamy led 7 Platoon forward to an orchard overlooking the valley south of the village. A dry river bed lined by trees on either side, the depression was a natural anti-tank obstacle. It had been identified on aerial photographs but, aside from the road leading up to Lebisey, there was no certainty about how easily it might be crossed by armour. Rather than take a patrol, Bellamy decided to recce the depression himself and cautiously crept forward from the orchard until he reached the line of trees. Taking note of the width of the hollow and the slopes on either side, he suddenly came

---

[*] In the accounts of fighting in both towns, it is clear that some people mixed up the two villages – hardly surprising given their proximity and similar names.
[†] Many KSLI accounts believed 736 HQ to have been in Biéville Château when it was actually in Beuville, which the KSLI had just bypassed.

across a German machine gun position. His Sten clattered as he tried to suppress it but a burst of fire caught him in the arm and knee and he went to ground. Hearing the commotion, his platoon sergeant rushed forward and managed to extract the wounded officer, who was able to brief Lieutenant Colonel Maurice before he limped off to the rear.

Behind 7 Platoon, Lieutenant Harry Jones had just paused on the southern outskirts of Beuville to consult with Major Guy Thornycroft, and the two officers studiously examined a map to decide the best way forward. Suddenly, and without warning, there was an earth-shattering explosion nearby as a German shell detonated mere yards away. By a slight miracle neither man was injured, and after jumping to cover Jones looked south towards the likely origin of the shell. What he saw shook him: on the right flank were five or six German tanks advancing north. He shouted to his platoon and they immediately dispersed into cover behind the road.

Across the Staffordshire Yeomanry radio net new cries of alarm buzzed through the air. The recce troop and two troops of C Squadron had just raced down the right flank of the advance towards Lebisey, successfully crossing the hollow just south of Biéville on the west side of the road, and now they spotted the approaching threat. The moment Lieutenant Colonel Jim Eadie heard the warning he asked for the release of A Squadron, which was still back on Périers Ridge waiting to support the attack on Hillman. Minutes later the squadron was racing south along the road and pulled into the fields north-west of Biéville.

Hauptmann Herr and 5 Company were advancing fast. Driving into the hollow between Lebisey and Biéville they turned west, probing for the end where they could get across. As soon as they reached the western end they came under the combined fire of the KSLI's 6-pounder anti-tank guns that had been brought forward from Beuville, and the Shermans of 1 and 2 Troops of C Squadron the Staffordshire Yeomanry. As heavy and accurate fire ripped into the battlegroup, Herr quickly led his tanks further west towards some wooded country that should temporarily shield them from the Shermans' view. Firing as they fled, they quickly discovered that their own 75mm guns lacked the penetrative power the Shermans enjoyed at the same range. One of their luckier rounds hit the Sherman Firefly of Sergeant Billings and his crew; they had themselves just slammed a 17-pounder anti-tank round into one of the German Panzers when their own tank started to burn. The crew jumped out but quickly realized that the fire was only external, and after dousing it, they jumped back in. But by then the Germans had escaped into the wood, leaving two burning Panzer IVs behind them with wrecked men and equipment inside.

A Squadron was by now charging across the fields west of Biéville, and when Herr and his tanks emerged from the north side of the trees, 1 Troop was already moving into position to intercept, albeit inadvertently. Sergeant Leslie Joyce was moving into position at the far west end of the squadron and had just reached good cover at a spot overlooking the open ground to the right of the woods. To his amazement he suddenly found the line of German tanks moving across his front only 600 yards away. Patiently, he allowed the line to come well into the open and then targeted the rear tank, scoring a direct hit with the first shot. Calmly he directed his layer to traverse right and began engaging the tanks from left to right. With four more shots he disabled another three tanks. Two more succumbed to other guns, and after losing six tanks – including Herr's – in quick succession, the rest of the group scuttled back to cover. Oppeln-Bronikowski realized they could not get through this way and ordered the group to retire until a new route could be established.

Learning the fate that had befallen his CO, Major von Gottberg took his own unit further west towards Epron, driving across the fields on either side of the Château de la Londe and then aiming for the gap between Mathieu and Périers-sur-le-Dan. While the open fields allowed them to race quickly across the landscape, it also made them obvious to the units of the KSLI, M20s of 20 Anti-Tank Regiment and A Squadron of the Staffordshire Yeomanry arrayed east of them. The British rained fire upon the tanks from 1,200 yards away and B Squadron, now positioned near Point 61 on the ridge, was alerted. Within minutes six German tanks were destroyed, even before B Squadron sent three of their 17-pounder anti-tank gun-equipped Fireflys forward along with a regular Mk III equipped with a 75mm gun. They proceeded to engage von Gottberg's force head on and quickly knocked out three more tanks and damaged several others for the loss of two of their own and one of the M20s. Faced with such furious firepower from much better deployed tanks, von Gottberg had little choice but to wheel his armour around and withdraw.

Further west, Oberst Josef Rauch's battlegroup was enjoying more success. After he had left Oppeln-Bronikowski, General Marcks had visited the commander of 192 Panzer Grenadier Regiment and decided to personally lead the initial advance. Driving north from Saint-Contest,

Marcks led the battlegroup east of Cambes and Mathieu, exploiting the full width of the gap between the advancing Canadian forces to the west and the KSLI to the east. After a short while he peeled away and left 192 Regiment's 1 Battalion to continue the advance. Grenadier Walter Hermes, a despatch rider, was one of the men who then moved into the lead on his motorcycle. He raced ahead of the armoured cars and trucks and self-propelled guns, roaring across fields, joyfully surprised not to have yet been fired upon. At any moment, he thought, he should be able to see the tanks of 22 Panzer Regiment ahead of him and, after linking up, they could race to the coast and play merry hell with the landings there. He had no idea that even as he rushed north, 22 Panzer Regiment's advance had been completely blunted. Had any of Rauch's group cared to mention the sizeable gap between the British and Canadians that they had found to Oppeln-Bronikowski, they may well have been able to count on his armoured support. But as it was, the oberst had by then concluded that there was no way through the Allied armour, and he was already starting to form a defensive line at Lebisey.[1]

At 17:00, Major General Rennie strode into Brigadier Smith's HQ in Colleville. Time was marching on and 3 Division's CO was alarmed to see that the Warwicks were still in the orchards outside the village rather than advancing south. Having just been contacted by 6 Airborne Division, who had pleaded for reinforcement of the bridges, he knew that 185 Brigade needed to get moving. But Smith was still reluctant to send the battalion through Saint-Aubin – if the village was well defended then he did not want them to become bogged down trying to clear it. His latest information was that the village was in German hands and, even worse, rumours abounded that the Germans had already recaptured the canal and river bridges. His plan was to wait for 8 Brigade to report Saint-Aubin clear and then move the Warwicks through, preparatory to a possible counter-attack on the bridges. Rennie was unimpressed, pointing out that he had just driven through Saint-Aubin in his jeep and it had seemed clear enough. Suitably persuaded, Smith ordered Lieutenant Colonel Hugh Herdon to get moving at once.

Meanwhile, south of Colleville, Arthur Heal hadn't stopped working on the gap through the minefield. Despite Brigadier Cass's assurances that two Crabs would soon join him, Lieutenant Colonel Goodwin wanted to be doubly certain of getting tanks into Hillman and had the RE officer continue his task. The fact that no Crabs had been forthcoming so far, and that A Squadron of the Staffordshire Yeomanry had already been recalled, seemed to validate his decision – although he was hardly surprised at the latter's disappearance after he had heard the enemy armour alarm flashed across the divisional wireless.

At 16:15, Captain Heal returned to the sunken lane and updated Goodwin. The charge was ready to blow, hopefully detonating enough mines for the tanks of C Squadron 13/18 Hussars to get through. Goodwin decided another bombardment would make doubly sure and prepared for another 'Grab' as soon as the minefield went up. Priming the detonator and gripping it tightly, Heal twisted the handle, and a split second later there was an almighty explosion. Grey smoke, stained brown by the Norman earth, erupted ahead of them, barbed wire was thrown into the air, and numerous smaller explosions confirmed that at least some of the mines were detonating. Goodwin ordered 'Grab' and immediately the combined fire of 76 and 33 Field Regiments, both of whom had now moved to positions inland, fell on to the strongpoint. For five minutes Hillman was ravaged as 105mm shells fell among its bunkers, while the first tanks of 13/18 Hussars lumbered up the road towards the wire.

Almost too quickly the deafening sounds of hurtling shells and explosions faded away, and two sections of 8 Platoon leapt from the sunken lane and pursued the lead tank to the wire. As he closed on it, Corporal Robert Lawson suddenly saw the tank slow to a halt. Coming alongside, he shouted up at the turret asking what was going on, whereupon the commander indicated the dead men lying in the gap in the wire. Lawson didn't intend to add to the number of men lying there and shouted ferociously for the tank to get moving; grudgingly the commander acquiesced and drove forward.

Watching from the sunken lane, Heal and Goodwin held their breath as the tank crawled forward, barely willing to blink until they had seen it cross the minefield unharmed. To their relief there was no explosion – the tank made it through the inner wire, and immediately another followed it in. The two sections of 8 Platoon raced through and fanned out behind the inner wire, whereupon the nearest cupola again opened fire and the men went to ground, returning fire ineffectually. The lead tank traversed its turret and fired a shell at the cupola, but with no visible effect. Meanwhile, Major Sir Delaval Cotter had advanced his tank further into the strongpoint, firing at any viable target with its machine gun and 75mm. As the tank moved further forward, Cotter suddenly felt it lurch as it slipped into a depression, breaking a track in the process.

Having collapsed a latrine they were stuck but safe inside their Sherman, and Cotter only opened the turret hatch enough to lob grenades down the trench and keep any curious Germans away.

8 Platoon's Bren gunners were filtering through the gap and laying suppressing fire on the cupola. Private James Hunter dropped into a small shell hole just inside the wire; two more men fell in behind him and the machine gunner in the cupola quickly gave them some attention. As small explosions started to erupt around them, Hunter started to suspect mortar fire and decided that the risks of staying where he was were greater than moving. As soon as the machine gun panned away he jumped to his feet and, firing from the hip, advanced towards the cupola. After a few bursts the machine gun was silenced, and as he closed on it Hunter was able to fire directly inside the loophole. A few more men rushed to join him and together they fired into the adjacent trenches. Just as he was moving forward down the trench, a lone German fired at him and the bullet smashed Hunter's skull, wounding him and spraying blood across his face. One of his colleagues slapped a shell dressing over the wound and they carried on, thrusting grenades down the ventilation shafts of the nearest bunkers until their dazed occupants emerged to surrender.*

With the most dangerous cupola overpowered, 9 Platoon now poured through the wire and fanned out to start mopping up the other positions. At the wire, Lieutenant Smith, still furious after his losses on the left flank not long before, fired wildly into the strongpoint. His crew neutralized one of the machine gun posts and then hit one of the anti-tank guns that had given them so much trouble earlier, killing the crew with a spray of machine gun fire and setting fire to a store of petrol nearby.

Inside the HQ bunker the soldier peering through the observation turret had been shouting a narrative down to Ludwig Krug. Immediately he heard that tanks had entered the strongpoint the oberst had ordered his men to get out into the trenches and counter-attack. Hans Sauer grabbed a box of grenades and followed the men out of the main door. Following a sergeant up the trench, the sounds of explosion and small arms fire coming from the north, they suddenly found a section coming the other way. There was a tank on top of the kitchen behind them, they exclaimed, lobbing grenades into the bunker air ducts. Quickly the men

---

* James Hunter was awarded the Distinguished Conduct Medal for his actions on D-Day.

beat a retreat to the HQ bunker where, by now, some seventy men were gathered. Inside, an oppressive silence descended. It was clear to the defenders that they were beaten and they hurriedly closed the various hatches and sealed the main armoured door, wondering what Krug would do next.

Very soon the Suffolks and 13/18 Hussars controlled the surface of Hillman, but the bunkers continued to hold out. Royal Engineers with Beehive demolition charges were brought up to destroy some of the concrete defences, but it took time to overcome the individual positions. Eventually, at approximately 20:00, the position appeared to be taken as the last defenders still daring to fire were silenced.

D Company passed through to occupy a farm about 500 yards further south; as they advanced through the field two riflemen opened up at them and were quickly dealt with. Movement was seen at the farm and 17 Platoon went forward to clear the buildings. The platoon's Bren guns quickly advanced to the right side to provide covering fire and the sections prepared to rush across the yard. After several bursts of covering fire the assault began, but no sooner had the platoon burst across the open space than men started to emerge from trenches on the left flank with their arms in the air. Altogether fifty men emerged, willingly surrendering themselves to D Company and abandoning four machine guns as well as their small arms and cases of grenades. Had they decided to fight they would have proved a difficult obstacle. In fact they had decided long ago not to – the British noted with interest that the weapons were all laid out ready to be turned over as soon as the attackers arrived. D Company's commander, Major Phillip Papillon, knew what was coming next and withdrew to Hillman. They watched as German artillery and mortars pounded the farm, and only once darkness had fallen did they move forward to reoccupy it.[2]

Had von Gottberg managed to get up the slope on to Périers Ridge, his battlegroup might have been able to offer some support to the embattled defenders of Hillman, or at the very least strongpoint 21A. At that moment, Z Company of the KSLI, using mortars and PIATs, had succeeded in capturing one of 2 Battery 155 Artillery Regiment's MG 34s. Even so, accessing the centre of the battery seemed impossible until one of the prisoners taken outside the wire, a Polish Volksdeutscher, offered to show the attackers a way through the wire at the back of the battery. As one platoon fed through the barbed net, the strongpoint's garrison finally broke and ran, deserting the guns and falling back into thick woods down the slope behind the battery. While the attackers pursued them an RE officer, although badly wounded, set about spiking the guns and quickly rendered them useless.

It was 22:00 and growing dark when Major Peter Wheelock gathered his company and prepared to withdraw. They had successfully knocked out the battery, the last enemy defence on Périers Ridge, but it had not been without loss: Z Company had taken thirty-two casualties, including six killed, three missing and twenty-three wounded. They withdrew to a copse for the night and waited for daylight before rejoining the battalion.*[3]

By 19:00, Josef Rauch's battlegroup had sailed through the gap between 3 Division at Sword and 3 Canadian Division at Juno, swept past Cresserons and arrived at the coast between Lion-sur-Mer and Luc-sur-Mer. Rauch was pleased to find the shoreline deserted of enemy vessels, although he could see vast armadas to the east and west. But he was more concerned to find that there was no trace of Oppeln-Bronikowski's battlegroup. Quickly he sent men to make contact with the château, strongpoint 21 and strongpoint 24 at Luc-sur-Mer. Then he settled down to plan his next advance along the coast.

More than a mile away in Lion-sur-Mer, Rauch's arrival had gone unnoticed by 41 Commando. But while their defensive line had been reasonably quiet for the last few hours, Captain Dixon had been able to call on ORP *Ślązak* again and make life a little more uncomfortable for the Germans ahead of them. For a full hour from 17:00 to 18:00 the Polish destroyer poured shells on to the château and Trout. By 18:00, *Ślązak*'s gunnery officer reported to Romauld Nalecz-Tyminski that they had expended 986 rounds of 4-inch ammunition and there were only fifty-nine rounds remaining in the magazines. With so little left, the captain knew it was time to break off and reluctantly Captain Booth informed Dixon. For his part, Dixon passed on the enthusiastic thanks of the Royal Marines, who felt the destroyer had probably saved them from being overrun.

The bombardment also provided enough cover for the missing section from A Troop to make their way back to the main defensive line. At 19:30, Lieutenant Stevens wearily marched into Gray's HQ and reported that

---

* Wheelock was awarded an MC for this action. He was killed in action six weeks later.

during the initial withdrawal they had been cut off at the crossroads A Troop had been holding. A strong enemy presence had obliged them to remain there until it appeared quiet enough to move, but even so, an armoured car had appeared as they withdrew. Stevens had despatched it himself with a grenade.[4]

As soon as the tank threat had passed, Major Steel had led Y Company of the KSLI out of Biéville. They crossed the deep hollow just south of the village and advanced up the slope towards the woods less than a mile away. To their right, 1 Troop of the Staffordshire Yeomanry's C Squadron had positioned itself at the road crossing the hollow, but they had come under heavy fire from artillery and tanks in the woods and sustained damage to some of the Shermans. On the left 4 Troop were held up after they had failed to find any way across the obstacle and the infantry were alone as they approached the northern face of Lebisey orchards at the top of the ridge at 17:30. Above them they could see the water tower that served the small village set behind the trees – an ideal spotter's position if ever there was one. But walking up an open field, the Germans hardly needed spotters, and Y Company quickly came under fire as they approached the tree line. Machine guns swept the fields as the company fanned out and scurried forward in quick bursts to infiltrate the tree line, but Major Steel was hit by a burst and killed. Captain Dane, the company second in command, rallied the men, but the defenders were well ensconced in the orchards and it was obvious that more than a company would be needed to push through.

Back at Biéville, Lieutenant Colonel Maurice concurred, but he had little else that he could commit to the fight. In the original plan, at least some elements of the Norfolks and Warwicks should be up with his battalion by now, but Brigadier Smith could only report that both regiments were still negotiating Périers Ridge. The Staffordshire Yeomanry was still deployed for a potential repeat round with German armour. With no support behind him, he needed to establish a firm position for defence in case of a counter-attack, rather than trying to capture another feature, and reluctantly he decided that they would have to abandon the attack on Lebisey. He instructed Dane to sit tight and pull back once it was dark.

15

DARKNESS FALLS

AT 20:50, THE BRIDGE CREW ON HMS *SCORPION* CAUGHT THE faint sounds of an unmelodic drone to the north. In the distance Tony Ditcham could make out a hazy blur on the horizon; to Colin Lawton on the deck of HMS *Serapis* it looked like a dark cloud that floated south, growing and growing until it spread itself across the fleet. And then, as the drone increased to a roar, the first of hundreds of aircraft and glider tows flew over the fleet. Ditcham marvelled at the spectacle as endless streams of RAF Dakotas, Stirlings, Halifaxes and Albemarles towed 250 Horsa and Hamilcar gliders above him.

Activity on the beach briefly paused as the stream passed overhead, until sporadic fire once again emanated from some of the houses that were yet to be cleared. On the dozens of landing craft that lay beached on the sand waiting for the next high tide, Oerlikon gunners opened up, spewing tracer at the windows wherever they saw movement. In Lion-sur-Mer, 41 Commando watched with delight as the vast armada soared overhead. Douglas Grant cheered as line after line went by, others waved at the pilots and passengers in the gliders. The huge display of strength changed the mood among the weary Royal Marines. Although they had been reinforced by the Lincolns a few hours ago, they had become so disconnected in their street fighting that they had barely seen any other units since they had left the beach that morning. They had taken 140 casualties during the day, including twenty-six killed. Now they no longer felt alone.

The appearance of such a huge airborne force alarmed the German defenders at Lion-sur-Mer. The infantry brought all the weapons they had to bear on the low-flying aircraft, men even lying on their backs and firing their rifles into the air, but there was little they could do in the face of such a display. They noted bitterly that there was no sign of friendly aircraft to attack the lumbering formation – it would have presented an easy target had the Luftwaffe had more presence. Now it appeared to Josef Rauch that he had inadvertently led his battlegroup into a trap. Having driven hard for the coast, the British would now land in his rear, join the forces landing to the east and west, and cut him off entirely from Caen.

Behind him, Edgar Feuchtinger had reached the same conclusion. As his armoured car raced north towards Cresserons the sight of hundreds of gliders being released ahead of him was an obvious threat to his forces on the coast. The airwaves of the Germans' limited wireless communication hummed as warnings were sent to Rauch's battlegroup and as quickly as possible the group assembled themselves, engines were fired up and orders hurriedly rapped out. The drone of the departing tug aircraft had barely receded before the first vehicles were roaring back inland. Rudolf Schaaf had been without orders for several hours when Hauptmann Mikisch told him that he too had been ordered to fall back to Caen. Seeing little sense in staying, Schaaf led the Graf Waldersee Battery racing back inland, abandoning one of their guns when it threw a track. At first the units pulled back to a line between Mathieu and Anguerny, but in the confusion of dozens of vehicles pouring along the limited tracks south, 1 Company of 192 Regiment found themselves at Douvres-la-Délivrande's Luftwaffe radar station, where they would remain until the Allies overran it eight days later. Nevertheless, the bulk of Rauch's battlegroup withdrew in good order, taking with them the wounded and many of the men who had defended Trout all day.[*1]

As it was, the gliders were not coming to reinforce the western end of Sword; rather, 6 Airlanding Brigade was destined for the bridgehead across the Orne. Once they had crossed the coast, the towing aircraft started to release their gliders, some of which gently drifted down to a

---

[*] Schaaf's men continued south until, at length, they came to a roadblock. Recognizing British uniforms in the distance, he quickly ordered his men to doff their helmets and a tarpaulin was thrown over the German crosses on the hull. The self-propelled guns accelerated and tore through the roadblock before the shocked British infantry could react, then raced down the road until, several miles later, they came upon columns of infantry and vehicles pulling back to Caen. The exhausted gunners joined the throng and wearily took up positions north of the city.

field east of Saint-Aubin, others to the fields north of Ranville on the other side of the River Orne. Inland, heavier flak started to bite at the aircraft and gliders, but they ignored all distractions and eventually 248 safely reached their landing zones.*

In the grounds of Hillman the Suffolks, still euphoric from their hard-fought victory, were delighted to see such a powerful show of force. Their recently taken prisoners stared in disbelief. The spectacle was equally impressive for the Norfolks, still holding their slender little position on Périers Ridge at Rover. By now A and B Companies had managed to disentangle themselves from Hillman and had come up to join C and D, but they had sustained heavy casualties in doing so – fifty men were killed or wounded moving from Colleville on to the ridge. The sight of the vast airborne force droning overhead and the gliders coming down only a mile and a half away past Saint-Aubin greatly cheered the weary men, but it also brought a threat of a different kind. Once free of their gliders that had dragged behind them like giant aerial anchors, the tug aircraft pulled away to the left and right. As they crossed Périers Ridge they dropped their heavy tow ropes, many of which fell into Rover, forcing the men to dive and dodge the huge, deadly snakes.

The gliders came much closer to the Warwickshire battalion. By now, after the Norfolks' struggle to reach Rover, Brigadier Smith had decided that the most sensible route for the Warwicks to take was along the canal, passing through Bénouville and Blainville and approaching Lebisey from the east. B Company had led the battalion through Saint-Aubin, finding it largely deserted of German forces. Now A Company led a column of the battalion, supporting arms and F Troop of 92 Light Anti-Aircraft Regiment – towing Bofors guns – along the road towards le Port that Lovat and the commandos had followed earlier. Some rifle fire started to emanate from the nearest houses and the advance halted while Major John Lister of 7 Field Regiment tried to establish the range to the village. He was nearly ready to coordinate with the regiment back at Hermanville when the aerial armada descended from above, and he wisely decided to postpone the bombardment. The gliders floated silently from the sky and ploughed through the fields on the north side of the road where two

---

* The most commonly reported figures for Operation Mallard are that 258 tug-glider combinations took off from England and 248 gliders safely landed. Some of the combinations will have aborted over England. The official 6th Airborne report of operations in Normandy records 250 gliders taking part (CAB 106/970).

signallers with B Company, tuned into the wireless net with their headphones muffling all other noise, missed the warnings of their colleagues and were crushed beneath the weight of a Horsa. And this wasn't the only danger. As the gliders slewed to a stop, their occupants leapt out of the side doors firing wildly at any potential enemy. The Warwicks ducked as small fusillades of fire came from the nearest gliders and some men fell wounded. Only hasty shouting prevented more casualties.

The glider landings were sufficient to quell the sniper fire from le Port and A Company continued into the village. With no organized enemy units in occupation, the men quickly linked up with the small numbers of airborne forces still holding the southern side. But as the column followed them in, isolated Germans were soon sniping at them from house windows. Driver Jim Holder-Vale of 92 LAA Regiment had just gone to the back of his truck to find their camouflage nets when he suddenly heard a dull thump. With a start he realized a bullet had just missed his head and struck the vehicle, and in a flash he flew round to the other side of the truck. Glancing back, he could see the most obvious spot the bullet had come from and shouted out, 'Sniper in the church tower!' The mixed units in the village square dived for cover and a fusillade of bullets struck the tower, already plastered by the fighting earlier in the day. Eventually Sergeant Clements brought the troop's Number 1 gun to bear on the tower and fired several 40mm rounds into the belfry, further demolishing its fragile stonework. As the crashing of the Bofors' shells echoed around the square, the small arms fire slackened. A party of men rushed the church and emerged a few minutes later with a young, dazed and terrified-looking German. Buoyed by their success, the LAA troop brought their guns to bear on other windows that had brought trouble to the square and had soon amassed a number of prisoners.

With the East Yorks delayed in their progress at Daimler, D Company of the Warwicks were ordered to relieve the airborne forces still defending the perimeter of the two bridges across the Caen Canal and the River Orne. It was getting late when Major Thomas Bundock led his company to the bridge and sought out Major John Howard. The relieved airborne forces wearily gathered their kit and marched off towards Ranville while Bundock's men took over their positions, aghast at the size of the perimeter they now needed to defend.

The rest of the Warwicks still needed to push south along the canal, their next obstacle the village of Bénouville. Throughout the day the village had been held by a small battlegroup built around 8 Company,

2 Battalion of 192 Panzer Grenadier Regiment under Oberleutnant Braatz. In charge of the company's anti-tank platoon and three self-propelled 75mm guns, Leutnant Hans Hoeller had just watched the mass landings to the north, the gliders swooping down like giant black birds. They had fired every weapon that could be brought to bear on the armada but the sheer scale of the landings was simply too much. Then worse news had arrived from Braatz, who had just been made aware of the enemy advance on Biéville. The British were already further south than they were; all they needed to do was advance east for a mile and a half to the canal and they would cut off the small German force entirely. There was no question in Braatz's mind about what needed to be done now and he ordered a full retreat towards Hérouville.

To the north, Captain Illing had just reached the first buildings of Bénouville and was forming his company up to sweep the village. Round the corner of the building he was surprised to see two armed German soldiers jogging up the road towards them, apparently unaware of their presence. His men stepped into the road and the two startled Germans dived for a hedge, but were shot down before they could make it. Now the men raced forward, but only odd snipers seemed to be about to bother them.

Captain Gregory of 7 Field Regiment pushed his Observation Post tank forward through the village. Ahead of him, round a gentle bend in the road, Hoeller heard the tank engine revving and held his breath – the British were already here. Then, less than 100 yards ahead of him, a Sherman rounded the bend. After quickly training their anti-tank gun, all the time expecting the Sherman to open up at them, they fired at the tank. A bright explosion illuminated the gathering gloom and left the tank in flames. Satisfied, Hoeller ordered his crew to withdraw as quickly as possible and the self-propelled gun roared south while, behind him, Gregory and some of his crew, badly wounded, crawled from the tank. Some would never leave it alive.

By now the gloom of night was settling across Normandy, and the woodland alongside the road only hastened its descent. B Company took the lead again as the battalion pressed on through Bénouville, skirting around a machine gun position that further hindered progress. Lieutenant Field led the forward platoon towards Blainville where they engaged some defenders at the northernmost buildings in the town. Realizing that Blainville was occupied, and as they were now in complete darkness and unable to call on artillery support, Lieutenant Colonel Herdon decided it was time to call a halt. The battalion settled down astride the road between Bénouville and Blainville, unaware that even as they did so the Germans were pulling out of the latter village and withdrawing to Hérouville, more than a mile further south.[2]

In Biéville, the KSLI were out on a limb. W Company had dug in around the orchard above the depression south of the village. It was not an ideal position – the orchard was small and overlooked from Lebisey to the south – but there was nowhere else to go if they wanted to observe the enemy front. With 9 Platoon facing forward, 8 on the left side and 7 on the right, Captain Robert Rylands could only hope the thin screen of trees might hide them enough before darkness fell, but there was no hope of it resisting tanks – and there were no anti-tank guns to aid their defence. As darkness fell, Y Company carefully and noiselessly withdrew from Lebisey and took position on W Company's left flank. To their rear, X Company were digging in near the farm buildings of the village, where Lieutenant Jones was equally concerned about the lack of defensive power. He toured his men's positions where men were digging 6-foot trenches in expectation of an artillery bombardment and tank attack. Seeing one of the battalion's knocked-out 6-pounder guns, he was disturbed to find the arm of one of its former crew lying on the track, its hand pointing to the sky. He shook off the disturbing urge to shake the hand and retreated to cover for the night. Nervously, the battalion settled down to await the inevitable counter-attack.

Behind them, 2 East Yorks wearily advanced in Saint-Aubin. By now multiple battalions had passed through the village and there was little mopping up for them to do. They were relieved when 1 KOSB marched into the village from the other end to take up their position guarding the western approaches to the bridges, and the Yorkshiremen moved into the fields behind the Norfolks to recover. They had taken 209 casualties on D-Day, including sixty-five killed.

But to the south, the Germans had little thought of offensive action. Colonel Hermann von Oppeln-Bronikowski was already digging his tanks in along the Lebisey ridge – giant pits were scraped out into which the tanks drove so that only their turrets peeked out above ground level. To further strengthen a new line of defence Feuchtinger ordered Rauch to move his battlegroup back even further, and under cover of darkness they pulled back to their starting positions, joining the end of Oppeln-Bronikowski's line at Lebisey and stretching out to Cairon. They had given up all the land they had taken in their all too brief joyride to the coast.

Nearly 4 miles north of them, Ludwig Krug sat in his HQ bunker at Hillman. His regiment appeared to have been totally destroyed, the British were in full control of the surface above them, and they were probably well inland by now as well. At 21:00 he called General Richter, related the fall of the strongpoint to him and asked for tanks to be sent to his position to regain the advantage. Tired, uncertain of exactly where the enemy were, but knowing that one armoured counter-attack had already failed, Richter could only tell Krug to wait.

Three hours later, Richter sat in his command bunker in the old quarry at St Julien. To the south-east Caen was being bombed again – bright flames licked the sky as buildings crashed down into the road, blocking streets and junctions. The HQ's bunkers had been transformed into emergency medical shelters – wounded men were operated on by overworked surgeons while staff officers rushed by, trying to respond to urgent requests and orders flung around by bewildered men. Inside Richter's office SS-Standartenführer Kurt Meyer,[*] commander of 25 SS Panzer Grenadier Regiment of 12 SS Panzer Division, listened forlornly as the general outlined the situation. Meyer had just arrived. After the division was finally ordered to move at 16:00, he had spent a large proportion of his time under air attack and had only now reached Caen. But Richter had little he could tell him. As far as he knew only the strongpoints at Colleville and Douvres-la-Délivrande were holding out in 736 Regiment's sector and a handful on the coast in 726 Regiment's area. But there was hardly any contact with individual formations and only two artillery units were still firing. As far as Richter could tell, the rest had probably already been destroyed.

The telephone rang. Richter picked it up and Meyer heard the voice of Ludwig Krug on the other end of the line. He listened as the oberst outlined his predicament – that British forces now controlled the surface of his HQ, that he was trapped below ground with no means to fight back. He understood his obligation to fight, but he did not know how. What, he asked his general, were his orders?

Richter listened impassively. Krug did not realize the full extent of the defeat that had overtaken 716 Division, but with one counter-attack having failed and few units of his own division left to command there

---

[*] SS-Standartenführer was a rank broadly equivalent to colonel.

was now nothing the general could do. 'I cannot give you any further orders,' he told Krug. 'You must do what you have to do. Goodbye.' He replaced the receiver and sat in silence.

Bobbing around astern of HMS *Scylla*, the four MTBs of Lieutenant Commander Anthony Law's little division prepared to cast off. Law had led them out of Portsmouth Harbour at 14:00 and, bounding their way through pitching seas, they had followed seemingly endless convoys to the south. As they crossed the minefield they saw other convoys, this time steaming north. Ragged formations of LCTs and LCIs passed them, some still lightly smouldering from blackened patches on their hulls. The large troopships looked almost naked without their flotillas of LCAs hanging from the davits. Eventually they had reached the beaches and, after getting directions from various destroyers, had found their parent ship in Force S's anchorage.

Convoys had continued to arrive in the anchorage all evening. The first vessels of follow-up Force L, merchant ships, were already craning vehicles off their decks and on to landing craft alongside. All around *Scylla* the sea bustled as boats scurried one way and the other. But such activity was a tempting target for the Luftwaffe which would doubtless visit once darkness fell, and already preparations were being made for their arrival. Ships were already making smoke, sending thick plumes of dirty clouds into the sky in an attempt to shield the fleet from above.

On the MTBs crewmen donned their dark oilskin jackets and wrapped themselves in their distinctive dark blue Canadian lifejackets. One by one engines were fired up, exhaust smoke streaming across the boat decks and choking the men on the bridges as they gulped their last mouthfuls of tea and cocoa. As each skipper signalled he was ready, Law ordered the boats cast off and, one by one, the MTBs slipped their leashes and backed away from their parent cruiser like inquisitive ducklings slipping away from their mother.

Powering through the rolling waves, the boats headed north. The late summer sunlight had finally faded; by 22:30 gloom had enveloped the boats and, as if sensing the change in atmosphere, the darkened seas became rougher. Reaching their designated area, some 12 miles west of Cap de la Hève,* the boats cut their engines and tossed around in the pitching waves.

---

* The westernmost point of land on the Le Havre headland.

The last vestiges of natural light evaporated and the boats lost sight of one another. But overhead, even against the sound of the waves slamming against the hulls, the thunderous drone of dozens of aircraft marked the passing of time. Then lights flickered to the south and the crews turned to watch dozens of AA guns sending fingers of tracer into the air and small explosions blinking in the sky. Slowly, out of sync with what the crews could see, the rattle of gunfire and the shallow booms of blasts rolled across the sea, adding a surreal air to the show. Eventually the gunfire died out, the twinkling faded away and the last sounds of battle were whipped away by the wind. The boats resumed their silent waiting.

Two or three miles north lay four more boats, larger Fairmile D 'Dog Boats' of 55 MTB Flotilla. Lieutenant Commander Donald Bradford, the flotilla's senior officer, had led his division to a position on the very edge of the Allied minefield around Le Havre. Now they too waited in the water, waves crashing against the hulls and spraying foam over the teeth of the shark mouths proudly painted on each boat's bow. The crews sipped at their cocoa thoughtfully, the recently finished fireworks to the south a reminder that the night did not mean an end to the day's fighting. At midnight they were reminded again.

To the east, eleven R-boats from 4 and 10 Räumboot Flotillas ploughed through the waves, groping in the dark to reach and mine the area codenamed Blitz 25. Cautiously the boats advanced into their operations area, adjusted their formation and began sowing their deadly crop, the crews straining to push the sea mines over the stern rails as the rough seas tossed the heavily laden small boats around. As the boats slowly crawled south-west, four men were swept overboard when a mine crashed through the railings on the stern deck of R 46. As the sailors desperately tried to keep themselves above water R 115 pulled out of line and manoeuvred towards them. Clinging to their own railings, the crew gingerly plucked their comrades from the foaming sea one by one.

After an age, the R-boats completed their first line and the crews turned their boats to begin another. Then their dreary mood was shattered as the nearby gloom was suddenly lit up. The crews stared as bright flashes and daisy chains of light ascended into the sky, doubtless an air attack on someone at sea. But who was attacking? The crews' minds puzzled over the nearby spectacle as the boats pressed on to begin the next line of mines.

Nearby, Tony Law's flotilla were jerked alert when their radio transmitters crackled. Don Bradford's signaller had broken radio silence to let

Scylla know that they were investigating a radar contact. The Fairmile Ds fired up their engines and turned north, their shark snout bows barging through the waves, their eyes staring into the darkness. Bradford led his group north, hoping to reach the radar contact's line of advance well ahead of them and lie in wait. After half a mile his navigator called up welcome news and the flotilla prepared to spring its trap.

It was a dark night, the moon was clouded out of the sky, but there was no mist or fog and soon, at less than 1,000 yards, the enemy boats could be seen approaching the MTBs. Bradford watched through his binoculars – there looked to be five small boats, probably R-boats, and perhaps something larger, a Marinefährprahm[*] perhaps. There was no time to lose and Bradford signalled his boats to turn on an intercept course, the flotilla quickly forming into a well-rehearsed quarter line.[†] At 500 yards the bow guns of each boat launched rocket flares into the sky and almost immediately followed them with heavy gunfire. Tracer lurched across the waves as 6-pounders, 0.5-inch Vickers and .303 K-guns let fly.

But if the Royal Navy thought they had caught the Kriegsmarine totally off guard they were wrong. The R-boats immediately returned fire, and shells and bullets whizzed past the Dog Boats. Even so, the German skippers were dazzled by the gunfire coming their way and briefly seemed unsure what to do. There were still mines on deck, each well over a ton of delicate explosive. Turning away would expose them to the full force of the Royal Navy's gunfire. But to continue into the maelstrom was obviously suicide and hastily the boats came about, scattering away from the Dog Boats' path and desperately scurrying into the darkness. Bradford saw the larger boat pull away to the south, but decided to let it go so he could concentrate on the R-boats.[‡]

---

[*] A German landing craft comparable to an Allied LCT.
[†] A naval formation where the lead boat is followed by the next in line, positioned alongside with its bow level with the lead boat's quarter (its aft half). The next boat assumes the same position on the second boat and so on.
[‡] From the Kriegsmarine reports, it's evident that there was no larger vessel accompanying the R-boats. Fought at high speed in poor light, Coastal Forces actions are replete with such misidentifications. Famed commander of 21 MTB Flotilla Peter Dickens commented that 'If you know what you are looking at on a dark night you can guess the range; or if you know the range you can guess the size of what you are looking at; but if you know neither and guess one wrongly, the other will be wrong too' (Dickens, p.77).

The little boats raced towards the gloomy east, the occasional splash at their sterns showing the crews' hasty efforts to ditch their mines. Bradford's flotilla gave chase, driving their engines harder, the bows lifting out of the water and the sharks grinning at their prey. The 6-pounder bow guns thumped away, a round blasting out of the muzzle every second as the loaders desperately tried to keep up with the layers' enthusiasm. Ahead of them the R-boats started to make smoke, but the westerly wind whipped it ahead of the boats and silhouetted them against the dark night, making them even more visible to the Dog Boats. Then the navigator shouted a warning that chilled Bradford's blood: 'Sir, we are a mile inside!' In the excitement, Bradford had forgotten all about the hidden menace they'd been lying on the edge of. But if he was inside the minefield then so were the R-boats – and they'd run over the mines first. He decided to continue the pursuit.

On the R-boats the crews had realized the folly of making smoke and had switched the generators off. Even so, two of the boats continued to make smoke – flames licked up from their sterns and they dropped behind their comrades as Admiralty shells started to make themselves felt.

Bradford was feeling confident. They were gaining now, the two lame ducks would soon be at their mercy, and it wouldn't take all four of his boats to finish them off – some could press on against the rest of the enemy flotilla. Then a sickening blast awakened him from his imagination. A second followed moments later, a great geyser thrown up in the water alongside. Mines. Bradford hurriedly weighed up his options: he could press on and risk all his boats to the underwater peril, or he could slow down and withdraw from the minefield – and lose the R-boats. Another mine detonated nearby, warning him, and then another near the R-boats, goading him. But then, just as the agony of choice was clawing at him, a new explosion rent the air as the nearest R-boat detonated in a sheet of flame. Either his gunners had detonated a mine on the stern or the German boat had hit one just below the surface. Either way, the sight of a boat aflame was enough to make up Bradford's mind. He signalled to the group and they slowed and turned away to starboard.

To British eyes the luckless R-boat was doomed, but aboard R 49 the crew were fighting to save her. A hit in the bow had started a fire and left a large hole in the hull, the port engine was ablaze, and nine men lay around the boat, some nursing injuries, three already beyond help. Lagging near her was R 234, damaged and with three casualties on board.

The relieved crews watched as their pursuers pulled away and gratefully waited for their companions to put about and come to their aid.*

Bradford's flotilla crawled south, groping for a way out of the minefield. Holding their breath and involuntarily walking on tiptoes as if their lighter feet would make the difference, the four boats daintily made their way through the treacherous waters. Even so mine after mine detonated, some uncomfortably close, others much further away – seemingly exploding in sympathy with their neighbours. By the time they emerged from the minefield, Bradford's crews had counted twenty-three detonations.

Once free of the danger, Bradford carried on south, back towards the fleet. Some 200 yards away, silent and darkened, Law's flotilla watched their shadowy progress across their bows. But to the north-east, radar revealed the presence of other ships. As Bradford was seemingly oblivious to their presence, Law decided it was his turn and hurriedly led his MTBs towards them. Radios crackled to life as he signalled his intentions to *Scylla* and the boats hastened north-east to intercept the fleeing prey.

A few minutes later, the leading group of R-boats found themselves illuminated by starshell once again. Charging from the south-west came another flotilla of Allied ships, tracer already accelerating towards them and whipping past the boats. Instantly the deck guns came into action and a fusillade of fire was returned to the new aggressors.

Several lines of tracer flicked through the air as German gunners steadied their weapons while the boats twisted and turned beneath them. Like powerful hoses being brought under control, the flickering streams of tracer were slowly manhandled on to their targets. Law observed that the returning fire was quickly becoming increasingly accurate and then, to his horror, noticed the streams heading towards him. Lingering in the air, the tracer seemed suspended in slow motion until suddenly, as it neared MTB 459, it whipped up a new pace and quicker than the eye could perceive it struck the boat. A quick series of stark thuds and the crackling of split timbers echoed around Law as rounds pummelled into his boat and, along with his small bridge crew, he dived down and into the frail shelter offered by the deckhouse. Ahead of him one of the gun crew was badly wounded and very briefly 459 was hors de combat. She wasn't the only one – all four of Law's boats took damage in the initial fusillade.

---

* Despite the damage R 49 and R 234 sustained, they, along with all the other R-boats, were able to limp back into Le Havre in the early hours of the morning.

Nonetheless, the R-boats were obviously not interested in sticking around, and as they fled further east Law's boats arced round and gave pursuit. Now able to sting the enemy from behind, the Canadians launched their own fusillade of fire, pouring shot and shell into the small boats until, as Bradford had experienced, reality made itself known. A mine exploded, followed by another, and Law realized their predicament. Wasting no time he led his boats in a turn away and made smoke to cover their escape from the minefield.

For a tense few minutes the boats puttered through the dangerous seas until the navigator finally reported that they were outside the known mined area and everyone breathed a sigh of relief. The first glows of light were appearing to the north-east and, their duty done, the MTBs sailed south to find *Scylla* and hopefully medical treatment for their casualties.[3]

A damaged German casemate situated at the east end of strongpoint 8 (Bass) next to the mouth of the Caen Canal. The casemate housed a 50mm anti-tank gun but was probably knocked out during the pre-landing bombardment.

A B-26 Marauder – most likely from 323 Bomb Group – passes over Sword sector while returning from a raid on Caen at approximately 16:40 on D-Day. Numerous beached landing craft litter Queen Beach.

PART 5
THE FOLLOW-UP FIGHTS

16

JOINING JUNO, CLOSING ON CAEN

AT 06:45, AS LIGHT BEGAN ONCE AGAIN TO ILLUMINATE THE fields inland of Queen Beach, Oberst Ludwig Krug stepped out of his command bunker's main door. Rifles were trained on him from above, but with as much dignity as he could muster he marched up the steps out of the trench. As the Suffolks watched, scarcely able to believe their eyes, seventy-two men followed him out of the door, the whole procession taking nearly twenty minutes to exit the bunker. Lieutenant Colonel Goodwin allowed Krug to review his men: the soldiers formed up and Krug spoke briefly, praising their dedication and thanking them for their service. Then he and two of his officers were escorted away and to the beaches. 736 Regiment was no more.

At 08:35 the port engine of LCT 898 shuddered briefly and then ground to a halt. Exhausted as they were, Stokers Swordy and Hutchings set about stripping it down to find the fault, while Sub Lieutenant Charles Flynn, his eyes blood-stained through exhaustion, slumped on the bridge as the lonely landing craft swayed in the morning swell. They had done well to get this far: no sooner had they left the beach yesterday morning than the one remaining winch wire holding up the bow ramp had given way, and it now hung uselessly below the surface like a giant sea anchor, mocking their slow progress home. Sub Lieutenant Willis had begun treating the wounded as soon as they were off the beach – he had been forced to amputate two of George Wells's fingers there and then with a pair of scissors. Two hours later they made it alongside HMS *Princess*

Astrid, where Wells, McKinnon and the body of Batty were transferred, and then they had begun the plodding journey back to England.

After what felt like an age, the port engine choked back into life and 898 limped on. Finally, almost twenty-nine hours after they had left the beach, they pulled into the Solent. After arranging for Willis and Leading Seaman Tyson to be taken ashore, Flynn staggered to the wardroom and collapsed into a chair, letting the events of the last three days slowly sink in. There was a knock on the thin wooden door, and wearily Flynn called in the intruder on his thoughts. It was Able Seaman Fowler, who stood erect in the doorway. 'Sir,' he began, 'I have been chosen by the remainder of the crew to thank you for getting us back.' Stunned and barely able to comprehend the message, Flynn thanked Fowler and dismissed him. As the door closed, he put his head in his hands on the wardroom table and wept.*

After the tribulations of the day, the night of 6/7 June passed relatively quietly for 41 Commando. The much anticipated counter-attack had failed to materialize – they had no real way of knowing that the vast majority of the units they had faced had withdrawn late in the evening in the wake of 6 Airlanding Brigade's arrival. But there was still the expectation of hard fighting on the 7th. In fact, it got harder much faster than expected.

Occasional sniper's bullets and the odd mortar round bothered the unit after stand-to, but with no orders to move forward yet the commandos waited in their foxholes. Then, at 11:05, everything changed when three Heinkel bombers suddenly swooped along the coast, a number of Spitfires on their tails. Despite their likely destruction at the hands of the overwhelming fighter cover, one of the bomber's pilots concentrated on a run and, as it passed over Lion-sur-Mer, sticks of anti-personnel bombs descended from its belly. The commandos, looking up and expecting to see a short aerial engagement, found themselves staring in wonder at the falling objects instead. Then realization dawned. Screaming warnings, men dived to the ground, seeking out foxholes, ditches and alleys. The bombs scattered as they fell, crashing down among the streets and gardens at the east end of the town; one or more fell on the small wood where HQ were based with devastating results, killing Captain Dixon

---

* George Wells received a Distinguished Conduct Medal for his actions on D-Day, while Flynn and Swordy were both mentioned in despatches. Lawrence Batty was buried at sea and is commemorated on the Chatham Naval Memorial.

and two others and wounding eleven men, including Lieutenant Colonel Gray. A signaller who had dived into a slit trench actually survived one of the bombs following him in, although it cost him a leg. Captain Cregan, 41 Commando's medical officer, was quickly on the scene again, and he had no choice but to order Gray's evacuation. With second in command Major Barclay already dead, command passed to Major John Taplin.

Taplin had barely learned of his new responsibility before Lieutenant Colonel Christopher Welby-Everard visited. After passing on his condolences, he explained that Brigadier Cass of 8 Brigade, who now had the Lincolns under his command after losing the Suffolks to 9 Brigade, had placed 41 Commando under his command. The Lincolns were to clear the way to the west, although it wasn't until the afternoon that more detailed plans came through: the Lincolns with 41 Commando in reserve were to clear Lion-sur-Mer by flanking Trout, capturing the château, and then sweeping back to Trout and clearing the rest of the town. The objective sounded simple, but Taplin was able to advise Welby-Everard on just how tough a nut the château was. With its surrounding 10-foot wall and views in all directions across the surrounding flat fields, the defenders enjoyed a significant advantage.

It wasn't until gone 15:00 that the Lincolns' attack went in. Advancing from their positions on the left flank, Major Leslie Colvin led B Company along the tree-lined lane from the communal cemetery towards the château – the same lane that John Sturgis and James Kelly had fired on the previous day. Mortar fire hit the company as they advanced and machine gun fire quickly pinned them down, but B Company established a base of fire and suppressed the defenders enough to allow C Company to move up on their right. Once they reached the château walls it didn't take long for the company to break through, where they found limited opposition. It quickly became evident that most of the defenders had made good their escape and C Company rounded up the rest. In contrast to 41 Commando's efforts the previous day, the attack had cost only nine wounded.

The battalion prepared to wheel right and turn on Trout from behind, but just as C and D Companies were forming up a change in plans came down from 8 Brigade: the battalion were to move south-east to Saint-Aubin and Bénouville and protect the left flank on the River Orne. It was a 4-mile trip so motor transport was laid on for the battalion, although not entirely to their liking. A number of trucks arrived in Hermanville to transport them, but most were filled with 'flimsy' petrol containers that the troops had to sit on top of. For those familiar with the leaky containers, the consequences of another air attack didn't bear thinking about. Fortunately one never developed and the battalion deployed along the Orne without difficulty.

Meanwhile, 41 Commando were instructed to proceed west. With Trout flanked, progress was easy, and after advancing into Luc-sur-Mer at 18:20 the men met up with 46 Commando, who had landed at Juno that morning. The two neighbouring beaches were joined.[1]

While the Lincolns and 41 Commando were securing the coast, the rest of 3 Division were looking to fulfil their tasks from D-Day. To everyone's surprise a night attack had not come and, although it had been a tense night, the battalions had had a chance to recover and reorganize. Striking west from Hermanville, the South Lancs advanced towards Cresserons and Plumetot as a naval bombardment fell on the two villages, and at 13:00 they moved into them practically unopposed. B Company advanced as far as Douvres-la-Délivrande and moved north to help the commandos clear Luc-sur-Mer. The following day, after another intense naval bombardment, they returned to Lion-sur-Mer and silenced Trout. The defenders from 10 Company 736 Regiment had held out for two days before, short of ammunition and supplies, they accepted the inevitable. Eighty of them were marched from the strongpoint to the beaches and piled on to LSTs to be taken to England.

The East Yorks, still severely understrength, moved along Périers Ridge to take over the Royal Ulster Rifles' position near Point 61. The Rifles, who had yet to engage the Germans, passed through Périers-sur-le-Dan, reporting it clear, and 1 KOSB followed through and moved into Mathieu, which was similarly deserted. Hoping to push even further south, Dennis Orr, now a temporary brigadier, instructed 2 RUR to prepare to assault Cambes. That afternoon the battalion, supported by A and B Squadron of the East Riding Yeomanry, advanced towards the tiny settlement of Le Mesnil, where they first started to come under fire. The tanks raced ahead along with D Company, crossing the 700 yards of open ground between the two villages and infiltrating into the northern corner of Cambes. The two tank squadrons worked their way around the edges of the village, seemingly surprising the enemy occupants but quickly realizing that they themselves had wandered into a beehive. In a wild and uncoordinated action, the East Riding Yeomanry destroyed three enemy tanks, a half-track and four ammunition trucks for the loss of only one of their own. But the village was too strongly held and, as darkness fell, they withdrew to Le Mesnil for the night. Cambes eventually fell to 2 RUR on 9 June, but it would be much longer before the Allies made any more movement from the village towards Caen.[2]

To the east, Major General Rennie's greatest ambition was to push through Lebisey and on to Caen. 2 Warwick secured Blainville early in the morning and reconnaissance further south quickly revealed that the German forces had withdrawn from their immediate front. Under orders from Brigadier Smith to attack Lebisey at 09:45, the battalion's three companies moved forward, but were delayed when they came under fire from a German position at Beauregard. Smith decided to postpone the attack by thirty minutes, but B and C Companies didn't receive the message and, when the men arrived at the forming-up position in time to attack as originally scheduled, they pressed forward – but without support. Hearing what had happened, Lieutenant Colonel Herdon pushed A Company forward on their left flank to support them. Progress to the tree line was good but as soon as they entered the woods the companies were heavily engaged by 21 Panzer Division's well-entrenched defenders. Struggling to cross the natural hollow south of Biéville, tanks and anti-tank guns were forced to use the road and fell victim to ambushing tanks and artillery. To make matters even worse for the infantry their CO was killed as he advanced into the woods.

All morning the battalion struggled to gain ground through the woods. In mid-afternoon Smith committed 1 Norfolk to the fight, supported by A Squadron of the Staffordshire Yeomanry. A full nine hours after the Warwicks had attacked, the Norfolks joined the fray, but their CO quickly realized that in the thick woods there was little hope of a coordinated action. At 22:30 the Warwicks started to fall back in the face of fresh tank attacks and the Norfolks followed as they withdrew to Biéville for the night. The Warwicks had sustained 154 casualties after more than twelve hours of fighting – in fact they had almost made it through the woods, and for the briefest of moments the men had seen Caen just a few miles to the south.

But it would be a full month before the Allies moved any closer to Caen. When the Allies launched Operation Charnwood on 8 July, 3 Division were still covering the city's northern flank, and that day the Norfolks finally made it through Lebisey and found the month-old wreckage of the Warwicks' attack deep in the woods. The next day the division entered Caen's northern suburbs.[3]

17

SECURING SWORD

BY THE TIME MAJOR GENERAL THOMAS RENNIE HIT THE SAND ON D-Day, Queen Beach was largely secure. Strongpoints 18, 20 and 20A had been overwhelmed by the arrival of Assault Group S3's 170-odd landing craft, which had put approximately 8,500 men and 1,200 vehicles ashore in the first two and a half hours.

This achievement by both the naval and land forces is one that rarely gets the praise it deserves. After the landing areas had been secured, observers, intelligence officers and specialists in artillery, fortifications and enemy weapons pored over the beaches, assessing the strength of the defences and the impact of the pre-landing bombardment and the assault techniques used. Their observations were naturally restricted by what evidence remained – many craters had already been filled, ammunition removed, machine guns liberated, and witnesses killed or moved on. But their reports provide some insight into the differences between the five landing beaches and the achievements on each.

Of the three British and Commonwealth beaches, Gold, Juno and Sword, Sword was perhaps the most hotly defended. At just under a mile wide it was also the smallest landing area. To the west, Force G1 at Jig Green and Red Beaches was landing on a 1.7-mile front and G2 at King Green and Red on some 1.3 miles of beach. Force J1 landed on approximately 1.7 miles of Mike and Nan Green Beaches, and J2 came ashore on 1.5 miles of beach at Nan Green and Red. Of these five areas, Sword had significantly more anti-tank guns, mortars and machine guns in fixed positions per mile. Only Force J1's landings on the west flank of Juno Beach faced comparable defences and even then there were significantly fewer mortars in waterfront positions.

The source of much of the additional armament was of course strongpoint Cod, stretching across almost a third of the landing area. But Skate and strongpoint 20A were equally significant, and in addition to the seven AT guns these three positions housed, another four were located less than a mile to the east and west of the landing area at strongpoints 10 and 21. Both had good views of the Queen White and Red Beaches, and while strongpoint 10's 75mm could not traverse sufficiently to fire directly on to Queen Red, it had excellent views of the waters in front of it and most likely was the source of the shots that knocked out LCTs 2191 and 2052.

It is unsurprising, then, that the easternmost beach was found to be one of the bloodiest for the infantry. An analysis of the casualties sustained by the first two waves suggested that 8 Infantry Brigade and its attached formations had sustained approximately 25.2 per cent casualties on the beaches, nearly double that at Juno (13.7 per cent) and three times that at Gold (8.1 per cent). When looking at casualties sustained in the first forty-five minutes of the assault, Sword was estimated to have claimed 9.7 per cent casualties, Juno 5.2 per cent and Gold 4.25 per cent. For the entire assault division casualties sustained on the beaches, this dropped to 2.7 per cent casualties at Sword, 3.5 per cent at Juno and 1.8 per cent at Gold.

Such figures are of course simply statistics. It would be wrong to say that Gold was not a struggle – the forced closure of Jig Green Beach for most of the day is testament to the ferocity of the fighting there. At Juno, when the individual beaches are considered separately, Nan Red and White Beaches were estimated to have seen 6.2 per cent casualties among the assault wave, higher than Sword's 5.2 per cent. Juno also sustained far more casualties on the beaches throughout D-Day, owing in part to the delay in securing the strongpoints.

Even so, it's quite plain that the losses at Sword were significant and much higher in the first two waves of infantry than at Juno and Gold – this is despite the DD tanks of 13/18 Hussars successfully coming ashore almost to schedule, while at the other two beaches they were somewhat delayed. In their war diary, 2 East Yorks reported that 209 casualties had been sustained by the morning of 7 June – five officers and sixty other ranks killed, four officers and 137 other ranks wounded, and three other ranks missing. While some of these casualties were from their attacks on inland defences later in the day, the vast majority were sustained on the beach – as Lieutenant Rutherford discovered.

Even next to the most famous beach of D-Day, Sword is shown to have been no cakewalk. In fact, the number of fixed defensive weapons per mile at Sword and Omaha were very similar, with machine guns at the latter being the only weapon type that was more numerous. An attempt to establish a generic defensive measure based on equivalenting mortars to machine guns found that per 1,000 yards, Sword's defenders were in fact marginally better equipped than at Omaha, and significantly better than at any of the other beaches.* The same survey estimated approximately 3,000 casualties on Omaha and 630 on Sword, or 790 and 525 per mile respectively.

But such studies should be treated with considerable caution. The survey referred to above is based on landing areas that are somewhat larger than the beach limits (the statistics for Utah, where the landing area was only about a mile wide, appear to be based on a length of 5.5 miles), and freely admits that the statistics for Omaha included casualties sustained inland, while those for Sword only include the beach. Other conclusions in the report are based on incomplete or often questionable data.

In the present day, trying to establish the exact statistics is no easier, although revisiting the details does allow for what might be some more accurate comparisons. We know, for instance, that the number of casualties at Omaha Beach was probably closer to 2,500 than 3,000, which would reduce the average number per mile to 657. Steven Zaloga reviewed the likely number of fixed defences at Omaha, finding significantly higher numbers of mortars than the wartime estimates, although there were probably fewer fixed machine guns, perhaps as few as fifty. Reviewing the statistics for Sword, it appears the 1944 observers may have counted weapons pits as indicating the presence of weapons when in reality they may not have been present, especially at two of the mortar pits.

Even so, taking the newer numbers, the number of fixed defences is broadly the same at both beaches, with an average of 1.9 concrete gun casemates, 3.3 anti-tank guns, 2.3 mortars and 6.6 machine guns per

---

* The statistic was created by establishing the rough casualty rate caused by mortars. 8.1cm mortars were found to have caused approximately three times the number of casualties that machine guns caused, while 5cm mortars were on a par with machine guns. A mortar was therefore equivalent to three machine guns, and by extrapolating this across the beaches, a defensive 'score' could be arrived at. At Omaha, the score was 14 equivalent machine guns per mile, at Sword it was 17.7. It is not a precise measure, though, and does not account for other factors such as the presence of rockets used against the US forces at Omaha, or the terrain there, which significantly aided the defence.

1,000 metres on Sword and 1.8 gun casemates, 2.7 anti-tank guns, 3.5 mortars and 5.4 machine guns per 1,000 metres at Omaha. This still overlooks significant other factors like the terrain at Omaha, and the flanking strongpoints at Sword. Zaloga attempted to establish the average number of defending troops, estimating approximately 113 troops per 1,000 yards at Omaha and only sixty-eight at Sword. However, he appears to have underestimated the force at Sword while considerably exaggerating the landing area: were we to count the entire frontage of 5,500 yards he uses, it would include three additional companies of men and troops at strongpoint Bass, increasing the number of troops per 1000 yards to somewhere closer to a hundred.

But such statistics can only ever act as a guide to the strength of defences and should never be taken literally. What we can ascertain from them is that Sword's fortifications were not insignificant and that they were nearly as deadly as Omaha's. The capture of the landing area was certainly not the easy walk ashore that is so often assumed – man for man, the attackers faced a stretch of coast that was roughly as well defended as the other four beaches. The systematic neutralization of those defences, first from the air, then the sea, and finally by putting men and vehicles ashore, was just as hard a task as anywhere else.

Superlatives abound when describing D-Day – Omaha was the deadliest beach, Courselles-sur-Mer was the most strongly defended part of the British and Commonwealth beaches, and the Canadian units who assaulted it suffered the heaviest average casualties. Such statements and comparisons are rarely accurate or helpful – each beach was a separate battle, fought for in individual circumstances. Our judgement of the severity of fighting at Sword – or any other beach – should not be influenced by the events at another and we should certainly not allow ourselves to be misled into thinking that any beach was 'easy' simply because statistics can make it look like others were more strongly defended. The capture of Sword Beach speaks for itself and does not need to be told in association with the beaches to the west.

Inland, the situation was different. There were considerably more strongpoints behind the beach at Sword than there were anywhere else, part of the thicker defences protecting Caen from the sea. The accusation most commonly levelled at 3 Division is that they failed to move quickly enough to capture Caen, stalling at Hillman in particular. It was the journalist Chester Wilmot who first gave voice to these accusations in his 1952 book *The Struggle for Europe*, and in it he singled out Rennie, Cass and Goodwin in particular, accusing them of having insufficient drive. To level this accusation at the assault brigade only showed Wilmot's lack of familiarity with the events at Sword, something further exemplified by the fact he described the capture of Queen White Beach in a single sentence: 'Under covering fire from the armour, the South Lancs quickly cleared the foreshore and plunged into the network of fortifications along the dunes.' There was another sentence for Queen Red: 'The East Yorks were engaged in a bitter struggle from strongpoint to strongpoint and the beach was freed of small-arms fire only after No.4 Commando had taken the western edge of Ouistreham.' In contrast, Wilmot dedicates almost six pages to the landings on Omaha, outlining the difficulties the attackers faced and giving yet more space to describing the defences, something that he does not do at Sword. It is not difficult to see how such a simple description of the events on Queen Beach can allow the reader to believe that the landings there were relatively straightforward, and this impression can only have been strengthened among the public ten years later with the cinematic release of *The Longest Day*, in which Peter Lawford as Lord Lovat strides ashore with little more danger than the occasional shell. Ironically, of course, this was relatively true for 1 Special Service Brigade, but it overlooks the initial landings seventy-five minutes earlier.

Wilmot's chief criticism was the failure to take Hillman, seeing this as the cause for the delays that prevented 3 Division from taking Caen. This understanding has become part of the generally accepted historiography of Sword ever since, which is why Hillman has become part of the usual narrative as outlined at the start of this book. But is it fair? And how accurate is it really?

First and foremost, it should be realized that Hillman was a much tougher objective than the Allies had expected. A sizeable strongpoint with a dominating position and boasting strengthened defences, it could not be overcome easily. Wilmot criticized Goodwin for indulging in lengthy complicated plans with plenty of pre-prepared fire support, taking time that the attackers could ill afford. He then blames Rennie for telling Goodwin he needed to take the strongpoint by dark, as if this was some sort of permissive schedule. In reality, Goodwin was working as fast as circumstances would allow. It simply wasn't possible to attack Morris and Hillman at the same time – Morris needed to be taken first, and in order to do that Colleville needed to be cleared. Having only assembled a mile north of the village at 09:30, it is hard to see how the attack on Hillman could have been achieved any earlier than the first effort at 13:10. The necessity of clearing the minefield before the second attack was a delay that couldn't be ignored – and the fact that Goodwin instructed Heal to continue clearing by hand rather than idly waiting for Sherman Crabs to arrive is proof of the urgency with which he approached the task. Given the strength of the defences the Suffolks faced, it is hard to see how the strongpoint could have been overcome any quicker without the battalion suffering critical casualties.

But how much did Hillman hinder the advance anyway? While the position certainly delayed the Norfolks during their advance to the east, it had little impact on the KSLI as they advanced on the west side. This was in part because Hillman was itself under attack as the KSLI went past, but that proves that when suppressed, the strongpoint could be bypassed. Had it been under attack when the Norfolks passed, their advance may have been more successful. So as events transpired, Hillman did hinder the advance, but certainly didn't stop it.

So what did 'go wrong' on Sword? Well, first, we should open our minds to the possibility that nothing actually did, that the events at Sword were part and parcel of an amphibious assault against an occupied country. But if we were to try and establish why the Allied advance failed to reach Caen, then we need to look back much earlier. We can look back to the storm that swept the Channel the previous day, the lingering residue of which pushed the tide much higher up the beach than was anticipated on D-Day. The rapid narrowing of the available dry sand in the morning was perhaps one of the most significant factors that impacted the advance – there simply wasn't space on the beach for all the vehicles that were arriving. To be added to this was the problem in securing sufficient exits from the beach. In the past, various people have levelled complaints at different units for the failure to secure the beach quickly enough – Lovat and many of his men variously blamed 2 East Yorks for failing to secure Queen Red, with their accounts full of descriptions of seeing the Yorkshiremen digging in on the beach and of failing to overcome their allocated targets. As can be seen in chapters 6 and 7, this is nonsense. The first two assault companies were heavily engaged and, supported by armour, did overpower elements of Skate and Cod. The two reserve companies, through no fault of their own, did not arrive until after 4 Commando, and it was only that commando unit that had to undertake any significant fighting as they landed. In reality the men the commandos saw digging in on the beach were almost certainly members of 5 Beach Group – who needed to dig in there. Lovat's account, while sadly influential, was ill informed and compounded already unjust criticisms.

Considering their lack of action between the summer of 1940 and the summer of 1944, many analysts (led by Wilmot) have stated that 3 Division lacked experience, while others have claimed it became unadventurous and lacked elan as a result of constant training without action. Training was an essential tool when not in battle and most of the division had, at one point or another, passed through not only numerous battle schools but the Combined Training Centre at Inveraray as well. Everyone had conducted exercises under fire. When they were earmarked for the liberation of Europe, that training only increased.

It is curious that this criticism is not levelled at other units that landed on D-Day which had similarly trained extensively but lacked any combat experience. Units of the US 101 Airborne Division, for example, had not seen combat since the war started and constantly trained both in the US and then in the UK after their move to Berkshire and Wiltshire, at about the same time as 3 Division was earmarked for the invasion. Yet despite that, 101 Division is frequently considered to have been an elite formation even before D-Day. Even if this assessment is judged on only a few of its units, the same principles apply: why would one unit be considered elite and another stale based on the same period of preparation for the invasion, and neither of them battle-tested? It is quite unfair to think that 3 Division was not ready for the role it would fulfil on D-Day.

The landing schedule at Sword was tight, a necessary evil born of the fact that there was only space to land one brigade at a time. This meant that even slight delays would quickly become compounded, as indeed they did. The failure to secure sufficient beach exits quickly meant that vehicles from the assault waves were still on the beach when 41 LCT Flotilla arrived forty-five minutes later with the next wave of vehicles. And as a result, they were still there when the next wave arrived thirty minutes after that. It was these delays that most significantly impacted the arrival of an entire armoured regiment three hours after the initial landing. The Staffordshire Yeomanry were trapped on the beach for over an hour, and it was because of this that the plan to capture Caen unravelled.

But another delay had already occurred before then. The problems 41 Commando experienced on the right flank were just the beginning of a near collapse of the plan for the west side of the landings. The German defence of Lion-sur-Mer and the subsequent reinforcement of the town by Schaaf and Gutsche prevented any exploitation in that direction for the rest of the day. It put 185 Brigade and 9 Brigade's forming-up positions in range of enemy mortars and snipers, and played a part in their movement to the east. When 9 Brigade arrived there was no easy way for them to press down the west flank as planned, especially when they lost their leader.

Brigadier Smith's decision to hold the Warwicks and re-route them east quite possibly saved them. At the time he had no way of knowing if their anti-tank guns would clear the beach, and had they advanced as planned on the right of the KSLI they would have been exposed on their right flank for the entirety of their advance and may well have run slap into von Gottberg's or Rauch's advances during the counter-attack. Smith has often been criticized for his decision. In his memoir, Robin Dunn of 7 Field Regiment, later a Lord Justice, was scathing. But his criticisms are confusing: in the same paragraph he notes that 'as K. P. Smith had predicted, German tanks attacked the right flank of the KSLI line in Biéville', but goes on to say that 'the fears of K. P. Smith of a tank attack on our right flank were shown to have been groundless'. While it's true that the attack was repulsed, Smith's fears were far from groundless – in fact he was proved right. While we can never know if the Warwicks would have survived the encounter, it is fair to assume they would have been in some trouble.

What is often overlooked is that the landings on Sword probably saved 6 Airborne Division. Had 21 Panzer Division's attack east of the Orne gone in as planned, before Marcks redeployed Oppeln-Bronikowski and Rauch to the west, it is quite possible they could have taken one or both of the bridges over the canal and river, and cut off the bridgehead entirely. That the attack came west of the Orne may have saved 6 Division, but it cost 3 Division instead. The counter-attack delayed the KSLI and Staffordshire Yeomanry from advancing into Lebisey and further cut off the west flank to Allied advances that day. But ironically, it was the blunting of Oppeln-Bronikowski's advance in particular that made the following attack on Lebisey, and that of the next day, almost doomed to fail. After their counter-attack was thwarted, Oppeln-Bronikowski's battlegroup dug in on the ridge, creating entrenched positions that the Allies could not hope to penetrate. Arguably, Smith made a grievous error in holding the Warwicks' advance back for so long that they could not reach Lebisey to support the KSLI attack on D-Day. As it was he was acting on poor intelligence, but even if he had released the Warwicks, it seems unlikely they could have penetrated all the way to Lebisey along the canal, and even if they had, whether their numbers would have made the difference in the woods is open to debate.

And this is the crucial element of the battle for Sword Beach that is so often overlooked – the defenders. It was the defences at Cod that held out against the initial landings and slowed the clearance of the beach and the creation of exits, which ultimately caused the delays. It was the German defence of Lion-sur-Mer that stalled the advance to the west, and the defenders of Hillman that tied up the Suffolks and the Norfolks. It was the units of 21 Panzer Division that hampered the advance at Périers Ridge and Lebisey, and at Cambes the next day. So often analysis of the battle concentrates on the failings of the British rather than acknowledgement that the Germans they were fighting did in fact influence events. Had 3 Division not been deployed as they were when 21 Panzer Division counter-attacked, had they advanced rapidly to seize Caen without securing their flanks as Wilmot would have had them do, the consequences do not bear thinking about.

Equally, had Oppeln-Bronikowski and von Gottberg's battlegroups got through to the beach, the chaos they might have been able to inflict could well have unhinged the landings there long enough for 12 SS Division to follow up. While it might not have thrown the Allies back into the sea, it would certainly have made the subsequent Battle of Normandy a much more difficult operation. And of course the same is true if 3 Division had not drawn 21 Panzer Division away from 6 Airborne Division.

Realistically, 3 Division achieved everything that was in their power to achieve given the opposition and difficulties they encountered on D-Day. Force S landed some 28,000 men on to a narrow beach, 8 Brigade secured the beaches, and 185 Brigade advanced as far south as possible in the time available and in the face of enemy forces. By the time 9 Brigade came ashore, their plan was already unrealistic; they could perhaps have been employed less conservatively, but it is hard to see how without suffering unnecessary casualties given the strides they made the next day. Most crucially, the division secured the left flank of the amphibious landings, made contact with and reinforced the airborne bridgehead, and established suitable positions from which to lay siege to Caen over the coming campaign. That in itself was a tremendous victory, one that has seemingly been forgotten until now.[1]

EPILOGUE

EARLY ON 8 JUNE, A GREAT BATTLESHIP APPEARED AT THE END of the swept channels north of the Sword Beach anchorage. She was far from out of place: HMS *Warspite* had passed by her in the night as she made her way to Portsmouth, *Ramillies* had just returned from the south coast, and *Rodney* was even then bombarding targets in Cambes. And so, as ships hurried past this way and that, no one paid the battleship much mind as she lay stately at anchor. But had they done so, they might have looked a little more quizzically. She was an older design, almost certainly a First World War battleship, evidenced by the amidships turrets on either side of her superstructure. She looked tired too – rust mottled her darkly painted and weathered hull, and her two attendant tugs suggested a ship that might not have made its own passage. And from her oversized tripod mast, the Free French flag fluttered in the sea breeze.

For hours the battleship *Courbet* sat at the end of the swept channel, and it wasn't until gone lunchtime that an observant ML crew spotted her and made enquiries. After some alarming discoveries, the ML scuttled south and sought out the cruiser HMS *Durban*, at anchor off Sword. The little boat's skipper went aboard, seeking out Captain Laurence Hill, curiously titled Senior Naval Officer, Corncob. Hill had only just settled down for his first sleep for some sixty hours and his deputy, Lieutenant Commander John Taylor, not enamoured with the thought of waking him, went to find out what was needed for himself.

The ML's commander passed on a confusing story. The captain of *Courbet* had instructions to put himself under Captain Hill and await orders. He had no desire to bring his great ship into the busy anchorage and search for Hill himself, so he had simply waited. But at some point he would need to enter the anchorage for protection before night fell. Taylor was dumbfounded that a ship the size of *Courbet* could have been sent south with the captain deprived of orders for what to do on arrival and instantly commandeered the ML for a trip back to the battleship.

On board, Captain Roger Wietzel greeted Taylor in impeccable English and with solemn formality in the faded splendour of the battleship's admiral's quarters. After Taylor had profusely apologized both for his captain's absence and their not knowing about *Courbet*'s stranding outside the anchorage, Wietzel kindly waved his entreaties aside. It did not matter, he told the lieutenant commander – he had orders to report to Hill, and as Hill's representative he was quite happy to report to Taylor. But what, he asked, were his orders?

Taylor explained the next day's tasks. *Courbet* would be moved into position almost 2,000 yards off the beach at La Brèche. At high water, when the tide was slack, she would be scuttled and her keel would touch French sand. For *Courbet* was a Corncob, the Allied codeword for the ships that would be sunk to create breakwaters off all five beaches and provide the bustling maritime traffic with some sheltered waters. Alongside *Courbet* at Gooseberry 5 would be six obsolete British merchant ships, the Dutch cruiser *Sumatra*, and Taylor's ship *Durban*. The sacrifice of his own ship would hopefully lessen the blow to the French captain, Taylor thought, for he knew that the scuttling of a ship of *Courbet*'s size, which had fought in the First World War and was one of the few Free French ships to have survived the German occupation of 1940, was far from a simple administrative matter for a proud Frenchman.

Wietzel nodded. He already knew *Courbet*'s part, of course. Four years earlier he had sailed along the Normandy coast in *Courbet* firing on German forces as they advanced on Cherbourg. He was proud to return on the same vessel, and that this old ship still had a part to play. It was different of course – he had been towed across the Channel by two Royal Navy tugs because the battleship no longer had any machinery aboard: her engine and boiler rooms were instead filled with concrete ballast. He knew that thirty-three years after she was launched, her time was at an end. 'It is good. That will be a fine end for this old ship. It is a magnificent idea.'

Out on deck, Taylor highlighted the anchorage where *Courbet* would need to rest for the night. Wietzel looked at the spot with no great delight, knowing that it would not be easy to manoeuvre his ship with two large tugs whose sole purpose was to generate pulling power. His eyes drifted instead to the shore.

EPILOGUE

'And now I have a request to make that you must take to your captain,' he announced. 'I must go ashore and gather a handful of French soil. I wish to send it to Mr Winston Churchill.* You will understand what this means to a Frenchman – it is four years.'

Taylor squirmed. Among his voluminous orders he knew there was a section forbidding any of the Corncob crews from going ashore under any circumstances. Choosing his words carefully, Taylor tried to allude to his own instructions, but with great presence Wietzel made his own position clear. 'I must do this. I must land on the soil of France with my men. I will give my word for them. They will all be with me and will return with me. This I must do, but I make the request for permission because I am under the orders of Captain Hill.' There was little Taylor could say in response, so he promised to pass the request on to Hill.

A few hours later, towed by two tugs, *Courbet* moved to the anchorage. It was stressful for both Wietzel and Taylor, watching HMS *Samsonia* and *Growler* pull the battleship with great power but little dexterity. Eventually Wietzel felt it better to stop just outside his designated area than to risk getting too close to some of the ships already anchored in it.

The next morning, Taylor took a launch back to *Courbet*, carefully following the course the battleship would need to take to reach her scuttling position. Coming alongside each ship that lay in the path, he cajoled or bullied the skipper into shifting his position until he had a suitably wide channel to move the unwieldy ship.

Aided by four more nimble tugs, *Courbet* weighed anchor and slowly, gracefully, began her final journey. As well as the Free French flag, Wietzel had raised an enormous tricolore on the stern mast, its bright colours seeming to illuminate the whole tired ship. She floated onwards, dwarfing the small launches and landing craft scuttling around in the shadow of her superstructure, while the occasional splashes from desultory shells fired from east of the Orne appeared tiny in her presence. Within thirty minutes she was at the line of merchant ships already scuttled at Gooseberry 5, looming over the bow of the *Empire Tamar*. Deftly, the tugs pushed and pulled the battleship this way and that, gently sliding her into the gap between *Tamar* and *Becheville*. The metal hulls of the ships ground and folded under the slow-motion collision. Once something

---

* Taylor is clear that Wietzel told him he wanted the soil for Churchill, although a memorial on shore suggests it was intended for General Charles de Gaulle. The latter seems more likely.

that would have seen disciplinary action, it no longer mattered for these obsolete vessels.

Once the giant ship was steady, the tugs moved away. An air of quiet reverence descended over the immediate area, the various officers of Corncob watching closely, satisfied the ship was ready. Then came a muffled explosion and a slight tremor across the water as the scuttling charges detonated. Unrushed, *Courbet* started to settle, her hull inching down until her keel hit the seabed a mere 3 feet below. *Courbet* lay still now, waves lapping at her hull. Her final voyage was over.

A landing craft lay alongside, steadily filling with men as the crew disembarked for the final time. When the last man was aboard, the boat pulled away and headed for the shore. When Taylor passed Wietzel's request on to Hill, the captain had assented to it immediately. There was no understanding of this sort of matter in the fleet orders, written by someone who would probably never visit Normandy and merely included such security details because they had done so for years. No harm could come from it – some things were better allowed than others, and this was clearly one. The landing craft ploughed on towards the shore, dodging moored and moving ships alike. Eventually it beached at the junction of Queen White and Red, dead centre of the landing area that had seen so much destruction only three days before. Now there were no bodies littering the shore, the wrecked tanks had been towed away, and the bunkers lay silent. The boom of artillery and the chatter of machine guns had moved further inland. The beach had been cleared, obstacles towed up to the dunes, barbed wire hauled away and dumped in the burned-out shell holes of beachside villas. There was nothing to impede the Frenchmen's progress as they stepped back on their home soil for the first time in four years.

As the crew danced around on the sand, giddy with the joy of being back in their home country, Wietzel walked up the beach and inland. Following the road that three days earlier the Suffolks had advanced along towards Hermanville, he passed a burned-out supply dump and reached the fields just beyond. Kneeling down on the side of the road, he plunged his hands into the soil, letting the dry earth work its way into the lines of his palms and under his fingernails. Pulling up a handful of this free French soil, he poured it into a tin and screwed the lid down, careful not to spill any of the precious contents. Gingerly he placed the tin into his pocket, stood up, and turned towards the beach, ready to deliver it to England.[1]

APPENDIX I:

THE ARRIVAL AT PEGASUS BRIDGE

EXACTLY WHEN THE COMMANDOS REACHED THE CANAL AND RIVER bridges is one part of the D-Day story that has never been satisfactorily answered. In his 1956 memoir, Mills-Roberts observed that 6 Commando 'were only two and a half minutes behind schedule' when they reached le Port (p.99). In his 1978 memoir, Lovat mentions making an apology for being two minutes late when he reached the River Orne bridge (p.322).

While it's theoretically possible that both of these statements could be true, what the authors do not make clear is what time they were meant to arrive, or what time they did arrive. At this juncture it's worth observing that they would only be late by their own timetable. They were not tasked with relieving the airborne forces at the bridges – indeed the airborne forces were required to hold the bridges until much later on D-Day.

The only surviving document to provide an intended commando schedule for D-Day is 3 Commando's Operational Order, which states that phase 1 (the move to the bridges) should be complete by H+240 (i.e. four hours after H-Hour, or 11:25). There are no documents that tell us if 6 Commando – who landed thirty minutes before 3 Commando – were expected to arrive earlier or not, but the orders issued to 5 Parachute Brigade state that '1 SS Brigade will pass through the bridge positions at approximately H+4 hours', which suggests that H+240 applied to all of the commando forces moving to the east flank (accepting that it would take time for an entire brigade to cross). This would allow 6 Commando and Brigade HQ, who were due to land at H+75 (08:40), two hours and forty-five minutes to reach the bridges, and 3 and 45 Commandos, due to land at H+105 (09:10), two hours and fifteen minutes.

In his memoir, Lovat claims to have allowed three hours to reach the bridges (p.304), which would have given 6 Commando and Brigade HQ until 11:40 – slightly later than the operational orders. Lovat's memoir doesn't provide a precise schedule, but he further commented that once ashore they had two and a half hours to reach the bridges (p.317). It seems that he hoped to reach the bridges before midday.

Neither 6 Commando's war diary nor the attached reports specify a time of arrival at le Port, although 2 Troop's report states they were in action in Saint-Aubin at 12:00 (WO 218/68, June). A lengthy report of 1 Special Service Brigade's activities in Normandy states that contact was made with airborne forces (presumably in le Port) at 12:30 (IWM Documents.22991) while the war diary states that the bridges were reached at 12:30 (DEFE 2/53). 45 (RM) Commando's war diary reports reaching the Caen Canal bridge at 14:15 (ADM 202/82). 3 Commando's war diary notes that the unit was following 45 Commando and reached Colleville-sur-Orne at 12:00 (WO 218/65), where Peter Young's memoir states he took a small party ahead of the Royal Marines to see progress further ahead (p.149). The war diary then states they 'moved on the bridges' at 12:30 and most of their troops crossed at 15:30. 5 Parachute Brigade's war diary states that 1 Special Service Brigade reached and crossed the bridges at 13:00 (WO 171/595). 7 Battalion's war diary states that a commando battalion passed through their positions at 13:25 (WO 171/1239). It's worth noting that all of these times are later than other seaborne units that arrived at the bridges, including 71 Field Company RE and, quite likely, Major William Purchase-Rathbone of 20 Anti-Tank Regiment RA, who went well ahead of the landing forces to recce the approaches to the bridge.

Neither Lovat's, Mills-Roberts's or Young's memoirs give a time, although Poett's 1991 memoir claims that they heard bagpipes 'towards 12 noon' (p.70). In his post-war diary, Howard states that Lovat reached the Caen Canal bridge at about 13:00 (p.137), while Pine-Coffin's 1947 diary recalled that Lovat crossed the bridge in great ceremony at around 14:00 (p.51). Aside from Lovat, only Howard recalls joking about lateness, telling Lovat, 'About bloody time.'

What can we conclude from this? Aside from the fact that war diaries and memoirs should always be treated with a certain amount of caution, the wide disparity of timings tells us that the authors probably saw different things happening. The passage of three commando units and a Brigade HQ across the bridges naturally took some time – different people saw different parts of this procession and recalled what happened, and when, differently as a result. At any rate they are all fairly unreliable. Howard refers to Churchill tanks accompanying the commandos, Pine-Coffin's belief that a special ceremonial crossing of the bridge was made is not supported by anyone else (and effectively denied by Lovat), and Lovat confessed in the copy of his memoir that he gave to Howard that it was 'full of mistakes'.*

What we can conclude from every time given in primary source documents and memoirs is that the first commandos arrived substantially later than 11:25 and the vague three-hour timeframe Lovat referred to in his memoir. In all likelihood 6 Commando, with leading elements of HQ, reached le Port and then the bridges between about 12:30 and 13:00. 45 and 3 Commandos followed between 14:00 and 15:30.

With this in mind we can also conclude one more thing: the commandos were substantially later than two minutes. The 'I'm sorry we're two minutes late' comment supposedly made by Lovat to one of the airborne officers (variously Howard, Pine-Coffin, Poett or Gale, depending on the book it's in) has become the basis for numerous post-war books' claims that the statement was factual, and the commandos were literally only two minutes behind schedule. In all likelihood, Lovat even saying it is probably a fiction. He was much later than a mere two minutes and doesn't mention the comment in any great detail in his memoir, only stating that 'apologies for the two-minute late arrival came at the wide river' after they'd crossed the canal (p.322). He does not specify who this apology was made to, but implies it was Pine-Coffin or Poett who, he says, were waiting on the east riverbank – although neither recalled it in their writing. In reality he almost certainly got the idea from Mills-Roberts's memoir, which he liberally quoted in his own. For his part, Mills-Roberts claims that Lovat had raced down the road to join him and they arrived at 7 Battalion's positions two and a half minutes late, where Lovat hailed Pine-Coffin – before crossing the canal bridge (p.99). Obviously both of these statements can't be true, and 2 Troop's report contradicts Mills-Roberts's timing. But at any rate, it's fairly safe to assume from the detail in his book that Mills-Roberts wrote it with the benefit of 6 Commando's war diary. In it is 3 Troop's D-Day report, compiled by Leaphard and Colquhoun on 2 July 1944. They clearly had some familiarity with their CO's sense of humour when they wrote: 'The Brigadier

---

* In a letter from Howard to Lovat kindly supplied by Dave Chisholm.

[Poett] said to our Troop Commander, "We are very pleased to see you." The Troop Commander [Pyman] characteristically answered, looking at his watch: "I am afraid we are a few minutes late, Sir!"' (WO 218/68).

It was a joke – a bit of British light-hearted humour. Similarly, Julius Neave of B Squadron 13/18 Hussars relates a story that 2 Troop's CO Douglas Coker apologised to Gale for being fifteen minutes late (IWM 27183). This might even be true, but the two-minute line seems to have taken on a life of its own in the years after D-Day. In all likelihood it was 'acquired' by Mills-Roberts and then by Lovat in their memoirs. It then went on to become the basis for the claim that the commandos' arrival was only two minutes behind schedule, when in reality it was at least an hour behind their intended timetable. The chances that both Pyman and Lovat made an almost identical joke to both Poett *and* Pine-Coffin within about thirty minutes of each other, but it didn't stick in either of the airborne officer's minds enough to recall it later, seem pretty slim.

Sadly Captain Pyman did not survive D-Day – he was shot by a sniper in Bréville a few hours later. It seems that his joke has not really survived either.

APPENDIX 2:

MILITARY RANKS

IN AN IDEAL WORLD, THE RANKS USED BY THE GERMAN ARMED forces during the Second World War would have direct equivalents in the British armed forces. In reality this was rarely the case. Not only did the British use a baffling number of different titles for their ranks (private might become bombardier, driver, marine, trooper, guardsman etc. in different regiments), but so too did the Germans. As might be expected, these ranks did not always perfectly align and there were some that had no direct equivalent. Additionally, the German army's structure meant that even equal ranks might have different responsibilities within their units.

These tables are therefore only meant to be taken as a guide and are provided simply to help gain some understanding of an individual's position and level of responsibility during the events of 6 June.

BRITISH ARMY	GERMAN ARMY
Private	Soldat / Grenadier / Schütze
	Obersoldat / Obergrenadier / Oberschütze
Lance Corporal	Gefreiter
	Obergefreiter
Corporal	Unteroffizier
Sergeant	Unterfeldwebel
Company Sergeant Major	Feldwebel
Regimental Sergeant Major	Oberfeldwebel

Second Lieutenant	Leutnant
Lieutenant	Oberleutnant
Captain	Hauptmann
Major	Major
Lieutenant Colonel	Oberstleutnant
Colonel	Oberst
Brigadier	Generalmajor
Major General	Generalleutnant
Lieutenant General	General
General	Generaloberst
Field Marshal	Generalfeldmarschall

ROYAL NAVY	KRIEGSMARINE
Midshipman	Leutnant zur See
Sub Lieutenant	Oberleutnant zur See
Lieutenant	Kapitänleutnant
Lieutenant Commander	Korvetten-Kapitän
Commander	Fregattenkapitän
Captain	Kapitän zur See
	Kommodore
Commodore	Konter-Admiral
Rear Admiral	Vize-Admiral
Vice Admiral	Admiral
Admiral	Generaladmiral
Admiral of the Fleet	Großadmiral

APPENDIX 3:

ORDERS OF BATTLE AND COMMON ABBREVIATIONS

ALLIED ORDER OF BATTLE

3 INFANTRY DIVISION

3 INFANTRY DIVISION HQ	3 Division
Recce Regiment	
2 Middlesex Regiment (Machine Gun Battalion)	2 Middlesex

8 INFANTRY BRIGADE	8 Brigade
2 East Yorkshire Regiment	2 East Yorks
1 South Lancashire Regiment	1 South Lancs
1 Suffolk Regiment	1 Suffolk

185 INFANTRY BRIGADE	185 Brigade
2 Warwickshire Regiment	2 Warwick
1 Norfolk Regiment	1 Norfolk
2 King's Shropshire Light Infantry	2 KSLI

9 INFANTRY BRIGADE	9 Brigade
2 Lincolnshire Regiment	2 Lincoln
1 King's Own Scottish Borderers	1 KOSB
2 Royal Ulster Rifles	2 RUR

ROYAL ARTILLERY	RA
7 Field Regiment	
33 Field Regiment	
76 Field Regiment	
20 Anti-Tank Regiment	
16 Field Battery	
92 Light Anti-Aircraft Regiment	

ROYAL ENGINEERS	RE
246 Field Company	
253 Field Company	
17 Field Company	
15 Field Park Company	
2 Bridging Platoon	

ROYAL ARMY MEDICAL CORPS	RAMC
8 Field Ambulance	
9 Field Ambulance	
223 Field Ambulance	

ATTACHED UNITS

27 ARMOURED BRIGADE HQ	
13/18 Royal Hussars (Queen Mary's Own)	13/18 Hussars
Staffordshire Yeomanry	Staff Yeo
1 East Riding Yeomanry	1 ERY

I SPECIAL SERVICE BRIGADE	1 SS Brigade
3 Commando	

ORDERS OF BATTLE AND COMMON ABBREVIATIONS

4 Commando	
6 Commando	
10 Commando	
45 (Royal Marines) Commando	
41 (Royal Marines) Commando	

79 ARMOURED DIVISION	
22 Dragoons	
5 Assault Regiment RE HQ	
77 Assault Squadron RE	
79 Assault Squadron RE	
71 Field Company RE	
263 Field Company RE	
629 Field Company RE	

ROYAL MARINES	
5 Royal Marine Armoured Support Group	5 RMASG
RM Engineer Commando	

ROYAL ARMY SERVICE CORPS	RASC
90 Armoured Brigade Coy RASC	
106 Bridge Coy RASC	

ROYAL ARTILLERY	
53 Regiment RA HQ	
73 LAA Regiment RA	
93 LAA Regiment RA	
652 Air Observation Point Sqn	

A Squadron 'Phantom' GHQ Liaison	

101 BEACH SUB AREA

Royal Engineers	101 Beach Group HQ
	18 GHQ Troop Engineers
	9 Port Operating Company
	999 Port Operating Company

5 BEACH GROUP	
Royal Navy	Beach Commando Unit F, 13 Beach Signals
Infantry	5 King's Regiment (Liverpool)
Royal Army Medical Corps	20, 21, 30 Field Dressing Stations, 1 Field Sanitary Section, 39, 40, 55 Field Surgery Units, 21, 29 Field Transfusion Units, 16 Casualty Clearing Station
Royal Army Ordnance Corps	44 Ordnance Ammunition Company, 11 Ordnance Beach Detachment
Pioneers	53, 102, 129, 267, 292, 303 Pioneer Companies
Royal Electrical Mechanical Engineers	20 Beach Recovery Section
Royal Army Service Corps	HQ 21 Transport Column, 96 Detail Issue Depot, 39, 101, 635 General Transport Companies, 237 Petrol Depot
Royal Engineers	84 Field Company, 940 Inland Waterway Transport, 8 Stores Section, 20 Port Detachment
Provost	241 Provost Company
Royal Air Force	101 RAF Beach Flight

ORDERS OF BATTLE AND COMMON ABBREVIATIONS

6 BEACH GROUP	
Royal Navy	Beach Commando Unit R, 18 Beach Signals
Infantry	1 Buckinghamshire
Royal Army Medical Corps	9, 12 Field Dressing Stations, 2 Detachment Field Sanitary Section, 37, 38 Field Surgery Units
Royal Army Ordnance Corps	12 Ordnance Beach Detachment
Pioneers	85, 149 Pioneer Companies
Royal Electrical Mechanical Engineers	21 Beach Recovery Section
Royal Army Service Corps	299 General Transport Company, 138 Detail Issue Depot, 238 Petrol Depot
Royal Engineers	91 Field Company, 9 Stores Section, 50 Mechanical Equipment Section, 1028 Port Operating Company
Provost	245 HQ Provost Company
Royal Air Force	102 RAF Beach Flight

FORCE S

ASSAULT GROUP S3	
HMS *Goathland*	43 LCT Flotilla
LCHs 185 and 269	45 LCT Flotilla
HMS *Glenearn* (535 & 543 Assault Flotilla)	100 LCT Flotilla
SS *Empire Battleaxe* (537 Assault Flotilla)	261 LCI(L) Flotilla
SS *Empire Broadsword* (538 Assault Flotilla)	321 LCT(R) Flotilla
SS *Empire Cutlass* (536 Assault Flotilla)	330 Support Flotilla
14 LCT Flotilla	592 LCA(HR) Flotilla
32 LCT Flotilla	704 Assault Flotilla
38 LCT Flotilla	707 Assault Flotilla
41 LCT Flotilla	

INTERMEDIATE GROUP S2	
HMS *Dacres*	251 LCI(L) Squadron
40 LCT Flotilla	263 LCI(L) Squadron
42 LCT Flotilla	US Navy LCI(L) Group IV
48 LCT Flotilla	

RESERVE GROUP S1	
HMS *Locust*	39 LCT Flotilla
1 LST Flotilla	47 LCT Flotilla
3 LST Flotilla	265 LCI(L) Squadron
5 LST Flotilla	266 LCI(L) Squadron

BUILD-UP SQUADRONS	
C Build-Up Squadron	
D Build-Up Squadron	
U Landing Barge Squadron	

MINESWEEPERS	
1 Minesweeping Flotilla	137 Minesweeping Flotilla
15 Minesweeping Flotilla	165 BYMS Flotilla
40 Minesweeping Flotilla	

ESCORTS	
HMS *Saumarez*	HMS *Serapis*
HNoMS *Svenner*	HMS *Virago*
HNoMS *Stord*	HMS *Verulam*
HMS *Swift*	HMS *Middleton*
HMS *Scorpion*	HMS *Kelvin*
HMS *Scourge*	ORP *Ślązak*
HMS *Eglington*	

FORCE D	
115 Minesweeping Flotilla	HMS *Danae*
HMS *Mauritius*	HMS *Arethusa*
HMS *Ramillies*	ORP *Dragon*
HMS *Warspite*	HMS *Roberts*
HMS *Frobisher*	

GERMAN ORDER OF BATTLE

716 INFANTRY DIVISION

716 Division HQ (General Wilhelm Richter)	HQ at St Julien
726 GRENADIER REGIMENT (OBERST WALTER KORFES)	
1 Battalion (1, 2, 3 and 4 Companies)	In Gold Area
2 Battalion (5, 6, 7 and 8 Companies)	In Juno Area
3 Battalion (9, 10, 11 and 12 Companies)	In Omaha Area
439 Ost Battalion (1, 2, 3 and 4 Companies)	In Omaha Area
736 GRENADIER REGIMENT (OBERST LUDWIG KRUG)	Strongpoint 17 (Hillman)
1 Battalion	HQ at strongpoint 14 (Sole)
1 Company	HQ at Franceville Plage
2 Company	HQ at Ouistreham
3 Company	HQ at Franceville
4 Company	HQ at Colleville
2 Battalion (5, 6, 7 and 8 Companies)	In Juno Area
3 Battalion	HQ at Cresserons
9 Company	HQ at strongpoint 20 (Cod)

10 Company	HQ at strongpoint 24
11 Company	HQ at Cresserons
12 Company	HQ at Douvres
642 Ost Battalion (1, 2, 3 and 4 Companies)	3 Company in Hermanville

1716 ARTILLERY REGIMENT (OBERLEUTNANT KNUPE)	
1 Battalion	
1 Battery	Strongpoint 1 (Merville)
2 Battery	Strongpoint 16 (Morris)
3 Battery	Bréville
4 Battery	Strongpoint 12 (Daimler)
2 Battalion (5, 6, 7 and 8 Batteries)	In Juno and Gold Areas
3 Battalion (9, 10, 11 and 12 Batteries)	11 Battery at Plumetot

716 Anti-Tank Battalion	
1 Company	Biéville
2 Company	Biéville area
3 Company	Franceville Plage

716 Engineer Battalion	Caen area
716 Signals Battalion	
716 Fusilier Battalion	
441 Ost Battalion (1, 2, 3 and 4 Companies)	In Juno and Gold Areas

21 PANZER DIVISION

21 Panzer Division HQ (Generalmajor Edgar Feuchtinger)	HQ at Saint-Pierre-sur-Dives

22 PANZER REGIMENT (OBERST HERMANN VON OPPELN-BRONIKOWSKI)	
1 Panzer Battalion (1, 2, 3 and 4 Companies)	South of Caen
2 Panzer Battalion (5, 6, 7 and 8 Companies)	South of Caen

125 PANZER GRENADIER REGIMENT (MAJOR HANS VON LUCK)	
I Panzer Grenadier Battalion (1, 2, 3 and 4 Companies)	South-east of Caen
II Panzer Grenadier Battalion (5, 6, 7 and 8 Companies)	East of River Orne
9 and 10 Companies	East of River Orne

192 PANZER GRENADIER REGIMENT (OBERST JOSEF RAUCH)	
I Panzer Grenadier Battalion (1, 2, 3 and 4 Companies)	West of Caen
II Panzer Grenadier Battalion (5, 6, 7 and 8 Companies)	North of Caen
9 and 10 Companies	South of Caen

155 PANZER ARTILLERY REGIMENT	
I Panzer Artillery Battalion	
1 Battery	Beuville
2 Battery	Strongpoint 21A
3 Battery	Colomby-sur-Thaon
II Panzer Artillery Battalion (4, 5 and 6 Batteries)	South of Caen

III Panzer Artillery Battalion (7, 8, 9 and 10 Batteries)	South of Caen

200 ASSAULT GUN BATTALION	
1–4 and 6 Batteries	South of Caen
5 Battery	Epron, north of Caen

200 Anti-Tank Battalion	
1–2 Companies	Juno Area
3 Company	Basly

21 Panzer Reconnaissance Battalion	South of Caen
220 Panzer Engineer Battalion	South of Caen
305 Flak Battalion	Caen

OTHER UNITS

989 HEAVY ARTILLERY BATTALION	
1 Battery	Basly
2 Battery	Juno Area
3 Battery	Gold Area

1260 COASTAL ARTILLERY REGIMENT	
1 Battery	Strongpoint 8 (Bass)
2 Battery	Gold Area
3 Battery	Gold Area

APPENDIX 4:

LANDING TIMETABLE

GROUP	TIME		MAIN NAVAL UNIT	MAIN ARMY UNIT
1	H-7.5	07:17:30	14 LCT Flotilla	A & B Sqn 13/18 Hussars DD Tanks
2	H-Hour	07:25	45 LCT Flotilla	77 & 79 Assault Squadrons RE
			100 LCT Flotilla	5 (Independent) Armoured Support Battery
			536 LCA Flotilla	2 East Yorks Assault Companies
			535 LCA Flotilla	1 South Lancs Assault Companies
5	H+20	07:45	543 & 538 LCA Flotillas	2 East Yorks Reserve Companies
			537 & 536 LCA Flotillas	1 South Lancs Reserve Companies
6	H+25	07:50	LCI(S)s 523 & 527	No. 1 Free French Commando
	H+30	07:55	500 LCA Flotilla	4 Commando
	H+35	08:00	514 LCA Flotilla	4 Commando

7	H+45	08:10	41 LCT Flotilla	C Sqn 13/18 Hussars, 8 Infantry & Priority Vehicles
8	H+60	08:25	3x LCI(L)s, 538 & 537 LCA Flotillas	1 Suffolk Battalion
9	H+75	08:40	200 & 201 LCI(S) Flotillas	6 & 41 Commando
4	H+75	08:40	38 LCT Flotilla	76 Field Regiment RA SP Artillery
9A	H+105	09:10	200 & 201 LCI(S) Flotillas	45 & 3 Commando
4A	H+105	09:10	32 LCT Flotilla	33 Field Regiment RA SP Artillery
10	H+120	09:25	43 LCT Flotilla	8 Infantry Brigade & Priority Vehicles
11	H+150	09:55	263 LCI(L) Flotilla	185 Infantry Brigade
12	H+185	10:30	40 LCT Flotilla	Staffordshire Yeomanry Armoured Regiment
4B	H+195	10:40	32 LCT Flotilla	7 Field Regiment RA SP Artillery
13	H+215	11:00	USN LCI(L) Group 4	Beach Group Infantry
14	H+230	11:15	251 LCI(L) Flotilla	Beach Group Infantry
15	H+250	11:35	42 & 48 LCT Flotillas	185 Infantry Brigade & Priority Vehicles
16	H+270	11:55	266 LCI(L) Flotilla	9 Infantry Brigade
17	H+330	12:55	1 LST Flotilla	Priority Vehicles, via Rhino Ferry from 1,000 yards off beach
18	H+330	12:55	39 LCT Flotilla	East Riding Yeomanry Armoured Regiment
19	H+360	13:25	47 LCT Flotilla	9 Infantry Brigade & Priority Vehicles

APPENDIX 5:
FIRST MISSION EIGHTH AIR FORCE TARGETS

TARGET ID	LOCATION	TARGET	BOMB GROUP	TIME	AIRCRAFT ASSIGNED	AIRCRAFT ATTACKED	BOMBS DROPPED
16	Caen	Chokepoint 3	384	08:06 to 08:30	30	30	360x 500lb HE, 55x 1,000lb HE
16	Caen	Chokepoint 4	303	08:06 to 08:30	36	17	202x 500lb HE, 28x 1,000lb HE
17	Bernières-sur-Mer	Strongpoint 28	96, 388 & 452	06:55 to 07:20	30	29	1,005x 500lb HE, 12x 1,000lb HE
18	Saint-Aubin-sur-Mer	Strongpoint 27	96, 388 & 452	06:55 to 07:20	42	41	462x 1,000lb HE
19	Périers-sur-le Dan	Strongpoint 21A	385	06:55 to 07:20	12	12	136x 500lb HE on alternate target
20	Luc-sur-Mer	Strongpoint 24	94 & 388	06:55 to 07:20	24	24	288x 500lb HE
21	Lion-sur-Mer	Strongpoint 21 (Trout)	94, 385 & 447	06:55 to 07:20	43	37	408x 500lb HE

22	Ouistreham	Strongpoint 20 (Cod)	94, 385 & 447	06:55 to 07:15	30	30	1,101x 100lb HE, 4x 500lb HE
23	Ouistreham	Strongpoint 10	100	06:55 to 07:20	42	41	461x 500lb HE, 46x 1,000lb HE
24	Merville-Franceville	Strongpoint 5	390	06:55 to 07:25	36	36	412x 500lb HE, 54x 1,000lb HE
25	Merville-Franceville	Strongpoint 3	95	06:55 to 06:59	37	37	424x 500lb HE, 50x 1,000lb HE
26	Molineaux	Battery	96	07:15 to 07:35	12	12	72x 500lb HE
27	Colleville-sur-Orne	Strongpoint 16 (Morris)	447	07:15 to 07:35	13	6	72x 500lb HE
28	Ouistreham	Strongpoint 12 (Daimler)			2x squadrons reassigned to targets 24 and 25		
29	Tailleville	Battalion HQ	452	07:25 to 07:28	7	3	76x 100lb HE, 6x 500lb HE, attacked alternate target
30	St Julien	Divisional HQ	388	07:25 to 07:28	6	1	38x 100lb HE on alternate target
31	Biéville	Regimental HQ	94	07:25 to 07:28	7	0	

32	Colleville-sur-Orne	Strongpoint 17 (Hillman)	94	07:25 to 07:28	6	0	
33	Tailleville	88mm Battery	452	06:55 to 07:20	13 total	13	14x 100lb HE, 108x 500lb HE
34a	Caen	Chokepoint 1	486 & 487	07:30 to 08:02	48	0	
34	Caen	Chokepoint 2	34 & 490	07:30 to 08:02	49	0	

NOTES

CHAPTER 1: A SEASIDE RESORT

1   Rommel's tour on 30 May is related by Ruge (pp.167-8), Kortenhaus (pp.68-70), Hoeller (pp.116-18), who formed up at Lebisey, and by Willi Hornack in Weight (p.149). Although the location is frequently described as Riva Bella, photographs taken on the shore quite clearly show the reinforced houses at strongpoint 21. Ysker and Fischer's deployment to the coast is recounted in their PoW interviews (WO 208/3621). The state of the anti-landing obstacles on the beach comes from Allied intelligence assessments in 79 Assault Squadron's war diary (WO 171/1807) and a post-landing Allied assessment of defence preparedness (CAB 146/482).

2   The destruction of the oil installations in Ouistreham is well described in Brazier (pp.75-9).

3   Much of the information on 716 Division's deployment comes from a map and Order of Battle captured after D-Day (CAB 146/482). 21 Division's deployment is well described in Kortenhaus.

4   Mademoiselle Pigache related her story to Donald Gilchrist, adjutant of 4 Commando, who included it in his memoir (pp.88-90). While Gilchrist couldn't confirm or deny her story, in reality it's highly unlikely that British agents masqueraded as German officers in Ouistreham and Sallenelles.

CHAPTER 2: A FORCE IN WAITING

1   Barber describes the desertion of his Royal Marines and his subsequent meeting with Bush in his memoir (pp.74-81). Bush describes his appointment as SOAG S3 in his memoir (p.251), although he does not mention his meeting with Barber.

2   The plan for Sword is well detailed in the Force S orders (DEFE 2/403) and the Operation Orders for 3 Division (WO 171/409), 8 Brigade (WO 171/611), 185 Brigade (WO 171/702) and 9 Brigade (WO 176/616).

3   Law's trials and tribulations are recorded in his memoir (pp.61-3). The unveiling of orders on *Scorpion* and *Scourge* is detailed by Ditcham (pp.205-8). The French recognition of their objectives is detailed in Dear (pp.204-5). Montlaur's comment is in Ryan (p.60), but it is unclear where he

sourced it from, as neither Kieffer nor Montlaur appear to have submitted information to him.

4   A fascinating book about the preparation for the embarkation is Dalgleish's account, published in 1945.

5   Churchill's visit is recounted in his account of the Second World War (vol.10, p.269), in Ditcham (pp.208-9) and in contemporary footage (IWM ADM 1252). The ceremony on HMS *Glenearn* comes from Nightingale (p.170), and Curtis's time in sick bay is described in papers in the D-Day Story collection (1992/275/101).

6   The Reverend Derrick Lovell Williams's tragic story is related by Mills-Roberts in an unpublished excerpt from his memoir (Liddell Hart Archive), Lovat (p.303) and Campbell (pp.61-2). According to Mills-Roberts, Lovat was not actually at the service but quickly learned of its impact on the men. Williams was recorded as a battle casualty and is buried at Southampton's Hollybrook Cemetery (www.cwgc.org/find-records/find-war-dead/casualty-details/2350467/the-rev-derrick-lovell-williams/).

CHAPTER 3: THE WAITING ENDS

1   The details of the sailings are taken from the Force S fleet orders (DEFE 2/403) and subsequent reports by Talbot (DEFE 2/419), and the various accounts in DEFE 2/420. Clouston's reaction was recorded by Ditcham in his memoir (p.212). 45 LCT Flotilla's departure from Portsmouth Harbour was recorded by Joe Williams (in Welch).

2   The commando accounts from Southampton Common and embarking at Warsash come from the unit war diaries, Lovat's memoir (pp.303-4) and Peter Young's memoir (pp.144-5). Accounts of the sailing come from Jim Brooker's account in the D-Day Story archive (2014/58/101), Denis Glover's account (in Winton, p.337), Rupert Curtis's unpublished account *We Landed the Commandos* (p.3) and Bill Millin's memoir (pp.63-5).

3   The narrative of the convoys is largely told in Commander Bush's report (DEFE 2/420), most notably the section on the passage (pp.173-83), and Edmund Currey's report written on 7 June (pp.309-10). Currey does not appear to have originally been aware of the fate of LCP(L) 272, but it is well described by Bush in his account of 30 June.

4   1 Minesweeping Flotilla's passage is covered in Talbot's report (DEFE 2/419, pp.19-21), by Williams (pp.75-7) and by Maher in his memoir (pp.114-19). Eric Smith's account comes from his unpublished reminiscences.

CHAPTER 4: ON THE MIDNIGHT SWELL

1   The minesweeping plan for 1 Flotilla is well described by Williams (pp.35-6) and in the Force S Orders (DEFE 2/403, Enclosure ONEAST/S.6). Maher

describes his experience in his memoir (pp.114-17). The experiences of the convoys are best described in the Force S report (DEFE 2/420, pp.178-83). Dickinson describes his unpleasant voyage in the reports submitted by 77 Assault Squadron, contained in Brigadier Cass's papers (IWM Documents.1471).

2   John Madden recorded his D-Day experiences only two years later in the *McGill Daily* (13 and 20 June 1946). Earl Rice's account appears in Boegel (pp.152-60). Details of Kirkham's flight and crew are taken from the RAF record books of 570 Squadron (Kirkham) and 295 Squadron (Rice's pilot was most likely Flight Officer Jones).

3   Ludwig Krug's experience comes from his interrogation statement (WO 208/3590), secret recordings of his conversations with fellow PoWs (WO 208/4618) and Dudignac, who also describes Sauer's patrol (pp.64-5). The naval response is covered by Tarrant (pp.56-7), with additional details from FS Gkdos 18961, Report concerning 5th Torpedoboot Flotilla, 6 June, *KTB 2nd Sicherungsdivision*, and in Krancke's information supplied to Cornelius Ryan (Box 26, Folder 24).

4   1 Minesweeping Flotilla's passage is covered in Talbot's report (DEFE 2/419, pp.19-21), by Williams (pp.75-7) and by Maher in his memoir (pp.114-19). The death of Sergeant Ibbetson is recounted by Arthur Smith (IWM Documents.21902) and in Craggs (p.117).

5   Taken from Madden's account in the *McGill Daily*.

6   Taken from Operation Gambit reports in DEFE 2/419 (pp.61-5), DEFE 2/420 (pp.229-31) and ADM 179/475.

CHAPTER 5: OPENING SHOTS

1   Bob Armit recounts his D-Day experience in Hepworth, Porrelli & Dison (pp.138-40). Further details are taken from 514 Squadron's Operations Record Books.

2   Odette Mousset relayed her experience of D-Day to Howarth (pp.212-13) fifteen years later.

3   Report on the Bombing of Targets in the British Sector, Normandy (DEFE 2/487).

4   Richter's account is taken from the post-D-Day Operations report on the invasion in the sector of 716 Infantry Division. Krug's sighting of Force S comes from Dudignac (pp.67-9).

5   The actions of 5 Flotilla are detailed in FS Gkdos 18961, Report concerning 5th Torpedoboot Flotilla, 6 June, *KTB 2nd Sicherungsdivision*. Hoffmann's reaction is quoted in Ryan (p.152). More information on German Torpedoboote can be found in Whitley. 88 Squadron's smoke-laying mission is detailed in their Operations Record Books.

6   HMS *Ramillies*'s actions are contained in her log for 6 June (ADM 53/120330) and HMS *Roberts*'s in her Report of Proceedings (ADM 179/507). Details on the torpedo boat attack are contained in the Report by Naval Commander, Force S (DEFE 2/419), the report from HMS *Virago* (DEFE 2/420) and HNoMS *Svenner*'s Report of Loss (ADM 179/507). Lieutenant Desmond Lloyd's experience is recounted in Ryan (p.152) and Kenneth Wright's in Ambrose (p.266). Gower describes his actions in ADM 179/507.

7   15th Vp Flotilla's action is recorded in FS Gkdos 18897, Report concerning 15th Vp Flotilla, 6 June, *KTB 2nd Sicherungsdivision*. HMS *Warspite*'s response is contained in her Report of Proceedings (ADM 179/507).

8   The trials and tribulations of LCA 791 are described in the survivor statements given by Foden and Betts (ADM 199/1650, p.264 and p.429). Bateman describes LCA 1383's experience in his post-invasion report (DEFE 2/420, pp.330–1).

9   Reports from the bombardment ships come from HMS *Danae*'s log 6 June 1944 (ADM 53/119197), HMS *Scylla*'s log (ADM 53/120451) and HMS *Arethusa*'s log (ADM 53/118866). Law's account is in A. Price (p.110). Further details of the bombardment come from the Report by the Naval Commander, Force S. The Bombardment (DEFE 2/419). Odette Mousset's experience comes from Howarth (pp.212–13). HMS *Scorpion*'s actions on D-Day come from Ditcham (pp.211–20), and her two Reports of Proceedings (ADM 179/507 and IWM Documents.7683). Schmidt and Bonna's experiences come from their interrogation reports (WO 208/3621 p.8 and p.31).

10 Currey's responsibilities and actions are outlined in Force S's orders (Enclosure S1. General, and Enclosure S7. The Assault, both in ADM 199/1561) and reports (Force S Reports, Report of Commander, Support Group. DEFE 2/420). Further detail comes from Talbot's Report by Naval Commander, Force S (DEFE 2/419) and Bush's Force S Reports: The Assault (DEFE 2/420). Stephenson's navigation report is contained in DEFE 2/420 and Muskett recounts his memory of the beach in his memoir (p.50). X-23's achievement is in the Force S Reports: Operation Gambit (DEFE 2/420).

11 The bulk of the launching reports are taken from C. Miller (pp.182–5) and the Force S Reports: The Assault (pp.185–6). The actions of COPP 6 are found in the Force S Reports (DEFE 2/420, pp.240–3).

12 The action of HMS *Virago* is found in Force S Reports (DEFE 2/420 pp.270–3) and *Middleton*'s in Alston (pp.170–1).

13 Bruce recounted his experience in a report filed in 7 Field Regiment's war diary (WO 171/969). Toni Kresken recounts his experience in his interrogation report (WO 208/3621).

14 The actions of 388 Bomb Group in advance of the operation come from D. Price (pp.15–22). Additional detail comes from the *History of the 4th*

Combat Wing, June 1944. Scannell recorded his experience in his memoir (pp.197-200) with supplementary information on 94 Bomb Group taken from 94th Bomb Group Database (Facebook). Rohmer recorded his experience in his memoir (pp.70-1). The full details of the bombing mission are found in the Eighth Air Force's *Tactical Operations in Support of the Allied Landings in Normandy* (pp.52-60 and pp.236-48). The last-minute change of plans is revealed by Bourque (pp.44-8). The French civilian experience comes from Howarth (p.213).

15 Damage to the bunkers is taken from the bombardment special observer report (DEFE 2/433, pp.8-13). Koza's brief interrogation report is in WO 208/3621.

16 The decision to press 45 Flotilla through the DD tanks is described in Talbot's report (DEFE 2/419, p.31), Lieutenant Commander James's report (DEFE 2/420, p.321) and Bush's report (DEFE 2/420, p.187). The impact on the DDs is recorded in C. Miller (pp.97-8 and p.184). The LCT(R) attack is detailed by the commanders in Force S Reports, The Assault (pp.197-8 and p.315) and the effect on 45 Flotilla is taken from Talbot's report (p.27) and an account by Joe Williams, one of Sergeant Wingate's crew (in Welch). Lawton's account comes from his midshipman diary (http://samilitaryhistory.org/vol095cl.html).

17 Badenoch's experiences are found in a brief personal account at IWM (Documents.13113). Jack Tear's are from a handwritten account in the D-Day Story's archive (2014/58/174).

18 440 Squadron's attack is detailed in their squadron logs (AIR 27/1880/7 and AIR 27/1880/8), with additional information from Delve (pp.106-7) and Milne (p.177).

19 The final approach is well described by Amer and Wild in their reports (DEFE 2/420, pp.240-3).

CHAPTER 6: H-HOUR

1 LCT 947's fateful landing is recounted by Birt (pp.168-70), Burn (pp.213-15), the report filed by Fairie (80 Assault Squadron War Diary, WO 171/1808), Joe Williams (in Welch) and James's report (DEFE 2/420, p.321).

2 The landing of 9 Platoon and A Company HQ is related in Butler (pp.35-7).

3 Wormald and Hennessey's accounts are contained in an unpublished diary produced by A Squadron's commander.

4 Jones's account comes from his oral archive (IWM 13670) and Butler (pp.33-5). Knapp's sweep of the road to Hermanville is detailed in his account of D-Day (IWM Documents.22330). All the AVRE experiences come from the individual accounts in 77 Assault Squadron's post-D-Day reports, found in 80 Assault Squadron's June war diary (WO 171/1808). Additional detail comes from Birt (pp.167-70) and Anderson (pp.96-101).

5   A Company's account comes primarily from Major King's correspondence with Blenkhorn and Blenkhorn's mother (IWM Documents.2840) and Blenkhorn's oral archive interview (IWM 13263).

6   Reginald Rutherford recorded his D-Day experiences in 1993 (IWM 13153). Ron Major wrote his experiences down in a 1991 account for his family and again in 1996 (IWM Documents.4730). Additional details are from Craggs, including a list of the men in Rutherford's platoon (pp.261-2).

7   The AVRE accounts come from the individual reports in 79 Assault Squadron's post-D-Day reports, found in 80 Assault Squadron's June war diary (WO 171/1808).

8   Carruthers and Dickinson each provided two accounts of the landings, one for the squadron's war diary (WO 171/1808) and one for a staff tour in 1946 (IWM Documents.1471). Additional information comes from Bush's report on the landings (DEFE 2/420, p.193).

9   The story of LCT(A)s 2123, 2052 and 2191 is relayed in the Admiralty post-landing reports (DEFE 2/420, pp.194-5), as well as letters written by Albert Smith (D-Day Story, 2014/58/68), Peter Hutchins (D-Day Story 2014/58/27) and Victor Orme's wife (D-Day Story, 2014/58/30). Some supplementary information can be found on the Combined Operations website (www.combinedops.com/LCT_PAGE.htm).

10 Urquhart and 629 Field Squadron's actions are recounted in the unit war diary (WO 171/1666), a report on 3 Division's engineer activities on D-Day (WO 171/415) and Urquhart's citation for a decoration. Major General Thomas Rennie recommended Urquhart for an immediate Distinguished Service Order, which he received (WO 373/48/16).

11 Corporal Oddie recounted his D-Day experience shortly after he returned to the UK at the end of June (ADM 199/1650, pp.479-80). LCA 791's woes are found in Foden and Bett's survivor statements (ADM 199/1650, p.264 and p.429).

12 Rouse recounts the death of Bell-Walker and Burbury in his 1994 interview with IWM (IWM 14255).

13 A Company's account comes primarily from Major King's correspondence with Blenkhorn and Blenkhorn's mother (IWM Documents.93/39/1) and Blenkhorn's oral archive interview (IWM 13263). The silencing of the 75mm bunker comes from the post-battle analysis of Cod's defences (DEFE 2/433, p.11). Kresken and Sommer's accounts come from their PoW interviews (WO 208/3621).

CHAPTER 7: THE COMMANDOS ARRIVE

1   Berry's account of landing the French commandos comes from his recollections in Warner (pp.230-2), with additional information from Rupert Curtis's unpublished memoir submitted to Ian Dear, likewise Lofi's

account and a copy of Kieffer's report written shortly after D-Day (IWM Documents.22991). Additional detail comes from Kieffer's recollections of the landing in his memoir and Vourc'h's conversations with Dear, and used in his book (pp.210-11).

2   Gilchrist and McDougall recounted their experiences in their memoirs (pp.50-3 and pp.64-75 respectively), while Patterson wrote a lengthy, sadly unpublished, account of his war experiences, especially D-Day (IWM Documents.13225). Additional detail comes from the Force S reports for Group 6 (DEFE 2/420, pp.210-13 and pp.328-9).

3   Gueritz described his experience of D-Day at length in his 1997 interview (IWM 17394). Lieutenant Scarfe's action is described in the 5 King's war diary (WO 171/1316), with additional details from Mileham (pp.165-6).

4   The account of the landing of the reserve companies of 2 East Yorks comes from Bateman's lengthy report on 543 Flotilla's D-Day experience (DEFE 2/420, pp.330-1), with some additional details from Bicknell in his survivor statement (ADM 199/1650, p.468). The infantry experience comes from the battalion war diary (WO 171/1397), Hugh Bone's correspondence written in July 1944 (IWM Documents.1464), accounts from Arthur Smith and John Scruton (IWM Documents.21902), and Thompson's 1993 interview (IWM 13370).

5   LCOCU 7 and 8's actions are well described by Jackson in his post-D-Day report (DEFE 2/420, pp.326-7). Information on LCA 352 is in the report of 543 LCA Flotilla (DEFE 2/420, pp.330-1).

6   The mission to bomb the Caen chokepoints is well described in Eighth Air Force's *Tactical Operations in Support of the Allied Landings in Normandy* (pp.52-60). Additional information comes from 303 Bomb Group's Mission 172 summary (http://www.303rdbg.com/missions.html) and Cronkite's memoir (pp.103-4).

7   41 LCT Flotilla's landing is described in Bush's Force S reports (DEFE 2/420 pp.214-16). Flynn described his D-Day experience in Shaw & Shaw (pp.239-40), LCT 898's last-minute addition to the invasion was established through comparison with the original fleet orders and Bush's report (DEFE 2/420, p.174), and Batty's injuries are recounted by Stanley Hough on the BBC's WW2 People's War (www.bbc.co.uk/history/ww2peopleswar/stories/67/a1979067.shtml). The experience of LCT 980 is taken from www.combinedops.com/LCT_980.htm while that of 854 is relayed in the Force S reports, photographs held by the D-Day Story and IWM, as well as Herbert Jankel's testimony given to Ryan (Box 21, Folder 26).

8   Priller's brief attack is taken from Ryan (pp.200-1). Although Ryan suggests the two Fw 190s attacked the entire length of the beaches from Sword to Omaha, this would have been suicidal and involved flying over dozens of miles of empty beach without knowing what lay ahead. Barnard's death is described in 186 Squadron's logs (AIR 27/1093/36).

9 6 and 41 Commandos' landing is well described in the Force S reports (DEFE 2/420, pp.222-5 and pp.316-20), the unit war diaries (6 Commando WO 218/68 and 41 Commando ADM 202/103) and in several memoirs: Lovat (pp.309-12), Millin (pp.67-9), Mills-Roberts (pp.93-4), Glover (in Winton, pp.341-4), Mitchell (pp.36-9) and Curtis's unpublished account (pp.5-10).

10 76 Field Regiment's landing is well covered in their war diary (WO 171/976) and in the Force S Reports (pp.201-2). 32 Flotilla's landing is recounted in the Force S reports (p.203 and Jewsbury's report pp.322-3) and 33 Field Regiment's war diary (WO 171/971). Assault Group 9A's landing is detailed in the Force S reports (DEFE 2/420 pp.222-5). Young described his landing in his memoir (pp.146-7) and Grant in his (pp.46-9).

11 Glover's experiences once he left the beach are detailed in Winton (pp.345-7), with additional details in the Force S reports (DEFE 2/420, pp.218-19 and p.233). The story of LCI(S) 524 is outlined in a two-page report Curtis submitted to Talbot, and Clark's rescue is detailed in Ostrom (p.122).

CHAPTER 8: THE BATTLE OF OUISTREHAM

1 8 Troop's assault on strongpoint 10 is not one that has been particularly well documented in the past, with many authors assuming they attacked the casino with Kieffer. Dear gives the most accurate account (pp.212-13), but much additional detail comes from Lofi's original account of the assault, written in 1986 at the behest of Dawson for Dear's book (Documents.22991). His and Dawson's accounts are in the files of Dear's correspondence in the IWM archive. The identity of the German defenders is taken from PoW reports in WO 208/3590 and WO 208/3621, whose presence at the strongpoint is plain from their descriptions of the weapons. Post-battle observers noted the large quantity of ammunition its guns had expended in DEFE 2/433.

2 1 Troop's battle at the casino is best told by Kieffer himself in his report dictated from his hospital bed on 14 June 1944. Additional detail comes from his memoir, and from Guy de Montlaur's account written some time after the war (although it is possibly the least reliable of the three). All are contained in Ian Dear's papers (Documents.22991). Faure's experience comes from an interview conducted by Catherine Trouiller for the French magazine *Espoir* (www.charles-de-gaulle.org/blog/2021/05/24/hubert-faure-membre-du-commando-kieffer-par-catherine-trouiller/). Some information comes from Dear (pp.214-17) and Stasi (pp.46-51), whose account includes detail from several French-language memoirs.

3 4 Commando's battle is told in their War Diary (DEFE 2/40). Additional detail comes from McDougall's memoir (pp.80-90), Gilchrist's memoir (pp.53-9), Bidmead's unpublished memoir (pp.47-8), Patterson's account of

D-Day (Documents.13225) and Portman's oral archive (IWM 9766, reels 3 & 4). More information and the experiences of Byrne come from Dunning (pp.137-40) while Porteous's all too brief account is in Bowman (p.143). The brief German accounts come from the PoW reports in WO 208/2621, and observations on the strongpoint come from DEFE 2/433 and DEFE 2/487. Further important additional detail regarding locations, especially of the bag drop and E and F Troops' route, can be gleaned from Sergeant George Laws' film of the attack (IWM A 7031-3) and aerial photographs of Ouistreham taken on D-Day (NCAP). Porteous does not name the officer who fell at the base of the tower. Positive identification of Michael Burness comes courtesy of my mother, who is much better at genealogy than I am and confirmed that Burness was the only officer of 4 Commando killed on D-Day who had married in early 1944.

4 Odette Mousset's move to the church is described in Howarth (pp.213-14) and the *Ouest France* article 'Blanche Boulet devenue infirmière au D-Day' (www.ouest-france.fr/normandie/ouistreham-14150/ouistreham-blanche-boulet-devenue-infirmiere-au-d-day-6480652).

CHAPTER 9: THE RACE TO PEGASUS BRIDGE

1 6 Commando's advance to Colleville is recounted in their June war diary, particularly in additional reports filed by 2 and 3 Troops (WO 218/68). Additional detail, particularly regarding Coade, is provided by Mills-Roberts in his memoir (pp.94-6) and Lovat in his (pp.317-18). The German defence, including the story of Ferdinand Krug, is recounted by Josef Häger in his original interview for Cornelius Ryan, which was retold in *The Longest Day* (pp.192-5). Some more information is provided by Feldwebel Wilhelm Dohmen in his PoW interview (WO 208/3621). The locations of the various actions are well defined by the grid references given in the war diary and from the descriptions given by the participants. It is highly unlikely that the men from opposing sides knew or ever met one another, and they certainly don't refer to each other in their accounts. But they agree on key details, and every aspect of the action is corroborated by people on both sides. There can be no doubt that they were all involved in the same action.

2 Pritchard describes his first experience of calvados in Warner (p.228).

3 The brief action in Saint-Aubin is only recounted by Lovat in his memoir (pp.319-21). I/736 Battalion's ration train's presence in the town is confirmed by the map of 716 Division's dispositions, captured shortly after D-Day (CAB 146/482).

4 Masters' story of the advance inland is taken from the four different versions he provided after the war, the first to Ryan (Box 21, Folder 46: Peter Masters), then Ian Dear (IWM Documents.22991), Ambrose (pp.560-4) and finally in his own memoir (pp.152-60).

5   Lovat and Millin's arrival at le Port is recounted slightly differently in both their memoirs (pp.321-2 and pp.72-5 respectively).

CHAPTER 10: BUILDING A BEACHHEAD

1   Madden's account first appeared in the *McGill Daily*.
2   The main narrative of the Suffolks' assault on Colleville-sur-Orne and Morris comes from their June war diary (WO 171/1381) and Goodwin's account of D-Day written in the summer of 1944 (DEFE 2/478). Additional detail and personal accounts come from Nicholson (pp.99-100), Lummis (pp.11-16), Forsdike (pp.24-30) and Smith (*The Assault 6-23 June 1944*).
3   The East Yorks' movement inland is detailed in their war diary (WO 171/1397), with additional details from Hugh Bone's correspondence in the summer of 1944 (IWM Documents.1464). The advance from Colleville to Sole comes from John Scruton's account of D-Day (IWM Documents.21902) and McGregor's death is related by Peter Brown in his oral archive (IWM 13854). The German defence of strongpoint 14 is best told by Josef Häger in his account supplied to Cornelius Ryan and much of it is supported by PoW interviews. Feldwebel Briefs and Obergefreiter Bosseler (WO 208/3590) detail signalling information (including codewords), Hauptmann Gundlach's interview (WO 208/3590) provides additional details of the defence, and Günther Fischer (WO 208/3621) confirms the use of a flamethrower. Nimz (WO 208/3590) mentions that men in the bunker fainted owing to the conditions.

CHAPTER 11: THE FIGHT FOR LION-SUR-MER

1   Knapp's sweep of the road to Hermanville is detailed in his account of D-Day (IWM Documents.22330). Kilvert's journey into Hermanville comes from his own account in 77 Assault Squadron's post-D-Day reports, found in 80 Assault Squadron's June war diary (WO 171/1808). Additional details come from Freer and Tennent's reports. It's worth noting that while Freer records searching the farmhouse, he does not mention an armed assault on it. Tennent mentions the action on the road, although he was not present at it. Kilvert won a Military Medal for his actions on D-Day (WO 373/48/294) – it would be churlish to ignore his own testimony.
2   Wilson's account comes from Butler (pp.51-3), with additional details from Rouse's oral archive (IWM 14255).
3   The South Lancs' move into Lion-sur-Mer is recounted in Jones's oral archive (IWM 13670) and Butler (pp.53-6).
4   41 (RM) Commando's initial push into Lion-sur-Mer is well described in the unit war diary (ADM 202/103), by Mitchell in both his history of the unit (pp.90-2) and his memoir (pp.39-43), in Grant's memoir (pp.163-7) and

by Sturgis in his Legasee interview (www.legasee.org.uk/veteran/john-sturgis/).

5   77 Assault Squadron's attack on Trout is detailed in the reports written by Low, Tennent and an unnamed crew member in McLennan's AVRE (WO 171/1808). Despite all being involved in the same action in the same vicinity, the three men provide quite contradictory information and there is uncertainty as to whether a second AT shot or the exploding Petard knocked out McLennan's AVRE, whether Low's AVRE succumbed to a mine or the AT gun, and the order in which Low and Tennent's AVREs were knocked out. The most likely sequence of events is probably related by Low, whose account is more detailed and who was in a better position to appreciate the overall situation. Even so, their different accounts offer an insight into how battles are perceived and recorded, and the problems faced by historians in trying to make sense of them.

6   The German plan to counter-attack is described by General Wilhelm Richter in his 23 June 1944 report and by Schaaf, who was interviewed by Max Hastings for his book *Overlord* (pp.104-5).

7   41 Commando's withdrawal is recounted in the war diary, Grant's memoir (pp.167-70) and James Kelly's oral archive (IWM 11281). My grateful thanks to Stuart Bertie for establishing the height of Lion-sur-Mer's church tower. Kelly does not name Sturgis – he did not know him – but noted the officer was red-haired, as Sturgis was. No other troop was near to A and B Troops at this time, so his mystery assistant must have been Sturgis. His presence there somewhat contradicts the war diary, which implies B Troop had made it another 100 yards or so west, but in reality this was probably either a very brief incursion or a simple typo in the grid reference recorded.

8   As well as Schaaf's description of events, the brief counter-attack towards the church is implied in Richter's report of 23 June 1944 and by Grant (pp.171-2).

CHAPTER 12: THE GERMAN PARRY

1   Brigadier Smith's landing is recounted in his memoir (pp.104-7), the report filed by Colonel Tapp of 7 Field Regiment RA (WO 171/969) and the report of Assault Group 9 (DEFE 2/420, p.224). The landing of 185 Brigade is related in the reports of Captain Group S2 and Intermediate Group 11 (DEFE 2/420, pp.248-51 & p.304), the war diaries of 2 Warwick (WO 171/1387), 1 Norfolk (WO 171/1350) and 2 KSLI (WO 171/1325), and the reminiscences of Bob Littlar (www.bbc.co.uk/history/ww2peopleswar/stories/39/a2524439.shtml).

2   The landing of Intermediate Group 12 comes from their reports (DEFE 2/420, pp.307-8), the Staffordshire Yeomanry war diary (WO 171/863) and the recollections of Ralph McClure (recounted in the ITV programme *Vicky*

McClure: *My Grandad's War*, which the author contributed to). The decision to close the beach is given in Leggatt's report (DEFE 2/420, pp.252-3).

3   The decisions of 185 Brigade are outlined in the brigade war diary (WO 171/702), Smith's memoir (pp.105-7) and the reports filed by Tapp and Cameron of 7 Field Regiment (WO 171/969). The French civilian's report of tanks is in 3 Division's G (Operations) war diary (WO 171/410, 6 June, serial 40). Smith's actions during Fabius are described by Robin Dunn (p.54).

4   The first attack on Hillman is described by Goodwin in his post-landing report (DEFE 2/478), the Suffolk war diary (WO 171/1381), Lummis (pp.17-20) and Forsdike (pp.31-40). Earl Rice's account is in Boegel (pp.152-60) and Sauer's account comes from Dudignac (p.85).

5   The KSLI advance is detailed in the unit war diary, with extra appendices covering X and Z Companies' actions (WO 171/1325), and the Staffordshire war diary (WO 171/863). Additional information comes from Radcliffe (pp.14-16) and the Soldiers of Shropshire Museum's account of D-Day (www.soldiersofshropshire.co.uk/wp-content/uploads/2023/07/2-KSLI-V-27.7.2023-PDF-1.pdf), and Harry Jones's account comes from War Chronicle (https://warchronicle.com/harry-g-jones-2nd-battalion-ksli/).

6   The stalemate at Hillman and the Norfolks' advance is recounted in Lummis (pp.21-3), Forsdike (pp.40-1), Lincoln (pp.24-5) and the reports filed by Tapp and Dunn (WO 171/969).

CHAPTER 13: THE SLOG INLAND

1   9 Brigade's landing, especially from the landing craft perspective, is well described in the reports of Reserve Group 16 (DEFE 2/420, pp.278-89) and the war diaries of 2 Lincoln (WO 171/1334), 1 King's Own Scottish Borderers (WO 171/1318) and 2 Royal Ulster Rifles (WO 171/1384). Additional information comes from Cyril Rand's unpublished memoir (pp.60-2).

2   The story of LST 302 is related in Airth (pp.13-26).

3   The Lincolns' advance to Lion-sur-Mer is described in their war diary (WO 171/1334) and in Weight (pp.148-53). The bombing of 9 Brigade HQ and their change in command and orders is described in the brigade war diary (WO 171/616) and Grant (pp.174-5). Ślązak's bombardment is detailed in Ambrose (p.552). The deployment of 2 RUR is covered in their war diary (WO 171/1334).

4   The assault on Daimler is described in the unit war diary (WO 171/1397) and accounts by Lionel Roebuck (IWM Documents.2832), Scruton and Crauford (IWM Documents.21902).

5   The action at Ouistreham locks is taken from 79 Assault Squadron's June war diary and the personal testimonies in 80 Assault Squadron's June war diary (which includes the reports of tank commanders from 5 Assault

Regiment RE). Beeton's account is in Shaw & Shaw (p.37). Odette Mousset's evacuation is described in Howarth (pp.214-15).

CHAPTER 14: THE PANZER RIPOSTE

1 Details of the German counter-attack are taken from Kortenhaus (pp.101-9), with additional information from Oppeln-Bronikowski's recollections supplied to Cornelius Ryan (Box 027, Folder 19). Hermes' account comes from Ryan (p.220). The British reaction comes from the KSLI war diary (WO 171/1325) and Staffordshire Yeomanry war diary (WO 171/863). Additional information comes from the Soldiers of Shropshire Museum's account of D-Day (https://www.soldiersofshropshire.co.uk/wp-content/uploads/2023/07/2-KSLI-V-27.7.2023-PDF-1.pdf). Harry Jones's account comes from War Chronicle (https://warchronicle.com/harry-g-jones-2nd-battalion-ksli/), while the actions of Sergeants Billings and Joyce are related in the *West County Bugle* ('Troopers of the Staffordshire Yeomanry', 19 June 2019) and Underhill (p.26).

2 The second attack on Hillman is described by Goodwin in his post-landing report (DEFE 2/478), the Suffolk war diary (WO 171/1381), Lummis (pp.21-6) and Forsdike (pp.41-5), and Eric Smith's unpublished account. Sauer's account comes from Dudignac (pp.87-9).

3 The KSLI capture of strongpoint 21A is detailed in the Z Company appendix in the unit war diary (WO 171/1325). Additional information comes from the Soldiers of Shropshire Museum's account of D-Day (www.soldiersofshropshire.co.uk/wp-content/uploads/2023/07/2-KSLI-V-27.7.2023-PDF-1.pdf) and Radcliffe (p.15).

4 Rauch's arrival at Lion-sur-Mer is detailed in Kortenhaus (pp.108-9). The bombardment by Ślązak is detailed in Ambrose (p.552), with additional identities and details established through Force S's orders (DEFE 2/403). Lieutenant Stevens' return is detailed in 41 Commando's war diary (ADM 202/103).

CHAPTER 15: DARKNESS FALLS

1 The arrival of 6 Airlanding Brigade is detailed in Ditcham (p.220), Colin Lawton's diary (http://samilitaryhistory.org/vol095cl.html) and Grant's memoir (p.173). The German response is covered in Kortenhaus (pp.109-10).

2 The Norfolks' experience is described in Lincoln (pp.25-6). The Warwicks' advance on Bénouville is covered in their war diary (WO 171/1387) and Cunliffe (pp.79-80), with additional details from Captain Lister of 7 Field Regiment (WO 171/969), and the experiences of 92 LAA Regiment in Barber (pp.262-6).

3 Captain Rylands' account comes from War Chronicle (https://warchronicle.com/from-w-company-2nd-bn-ksli/). Richter's final message to Krug is

related by Meyer in his memoir (pp.217-18). The naval action on the night of 6/7 June is assembled from Law's description in his memoir (pp.72-6) and Bradford's account in Scott (p.194). The German experience is taken from FS Gkdos 19027 from Chief 10th R Flotilla, 7 June, *KTB 2nd Sicherungs division*.

CHAPTER 16: JOINING JUNO, CLOSING ON CAEN

1. The actions of 7 June are detailed in the war diaries of the Lincolns (WO 171/1334) and 41 Commando (DEFE 2/48), with extra details from Weight (pp.155-60) and Grant (pp.175-7).
2. The attack on Cambes is described in the war diaries of 2 RUR (WO 171/1384) and the ERY (WO 171/862), as well as Mace (pp.128-30).
3. The defeat at Lebisey is best related in the Warwicks' war diary (WO 171/1387).

CHAPTER 17: SECURING SWORD

1. The statistical data of the landings on Sword is primarily drawn from special observations made after the landings, in particular DEFE 2/490, DEFE 2/491 and DEFE 2/492. Wilmot's account of Sword Beach makes up thirteen pages of his book (pp.302-15) and Dunn's criticisms of Smith come from his memoir (p.61).

EPILOGUE

1. *Courbet*'s story is well told by Taylor in his own account of the Gooseberries (pp.94-105).

GLOSSARY

AFPU	Army Film and Photographic Unit
AP	armour piercing – a type of shell used by tanks, warships and artillery
AT gun	anti-tank gun
AVRE	Armoured Vehicle Royal Engineers
Bangalore torpedo	an explosive stick charge designed to destroy barbed-wire obstacles
BARV	Beach Armoured Recovery Vehicle
Beehive charge	an explosive charge designed for blowing holes in walls
Boase Bangalore	a pair of Banglarore torpedoes mounted on a frame attached to AVREs to be pushed into sand dunes or barbed wire in order to clear vehicle lanes
CO	commanding officer
COPP	Combined Operations Pilotage Party
COSSAC	Chief of Staff to the Supreme Allied Commander
DD	Duplex Drive (swimming tank)
FOB	Forward Officer Bombardment
FOO	Forward Observation Officer
HDML	Harbour Defence Motor Launch
HE	high explosive – a type of shell used by tanks, warships and artillery
HNoMS	His Norwegian Majesty's Ship
LCA	Landing Craft Assault
LCA(HR)	Landing Craft Assault (Hedgerow)
LCF	Landing Craft Flak
LCG(L)	Landing Craft Gun (Large)
LCH	Landing Craft Headquarters
LCI(L)	Landing Craft Infantry (Large)
LCI(S)	Landing Craft Infantry (Small)
LCM	Landing Craft Mechanized
LCN	Landing Craft Navigation
LCOCU	Landing Craft Obstacle Clearance Unit
LCP(L)	Landing Craft Personnel (Large)
LCP(L)(S)	Landing Craft Personnel (Large) (Smoke)
LCP(SY)	Landing Craft Personnel (Survey)

LCS(L)	Landing Craft Support (Large)
LCS(M)	Landing Craft Support (Medium)
LCS(S)	Landing Craft Support (Small)
LCT	Landing Craft Tank
LCT(A)	Landing Craft Tank (Armoured)
LCT(CB)	Landing Craft Tank (Concrete Buster)
LCT(HE)	Landing Craft Tank (High Explosive)
LCT(R)	Landing Craft Tank (Rocket)
LOB	Left out of Battle: infantry troops left out of the first wave during the assault
LSH	Landing Ship Headquarters
LSI	Landing Ship Infantry
LST	Landing Ship Tank
ML	motor launch
MTB	motor torpedo boat
Nebelwerfer	a German multi-barrelled mortar, known to the Allies as a 'moaning Minnie' on account of the sound the projectiles made
ORP	Polish Navy ship prefix (Okręt Rzeczypospolitej Polskiej)
Petard mortar	a spigot mortar fitted to AVREs: the projectile was fitted to a rod (the spigot) and could be fired from a short barrel
PIAT	a portable anti-tank weapon (Projector, Infantry, Anti-Tank)
Porpoise	an ammunition sled towed by tanks and self-propelled artillery during the initial landings
RA	Royal Artillery
RAMC	Royal Army Medical Corps
RAOC	Royal Army Ordnance Corps
RAP	Regimental Aid Post
RASC	Royal Army Service Corps
Räumboot	R-boat – minesweeper/minelayer
RCNVR	Royal Canadian Naval Volunteer Reserve
RE	Royal Engineers
REME	Royal Electrical Mechanical Engineers
RM	Royal Marines
RMASG	Royal Marine Armoured Support Group
RN	Royal Navy
RNVR	Royal Naval Volunteer Reserve
RNZNVR	Royal New Zealand Naval Volunteer Reserve
Schnellboot	German motor torpedo boat, usually abbreviated to S-boat but more commonly known to the Allies as an E-boat
SHAEF	Supreme Headquarters Allied Expeditionary Force

SP gun	self-propelled gun – essentially an artillery or AT gun mounted on its own vehicle, as opposed to being towed
Stützpunkt (StP)	German for 'base' or 'strongpoint', typically a company-sized defensive point
Stützpunktgruppe	German for a group of stützpunkte
Torpedoboot	a German class of warship equivalent to a small destroyer
Volksdeutscher	a soldier who according to the Nazis was of German origins but who did not hold German citizenship
Vorpostenboot	a German boat tasked with patrol, escort and combat duties
Wehrmachthelferin	women 'helpers' (a Nazi auxiliary corps)
Widerstandsnest (WN)	German for 'resistance nest', typically a platoon-sized defensive point
Zollverwaltung	German customs and border guard service

BIBLIOGRAPHY

PUBLISHED SOURCES

Airth, G., *HMLST 302 Diary* (privately published, 2005)

Alston, M., *Destroyer & Preserver: The Story of HMS Middleton & Her Ship's Company* (privately published, 1993)

Ambrose, S., *D-Day: June 6, 1944* (Simon & Schuster, 1994)

Anderson, R., *Cracking Hitler's Atlantic Wall: The 1st Assault Brigade Royal Engineers on D-Day* (Stackpole, 2010)

Anon., *The Story of 79th Armoured Division* (privately published, 1945)

Barber, N., *The Pegasus & Orne Bridges: Their Capture, Defence and Relief on D-Day* (Pen & Sword, 2009)

Barber, P., *Some War* (privately published, 1998)

Bastable, J., *Voices From D-Day: Eyewitness Accounts of 6th June 1994* (David & Charles, 2004)

Belcham, D., *Victory in Normandy* (Chatto & Windus, 1981)

Birt, R., *XII Dragoons 1760-1945: The Story of a Regiment* (Gale & Polden Limited, 1950)

Boegel, G., *Boys of the Clouds: An Oral History of the 1st Canadian Parachute Battalion 1942-1945* (Trafford Publishing, 2007)

Bourque, S., *D-Day 1944: The Deadly Failure of Allied Heavy Bombing on June 6* (Osprey, 2022)

Bowman, M., *Air War D-Day: Gold, Juno, Sword* (Pen & Sword, 2013)

Brazier, C., *XD Operations: Secret British Missions Denying Oil to the Nazis* (Pen & Sword, 2004)

Brown, D. (ed.), *Battle Summary No.39. Operation Neptune: Landings in Normandy, June 1944* (HMSO, 1994)

Burn, L., *Down Ramps! Saga of the Eighth Armada* (Carrol & Nicholson, 1947)

Bush, E., *Bless Our Ship* (George Allen & Unwin, 1958)

Butler, D., *Fighting Iron: 1st South Lancashire Regiment from D-Day to Normandy* (privately published, 2021)

Caddick-Adams, P., *Sand and Steel* (Hutchinson, 2019)

Campbell, D., *Magic Mistress: A Thirty Year Affair with Reuters* (Tagman, 2000)

Churchill, W., *The Second World War, Vol. 10: Assault from the Air* (Cassell, 1964; first published 1952)
Collingwood, D., *The Captain Class Frigates in the Second World War* (Leo Cooper, 1998)
Cunliffe, M., *History of the Royal Warwickshire Regiment, 1919-1956* (William Clowes & Sons, 1956)
D'Este, C., *Decision in Normandy* (Robson Books, 2000; first published 1983)
Dalgleish, J., *We Planned the Second Front* (Victor Gollancz, 1945)
Dear, I., *Ten Commando, 1942-1945* (Leo Cooper, 1987)
Delve, K., *D-Day: The Air Battle* (The Crowood Press, 1994)
Dickens, P., *Night Action: MTB Flotilla at War* (Seaforth, 2008; first published 1974)
Ditcham, A., *A Home on the Rolling Main: A Naval Memoir, 1940-1946* (Seaforth, 2012)
Dudignac, G., *La Vie Du Colonel Krug* (privately published in French, 2011)
Dunn, R., *Sword and Wig* (Quiller, 1993)
Dunning, J., *The Fighting Fourth: No.4 Commando at War 1940-45* (Sutton, 2003)
Eisenhower, D., *Crusade in Europe* (Heinemann, 1958)
Ellis, L., *History of the Second World War: Victory in the West, Volume 1: The Battle of Normandy* (HMSO, 1962)
Ford, K., *D-Day 1944: Sword Beach & The British Airborne Landings* (Osprey, 2002)
Ford, K., *Battlezone Normandy: Sword Beach* (Sutton, 2004)
Foreman, J., *1944: The Air War Over Europe, June 1st-30th: Over the Beaches* (Air Research Publications, 1994)
Forsdike, M., *Fighting Through to Hitler's Germany: Personal Accounts of the Men of 1 Suffolk, 1944-45* (Pen & Sword, 2020)
Gilchrist, D., *The Commandos: D-Day and After* (Robert Hale, 1982)
Grant, D., *The Fuel of the Fire* (Cresset Press, 1950)
Grant, I., *Cameramen at War* (PSL, 1980)
Hastings, M., *Overlord: D-Day and the Battle for Normandy, 1944* (Book Club Associates, 1984)
Hepworth, S., Porrelli, A. & Dison, H., *Nothing Can Stop Us: The Definitive History of 514 Squadron RAF* (Mention the War Publications, 2015)
Hewitt, N., *Normandy: The Sailors' Story: A Naval History of D-Day and the Normandy Campaign* (Yale University Press, 2024)
Hoeller, H., *D-Day Tank Hunter* (privately published, 2022)
Howard, J. & Bates, P., *The Pegasus Diaries: The Private Papers of Major John Howard DSO* (Pen & Sword, 2006)
Howarth, D., *Dawn of D-Day* (The Companion Book Club, 1959)
Illing, H., *No Better Soldier* (The Royal Regiment of Fusiliers Museum, 2001)
Kieffer, P., *Beret Vert* (France-Empire, 1974)
Kilvert-Jones, T., *Battleground Europe: Sword Beach* (Pen & Sword, 2001)

Kortenhaus, W., *The Combat History of the 21 Panzer Division* (Helion, 2014)
Kronkite, W., *A Reporter's Life* (Atlantic Books, 1997)
Law, A., *White Plumes Astern: The Short, Daring Life of Canada's MTB Flotilla* (Nimbus, 1989)
Lewis, J., *Eyewitness D-Day* (Robinson, 1994)
Lincoln, J., *Thank God and the Infantry: From D-Day to VE Day with the 1st Battalion The Royal Norfolk Regiment* (Alan Sutton, 1994)
Lovat, Lord, *March Past: A Memoir by Lord Lovat* (Weidenfeld & Nicolson, 1978)
Lummis, E., *1 Suffolk and D-Day* (privately published, 1989)
Lummis, E., *An Illustrated Guide to Sword Beach* (privately published, 1994)
Mace, P., *Forrard: The Story of the East Riding Yeomanry* (Pen & Sword, 2001)
Maher, B., *A Passage to Sword Beach: Minesweeping in the Royal Navy* (Naval Institute Press, 1996)
Masters, P., *Striking Back: A Jewish Commando's War Against the Nazis* (Presidio, 1997)
McDougall, M., *Swiftly They Struck: The Story of No. 4 Commando* (Arms & Armour Press, 1954)
McNish, R., *Iron Division: The History of the 3rd Division* (Ian Allan, 1978)
Meyer, K., *Grenadiers: The Story of Waffen SS General Kurt 'Panzer' Meyer* (Stackpole Books, 2005; first published 1957)
Mileham, P., *Difficulties Be Damned: The King's Regiment* (Fleur de Lys, 2000)
Miller, C., *History of the 13th/18th Royal Hussars (Queen Mary's Own) 1922–1947* (Chisman Bradshaw, 1949)
Miller, R., *Nothing Less Than Victory: The Oral History of D-Day* (Michael Joseph, 1993)
Millin, B., *Invasion* (privately published, 1991)
Mills-Roberts, D., *Clash by Night* (William Kimber, 1956)
Milne, R., *Sailor Boy to Typhoon Pilot* (privately published, 1988)
Mitchell, R., *They Did What Was Asked of Them: 41 (Royal Marines) Commando* (Firebird Books, 1996)
Mitchell, R., *Commando Despatch Rider: From D-Day to Deutschland 1944–1945* (Pen & Sword, 2001)
Montgomery, B., *The Memoirs of Field-Marshal Montgomery* (Collins, 1958)
Muskett, D., *Tubal Cain: The Sinking of HMS Barham* (The Book Guild Ltd, 1986)
Nicholson, W., *The Suffolk Regiment, 1928 to 1946* (East Anglian Magazine, 1946)
Nightingale, P., *The East Yorkshire Regiment (Duke of York's Own) in the War 1939/45* (privately published, 1952)
Nolan, B., *Airborne: The Heroic Story of the 1st Canadian Parachute Battalion in the Second World War* (Turner Books, 2002)
Orr, D. & Truesdale, D., *The Rifles Are There: The Story of the 1st and 2nd Battalions The Royal Ulster Rifles 1939–1945* (Pen & Sword, 2005)

Ostrom, T., *The United States Coast Guard in World War II: A History of Domestic and Overseas Actions* (McFarland & Co., 2009)

Patterson, L., *Hitler's Forgotten Flotillas: Kriegsmarine Security Forces* (Seaforth, 2017)

Pine-Coffin, R. & Maddox, R., *The Tale of Two Bridges* (privately published, 2003)

Poett, N., *Pure Poett: The Autobiography of General Sir Nigel Poett* (Leo Cooper, 1991)

Price, A., *Spitfire: A Complete Fighting History* (Productivity Press, 1998)

Price, D., *A Bomber Crew Mystery: The Forgotten Heroes of 388th Bombardment Group* (Pen & Sword, 2016)

Radcliffe, G., *2nd Battalion The King's Shropshire Light Infantry, 1944-1945* (Basil Blackwell, 1947)

Reynolds, M., *Eagles & Bulldogs in Normandy 1944* (Spellmount, 2003)

Rohmer, R., *Patton's Gap: An Account of the Battle of Normandy* (Arms & Armour, 1981)

Ross, P., *Hampshire at War: An Oral History, 1939-1945* (King's England Press, 2013)

Ruge, F., *Rommel in Normandy* (MacDonald & Jane, 1979)

Rush, R., *The Last Man Standing* (Camera Journal, 2020)

Ryan, C., *The Longest Day* (Victor Gollancz, 1960)

Sanders, G., *Soldier, Sailor* (The Bombardment Units Association, 1947)

Scannell, F., *One Man's War: Remembrances of WWII* (privately published, 2019)

Scarfe, N., *Assault Division* (Collins, 1947)

Scott, P., *The Battle of the Narrow Seas* (Country Life, 1945)

Shaw, F. & Shaw, J., *We Remember D-Day* (privately published, 1994)

Smith, K. P., *Adventures of an Ancient Warrior* (privately published, 1984)

Stasi, J., *Kieffer Commando: The Free French Landings in Normandy* (Heimdal, 2014)

Stewart, A., *Caen Controversy: The Battle for Sword Beach 1944* (Helion, 2014)

Sykes, S., *Deceivers Ever: The Memoirs of a Camouflage Officer* (Spellmount, 1990)

Tarrant, V., *The Last Year of the Kriegsmarine* (Arms & Armour, 1994)

Taylor, J., *The Last Passage* (George Allen & Unwin, 1946)

Thurlow, D., *Attack on Concrete: Driving the Germans from their Concrete Defences in Northwest Europe* (privately published, 2022)

Tute, W., Costello, J. & Hughes, J., *D-Day* (Sidgwick & Jackson, 1974)

Underhill, D. F., *The Queen's Own Royal Regiment, the Staffordshire Yeomanry: An Account of the Operations of the Regiment During World War II, 1939-1945* (Staffordshire Libraries, Arts and Archives, 1994)

Vian, P., *Action This Day: War Memoirs of Admiral of the Fleet* (Muller, 1960)

Warner, P., *The D-Day Landings* (Pen & Sword, 2004; first published 1980)

Weight, G., *Mettle and Pasture: The History of the Second Battalion of the Lincolnshire Regiment During World War II* (Helion, 2015)

Whitley, M., *German Destroyers of World War Two* (Arms & Armour, 1991)
Williams, J., *They Led the Way: The Fleet Minesweepers at Normandy, June 1994* (privately published, 1994)
Wilmot, C., *The Struggle for Europe* (The Reprint Society, 1954; first published 1952)
Winton, J., *Freedom's Battle, Volume I: The War at Sea, 1939-1945* (Hutchinson, 1967)
Young, P., *Storm from the Sea* (Wren's Park Publishing, 2002; first published 1958)
Zaloga, S., *D-Day Fortifications in Normandy* (Osprey, 2005)

NEWSPAPER ARTICLES

Anon., 'Troopers of the Staffordshire Yeomanry', *West Country Bugle*, 19 June 2019
Madden, J., 'Ex Coelis, Part 1', *McGill Daily* (Montreal), 13 June 1946
Madden, J., 'Ex Coelis, Part 2', *McGill Daily* (Montreal), 20 June 1946

UNPUBLISHED SOURCES

Anon., *C Squadron 13/18th Royal Hussars War Diary: From 6th June 1944 to 8th May 1945* (available from www.lightdragoons.org.uk/downloads.html)
Anon., *Eighth Air Force: Tactical Operations in Support of Neptune, June 2-17* (1944)
Anon., *History of the 4th Combat Wing, June 1944* (available from Fold3.com)
Anon., *KTB 2nd Sicherungsdivision War Diary* (German)
Bidmead, W., *Hail the Young Soldier* (available from the National Army Museum, 2007-12-17)
Craggs, T., *An 'Unspectacular' War?: Reconstructing the History of the 2nd Battalion East Yorkshire Regiment during the Second World War* (a 2007 thesis submitted for the degree of Doctor of Philosophy, University of Sheffield, available from: https://etheses.whiterose.ac.uk/3626/)
Curtis, R., *We Landed the Commandos* (available from the National Army Museum, 9107-238)
Feuchtinger, E., *History of the 21st Panzer Division from the Time of its Formation until the Beginning of the Invasion* (1947, available from Fold3.com)
Major, R., *The War Years by Pte. Ronald Major* (kindly supplied by Nigel Walworth)
Neave, J., *The War Diary of Julius Neave* (available from www.lightdragoons.org.uk/downloads.html)

Rand, C., *From Sword to Troan* (kindly supplied by Paul Woodadge)

Richter, W., *Operations Report on the Action in the Sector of the 716. Infantry Division on 6 June 1944* (1944, available from Fold3.com)

Smith, E., *The Assault 6-23 June 1944: The Story of C Squadron – 13th/18th Royal Hussars (QMO)* (available from www.lightdragoons.org.uk/downloads.html)

Welch, P., *A Breaching Time on D-Day* (kindly supplied by Paul Welch)

Welch, P., Interview with Joe Smith (aged 80), 77 Assault Squadron. 18 February 2001 (kindly supplied by Paul Welch)

Wormald, D., *Introduction to Recollections of the Operations Undertaken by a Squadron of the 13th/18th Royal Hussars (QMO) During the 1944-45 Campaign in Europe* (available from www.lightdragoons.org.uk/downloads.html)

WAR DIARIES HELD IN THE NATIONAL ARCHIVES

3 Infantry Division HQ	WO 171/409
3 Infantry Division HQ G	WO 171/410
3 Infantry Division AQ	WO 171/413
3 Infantry Division CRA	WO 171/414
3 Infantry Division CRE	WO 171/415
3 Infantry Division Signals	WO 171/417
Recce Regt	WO 171/418
2 Middlesex Machine Gun Battalion	WO 171/1341
3 Infantry Division CRASC	WO 171/419
3 Infantry Division CREME	WO 171/420
3 Infantry Division ADOS	WO 171/421
3 Infantry Division Ordnance Field Park	WO 171/422
3 Infantry Division Provost Company	WO 171/423
3 Infantry Division Postal Unit	WO 171/424
7 Field Regiment RA	WO 171/969
33 Field Regiment RA	WO 171/971
76 Field Regiment RA	WO 171/976
20 AT Regiment RA	WO 171/913
16 Field Battery	WO 171/1005
92 LAA Regiment	WO 171/1123
246 Field Coy RE	WO 171/1604

253 Field Coy RE	WO 171/1606
17 Field Company	WO 171/1518
15 Field Park Company	WO 171/1516
8 Field Ambulance RAMC	WO 177/688
9 Field Ambulance RAMC	WO 177/690
223 Field Ambulance RAMC	WO 177/830
8 Infantry Brigade	WO 171/611
2 East Yorkshire Regiment	WO 171/1397
1 South Lancashire Regiment	WO 171/1332
1 Suffolk Regiment	WO 171/1381
185 Infantry Brigade	WO 171/702
2 Warwickshire Regiment	WO 171/1387
1 Norfolk Regiment	WO 171/1350
2 King's Shropshire Light Infantry	WO 171/1325
9 Infantry Brigade	WO 171/616
2 Lincolnshire Regiment	WO 171/1334
1 King's Own Scottish Borderers	WO 171/1318
2 Royal Ulster Rifles	WO 171/1384
27 Armoured Brigade HQ	WO 171/623
Signals	WO 171/624
27 Armoured Brigade Signals	WO 166/15542
Ordnance Field Park	WO 171/625
REME Workshop	WO 171/626
13/18 Hussars	WO 171/845
Staffordshire Yeomanry	WO 171/863
1 East Riding Yeomanry	WO 171/862
1 SS Brigade HQ	DEFE 2/53
3 Commando	WO 218/65
4 Commando	DEFE 2/40
6 Commando	WO 218/68
10 Commando	WO 218/70
41 (RM) Commando	DEFE 2/48
45 (RM) Commando	ADM 202/82
45 (RM) Commando	DEFE 2/51
Commandos in action: reports 1943–1945	DEFE 2/1091

22 Dragoons   WO 171/841
5 Assault Regiment RE HQ   WO 171/1800
77 Assault Squadron RE   WO 171/1806
79 Assault Squadron RE   WO 171/1807
80 Assault Squadron RE   WO 171/1808
71 Field Coy RE   WO 171/1528
263 Field Coy RE   WO 171/1611
629 Field Coy RE   WO 171/1666

5 RMASG   ADM 202/304
RM Engineer Commando   DEFE 2/49

90 Armoured Brigade Coy RASC   WO 171/2377
106 Bridge Coy RASC   WO 171/2383

53 Regiment RA HQ   WO 171/1055
73 LAA Regiment RA   WO 171/1121
93 LAA Regiment RA   WO 171/1124
652 Air Observation Point Sqn   WO 171/1223

A Squadron GHQ (Phantom) Liaison   WO 171/3459

101 Beach Group Jan-May 1944   WO 171/813
101 Beach Group Jun-Dec 1944   WO 171/814
18 GHQ Troop Engineers   WO 171/1491

Beach Commando Unit F   DEFE 2/987
5 Battalion The King's Regiment   WO 171/1316
20 Field Dressing Station   WO 177/905
21 Field Dressing Station   WO 177/906
30 Field Dressing Station   WO 177/916
1 Field Sanitary Section   WO 177/1560
39 Field Surgery Unit   WO 177/1620
40 Field Surgery Unit   WO 177/1621
55 Field Surgery Unit   WO 177/1636
21 Field Transfusion Unit   WO 177/1795
29 Field Transfusion Unit   WO 177/1802
16 Casualty Clearing Station   WO 177/649
44 Ordnance Ammunition Company   WO 171/2736
11 Ordnance Beach Detachment   WO 171/2689

53 Pioneer Company	WO 171/3054
102 Pioneer Company	WO 171/3090
129 Pioneer Company	WO 171/3109
267 Pioneer Company	WO 171/3200
292 Pioneer Company	WO 171/3214
303 Pioneer Company	WO 171/3221
20 Beach Recovery Section	WO 171/2960
96 Detail Issue Depot	WO 171/2117
HQ 21 Transport Column RASC	WO 171/2232
39 General Transport Company	WO 171/2362
101 General Transport Company	WO 171/2381
635 General Transport Company	WO 171/2507
237 Petrol Depot	WO 171/2288
84 Field Company	WO 171/1534
940 Inland Waterway Transport	WO 171/1740
8 Stores Section	WO 171/1934
241 Provost Company	WO 171/3386
101 RAF Beach Flight	AIR 29/438/4
Beach Commando Unit R	DEFE 2/987
1 Buckinghamshire	WO 171/1269
9 Field Dressing Station	WO 177/894
12 Field Dressing Station	WO 177/897
2 Detachment Field Sanitary Section	WO 177/1561
38 Field Surgery Unit	WO 177/1619
12 Ordnance Beach Detachment	WO 171/2690
85 Pioneer Company	WO 171/3076
149 Pioneer Company	WO 171/3124
21 Beach Recovery Section	WO 171/2961
138 Detail Issue Depot	WO 171/2143
299 General Transport Company	WO 171/2429
238 Petrol Depot	WO 171/2289
91 Field Company	WO 171/1539
9 Stores Section	WO 171/1935
50 Mechanical Equipment Section	WO 171/1870
1028 Port Operating Company	WO 171/1777
245 HQ Provost Company	WO 171/3390
102 RAF Beach Flight	AIR 29/438/4
999 Port Operating Company	WO 171/1770

OTHER FILES HELD IN THE NATIONAL ARCHIVES

Force S Orders	ADM 199/1561
Force S Orders	DEFE 2/403
Force S Landing Tables	WO 219/3075
Report by Naval Commander Force S	DEFE 2/419
Report by Naval Commander Force S	DEFE 2/420
Operation Gambit	ADM 179/475
HMS *Arethusa* Log June 1944	ADM 53/118866
HMS *Danae* Log June 1944	ADM 53/119197
HMS *Frobisher* Log June 1944	ADM 53/119464
HMS *Mauritius* Log June 1944	ADM 53/119862
HMS *Ramillies* Log June 1944	ADM 53/120330
HMS *Rodney* Log June 1944	ADM 53/120411
HMS *Scylla* Log June 1944	ADM 53/120451
HMS *Warspite* Log June 1944	ADM 53/120730
HMS *Roberts* report	ADM 179/507
Green List 29 May 1944	ADM 210/7
Survivor Reports	ADM 199/1650
Survivor Reports	ADM 199/1651
Survivor Reports	ADM 199/1652
The German Defences in the Courselles–Saint-Aubin Area on the Normandy Coast (Information from German Sources)	CAB 146/482
Report on the Operations of 6th Airborne Division in Normandy, 6 June – 27 August 1944.	CAB 106/970
Report of Special Observer Party Investigating the Effect of Fire Preparation – Operation Neptune	DEFE 2/433
Various D-Day Reports	DEFE 2/478
Reports by various authorities on special phases of the operation	DEFE 2/484
Observations on Air Attacks on Coastal Defences	DEFE 2/487
Opposition Encountered Commonwealth Beaches	DEFE 2/490
Comparison of British and US Assault Areas	DEFE 2/491
Casualties and Fire Support British Beaches	DEFE 2/492
D-Day Beach Intelligence Report	DEFE 2/494
3 Division from D-Day to D+24	WO 205/903
PoW Interrogations	WO 208/4618
PoW Interrogations	WO 208/3621
PoW Interrogations	WO 208/3590
Recommendation for Award for Kilvert, Thomas	WO 373/48/294
Recommendation for Award for Urquhart, Ronald	WO 373/48/16

15 Squadron RAF	AIR 27/204/11
15 Squadron RAF	AIR 27/204/12
75 Squadron RAF	AIR 27/647/11
75 Squadron RAF	AIR 27/647/12
105 Squadron RAF	AIR 27/827/35
105 Squadron RAF	AIR 27/827/36
109 Squadron RAF	AIR 27/854/11
109 Squadron RAF	AIR 27/854/12
115 Squadron RAF	AIR 27/891/11
115 Squadron RAF	AIR 27/891/12
514 Squadron RAF	AIR 27/1977/15
514 Squadron RAF	AIR 27/1977/16
622 Squadron RAF	AIR 27/2137/21
622 Squadron RAF	AIR 27/2137/22
440 Squadron RCAF	AIR 27/1880/7
440 Squadron RCAF	AIR 27/1880/8
570 Squadron RAF	AIR 27/2041
570 Squadron RAF	AIR 27/2043
295 Squadron RAF	AIR 27/1644
295 Squadron RAF	AIR 27/2583
168 Squadron RAF	AIR 27/1093/36

DOCUMENTS, PRIVATE PAPERS, ORAL ARCHIVES AND FILM FOOTAGE IN THE IMPERIAL WAR MUSEUM COLLECTION

Private Papers of A. C. Badenoch	Documents.13113
Private Papers of Lieutenant H. T. Bone	Documents.1464
Private Papers of Brigadier E. E. E. Cass CBE DSO MC	Documents.1471
Private Papers of Commander W. S. Clouston DSC RN	Documents.7683
Private Papers of Ian C. B. Dear	Documents.22991
Private Papers of Major C. K. King DSO	Documents.2840
Private Papers of Lieutenant D. R. Knapp	Documents.22330
Private Papers of R. Major	Documents.4730
Private Papers of Captain J. H. Patterson	Documents.13225
Private Papers of L. A. Roebuck	Documents.2832
Five Memoirs from 2nd Battalion East Yorkshire Regiment in North-West Europe, 1944-45	Documents.21920
Blinkhorn, James (Oral history)	IWM 13263

Brown, Peter (Oral history)   IWM 13854
Gueritz, Edward Findlay (Oral history)   IWM 17394
Jones, Edward (Oral history)   IWM 13670
Kelly, James Anthony (Oral history)   IWM 11281
Neave, Julius Arthur (Oral history)   IWM 27183
Portman, Irving (Oral history)   IWM 9766
Rouse, Arthur (Oral history)   IWM 14255
Rutherford, Reginald (Oral history)   IWM 13153
Force S Assembles for Operation Neptune   IWM ADM 684
Departure from UK for Normandy Invasion (Part 1)   IWM A70 23-3
Departure from UK for Normandy Invasion (Part 2)   IWM A70 25-1
HMS *Largs* at Portsmouth and off Sword Beach   IWM ADM 1252
Force D Bombards Sword Beach   IWM ADM 1258
Onboard HMS *Largs*, HQ Ship for Force S   IWM ADM 1260
Landings On 'Sword' Beach, 6 June 1944 (Part 1)   IWM A70 29-1-2
Landings On 'Sword' Beach, 6 June 1944 (Part 2)   IWM A70 31-1
Landings On 'Sword' Beach, 6 June 1944 (Part 3)   IWM A70 31-2
Landings On 'Sword' Beach, 6 June 1944 (Part 4)   IWM A 70 31-3
Landings On 'Sword' Beach, 6 June 1944 (Part 5)   IWM A70 32-2
Landings On 'Sword' Beach, 6 June 1944 (Part 6)   IWM A70 36-1
185 Brigade Prepares to Go Ashore at Sword Beach   IWM ADM 1259

DOCUMENTS IN OTHER ARCHIVES

CORNELIUS RYAN ARCHIVE

Peter Masters   Box 21, Folder 46
Hermann von Oppeln-Bronikowski   Box 27, Folder 19
Edgar Feuchtinger   Box 26, Folder 13
Wilhelm von Gottberg   Box 27, Folder 17
Herbert Jankel   Box 21, Folder 26
Theodor Krancke   Box 26, Folder 24

THE D-DAY STORY

Jim Brooker's Correspondence   2014/58/101
Rupert Curtis Collection   1992/275/101
Albert Smith's Correspondence   2014/58/68

Peter Hutchins's Correspondence   2014/58/27
Victor Orme's wife's Correspondence   2014/58/30
Jack Tear's Correspondence   2014/58/174

UNIVERSITY COLLEGE LONDON, LIDDELL-HART COLLECTION

Derek Mills-Roberts: Papers relating to his service
with the Commandos, 1942-1945,   MILLS-ROBERTS

WEBSITES

94th Bomb Group Database, *History of the 94th Bomb Group* (available from www.facebook.com/94thBombGroup/)

100th Bomb Group Foundation, *Sharing the Legacy of the Bloody Hundredth* (available from https://100thbg.com/)

BBC People's War / Hough, S., *HMS Princess Astrid 1942 to 1944* (available from www.bbc.co.uk/history/ww2peopleswar/stories/67/a1979067.shtml)

BBC People's War / Littlar, B., *Bob Littlar's D-Day: 2nd Battalion King's Shropshire Light Infantry* (available from www.bbc.co.uk/history/ww2peopleswar/stories/39/a2524439.shtml)

Combined Operations, *D-Day Landing Craft and Normandy Beaches* (available from www.combinedops.com/LCT_PAGE.htm)

Combined Operations, *Landing Craft Tank (4) 980 – LCT (4) 980* (available from www.combinedops.com/LCT_980.htm)

Fondation Charles de Gaulle / Trouiller, C., *Hubert Faure, membre du commando Kieffer* (available from www.charles-de-gaulle.org/blog/2021/05/24/hubert-faure-membre-du-commando-kieffer-par-catherine-trouiller/) (French)

Hell's Angels 303rd Bomb Group, *364 Combat Missions of the 303rd Bomb Group* (available from http://www.303rdbg.com/missions.html)

Legasee, the Veteran's Video Archive / Sturgis, J., *John Sturgis Interview* (available from www.legasee.org.uk/veteran/john-sturgis/)

Ouest-France, Ouistreham, *Blanche Boulet devenue infirmière au D-Day* (available from https://www.ouest-france.fr/normandie/ouistreham-14150/ouistreham-blanche-boulet-devenue-infirmiere-au-d-day-6480652) (French)

Soldiers of Shropshire Museum, *2nd Battalion King's Shropshire Light Infantry (1939-1945): D-Day 6th June 1944* (available from www.soldiersofshropshire.co.uk/wp-content/uploads/2023/07/2-KSLI-V-27.7.2023-PDF-1.pdf)

The South African Military History Society / Lawton, C., *In a Royal Navy Destroyer on D-Day: The experience of a young South African as recorded in his Midshipman's Journal* (available from http://samilitaryhistory.org/vol095cl.html)

War Chronicle / Jones, H., *Harry G. Jones 2nd Battalion KSLI British 3rd Division World War II* (available from https://warchronicle.com/harry-g-jones-2nd-battalion-ksli/)

War Chronicle / Rylands, R., *From W Company 2nd BN KSLI* (available from https://warchronicle.com/from-w-company-2nd-bn-ksli/)

ACKNOWLEDGEMENTS

I am indebted to a number of people – friends and colleagues – without whose kind support and encouragement this book would not have been possible.

First and foremost I must thank my much better half Caroline, who has supported me throughout and given me the space and encouragement to undertake this work. Without her very few of the things I now take for granted would have been achievable.

I am also indebted to author and broadcaster James Holland, who was kind enough to support me when I first looked for a publisher for this book. After I supplied him with useful information about Gold Beach while he was writing his book *Brothers in Arms*, James was kind enough to promote my proposal and put me in touch with the people who could bring it to life. I am deeply indebted for his support. I'm also grateful to his fellow host on the *We Have Ways of Making You Talk* podcast, Al Murray, both having been kind enough to let me ramble on about my interest in D-Day online and in person at their annual festival.

I am also deeply indebted to my agent Trevor Dolby who, at James's suggestion, took on a new and unknown author based on a few pages of text. I have no doubt that since then he has been pulling out his hair at the length of time it takes me to reply to anything, but I am incredibly grateful for his steering me through the complicated world of publishing. I'm similarly grateful to Bill Scott-Kerr of Penguin Random House. After approaching him at an event and, fortified by wine, outlining just how great my book idea was, he was willing to give me the chance to prove it when a more sober proposal landed on his desk. I hope that I didn't let him down too badly by submitting my manuscript as late as I did.

ACKNOWLEDGEMENTS

I'm incredibly grateful to all of the staff at Penguin Random House who rallied round when I handed in my manuscript and have worked evenings and weekends to get it ready to publish. In particular I must thank Philip Lord, who worked so diligently on the maps and images, and Daniel Balado, who copyedited my text and polished it to something far better than I submitted. My thanks also to Katrina Whone, Barbara Thompson, Nicole Whitmer, Tom Hill and Melissa Kelly – the way they have come together for the final push has been truly wonderful.

A number of other very notable people have been kind enough to support this unknown entity. As well as giving me free rein on some of his *History Hit* shows, Dan Snow was good enough to vouch for me when I first proposed this book. Peter Caddick-Adams and Robert Lyman have similarly shown great interest in my work and promoted it whenever they get the chance.

Among my friends and colleagues, I am grateful to many people I know in person or interact with in the digital world. In my archaeology and history career, many people have given me the chance to further hone my skills and expertise to the point where I am qualified to tackle a subject like Sword Beach. In particular I am grateful to my old employer the Maritime Archaeology Trust, and to Nick Hewitt who, when Head of Collections and Research at the National Museum of the Royal Navy, employed me as archaeologist and historian during the restoration of the last surviving D-Day landing craft tank, LCT 7074.

There is a whole online history community who have all helped in their own special ways. The historians and enthusiasts I have met or cooperate with on Twitter, WW2Talk and the *We Have Ways of Making You Talk* community especially have my thanks. In particular I'm grateful to battlefield guides Paul Woodadge and Sean Claxton for sharing numerous valuable historical sources and important insights into Normandy, and Paul especially for sharing his uncle's story with me. Additionally I must thank Lieutenant Colonel Ingram Murray (Al's father) for his assistance with sources, Robert Glennie for his kind help with tank details, Paul Welch for sharing his knowledge of the assault wave, especially his interview with and subsequent article about Sapper Joe Williams, and for sharing images with me, Ben Mayne for his insight and regular sharing of copies of documents, Jeffrey Street for his valuable assistance in understanding the story of 1 Canadian Parachute Battalion on D-Day, and Nigel Walworth for supplying a short autobiography by his uncle Ron Major. Danny Lovell, too, for his very kind assistance in all things landing craft,

ACKNOWLEDGEMENTS

Michel Sabarly for his incredible understanding of the landings, Niels Henkemans for his assistance with German units and for gently steering me on to the correct path when I started to wander away from it, Craig Moore for kindly explaining the difference between a 29mm and a 290mm Petard mortar on the AVREs (quite simply that the latter didn't exist), Nick Stanley and Rob Crane for sharing their expertise on minesweeping and COPP respectively with me, Taff Gillingham for his help with Suffolk Regiment particulars, David Maréchal for helping me with French naval ranks, Mike Anton for selflessly offering to copy documents, Stuart Bertie for happily going out of his way to measure the height of Lion-sur-Mer's church tower, Lawrence Waller, Paul Reed, Romain Bréget, Jon Lander, Dave Chisholm, Tony Todd, Merryn Walters, Ian Pegg and Felix Pedrotti. Jasmine Noble-Shelly, too, for her support when writing my original proposal, my dog Flynn for making me take walking breaks, and thanks to my cat Stellar for keeping her keyboard wanderings to a minimum. If I have missed anyone I can only apologize profusely.

Additionally, it would be remiss not to acknowledge the many people and organisations that have made access to so many personal accounts possible. There are too many to list here, but their names are included in the references. I decided early that there was no real advantage in speaking to veterans myself – for one I'm painfully shy about doing so, but more importantly, almost every veteran still with us has already expressed his or her memories of D-Day in a variety of means. Whether that be through oral archiving conducted with staff and volunteers from a number of museums over many decades, museums and archives that have collected and preserved original documentation, private papers, letters, transcripts and unpublished memoirs, or families and collectors who have made documents accessible to the public, the preservation of memories of major events in history is a vital contribution to the historical record and one that we must seek to maintain.

Last but not least, I must thank my family. From an early age my parents instilled a fascination of history in me and did nothing but encourage it, with regular trips to Normandy during family holidays. And again I thank my much better half Caroline, who has supported me throughout, tolerated my endless trips to archives, and fed the pets while I've been at my desk. I couldn't have done it without her.

PICTURE ACKNOWLEDGEMENTS

MAPS

Original maps on pp. xxvi, xxvii and xxxviii and other linework by Lovell Johns Ltd

PART-OPENER PICTURES

Pages 6–7 Men of C Squadron 13/18 Hussars: © IWM H 38986
Pages 66–7 Beach group personnel and infantry: © IWM B 5091
Pages 194–5 Troops from 4 Commando: © **IWM MH 2011**
Pages 270–1 Troops of 1 Norfolk: © IWM B 5078
Pages 334–5 A B-26 Marauder: Smithsonian: USAF-51988AC

IN-TEXT PICTURES

Page VI HMS *Roberts*: © IWM A 23920
Page XXIV A graphic from the Force S orders: Public domain
Page LIX Commandos of 1 Special Service Brigade HQ: © IWM B 5057
Page LX X class midget submarine: © IWM A 21699
Page 5 Page from the Force S orders: Courtesy National Archives and Records Administration, USA
Pages 126–7 Cross section diagram of Queen Red Beach: Compiled using navigational data contained in the Force S orders (DEFE 2/403) and after-action reports on the defences (DEFE 2/490)
Page 333 A damaged German casemate: Courtesy National Archives and Records Administration, USA (Photo no. 204896459)
Page 429 Piper Bill Millin plays to men of 45 Commando: © H IWM 39039

PICTURE ACKNOWLEDGEMENTS

Page 430–1 A German photograph taken from Franceville a few days after the landings: Siedel/Bundesarchiv, bild: 101I-493-3363-13
Page 432 Landing craft manoeuvre on Queen White Beach: © Crown Copyright/Ministry of Defence. Courtesy of Air Historical Branch (RAF)
Page 433 Commandos of 1 Special Service Brigade march off the beach: © IWM B 5071
Page 434 Commandos of 1 Special Service Brigade push Italian PoWs on the way to le Port: © IWM B 5059

PLATE SECTION PICTURES

Page 1, top Allied bombs fall: Courtesy National Archives and Records Administration, USA (Photo no. 204894260)
Page 1, centre Rommel inspects: Bundesarchiv, Bild 101I-300-1865-06/Speck/CC-BY-SA 3.0. https://creativecommons.org/licenses/by-sa/3.0/de/deed.en
Page 1, bottom left Rommel and his fellow officers: Bundesarchiv, Bild 101I-300-1863-26/Speck/CC-BY-SA 3.0. https://creativecommons.org/licenses/by-sa/3.0/de/deed.en
Page 1, bottom right A Somua gun tractor: Bundesarchiv, Bild 101I-300-1863-14/Speck/CC-BY-SA 3.0. https://creativecommons.org/licenses/by-sa/3.0/de/deed.en
Page 2, top Strongpoint 20 (Cod): The National Archives, ref. WO 205/1108
Page 2, bottom Aerial view of Ouistreham: Courtesy National Archives and Records Administration, USA (Photo no.195952885)
Page 3, top Aerial view of Queen Red Beach: Courtesy National Archives and Records Administration, USA (Photo no. 195952891)
Page 3, centre Aerial view of Queen White Beach: Courtesy National Archives and Records Administration, USA (Photo no. 195952893)
Page 3, bottom Rommel inspects beach defences: Bundesarchiv, Bild 101I-719-0243-33/Jesse/CC-BY-SA 3.0. https://creativecommons.org/licenses/by-sa/3.0/de/deed.en
Page 4, top left German machine gun position: Bundesarchiv, Bild 101I-291-1213-34/Müller, Karl/CC-BY-SA 3.0. https://creativecommons.org/licenses/by-sa/3.0/de/deed.en
Page 4, top right Juno Beach machine gun position: The National Archives, ref. DEFE 2/430
Page 4, bottom left Tanks of C Squadron 13/18 Hussars: © IWM H 39000
Page 4, bottom right Major General Thomas Rennie: © IWM H 39002
Page 5, top Men of 3 Commando LCI(S)s: © IWM H 39041
Page 5, centre Force S sails: © IWM HU 72031
Page 5, centre left German torpedo boat *Jaguar*: Siegfried Raap/Peter Raap/CC-BY-SA 3.0. https://creativecommons.org/licenses/by-sa/3.0/de/deed.en

PICTURE ACKNOWLEDGEMENTS

Page 5, centre right HMS *Scorpion*: Courtesy National Archives and Records Administration, USA (Photo no. 80-G-253421)
Page 5, bottom HMS *Warspite*: © IWM A 23916
Page 6, top, centre and bottom Sequence of images taken by Lambton Burn: Courtesy of the Lambton Burn family
Page 7, top 77 Assault Squadron: © IWM HU 72031
Page 7, 2nd row, left Submarine HMS X-23: © IWM ADM 1260
Page 7, 2nd row, right Leutnant Nessel's HQ bunker: © IWM 9702-02
Page 7, centre The 75mm bunker at strongpoint 18: © IWM B 6381
Page 7, bottom Medics attending to wounded: © IWM B 5095
Page 8, top left Interior of the 75mm gun bunker at Skate: © IWM B 6380
Page 8, top right Heavily laden men from 4 Commando: © IWM A70 31-3
Page 8, centre Self-propelled 105mm Priest guns: The National Archives, ref. DEFE 2/419
Page 8, bottom Looking towards the twin villas of Quinquin and Tancrède: © IWM B 5111
Page 9, top Vehicles on the tank deck of LCT 854 burn: © IWM B 5112
Page 9, 1st row centre Photograph taken by Lieutenant William Winkley from the bridge of LCT 979): Courtesy The D-Day Story, Portsmouth; © Portsmouth City Council
Page 9, 2nd row centre Sherman Tanks of C Squadron 13/18 Hussars: The National Archives, ref. DEFE 2/419
Page 9, bottom Troops and vehicles advance up Queen Red Beach: © IWM MH 2021
Page 10, top Commandos from HQ 1 Special Service Brigade: © IWM B 5103
Page 10, centre Commandos race ashore: National Army Museum
Page 10, bottom left LCI(S)s carrying 45 (RM) Commando: © IWM A70 31-2
Page 10, bottom right Lieutenant John Allen's crab: © IWM A70 31-2
Page 11, top Infantry advance down exit 23: © IWM B 5087
Page 11, centre The 75mm bunker at strongpoint 10: The National Archives, ref. DEFE 2/487
Page 11, bottom left Patch of burning sea: © IWM A 24102
Page 11, bottom right Major General Tom Rennie: © IWM ADM 1260
Page 12, top Commandos advance towards strongpoint 8: © IWM A70 31-3
Page 12, centre 50mm gun bunker at strongpoint 10: The National Archives, ref. DEFE 2/487
Page 12, centre right Commandos of 1 Special Service Brigade: © IWM B 5055
Page 12, centre left The range-finding tower at strongpoint 8: The National Archives, ref. DEFE 2/487
Page 13, top Two wounded South Lancs men: © IWM B 5029
Page 13, centre LCTs of Group 10 and LCI(L)s of Group 11 try to unload: Courtesy National Archives and Records Administration, USA (Photo no. 214987619)

PICTURE ACKNOWLEDGEMENTS

Page 13, bottom Tanks of the Staffordshire Yeomanry are disgorged from LCTs: Courtesy National Archives and Records Administration, USA (Photo no. 195956840)
Page 14, top left An M10 self-propelled gun: © IWM B 5088
Page 14, top right A self-propelled 105mm Priest gun: © IWM B 5032
Page 14, centre British infantry advance past a First World War memorial: © IWM B 5018
Page 14, bottom The Suffolks' attack on Hillman begins: Courtesy National Archives and Records Administration, USA (Photo no. 49.27313369, 0.303133347). This image was produced through a partnership with the National Collection of Aerial Photography (NCAP). https://ncap.org.uk/
Page 15, top Anti-tank gunners of 1 South Lancs: © IWM B 5020
Page 15, centre Sherman tanks of the Staffordshire Yeomanry: © IWM B 5021
Page 15, bottom Troops and vehicles advance inland: © IWM B 5080
Page 16, top A photograph taken by Lieutenant Peter Wild (COPP 6): © IWM HU 72039
Page 16, centre A German Panzer IV of 21 Panzer Division: © IWM B 7056
Page 16, bottom 6 Airlanding Brigade: © IWM A 24096

INDEX

Agnew, Corporal 139
Allen, Lieutenant Bill 128
Allen, Lieutenant John 141, 187–8
Amaury, Lieutenant 198
Ambrose, Stephen: *D-Day: June 6, 1944* xx, 96*n*
Amer, Lt Commander Donald 58, 101, 104, 123
Anderson, Lieutenant 105
Applin, Corporal 131
Arethusa, HMS 72, 87, 91, 95, 96
Armit, Flight Sergeant Bob 81, 82, 307
Aschenbrenner, Leutnant 201, 203*n*
Ashby, Corporal Fred 239
Ashcroft, Lieutenant Eric 149–50
Ashcroft, Lord Michael 149*n*
Atlantic Wall, the 14, 15, 117
Attwood, Commodore Marcel 92 *and n*

Backlog, Lieutenant Frederick 183, 184
Badenoch, Lieutenant Cameron 120–21
Bagot, André 201, 202, 203
Baker, Lieutenant 178
Balaclava (AVRE) 132, 250, 260
Balfour, Lt Commander Ian 48
Band Sector 26 *and n*, 235
Barbarian (AVRE) 126, 127

Barbaric (AVRE) 134, 135, 260, 262
Barber, Lieutenant Philip 21–2, 122, 160–61
Barber, Major Robert 163, 242
Barclay, Major David 255, 256, 339
Barnard, Flying Officer Stanley 179
Barracuda (AVRE) 260, 261–2
Barrow, Major David de Symons 243, 245, 301, 302 *and n*
Barter, Able Seaman 296
Bartley, Lance Sergeant 139–40, 141*n*
Barton, Second Lieutenant Arthur 14
Barton, Able Seaman Harold 189
Basly 276
Bass (German strongpoint 8) 27, 42, 44, 83, 97–8, 109, 198, 204, 216, 217, 221, 276, 345
Bateman, Captain Reginald 95, 161–2, 165
Battleaxe (AVRE) 126, 127
Batty, Able Seaman Lawrence 172, 173, 338 *and n*
Bayeux Memorial 133*n*
BBC radio broadcast 76
Beach Groups x*n*, 38–9, 45, 58, 159, 176, 178, 188, 347
Beauregard 341
Becheville (ship) 353–4

INDEX

Beeton, Sapper Edward 306
Beirness, Private 72–3, 74
Belec, Private 73, 74, 236
Bellamy, Lt Colonel Robert 291, 292, 293, 311–12
Bell-Walker, Lieutenant Robert 150
Benerville 15; Battery 96
Bénouville 20, 75, 299, 322, 323–4, 325, 339
Beresford, Lieutenant Stephen 97
Berg, Lieutenant Christopher 182, 273, 275
Bernières-sur-Mer 84
Berry, Sub Lieutenant John 153, 154
Berryman, Bombardier Hazel 'Dick' 268
Bett, Marine Geoffrey 94
Beuville 9, 45, 287, 288, 301, 311, 312; Château 18
Bevin, Ernest 54
Bicknell, Corporal Maurice 162, 165
Bidmead, Bill 212
Bielefeld 16
Biéville 9, 45, 277, 285, 286, 288, 311, 312, 313, 319, 325, 341
Billings, Sergeant 312
Bismarck (German ship) 28
Blainville 322, 324, 325, 341
Blenheim (AVRE) 132, 249
Blenkhorn (Blinkhorn), Private James 136–7 *and n*
Board, Lt Colonel David 58, 158–9
Bois du Caprice 227
Bolloré, Matelot-Breveté 206, 207
Bone, Lieutenant Hugh 164, 242–3, 301
Bonna, Clemens 98
Booth, Captain 318
Booth, Lieutenant Jim 79
Bosseler, Obergefreiter 244, 246, 247
Boulet, Blanche 218
Boulton, Lance Corporal 290
Boycott, Major Charles 239
Braatz, Oberleutnant 324
Bradford, Lt Commander Donald 328–32

Brawny (AVRE) 135
Brèche, La 12, 13, 14, 17, 18, 117, 220, 222, 244, 249, 254, 263, 264, 352
Bréville 358; Ridge 235
Bridge Too Far, A (film) 230*n*
British Army
  20 Anti-Tank Regiment RA 36, 275, 287, 313, 356
  27 Armoured Brigade 37, 58
  79 Armoured Division 37–8
  21 Army Group 24
  5 Assault Regiment RE 58
  77 Assault Squadron RE 131, 133, 252, 259
  79 Assault Squadron RE 37–8, 139, 141, 175*n*, 305
  AVREs 38, 43, 44, 70, 71, 118, 119, 124*n*, 126 *and n*, 127, 130, 131–3, 134–5, 139–41, 142–3, 151, 160, 167, 188, 250, 252, 256, 259, 260–63, 305–6
  3 Commando 45, 60, 187, 230–31, 355, 356, 357
  4 Commando xxi, 44, 59, 60, 90, 137, 153*n*, 155–6, 161–2, 163, 194, 198, 203 *and n*, 204*n*, 208–10, 213, 216, 217, 228, 237, 242, 305 *and n*, 346, 347
  6 Commando xx, xxi, xxiii, 45, 56, 60, 180, 182, 219, 222–5, 226–7, 228–9, 231–2, 239, 242, 243, 244, 355–6, 357
  10 Commando xx, 232
  41 (Royal Marines) Commando 340
  45 (Royal Marines) Commando 45
  22 Dragoons 38, 43, 125, 139
  1 East Riding Yeomanry 37, 301
  2 East Yorkshire Regiment xiii, 35, 36, 43–4, 54, 78, 94, 135, 234*n*, 237, 242, 246*n*, 301, 325, 343, 347
  Eighth Army 34
  71 Field Company RE 356
  246 Field Company RE 37, 251*n*, 290
  15 Field Park Company RE 37

British Army – *cont'd*
  7 Field Regiment RA 36, 45, 106, 108, 109, 273, 277–8, 279, 289, 293, 297, 322, 324, 349
  33 Field Regiment RA 36, 44, 106, 108, 185, 186, 238, 241, 286, 315
  76 Field Regiment RA 36, 44, 106, 108, 184, 185, 245, 281, 302
  629 Field Squadron RE 146, 167 *and n*
  Forces: B 25; D 32, 41, 42–3, 63, 77, 273; G 25, 26*n*, 51, 55, 61 *and n*, 342; H 28; J 25, 26*n*, 28, 30, 51, 58, 61, 63, 84*n*, 342; L 25, 41, 51; O 25, 26*n*, 28, 327; S xxii, 21, 23, 24, 25, 26*n*, 27, 28, 29–30, 31, 32, 39–40, 41–2, 47–8, 51, 52, 55, 57–8, 63, 64, 72, 77, 86, 99, 106, 123, 124*n*, 170, 180, 302, 327, 350; U 25, 26*n*, 31; Z 28
  13/18 Hussars xiii, xvii, xxi, 30, 37, 40, 43, 44, 93, 100*n*, 223, 235, 245*n*, 246*n*, 248*n*, 304*n*, 343; A Squadron 102; B Squadron *194*, 199, 222, 245, 358; C Squadron 6–7, 49, 65, 170, 175, 185, 238–9, 241, 275, 281, 289, 291, 292, 315, 317
  22 Independent Parachute Company 72
  7 Infantry Brigade 33
  8 Infantry Brigade xiii, 33, 34, 35, 36, 37, 43, 45, 66, 185, 237, 248*n*, 300, 302*n*, 304*n*, 314, 339, 343, 350
  9 Infantry Brigade 33, 34, 35, 36, 37, 40, 46, 55, 58, 295, 298, 299, 300, 301, 339, 348–9, 350
  185 Infantry Brigade 34, 36, 37, 40, 45–6, 47, 52, 275, 278, 291, 314, 348, 350
  3 Infantry Division 24, 32–8, 307
  46 Infantry Division 35
  50 Infantry Division 35, 54
  1 King's Own Scottish Borderers (1 KOSB) 36, 295, 301, 325, 340
  5 King's Regiment (Liverpool) 58, 158
  2 King's Shropshire Light Infantry (2 KSLI) 36, 45, 274, 277, 279, 284, 286, 288, 289, 301, 311 *and n*, 312, 313, 314, 317, 319, 325, 347, 349
  92 Light Anti-Aircraft Regiment RA 322
  2 Lincolnshire Regiment 36, 295, 298, 300, 320, 339, 340
  2 Middlesex Regiment 175
  1 Norfolk Regiment 36, 45, 46, 47, 270, 289, 291, 341
  9 Parachute Battalion 72, 96*n*
  5 Parachute Brigade 234, 355, 356
  Royal Army Medical Corps (RAMC) 37, 39, 307
  Royal Army Ordnance Corps (RAOC) 37, 39
  Royal Army Service Corps (RASC) 37, 39
  Royal Engineers 13, 36–7, 43, 70, 130, 131–2, 146–7, 165, 166, 167, 251, 278, 285, 296, 305, 317
  5 Royal Marine Armoured Support Group (5 RMASG) 30, 38, 43, 62, 207*n*, 212*n*, 258
  2 Royal Ulster Rifles (2 RUR) 36, 294, 295, 299, 301, 340, 341
  1 South Lancashire Regiment 36, 43, 44, 95, 127, 130, 251, 256
  1 Special Service Brigade xvii, xxi, 38, 44, 55, 59, 180, 181, 219–20, 305*n*, 346, 355, 356
  4 Special Service Brigade 38, 55
  Staffordshire Yeomanry 37, 45, 47, 52, 275, 276, 277, 279, 286, 291, 301, 311, 312, 319, 348, 349; A Squadron 313, 315, 341; C Squadron 312, 319
  1 Suffolk Regiment 36, 43, 44, 55, 176, 177, 178, 179, 226, 237 *and n*, 241, 242, 276, 283, 288, 289, 300, 301, 317, 322, 337, 339, 347, 350, 354; A Company 238; B Company 238, 353; C Company 238, 279; D Company 238, 253 *and n*

2 Warwickshire Regiment 36, 45, 46, 47, 289, 341
see also landing craft
British Expeditionary Force (BEF) 33–4
Brooker, Able Seaman Jim 60
Brotherton, Corporal Ernest 125, 127
Brown, Flying Officer Ernest 72
Brown, Peter 242
Brownrigg, Captain Thomas 95
Bruce, Captain Hendrie 108–9
Brutal (AVRE bridge-layer) 134–5
Bryson, Able Seaman Robert 145, 164
Bundock, Major Thomas 323
Bunting, Signaller Corporal George 311
Burbury, Lt Colonel Richard 149, 150, 251
Burgess, Lieutenant Roy 120
Burn, Lambton 126–7 *and n*
Burness, Lieutenant Michael 214
Busaco (AVRE) 132, 249, 260
Bush, Captain Eric 21–2, 23, 43, 57, 58, 99, 100*n*, 105*n*, 118, 120, 275
Bush, Private Raymond 135, 136
Byatt, Corporal Eddie 242
Byrne, Sergeant Patrick 212

Cabieu, Michel 12
Caborg 16, 91
Caen 12, 13, 14, 16, 18, 19, 20, 24, 41, 46, 49, 71, 76, 84, 112, 115, 168, 169 *and n*, 170, 199, 203, 277, 301, 308–10, 321, 326, 341, 345–7, 350; Caserne Lefèbvre 14, 244
Caen Canal 14, 15, 17, 18, 26, 45, 49, 71, 107, 300, 305, 306*n*, 323; bridge 74, 75, 356
Cairon 325
Calvados 23, 24
Cambes 46, 295, 314, 340–41, 350, 351
Cameron, Major Alistair 277, 278
Canadian Forces x*n*, 246*n*, 314, 345
 Air Force: 430 Squadron 112; 440 Squadron 121–2
 8 Infantry Brigade 279

1 Infantry Division 34
3 Infantry Division 24, 25*n*, 34, 41, 46, 84*n*, 318
MTB Flotillas 47, 327, 332
1 Parachute Battalion 72, 73–4, 78–9
paratroopers 237–8, 239
Carentan 16
Carr, Captain Knyvet 157–8
Carruthers, Captain William 142–3, 260
Carson, Major Frederick 146, 167
Cash, Sub Lieutenant George 185
Cass, Brigadier Edward 34, 291, 300, 314, 339, 345
Castle, Colonel Frederick 113
Cazalet, Captain Peter 88, 106–7
Chandler, Lieutenant 71
Channel Islands 111, 170
Chappelle, Lieutenant Victor 107–8
Cherbourg 13, 14, 23, 85*n*, 91, 352
Chisholm, Dave 357*n*
Chivers, Frank 240
Churchill, Winston 24, 54, 353 *and n*
Clague, Sergeant Norman 230*n*
Clark, Lieutenant George 189–90, 191*n*
Clements, Sergeant 323
Clouston, Lt Commander William 48, 57, 97, 98, 107
Coade, Major Bill xxiii, 222–3, 224
Cochran, Sergeant 139
Cocks, Lt Colonel Arthur 58, 120, 126, 167
Cod (German strongpoint 20) 44, 46, 66, 107–8, 109, 117, 119, 122, 124, 125, 126*n*, 135–6, 149–52, 174, 175, 178, 181, 183, 192, 274, 276, 342–3, 347, 350
Coker, Douglas 358
Colleville-sur-Orne xxii, xxiii, 18, 44, 75, 117, 118, 220–22, 224, 226, 228 *and* n, 231, 237, 238, 239–40, 241, 243 *and n*, 245, 248, 279, 280, 281, 289, 291–3, 322, 326, 346, 356; 9 Brigade HQ 300, 301, 314; Château de 180, 197, 199*n*

Colquhoun, Lieutenant Donald 219, 220, 234*n*, 357
Colvin, Major Leslie 339
Combined Operations Pilotage Parties (COPPs) 1–3, 43, 58, 93, 103
Cook, Lieutenant 58, 158
COPPs *see* Combined Operations Pilotage Parties
Corrin, Lieutenant 104–5 *and n*
COSSAC 23, 24, 25, 26, 27, 40
Cotter, Major Sir Delaval 238, 291, 315–16
Coulson, Captain Len 157, 200, 216
Courbet, HMS 351, 352–4
Courselles-sur-Mer 17, 18, 345
Cowan, Electrical Lieutenant J., RCNVR 119, 120
Cox, Lieutenant Cyril 13–14
Cox, Lieutenant Ian 107
Cranshaw, Freddie 60
Crauford, Captain Clive 302, 303–4
Craven, Lieutenant Charles 60, 153, 154
Cregan, Captain 299, 339
Cresserons 18, 109, 264, 295, 298, 299, 300, 318, 321, 340
Crichton, Lt Commander 102
Crocker, Lt General John 278
Cromar, Lieutenant Alan Nigel 189, 190 *and n*
Cronkite, Walter 168, 169; *A Reporter's Life* 169*n*
Cruden, Lieutenant Peter 227
Cunningham, Brigadier James xix, 34, 295, 298–9
Cunningham, Lieutenant Redmond 307
Currey, Commander Edmund 58, 62, 84, 98–104, 105*n*, 141, 158, 188
Curtis, Lt Commander Rupert 54–5, 59, 61, 179–81, 189

Dacres, HMS 31, 273
Daimler (German strongpoint 12) 44, 95 *and n*, 96, 125, 237, 301, 302–3, 304*n*, 323
Dalrymple-Smith, Captain 96
Danae, HMS 87, 95, 96, 97
Dane, Captain 319
Dann, Commando Sid 234*n*
Darrington, Sapper 140
Dawson, Kenneth 153, 155
Dawson, Lt Colonel Robert 153*n*, 157, 197–8, 200, 203, 217, 305 *and n*
Dean, Corporal Gerald 177
Dear, Ian 153*n*; *10 Commando* xx
Denny, Captain Noel 119 *and n*
Deptolla, Hauptmann 84
Desange, Captain Geoffrey 140
Desoubeaux, Pierre 218
Devager, Matelot 206, 207
Dickens, Commander Peter 329*n*
Dickinson, Lieutenant Ivan 70, 78, 142
Dignam, Art 112, 114
Ditcham, Sub Lieutenant Tony 53–4, 57, 97–8, 320
Dixon, Captain Peter 258, 268, 300, 318, 338
Dohmen, Feldwebel Wilhelm xxiii, 223
Douvres-la-Délivrande 2, 18, 255, 321, 326, 340
Dragon, HMS 87
Dragon, ORP 32, 118, 177, 238
Drummond, Lance Bombardier Robert 184–5
Dunbar (tank) 125, 127, 141
Duncan, Private Geoffrey 292
Dunkirk, evacuation of (1940) 34
Dunn, Major Robin 293, 349
Durban, HMS 351, 352
Durbo (Italian submarine) 99
Dushinski, Zenon 217

Eadie, Lt Colonel Jim 286, 289, 291, 312
Eastern Task Force 25, 51, 87, 95
Edwards, Lieutenant 71, 139
Eisenhower, General Dwight D. 3, 4, 24–5, 40
Elliott, Captain Edward 143, 144, 164
Empire Cutlass, SS 94, 106
Empire Tamar 353–4

INDEX

Epron 313
Escoville 308
Escuat, River 34
Euryalus, HMS 21
Evans, Captain 229*n*
Evans, Private 292

Fairie, Captain Thomas 126, 127, 141
Fairlie, Lance Corporal Walter 132, 133 and *n*
Farnese, Orlando 209
Faure, Maître-Principal Hubert 204 and *n*, 205, 206, 207
Fenwick, Lance Sergeant Robert 138
Feuchtinger, Generalmajor Edgar 9, 19, 76, 308, 309, 310, 321, 325
Field, Lieutenant 324
Field, Major 302*n*
Firedrake, HMS 99
Fischer, Günther 11, 237*n*, 246 and *n*
Flynn, Sub Lieutenant Charles RNVR 170–72 and *n*, 337, 338*n*
Flynn, Petty Officer 170
Foden, Corporal 94, 147, 148
Foster, Lt Commander Edward 62, 143
Fowler, Able Seaman 338
Fox, Marine Stanley 162
Franceville 12, 115
Franceville Plage 13, 18
Francis, Sub Lieutenant 144
Fraserburgh, HMS 77
Freer, Lance Sergeant 250
French Resistance 76, 204
Frobisher, HMS 87, 96
Furguson, Major 259–60
Furnes 34

Gale, Brigadier Richard 357, 358
Garrod, Wireman Denis 173–4
Gaulle, General Charles de 353*n*
Gaunt, Sub Lieutenant Joe 192
Gee, Trooper 174
Gem Sector 26
George VI 28
Gérandier, Paule 218

German Army
 7 Army 15, 16
 15 Army 15
 1716 Artillery Regiment 125, 241, 263, 264, 276, 304
 1260 Coastal Artillery Regiment 19, 216
 726 Grenadier Regiment 18, 326
 736 Grenadier Regiment xiv, xxiii, 10, 18, 19, 73, 84, 115, 117, 221, 229*n*, 244, 264, 280, 311*n*, 326, 337, 340
 989 Heavy Artillery Battalion 125, 276
 352 Infantry Division 16
 716 Infantry Division xiv, 10, 16, 19, 20, 244, 286*n*, 310, 326
 155 Panzer Artillery Regiment 309–10
 1 Panzer Corps 19
 21 Panzer Division 9, 10, 11, 19–20, 76, 117, 125, 286, 309, 310, 341, 349, 350
 125 Panzer Grenadier Regiment 76, 310
 192 Panzer Grenadier Regiment 9, 11, 310, 313, 324
 22 Panzer Regiment 308–9, 314
 100 Tank Regiment 11
GI Jane (B-17) 115
Gibbons, Lieutenant 143
Gilchrist, Captain Donald 156–7, 197, 199*n*, 204*n*, 209–10, 215–16
Glass, Lieutenant Donald 158
Glenearn, HMS 29, 54, 78, 93, 94, 95, 106, 130, 160
Glover, Lieutenant Denis 60, 180, 182, 188–9, 191–2
Glover, Wing Commander L. 96*n*
Goathland, HMS 31, 57, 100*n*, 118, 120, 275, 277
Gold Sector 24, 26 and *n*, 35, 41, 110, 342, 343; casualties 343
Goodwin, Lt Colonel Richard 176, 178, 226, 229*n*, 237–8, 239, 241, 279, 280, 281, 289–91, 314–15, 337, 346–7

Gosport 41, 52, 53; ferry 58, 171
Gottberg, Major Wilhelm von 309, 313, 317, 349, 350
Gotto, Captain Renfrew 273
Gough, Major James 176, 189, 191, 238
Gower, David 90*n*
Gower, Lt Commander John 90, 107
Grant, Captain Douglas xix, 183, 257, 266, 267, 268, 298, 320; *The Fuel of the Fire* xix, xx
Grant, Sergeant Ian 186, 187–8
Gray, Lt Colonel Thomas 183, 255–6, 257–9, 260, 265, 267–8, 298–9, 318–19, 339
Green, Sub Lieutenant Sidney 145
Greenock 41
Gregory, Captain 324
Gregory, Corporal 135
Griffin, Major Patrick 286
Grindle, Lt Commander 13
Growler, HMS 353
Gueritz, Lt Commander Edward 58, 158–60 *and nn*, 276–7
Gundlach, Hauptmann 243–4 *and n*, 245, 246–8
Gurnsey, Sub Lieutenant Peter RNZNVR 173
Guswich, Unteroffizier 98, 217
Gutsche, Leutnant Hans 264, 266, 298, 348

H2X radar 113, 117, 168, 169
Häger, Obergefreiter Josef xxiii, 221–2, 223–4, 243*n*, 244*n*, 245*n*, 246 *and n*, 247
Haines, Captain John 95, 97
Haldane, General Aylmer 33
Hamble, River 41, 54
Hand, Sapper 250–51
Hanke, Leutnant 75
Hannah, Cox'n Norman 144
Hanson, Major John 305, 306, 307
Harbottell, Lt Commander James 295
Hardey, Captain Ronald 222, 226
Harper-Gow, Captain Max 180, 181, 229

Harrier, HMS 64, 69
Harris, Lt Colonel Ian 299, 300
Harrison, Lieutenant 274
Harrison, Major Robert 150 *and n*
Harward, Major John 128–9 *and n*, 254
Havre, Le 14, 15, 23, 27, 42, 76, 92, 179, 328
Haygarth, Sergeant 292
Heal, Captain Arthur 290–91, 314, 315, 347
Hennessey, Lance Corporal Patrick 100–1, 129–30
Henry, Lieutenant 298
Herdon, Lt Colonel Hugh 274, 291, 314, 324–5, 341
Hermanville-sur-Mer xxi, 44, 49, 109, 131, 237, 238, 239, 249, 250, 251, 252 *and n*, 253, 259–60, 275, 276, 278, 284–5, 295, 298, 300, 339–40, 354; War Cemetery 129*n*, 133*n*
Hermes, Grenadier Walter 314
Hérouville 324, 325
Herr, Hauptmann 311, 312, 313
Herrlingen, Germany 76
Higham, Lieutenant 155
Hill, Captain Laurence 351, 352, 353, 354
Hillman (German strongpoint 17) xvii, 44, 46, 115, 237–8, 241, 244, 279–80, 285, 288, 289–90, 291–3, 301, 312, 314–15, 317, 322, 326, 345, 346–7, 350
Hitler, Adolf 15, 309
Hobert, Major General Percy 37
Hoeller, Leutnant Hans 324
Hoffmann, Korvetten-kapitän Heinrich 77, 85–7 *and n*, 89, 90 *and n*, 91, 92 *and n*, 95
Hogg, Trooper John 134
Holder-Vale, Jim (driver) 323
Holmes, Captain Robert 229
Holmshaw, Albert (REME fitter) 297
Holthe, Lt Commander Tor 89, 90
Honour, Lieutenant George 1, 2–3, 65
Houghton, Lieutenant Jack 294–5, 296
Houlgate 15; Battery 88

INDEX

Howard, Major John 74 *and n*, 323, 356, 357 *and n*
Howes-Dufton, Captain Peter 260–61, 262
Hubert, Sous Lieutenant Louis 201, 203
Hulot, Sous Lieutenant Leopold 200, 201–2
Humphrey, Lt Commander Frederick 275, 276
Hunter, Private James 316 *and n*
Hurn, RAF 121
Hutchings, Stoker 170, 337
Hutchins, Lieutenant Leslie 69
Hutchins, Peter (signaller) 145–6
Hutchinson, Lt Colonel Charles 54, 95, 161–2, 164, 243, 248*n*, 301, 302
Hutchinson, Lieutenant 175*n*, 305, 307 *and n*
Hutchison, Captain Colin 54

Ibbetson, Sergeant Eric 78
Illing, Captain 324
Inverary: Combined Training Centre 348
Inverness: Cameron Barracks 28
Ismay, General Hastings 54

Jackson, Captain Archibald 165–7 *and n*
Jaguar (German ship) 85
James, Able Seaman 296
James, Lt Commander Robert 118, 123, 126*n*, 141–2
Jankel, Captain Herbert 174, 175
Jeff, Lt Commander Cecil 57
Jeffrey, Colonel Thomas 115–16
Jewsbury, Lieutenant Ernest 185–6
Johnson, Corporal 141
Johnson, Major Eric 135–6
Jones, Corporal Edmund 282
Jones, Lieutenant Edward 130–31, 133, 254, 255, 259
Jones, Sergeant George 144 *and n*
Jones, Lieutenant Harry 285, 287–8, 312, 325

Joyce, Sergeant Leslie 313
Juno Sector 3, 17, 24, 25*n*, 27, 41, 88, 110, 111, 318, 342, 343; casualties 343

Keel, Sergeant 73, 74, 79, 113–14
Kelly, Leading Stoker 296
Kelly, Private James xxi, xxii, 265–6, 267, 339
Kelvin, HMS 89, 177, 238
Kieffer, Commandant Philippe 49 *and n*, 60, 155, 197, 198, 199, 203, 204 *and n*, 205–8 *and n*
Kilvert, Sergeant Thomas xxi, 132 *and n*, 133, 249–50, 251, 252*n*, 259, 277
King, Major Charles 'Banger' 94, 136–7 *and n*, 151, 175*n*, 302
Kirkham, Pilot Officer William 71–2
Klug, Ferdinand xxiii, 223, 224
Knapp, Lieutenant David 131, 132, 133, 249–50
Knettishall, RAF 111
Koza, Franz 117–18
Kramarczyk, Obergrenadier Johann 225–6
Krancke, Vize-Admiral Theodor 76 *and n*
Kresken, Obergefreiter Toni 109, 152
Krug, Oberst Ludwig 18, 73 *and n*, 75, 84–5, 264*n*, 280, 316, 326–7, 337
Kuhtz, Hauptmann Heinrich 109*n*

Labas, Marcel 203
Lacy, Lieutenant Wilfred 149
landing craft ix–x, xi, xiii, 11, 165–7, 176–7, 251, 327
  Landing Craft Assault (LCA) 29, 43–4, 60, 93–5, 106, 118, 120, 121, 123, 124, 127, 129, 130, 136–7, 139, 146–9, 155–6, 158–62, 165–7, 176–7, 251, 327
  Landing Craft Assault (Hedgerow) (LCA(HR)) 32, 71, 105
  Landing Craft Flak 31–2; (LCF 34) 21–3, 122, 160–61
  Landing Craft Gun (LCG) 31

421

landing craft – *cont'd*
- Landing Craft Infantry (LCI) 29
- Landing Craft Tank (LCT) ix, xiii, 25, 30–32, 43–5, 50, 53, 55, 57, 58, 62–5, 70, 71, 78, 84, 93, 100–6, 108–9, 118–19, 120, 121, 123, 124–7, 130–34, 139–43, 144, 147–8, 165–6, 170–76, 180, 184–6, 275–6, 298, 327, 337, 343, 348
- Landing Craft Tank (Armoured) (LCT(A)) 61, 62, 106, 118, 120, 121, 143, 144, 162, 164
- Landing Craft Tank (Rocket) (LCT(R)) 32, 43, 70–71, 106, 119–20

Langrune-sur-Mer 2, 17
Lanternier, Second-Maître 208
Laot, Matelot Guy 202, 203
Lardennois, Maître Abel 205, 207
Largs, HMS 31, 54, 58, 63, 89, 93, 192, 300
Laurie, Captain James 163 *and n*
Law, Lt Commander Anthony 47–8, 57, 327, 328, 331–2
Law, Lieutenant Dick 95–6 *and n*
Lawford, Peter 346
Laws, Sergeant George xxi, 199*n*
Lawson, Corporal Robert 315
Lawton, Midshipman Colin 119, 320
Leaphard, Lieutenant Marshal 220, 234*n*, 357
Lebisey 9, 45, 47, 277, 287, 310, 312, 319, 322, 325, 341, 349, 350; Wood 287, 311
Lefauconnier, Charles 304–5
Lefèvre, Marcel 204 *and n*, 209*n*
Leggatt, Captain William 276
Le Mans 16
Lemon, Cox'n Francis 145
Lenauld, Alphonse 240
Letang, Jean 202–3
Lewis, Commander Herbert 42, 77
Lewis, Sergeant Major Taff 212
Lion, Médecin-Capitaine Robert 206–7
Lion-sur-Mer xi, xxi, 9–10, 13, 18, 26, 44, 45, 49, 101, 103, 109, 123, 179, 249, 254, 255, 256, 260, 264 *and n*, 265, 267–9, 276, 297–300, 318, 320, 338, 339, 348, 350; Château xxii, 10, 255
Lister, Major John 322
Littlar, Corporal Robert 274–5, 284–5, 287
Llewellyn, Royal Artillery Captain Glyn 177 *and n*, 238, 281
Lloyd, Lieutenant Desmond 89, 90
Lockett, Private William 128
Lofi, Officier des Équipages Alexandre 154, 155, 197, 198, 199 *and n*, 200, 201, 202, 203
Longest Day, The (film) 207*n*, 230*n*, 346
Louis XVI, of France 12–13
Lovat, Simon Fraser, Brigadier the Lord xix, xxi, 38, 49*n*, 56, 59, 60, 61, 179–80, 181, 182, 204*n*, 219, 223, 224–5, 226 *and n*, 227, 228*n*, 229–30 *and n*, 231*n*, 234–5, 239, 346, 347, 355, 356, 357*and n*, 358
Low, Captain Arthur 133–4, 135, 259–61, 262–3
Luc-sur-Mer 13, 17, 115, 318, 340
Luck, Major Hans von 308
Luke, Oberleutnant 221, 224, 243, 247
Lumb, Lieutenant 71
Lyle, Lt Colonel Lewis 168, 169–70 *and n*
Lyne, Lieutenant Geoffrey 1, 79, 80, 99, 102
Lyon, Captain Peter 103, 104

McCaffrey, Major Dennis 241, 242
McClure, Able Seaman Ralph 276
MacDonald, Corporal 73, 74
McDougall, Lieutenant Murdoch xxi, 157, 199*n*, 200, 204*n*, 210, 211–12, 215, 216
McGregor, Captain James 246 *and n*, 302
McKinnon, Able Seaman 172, 338
MacLean, Lieutenant 185
McLennan, Captain George 131, 132, 249, 250, 260, 261, 262, 263

McNamara, Lance Corporal 132
McReynolds, Lt Commander 297
Madden, Lieutenant John 72, 73–4, 78–9, 113–14, 219*n*, 236, 237–8 *and n*
Maher, Sub Lieutenant Brendan 64, 69, 86
Major, Private Ron 137, 138
Mapham, Sergeant James 175*n*
Marcks, General Erich 10–11, 75, 309, 310, 313–14, 349
Masters, Corporal Peter (*formerly* Peter Arany) xx, 226*n*, 231–3, 235
Mathieu 46, 313, 314, 340
Maurice, Lt Colonel 277, 279, 285, 286, 287, 312, 319
Mauritius, HMS 87, 91, 92*n*
Melville, Alan 296*n*
Menday, Major Ronald 209–10, 217, 218
Merville 18; Battery 72, 96 *and n*
Mesnil, Le 340, 341
Meyer, SS-Standartenführer Kurt 326
Middleton, Captain 92*n*
Middleton, HMS 107, 108, 109, 110, 118
Mikisch, Hauptmann Kurt 109 *and n*, 264, 321
Miller, C.: *History of the 13th/18th Royal Hussars...* 100*n*
Millin, Piper Bill xxi, 60, 61, 181, 182, 219, 235
Mills-Roberts, Lt Colonel Derek xx, 180, 182, 222–3, 224, 226–8, 229*n*, 230*n*, 235; *Clash by Night* xx, xxiii, 56, 355, 356, 357, 358
Milne, Lieutenant Anthony 175 *and n*
Milne, Flying Officer Ramsey 121–2
Mitchell, Corporal Raymond 183, 184, 256–7
Moakler, Sergeant Patrick 84
Monck, HMS 99
Monk, Frederick (signaller) 240
Montgomery, General Bernard Law 4, 24–5, 26, 33, 34, 40
Montlaur, Sergent Guy de 49, 204*n*, 207, 208

Moore, Private Arnie 162, 163, 242
Moray Firth 39, 40
Morgan, Lt General Frederick 23–4, 26
Morocco 24
Morris (German strongpoint 16) 44, 118, 125, 237, 238–9, 240–41, 242, 253*n*, 276, 346
Morris, Captain 257
Mousset, Odette 83, 96, 116, 218, 307
Mousset, Raoul 307
Möwe (German ship) 85
Mullen, Lance Corporal Brian 156 *and n*
Murdock, Flying Officer 81
Musketeer, HMS 99
Muskett, Chief Engine Room Artificer 101
Myhill, Sergeant Albert 134–5

Nalecz-Tyminski, Captain Romauld 300, 318
Napoleon Bonaparte 13
Naurois, Capitaine René 208
Neave, Captain Julius 49, 199*n*, 358
Nessel, Leutnant 10, 109 *and n*
Newhaven 41, 52
Newman, Lt Commander Frederick 274
Nicholl, Commander Rowley 58, 159 *and n*, 160
Nicholls, Commander Harry 42, 64
Nicholson, Lieutenant 140–41 *and n*
Nimz, Hilfszollassistent 246*n*
Nix, Lieutenant 71
Northern Sky, HMS 57
Norwegian Navy, Royal 88

Oddie, Corporal Jas 147–8 *and n*
Oldham, Lieutenant 184
Omaha Sector 24, 26 *and n*, 110, 169*n*, 344 *and n*, 345; casualties 344
Operation Charnwood 341
Operation Husky 31, 34
Operation Jubilee 28
Operation Mallard 322*n*

Operation Neptune ix, x, 4, 25 *and n*, 28, 49, 52
Operation Overlord 23, 24, 25*n*
Operation Rutter 28
Operation Torch 31
Oppeln-Bronikowski, Oberst Hermann von 308–11, 313, 314, 318, 325, 349, 350
Ordnance Express (B-17) 111, 114
Organization Todt 217
Orkan, ORP 99
Orme, Stoker Victor 145, 164
Orne, River/Orne valley 13, 15, 18, 46, 49, 71, 76, 170, 232, 234, 309, 322, 339, 340, 349; bridges 41, 45, 74, 75, 168, 170, 238, 300, 305, 308, 321, 323, 355; Estuary 12, 25, 26, 82, 115
Orr, Colonel Dennis 299, 301, 340
Ouistreham xi, xxi, 1–2, 12–16, 17, 18, 20, 26–7, 40, 42, 44, 45, 49, 77, 83, 84, 85, 91, 95, 96–8, 107, 112, 115, 179, 187, 191*n*, 197–218, 228, 237, 244, 245, 254, 260, 305, 307, 346; Hôtel de Normandie 83, 116, 218; lighthouse 2, 123, 211
Owen, Private Edward 288

Palmbern, Korvetten-Kapitän 77
Papillon, Major Phillip 238–9, 240–41, 317
Parkinson, Stoker 145
Parsons, Lance Corporal 306
Patterson, Captain Joseph 155–6, 158, 200, 203*n*, 208, 218, 305 *and n*, 307
Pearce, Lieutenant Robert 130, 254, 259
Penewitz, Franz 11, 117
Penter, Corporal Gordon 252
Pentland, Squadron Leader William 122
Percival, Lieutenant Frederick 289 *and n*
Périers Ridge 115, 237, 241, 277, 285, 286, 287, 289, 301, 310, 312, 317, 318, 319, 322, 340, 350; *see also* Hillman (strongpoint 17)

Périers-sur-le-Dan 9, 18, 45, 125, 279, 287, 288–9, 313, 340
Phillips, Lieutenant Tom 119, 141*n*
Pickles, Corporal 292
Pidleburg, Private 73, 74
Pigache, Mademoiselle 20
Piggot, Stoker 145
Pine-Coffin, Lt Colonel 234*n*, 356, 357
Plimer, Corporal 131
Plumetot 45, 125, 263, 295, 340
Poett, Lt Colonel Nigel 234 *and n*, 357–8
Pollard, Captain Eric 305, 306
Ponsford, Captain Keith 230, 231
Pooley, Major 231
Port, Le xix, xx, 234, 235, 322, 323, 355, 356, 357
Port-en-Bessin 25, 77
Porteous, Captain Patrick 209, 213, 214
Porter, Able Seaman 170, 172, 173
Portman, Sergeant Major Irving 209, 213
Portsmouth 3, 41, 47, 52, 55, 58, 62, 63, 351; Harbour 53, 54, 57, 58, 327
Potts, Surgeon Lieutenant Geoffrey 54–5
Poucher, Lt Commander Herman RNVR 170, 171, 175
Poulain, Dr Charles 218, 307
Powell, Captain Caryll 265, 267
Powell, Lieutenant John 282–3, 284 *and n*
Price, Reverend Victor 164
Price, Sapper 140
Priller, Oberstleutnant Josef 'Pips' 178–9, 296*n*
Prince of Wales, HMS 28
Princess Astrid, HMS 90, 337–8
Prior-Palmer, Brigadier George Erroll 58, 99, 100 *and n*, 101, 102, 103
Pritchard, Philip 228
Pummell, Lance Corporal 141
Purchase-Rathbone, Major William 356
Purkiss, Lance Sergeant 140

Putot-en-Bessin 41
Pyman, Captain Alan 219, 220, 234 *and n*, 358

Quadrant Conference, Quebec (1943) 23
Queen Beaches 26, 122, 124, 125, 192, 334, 342, 347, 354; Green 26, 27, 276; Red 26, 27, 32, 41–4, 136–7, 146, 151, 160–61, 175, 179–80, 184, 186, 192, 203*n*, 237, 274, 275, 276–7, 343, 346, 347, 354; White 26, 27, 32, 41–4, 110, 120, 125, 129, 131, 135–6, 146, 147–52, 160, 175, 176, 179, 183, 184, 185, 186, 251, 273–5, 276, 295–6, 302, 343, 346, 354

Rae, Major Ian 289
Rall, Korvetten-Kapitän Viktor 77, 90, 91, 92*n*
Ramillies, HMS 32, 87, 88, 91, 92*n*, 95, 96, 351
Ramsay, Admiral Bertram 3, 28, 52
Ramsey, Lieutenant 102
Rand, Lieutenant Cyril 294, 295, 299
Ranville 308, 322, 323
Rauch, Oberst Josef 310, 313, 314, 318, 321, 325, 349
Reed, Ed (pilot) 114
Renault, Emil 206
Rennie, Major General Thomas 28, 39, 54, 192–3, 279, 290, 300, 314, 341, 342, 345, 346
Repulse, HMS 28
Rice, Sergeant Earl 74, 279
Richter, General Wilhelm 16 *and n*, 18, 76, 84, 115, 264*n*, 286*n*, 309, 310, 326–7
Ries, Lt Colonel Norman 56
Riva Bella zone 13, 17, 18
Roberts, HMS 32, 87, 88, 95
Roberts, Sergeant Major 311
Robinson, Lieutenant Donald 125, 141
Robinson, Captain Douglas 225, 228–9, 231–2

Robinson, Leading Motor Mechanic 143
Rodney, HMS 351
Roebuck, Lionel xxii, 301–2, 303
Roger Sector 26, 27, 180
Rohmer, Flying Officer Richard 112, 115
Rollin, Matelot-Breveté Paul 206–7
Rommel, Generalfeldmarschall Erwin 9–11, 15, 16, 19, 76, 310
Roney, Sub Lieutenant Julian 145
Roubaix 34
Rouse, Captain Arthur 149–51, 252, 253
Rowland, Private Eric 283
Royal Air Force 39, 119, 178, 320
   Bomber Command 39, 42, 81–4, 97, 115, 216
   Second Tactical Air Force 39
   26 Squadron 96*n*
   88 Squadron 86
Royal Engineers *see under* British Army
Royal Navy *see specific ships*; *see also* landing craft
Rugge-Price, Major 104
Rundstedt, Feldmarschall Gerd von 14–15, 19
Russell, Lieutenant Mike 281, 282
Ruter, Sergeant 224
Rutherford, Lieutenant Reginald 137, 138–9, 343
Ryan, Cornelius: *The Longest Day* xx
Rylands, Captain Robert 288, 325
Ryley, Captain Geoff 280–81, 284

Saeren, Second-Maître Robert 202
St Adrian, HMS 90
Saint-Aubin-d'Arquenay 2, 18, 227, 228–31, 233, 239, 291, 292, 301, 314, 322, 325, 339, 356
Saint-Aubin-sur-Mer 17
Saint-Contest 46, 310, 313
St Julien 115; quarry 76, 326
Saint-Nazaire 16
Sallenelles 12, 20
Samsonia, HMS 353

Sauer, Obergefreiter Hans 75, 281, 316
Saumarez, HMS 88, 106–7
Scannell, Frank (pilot) 110, 111, 112, 113, 114
Scarfe, Lieutenant Peter 159–60
Scarlett, Lieutenant 289
Schaaf, Leutnant Rudolf 264, 266–7, 268, 298, 321 *and n*, 348
Scharnhorst (German ship) 88
Schmidt, Unteroffizier Helmut 98, 214
Schnellboote 85*n*
Schulz, Oberleutnant zur See 91, 92 *and n*
Scorchy II (tank) 168
Scorpion, HMS 48, 53, 54, 57, 89, 97, 98, 106–7, 216, 320
Scotson, Commando Geoffrey 234*n*
Scott, Captain J. D. 143
Scourge, HMS 48, 89
Scruton, Corporal John xxii, 162, 242, 244, 245, 302, 303
Scylla, HMS 95, 96, 327, 329, 331, 332
Seine Bay 77
Seine Estuary 82
Sellars, Commander Kenneth 'Monkey' 105, 106, 118
Serapis, HMS 89, 119, 177*n*, 320
Seymour, Lieutenant John 181
SHAEF 3
Shark, HMS 88
Sharp, Leading Seaman Philip 276
Sheath, Major 302 *and n*
Sheets, Captain Robert 168
Shephard, Lieutenant 99
Shoo Shoo Baby (B-17) 168, 169
Shoreham-by-Sea 41, 52
Sicily 28, 34
Simmons, Bob (bombardier) 115
Skate (German strongpoint 18) 44, 124, 137, 141, 151, 157–8, 161, 181, 276, 343, 347
Slater, Lieutenant Donald 58, 103
Slatter, Major 288

Ślązak, ORP 107, 109, 110, 118, 258, 268, 300, 318
Sloley, Captain Basil 256
Smith, Albert 144
Smith, Private Arthur 162, 163, 242
Smith, Lance Corporal Eric 222, 224
Smith, Lieutenant Eric 64–5, 174, 239, 240 *and n*, 292, 316
Smith, Brigadier Kenneth Pearce 34, 273, 277, 279, 284–5, 289, 291, 314, 319, 322, 341, 349
Smith, Private Leslie 254–5
Smuts, Field Marshal Jan 54
Smyth, Sergeant Walter 134
Sole (German strongpoint 14) xi, 44, 224, 237, 246–8*nn*, 301, 302, 303
Solent, the 41, 42, 47–8, 53, 55, 57, 63, 70, 104, 171
Somerset, Sub Lieutenant Shan 103
Sommer, Obergefreiter Herbert 151
South Downs 52, 53
Southampton Common 55, 59
Southampton Water 59, 61
Southsea Pier 55, 58
Southwick House, nr Portsmouth 3–4, 57
Spiedel, General Hans 309
Spithead 58, 62; Gate 63
Stagg, Group Captain James 3, 4
Steel, Major Peter 288, 319
Steinjan, Oberleutnant zur See 92 *and n*, 95
Stephenson, Lieutenant John 99, 101, 102
Stevens, Lieutenant 318–19
Stewart, Squadron Leader Derek 81–2
Stiles-Cox, Lieutenant 276
Stokes Bay 61, 63
Stone, Major Jack 150, 178
Storcheil, Lt Commander 98
Stord, HNoMS 88–9, 98, 106–7
Stornoway (tank) 125
Stratford, Captain 257

INDEX

Sturgis, Lieutenant John 257, 258–9, 266, 267, 339
Style, Captain David 198, 212
Success, HMS 88, 90
Sumatra (Dutch cruiser) 352
Surtees, Sub Lieutenant Harold 134, 142
Svenner, HNoMS 88 *and n*, 89, 90, 93, 98
Sweetapple, Sergeant 104
Swift, HMS 88, 90, 107
Sword Beach x, xi–xii, xvi, xvii, xx, xxiii, 26 *and n*, 27, 29, 30, 38, 39, 40–41, 44–5, 46–7, 48–9, 110, 111, 116, 117, 168, 318, 342, 343–4, 345–7, 348, 349–50, 351; casualties 343, 344
Swordy, Stoker 170, 337, 338*n*
Sykes, Captain John 176
Sykes, Steven 205*n*

Tailleville 84, 280
Tait, Sub Lieutenant John 173–4
Talbot, Rear Admiral Arthur 27–8, 31, 39, 54, 58, 63, 89, 100*n*, 105*n*, 192, 296*n*
Taplin, Major John 265, 339
Tapp, Lt Colonel Nigel 273, 278, 279
Taylor, Flight Lieutenant Jack 112
Taylor, Lt Commander John 351–3 *and n*, 354
Tear, Jack (tank crew) 62, 121, 144
Temeraire (Centaur tank) 121, 144, 164
Tennent, Lieutenant Charles 132, 250, 260, 261, 262
Terkowitz, Abe 111, 112
Thompson, Lance Corporal Arthur 162–4
Thompson, Captain John 72, 96
Thonber, Sub Lieutenant Richard 145
Thornycroft (company) 29, 30
Thornycroft, Major Guy 287, 288, 312
Tilbury 41
Tommy (B-17) 114
Tooley, Lieutenant Trevor 284 *and n*
Tormentor, HMS 54, 101

Trendell, Wireman Edward 145
Tresckow, Konter-Admiral Hans-Udo von 76–7
Tribolet, Leon 218
Trout (German strongpoint 21) 45, 107, 124, 172*n*, 254, 255, 258–9, 263, 268, 269, 274, 276, 300, 318, 321, 339–40
Turner, Major George 286
Tyson, Leading Seaman 171, 338

Umphress, Lieutenant 169
Unite, Lt Commander Tom 184
United States Army Air Force 39
  Eighth Air Force 34, 39, 43, 110–12, 113, 116–17, 168–70
Universal Carriers (Bren Carriers) 36, 124*n*, 175, 245 *and n*, 253, 275
Urquhart, Lt Colonel Ronald 146–7, 167*n*
Utah Sector 26 *and n*, 74*n*, 344

Vale, Sub Lieutenant 131
Van Heems, Lieutenant Martin 61, 121
Varaville, France 71, 74
Varley, Signaller Frank 284
Vaughan, Sapper 251
Vaughan, Sergeant 132–3
Vernon, HMS 57
Verulam, HMS 89, 258, 268
Vian, Rear Admiral Philip 95
Villers-sur-Mer 25
Villerville 15
Virago, HMS 89, 107
Vourc'h, Enseigne de Vaisseau 154–5

Wall, Lt Commander 176, 188
Wallrabe, Major 243
Walsh, Corporal 133
Walsh, Lieutenant Myles 168
Warsash 41, 54, 59–60; Rising Sun pub 59, 60
Warspite, HMS 32, 87 *and n*, 91, 92*n*, 95, 96*n*, 351
Wavell, General Sir Archibald 33

weapons 9, 10
  Bangalore torpedoes 281–2
  Boase Bangalores 126n, 132, 134, 135, 139, 142
  flamethrowers 17, 204n, 221, 224
  'Hedgehog' spigot mortars 32
  machine guns 303, 344 and n
  mortars/mortar bombs xvi, 10, 17, 36, 38, 121, 136, 137, 172, 344 and n
  Petard mortars 38, 139, 261, 306
  PIAT anti-tank weapons 35, 38, 202, 205, 208, 214, 282–3, 317
  Priests 108, 184, 185, 186, 241, 278, 288
  torpedoes 77, 85–6, 87, 88 and n, 89–90
  Vickers K-guns 38
  Vickers machine guns 38
Weedy, Captain, RM 101
Welby-Everard, Lt Colonel Christopher 300, 339
Wellings, Private Bill 128–9
Wellington, Arthur Wellesley, Duke of 32–3
Wells, Able Seaman George 172–3, 337–8 and n
Westcliff, HMS 22–3
Western Task Force 25
Weston, Marion (tail gunner) 111
Wheelock, Major Peter 286–7, 288, 318
White, Lt Commander Archibald 89, 107
White, Captain Brian 230
Whitworth, Lieutenant Peter 187
Wietzel, Captain Roger 352–3 and n, 354
Wight, Isle of 57, 61, 63, 65
Wigley, Lieutenant 133–4

Wild, Lieutenant Peter 103, 104, 110, 123
Williams, Reverend Derrick 55–6, 59
Williams, Sapper Joe 126
Williams, Private Samuel 138n
Williams, Sub Lieutenant 295
Willis, Sub Lieutenant 172, 173, 337, 338
Willoughby, Lieutenant Francis 294, 295–6
Wilmot, Chester 350; *The Struggle for Europe* 345–6, 348
Wilson, Lieutenant George 251, 252–3 and n, 278
Wilson, Major Humphrey 274, 291–2
Wingate, Sergeant James 120
Winkley, Sub Lieutenant William 174
Winstanley, Frank (tank driver) 126, 127
Wodarczyk, Unteroffizier Heinz 179, 296n
Woodham, Lieutenant 145
Wormald, Major Derek 102, 103–4, 123, 129
Wrestler, HMS 99
Wright, Captain Kenneth 90
Wright, Sub Lieutenant 105

X-20, HMS 3
X-23, HMS 1–3, 4, 42, 43, 65, 79–80, 99, 102, 107

Young, Lieutenant Peter 187 and n, 231 and n, 356
Yser Canal 34
Ysker, Oberschütze 11, 117, 246

Zaloga, Steven: *D-Day Fortifications in Normandy* 344, 345

Piper Bill Millin plays to men of 45 Commando on Strawberry Field, Warsash, next to the embarkation area on the River Hamble, on 5 June.

A German photograph taken from Franceville a few days after the landings. The assembled ships of Force S dominate the horizon.

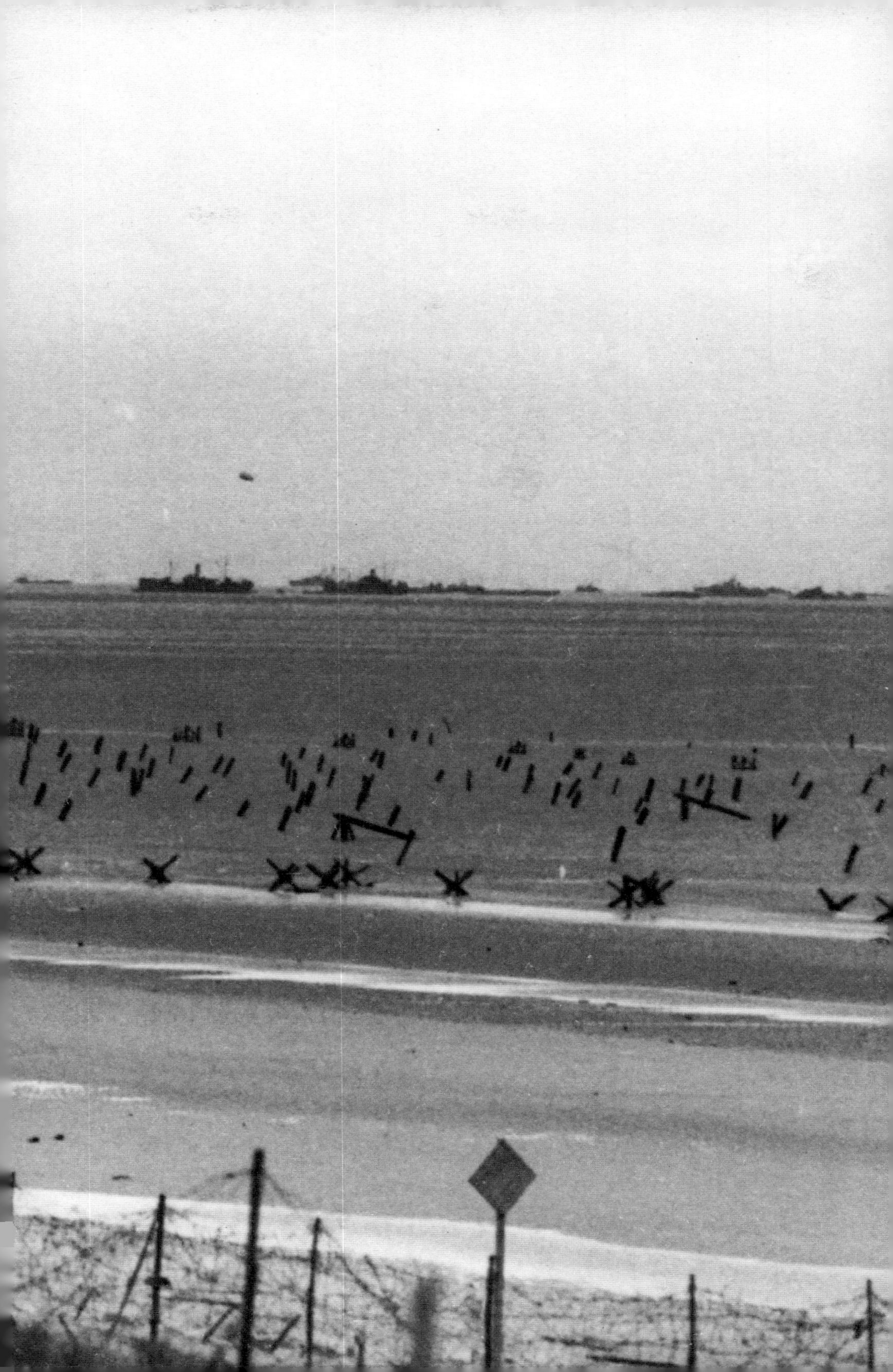

Landing craft manoeuvre in front of exits 12 to 16 on Queen White Beach.

Commandos of 1 Special Service Brigade march off the beach between exits 25 and 26. In the background an AVRE of 4 Troop 79 Squadron Royal Engineers prepares to lay a steel box girder bridge on the dunes.

Commandos of 1 Special Service Brigade push Italian PoWs down the road ahead of them as they make their way to le Port.

ABOUT THE AUTHOR

Stephen Fisher is an archaeologist and historian specializing in twentieth-century warfare and maritime history. He has been researching landing craft and the D-Day fleets for a number of years, working on a huge range of projects which have made him uniquely qualified to write this book.

Previous work has included advising on the restoration of LCT 7074, the world's last surviving D-Day landing craft tank, and compiling a comprehensive assessment of the Second World War archaeology of the New Forest National Park. At present he undertakes archaeological surveys of the New Forest and sails with National Geographic/Lindblad Expeditions as a historian.